# Greek Dialogue in Antiquity

# Greek Dialogue in Antiquity

*Post-Platonic Transformations*

KATARZYNA JAŻDŻEWSKA

# OXFORD
UNIVERSITY PRESS

Great Clarendon Street, Oxford, OX2 6DP,
United Kingdom

Oxford University Press is a department of the University of Oxford.
It furthers the University's objective of excellence in research, scholarship,
and education by publishing worldwide. Oxford is a registered trade mark of
Oxford University Press in the UK and in certain other countries

© Katarzyna Jażdżewska 2022

The moral rights of the author have been asserted

First Edition published in 2022

Impression: 1

All rights reserved. No part of this publication may be reproduced, stored in
a retrieval system, or transmitted, in any form or by any means, without the
prior permission in writing of Oxford University Press, or as expressly permitted
by law, by licence or under terms agreed with the appropriate reprographics
rights organization. Enquiries concerning reproduction outside the scope of the
above should be sent to the Rights Department, Oxford University Press, at the
address above

You must not circulate this work in any other form
and you must impose this same condition on any acquirer

Published in the United States of America by Oxford University Press
198 Madison Avenue, New York, NY 10016, United States of America

British Library Cataloguing in Publication Data

Data available

Library of Congress Control Number: 2021951163

ISBN 978–0–19–289335–2

DOI: 10.1093/oso/9780192893352.001.0001

Printed and bound by
CPI Group (UK) Ltd, Croydon, CR0 4YY

Links to third party websites are provided by Oxford in good faith and
for information only. Oxford disclaims any responsibility for the materials
contained in any third party website referenced in this work.

# Acknowledgments

This book was written with support from several institutions. The research was financed by the Polish National Science Center (Sonata grant 2015/17/D/HS2/01438), which allowed me to spend many summer weeks in the Institute of Classical Studies Library in London. I greatly thank the staff of the library, and especially Sue Willets, for their help and hospitality over the years. Since August 2020 I have received funding from the European Union's Horizon 2020 research and innovation programme under the Marie Skłodowska-Curie grant agreement No 754513 and The Aarhus University Research Foundation. The project was also generously supported by the Alexander von Humboldt Foundation, whose Fellowship for Experienced Researchers permitted me to spend ten productive months in the libraries of Katholische Universität Eichstätt-Ingolstadt. I heartfully thank my Eichstätt host and friend Gernot Müller for his enthusiasm for my project and many stimulating discussions. I am also grateful to Anna Ginestí Rosell and Johannes Sedlmeyr, my Eichstätt colleagues, for our conversations on the dialogues of Plutarch and Cicero. Special thanks are due to Sandrine Dubel, Anne-Marie Favreau-Linder, and Jean-Pierre de Giorgio of the Centre de Recherches sur les Littératures et la Sociopoétique at Université Blaise-Pascal Clermont-Ferrand, who invited me to participate in lively workshops and conferences on the ancient dialogue, and to Krystyna Bartol for providing me with the opportunity to present my research before the Committee on Ancient Culture of the Polish Academy of Sciences.

I am most grateful to Christopher van den Berg, Jan Kwapisz, and Geert Roskam for reading parts of the manuscript and providing me with constructive criticism. I am indebted to the anonymous readers of Oxford University Press, whose careful reading and valuable comments helped to improve the manuscript. I owe very special thanks to Krystyna Stebnicka, whose friendship, advice, and encouragement meant a great deal to me during this lengthy journey. To my family team, Krystian, Robert, and Maja, I owe more than I can acknowledge: thank you for cheering me on and for being curious, and for enduring books and papers spilling over tables and sofas.

# Contents

| | |
|---|---|
| *List of Abbreviations* | xi |
| Introduction | 1 |
|   0.1 Re-examining the History of Dialogue | 1 |
|   0.2 A "Genre" of Dialogue? | 7 |
|   0.3 Structure of the Book | 11 |
| 1. Dialogic Entanglements | 13 |
|   1.1 Introductory Remarks | 13 |
|   1.2 Dialogue and Anecdote | 13 |
|   1.3 Dialogue and Epistolography | 28 |
|   1.4 Dialogue and Extended Biographies | 41 |
|   1.5 Conclusion | 42 |
| 2. Dialogues in Papyri | 43 |
|   2.1 Introductory Remarks | 43 |
|   2.2 Philosophical Dialogues | 45 |
|     2.2.1 On *Eros* (PErl. 4 [MP³ 2103]) | 45 |
|     2.2.2 The Art of Speaking in Democracy and Oligarchy (PSI XI 1215 [MP³ 2098]) | 48 |
|     2.2.3 Socrates and Hedonists: A Fragment of Hegesias of Cyrene? (PKöln 5.205 [MP³ 2587.01]) | 50 |
|     2.2.4 A Protreptic Dialogue: Nothing Is Useful for a Bad Man (POxy. 53.3699 [MP³ 2592.610]) | 52 |
|     2.2.5 Dialogue on Ideas (PAï Khanoum inv. Akh IIIB77P.O.154 [MP³ 2563.010]) | 57 |
|     2.2.6 On Animals and their Affinity with Humankind(?) (PPetr. 2.49e (= PLit.Lond. 159a) [MP³ 2593]) | 59 |
|   2.3 Dialogues on Literature | 61 |
|     2.3.1 Satyrus' *Life of Euripides* (POxy. 9.1176 [MP³ 1456]) | 61 |
|     2.3.2 Dialogues on Homeric Topics (PGiss.Univ. 4.39, PLit.Lond. 160, PSchub. 4 [MP³ 1215, 1214, 1229]) | 66 |
|   2.4 Historical Dialogues | 69 |
|     2.4.1 "Peisistratus' Dialogue" (POxy. 4.664/50.3544 [MP³ 2562]) | 70 |
|     2.4.2 "Trial of Demades" (PBerol. inv. 13045 [MP³ 2102]) | 75 |
|   2.5 Dialogized Anecdotes | 78 |
|     2.5.1 Ethical Views of Socrates (PHibeh 182 [MP³ 2084]) | 78 |
|     2.5.2 Anecdotes about Diogenes the Cynic (PVindob. G 29946 [MP³ 1987]) | 79 |
|     2.5.3 Conversation between Stilpo of Megara and Metrocles(?) (POxy. 52.3655 [MP³ 2592.200]) | 82 |

| | |
|---|---|
| 2.6 School Compositions | 85 |
| 2.6.1 Alexander the Great and Gymnosophists (PBerol. inv. 13044 [MP³ 2099]) | 85 |
| 2.6.2 Prose Animal Fables (PMed. inv. 70.01 recto, MPER 3.30 (= PVindob. inv. G 29813–14) [MP³ 2652.100 and 2652]) | 86 |
| 2.7 Other Fragments | 86 |
| 2.7.1 PIen. inv. 660 [MP³ 2584.010] | 86 |
| 2.7.2 PBerol. inv. 21256 (= BKT 9.160) [MP³ 2099.010] | 87 |
| 2.7.3 PKöln 9.360 [MP³ 2103.010] | 87 |
| 2.7.4 PRein.1.5 (= PSorb. inv. 2014) + PBerol. inv. 9869 (= BKT 2.55) [MP³ 2444] | 87 |
| 2.7.5 PHeid. G inv. 28 + PGraec.Mon. 21 [MP³ 1389.100, previously 2560 + 2561] | 87 |
| 2.8 Conclusion | 87 |
| 3. Dialogue in the Academy | 89 |
| 3.1 Introductory Remarks | 89 |
| 3.2 Heraclides of Pontus | 92 |
| 3.3 Speusippus | 109 |
| 3.4 Eudoxus of Cnidus | 113 |
| 3.5 Xenocrates | 114 |
| 3.6 Crantor | 115 |
| 3.7 The New Academy | 119 |
| 3.8 Conclusion | 124 |
| 4. Platonic *Dubia* and the *Appendix Platonica* | 126 |
| 4.1 Introductory Remarks | 126 |
| 4.2 Selected *Dubia* in the Thrasyllan Canon | 128 |
| 4.2.1 The *Epinomis* | 128 |
| 4.2.2 *Hipparchus or The Lover of Gain* | 132 |
| 4.2.3 *Minos or On Law* | 134 |
| 4.2.4 *Theages or On Philosophy* | 136 |
| 4.2.5 *Cleitophon or Exhortation* | 138 |
| 4.2.6 *Alcibiades II or On Prayer* | 140 |
| 4.2.7 *Rival Lovers or On Philosophy* | 142 |
| 4.3 Dialogues from the *Appendix Platonica* | 143 |
| 4.3.1 *Sisyphus* | 143 |
| 4.3.2 *Eryxias* | 145 |
| 4.3.3 *On Justice* | 147 |
| 4.3.4 *On Virtue* | 148 |
| 4.3.5 *Demodocus* | 150 |
| 4.3.6 *Axiochus* | 153 |
| 4.3.7 *Halcyon* | 157 |
| 4.4 Conclusion | 160 |

5. Aristotle and Peripatetics ............................................. 164
   5.1 Introductory Remarks ............................................ 164
   5.2 Aristotle ............................................................... 165
   5.3 Theophrastus ....................................................... 179
   5.4 Clearchus of Soli .................................................. 181
   5.5 Dicaearchus of Messana ...................................... 185
   5.6 Aristoxenus of Tarentum ..................................... 187
   5.7 Demetrius of Phaleron and Chamaeleon of Heraclea ... 188
   5.8 Praxiphanes of Mytilene ...................................... 188
   5.9 Prytanis and Hieronymus of Rhodes, Aristo of Ceos,
       Satyrus of Callatis ............................................... 190
   5.10 Conclusion ......................................................... 191

6. Other Schools and Authors ........................................ 193
   6.1 Introductory Remarks ............................................ 193
   6.2 Megarians ............................................................ 194
   6.3 Cyrenaics ............................................................ 199
   6.4 Cynics ................................................................. 202
   6.5 Stoics .................................................................. 215
   6.6 Epicureans .......................................................... 219
   6.7 Timon of Phlius ................................................... 230
   6.8 Eratosthenes of Cyrene ....................................... 232
   6.9 The *Tablet of Cebes* ......................................... 234
   6.10 Philo of Alexandria ............................................ 236
   6.11 Conclusion ......................................................... 238

Epilogue ............................................................................ 241

*References* ..................................................................... 247
*Index Locorum* .............................................................. 273
*Index of Greek Terms* .................................................... 289
*General Index* ................................................................ 290

# List of Abbreviations

The list contains abbreviations of editions of fragments, databases, and translations referred to by the translator's name. If no translator is named (either below the translated text or in an accompanying footnote), the translation is my own.

For references to ancient texts, I have mostly used the abbreviations of the *Oxford Classical Dictionary* (4th ed.) or *A Greek-English Lexicon* by H. G. Liddell, R. Scott, and H. S. Jones (9th ed.). The abbreviations of journal titles follow *L'Année philologique*.

| | |
|---|---|
| Arrighetti | G. Arrighetti, *Epicuro. Opere. Nuova edizione riveduta e ampliata*. Turin 1973² [1960]. |
| BNJ | I. Worthington (ed.), *Brill's New Jacoby*. Brill's online reference. |
| CMG | *Corpus medicorum Graecorum*. Berlin 1908–. |
| Cousin | V. Cousin, *Procli philosophi Platonici opera inedita*. Paris 1864. |
| Coxon | A. H. Coxon, *The Fragments of Parmenides. A Critical Text with Introduction and Translation, the Ancient Testimonia and a Commentary. Revised and Expanded Edition with New Translation by R. McKirahan and a New Preface by M. Schofield*. Las Vegas and Zurich 2009. |
| Diehl | E. Diehl, *Procli Diadochi in Platonis Timaeum commentaria*. Vols. 1–3. Leipzig 1903–6. |
| Döring | K. Döring, *Die Megariker. Kommentierte Sammlung der Testimonien*. Amsterdam 1972. |
| Düring | I. Düring, *Aristotle's Protrepticus. An Attempt at Reconstruction*. Göteborg 1961. |
| Fuentes González | P. P. Fuentes González, *Les diatribes de Télès*. Paris 1998. |
| Gow | A. S. F. Gow, *Machon. The Fragments. Edited with an Introduction and Commentary*. Cambridge 1965. |
| Isnardi Parente | M. Isnardi Parente, *Senocrate–Ermodoro. Frammenti*. Naples 1982. |
| K–A | R. Kassel and C. Austin, *Poetae comici Graeci*. Berlin and New York 1986–. |
| Kindstrand | J. F. Kindstrand, *Bion of Borysthenes. A Collection of the Fragments with Introduction and Commentary*. Uppsala 1976. |
| Körte | A. Körte, *Metrodori Epicurei fragmenta*. Leipzig 1890. |
| Kroll | G. Kroll, *Procli Diadochi In Platonis Rem Publicam commentarii*. Vols. 1–2. Leipzig 1899–1901. |

xii LIST OF ABBREVIATIONS

| | |
|---|---|
| Kühn | C. G. Kühn, *Claudii Galeni opera omnia*. Vol. 4. Leipzig 1822. |
| Merkelbach and West | R. Merkelbach and M. L. West, *Fragmenta Hesiodea*. Oxford 1967. |
| Mette | H. J. Mette, "Zwei Akademiker heute: Krantor von Soloi und Arkesilaos von Pitane." *Lustrum* 26 (1984): 7–94. |
| MP³ | Mertens-Pack 3, online database of papyri: http://cipl93.philo.ulg.ac.be/Cedopal/MP3/dbsearch_en.aspx. |
| Olson and Sens | S. D. Olson and A. Sens, *Archestratos of Gela. Greek Culture and Cuisine in the Fourth Century BCE*. Oxford 2000. |
| Rose³ | V. Rose, *Aristotelis qui ferebantur librorum fragmenta*. Leipzig 1886³. |
| Schorn | S. Schorn, *Satyros aus Kallatis. Sammlung der Fragmente mit Kommentar*. Basel 2004. |
| Schütrumpf | E. Schütrumpf, *Heraclides of Pontus: Texts and Translation*. New Brunswick 2008. |
| SH | H. Lloyd-Jones and P. J. Parsons, *Supplementum Hellenisticum*. Berlin and New York 1983. |
| Smith | W. D. Smith, *Hippocrates. Pseudepigraphic Writings. Letters. Embassy. Speech from the Altar. Decree*. Leiden 1990. |
| M. F. Smith | M. F. Smith, *The Epicurean Inscription*. Naples 1993. |
| SSR | G. Giannantoni, *Socratis et Socraticorum Reliquiae*. Vols. 1–4. Naples 1990. |
| Sudhaus II | S. Sudhaus, *Philodemi Volumina Rhetorica*. Vol. 2. Leipzig 1896. |
| SVF | H. von Arnim, *Stoicorum veterum fragmenta*. Vols. 1–4. Leipzig 1903–24. |
| Tarán | L. Tarán, *Speusippus of Athens. A Critical Study with a Collection of the Related Texts and Commentary*. Leiden 1981. |
| TrGF | B. Snell, R. Kannicht, and S. Radt, *Tragicorum Graecorum fragmenta*. Vols. 1–5. Göttingen, 1971–2004. |
| Wehrli (for Clearchus) | F. Wehrli, *Die Schule des Aristoteles. Texte und Kommentar. III: Klearchos*. Basel 1969². |
| Wehrli (for Praxiphanes) | F. Wehrli, *Die Schule des Aristoteles. Texte und Kommentar. IX: Phainias von Eresos, Chamaileon, Praxiphanes*. Basel 1969². |
| Westerink | L. G. Westerink, *Proclus Diadochus. Commentary on the First Alcibiades of Plato*. Amsterdam 1954. |

## Translations referred to by the translator's name

| | |
|---|---|
| J. Annas and J. Barnes | J. Annas and J. Barnes, *Sextus Empiricus. Outlines of Scepticism*. Cambridge 2000. |
| J. M. G. Barclay | J. M. G. Barclay, *Flavius Josephus, Against Apion. Translation and Commentary*. Leiden and Boston 2007. |

## LIST OF ABBREVIATIONS xiii

| | |
|---|---|
| J. Barnes | J. Barnes, *[Plato]. Demodocus*. In J. M. Cooper, D. S. Hutchinson (ed.), *Plato. Complete Works*, 1699–1706. Indianapolis and Cambridge 1997. |
| J. Barnes and G. Lawrence | J. Barnes and G. Lawrence, *Aristotle. Fragments*. In J. Barnes (ed.), *The Complete Works of Aristotle. The Revised Oxford Translation*. Vol. 2, 2384–462. Princeton 1984. |
| R. Bett | R. Bett, *Sextus Empiricus. Against the Ethicists (Adversus Methematicos XI)*. Oxford 1997. |
| M. L. Chiesara | M. L. Chiesara, *Aristocles of Messene. Testimonia and Fragments. Edited with Translation and Commentary*. Oxford 2001. |
| S. M. Cohen, G. B. Matthews | S. M. Cohen and G. B. Matthews, *Ammonius. On Aristotle's Categories*. Ithaca, NY 1991. |
| S. Drake | S. Drake, *Galileo Galilei. Dialogue Concerning the Two Chief World Systems—Ptolemaic & Copernican*. Berkeley and Los Angeles 1967². |
| B. Einarson and P. D. De Lacy | B. Einarson and P. D. De Lacy, *Plutarch. Moralia*. Vol. 14. Cambridge, MA 1967. |
| W. H. Fyfe | W. H. Fyfe, *Longinus. On the Sublime*. Revised by D. A. Russell. In S. Halliwell, W. H. Fyfe, D. A. Russell, and D. C. Innes, *Aristotle: Poetics. Longinus: On the Sublime. Demetrius: On Style*. Cambridge, MA 1995. |
| M. Graver | M. Graver, *Cicero on the Emotions. Tusculan Disputations 3 and 4*. Chicago and London 2002. |
| C. R. Haines | C. R. Haines, *Fronto. Correspondence*, Vols. 1–2. Cambridge, MA 1919–1920. |
| W. C. Helmbold | W. C. Helmbold, *Plutarch. Moralia*. Vol. 6. Cambridge, MA 1939. |
| R. D. Hicks | R. D. Hicks, *Diogenes Laertius. Lives of Eminent Philosophers*. Vols. 1–2, Cambridge, MA 1925. |
| D. C. Innes | D. C. Innes, *Demetrius. On Style*. In: S. Halliwell, W. H. Fyfe, D. A. Russell, D. C. Innes, *Aristotle: Poetics. Longinus: On the Sublime. Demetrius: On Style*, Cambridge, MA 1995. |
| G. A. Kennedy | G. A. Kennedy, *Invention and Method. Two Rhetorical Treatises from the Hermogenic Corpus. Translated with Introductions and Notes*. Atlanta 2005. |
| R. Kent Sprague | R. Kent Sprague, *Plato. Charmides*. In: J. M. Cooper, D. S. Hutchinson (ed.), *Plato. Complete Works*, 640–663. Indianapolis and Cambridge 1997. |
| J. E. King | J. E. King, *Cicero. Tusculan Disputations*. Cambridge, MA 1927. |

| | |
|---|---|
| E. C. Marchant | E. C. Marchand, *Xenophon. Memorabilia*. In E. C. Marchant and O. J. Todd, *Xenophon. Memorabilia. Oeconomicus. Symposium. Apology*. Revised by J. Henderson. Cambridge, MA 2013. |
| R. D. McKirahan, Jr. | R. D. McKirahan, Jr., *[Plato]. Epinomis*. In J. M. Cooper and D. S. Hutchinson (ed.), *Plato. Complete Works*, 1617–33. Indianapolis and Cambridge 1997. |
| S. D. Olson | S. D. Olson, *Athenaeus. The Learned Banqueters*. Vols. 1–8. Cambridge, MA 2006–12. |
| R. J. Penella | R. J. Penella, *The Private Orations of Themistius*. Berkeley and Los Angeles 2000. |
| W. A. Pickard-Cambridge | W. A. Pickard-Cambridge, *Aristotle. Sophistical Refutations*. In J. Barnes (ed.), *The Complete Works of Aristotle. The Revised Oxford Translation*. Vol. 1, 278–314. Princeton 1984. |
| D. R. Shackleton Bailey | D. R. Shackleton Bailey, *Cicero. Letters to Atticus*. Vol. 4. Cambridge, MA 1999. |
| W. D. Smith | W. D. Smith, *Hippocrates. Pseudepigraphic Writings. Letters. Embassy. Speech from the Altar. Decree*. Leiden 1990. |
| P. Stork, J. van Ophuijsen, S. Prince | E. Schütrumpf, P. Stork, J. van Ophuijsen, and S. Prince, *Heraclides of Pontus: Texts and Translation*. New Brunswick 2008. |
| B. G. Wright | B. G. Wright, III, *The Letter of Aristeas. "Aristeas to Philocrates" or "On the Translation of the Law of the Jews."* Berlin and Boston 2015. |

# Introduction

## 0.1 Re-examining the History of Dialogue

This aim of this book is to re-examine and reassess evidence for Greek dialogue between the mid-fourth century BCE and the mid-first century CE— that is, roughly from Plato's death to the death of Philo of Alexandria. The genre of dialogue in this period has not been subject to a thorough examination since Rudolf Hirzel's 1895 monograph *Der Dialog. Ein literarhistorischer Versuch*; however, since that time, not only have conceptual frameworks and methodological approaches in the field shifted, but new evidence—including papyri-fragments—has also emerged.

There are a number of reasons why dialogue in this period has not been comprehensively studied since the end of the nineteenth century. There is the obvious problem of scarcity of evidence: very little is extant of Hellenistic prose and almost all Greek dialogues composed between Plato and the first century CE— apart from difficult-to-date Platonic *spuria*—have been lost. There is, however, another reason for its being overlooked, namely the widespread assumption that dialogue went into disuse in the Hellenistic period. The dialogue format, modern scholars say, went through a period of "decline," experienced an "almost total eclipse," or "fell out of fashion," only to be revived in the Roman period: in Latin by Cicero in the mid-first century BCE, and in Greek by Plutarch over a century later.[1]

At first sight, such a narrative appears persuasive. It relies not only on the pattern of survival of ancient dialogues but also on the known fact that in the late Classical and Hellenistic periods prose genres, philosophical genres included, multiplied. With the emergence of other formats—the treatise, continuous

---

[1] See e.g. Pade 2007, 45: "[a]fter a long period of almost total eclipse the dialogue had reappeared with Plutarch" (following Robinson 1979, 9); Gutzwiller 2007, 141: the "livelier genre of dialogue...fell out of fashion, but some of Cicero's philosophical works, which adapt Hellenistic philosophy for a Roman audience, return to the dialogue form"; Grafton et al. 2010, 266: "[a]fter a period of decline the Greek dialogue was revived by Plutarch"; more cautiously, White 2010, 371: "apart from some diehard Socratics and minor Peripatetics, dialogues are securely attested for very few after the fourth century." This model is also reflected in recent edited volumes on the ancient dialogue (Goldhill 2008; Föllinger and Müller 2013; Dubel and Gotteland 2015) which contain very little material from the Hellenistic period. The reasons for the dialogue's purported loss of appeal for Hellenistic authors and audiences are not made clear; White 2010, 371 suggests that the decline was due "in part to the continuing popularity of fourth-century works" and to the fact that "interest shifted to supplying its larger audience with portraits of philosophers in action," which led to the development of biographico-anecdotal writings.

discourse of a protreptic or paraenetic character, the philosophical letter, the commentary, etc.—dialogue was displaced from the special position it enjoyed in the first half of the fourth century BCE in the hands of Plato and other Socratics. However, displacement from a privileged position is not tantamount to its abandonment, and the diversification of prosaic genres does not preclude that dialogues continued to be produced alongside other formats and that the genre, freed from its Socratic backgrounds and tropes, flourished in the hands of the Hellenistic authors—as it did in Cicero's times in Rome and later in Greek and Roman literature in the imperial period. In fact, there are indications in Greek imperial period literature that the narrative of the dialogue's discontinuity is not accurate. Plutarch, for instance, in the opening of the *Table-Talk* lists several "highly reputed philosophers" (τῶν φιλοσόφων τοὺς ἐλλογιμωτάτους) as models for his dialogue: they include, apart from Plato and Xenophon, also Aristotle, Speusippus, Epicurus, Prytanis, Hieronymus, and Dion of the Academy (*Quaest. conv.* 612d–e). He therefore postulates a continuous tradition of the sympotic dialogue running from the Socratics to the first century BCE (Dion), a tradition alive not only in the Academy but also in the Peripatos and the Epicurean school. Our knowledge, however, of this tradition is extremely limited: no substantial fragments of the sympotic works by Aristotle, Speusippus, and Epicurus are extant, and about Prytanis, Hieronymus, and Dion (whom Plutarch was comfortable to name together with such authoritative figures as Plato and Aristotle) we know almost nothing, which clearly shows how limited our knowledge of the Hellenistic dialogue is. On the other hand, the narrative associating the revival of the Greek dialogue with Plutarch specifically is oblivious to dialogues composed by Philo of Alexandria and Dio Chrysostom, whose dialogues either slightly preceded or were contemporaneous with Plutarch's and provide independent testimony to the genre's persistence in the early imperial period.

It should be noted that from a methodological perspective, it would be difficult to produce strong evidence for a break in dialogue-writing in Hellenistic times. While a shortage of data on dialogue composition during this period is suggestive,[2] it does not prove the decline of the genre. We are dealing with literature that suffered immense losses: thousands of prose works—philosophical, technical, didactic, and literary—have completely vanished, and in the case of the small percentage of texts we know about, our understanding of their literary forms is extremely limited. Ancient authors from later periods who have preserved for us bits and pieces of earlier works usually betray little interest in formats and rarely make an explicit note of them. When they quote or paraphrase a dialogue, they frequently abandon the dialogue format and extract the contents they find of

---

[2] Cf. a note by Momigliano 1970, 140–1 on Droysen's creation of the concept of the Hellenistic period: "The other factor is the paucity of the literary evidence about the third century B.C. The literary fragments of the third and second centuries B.C. seemed to confirm by their very nature the impression of decline and fall.... it is difficult to resist the first impression that there is something wrong with an age which has left an insufficient account of itself."

interest, be it a philosophical argument, a playful saying, or a piece of information. Dialogic utterances, i.e. those expressed by dialogue interlocutors, were frequently assigned to the author of a given work. We see this in the case of Plato's dialogues, where the utterances of Socrates and other speakers are routinely quoted by ancient writers as if they were said by Plato *in propria voce*. Eusebius of Caesarea quotes twice from Philo of Alexandria's *On Providence*, a dialogue between Philo and his nephew Alexander, without acknowledging its format or mentioning Alexander, even though he quotes words assigned to him by Philo.

Scholars frequently hypothesize about the formats of lost works based on transmitted titles, preserved, for instance, in doxographical texts such as Diogenes Laertius' *Lives and Views of Philosophers*. The value of this evidence is limited, both for identifying dialogues and denying the dialogue format. Many works circulated under several different titles whose provenance remains unclear—they might have originated with the author, but also might have come from readers or ancient scholars cataloging the author's works, who were influenced by contemporary conventions and individual inclinations.[3] Moreover, there were no strict conventions for dialogue titles. While a work titled *Symposion* would have been with reasonable probability a dialogue, name titles, familiar from the Platonic corpus, are more elusive and may signify not only dialogues but also works of a biographical or panegyric character. On the other hand, it is sometimes presumed that philosophical works with *peri*-titles—that is, starting with περί, "on," followed by a noun designating the topic—were continuous expositions,[4] but that is certainly incorrect, as the case of Aristotle's dialogues *On Noble Birth* and *On Poets* (Περὶ εὐγενείας, Περὶ ποιητῶν), for example, demonstrates. Dialogues also circulated under unusual titles—such as Heraclides of Pontus' *On the Woman Not Breathing* (Περὶ τῆς ἄπνου or Ἄπνους)—or titles misleadingly suggestive of other prose-genres, such as Satyrus of Callatis' *Life of Euripides*. In fact, it seems that name titles became less popular with time, and by the time of Dio Chrysostom and Plutarch, they were little used.

Furthermore, ancient generic terminology is frequently blurry. The word διάλογος or *dialogus* would typically indicate a dialogue format, though the case of Seneca's *Dialogues* (*Dialogi*) suggests that caution is warranted. Other terms tend to be non-specific—such as λόγος or βιβλία—or ambiguous. To the latter group belong συγγράμματα and ὑπομνήματα, which, though in translation they are frequently rendered, respectively, as "treatise" and "commentary/memoir," in reality are fluid and may simply mean "writing(s)."[5] Another hazy term is διατριβή

---

[3] The early history of Greek titles is obscure. There is little doubt that by the time of Plato, titles were in common use (as Plato's reference to his own work as *Sophist* in Plt. 284b shows); still, a work might have circulated under various titles, and an original title might have been later changed in the Hellenistic period by philologists and scholars who classified and categorized works of literature. See Nachmanson 1941 and observations on the titles of Plato's dialogues in Mansfeld 1994, 71–4.

[4] e.g. Fortenbaugh 1984, 120.

[5] Cf. e.g. two partially overlapping lists of Aristippus' works, once referred to as διάλογοι, once as συγγράμματα in Diogenes Laertius 2.83–5, as well as Diogenes' references to Plato's works as συγγράμματα (3.37, 3.80). For the non-specific meaning of ὑπομνήματα cf. Diogenes Laertius 1.16,

which, as Jan Kindstrand noted, "tells us nothing of the literary form."[6] An instructive case in point is a passage in Diogenes Laertius where Praxiphanes is said to have written "a διατριβή about poets, which took place in the country, when Isocrates was entertained by Plato" (3.8: ἀνέγραψε διατριβήν τινα περὶ ποιητῶν γενομένην ἐν ἀγρῷ παρὰ Πλάτωνι ἐπιξενωθέντος τοῦ Ἰσοκράτους); this διατριβή, in all probability, was a dialogue between Plato and Isocrates.

Contemplation of the exceedingly fragmentary character of the available evidence should "humble our attempts to create totalizing reconstructions."[7] Grand-scale narratives of the Hellenistic-period dialogue are inevitably highly speculative, and while they are not necessarily without merit, they should be phrased with due caution and originate as a result of a thorough examination of surviving material. The last comprehensive study of the remains of the post-Platonic dialogue was the above-mentioned 1895 monograph by Hirzel, and it is probable that the narrative of the dialogue's decline and subsequent revival, lingering still in modern scholarship, ultimately derives from it. The model of a bloom, decline, and revival is strongly reminiscent of nineteenth-century philology and its perception of the Hellenistic times as a period of regression.[8] Histories of Greek literature produced at the time postulated a relapse in literary production after the Classical period and a subsequent revival spurred by the emergence of the Romans on the political and cultural scene. While this model, as a whole, has been rejected, its influence remains palpable in various segments of scholarship. The editors of a recent volume dedicated to Hellenistic period note that:

> Hellenistic literature often fares poorly in histories of Greek literature, most of which explicitly or implicitly offer a rise-and-fall narrative that privileges the Classical period and sees the Hellenistic period as a time of decline. The almost complete loss of much of the period's prose literature makes it even easier to give it short shrift.[9]

---

where a distinction is made between philosophers who did not write and philosophers who left writings (κατέλιπον ὑπομνήματα). While both συγγράμματα and ὑπομνήματα may have been used in a specific meaning, it is frequently difficult to decide when this is the case. Translators routinely overinterpret these terms, cf. e.g. Hicks's translation of Diogenes Laertius in Loeb, where Xenocrates' συγγράμματα, ἔπη καὶ παραινέσεις are translated as "treatises, poems and addresses" even though several items on the list suggest a dialogue format (4.11–12); he also renders καταλέλοιπε δὲ πάμπλειστα ὑπομνήματα καὶ διαλόγους πλείονας as "he has left behind a vast store of memoirs and numerous dialogues" (in a section about Speusippus), while τάξεις ὑπομνημάτων in the list that follows—as "arrangements of commentaries" (4.4–5).

[6] Kindstrand 1976, 23.    [7] Armstrong 2016, 32, speaking about Greek literature in general.

[8] The narrative of the decline and revival originated in antiquity as a part of a classicizing self-fashioning of late Hellenistic and imperial writers; cf. Dionysius of Halicarnassus, Orat. vett. 1; [Longinus], Subl. 44; Philostratus, VS 511; see also studies by Heldmann 1982; de Jonge 2014; Kim 2014.

[9] Clauss and Cuypers 2010a, 13; see also Cuypers 2010 on some aspects of Hellenistic prose. For changing perceptions of Hellenistic literature, see Kassel 1987; Rengakos 2017.

As the widely accepted narrative of the dialogue's evolution, postulating the genre's decline in the Hellenistic times, mirrors this outdated model of the history of Greek literature, its origins merit a closer inspection.

Hirzel's two-volume comprehensive treatment of the ancient dialogue is certainly a treasury of information, and as such remains an important reference for anyone working on the genre. Yet, his ambition was not merely to collect and discuss the evidence but to produce a grand history of the dialogue, a comprehensive account of its development set against the background of the social and political history of the ancient world. Briefly speaking, he came up with the following model: the dialogue enjoyed *Blüthe*, its blooming-period, under Socratics and reached its high point with Plato. The genre then experienced a gradual decline, *Verfall*, the first symptoms of which were already manifest in the works of Aristotle and his contemporaries. Around this time, dialogue (and philosophy in general) withdrew from public space into scholars' quarters, lost its rapport with life as well as its vitality and freshness, and began to "ail in the air of a classroom." This is the point when other genres, such as the letter and the treatise, began to evolve. These shifts had to do with Aristotle's development of a new scientific method and with changes in the interests of philosophers, who moved from examining people's opinions to an impersonal examination of truth. Even though Aristotle and his contemporaries occasionally composed dialogues out of respect for and in acknowledgement of the genre's previous eminence, the dialogic format remained at odds with what was essentially monologic and dogmatic content.[10]

Hirzel dedicated about sixty pages to what he called "Ueberreste bei den Alexandrinern" ("Remains of the Alexandrians"), where he discussed prose-genres in use in the Hellenistic period. He thought that dialogue suited the intellectual life of fifth-century Athens, but did not fit the geographically expanded world after Alexander the Great—here, a letter was more convenient. He admitted that some types of dialogue persisted, in particular ones that were not cut off from real life—such as, for instance, *symposia*; however, even in this case the genre lost its lofty and free spirit and either focused on specialized knowledge or on crude accounts of sympotic revelry. As a result, "pedants and barbarians reigned where the Hellenic spirit of the good times had yielded such noble blossoms." While Hirzel acknowledged the development of new genres out of dialogue, he did not think that they managed to retain the dialogue's "true spirit": for instance, in the Menippean satire the fine and noble Socratic irony was substituted with a farcical humor that left no space for philosophy or serious investigation.[11] The revival of the dialogue, its *Wiederbelebung*, was possible when the political and social

---

[10] Hirzel 1895a, 273, 307, 309.   [11] Hirzel 1895a, 369, 360, 385.

conditions that allowed for its original development recurred.[12] The key moment, Hirzel thought, came when Greek philosophy entered Rome in the mid-second century BCE. The fruits of this encounter ripened in the late Roman Republic: in its intellectual and political ferment, the dialogue became a peaceful reflection of the civil wars. In the Greek world, dialogue was strengthened under Trajan and Hadrian thanks to the spirit of freedom of the era.[13]

The narrative of the dialogue's evolution and of its three phases (a blooming under Plato and the Socratics, a relapse in the Hellenistic period, and a revival under the Romans) persistent in current scholarship largely overlaps with Hirzel's model. As there has been no comprehensive examination of the genre and its diachronic evolution after Hirzel, it appears probable that the present model owes its existence to the work of the German scholar. Its persistence has been facilitated by the reinterpretation of Hirzel's qualitative degeneration of the dialogue as a mostly quantitative decline. While in 1961 Ingemar Düring still very much followed Hirzel when he noticed that the development of the scientific method by Aristotle was "a turning point in the history of the dialogue" because at this moment the genre lost its main purpose and soon degenerated,[14] scholars later rephrased the narrative and postulated the gradual abandonment of dialogue-writing; as a consequence, the decline narrative acquired an "objective"—and therefore more palatable from a modern perspective—tone.

With the field of post-Classical scholarship flourishing, it is the right time for a reevaluation of the evidence.[15] The purpose of this book is to reassess the notion of the dialogue's decline and argue for its unbroken continuity from the Classical period to the Roman Empire; from the *Sokratikoi logoi* and Plato to Philo of Alexandria, Dio Chrysostom, and Plutarch and other early imperial period authors. This does not mean that the dialogue was a dominant prose form, nor that the majority of philosophical authors composed dialogues. However, evidence demonstrates that dialogues and texts creatively interacting with dialogic conventions were composed throughout Hellenistic times; consequently, the imperial period dialogue should be reconceptualized as evidence not of a resurgence, but of continuity in this literary tradition. As such, the project follows

---

[12] Hirzel 1895a, 417–18. His view that the quality of literature depends on political conditions, and in particular on freedom, is rooted in antiquity; cf. [Longinus], *Subl.* 44 on the potential reasons for literature's decline: "Are we really to believe the hackneyed view that democracy is the kindly nurse of genius and that—speaking generally—the great men of letters flourished only with democracy and perished with it? Freedom, they say, has the power to foster noble minds and fill them with high hopes, and at the same time to rouse our spirit of mutual rivalry and eager competition for the foremost place" (trans. W. H. Fyfe).

[13] Hirzel 1895a, 433; Hirzel 1895b, 84.   [14] Düring 1961, 31.

[15] For a recent reconsideration and reappreciation of late antique Christian dialogues, see Rigolio 2019.

the efforts of other scholars of Hellenistic literature who have stipulated such continuity for various literary forms.[16]

## 0.2 A "Genre" of Dialogue?

Before moving forwards, however, it is necessary to problematize the notion of the dialogue. I have been referring to it as a "genre" and "format," implying a fixed and definable identity and generic stability. Yet it needs to be acknowledged that not only was there no coherent sense of the dialogue as a genre in antiquity, but also that the corpus of ancient texts generally considered dialogues is widely diverse. This does not mean that there were no efforts to create normative definitions postulating the dialogue's generic fixity that would rescue it from becoming an overly baggy category with little taxonomic usefulness. An ancient definition preserved by Diogenes Laertius and Albinus characterizes διάλογος as a discourse consisting of questions and answers (λόγος ἐξ ἐρωτήσεως καὶ ἀποκρίσεως συγκείμενος) on a philosophical or political subject, with proper characterization of the interlocutors and choice of diction.[17] Albinus emphasizes that the question-and-answer format is a feature characteristic of the dialogue (ἴδιον τοῦ διαλόγου ἐρωτήσεις καὶ ἀποκρίσεις) and distinguishes it from other types of spoken discourse, such as narration (ὁ κατὰ διέξοδον λεγόμενος) and verbal exchanges in other genres, for instance, historiography (exchanges in Thucydides are not dialogues, but "speeches set against each other," δημηγορίας κατ' ἐνθύμησιν ἀλλήλαις ἀντιγεγραμμένας). Albinus makes it explicit that his definition is normative when he notes that if a text is called a dialogue, but lacks the features specified, then it has not been rightly assigned the name.[18]

The ancient definition postulates that the dialogue can be defined as a genre by a combination of formal, thematic, stylistic, and linguistic criteria. Such fixity, however, comes at a price. Describing a dialogue as consisting of questions and answers is problematic even when considering Plato's corpus, in which the question-and-answer format is not necessarily a predominant type of speech

---

[16] Cf. Cuypers 2010, 318 on "continuity and shared ground among forms of literary expression and types of intellectual activity across the cultures of the Mediterranean world from the Classical period through the Hellenistic period to the Empire"; this is a common thread among contributions in Clauss and Cuypers 2010b.

[17] Diogenes Laertius 3.48; Albinus, *Intr.* 1. For a discussion, see Nüsser 1991; Ford 2008, 34–5; Charalabopoulos 2012, 24–9; Jazdzewska 2014, 31–2. Other authors alluding to this definition are Theodoretus of Cyrus, *Eranistes* 62: Διαλογικῶς μέντοι ὁ λόγος προβήσεται, ἐρωτήσεις ἔχων καὶ ἀποκρίσεις καὶ προτάσεις καὶ λύσεις καὶ ἀντιθέσεις, καὶ τὰ ἄλλα ὅσα τοῦ διαλογικοῦ ἴδια χαρακτῆρος; the anonymous author of the *Prolegomena in Platonic Philosophy* 14.3–4 and 15.31–2; *Suda* s.v. διαλεκτική (δ 627); Ps.-Zonaras s.v. διαλεκτική; Tzetzes, *Chil.* 10.355.783–5. See also the association between the dialogue and the question-and-answer in Lucian, *Bis acc.* 34 and Proclus, *In Alc. I* 274.3–4 Westerink.

[18] For other ancient remarks on the dialogue, see Aygon 2002; Dubel 2015.

representation. In some dialogues, speeches, myths, and non-erotapocritic exchanges dominate over the question-and-answer format or even replace it—think of *Symposion* or *Timaeus*—but one would hardly hesitate to call them dialogues for that reason.[19] From the perspective of a modern scholar studying the ancient dialogue, other criteria appearing in Albinus and Diogenes Laertius seem likewise overly restrictive. Insisting on "a philosophical or political subject," even broadly conceived,[20] would exclude some of Lucian's dialogues. The criteria of "proper characterization" and "proper diction" obfuscate the wide spectrum of ethopoietic and stylistic strategies employed by ancient authors. As my aim is to explore diachronic developments in the dialogue—and therefore, in particular, its metamorphoses, transmutations, and deviations from earlier traditions—a rigid, normative approach will not do; a broader perspective is needed.

In recent scholarship, in which a diversity of ancient dialogue formats has been increasingly acknowledged, dialogue has been defined as a prose work reporting a conversation between a number of characters in direct speech.[21] Such a definition, focusing on external form without specifying thematic and stylistic criteria, appears straightforward and practicable. However, if used as a taxonomic yardstick, it proves less helpful than one would wish. In particular, the distinction between a dialogue and a narrative *diegesis* with embedded dialogized sections remains problematic.[22] This is not an imagined dilemma, but one exemplified by several imperial period works—which are instructive insofar as they represent potentialities in lost Hellenistic prose. Is the first half of Dio Chrysostom's *Euboean Oration* a dialogue or a narrative with dialogic exchanges? What about his *Oration 8*, the majority of which consists of a conversation between Diogenes

---

[19] As Ford 2008, 35 observes, "Albinus' identification of dialogue with the exchange of question and answer is logical and etymologically sound, but seems to reflect the philosophy teacher's need to bear down on the arguments in such texts at the expense of their formal variety."

[20] For the problem as to what constitutes a philosophical subject, see Hösle 2006, 54–5 who defines the philosophical dialogue as "ein literarisches Genre, das eine Unterredung über philosophische Fragen darstellt" and the philosophical questions very broadly as "Fragen, die die Prinzipien unseres Wissens und Handelns betreffen."

[21] On dialogue as a polymorphic genre, see Dubel 2015, 12; Rigolio 2019, 8–9. For various definitions, see e.g. Görgemanns 1997, 517: "eine Gattung der Prosalit.... welche in direkter Rede ein Gespräch zwischen mehreren Personen wiedergibt"; Föllinger and Müller 2013, 2: "ein im Medium der Schrift gestaltetes Gespräch in direkter Rede zwischen verschiedenen Figuren"; Cox 1992, 2: "It may be safe to venture a definition of the dialogue as an exchange between two or more voices, but, beyond this unhelpfully low common denominator, even the most cautious generalizations are doomed to founder under the weight of the exceptions they create."

[22] For a narratological perspective on the relationship between the dialogue and the narrative, cf. e.g. Whitmarsh 2004, 470 who observes that in case of Lucian "too firm a distinction should not be drawn between the dialogic and non-dialogic works" as "there is a substantial degree of crossover between the roles of narrators and narratees." De Jong 2004, 7–8 proposes to consider even dramatic dialogues as "narratives with a suppressed primary narrator and suppressed primary narratees"; this is the perspective assumed by Morgan 2004, 358 who considers all Plato's dialogues as narratives; see also Finkelberg 2018, 2 who emphasizes that "Plato unambiguously classifies mimetic genres as a subcategory of diegesis" and therefore "his dramatic dialogues should be approached as no less diegetic than the narrated ones." While this approach allows one to apply narratological tools to dialogues, it risks obfuscating the distinctiveness of dialogized works.

the Cynic and an anonymous passer-by at the Isthmian Games? If nothing else, are they not noteworthy as belonging to the fringes of dialogue literature? Other fringe cases include longer *chreiai* and dialogized anecdotes, as well as prose mimes.[23] On the other hand, scholars feel uneasy about labeling as dialogues works which formally belong to this category, but betray little conversational dynamics and are filled mostly by lengthy continuous speeches by a particular interlocutor. For this reason, some of Plutarch's texts with dialogic openings (therefore formally framed as reports of conversations) yet consisting mostly of one character's lengthy excursus are frequently referred to as "treatises" or "essays."[24]

Bearing these difficulties in mind, I will not focus on taxonomy or establish a demarcation line between a dialogue and other prose forms. In fact, I think it is important to acknowledge that volatility and change marked dialogue literature since its emergence. Writing about the Renaissance dialogue, Virginia Cox observed that the dialogue had eluded "the net of traditional genre criticism" because of the "sheer variety of different 'kinds' of writing encompassed by this most slippery of terms."[25] This is no less true of the ancient dialogue, even in its early phase of development. From its beginnings, the dialogue has been characterized by fluidity and a Protean character rooted in and conditioned by its Socratic origins, when numerous competing students of Socrates took on the task of writing down, in their own styles and manners, divergent versions of Socrates' conversations. The Platonic corpus itself, which bears witness to Plato's untiring intellectual, formal, and stylistic experimentation, ratified and encouraged the dialogue's flexibility: besides works such as *Crito* or *Euthyphro*, consisting of lively exchanges, it encompasses works dominated by speeches and long utterances, such as *Timaeus*, *Critias*, and *Laws*. Early dialogues blended, in various proportions and configurations, internal or external narration, dialectical exchanges, casual conversations, continuous speeches, and stories.[26] The number

---

[23] For discussion of prose mime and its mimetic character in the context of dialogue literature, see Ford 2010; Charalabopoulos 2012, 47–9. Hösle 2006, 53 n. 64 proposes that most of Lucian's dialogues are closer to mime than to philosophical dialogues understood as accounts of discussions.

[24] Dillon 1996², 187 includes several of Plutarch's works framed as conversations among "serious philosophical treatises" and "treatises of a polemical nature"; Flacelière 1987, ccxvi–ccxvii in his typology of Plutarch's dialogues distinguishes "treatises introduced by a short dialogic exchange between two characters"; Van der Stockt 2000, 105 defines a dialogue as "the act of organizing many voices involved in a quest" and distinguishes between Plutarch's "dialogical" and "monological" dialogues; the latter category contains seven "dialogues" that "do not hold up the fiction of *altercatio*" (116).

[25] Cox 1992, 2.

[26] One conventionally distinguishes three types of dialogue, based on formal criteria: (1) diegetic (also referred to as narrated or reported), (2) dramatic (consisting exclusively of direct speech), and (3) mixed (a narrated conversation is nested within a dramatic-dialogue frame). For ancient categories of dramatic, diegematic, and mixed dialogues, cf. Diogenes Laertius 3.50; Plutarch, *Quaest. conv.* 711b-c; for ancient classifications and their unclarities, Nüsser 1991, 187–204, 238–42. For the rhetorical efficacy of mixing conversational and exploratory exchanges cf. [Hermogenes], *Meth.* 36.455: dialogue combines "ethical and investigative speeches. Whenever you intermingle conversation and inquiry, the

of interlocutors varied as well as the degree of their characterization. As far as length is considered, dialogue writers took great liberty, as a comparison between Plato's *Ion* (around four thousand words) and his *Laws* (more than one hundred thousand words) demonstrates. Xenophon's *Apomnemoneumata* are affiliated with memoir literature and anecdote and collate numerous conversations within one work, with narration acting as a unifying factor. Socratic dialogues examined a diversity of themes, including ethics and politics, music and literature, education and sciences, religion, love, etymology, theology, cosmology, and more. They fostered methodical intellectual inquiry, but also permitted miscellaneous digressions;[27] they could be aporetic or dogmatic, they could question and problematize or provide positive instruction. They pursued the truth by means of argument, while at the same time engaging in the process of fiction-writing; they advanced the development of artistic prose and were capable of a broad stylistic range, even within a single work.[28] In addition, from early on the dialogue interacted with a variety of other literary formats, both prosaic and poetic, and enthusiastically absorbed them, becoming a form particularly "hospitable to other prose genres."[29] As a consequence, the early phase of the dialogue's development did not provide subsequent authors with a stable, uniform generic matrix to engage with, but rather with a miscellany of works whose common denominator was that at their core there was a record of a conversation or discussion (or a series of them), originally probably with Socrates as the interlocutor, though both Plato and Xenophon also wrote non-Socratic dialogues.

The diversity of the early dialogic tradition invited and spurred further innovations. As next generations of dialogue writers parted with the Socratic backdrop, the author-figure and his intellectual environment gained significance; or alternately, other historical and mythical backgrounds were put to work, allowing a

---

ethical speeches that are interspersed refresh the mind, and when one is refreshed, the inquiry is brought in, like the tension and relaxing of an instrument" (trans. G. A. Kennedy). "Ethical" passages are ones that reflect a speaker's character.

[27] Cf. a remark by Galileo, who in the *Dialogue Concerning the Two Chief World-Systems* notes that he chose the dialogue form because it is not "restricted to the rigorous observance of the mathematical laws," but "make[s] room also for digressions which are sometimes not less interesting than the principal argument" (trans. S. Drake).

[28] The stylistic complexity of the dialogue was according to Diogenes Laertius acknowledged by Aristotle, who said that in terms of style the dialogue partook of both poetry and prose (3.37: μεταξὺ ποιήματος εἶναι καὶ πεζοῦ λόγου). For the stylistic freedom, cf. Quintilian on *dialogorum libertas* (*Inst.* 10.5.15); for the diversity of styles used by Plato, see Thesleff 1967.

[29] Ford 2008, 41. For Plato's dialogues' easy absorption and interaction with other genres, see Nightingale 1995, 2 who observes that Plato "exhibits a positive hankering for the hybrid in so many of his texts" and "mixes traditional genres of discourse into his dialogues and disrupts the generic boundaries of both his own texts and the texts that he targets." For Segoloni (2012, 339 and 349) dialogue is "un ibrido o un incrocio...un genere che anche probabilmente per questa sua natura ambivalente e ibrida è per così dire sfugitto nell'insieme all'attività descrittiva e normativa di retori, critici letterari e eruditi antichi"; he argues that "l'intreccio e la mescolanza di generi diversi, sia sul piano letterario la cifra e il gene constitutive del dialogo." Averintsev 2001 emphasizes the fluidity of many Greek "younger genres" (that is, genres other than epic, tragedy, comedy, lyric formats, and certain rhetorical ones), but argues against the notion of their hybridization, which presupposes clear generic identities (for a critique of the concept of hybridity, see also Allen 2013).

writer to imagine characters deliberating and debating in a variety of political and historical circumstances. The early dialogue's propensity to absorb and assimilate other genres persisted in later centuries, when it readily interacted with newly developed formats such as, for instance, *zetemata*, consolation, and paradoxography, as we will see in the book. Substantial dialogized sections, on the other hand, were incorporated in other types of prose narratives, for example, in letters and works of a biographical or anecdotal character. Such mergers of various templates and discursive strategies belong to the history of the dialogue and constitute significant contributions to its transformations.[30]

## 0.3 Structure of the Book

The book is conceived as a study of the Greek dialogue in the period of its putative decline. The time covered spans four centuries, from the mid-fourth century BCE to the mid-first century CE. While I use "Hellenistic" as a shorthand term for this period, the time frame does not overlap with what is customarily referred to as the Hellenistic era (stretching from Alexander's death in 323 BCE to the battle of Actium in 31 BCE), but extends back into the fourth century to accommodate early successors of Plato and into the mid-first century CE to allow for inclusion of little-known dialogues by Philo of Alexandria, predating works by Plutarch and Dio Chrysostom. The chronological boundaries are to be considered somewhat fluid, as it is frequently impossible to attach a firm date to fragments, anonymous texts, and less-known authors.

Greek literature in the period examined in this book was widely heterogenous. The societal and political circumstances behind the writing of the literature examined here were changing throughout this period as the power balance shifted from Athens to other Greek cities and next to new political centers established outside of mainland Greece by Hellenistic monarchs, many of whom stimulated, encouraged, and influenced literary production in their regions. There followed the gradual military and political expansion of Rome and consolidation of the Mediterranean world under the Roman Empire. Use of the Greek language and education spread east and west throughout this multi-ethnic, heterogenous world. Greek literature was shaped by a shared education and literary tradition on one hand, and by distinctive regional social and political stimuli on the other, though

---

[30] For recent discussions on genre-blending in antiquity, see Gallo 1998, 3520; Papanghelis et al. 2013; Greatrex and Elton 2015. Morgan 2011, 49 talks of the "fertility of genres" and notes of the imperial period that: "Genres freely cross-bred: history with philosophy, biography, or apologetic; epic with fable; grammar with dialogue." For incisive examination of Lucian's dialogues as generic hybrids, see Baumbach and von Möllendorf 2017, 176–209. Fowler 1982, 45 considers generic blending an essential trait of European literature: "...if we describe the genres in fuller detail, we find ourselves coming to grips with local and temporary groupings, perpetually contending with historical alterations in them. For they everywhere change, combine, regroup, or form what seems to be new alignments altogether."

the scarcity of evidence makes it difficult to trace these evolutions and regional characteristics in detail. Literature in this period was erudite and conspicuously aware of its predecessors, yet also excitingly innovative and marked by stylistic and formal experimentation. Its learnedness, allusivity, and fondness for antiquarian knowledge was paralleled by self-reflexivity, irony, and liking for generic hybridization. Prose and poetry stimulated and influenced each other; scientific, scholarly, and philological interests, both linguistic and literary, as well as literary criticism, were vigorously pursued.[31] In philosophy, it was a period marked by the crystallization and evolution of philosophical schools as well as by the popularization of new formats of philosophical writings, as has already been mentioned, such as the systematical or polemical treatise and continuous discourse of a protreptic or paraenetic character, as well as the consolation, philosophical letter, and commentary.[32] It is against the backdrop of this vibrant and shifting literary and intellectual culture that the remains of Hellenistic dialogue literature collected and examined in the book should be considered.

The book consists of six chapters. The first one, titled "Dialogic Entanglements," traces some of the ways in which the post-Platonic dialogue interacted and blended with other prose forms: anecdote, letter, and biography. Its goal is to widen our understanding of the dialogue and examine cases in which boundaries become fluid—as when anecdotes are conversed into dialogues and dialogue snippets into anecdotes, or when letter authors and biographers report conversations and philosophical discussions. Chapter 2 provides an overview and examination of dialogue fragments in papyri. Despite difficulties encountered when studying this evidence, papyri fragments provide a significant contribution to our knowledge about the use of the dialogue, which was not limited to philosophical inquiry: apart from philosophical dialogues we find in the papyri also, for instance, dialogues on literature, which betray the influence of Peripatetic and Alexandrian scholarship, and historical dialogues with a rhetorical flavor. Chapters 3–6 systematically examine various post-Platonic philosophical traditions: the employment of the dialogue in the Academy and by authors of the pseudo-Platonica (Chapters 3 and 4); by Aristotle and his followers (Chapter 5); and in other intellectual environments, from the Minor Socratic schools of the Megarians and Cyrenaics, to the major Hellenistic traditions—the Cynics, Stoics, and Epicureans—and from Timon of Phlius and Eratosthenes of Cyrene to Philo of Alexandria and the *Tablet of Cebes* (Chapter 6). In the Epilogue, I identify some emergent trends and lines of development in the post-Platonic dialogue and point to recurrent literary strategies which affiliate the post-Platonic dialogue with broader trends of Hellenistic literature and its aesthetics.

---

[31] For general discussions of the most salient features of Hellenistic literature, see recent discussions: Krevans and Sens 2006; Gutzwiller 2007; contributions in Clauss and Cuypers 2010b; and Hutchinson 2014.

[32] White 2010.

# 1
# Dialogic Entanglements

## 1.1 Introductory Remarks

The purpose of this chapter is to expand our understanding of the dialogue by tracing some of the ways in which it interacts and blends with other prose forms: anecdote, epistolography, and biography. The dialogue's relationship with anecdotal and biographical literature is multifaceted. As Arnaldo Momigliano observed in *The Development of Greek Biography*, Socratic dialogues were essentially an experiment in biography, as the Socratics were preoccupied, at least at some level, with recollecting and recreating the life, words, and deeds of Socrates. At the same time, they moved beyond the factual realm and explored the potential rather than the real Socrates, thus situating themselves in the ambiguous space between truth and imagination.[1] Xenophon's *Apomnemoneumata* ("recollections"), with their episodic structure and anecdotal modules, proved to be a particularly important precedent for Hellenistic prose and its oscillation between biography, anecdote, and dialogue; for this reason I will begin with it.

## 1.2 Dialogue and Anecdote

It has been long recognized that Xenophon's *Apomnemoneumata* have been influenced by earlier biographical literature formats. The work is a collection of dialogues and short exchanges between Socrates and named or anonymous interlocutors, interwoven with his sayings and speeches as well as interventions by the narrator of various lengths. Apart from the Socratic dialogue, two chief influences have been identified, namely the *chreia*[2] and memoir literature. The influence of *chreia* on Xenophon's work is particularly apparent in passages in which Xenophon quotes Socrates' responses or sayings without quoting in direct speech the words of the other person engaged in the interaction—as when he precedes Socrates' responses with the participle ἐρωτώμενος ("when asked," *Mem.* 3.9.1) or

---

[1] Momigliano 1971, 46. For the importance of Socrates for development of biographical literature, see Dihle 1956, 13–20, 29–34; Gallo 1980, 169–76.
[2] The term *chreia* (χρεία) was fluid in antiquity and at times synonymous with *apophthegma, gnome,* and *apomnemoneuma* (Searby 2019). I will use it in the meaning codified by late antique rhetorical textbooks, and conventional in modern scholarship, that is in reference to a short anecdote involving a historical person of interest, usually containing a memorable, pointed saying.

with genitive absolute constructions such as ἐρομένου δέ τινος αὐτόν ("when someone asked him," *Mem.* 3.9.14), ἄλλου λέγοντος ("when someone else said," *Mem.* 3.13.2, 3.13.3, 3.13.6), φοβουμένου τινος ("when someone was afraid," *Mem.* 3.13.5).[3] Consider, for instance, the anecdote in *Mem.* 3.13.1:

> Ὀργιζομένου δέ ποτέ τινος, ὅτι προσειπών τινα χαίρειν οὐκ ἀντιπροσερρήθη, "Γελοῖον," ἔφη, "τό, εἰ μὲν τὸ σῶμα κάκιον ἔχοντι ἀπήντησάς τῳ, μὴ ἂν ὀργίζεσθαι, ὅτι δὲ τὴν ψυχὴν ἀγροικοτέρως διακειμένῳ περιέτυχες, τοῦτό σε λυπεῖ."

> On a man who was angry because his greeting was not returned: "Ridiculous!" he exclaimed; "you would not have been angry if you had met a man in worse health; and yet you are annoyed because you have come across someone with ruder manners!"[4] (trans. E. C. Marchant)

This passage has several features recurrent in ancient *chreiai*: there is an anonymous person whose behavior, rendered in a genitive absolute construction, spurs Socrates' reaction. Socrates' comment takes the form of a succinct saying and relies on analogical reasoning. The reaction of the unnamed man is not recorded, and therefore the reader's attention remains focused on the essential part of the anecdote, that is, Socrates' words.

At the same time, Xenophon's work gives the impression of being a memoir of sorts. The Greek title under which it has been preserved—namely, Ἀπομνημονεύματα ("memories, recollections")—reflects Xenophon's purpose to preserve the remembrances of Socrates.[5] The episodic and relaxed structure of the text reinforces the feeling that we are being provided with a memoir, as does the first-person voice of the narrator. This aspect of Xenophon's text might have informed the ancient opinion preserved in Diogenes Laertius that Xenophon in the *Apomnemoneumata* "was the first to note down (ὑποσημειωσάμενος) and circulate among people the conversations of Socrates" (2.48). In this respect, Xenophon's work is reminiscent of Ion of Chios's *Epidemiai*, which described

---

[3] For the *chreia* and Xenophon's *Apomnemoneumata*, see Hirzel 1895a, 145; Momigliano 1971, 53; for the influence of pre-Socratic anecdotal tradition on *Sokratikoi logoi* and philosophical biography, Wehrli 1973. For collections of sayings before Xenophon, see Gray 1998, 174–7 who argues for the chief influence of *chreia* and wisdom literature on the *Apomnemoneumata* (according to her, Xenophon is "Socratizing" the *chreia*; see pp. 179–80).

[4] For the Greek text of Xenophon's *Apomnemoneumata* I follow Bandini and Dorion 2000a.

[5] The provenance of the title is unclear; it might have come from Xenophon himself or from a (Hellenistic?) editor of his work. Xenophon states the intention to write down his memories in *Mem.* 1.3.1: γράψω ὁπόσα ἂν διαμνημονεύσω (cf. *Mem.* 4.1.1: τὸ ἐκείνου μεμνῆσθαι and Bandini and Dorion 2000b, 124 n. 185). Koester 1989, 377 n. 3 argued that there is no evidence for the title before the imperial period and that ἀπομνημονεύματα "was not used for philosophers' memoirs before the Second Sophistic in the 2nd c. CE"; but relative consistency of the tradition concerning the title makes it unlikely that the text circulated under a different name in the Hellenistic period. There is also ample evidence for existence of other Hellenistic works titled *Apomnemoneumata* which I discuss later in this chapter.

the author's memories of famous people, including Aeschylus, Sophocles, and Cimon.[6] A passage from the *Epidemiai* quoted in Athenaeus' *Deipnosophists* describes Sophocles' stay at Chios, which Ion claims to have witnessed. The tragedian participated in a feast there. Ion says that he was witty and playful when drinking and reports in direct speech the poet's banquet conversations: first with a pretty slave boy and then with an anonymous guest from Eretria on the subject of the poetry of Phrynichus and Simonides (Athenaeus, *Deipn.* 13.603f–604d [*BNJ* 392 F 6]). From Plutarch (*Cim.* 9.1-6 [*BNJ* 392 F 13]) we learn that Ion also described a feast at Athens in which he participated as a young man together with Cimon; this passage also, in all probability, appeared in the *Epidemiai*. Plutarch's summary suggests that in this case as well Ion reported a banquet-conversation, this time with Cimon as a speaker. The *Epidemiai* have been rightly referred to as "proto-dialogic" and considered as a forerunner of the Socratic and Platonic dialogue; the resemblance between them and Xenophon's *Apomnemoneumata*—in terms of episodicity and the memoir-character—suggests that the format of the latter might have been informed by Ion's work.[7]

The deliberate formal variety and inconsistency of Xenophon's *Apomnemoneumata* as a collection of short dialogues, anecdotes, and sayings, as well as its ties with the anecdote and early biographical/memoir literature, on the other, provides an important precedent for Hellenistic literature. There is evidence that Xenophon's work influenced a host of subsequent writers.[8] Diogenes Laertius (7.1, 7.4) relates that after coming to Athens, Zeno of Citium went into a bookshop and started reading the second book of the *Apomnemoneumata*. He liked it so much that he asked the bookseller where such men can be found and was showed Crates of Thebes; later he authored *Apomnemoneumata of Crates*. Other authors said to have composed *Apomnemoneumata* include the Megarian Alexinus of Elis and the Stoics Persaeus and Aristo of Chios.[9] Philodemus in the *History of the Academy* (*Acad. ind.* col. vi.10) mentions that Erastus and Asclepiades wrote *Apomnemoneumata of Plato*. Diogenes Laertius (4.2) draws information about Speusippus' teachings from some Diodorus' *Apomnemoneumata*; we also have

---

[6] Ion might have referred to these stories as his memories; cf. Plutarch, *Cim.* 16.10 [*BNJ* 392 F 14], about Cimon: ὁ δ' Ἴων ἀπομνημονεύει καὶ τὸν λόγον, ᾧ μάλιστα τοὺς Ἀθηναίους ἐκίνησε.... For the format of the *Epidemiai*, dated to 430s or early 420s BCE, see West 1985, 75: a "pioneering work... [n]either biography nor dialogue literature, it had something to do with the origins of both." Dover 1986, 33–4 points to remarkable similarity with Xenophon's *Apomnemoneumata* and postulates that the *Epidemiai* "should be given a place in the genealogy of the Socratic dialogues of Plato." Jennings and Katsaros 2007, 5 characterize it as comprising of a series of anecdotes "whose proto-dialogic form sits tantalizingly between the scattered apophthegmatic vignettes about the Seven Wise Men (or Simonides) and the more fully developed 'biography' manifest in Xenophon's works, or the *Lives of the Poets*, or the Platonic dialogues."

[7] Interestingly, Ion also wrote about Socrates' journey to Samos with Archelaus (Diogenes Laertius 2.23).

[8] Untersteiner 1980, 66–8.

[9] Alexinus: Eusebius, *PE* 15.2.4; Persaeus and Aristo of Chios: Diogenes Laertius 7.36 and 7.163.

references to *Apomnemoneumata* by Dioscurides (which contained, among others, anecdotes about Solon and Plato), Empedus (from which we have a piece of anecdotal information about Zeno), and Lynceus of Samos, a pupil of Theophrastus and a brother of Duris.[10] Bacchius of Tanagra, a medical doctor from the third century BCE, wrote Ἀπομνημονεύματα Ἡροφίλου τε καὶ τῶν ἀπὸ τῆς οἰκίας αὐτοῦ, *Apomnemoneumata of Herophilus and Those of his School*, which collected anecdotes about his teacher Herophilus and his fellow students.[11] Some of these books (Zeno's *Apomnemoneumata of Crates*, Bacchius' text, perhaps also Erastus' and Asclepiades' *Apomnemoneumata of Plato*) presumably were, like Xenophon's work, students' memories of their teacher; other works might have been miscellaneous collections of anecdotes about various people.

Although it is difficult to determine how extensive the employment of the dialogue format was in these texts, some of them certainly reported extended conversations. Eusebius of Caesarea quotes a criticism of the Megarian Alexinus by Aristocles the Peripatetic (*PE* 15.2.4 [F 90 Döring]):

Καταγέλαστα δ' εἰκότως εἶναι φαίη τις ἂν καὶ τὰ Ἀπομνημονεύματα τὰ Ἀλεξίνου τοῦ Ἐριστικοῦ. ποιεῖ γὰρ Ἀλέξανδρον παῖδα διαλεγόμενον Φιλίππῳ τῷ πατρὶ καὶ διαπτύοντα μὲν τοὺς τοῦ Ἀριστοτέλους λόγους, ἀποδεχόμενον δὲ Νικαγόραν, τὸν Ἑρμῆν ἐπικληθέντα.

One may also reasonably say that the *Memoirs* of Alexinus the Eristic are ridiculous. For he makes Alexander when a boy, in conversation with his father Philip, pour contempt upon Aristotle's doctrines, while approving Nicagoras, called Hermes.   (trans. M. L. Chiesara)

The passage appears to be a direct quotation of Aristocles; it refers to a section in Alexinus' work which relates a conversation between young Alexander and his father.[12] We do not know what aspect of Aristotle's teachings Alexander was criticizing (literally "spat on"). It is also unclear what was Alexinus' aim: was it a polemic with Aristotle, a presentation of the character and early inspirations of young Alexander, or a discussion of monarchy?[13] The conversation might

---

[10] Dioscurides: Diogenes Laertius 1.63 and Athenaeus, *Deipn*. 11.507d; Empedus: Athenaeus, *Deipn*. 9.370c; Lynceus of Samos: Athenaeus, *Deipn*. 6.248d.

[11] For Bacchius and his work, see von Staden 1999, 158–60. Galen preserves an anecdote about a doctor Callianax, who, when a patient said "I am going to die," responded with a quotation from a tragedy: "Unless Leto, blessed with fair children, gave birth to you"; to another one he said: "Patroclus, too, died, and he was much better than you" (*In Hipp. Epid*. VI 4.10.145 *CMG*).

[12] The wording ποιεῖ γὰρ Ἀλέξανδρον παῖδα διαλεγόμενον Φιλίππῳ suggests that passage was not a short anecdote but a conversation of some length. For a similar phrase, cf. Plutarch, *Adv. Col.* 1109e-f: ἐν τῷ Συμποσίῳ Πολύαινον αὐτῷ διαλεγόμενον Ἐπίκουρος πεποίηκε.

[13] Alexinus, who belonged to the Megarian school and was known as *Elenksinos* (Diogenes Laertius 2.109), wrote an ethical work titled *On Self-Sufficiency* and a *paian* for Craterus (Athenaeus, *Deipn*. 10.418e, 15.696e). This suggests a diverse literary output and makes it difficult to narrow down possible options. On the Megarians, see also Chapter 6.2.

have implied Aristotle's didactic inaptitude (after all, his pupil was depicted as preferring Nicagoras, the tyrant of Zeleia), or exonerated the philosopher (and philosophy in general) from blame for influencing Alexander's future behaviors. Nicagoras appears to have claimed divine honors for himself; perhaps the young Alexander approved of his self-deification, which would foreshadow his later actions as a ruler.[14] Regardless of the actual scope, Aristocles' testimony indicates that a dialogue between Alexander and Philip was embedded in Alexinus' *Apomnemoneumata*.[15]

While we may assume that Hellenistic *apomnemoneumata*-texts included, following the example of Xenophon, longer dialogized sections, such sections certainly also appeared in works transmitted under other titles. In particular, there is evidence that works titled *Hypomnemata* and *Chreiai*, which included similar material of an anecdotal and biographical nature, also contained longer dialogized sections. For instance, Athenaeus quotes a fragment from the *Sympotic Hypomnemata* by the Stoic Persaeus reporting a visit by Arcadian delegates to the court of Antigonus Gonatas. The event was apparently narrated by someone who claimed to have witnessed it himself: this is suggested by the phrases ὃ καὶ πρώην ἐγένετο ("this happened the other day") and οὐχ ... ἡμῶν τινα προσβλέποντες ("not looking at any of us," of the Arcadian envoys) (*Deipn.* 13.607a–e [*SVF* 1.100 F 451]).[16] This suggests that the section was written in a dialogue form and that the narrator was relating events he had witnessed to other interlocutors.

As for *Chreiai*, we know that the term χρεία, which later meant a short anecdote with a pointed saying, did not have a fixed meaning in the early Hellenistic period. Diogenes Laertius ascribes *Chreiai* to many philosophers, including Aristippus of Cyrene, Demetrius of Phaleron, Diogenes the Cynic, Metrocles, Zeno, Persaeus, Aristo of Chios, and Hecato.[17] Although we do not have much direct evidence about the form of these works, some insight may be gained from a work by the comic poet Machon. He composed the poetic *Chreiai*, which are dated to the

---

[14] For the evidence on Nicagoras, see Schorn 2014b, with Aristocles' testimony discussed at 82–3.

[15] Such a dialogue, composed merely few decades after Alexander's death, is a noteworthy specimen of the Alexander-dialogue, a sub-category in dialogue literature known to us from papyri (see Chapter 2.6.1) and Dio Chrysostom, whose *Second* and *Fourth Kingship Oration* are dialogues with Alexander as interlocutor. The former depicts Alexander as a youth (μειράκιον ὄντα) in a conversation with Philip and ends with Philip's praise of Aristotle.

[16] Persaeus' *Sympotic Hypomnemata* might have been identical with the *Sympotic Dialogues* ascribed to him elsewhere (so Steinmetz 1994, 556 and Pohlenz 1980⁵, 15, who also thought that it is the same work as the *Apomnemoneumata* listed by Diogenes Laertius 7.36). The titles *Apomnemoneumata* and *Hypomnemata* were sometimes mixed on account of the phonetic and semantic similarity: Xenophon's *Apomnemoneumata* are titled *Hypomnemoneumata* (sic) in one manuscript, and Favorinus' *Apomnemoneumata* are once referred to as *Hypomnemata* (Diogenes Laertius 8.53); cf. Mensching 1963, 26.

[17] Aristippus: Diogenes Laertius 2.84, 2.85; Demetrius of Phaleron: 5.81; Diogenes the Cynic: 6.80; Metrocles: 6.33; Zeno: 6.91; Persaeus: 7.36; Aristo of Chios: 7.163; Hecato: 6.4, 6.32, 6.95, 7.26, 7.172.

mid-third century BCE; the work contained anecdotes about parasites, *hetairai*, poets, and musicians.[18] Substantial fragments preserved by Athenaeus indicate that Machon's work was intended as a parody of the philosophical counterparts; consequently, we may assume that it retained some formal features of the parodied genre.[19] The fragments preserved in Athenaeus typically contain a narratorial introduction followed by a direct-speech exchange between two interlocutors. The exchange is sometimes of considerable length, as in the anecdote about the poet Philoxenus, a glutton, who became ill after eating a big octopus. A doctor visited him and said (*Deipn.* 8.341b–d [F 9 Gow]):

"εἴ τί σοι ἀνοικονόμητόν ἐστι, διατίθου ταχύ, Φιλόξεν᾽· ἀποθανῇ γὰρ ὥρας ἑβδόμης." κἀκεῖνος εἶπε, "τέλος ἔχει τὰ πάντα μοι, ἰατρέ," φησί, "καὶ δεδιῴκηται πάλαι. τοὺς διθυράμβους σὺν θεοῖς καταλιμπάνω ἠνδρωμένους καὶ πάντας ἐστεφανωμένους, οὓς ἀνατίθημι ταῖς ἐμαυτοῦ συντρόφοις Μούσαις. Ἀφροδίτην καὶ Διόνυσον ἐπιτρόπους—ταῦθ᾽ αἱ διαθῆκαι διασαφοῦσιν. ἀλλ᾽ ἐπεὶ ὁ Τιμοθέου Χάρων σχολάζειν οὐκ ἐᾷ, οὐκ τῆς Νιόβης, χωρεῖν δὲ πορθμὸν ἀναβοᾷ, καλεῖ δὲ μοῖρα νύχιος ἧς κλύειν χρεών, ἵν᾽ ἔχων ἀποτρέχω πάντα τἀμαυτοῦ κάτω, τοῦ πουλύποδός μοι τὸ κατάλοιπον ἀπόδοτε."

"If you've got any business that needs to be taken care of, do it right away, Philoxenus; because you'll be dead by mid-afternoon." He responded: "My affairs are all in order, doctor," he said, "and have been settled for a while now. With the gods' help, the dithyrambs I'm leaving behind have all grown up and been awarded garlands, and I'm entrusting them to the care of the Muses I grew up with. That Aphrodite and Dionysus are my executors, my will makes clear. But since Timotheus' Charon, the one from his *Niobe*, is not allowing me to linger, but is shouting for me to proceed to the ferry, and my night-dark fate, which I must heed, is calling—so that I can run off to the Underworld with everything that's mine: give me the rest of that octopus!"    (trans. S. D. Olson)

The fragment reads like a parody of a philosophical dialogue on death, a subcategory of dialogue literature that originated with Plato's *Phaedo*, as it depicts the gluttonous Philoxenus as being philosophically unmoved by his imminent death—that is, as long as he gets to eat the rest of the octopus. As Pauline LeVen pointed out, his last words—τοῦ πουλύποδός μοι τὸ κατάλοιπον ἀπόδοτε—parody the famous last words of Socrates: Ὦ Κρίτων, ἔφη, τῷ Ἀσκληπιῷ ὀφείλομεν

---

[18] For a discussion of the fragments and dating of Machon's work, see Gow 1965.

[19] According to Davidson 1997, 93 Machon's work was "an ironic versified counterpart to the collection of philosophical anecdotes such as Xenophon's *Memoirs*." Kurke 2002, 23 speaks of "a parody or send-up of the philosophical tradition." On terminological grounds, it is noteworthy that Athenaeus twice refers to Machon's anecdotes as *apomnemoneumata* (*Deipn.* 8.348e, 13.579d).

ἀλεκτρυόνα· ἀλλὰ ἀπόδοτε καὶ μὴ ἀμελήσητε (Plato, *Phd.* 118a).²⁰ Philoxenus' death also mirrors the death of Diogenes the Cynic who, according to some sources, died after eating a raw octopus.²¹

Additional evidence that Hellenistic works of biographic and anecdotic nature included longer dialogized passages comes from two papyri, PVindob. G 29946 and POxy. 52.3655 (discussed in Chapters 2.5.2 and 2.5.3), which preserve anecdotes about Diogenes of Sinope and a conversation between Stilpo of Megara and Metrocles the Cynic. PVindob. G 29946 originates from the mid-third century BCE and is the earliest preserved text that speaks of Diogenes the Cynic. It includes several dialogized anecdotes, considerably longer and more complex than a standard *chreia*. POxy. 52.3655 contains an exchange between Stilpo and Metrocles, the character of which is reminiscent of Xenophon's *Apomnemoneumata*; while the papyrus itself comes from the imperial period, scholars agree that it preserves a text composed in early Hellenistic times. It might have been the same work from which Plutarch drew the following exchange between Stilpo and Metrocles (*De tranq. anim.* 468a [SSR II O 17]):

ὥσπερ οὐδὲ Στίλπωνα τῶν κατ' αὐτὸν φιλοσόφων ἱλαρώτατα ζῆν ἀκόλαστος οὖσ' ἡ θυγάτηρ· ἀλλὰ καὶ Μητροκλέους ὀνειδίσαντος "ἐμὸν οὖν" ἔφη "ἁμάρτημα τοῦτ' ἐστὶν ἢ ἐκείνης;" εἰπόντος δὲ τοῦ Μητροκλέους "ἐκείνης μὲν ἁμάρτημα σὸν δ' ἀτύχημα" "πῶς λέγεις;" εἶπεν "οὐχὶ τὰ ἁμαρτήματα καὶ διαπτώματ' ἐστί;" "πάνυ μὲν οὖν" ἔφη. "τὰ δὲ διαπτώματ' οὐχ ὧν διαπτώματα, καὶ ἀποτεύγματα;" συνωμολόγησεν ὁ Μητροκλῆς. "τὰ δ' ἀποτεύγματ' οὐχ ὧν ἀποτεύγματ', ἀτυχήματα;" πράῳ λόγῳ καὶ φιλοσόφῳ κενὸν ἀποδείξας ὕλαγμα τὴν τοῦ κυνικοῦ βλασφημίαν.

...the licentiousness of his daughter did not prevent Stilpo from leading the most cheerful life of all the philosophers of his time; on the contrary, when Metrocles reproached him, he asked, "Is this my fault or hers?" And when Metrocles replied, "Her fault, but your misfortune," he said, "What do you mean? Are not faults also slips?" "Certainly," said Metrocles. "And are not slips also mischances of those who have slipped?" Metrocles agreed. "And are not mischances also misfortunes of those whose mischances they are?" By this gentle and philosophic argument he showed the Cynic's abuse to be but idle yapping.

(trans. W. C. Helmbold)

---

[20] LeVen 2014, 139. Machon makes the intertext clear by leaving the verb ἀπόδοτε in the same grammatical form as in Plato, even though the second-person plural does not fit the context (cf. Gow 1965, 79 who notes the oddity of the form and proposes that Philoxenus here "turns from the doctor and addresses the servants in attendance").

[21] Athenaeus, *Deipn.* 8.341e (immediately after the quotation from Machon); Lucian, *Vit. auct.* 10; Diogenes Laertius 6.76; Julian, *Or.* 6.181a; see also Plutarch, *De esu I* 995c–d about Diogenes' reasons for eating the octopus raw.

The anecdote is reminiscent of Socrates' encounters with antagonistic interlocutors such as Antiphon or Aristippus in Xenophon's *Apomnemoneumata*: the protagonist is challenged by a philosophical rival, maintains his composure, and defeats the enemy. The anecdote mimics some outward features of the Socratic dialogue and its discursive strategies by employment of a question-and-answer format, repetition of words, and propelling an argument forward by identification of partially semantically overlapping terms (linked also by phonetic similarity: ἁμάρτημα, ἀτύχημα, διάπτωμα, ἀπότευγμα).[22]

We can see in these examples—the fragments of Machon, the papyri fragments, the conversation between Stilpo and Metrocles quoted by Plutarch—that the boundary between a dialogized anecdote and a dialogue is fluid: extended dialogized anecdotes are in fact miniature dialogues, frequently using the trademark techniques of the Socratic dialogue. But there is also fluidity between the two literary forms in another sense: namely, there is a widespread literary practice of converting one into the other, be that by means of abridgment and condensation of a dialogue into an anecdote, or by means of expanding an anecdote into a longer dialogue. Because of the loss of the great share of Hellenistic prose, it is impossible to trace the transformation and rearrangement of biographical and anecdotal material, but there is evidence that such processes were at work. The dissolute life of Stilpo's daughter, which was the theme of a conversation between Stilpo and Metrocles in Plutarch, becomes in Diogenes Laertius the topic of a *chreia* (2.114 [SSR II O 17]):

καὶ θυγατέρα ἀκόλαστον ἐγέννησεν, ἣν ἔγημε γνώριμός τις αὐτοῦ Σιμμίας Συρακόσιος. ταύτης οὐ κατὰ τρόπον βιούσης εἶπέ τις πρὸς τὸν Στίλπωνα ὡς καταισχύνοι αὐτόν· ὁ δέ, "οὐ μᾶλλον," εἶπεν, "ἢ ἐγὼ ταύτην κοσμῶ."

He had a profligate daughter, who was married to his friend Simmias of Syracuse. And, as she would not live by rule, someone told Stilpo that she was a disgrace to him. To this he replied, "Not so, any more than I am an honour to her."

(trans. R. D. Hicks)

In a manner typical of *chreiai*, Stilpo responds to an anonymous person rather than Metrocles, which prevents dissipation of focus: all the spotlight is on Stilpo's response, which owes its potency and memorability to contraposition of the notions of bringing disgrace upon or honor to someone. Although Plutarch and Diogenes Laertius probably took the anecdote from different sources (there is little

---

[22] Another protracted dialogized anecdote is about Diogenes the Cynic and Aristippus in which Diogenes ridiculed the hedonist for living with a *hetaira*. The short conversation mimics the Socratic dialogue by its employment of the question-and-answer format and argument by analogy (Athenaeus, *Deipn.* 13.588e–f; cf. also a slightly modified version in Diogenes Laertius 2.74).

verbal similarity between the passages), they appear to have preserved different elaborations of the same story, in a condensed and expanded version.

The process of abridging longer conversations into short anecdotal sayings can be observed in Athenaeus' *Deipnosophists*. Though the text comes from a later period than the one surveyed in this book, it is instructive to observe these strategies at work as a host of our evidence for Hellenistic prose comes in the form of quotations and paraphrases embedded in works of imperial period authors. In *Deipn.* 5.186d, we read that when Socrates noticed that someone (ἰδών τινα) was eating *opson* (that is, a dish intended to be an addition to bread) immoderately, he said "Fellow guests, which of you is consuming bread as if it were the fanciest dish [*opson*], and the fanciest dish as if it were bread?" (ὦ παρόντες, ἔφη, τίς ὑμῶν τῷ μὲν ἄρτῳ ὡς ὄψῳ χρῆται, τῷ δ' ὄψῳ ὡς ἄρτῳ; trans. S. D. Olson). This is a paraphrase of a passage from Xenophon's *Apomnemoneumata*, where a snippet from a meal conversation between Socrates and some unnamed people is related. In Xenophon we read (*Mem.* 3.14.4):

καὶ ὁ Σωκράτης καταμαθών, Παρατηρεῖτ', ἔφη, τοῦτον οἱ πλησίον, ὁπότερα τῷ σίτῳ ὄψῳ ἢ τῷ ὄψῳ σίτῳ χρήσεται.

When Socrates observed this, he said: "Watch that one, you who are near him, and see whether he treats the bread as his appetizer [*opson*] or the appetizer as his bread." (trans. E. C. Marchant)

In Xenophon, the sentence ends a report of a meal conversation between Socrates and some unnamed people, the topic of which was gluttony. Athenaeus detaches Socrates' words from their context, though not in a mechanical way. He first precedes this with the word ἰδών (an introductory participle recurrent in *chreiai*)[23] followed by the object (the glutton), instead of Xenophon's καταμαθών, which refers to the previous sentence. In addition, Socrates' words are separated from the context by substitution of the phrase οἱ πλησίον, "the ones who are near him," with the more general παρόντες, "the people present." While in the *Apomnemoneumata* Socrates urged other guests to keep an eye on the glutton, in Athenaeus he uses his behavior as a reminder and admonition for other guests to behave appropriately.

A further example of abridging a section of a dialogue appears in another passage of the *Deipnosophists* (13.588d), where Socrates is said to have reacted to someone's description of Theodote:

---

[23] Cf. for instance Diogenes Laertius 6.51-2, where five consecutive anecdotes about Diogenes the Cynic are introduced with the participle ἰδών (followed by the verb ἔφη); and PBour. 1 fol. 6–7, ll. 141–68, where we find five school *chreiai* about Diogenes the Cynic, all introduced with the participle ἰδών.

ὅτι δὲ καλλίστη εἴη καὶ στέρνα κρείττω λόγου παντὸς ἔχοι λέγοντός <τινος>, "ἰτέον ἡμῖν," ἔφη· "θεασομένοις τὴν γυναῖκα· οὐ γὰρ δὴ ἀκούουσιν ἔστιν κρῖναι τὸ κάλλος."

When someone observed that she was extremely beautiful and had a chest that was lovelier than words could describe, he said: "We have to go see this woman; because you can't judge beauty by hearing about it." (trans. S. D. Olson)

Athenaeus refers to the famous section in Xenophon's *Apomnemoneumata* in which Socrates' visit to and conversation with the *hetaira* Theodote is reported. In Xenophon, Socrates learns from a bystander that Theodote's beauty is "greater than words" (κρεῖττον λόγου) and that painters visit her to make her portraits, while she shows them "as much of herself as is decent" (οἷς ἐκείνην ἐπιδεικνύειν ἑαυτῆς ὅσα καλῶς ἔχοι). Upon hearing this, he urged everyone to go and see her because "it is not for those who heard to judge what is stronger than words" (*Mem.* 3.11.1 Ἰτέον ἂν εἴη θεασομένους ... οὐ γὰρ δὴ ἀκούσασί γε τὸ λόγου κρεῖττον ἔστι καταμαθεῖν). Socrates' response is closely tied to what he has just heard about Theodote's beauty: he repeats the phrase λόγου κρεῖττον, which was used by the speaker and notes that it is impossible for him and those present to judge it without seeing. Athenaeus, on the other hand, makes the reader visualize the beauty of Theodote's body (it is her chest, στέρνα, that is more beautiful than words can describe) and then reduces Socrates' response to a general *bon mot* (it is impossible to judge beauty by hearing).[24]

The two passages of Athenaeus exemplify the technique of rewriting dialogue utterances by exploiting their gnomic potential. Similar techniques of extraction and condensation, which made it possible to transform dialogue passages into *chreiai*, were certainly also at work in other cases, though, to be sure, *chreiai* could have originated not only as abridgments of dialogues and longer dialogized anecdotes but also from dialogized sections of other types of prose texts.[25] In the early imperial period we can also observe opposite strategies at work, namely ones allowing the expansion of anecdotes into dialogues.[26] For instance, Dio Chrysostom's *Fourth Kingship Oration* is a dialogue that amplifies and expands on a popular anecdote about the meeting of Alexander the Great and Diogenes the Cynic, and the philosopher's request that the king move out of the sun. Plutarch's

---

[24] For Athenaeus' rewriting of this passage, see Maisonneuve 2007, 93. In Xenophon, Theodote was posing for a portrait and "showed as much as decency allowed"; in Athenaeus it is not explained in what circumstances Theodote's beauty was observed.

[25] For a discussion of ancient anecdotes and their sources, see Gallo 1980, 12–14. Giannantoni 1990c, 468 speaks of a process in which "tradizioni letterarie di vario tipo furono riscritte secondo i canoni delle χρεῖαι, sia per la particolare efficacia rappresentativa sia per la possibilità di utilizzazione che retori, grammatici e filosofi vi videro a fini scolastici...." White 2010, 372 notes that many *chreiai* or anecdotes "plainly derive from continuous compositions like dialogues, 'lives', or even plays."

[26] As noticed by Giannantoni 1990c, 468; cf. also Theon, *Progymn.* 101, 103, who speaks of the techniques of compression and expansion of an anecdote.

*Symposion of Seven Sages* expands on the anecdotal tradition of wise men and their interactions. Here we should also include certain pseudepigraphic epistles with protracted dialogized sections, which I discuss later in this chapter, and which develop biographic anecdotal episodes into epistolographic reports of conversations.

A large subcategory of ancient anecdotes relates sympotic/deipnic sayings, verbal exchanges, and behaviors of philosophers and other persons of historical interest. Like other biographical anecdotes, some of them probably originated as abbreviations of longer dialogized passages occurring in self-standing dialogues or in *apomnemoneumata*-type works.

Starting with the Socratics, sympotic dialogues were composed throughout the centuries and across philosophical schools. In *Table Talk*, Plutarch locates his nine books of sympotic conversations within the tradition of the philosophical sympotic dialogue, which, he notes, was practiced by such highly reputed philosophers as Plato, Xenophon, Aristotle, Speusippus, Epicurus, Prytanis, Hieronymus, and Dion of the Academy (*Quaest. conv.* 612d–e). Only the *Symposia* of the first two authors are extant; we hear of existence of the sympotic writings by Aristotle, Speusippus, and Epicurus from elsewhere, but there are no substantial extant fragments or testimonies. We know nothing about the dialogues written by the last three authors.[27] Plutarch's list, to be sure, is not comprehensive. He himself mentions elsewhere sympotic works by Theophrastus and Aristoxenus of Tarentum (*Non posse* 1095e).

From Athenaeus we learn that the Stoic Antipater of Tarsus organized a *symposion* at which guests were supposed to solve *sophismata*, riddle-syllogisms; he may be referring to a text reporting the event (*Deipn.* 5.186c). The Cynic Menippus of Gadara is credited with writing a *symposion*, as is Meleager of the same city, who was influenced by Menippus (Athenaeus, *Deipn.* 14.629e–f, 11.502c); in both cases we may assume that the texts were parodies of philosophical compositions, like the *Cynics' Symposion* by Parmeniscus, which I discuss in the next section. Menippus also included a report of a drinking party in his *Arcesilaus*, where he included details about the food served and mentioned the drunkenness of some guests (Athenaeus, *Deipn.* 14.664e) (on Menippus and Meleager see Chapter 6.4). In the early first century BCE Heraclides of Tarentum, an Empiricist physician, wrote a *Symposion* in at least three books,

---

[27] Evidence for sympotic works by Speusippus, Aristotle, and Epicurus is discussed in later chapters. Athenaeus mentions a dinner in which Prytanis participated, at which the poet Euphorion urinated into a cup (*Deipn.* 11.477e), but it is unlikely that the story comes from Prytanis' dialogue: we would have to assume that Prytanis' text was a satirical *symposion*, hardly a model for Plutarch to follow (Martin 1931, 197). Hieronymus should probably be identified as the Peripatetic philosopher from Rhodes who lived in the third century BCE. Diogenes Laertius 4.41–2 mentions a gathering he held with friends to celebrate the birthday of Antigonus' son; whether there is a connection with a sympotic text authored by Hieronymus is unclear. Dion "of the Academy" is mentioned also by Athenaeus (*Deipn.* 1.34b).

probably in a dialogue format, where issues pertaining to diet (including proper sympotic consumption)—and, presumably, other medical matters—were discussed.[28] Imperial period miscellaneous sympotic dialogues of Plutarch and Athenaeus had Hellenistic predecessors: the sympotic dialogue by Aristotle's student Aristoxenus of Tarentum, mentioned by Plutarch in *Non posse* 1095e, is probably to be identified with Aristoxenus' Σύμμικτα συμποτικά, a sympotic miscellany (Athenaeus, *Deipn.* 14.632a–b preserves a quotation from this work). Towards the end of the first century BCE the grammarian Didymus Chalcenterus wrote *Symposiaca* in at least ten books.[29]

The sympotic setting was also probably used for historical dialogues that expanded on existing anecdotal traditions. Diogenes Laertius, when speaking of the Seven Sages, notes (1.40–1):

Ἀρχέτιμος δὲ ὁ Συρακούσιος ὁμιλίαν αὐτῶν ἀναγέγραφε παρὰ Κυψέλῳ, ᾗ καὶ αὐτός φησι παρατυχεῖν· Ἔφορος δὲ παρὰ Κροίσῳ πλὴν Θαλοῦ. φασὶ δέ τινες καὶ ἐν Πανιωνίῳ καὶ ἐν Κορίνθῳ καὶ ἐν Δελφοῖς συνελθεῖν αὐτούς.

Archetimus of Syracuse describes their meeting at the court of Cypselus, on which occasion he himself happened to be present; for which Ephorus substitutes a meeting without Thales at the court of Croesus. Some make them meet at the Pan-Ionian festival, at Corinth, and at Delphi.    (trans. R. D. Hicks)

There is no other evidence concerning Archetimus of Syracuse and the fact that he provided an eye-witness account of the meeting of the sages suggests that he might have been a fictitious character who played the role of a narrator in a dialogue rather than a historical person.[30] It is evident from Diogenes Laertius that there was a fertile tradition of reports of meetings between wise men, some of which probably had a sympotic setting. The only surviving specimen, Plutarch's dialogue *Symposion of the Seven Sages*, which takes place in the court of Periander, refers obliquely to its predecessors when its narrator Diocles tells his anonymous audience that he is about to correct false accounts circulating about the banquet of the sages.[31]

---

[28] For dating, see Guardasole 1997, 23.

[29] We also know of Cleanthes' Περὶ συμποσίου, *On Symposion* (Diogenes Laertius 7.175) and normative συμποτικοὶ νόμοι, "rules of symposion," composed by Aristotle and Xenocrates (Athenaeus, *Deipn.* 5.186b). There were parodies of such normative works; cf. Athenaeus, *Deipn.* 13.585b: the courtesan Gnathaena "composed a set of dinner-regulations (νόμον συσσιτικὸν), which her lovers were required to follow when they visited her and her daughter, in imitation of the philosophers who put together similar documents (κατὰ ζῆλον τῶν τὰ τοιαῦτα συνταξαμένων φιλοσόφων)."

[30] As suggested by Radicke 1999.

[31] For Plutarch's *Symposion of the Seven Sages* as "an expression of a continuing tradition" and "not just Plutarch's innovation," see Martin 1993, 123. See also Cazzato and Prodi 2016, 13 on the sympotic overtones in the tradition of the Sages' meeting, and Busine 2002, 15–85 on Plutarch's elaboration of the received tradition.

Apart from self-standing sympotic dialogues, there were also reports of snippets of conversations at meals and drinking parties embedded in prose works, which aimed to demonstrate a person's character as manifested in their attitudes toward food and wine. This tradition preceded the Socratics; as we saw, Ion of Chios described sympotic conversations with the participation of Sophocles and, probably, Cimon. Xenophon, apart from having written the *Symposion*, presented Socrates at meals in the *Apomnemoneumata*.[32] Athenaeus says that the Stoic Persaeus wrote sympotic dialogues (συμποτικοὺς διαλόγους) "compiled from the *apomnemoneumata* of Stilpo and Zeno" (συντεθέντας ἐκ τῶν Στίλπωνος καὶ Ζήνωνος ἀπομνημονευμάτων), in which (*Deipn*. 4.162b–c [*SVF* 1.101 F 452]):

ζητεῖ, ὅπως ἂν μὴ κατακοιμηθῶσιν οἱ συμπόται, πῶς ταῖς ἐπιχύσεσι χρηστέον πηνίκα τε εἰσακτέον τοὺς ὡραίους καὶ τὰς ὡραίας εἰς τὸ συμπόσιον καὶ πότε αὐτοὺς προσδεκτέον ὡραϊζομένους καὶ πότε παραπεμπτέον ὡς ὑπερορῶντας, καὶ περὶ προσοψημάτων καὶ περὶ ἄρτων καὶ περὶ τῶν ἄλλων ὅσα τε περιεργότερον περὶ φιλημάτων εἴρηκεν ὁ Σωφρονίσκου φιλόσοφος....

he tries to keep the guests at the symposium from falling asleep by asking how toasts should be made, and at what point good-looking young men and women should be introduced into the party, and when one ought to put up with their acting affectedly and when they ought to be kicked out for ignoring others, as well as questions about the items eaten along with the meal, and bread, and other matters, including whatever rather elaborate remarks Sophroniscus' son the philosopher made about kisses. (trans. S. D. Olson)

It remains unclear whether the phrase "*apomnemoneumata* of Stilpo and Zeno" refers to texts authored by these philosophers, to texts about them, written by their followers, or to Persaeus' own reminiscences and memories about them. Perhaps the latter was the case. Persaeus was a close associate of Zeno, who, in turn, might have been a student of Stilpo; therefore it would be fitting for Persaeus to write, after the model of Xenophon, memoirs in a dialogue format with his teacher and the latter's teacher as protagonists.[33] The plural used by Athenaeus, who refers to the text as συμποτικοὶ διάλογοι, suggests a collection of sympotic conversations with an episodic structure. The passage is noteworthy also because—apart from mocking Persaeus' work—it informs us about some of the topics that were discussed: wine, food, love, and their proper place at a *symposion*. As noted above, we do not know whether Persaeus' *Sympotic Dialogues* are identical with his *Sympotic Hypomnemata*, in which, as we also learn from Athenaeus, Persaeus proclaimed that it is appropriate to talk about erotic desire, τὰ ἀφροδίσια, at a *symposion* (*Deipn*. 13.607a) and in which proper sympotic themes and behavior

---

[32] Xenophon, *Mem*. 3.14; see also Socrates' comments on food in *Mem*. 3.13.2–4.
[33] Hirzel 1895a, 368 n. 1; Döring 1972, 151.

were probably discussed (it is unclear where Athenaeus' paraphrase of Persaeus ends; if it extended to *Deipn.* 13.607b, dialecticians discussing syllogisms while drinking were frowned upon, and merry drinking was deemed appropriate).

As with other biographical anecdotes, the original context of sympotic and deipnic ones is frequently difficult to determine. In some cases, however, there are hints suggesting they have originated from a dialogue or a dialogized section embedded in a longer prose text. Consider, for instance, the anecdotes about Arcesilaus related by Athenaeus (*Deipn.* 10.420c–d):

> Ἀρκεσίλαος δ' ἑστιῶν τινας, καὶ ἐλλιπόντων τῶν ἄρτων νεύσαντος τοῦ παιδὸς ὡς οὐκ ἔτ' εἰσίν, ἀνακαγχάσας καὶ τὼ χεῖρε συγκροτήσας "οἷόν τι," ἔφη, "τὸ συμπόσιόν ἐστιν ἡμῶν, ἄνδρες φίλοι· ἄρτους ἐπιλελήσμεθ' ἀρκοῦντας πρίασθαι. τρέχε δή, παῖ." καὶ τοῦτ' ἔλεγεν αὐτὸς γελῶν· καὶ τῶν παρόντων δ' ἄθρους ἐξεχύθη γέλως καὶ διαγωγὴ πλείων ἐνέπεσεν καὶ διατριβή, ὥστε ἥδυσμα γενέσθαι τῷ συμποσίῳ τὴν τῶν ἄρτων ἔνδειαν. ἄλλοτε δὲ ὁ Ἀρκεσίλαος Ἀπελλῇ τῷ γνωρίμῳ προστάξας καθυλίσαι τὸν οἶνον, ἐπειδὴ διὰ τὴν ἀπειρίαν ἐκεῖνος τὰ μὲν ἐτάραττεν, τὰ δ' ἐξέχει, καὶ πολὺ θολώτερος ἐφαίνετο ὁ οἶνος, ὑπομειδιάσας ἔφη· "ἐγὼ δὲ καθυλίσαι προσέταξα ἀνθρώπῳ μηδὲν ἑωρακότι ἀγαθὸν ὥσπερ οὐδ' ἐγώ. ἀνάστηθι οὖν σύ, Ἀρίδεικες· σὺ δὲ ἀπελθὼν † τὰ ἑκτὰ τρύπα †." ταῦτα δ' οὕτως εὔφραινε καὶ ἐξιλάρου τοὺς παρόντας ὡς εὐθυμίας πληροῦσθαι.

> When Arcesilaus had some people to dinner, and the bread ran out and the slave shook his head to signal that it was all gone, he burst out in laughter, clapped his hands, and said: "What a party we're having, my friends—we forgot to buy enough bread! Run, slave!" He was laughing as he said this, and all the guests also began to laugh, and the party became happier and more enjoyable, the result being that the shortage of bread added zest to the occasion. On another occasion Arcesilaus assigned his student Apelles to strain the wine, and when Apelles' lack of experience caused him to make some of it cloudy, and to spill the rest, and when the wine actually looked much murkier than it did before, Arcesilaus smiled gently and said: "I assigned someone to strain the wine who has no more idea of what the Good is than I do. So get off of your couch, Arideices! And as for you, go away † the qualities pierce!" † These remarks delighted and amused the other guests so much that they were in a very good mood.
>
> (trans. S. D. Olson)

There are notable circumstantial details in the first anecdote: the slave who makes a signal with his head, Arcesilaus' laughter and hand-clapping, his sending the slave to fetch the bread. This would be unusual for a story designed as an anecdote to begin with and rather suggests that the passage derives from a longer sympotic scene. The second anecdote likewise contains some details suggesting that it is a snippet from a longer description of a *symposion*. The last words of Arcesilaus in Athenaeus' passage, τὰ ἑκτὰ τρύπα, appear damaged; the corruption of the text (or, if the text is correct, its obscurity) is probably due to the fact that the passage has been taken out of context. The names of two of Arcesilaus' students, Apelles and Arideices, appear. They are not well-known philosophers and their identities add little to the anecdote—unless the anecdote was an episode of a longer text in which they played a part. Arideices, interestingly, appears in two other sympotic anecdotes: in Plutarch's *Table Talk* 634c, he makes an arrogant freedman of a king leave the dinner, and in Diogenes Laertius (4.42) he is proposing an investigation, τι θεώρημα, in sympotic circumstances, which Arcesilaus finds not fitting the occasion.[34] It is possible that these anecdotes originated from the same text.

Another example of a sympotic anecdote that might have originally come from a dialogue or an *apomnemoneumata*-type collection is a conversation between Stilpo and the *hetaira* Glycera, reported by Athenaeus, who found it in the *Lives* of Satyrus of Callatis (*Deipn.* 13.584a [F 19 Schorn]). Stilpo was said to have accused Glycera of corrupting young men to which she responded:

"τὴν αὐτήν," ἔφη, "ἔχομεν αἰτίαν, ὦ Στίλπων. σέ τε γὰρ λέγουσιν διαφθείρειν τοὺς ἐντυγχάνοντάς σοι ἀνωφελῆ καὶ ἐρωτικὰ σοφίσματα διδάσκοντα, ἐμέ τε ὡσαύτως."

"We get accused of the same thing, Stilpo. People claim you corrupt those who meet you, by teaching them your worthless erotic drivel; and they criticize me the same way." (trans. S. D. Olson, modified)[35]

The encounter of Stilpo and Glycera belongs to the tradition of depicting philosophers in conversation with *hetairai*, an early specimen of which is the Theodote-episode in Xenophon's *Apomnemoneumata*.[36] Like in Xenophon, here also a playful parallel is established between the activity of a philosopher and the activity of the *hetaira*. As in the anecdote about Arcesilaus, here also there is a textual problem, and the phrase ἀνωφελῆ καὶ ἐρωτικὰ σοφίσματα is sometimes corrected by editors who print ἐριστικά in place of ἐρωτικά. As Stefan Schorn observes, this difficulty may result from the separation of the anecdotal bit from a longer conversation; ἐρωτικά might have referred to something said before.[37] Stilpo was the protagonist of various dialogized stories, which makes a longer dialogic context of this anecdote probable.

---

[34] Arideices is also mentioned by Philodemus, *Acad. ind.* col. xx.7, and Apelles by Plutarch, *Quomodo adul.* 63d–e.

[35] For the Greek text, I follow Schorn 2004, 121 (F 19), who leaves the original ἐρωτικά instead of ἐριστικά (Hemsterhuys's conjecture). I have slightly modified Olson's translation ("erotic" instead of "eristic," and a different placement of quotation marks, as proposed by Schorn 2004, 401).

[36] Book 13 of Athenaeus' *Deipnosophists* is devoted to women (it is titled Περὶ γυναικῶν), in particular to *hetairai*, and exemplifies the popularity of the motif of an encounter of a famous man with a *hetaira*. For this tradition and Athenaeus' place in it, see McClure 2003a; and McClure 2003b, 288 for this specific passage.

[37] Schorn 2004, 400: "Die Anekdote stammt wahrscheinlich aus einem Gespräch, das hier zum Apophthegma verkürzt wird, woraus die Verständnisschwierigkeiten resultieren."

## 1.3 Dialogue and Epistolography

In a letter to Atticus, Cicero describes his meeting with a nephew Quintus (*Att.* 13.42.1):

> Venit ille ad me καὶ μάλα κατηφής. et ego "σὺ δὲ δὴ τί σύννους?" "rogas?" inquit, "cui iter instet et iter ad bellum, idque cum periculosum tum etiam turpe!" "quae vis igitur?" inquam. "aes" inquit "alienum, et tamen ne viaticum quidem habeo." hoc loco ego sumpsi quiddam de tua eloquentia; nam tacui. at ille: "sed me maxime angit avunculus." "quidnam?" inquam. "quod mihi" inquit "iratus est." "cur pateris?" inquam, "malo enim ita dicere quam cur committis?" "non patiar" inquit; "causam enim tollam." et ego: "rectissime quidem; sed si grave non est, velim scire quid sit causae." "quia, dum dubitabam quam ducerem, non satis faciebam matri; ita ne illi quidem. nunc nihil mihi tanti est. faciam quod volunt." "feliciter velim" inquam, "teque laudo. sed quando?" "nihil ad me" inquit "de tempore, quoniam rem probo." "at ego" inquam "censeo prius quam proficiscaris. ita patri quoque morem gesseris." "faciam" inquit "ut censes." hic dialogus sic conclusus est.

> He came to see me, "right down in the mouth." I greeted him with "You there, why so pensive?" "Need you ask," was the answer, "considering that I have a journey in front of me, and a journey to war, a dishonourable journey too as well as a dangerous one?" "What's the compulsion?" I enquired. "Debt," he answered, "and yet I haven't so much as my travelling expenses." At that I borrowed some of your eloquence—I held my tongue. He went on: "What distresses me most is my uncle." "How so?" "Because he's annoyed with me." "Why do you let him be annoyed? I prefer to say 'let be' rather than 'make'." "I shan't any more," he answered. "I shall do away with the reason." "Admirable," said I. "But if you don't mind my asking, I should be interested to know what the reason is." "It's because I couldn't make up my mind whom to marry. My mother was displeased with me, and so consequently was he. Now I don't care what I do to put things right. I'll do what they want." "Good luck then," said I, "and congratulations on your decision. But when is it to be?" "The time makes no odds to me," said he, "now that I accept the thing itself." "Well," I said, "I should do it before I left if I were you. That way you will please your father too." "I shall take your advice," he replied. Thus ended our dialogue.
>
> (trans. D. R. Shackleton Bailey)

While there is nothing odd in reporting a conversation in a letter to a friend, Cicero's extended use of direct speech and careful use of narratorial interventions (*inquam, inquit, et ego, at ille*) draws attention—as does the fact that he calls the exchange *dialogus*, suggesting that the passage was carefully structured. Its literariness is enhanced by echoes of Menander and by comic connotations of the figure of a fickle *adulescens* in need of money.[38]

When he wrote this miniature dialogue, Cicero was operating within an existing tradition of blending epistolography and dialogue. It is not clear how far back it goes, but Plato and Aristotle may be considered the patron figures of such a mixture. Plato was associated with both dialogue- and letter-writing, and some letters ascribed to him contain conversations related in direct speech.[39] Aristotle, apart from having written extant treatises, also composed dialogues and letters, though neither group has survived—and Artemon, the editor of Aristotle's letters, made a theoretical connection between a letter and a dialogue, remarking that a letter is one part of a dialogue ([Demetrius], *Eloc.* 223: εἶναι γὰρ τὴν ἐπιστολὴν οἷον τὸ ἕτερον μέρος τοῦ διαλόγου).

Several texts from the Hellenistic period exemplify the practice of embedding lengthy dialogized sections within an epistolographic frame. The *Letter of Aristeas*, composed probably in the mid- to late second century BCE, is a remarkable specimen of such generic blending.[40] This product of Jewish Hellenism, which contains the legendary account about the translation of the Septuagint into Greek, is framed as a letter by Aristeas to his brother Philocrates. It reports how Ptolemy II Philadelphus heard from Demetrius of Phaleron about Jewish Law and consequently dispatched the narrator to Judea to obtain the best possible copy. The text was provided by the Jewish High Priest Eleazar, who also sent to Alexandria seventy-two translators who could carry out the task. Within the frame of an epistolographic narrative (referred to by the narrator as διήγησις, *Ep. Arist.* 1), a variety of other formats are embedded: dialogic exchanges, a royal edict, a written report by Demetrius in his capacity as a librarian, letters between Ptolemy and Eleazar, an *ekphrasis* of royal gifts, a description of Jerusalem with its temple and surroundings, a speech by Eleazar on the Jewish distinction between clean and unclean animals, and an account of seven royal banquets during which Ptolemy entertained the Jewish translators.[41] The sections containing Eleazar's speech and the seven *symposia* have the largest proportion of direct speech, but there are also other dialogized passages. The narrative begins with an account of a conversation between Demetrius of Phaleron and Ptolemy (*Ep. Arist.* 9–11):

---

[38] Shackleton Bailey 1966, 397. Wynne 2019, 29 n. 68 suggests that Atticus might have also included such little dialogues in his letters.

[39] Cf. in particular [Plato], *Ep.* 7.346b–d (a lengthy utterance by Dionysius to Plato); 7.347b–c (Plato's response to Dionysius); 7.348c–e (conversation between Theodotes, Dionysius, and Plato); 7.348e–349b (conversation between Theodotes and Plato, and then also Dionysius); 7.350c–d (Plato's words to Dion); and in a different tone, a short conversation between Plato and Dionysius recorded in *Ep.* 13.360b.

[40] For arguments for dating of the letter to the second century BCE and an overview of earlier scholarship, see Wright 2015, 21–30; for the letter as an example of the Hellenistic generic eclecticism, see Honigman 2003, 13–35.

[41] For the letter's interaction with Hellenistic genres such as geographical and ethnographical treatise and utopian literature, see Gruen 2008, 141.

*Κατασταθεὶς ἐπὶ τῆς τοῦ βασιλέως βιβλιοθήκης Δημήτριος ὁ Φαληρεὺς ἐχρηματίσθη πολλὰ διάφορα πρὸς τὸ συναγαγεῖν, εἰ δυνατόν, ἅπαντα τὰ κατὰ τὴν οἰκουμένην βιβλία· καὶ ποιούμενος ἀγορασμοὺς καὶ μεταγραφὰς ἐπὶ τέλος ἤγαγεν, ὅσον ἐφ᾿ ἑαυτῷ, τὴν τοῦ βασιλέως πρόθεσιν. Παρόντων οὖν ἡμῶν ἐρωτηθείς· Πόσαι τινὲς μυριάδες τυγχάνουσι βιβλίων; Εἶπεν· Ὑπὲρ τὰς εἴκοσι, βασιλεῦ· σπουδάσω δ᾿ ἐν ὀλίγῳ χρόνῳ πρὸς τὸ πληρωθῆναι πεντήκοντα μυριάδας τὰ λοιπά. Προσήγγελται δέ μοι καὶ τῶν Ἰουδαίων νόμιμα μεταγραφῆς ἄξια καὶ τῆς παρὰ σοὶ βιβλιοθήκης εἶναι. Τί τὸ κωλῦον οὖν, εἶπεν, ἐστί σε τοῦτο ποιῆσαι; Πάντα γὰρ ὑποτέτακταί σοι τὰ πρὸς τὴν χρείαν. Ὁ δὲ Δημήτριος εἶπεν· Ἑρμηνείας προσδεῖται· χαρακτῆρσι γὰρ ἰδίοις κατὰ τὴν Ἰουδαίαν χρῶνται, καθάπερ Αἰγύπτιοι τῇ τῶν γραμμάτων θέσει, καθὸ καὶ φωνὴν ἰδίαν ἔχουσιν. Ὑπολαμβάνονται Συριακῇ χρῆσθαι· τὸ δ᾿ οὐκ ἔστιν, ἀλλ᾿ ἕτερος τρόπος. Μεταλαβὼν δὲ ἕκαστα ὁ βασιλεὺς εἶπε γραφῆναι πρὸς τὸν ἀρχιερέα τῶν Ἰουδαίων, ὅπως τὰ προειρημένα τελείωσιν λάβῃ.*

After he had been appointed over the king's library, Demetrius of Phalerum was furnished with much money in order to collect, if possible, all the books in the world, and making purchases and transcriptions, he brought to completion, as much as he could, the king's plan. Thus, while we were present, he was asked, "How many thousands of books have been obtained?" He said, "More than two-hundred thousand, O King; I will hasten in a short time to fulfill the remainder of five hundred thousand. But it also has been reported to me that the laws of the Jews are worthy of transcription and of inclusion in your library." "What is there, therefore, to prevent you from doing this?" he said. "For everything that you need has been provided to you." But Demetrius said, "Translation is still required; for in Judea they use their own characters, just as the Egyptians use their own arrangement of letters, inasmuch as they also have their own language. The Judeans are supposed to use Syrian. This is not so, but they use another style." After being informed of these things, the king proposed to write to the high priest of the Judeans so that Demetrius might bring to completion the aforementioned matters.   (trans. B. G. Wright)

The opening conversation is paralleled by another one at the end of the text (*Ep. Arist.* 312–13), in which Ptolemy, after having heard the Greek translation of the law, asks Demetrius why it was not translated earlier. It is apparent that the placement of the two conversations, which create a ring composition, was carefully planned.

Demetrius and Ptolemy, the protagonists of the conversations, are well-known historical characters; the author puts them in a fictitious or fictionalized story, engaging in what we call today historical fiction-writing.[42] He subtly marks his presence during the reported conversation (παρόντων ἡμῶν), emphasizing his

---

[42] On the question of fictionality and its role in Aristeas' letter, see Honigman 2003, 37–63; Rajak 2009, 38–43, 47–50.

eye-witness status. The identity of the narrator is carefully elaborated in later chapters: the Jewish author of the letter makes him a Greek official in the court of Ptolemy, interested in and amazed by Jewish wisdom. *Ego*-narratives, which aim at enforcing the veracity of a reported story, can be traced back to Herodotean historiography;[43] the literary strategy of blurring the distinction between fact and fiction through the device of a first-person account was popularized and conventionalized in narrated historical dialogues, which provide an important backdrop for the letter.[44]

The opening exchange between Ptolemy and Demetrius is an adaptation of the motif of an encounter between a ruler and a philosopher/wise man. In other examples of such conversations, rulers are given the opportunity to learn from representatives of knowledge: this is the case of Herodotus' report of a conversation between Croesus and Solon, Xenophon's dialogue between Hiero and Simonides, and similar texts.[45] Demetrius' role is reduced to informing Ptolemy of the existence of Jewish Law. Such a rewriting of the conventional motif is certainly not accidental: the limited role of Demetrius, a Greek philosopher, is paralleled by the repeated insistence further in the text that the Greek philosophers in Ptolemy's court were in awe of the Jewish translators and admitted their own inferiority (*Ep. Arist.* 200, 235, 296). The introductory conversation also introduces the familiar motif of a confrontation between Greek culture and philosophy with non-Greek, Eastern wisdom. In ancient dialogues, it was Persian wisdom and Persian sages that were most frequently discussed and represented, but Clearchus of Soli in the dialogue *On Sleep* has Aristotle tell his student Hyperochides of an encounter he had had with a sage from Judea (see Chapter 5.4).

There are other short exchanges embedded in the *Letter of Aristeas*, and a lengthy, partially allegorical speech by the Jewish priest Eleazar which provides the rationale for the distinction between clean and unclean animals (*Ep. Arist.* 130–69). But the influence of the dialogue is particularly palpable in a lengthy section describing banquets lasting seven days, by means of which Ptolemy celebrated the Jewish translators (*Ep. Arist.* 187–300).[46] The length of this part

---

[43] For strategies for enforcing veracity in the letter, see Honigman 2003, 67–91.

[44] Apart from the narrated Dialogues of Plato, two historical dialogues provide a particularly good parallel: "Peisistratus' Dialogue" (POxy. 4.664/50.3544), probably from the early Hellenistic period (see Chapter 2.4.1) and Plutarch's *Symposion of Seven Sages*. Presumably, by the time of the writing of the *Letter of Aristeas*, the literary device of a fictitious *ego*-narrative had become popular in a variety of genres, including novels and pseudepigraphic letters (Honigman 2003, 67).

[45] Other Dialogues which developed the *topos* include a dialogue by Heraclides of Pontus, in which the tyrant Gelon was visited by a Magus, and the same author's account of a conversation between the tyrant Leon and Pythagoras. The "Peisistratus' Dialogue" (POxy. 4.664/50.3544, see Chapter 2.4.1), offers a variation of this motif. Cf. also imperial period texts: Dio Chrysostom's *Fourth Kingship Oration* (Alexander and Diogenes the Cynic) and Plutarch's *Symposion of the Seven Sages*.

[46] The arrangement of the banquet and its relation to Hellenistic royal *symposion* is discussed in Murray 1996, 22–3.

of the letter—it occupies about one-third of it—signals its significance. At each banquet, Ptolemy asks the Jewish sages questions, seventy-two in all, so that every Jewish guest has the opportunity to give an answer. Many questions concern proper monarchical rule, though there is also a significant number of problems pertaining to ethical philosophy.[47] In their prudent answers, the sages manage each time, without fail, to refer to God, emphasizing the priority of a religious perspective. Their responses raise praise and acclamation, not only from Ptolemy but also, the author repeatedly emphasizes, from the Greek philosophers who were present.[48]

This erotapocritic, dialogized section demonstrates the wisdom of the Jewish sages as well as their superiority over the Greek philosophers. It belongs to the branch of dialogue exemplified in extant literature by the conversation between Alexander and the Indian Gymnosophists (PBerol. inv. 13044, second or first century BCE, see Chapter 2.6.1) and the section of Plutarch's *Symposion of Seven Sages* (152a–155d) in which the sages answer questions asked in a letter by the Egyptian king Amasis (notice that Plutarch also combines here, though in a different way, dialogue and epistolography).[49] Circumstances of these erotapocritic exchanges vary. In the encounter between Alexander and the Indian sages it is said that Alexander liked the answers of the Gymnosophists and therefore allowed them to leave unharmed—his interrogation, therefore, was a display of power. In Plutarch, the questions were sent by Amasis to Bias, and answered, in turn, by all the sages present at the banquet, which introduced an element of playful competition between them. Yet there are also considerable similarities. All three texts put a confrontation between political power and wisdom (the Gymnosophists and the Jewish sages represent foreign wisdom) in the spotlight: the rulers' questions challenge the wise men and allow for a display of wisdom and quick wit.

Dialogized sections might have also been embedded in "dinner-party letters" (δειπνητικαὶ ἐπιστολαί) by Hippolochus of Macedon and Lynceus, a pupil of Theophrastus. According to Athenaeus, the two men agreed to write to each other about all the expensive banquets they had attended.[50] Athenaeus provides

---

[47] For Murray 1967, 349 such questions not pertaining to kingship are due to the author's need to come up with seventy-two problems: "[d]oubtless if Aristeas could have thought of seventy-two questions on kingship alone, he would have not inserted these other questions." I think that this unnecessarily delimits the author's agenda, which is to highlight the universality of the wisdom of the sages and their superiority over the Greek philosophers.

[48] Cf. *Ep. Arist.* 200, where the philosopher Menedemus of Eretria voices his approval of the sages' responses, and 200, 235, and 296 in which the Jewish sages are explicitly compared with philosophers present at the *symposia*.

[49] For the similarity of the *symposia* in the *Letter of Aristeas* to the dialogue between Alexander and Gymnosophists, see Zuntz 1959a, 34; Zuntz 1959b, 440; Murray 1967, 348.

[50] Athenaeus, *Deipn.* 4.128a–b. Lynceus described a banquet given by the pipe-girl Lamia for Demetrius Poliorcetes and feasts given by Antigonus and Ptolemy (Soter or Philadelphus). For his letters, see Dalby 2000, 374–6. Martin 1931, 159–60 believes that Hippolochus is a fictitious figure and that the correspondence was fabricated in its entirety by Lynceus; Dalby 1988 rejects this hypothesis.

an overview of one of Hippolochus' letters, mostly paraphrasing it, though at times quoting directly. Hippolochus described a sumptuous wedding-feast given by a certain Caranus of Macedon and included details about the expensive tableware, lavish dishes, and various sympotic entertainments. A sense of satirical excessiveness and extravagance, not unlike the one we find in Petronius' *Dinner of Trimalchio*, permeates the account. The figures of a weeping guest (Athenaeus, *Deipn.* 4.129f), a jester (4.130c), and a heavy drinker (4.129a) are reminiscent of Plato's and Xenophon's *Symposia*, and there are several motifs that suggest the author's intertextual play with the latter's dialogue.[51] At the end of the epistle, Caranus' banquet is explicitly contrasted with a philosophical life in Athens, which encourages the reader to contemplate the difference between Macedonian extravagance and Athenian moderation.[52] The parodic tone and comic elements present in the letter have parallels in the poetic sympotic tradition, which exploited the humorous potential of the banquet-setting and the presence of food and wine.[53]

As the letter draws from and parodies the philosophical *symposion*, it is likely that it also included dialogized sections parodying philosophical sympotic conversations. Unfortunately, Athenaeus preserves a direct exchange between the banqueters only in one passage, in which a guest called Proteas drinks a big cup of almost undiluted Thasian wine and states: "The one who drinks the most, will also be the most cheerful" (ὁ πλεῖστα πίνων πλεῖστα κεὐφρανθήσεται). Caranus responds: "As you were the first to drink up your wine, you will be also the first to receive the cup as a gift. This will also be a reward for others when they finish their drink" (ἐπεὶ πρῶτος ἔπιες, ἔχε πρῶτος καὶ τὸν σκύφον δῶρον· τοῦτο δὲ καὶ τοῖς ἄλλοις ὅσοι ἂν πίωσιν ἔσται γέρας) (*Deipn.* 4.129f). It can be surmised that this was not the only section in the account of the *symposion* with direct speech, but the proportions of conversation and narration in the work remain impossible to determine.

In the same book, Athenaeus quotes another work that fuses epistolography with a sympotic dialogue, namely the *Cynics' Symposion* by Parmeniscus (*Deipn.*

---

[51] Martin 1931, 153. Mandrogenes the laughter-maker (γελωτοποιός, Athenaeus, *Deipn.* 4.130c) and his comic dance with his 80-year-old wife is reminiscent of Xenophon's Philip and his dancing performance in *Symposion* 2.22). Cf. also Xenophon, *Symp.* 2.26-7 where the company decides to drink from small cups (μικραῖς κύλιξι), but with wine-pourers driving the cups fast like good charioteers (θᾶττον περιελαύνοντας τὰς κύλικας), with Athenaeus, *Deipn.* 4.130c, where Caranus orders slaves to run fast with small cups (μικροῖς ἐκπώμασι περισοβεῖν ἐκέλευε).

[52] Martin 1931, 160. For representations of Macedonian *symposia* and their recurrent features (such as excessive drinking, violence, extravagant luxury), see Sawada 2010, 393-9.

[53] Cf. e.g. a parody of Philoxenus' Δεῖπνον by a comic poet Plato (Athenaeus, *Deipn.* 1.5b-d) and fragments of Matro of Pitane's mock-epic *Attic Dinner-Party* (c. 300 BCE) (Athenaeus, *Deipn.* 4.134e-137c). For the themes of food and wine in comedy and parody, see Wilkins 2000. Philosophers were clearly familiar with food-oriented poetry. Archestratus' gastronomic poem, for instance, elicited hostile responses from philosophers such as Clearchus of Soli from the Peripatos and Chrysippus the Stoic; the latter ridiculed Epicurus as a follower of Archestratus (Athenaeus, *Deipn.* 10.457c-e, 8.335b, 8.335d-336a, 3.104b and 7.278e-f [T 4-6 Olson and Sens]).

4.156d–158a). The text is difficult to date, but it has been ascribed tentatively to the first century BCE.[54] Like the letter of Hippolochus, it takes the form of a letter to a friend describing a feast. It is parodic in tone, with numerous comic elements. At the beginning the guests discuss the best type of water (rather than of wine), while deipnic ostentation takes the form of a variety of lentil dishes being served, which raises playful complaints from the company: one of them says "Zeus, let the one responsible for these lentils not escape you!" (Ζεῦ, μὴ λάθοι σε τῶνδ᾽ ὃς αἴτιος φακῶν) and another exclaims "May a bean-ful destiny and a bean-ful fate seize you!" (φακός σε δαίμων καὶ φακὴ τύχη λάβοι). The complaints are parodies of tragic lines: the symposiasts show off their learning and hilariously transform tragic lines by substituting φακός, "lentil," for κακός, "evil," which raises laughter from the other guests.[55] Two courtesans, Melissa and Nicion, join the company and laugh at the Cynic lentil-fare. Nicion starts a discussion on food with Carneius, called earlier the "dog-leader" (κύνουλκος)—that is, the chief Cynic (*Deipn.* 4.157a–d):

"οὐδεὶς ὑμῶν, ἄνδρες γενειοσυλλεκτάδαι, ἰχθὺν ἐσθίει; ἢ καθάπερ ὁ πρόγονος ὑμῶν Μελέαγρος ὁ Γαδαρεὺς ἐν ταῖς Χάρισιν ἐπιγραφομέναις ἔφη τὸν Ὅμηρον Σύρον ὄντα τὸ γένος κατὰ τὰ πάτρια ἰχθύων ἀπεχομένους ποιῆσαι τοὺς Ἀχαιοὺς δαψιλείας πολλῆς οὔσης κατὰ τὸν Ἑλλήσποντον; ἢ μόνον ἀνέγνωτε συγγραμμάτων αὐτοῦ τὸ περιέχον λεκίθου καὶ φακῆς σύγκρισιν; ὁρῶ γὰρ πολλὴν παρ᾽ ὑμῖν τῆς φακῆς τὴν σκευήν· εἰς ἣν ἀποβλέπουσα συμβουλεύσαιμ᾽ ἂν ὑμῖν κατὰ τὸν Σωκρατικὸν Ἀντισθένην ἐξάγειν ἑαυτοὺς τοῦ βίου τοιαῦτα σιτουμένους."[56]

"Don't any of you, beard-gathering sirs, eat fish? Or is it as your ancestor Meleager of Gadara said about Homer in his work entitled *The Graces*, that because he was a Syrian by birth he followed the customs of his country and represented the Achaeans as avoiding fish, even though there was an abundant supply of them in the Hellespont? Or is the only treatise by him you've read the one that includes a comparison of bean soup and lentil soup? Because I see that a lot of lentil soup has been prepared for you; and when I see it, my advice to you would be, to quote Socrates' associate Antisthenes, to export yourselves from life, if this is how you eat."     (trans. S. D. Olson)

In response, Carneius refers to Clearchus, who reported the Pythagoreans' doctrine of life as punishment of human souls and the sect's prohibition of suicide.

---

[54] Olson 2006, xiii. Parmeniscus mentions Meleager of Gadara as a Cynic ancestor (πρόγονος), which provides a terminus post quem. Sandin 2014b, 109 n. 97 proposes that the original text had "Menippus" instead of "Meleager," as the former makes better sense as a πρόγονος of the Cynics. For a thoughtful discussion of the letter, see Hobden 2013, 235–9.

[55] Euripides, *Med.* 332: Ζεῦ, μὴ λάθοι σε τῶνδ᾽ ὃς αἴτιος κακῶν; *Trag. Adesp.* TrGF F 92: κακός σε δαίμων καὶ κακὴ τύχη λάβοι.

[56] I follow Olson in Loeb in discriminating between Parmeniscus' text and the interventions of Athenaeus' interlocutors. For their unclear boundaries, see König 2012, 107–9.

"These are the doctrines we follow," τούτοις τοῖς δόγμασιν ἡμεῖς πειθόμεθα, he adds.

There is a sympotic display of knowledge here, but also an unmistaken element of the absurd. When Nicion mockingly suggests that it would be better for the Cynics to commit suicide than to keep eating lentils, Carneius quotes the Peripatetic Clearchus and his report on the Pythagorean doctrine forbidding suicide. His earnest reaction to Nicion's ridicule is ludicrous, and it is bizarre to have a Cynic quoting a Pythagorean doctrine with great solemnity. In addition, his response is conspicuously out of place in a sympotic dialogue: it reads as if it has been taken from a different dialogic realm, namely that of dialogues on death. The issue of suicide and its ethical permissibility as well as the idea that life is a punishment for the human race features famously in Plato's *Phaedo* (61c–62c), and while there was an ancient tradition of interweaving convivial texts with the notion of mortality, literary strategies employed to create such fusions were more subtle.[57] Parmeniscus seems to parody this tradition by having Carneius eagerly grasp onto the opportunity to "talk death" at the *symposion*.

Nicion responds (*Deipn.* 4.157d–f):

"ὑμῖν δὲ φθόνος οὐδὲ εἷς ἑλέσθαι ἕν τι τῶν τριῶν ἔχειν κακῶν. οὐ γὰρ ἐπίστασθε, ὦ ταλαίπωροι, ὅτι αἱ βαρεῖαι αὗται τροφαὶ φράττουσι τὸ ἡγεμονικὸν καὶ οὐκ ἐῶσι τὴν φρόνησιν ἐν αὐτῇ εἶναι." ... "Ἡμῖν δὲ αὐτάρκης μερὶς ἣν ἂν παρ' ὑμῶν λάβωμεν, καὶ οὐ χαλεπαίνομεν ὡς ἔλαττον φερόμενοι, καθάπερ ὁ παρὰ Ἀντικλείδῃ Ἡρακλῆς. φησὶ γὰρ οὗτος ἐν τῷ δευτέρῳ τῶν Νόστων· μετὰ τὸ συντελέσαι τοὺς ἄθλους Ἡρακλέα Εὐρυσθέως θυσίαν τινὰ ἐπιτελοῦντος συμπαραληφθέντα καὶ τῶν τοῦ Εὐρυσθέως υἱῶν τὰς μερίδας ἑκάστῳ παρατιθέντων, τῷ δ' Ἡρακλεῖ ταπεινοτέραν παραθέντων, ὁ Ἡρακλῆς ἀτιμάζεσθαι ὑπολαβὼν ἀπέκτεινε τρεῖς τῶν παίδων Περιμήδην, Εὐρύβιον, Εὐρύπυλον. οὐ τοιοῦτοι οὖν τὸν θυμὸν ἡμεῖς, εἰ καὶ πάντα Ἡρακλέους ζηλωταί."

"But no one begrudges you picking one of the three evils for your own.[58] You don't realize, you wretches, that these heavy foods impede the authoritative part of the soul and prevent your good sense from being fully conscious."... "Whatever share we get from you is enough for us, and we don't become angry because we got a smaller portion, as Anticleides' Heracles did. For he says in Book II of his *Homecomings*: After Heracles completed his labors, he was included in the party when Eurystheus made a sacrifice. Eurystheus' sons were serving each person his portion, and they served Heracles one of the poorer ones;

---

[57] For interweaving the sympotic texts with the theme of death, see Jażdżewska 2013.
[58] The "three evils" Nicion speaks about may be three methods of dying (ξίφος, βρόχον, κώνειον, "sword, noose, hemlock"; see Zenobius 6.11 and *Suda* s.v. τὰ τρία τῶν εἰς τὸν θάνατον (τ 154) or, more likely, three types of punishment (cf. Polyzelus F 3 K–A: τριῶν κακῶν γοῦν ἦν ἑλέσθ' αὐτῷ τι πᾶσ' ἀνάγκη, ἢ ξύλον ἐφέλκειν, ἢ πιεῖν κώνειον, ἢ προδόντα τὴν ναῦν ὅπως τάχιστα τῶν κακῶν ἀπαλλαγῆναι; the punishments presumably are prison, poison, exile); in the latter case, Nicion points out that if the gods were to punish Carneius for suicide, he would be able to choose the penalty.

he assumed that he was being insulted and killed three of the boys, Perimedes, Eurybius, and Eurypylus. Our temperament is different, even if we imitate Heracles in every way."  (trans. S. D. Olson)

Nicion suggests that the Cynics' diet negatively impacts their reasoning faculty; Carneius' answer again appears oddly out of place: he emphasizes the Cynics' temperance and reports a story about Heracles, the Cynic hero, but only to say that it exemplifies a comportment contrary to theirs.

Some of the incongruity in the exchange between Nicion and Carneius may be due to condensation and abridgment of the original text, but it seems that at least in part the letter was deliberately infused with a sense of the absurd and the bizarre. Assuming the first-century BCE dating is accurate, Parmeniscus' work, as a parodic *symposion*, precedes Petronius' *Dinner of Trimalchio* and Lucian's *Lexiphanes* and *Symposion, or the Lapiths*. On the other hand, the propensity of Parmeniscus' interlocutors to display their learnedness by erudite quotations sets a precedent to early imperial dialogues such as Plutarch's *Table Talk* and Athenaeus' *Deipnosophists*.[59]

An epistolary format with an embedded dialogue is also a recurrent feature in pseudepigraphic letters, which presently draw more scholarly attention than in the past, when they were scorned as "forgeries." These texts are difficult to date, but some appear to have originated in the late Hellenistic period. Such is the case of the pseudepigraphic letters of Hippocrates, which first emerge in a papyrus dated to the early first century CE (POxy. 1184).[60] *Letter* 17 belongs to a group of epistles that constitute a *Briefroman*, a novel in letters, as they all tell the story of Hippocrates' meeting with Democritus.[61] The first letter in the sequence is a request sent by the Abderites to Hippocrates, inviting him to come and heal the philosopher, who they fear is mad—and the most prominent symptom of his madness is his laughing at everything.

In *Letter* 17, addressed to a friend, Damagetus, Hippocrates provides an account of his visit to Abdera. After a short introduction detailing his arrival and a meeting with the citizens, Hippocrates narrates his encounter with Democritus. A report of their conversation—that is, a dialogue between Hippocrates and Democritus—takes up about eight out of nine pages in the recent

---

[59] For Parmeniscus' work as a challenge to and subversion of the learned and philosophical *symposion*, see Hobden 2013, 235; for its similarity with Athenaeus, Olson 2006, xiii–xiv.

[60] The late Hellenistic dating of *Letter* 17 discussed in this chapter remains tentative. For the dating of the Hippocratic letters, see Sakalis 1989, 86–9 (who proposes 40–30 BCE) and Smith 1990, 26–9, who points out several indications suggesting the first century BCE. Brodersen 1994 warns against considering the date of POxy. 1184 as terminus ante quem for all Hippocratic letters (it contains only letters 3–5 and 6a and the letters are not a homogenous corpus). The figure of the laughing Democritus was possibly known to Cicero (*De or.* 2.58.235) and certainly to Horace (*Epist.* 2.1.194) (Rütten 1992, 11–12), though this does not mean that they were familiar with the letters.

[61] Holzberg 1994, 22–8. He considers letters 1–9 and 10–17 as two sections of one narrative; see, however, Brodersen 1994 for arguments against their unity.

edition of the text by Smith.[62] Hippocrates describes how he approached Democritus, who was sitting under a "spreading low plane tree" (*Ep.* 17.2 [74.15–16 Smith]: ὑπό τινι ἀμφιλαφεῖ καὶ χθαμαλῇ πλατανίστῳ), with a small spring (λεπτόρρυτον ὕδωρ) and a shrine dedicated to Nymphs close by (τι τέμενος ... νυμφέων ἱδρυμένον). The landscape reminds the reader of Plato's *Phaedrus* with its "spreading and tall plane tree" (*Phdr.* 230b: πλάτανος αὕτη μάλ' ἀμφιλαφής τε καὶ ὑψηλή), a spring of cold water (πηγὴ χαριεστάτη ... μάλα ψυχροῦ ὕδατος), and a temple of the Nymphs (Νυμφῶν τέ τινων ... ἱερόν). By means of such an unambiguous gesture the author locates the conversation between Hippocrates and Democritus within the tradition of the philosophical dialogue. The passage splendidly exemplifies ancient mimetic literary strategies which entail a simultaneous echoing and transformation: the Platonic idyllic landscape is recreated, but at the same time, it is unsettled by the inclusion of details of Democritus' looks (he is pale, emaciated, and sloppily dressed) as well as by the alarming image of heaps of animal corpses, many of them cut up, that surround the philosopher (*Ep.* 17.2 [74.22–6 Smith]: σεσώρευντο ... ζῷα συχνὰ ἀνατετμημένα δι' ὅλων ...; and τὰ σπλάγχνα τῶν ζῴων in the next sentence).

The conversation itself plays with a variety of philosophical and dialogic *topoi*. The figures of the interlocutors—a physician and a philosopher—allow the author to highlight the association between philosophy and medicine: Hippocrates comes to Democritus in order to assess and heal him, but in the end, he is healed by the philosopher. When at some point Democritus laughs at Hippocrates, the latter seeks to understand the reason for his laughter (*Ep.* 17.4 [78.21–80.1 Smith]):

ὑποτυχὼν δ' ἐγώ, "ἀλλὰ μήν," ἔφην, "σοφῶν ἄριστε, Δημόκριτε, ποθέω γὰρ αἰτίην τοῦ περὶ σὲ πάθεος καταλαβέσθαι, τίνος ἄξιος ἐφάνην ἐγὼ γέλωτος ἢ τὰ λεχθέντα ὅκως μαθὼν παύσωμαι τῆς αἰτίης, ἢ σὺ ἐλεγχθεὶς διακρούσῃ τοὺς ἀκαίρους γέλωτας." ὁ δέ, "Ἡράκλεις, ἔφη, εἰ γὰρ δυνήσῃ με ἐλέγξαι, θεραπείην θεραπεύσεις οἵην οὐδένα πώποτε, Ἱππόκρατες." "Καὶ πῶς οὐκ ἐλεγχθείσῃ," ἔφην, "ὦ ἄριστε; ἢ οὐκ οἴει ἄτοπός γε εἶναι γελῶν ἀνθρώπου θάνατον ἢ νοῦσον ἢ παρακοπὴν ἢ μανίην ἢ μελαγχολίην ἢ σφαγὴν ἢ ἄλλο τι χέρειον ἢ τοὔμπαλιν γάμους ἢ πανηγύριας ἢ τεκνογονίην ἢ μυστήρια ἢ ἀρχὰς καὶ τιμὰς ἢ ἄλλο τι ὅλως ἀγαθόν; καὶ γὰρ ἃ δέον οἰκτείρειν γελᾷς καὶ ἐφ' οἷσιν ἥδεσθαι χρή, καταγελᾷς τούτων, ὥστε μήτε ἀγαθὸν μήτε κακὸν παρά σοι διακεκρίσθαι."

"But Democritus, wisest of men, I want to find out the reason for your affection why I or what I said seems to deserve laughter, so that, when I find out, I can cure my fault, or you, when you are proved mistaken, can repress your inappropriate laughter." He said: "By Heracles, if you can prove me mistaken you will have effected a cure such as you have never achieved for anyone, Hippocrates." "How

---

[62] For the dialogic character of the Hippocratic letters, see Hersant 1989, 14 who considers *Letter* 17 as a "bel exemple d'un mélange de diégétique et de mimétique."

shall you not be proved mistaken, oh best of men?" I said. "Don't you think you are outlandish to laugh at a man's death or illness, or delusion, or madness, or melancholy, or murder, or something still worse, or again at marriages, feasts, births, initiations, offices and honors, or anything else wholly good? Things that demand grief you laugh at, and when things should bring happiness you laugh at them. There is no distinction between good and bad with you."

(trans. W. D. Smith)

The triple use of the verb ἐλέγχω ("to question, refute") in this passage emphasizes a link with the tradition of the philosophical dialogue and discussion; at the same time, the topic of Hippocrates' conversation with Democritus slightly shifts from the particular problem of "why is Democritus laughing" and "is Democritus crazy" towards the moral question of the good and the bad. Democritus' explanation of his laughter takes the form of a lengthy excursus about human folly. He details the miseries of human existence and describes the wretched moral condition of the men whom he mocks and scorns with his laughter.[63] His denigration of human folly and wretchedness has a Cynic ring, and perhaps was influenced by Cynic *paraenesis*.[64]

By the end of the conversation, Hippocrates, swayed by Democritus, acknowledges Democritus' laughter as a remedy that has the power to bring people to reason (*Ep.* 17.10 [92.10 Smith]: σωφρονίζειν). The ending is abrupt, and perhaps ironic:[65] Hippocrates becomes convinced immediately after Democritus reminds him how ungrateful patients are towards physicians, which makes Hippocrates accept the philosopher's pessimistic view of human nature.

At the end of the conversation, Hippocrates promises to Democritus to come again to talk to him (*Ep.* 17.10 [92.4–6 Smith]): ἀπαλλάσσομαι.... αὔριον δὲ καὶ κατὰ τὸ ἑξῆς ἐν ταὐτῷ γενησόμεθα ("I shall go away.... But tomorrow and the day after we shall be in the same place," trans. W. D. Smith). Such promises of future conversations belong to the conventions of the ancient dialogue, which recurrently end with announcements that the discussion will be continued in the future.[66] They are among the dialogic conventions that help create an illusion of depth for the dramatic world, which appears to have a life of its own beyond the boundaries of literature.

The presence of recognizable dialogic strategies and motifs within an epistolographic frame clearly points to conscious intergeneric game. But dialogue and

---

[63] Democritus' laughter comes across not merely as derisive and reproachful, but also as disillusioned and desperate. For the lability of Democritus and his oscillation between the optimism and despair, see Hankinson 2019, 72.

[64] Stewart 1958; Smith 1990, 27–9; Temkin 1991, 62, 68–70.    [65] Hankinson 2019, 71.

[66] Plans to meet again at a specific time to continue the discussion are made at the end of Plato's *Theaetetus, Laches,* and the pseudo-Platonic *Axiochus*; unspecific later discussions are announced in *Cratylus, Protagoras,* and the pseudo-Platonic *Sisyphus*.

letter are not the only generic components the author reaches for. The epistle also interacts with Greek drama by means of the topography upon which the action unfolds. At the beginning of the letter we read that the Abderites take Hippocrates to a high hill (βουνὸς... ὑψηλός) shaded by large poplars (μακρῇσι... αἰγείροισιν) from which they watch Democritus and his house (ἔνθεν τε ἐθεωρεῖτο τὰ τοῦ Δημοκρίτου καταγώγια; later the place is referred to as "the lookout," σκοπιή, Ep. 17.10 [92.8 Smith]). Hippocrates asks the Abderites to stay on the hill, while he himself goes down a steep slope (Ep. 17.3 [76.5–6 Smith]: κατέβαινον ἡσυχῇ. ἦν δὲ ὀξὺ καὶ ἐπίφορον ἐκεῖνο τὸ χωρίον). His encounter with the philosopher is watched intensely by the citizens (who at one point strike their heads and pull their hair in reaction to Democritus' behavior, Ep. 17.4 [78.18–19 Smith]). The placement of the characters is reminiscent of the Greek theatre, with Democritus occupying the stage and the Abderites situated on a slope of a hill like the audience. That this topography is not accidental is confirmed by the mention of the poplars which grow on the hill: as Krystyna Bartol has observed, they are an allusion to a proverbial saying "a view/seat by the poplar," which meant a view from the back seats of the Athenian theatre, where a poplar once grew.[67] Moreover, the image of Democritus surrounded by animal carcasses, some of them cut up, is reminiscent of Sophocles' Ajax,[68] who in madness killed animals he brought to his hut (Aj. 233–44, 296–310), and according to scholia, was displayed on the *ekkuklema* surrounded by their corpses (note that the theme of madness permeates both the Ajax and Letter 17, in which Democritus not only is suspected of madness by his fellow citizens but also writes a treatise on the subject when Hippocrates approaches him).

Letter 17, skillfully blending the epistolary format with dialogue and theatrical topography, is the most elaborate and complex of the Hippocratic letters. On a smaller scale, interaction with the dialogue can be found in Letter 15, in which Hippocrates, prior to the visit to Abdera, narrates his dream to Philopoemen, his prospective host in the city. In the dream he saw Asclepius saying that his help will not be needed in Democritus' case; instead, another goddess will serve as Hippocrates' guide. The goddess, a tall and beautiful woman with a commanding look, then appeared, took Hippocrates by the hand, and said (Ep. 15 [68.22–6 Smith]):

---

[67] Bartol 2007a; Bartol 2007b, 41–2. The phrase is attested in several Greek lexica; see e.g. three entries in Hesychius s.v. αἰγείρου θέα (α 1695), θέα παρ' αἰγείρῳ (θ 166), and παρ' αἴγειρον θέα (π 513); Photius, Lex. s.v. αἰγείρου θέα καὶ ἡ παρ' αἴγειρον θέα (α 505) and θέαν παρ' αἴγειρον (θ 47); Suda s.v. ἀπ' αἰγείρου θέα καὶ ἐπ' αἴγειρον (α 2952) and αἴγειρος (αι 35). The verb θεωρέω used by the author of Letter 17 (βουνὸς... αἰγείροισιν ἐπίσκιος· ἔνθεν τε ἐθεωρεῖτο τὰ τοῦ Δημοκρίτου καταγώγια) echoes explanations of lexicographers (e.g. Hesychius s.v. θέα παρ' αἰγείρῳ: τόπος αἴγειρον ἔχων, ὅθεν ἐθεώρουν. εὐτελὴς δὲ ἐδόκει ἡ ἐντεῦθεν θεωρία).

[68] I thank an anonymous reviewer for drawing my attention to this point.

"αὔριόν σε παρὰ Δημοκρίτῳ καταλήψομαι." ἤδη δὲ αὐτῆς μεταστρεφομένης· "Δέομαι, φημί, ἀρίστη, τίς εἶ καὶ τίνα σε καλέομεν;" ἡ δὲ, "Ἀλήθεια," ἔφη, "αὕτη δὲ, ἣν προσιοῦσαν ὁρῇς," καὶ ἐξαίφνης ἑτέρη τις κατεφαίνετό μοι οὐκ ἀκαλλὴς μὲν οὐδ' αὐτή, θρασυτέρη δὲ ἰδέσθαι καὶ σεσοβημένη, "Δόξα," ἔφη, "καλεῖται. κατοικεῖ δὲ παρὰ τοῖσιν Ἀβδηρίτῃσιν."

"Tomorrow I shall find you at Democritus' house." As she turned away, I said: "I beg you, excellent one, who are you and what shall we call you?" "Truth," she said. "And this one you see approaching," and suddenly another woman appeared, not unhandsome herself, but bolder and agitated, "is named Opinion. She lives with the Abderites." (trans. W. D. Smith)

The dream, which comforts Hippocrates and convinces him that Democritus is well—which is why Asclepius' help is not needed—is a rewriting of the story of Heracles' meeting with Arete and Kakia in Xenophon's *Apomnemoneumata* (*Mem.* 2.1.21–34). The author of the letter creates a miniature, highly condensed rewriting of Xenophon's famous episodes, a rewriting which relies on the reader's familiarity with the hypotext and owes much of its meaning to it. At the same time, the opposition of Truth and Opinion is reminiscent of Parmenides (note that the gesture of Truth, who takes Hippocrates by the hand, mirrors that of the Goddess who speaks to Parmenides, F 1 ll. 22–3 Coxon).

Another set of pseudepigraphic epistles that combine epistolary and dialogic formats which merits a short mention are the letters of Diogenes the Cynic.[69] This is a heterogenous collection, composed by various anonymous authors at different times. Several of the letters, perhaps composed by the same person, include longer dialogized sections (*Ep.* 30, 35, 37–8) and three are dialogues in an epistolary frame as they consist almost entirely of Diogenes' report of his conversation (*Ep.* 31, 33, 36). Dating is uncertain; this particular segment of the letters might have been composed in the second century CE. They are, then, probably a product of the early imperial rather than the Hellenistic period. Still, in form and content they develop patterns and motifs familiar from earlier literature. In the epistolary dialogues *Letters* 31, 33, and 36 Diogenes writes to his addressees (Phaelynus, Phanomachus, and Timomachus, respectively) about conversations he had: in *Letter* 31, it is a conversation with a pancratist Cicermus; in *Letter* 33—with Alexander the Great; in *Letter* 36—with an unnamed passerby. The letters draw from a common anecdotal tradition concerning Diogenes. The format of the epistolary dialogue allows the author to have Diogenes himself narrate the conversations and extend familiar anecdotes into longer episodes—another exemplification of the processes discussed above, by which an anecdote might have been

---

[69] For Diogenes' letters in general, see Capelle 1896, 5–49; von Fritz 1926, 63–72; Emeljanow 1967; Malherbe 1977; a new critical edition appeared in Giannantoni 1990b, 423–64.

elaborated into a dialogue (or, alternatively, a dialogue might have been abridged and condensed into an anecdote).[70]

## 1.4 Dialogue and Extended Biographies

It should be briefly noted that interactions with the dialogue occurred also in extended Hellenistic biographies. First, ancient *bioi* could contain, besides short exchanges between the protagonist and other characters, also lengthy dialogized sections. Such is the case of Aristoxenus' *Life of Archytas*, a biography of the Pythagorean philosopher Archytas of Tarentum. Aristoxenus was a student of Aristotle and is considered to have been the first Peripatetic biographer.[71] A fragment of the biography preserved in Athenaeus' *Deipnosophists* (12.545a–546c [F 50 Wehrli]) relates a visit by ambassadors of the tyrant Dionysius the Younger to Tarentum, among whom was Polyarchus, nicknamed Ἡδυπαθής, "Voluptary," on account of his professed hedonism. Polyarchus used to listen to the conversations of Archytas and his followers, and on one occasion, when the problem of pleasure and desires was being discussed, he defended at length a life of pleasure as both natural and reasonable.[72] Athenaeus partially quotes, partially paraphrases his lengthy speech. Polyarchus' defense of pleasure must have been followed by a response by Archytas (the protagonist of the biography), which is not preserved in Athenaeus, but perhaps is summarized by Cicero's Cato the Elder in his dialogue on old age (*Sen.* 12.39–41). The connection of this section with the dialogue tradition goes beyond the employment of direct speech. As a discussion on a moral subject between a philosopher and someone associated with a tyrant, the conversation unfolds upon the background of dialogic literature representing encounters between wisdom and political rule—while, thematically, the figure of Polyarchus appears as a new incarnation of Plato's Callicles or Thrasymachus.

We encounter another, more surprising merger of dialogue and biography in *Life of Euripides* by the biographer Satyrus of Callatis. Preserved fragments, which I discuss in the next chapter (Chapter 2.3.1), demonstrate that the work, rather than being a continuous narration, was a dialogue, in which two or more interlocutors discussed the life and works of Euripides; moreover, at least one of them was a woman. This unusual format allowed Satyrus not only to present

---

[70] Another imperial period example of the combination of epistolography and a dialogue is the Epicurean inscription by Diogenes of Oenoanda, which contains Diogenes' letter to Antipater, in which he reports his conversation with Theodoridas on the infinite number of worlds; I discuss it briefly in Chapter 6.6.
[71] Momigliano 1971, 74–6. For Aristoxenus as a biographer, see Schorn 2012. See also Chapter 5.6.
[72] For a detailed discussion and commentary on the fragment, see Huffman 2005, 310–22.

biographical material but also to represent the reception of Euripides and the ongoing discussion about his legacy.

## 1.5 Conclusion

The chapter shows a diversity of interactions between the dialogue and anecdote, letter, and biography. In the case of the dialogue and anecdote, the boundaries were fluid. The ancient anecdote, *chreia*, typically contained a short verbal exchange or a memorable utterance related in direct speech, which associated it with the dialogue. In between the succinct *chreia* and the dialogue there is a continuum of shorter and longer dialogized conversational episodes and miniature dialogues, sometimes drawing from discursive strategies associated with the Socratic dialogue such as the question-and-answer format. This affinity allowed for the easy conversion of dialogue passages into anecdotes and the other way around.

The letter is immediately recognizable to the reader by its formal features, such as an epistolary prescript and greeting; therefore, it could embed and host a variety of other prose types without losing its generic affiliation. This is well exemplified by *The Letter of Aristeas*, which contains a variety of insets within the epistolographic frame, including longer and shorter dialogues. Such blending of a letter and dialogue was not unusual in pseudepigrapha, with some authors accentuating their intergeneric play by means of mimetic interaction with Plato (*Letter* 17 of Hippocrates). There is also a close affinity between such pseudepigraphic epistles and the anecdotal tradition, as seen in the letters of Diogenes the Cynic, which amplify anecdotes into longer conversations, at the same time "authorizing" them by making Diogenes their reporter.

Just as a letter could become a host genre for a dialogue; so could a biography, as probably happened in Aristoxenus' *Life of Archytas*, which referred to a philosophical discussion between Polyarchus and Archytas. An entirely different technique is employed by Satyrus, whose *Life of Euripides* appears to have had the outward form of a dialogue, but was filled with material conventionally providing the substance of a biography.

# 2
# Dialogues in Papyri

## 2.1 Introductory Remarks

Fragments of papyri offer us fascinating insight into dialogue production after the mid-fourth century BCE. The majority of the fragments discussed in this chapter were first published in modern times after the appearance of Rudolf Hirzel's 1895 monograph and therefore were not taken into account by him. In 1929, a survey of dialogues in papyri was published by W. M. Edwards.[1] Afterwards there was no general study examining the contribution of papyri to our understanding of the history of the ancient dialogue, and the material examined in the chapter is frequently overlooked even by scholars of Hellenistic prose.

There are numerous difficulties involved in studying fragments of dialogues extant in papyri, some inherent to any study of papyrological material, and some specific to an examination of the genre of dialogue itself. When dealing with a papyrus fragment, we usually do not know the identity of its author, his intellectual background and milieu, the title of the work or its length. Texts are damaged and lacunose, and often supplemented with the conjectures of editors, whose caution and restraint varies. Dating is highly conjectural: papyrologists usually tentatively identify the century in which a text was written down, which provides a terminus ante quem for its composition. In the case of Hellenistic period literature, such dating is particularly useful when a papyrus predates the imperial period; in the case of later papyri, one has to rely on slippery stylistic and linguistic criteria.

Identifying a papyrus fragment as coming from a dialogue is possible when it retains a sufficiently well-preserved section that includes an interlocutor change; if the lines in which a speaker change occurs are damaged, the format will most likely remain unrecognizable. In narrated dialogues, speaker changes are indicated by means of narrative interventions (ἔφη, εἶπεν, etc.); in dramatic ones, they are signaled with verbal forms indicative of conversation (names in the vocative, verbs in the first- and second-person, typical conversational phrases and responses such as πάνυ μὲν οὖν). Punctuation marks signaling speaker changes—*paragraphoi*, *dicola*, other types of dots—may also provide helpful clues.

---

[1] Edwards 1929.

Many of these features, however, are not exclusive to the dialogue format. First- and second-person verb forms and vocatives also appear in letters, oratory, continuous texts of a philosophical nature (in particular protreptic and moralizing texts as well as polemics), etc., while *paragraphoi* and other lectional signs have a variety of other functions. Consequently, one usually needs a combination of several elements to identify with confidence a text as a dialogue.

Even when one identifies a fragment as coming from a dialogue, extractable information about the text and its structure and argument is generally limited and potentially misleading. For instance, a dramatic format does not preclude the presence of narration in other parts of the text (narrated dialogues may omit narrative interventions in some sections),[2] while a narrated exchange may have come from a "mixed dialogue" and been embedded within a dramatic conversation. Likewise, the number of speakers in a preserved passage tells us little about the overall cast of characters, and if the papyrus is damaged, tracing the distribution of interlocutors within the fragment is difficult or outright impossible. The same caveat applies to themes and arguments: a topic discussed in a given fragment might differ from the overarching theme of the dialogue; a philosophical position might be presented by a character whose intellectual authority was not endorsed by the author and the argument made might have been abandoned, transcended, or refuted in subsequent sections.

Despite these difficulties, papyri fragments provide important and fascinating evidence about post-Platonic dialogue production. They may be divided into four main categories: philosophical dialogues, dialogues on literature, historical dialogues (i.e. dialogues set in the past and intended at reviving historical circumstances and characters), and dialogized anecdotes. This is by no means a consistent typology of dialogue literature, but rather a common-sense aggregation of kindred texts based on their most prominent features. Besides these groups, there are also remnants of what seem to be dialogized school exercises (animal prose fables and dialogues between historical characters). The discussed fragments include for the most part texts whose composition we may assign with reasonable probability to pre-imperial times. I am focusing on fragments substantial enough to allow for examination, even if provisional and tentative, of content and format (at the end of the chapter, I list some other papyri with post-Platonic dialogues). Throughout, I rely on published editions and, whenever possible, on digitized images of papyri. In quotations of the Greek text I reproduce only legible and relevant sections, and the layout may differ from that in a published edition.

---

[2] Cf. for instance a change of format in Plato's *Parmenides* 137c and very limited narration in the pseudo-Platonic *Axiochus*.

## 2.2 Philosophical Dialogues

Philosophical dialogues constitute a category that features most heavily in the history of the genre: Plato established the dialogue as *the* philosophical medium, and the format was continued, alongside other forms that developed subsequently, by philosophers throughout antiquity. We find two types of philosophical dialogues in papyri: Socratic dialogues and non-Socratic dialogues of Academic/Peripatetic origins. To the first category belong dialogues which depict Socrates as an interlocutor and dialogues that are reminiscent of *Sokratikoi logoi* in terms of style and themes. We know that Socratic dialogues were still being composed after the fervent period of activity of the first generation of Socratics, even well after the fourth century BCE: works such as *Halcyon* or *Axiochus* are certainly of a post-Classical date. The difficulties of dating encountered when examining the Platonic *dubia* and *spuria*—discussed in Chapter 4—are amplified when one turns to small fragments of Socratic dialogues surviving in papyri, and the distinction between fragments of "real" Socratic texts composed by Socrates' immediate successors and dialogues stylized as Socratic remains provisional. Two fragments I discuss in this chapter appear to belong to the former group and to date to the first half of the fourth century (PErl. 4 and PSI XI 1215). The third text, PKöln 5.205, appears to have been produced later, in the third century BCE, and some scholars argued that it may be the work of post-Aristippean hedonists, perhaps Hegesias of Cyrene or one of his followers.

The second group of papyri fragments of philosophical dialogues comes from the post-Platonic environment, most likely from Academic or Peripatetic circles. These fragments are the scanty remains of a substantial dialogue production by the post-Platonic Academy and Peripatos, discussed in Chapters 3 and 5. Among them are POxy. 53.3699, a fragment of a protreptic dialogue which bears a striking resemblance to a passage from Aristotle's *Protrepticus*; PAï Khanoum inv. Akh IIIB77P.O.154, discussing the Ideas; and PPetr. 2.49e, focusing on animals and arguing for their affinity with humankind.

### 2.2.1 On *Eros* (PErl. 4 [MP³ 2103])

The papyrus, dated to around 200 CE, contains a fragment of a dramatic dialogue between two speakers whose names are not preserved. Wilhelm Schubart, the editor, classified the text as either a letter or a dialogue; scholars today agree on its dialogue format, which is implied by a *paragraphos* at the beginning of col. ii.32 and this line's shortening.[3] The participants of the dialogue seem to have included

---

[3] For the genre, see Schubart 1942, 14; Merkelbach 1958, 107. Schubart's edition, with notes by Merkelbach 1958, 107 and Obsieger 2007, remains the most reliable, as the edition by Luz 2014, 166–8, though it has its merits, has transcription errors.

a handsome young man and his *erastes*, who is disappointed by the youth's character, which he finds at odds with his appearance. In the first, partially preserved sentence, the youth appears to have complained that his situation— presumably that of an *eromenos* followed by a lover—resembles that of the sons of prominent men (ὅπερ καὶ οἱ παῖδες πάσχουσι τῶν φανερῶν πατέ[ρων]), who can neither escape notice, nor be granted forgiveness ([ο]οὔτε ἀ[γνοί]ας δύνα[σθαι][4] τυχεῖν οὔτε συγγνώ[μ]ης), probably for their shortcomings (PErl. 4 col. ii.28–32). The other speaker answers (PErl. 4 col. ii.33–57):

> τὸ μὲν σύμπαν ἀληθές, ὅτι ὁ τρώσας εἰάσεται· ἄλλος δὲ ἄλλως· ὁ μὲν ἕκων ὁ δὲ ἄκων, ἐπεὶ καὶ σὺ ἰάσω με οὐ βουλόμενος. ἥδιστα μὲν οὖ[ν] ἰά[μ]ατα φιλανθρω[πί]α τοῦ καλοῦ, ἐνίοτε δὲ καὶ ἐξουσία· τὰ πικρὰ ὠφελεῖ· ἄλλον μὲν ὕβρις καὶ σκαιότης, ἤδη γὰρ καὶ ὑπὸ τούτων ἀπεστράφησαν, ὥσπερ ξίφους ἀκμὴ στερεωτέρωι πρ[οσ]πεσοῦσα· [ἐ]μὲ δὲ τὸ πα[ρ' ἐλ]πίδα, οἷόν σε ἐπελάτ[ρευον] ἐπὶ καλῶι τῶι προσώ[πωι] εὐρὺν τὰ στέρνα, ἡδ[ὺν ἅ]ψασθαι. σὺ δέ μοι ὤφ[θης ο]ὐκ ἀντὶ παρθένου [ἔλα]φος, ἀλλὰ ἀπρόσωπ[ος τὸ] ἔνδον· ὥστε ἐμα[υτοῦ ἠ]πίστουν τῆι ἐκ[στάσει] σε εἶναι οὕτω [καλὸν] τὸ πρόσωπον....

It is completely true that he who has inflicted the injury will also become the healer—one person in this way, one in another, one person willingly, one not willingly. And you have healed me unintentionally. For the most pleasant love-remedy is the kindness of a beautiful person (*unclear*), but sometimes bitter remedies also help. For someone it may be arrogance and clumsiness—for people have also turned away from persons of this sort, like the point of a sword that falls on a hard surface. To me, however, something unexpected happened: I (*unclear*) you for your beautiful face, and you were of a broad chest and pleasant to touch. But you appeared to me not like a fawn instead of a maiden, but like a person faceless inside, and I disbelieved my own astonishment that your face is so beautiful....[5]

The text is not bereft of literary ambition.[6] The style of the *erastes* is elaborate: in this short passage, he cites two proverbs (ὁ τρώσας αὐτὸς ἰάσεται and ἀντὶ παρθένου [ἔλα]φος) and makes use of a comparison ("like the point of a sword") and two metaphors ("bitter remedies," "faceless inside"). Judging from later literature, the proverb ὁ τρώσας αὐτὸς ἰάσεται ("he who has inflicted the injury, will also become the healer") was used in an erotic context to signify that the affection of the loved one provides a cure for the pains of love, but the author

---

[4] Or perhaps δύναμαι (Merkelbach) or δυνάμενοι (Luz).
[5] The text follows Schubart 1942 apart from Luz's conjecture [ἔλα]φος in place of [Σέρι]φος.
[6] Luz 2014, 188.

twists its meaning and considers disappointment with the character of the loved one as a true love-remedy.[7]

Although the interlocutors in the dialogue fragment remain unknown, its ties with Socratic literature are evident. The popular motif of Socratic erotics looms behind *erastes*' fascination with the beautiful boy, with Plato's *Charmides* 154d–e providing a particularly close parallel:

καὶ ὁ Χαιρεφῶν καλέσας με, Τί σοι φαίνεται ὁ νεανίσκος, ἔφη, ὦ Σώκρατες; οὐκ εὐπρόσωπος; Ὑπερφυῶς, ἦν δ' ἐγώ. Οὗτος μέντοι, ἔφη, εἰ ἐθέλοι ἀποδῦναι, δόξει σοι ἀπρόσωπος εἶναι· οὕτως τὸ εἶδος πάγκαλός ἐστιν. Συνέφασαν οὖν καὶ οἱ ἄλλοι ταὐτὰ ταῦτα τῷ Χαιρεφῶντι· κἀγώ, Ἡράκλεις, ἔφην, ὡς ἄμαχον λέγετε τὸν ἄνδρα, εἰ ἔτι αὐτῷ ἓν δὴ μόνον τυγχάνει προσὸν σμικρόν τι. Τί; ἔφη ὁ Κριτίας. Εἰ τὴν ψυχήν, ἦν δ' ἐγώ, τυγχάνει εὖ πεφυκώς. πρέπει δέ που, ὦ Κριτία, τοιοῦτον αὐτὸν εἶναι τῆς γε ὑμετέρας ὄντα οἰκίας. Ἀλλ', ἔφη, πάνυ καλὸς καὶ ἀγαθός ἐστιν καὶ ταῦτα.

And Chairephon called to me and said, "Well, Socrates, what do you think of the young man? Hasn't he a splendid face?" "Extraordinary," I said. "But if he were willing to strip," he said, "you would hardly notice his face, his body is so perfect." Well, everyone else said the same things as Chairephon, and I said, "By Heracles, you are describing a man without an equal—if he should happen to have one small thing in addition." "What's that?" asked Critias. "If he happens to have a well-formed soul," I said. "It would be appropriate if he did, Critias, since he comes from your family." "He is very distinguished in that respect, too," he said.

(trans. R. Kent Sprague)

Both the papyrus fragment and the *Charmides* passage use the term ἀπρόσωπος and draw a contrast between external and internal "looks"; in both passages the overall message is that the beauty of the soul is of greater importance than that of the body.[8] If the unknown author had *Charmides* 154d–e in mind, he wittily transposed the meaning of ἀπρόσωπος to the realm of the soul by qualifying it with [τὸ] ἔνδον, "inside." The situation in the *Charmides* is opposite to that in the papyrus: Charmides' good looks are accompanied by an upright character,[9] while the fragment, on the other hand, focuses on an unexpected discrepancy between

---

[7] Plato is alluding to the saying in *Grg*. 447b, where Chairephon, whom Socrates blames for being late to Gorgias' performance, answers: Οὐδὲν πρᾶγμα, ὦ Σώκρατες· ἐγὼ γὰρ καὶ ἰάσομαι. The ancient explanation of the proverb was that it originally referred to Telephus, whose wound, inflicted by Achilles, could have been healed only by him. In the context of love, see Chariton, *Callirh*. 6.3.7: φάρμακον γὰρ ἕτερον ἔρωτος οὐδέν ἐστι πλὴν αὐτὸς ὁ ἐρώμενος· τοῦτο δὲ ἄρα καὶ τὸ ᾀδόμενον λόγιον ἦν ὅτι ὁ τρώσας αὐτὸς ἰάσεται; in other contexts, see e.g. Plutarch, *De aud.* 47a; Lucian, *Nigr*. 38. For the proverbial "fawn instead of a maiden," cf. Achilles Tatius 6.2.3: θέαμα ἰδὼν παραδοξότατον τῆς κατὰ τὴν ἔλαφον ἀντὶ παρθένου παροιμίας.

[8] Obsieger 2007, 86. [9] For Plato's representation of Charmides, see Tuozzo 2011, 86–90.

appearance and character. Socrates' relationship with Alcibiades, repeatedly represented in Socratic literature, provides another parallel (the *erastes*' observation that people turn away from scornful youths is reminiscent of *Alcibiades I* 103b), and it has been speculated that the fragment depicts a conversation between Socrates and Alcibiades. The notion of the external and internal "looks" and the internal "facelessness" of the youth brings to mind Socrates' "internal appearance," famously discussed by Alcibiades in Plato's *Symposion* (215a, 216d). Compared to Plato's Socrates, however, the *erastes* of the papyrus is more direct and serious in revealing his attraction to the bodily beauty of the young man; there are no traces of Socratic self-effacing irony.

The text might have been composed by one of the Socratics in the first decades of the fourth century BCE, but the author could also have been a later emulator of Socratic literature or of Plato. The dating of the papyrus to around 200 CE indicates that the work was still being copied in the imperial period, which makes well-known Socratics probable candidates. Aeschines of Sphettus as well as Antisthenes or one of his followers have been proposed as potential authors.[10]

### 2.2.2 The Art of Speaking in Democracy and Oligarchy (PSI XI 1215 [MP³ 2098])

In the papyrus, dated to the second half of the first century CE, two unnamed interlocutors discuss whether the ability to speak is more useful in democracy or oligarchy. The format is that of a narrated dialogue: there is ἔφη in col. ii.2 and probably ἦ in col. ii.23. Two *paragraphoi* (col. ii.6 and ii.22) mark changes of speakers. Here is the best-preserved part of the text (PSI XI 1215 col. i.36–ii.36):

"ἔπειτα οἱ περὶ τῶν αὐτῶ[ν], ἔφη, βουλευό[μενοι] οὐ τῶν αὐτῶν δό[ξου]σιν λόγων καὶ γ[νώ]μης τῆς [αὐτῆς μετέχειν];" "πάνυ μ[έ]ν οὖν." "[τί δέ; ἔφη] χρησιμώτερον ἔσ[ται] τὸ εἰπεῖν δύνασθα[ι ἐν] δημοκρατίᾳ ἢ ἐν ὀ[λι]γαρχίᾳ; ἢ τί; ἐνθάδ[ε] μᾶλλον ἢ ἐν Λακεδ[αί]μονι; ἢ ταύτῃ δοκ[εῖ] σοι ἡ πολειτεία δια[φέ]ρειν ἡ ἐνθάδε τῆς [ἐν] Λακεδαίμονι, ὅτι ἐ[ν]θάδε μὲν πολλοί, ἐ[κεῖ] δὲ ὀλίγοι εἰσὶν οἱ β[ου]λευόμενοι καὶ λέγο[ν]τες; καὶ τὴν μὲν ἐ[νθά]δε δημοκρατίας, [τὴν] δ' ἐκεῖ ἀρ[ισ]τοκρατ[ίας] εἰκόνα ᾳ[ὐ] ποιε[ῖς];" "πάνυ μὲν οὖν", ἦ. "τί δέ; ἆρ' οὖν καὶ κιθάρισ[ιν] καὶ αὔλησιν ἄλλην [τι]νὰ ὑπολήψει εἶνᾳ[ι ἐ]ὰν πολλοὶ ὦσιν οἱ [κι]θαρίζοντες ἢ οἱ α[ὐλοῦν]τες, ἐὰν δὲ ὀλίγοι ἐ[τέ]ραν; ἔπειτ' ἔστ [[ι]] αι, ἔ[φη], ἡ μὲν δημοκρατι{κ}κὴ κιθάρισις ὅταν [οἱ] πολλοὶ κιθαρίζω[σιν], ἡ δ' ὀλιγαρχικὴ ὅταν ὀλίγοι ταὐτὸ τοῦτο πράττωσιν; ἔπειτα...

---

[10] Aechines: Merkelbach 1958, 107; Carlini 1989; Antisthenes or his followers: Luz 2014. The papyrus is not included in *SSR*.

"... then, do not the people," he said, "who deliberate about the same things, share the same words and the same opinions?" "Yes, of course." "Well," he said, "will it be more useful to have the ability to speak in democracy or in oligarchy? Here or rather in Sparta? Or does it seem to you that our government differs from the Spartan in that here many, while there few, participate in deliberating and speaking? And you would say that the government here is an image of democracy, while the other—of aristocracy?" "Yes, certainly," he said. "Well, do you think that playing a kithara or aulos is one thing when there are many musicians and another when there are few of them? Is not democratic kithara-playing like when there are many kithara-players, and oligarchic when there are few? Next...."[11]

The conversation takes place in Athens, to which ἐνθάδε in col. ii.10 and ii.14 refers; the interlocutors are Athenians. The interpersonal dynamics are reminiscent of Socratic dialogues: there is a dominant speaker who develops the argument and ensures that his partner follows and agrees. He addresses him in the second person (col. ii.12–13: δοκ[εῖ] σοι), phrases his statements as questions, and adds supplementary interrogatives to ensure his engagement (col. ii.23: τί δέ;). The other character's part is limited to assenting (col. ii.6: πάνυ μ[ὲ]ν οὖν, and probably the same phrase in col. ii.22–3), though in a preceding section he probably authored the thesis which is being challenged in the fragment, namely that the art of speaking is more useful in democracy than in oligarchy.

While the main speaker might have been Socrates, the identity of his partner is unknown. The narration is limited to several "he said" phrases (in most cases they are conjectures); we do not know whether the narration was external or internal, and if the latter, who the narrator was. Several features—language, style, a preoccupation with the polarities of oligarchy and democracy, and with Athens and Sparta—suggest an early date, probably the first half of the fourth century BCE. The author's seeming interchangeable use of "oligarchy" and "aristocracy" has led some scholars to stipulate a date preceding Plato's distinction of forms of government in the *Republic*, but Christian Vassallo in the new edition reads ἀρ[ισ]τοκρατ[ίας] ẹἰκόνα "an image of aristocracy" (ii.21-2), and argues that conceiving oligarchy as an *eikon* of aristocracy presupposes familiarity with Plato's delineation of the mimetic relations between the forms of government in the *Republic*.[12] The text has been variously interpreted as the work of an oligarch and a supporter of Sparta, written in an anti-democratic spirit;[13] as a dialogue on rhetoric and its usefulness;[14] and as a Socratic dialogue of political nature,

---

[11] The Greek follows Vassallo 2014, 203–4.
[12] Vassallo 2014, 211–12; earlier scholars read εἴποις instead of εἰκόνα.
[13] Gigante 1948; Gigante 1949.   [14] Bartoletti 1959.

discussing differences between democracy and oligarchy, and critical of the Athenian form of government, perhaps by Antisthenes.[15]

### 2.2.3 Socrates and Hedonists: A Fragment of Hegesias of Cyrene? (PKöln 5.205 [MP³ 2587.01])

While this fragment undoubtedly contains a Socratic dialogue—Socrates' name is preserved in the text—it has been persuasively assigned to the post-Classical period.[16] Two linguistic features confirm the post-Classical date of the composition. First, the term τέλος, "life goal," is used in the text in a way not altogether consistent with the use among Socratics; and the adjective ἐπίλυπος is not attested before Aristotle.[17] The text is set in a dramatic format; the identity of Socrates' companion remains unknown. Changes of speaker are marked by *paragraphoi*, high points, and blank spaces. Four columns are preserved sufficiently well to give us a sense of the text's setting and preoccupation.

The conversation takes place after Socrates' trial and therefore, presumably, in prison. It centers on a topic familiar from Socratic literature, namely why Socrates did not make a serious effort to escape death and did not defend himself more effectively. Socrates argues that a reasonable man does not fear death (PKöln 5.205 col. i.30–iii.36):

...ἀποθνήισκειν μέλλων οὐκ ἐνοχλήσεται τὸν ἡδύν τε καὶ σπου[δ]αῖον βίον καταλείπων· ἢ οὐ μνημονεύεις τούτ[ο]υ [γε ἕ]νεκ[εν] ἡμᾶς [εἰς τ]αύτην τὴν [θεωρ]ίαν ἀποκλί[ναν]τας;

– Ἀμέλει [μν]ημονεύω τε κ[αὶ ο]ἶδα ἀκριβῶς.

– Οὐκοῦν ἄχρι γε τοῦ νῦν κατ' οὐθένα τῶν λόγων δυνάμεθ' εὑρεῖν ὡς ὁ τοῦ νοῦν ἔχοντος βί[ο]ς ἡδίων ἐστὶ [........] ἢ ἐπιλυπότερος; οὐ γὰρ δή, μ[ὰ τὸν Δ]ία, οὐ τὰ ἰατρ[ρ.....].ᾳ [ἢ]ττον ἡδ[έα] .. [κα]ταλείπειν λυπ[οῖ]τ ἂν ὁ νοῦν ἔχῳ[ν], εἰ μέλλοι ἀποθ[νήισ]κειν.

– Ο ..[....]εται, ἐγὼ σοὶ .[...].

– Ἀλλὰ μὴν οὐ[δὲ ἐκ]είνου γε ἕνεκεν τοῦ μή τι ἐν Ἅιδου δυσχερὲς ἔπη[ται], ἀποκνήσει ἀποθνήισκειν· οἴομαι γὰρ ἡμῖν ἐν τοῖς ἔμπροσθεν δεδεῖχθαι, ὅτι οὐδενὶ οἷόν τ[έ] ἐστι τῶν ἐν Ἅιδου οὐθὲν δυσχερὲς [συμ]βαίνειν.

---

[15] Vassallo 2014, 217–31.

[16] Based on the script, the papyrus has been dated to the third century BCE. For a discussion on this, see Gronewald 1985; Barnes 1987, 365–6; Spinelli 1992; Lampe 2015, 136–42.

[17] Lampe 2015, 139 rightly observes that although τέλος happens to be used by Plato in this sense, "the formulation of 'ends' as ultimate reference points of positive and negative value, by which ethical systems could conveniently be encapsulated and compared, dates to a time after the debate among Socrates' immediate followers" and that "the casualness with which Socrates' interlocutor uses it ... suggests a date sometime after this technical term became central to ethical philosophy...." For τέλος and ἐπίλυπος, see also Gronewald 1985, 34 nn. 4, 43; Spinelli 1992, 12.

- Ἀμέ[λει κ]αὶ τοῦτό μοι δοκεῖ ἱκανῶς ὑπὸ ϙοῦ δεδεῖχθαι.
- [?] τ .[...ἐ]πιποθεῖς τιν[....]της ἀπολογ[ία- ἀ]κοῦσαι, ἥν ἀπ[....]υμεϱόν με . [....]αβες, δι' ἥν [αἰτία]ν οὐκ ἀπελ[ογ]ησάμην Ἀθη[ν]αίοις περὶ τῆς τοῦ θανάτου δίκης;
- Μὰ τὸν Δία οὐκέτι ἔγωγε ἀλλὰ ταῦτα μὲν ἄπαντα, ὦ Σώκρατες, ἐμοί τε καὶ σοὶ καὶ τοῖς νομίζουσιν ἡδονὴμ μὲν εἶναι [τέ]λος ἄριστον βίου, λύπην δὲ κάκισ[το]ν δόξειας ἂν κ[α]λῶς ἀπολελογῆσθαι, διότι οὐκ ἀπελογήσω περ[ὶ τ]ῆς τοῦ θαν[άτου] δίκης· . [].[. .]ν ἄλλοι γε τέλος τιθέμενοι τὸ καλόν τε καὶ τὸγ καλὸμ βίον ἄριστο[ν εἶ]ναι καὶ τὸ αἰσχρὸν [κ]αὶ τὸν αἰσχρὸμ β[ίο]ν κάκιστον οὐ β[ο]υλήσονται ἡμῖν συ[νο]μολογεῖν, ὡς ἄρ[α], ἐπειδὴ ἐν ἡδονῇ[ι κ]αὶ λύπῃ οὐθέ[ν] ἐλαττου [ ... ]

- ...who is about to die, will not be disturbed that he is leaving a pleasant and virtuous life. Or don't you remember that this is why we turned to this examination?
- Certainly, I remember and know very well.
- Isn't it that until now we were not able to find any argument that the life of a reasonable man is more pleasant [*lacuna*] than more painful? Not, by Zeus [*damaged*] A reasonable man, if he were to die, wouldn't be sorry to leave what is less pleasant.
- [*damaged*]
- But he will also not shrink from death because of fear that some unpleasant things will happen in Hades. For I think that we have shown before that it is not possible that anything unpleasant happens to anyone in Hades.
- Yes, I think that this also was sufficiently demonstrated by you.
- Do you wish [*damaged*] to hear a defense, which [*damaged*] why I did not defend myself in front of the Athenians against the death penalty?
- Not any more, by Zeus. However, this entire defense is well argued, Socrates, to me, to yourself, and to those who think that pleasure is the best goal in life and pain the worst—why you did not defend yourself against death penalty.... But other people, who believe that nobility itself is the aim and that the noble life is the best, while evil itself and the evil life are the worst, will not wish to agree with us that, when in pleasure and pain not less....[18]

Socrates' answer is not preserved.

Socrates' disregard for death and his half-hearted defense are recurrent topics in Socratic literature. The editor of the editio princeps proposed that the text was composed in the fourth century BCE by one of the immediate followers of Socrates, perhaps Aeschines of Sphettus or Aristippus of Cyrene. Spinelli has argued that in the fragment, Socrates and his interlocutor are associated with hedonists—those who consider pleasure to be τέλος—and juxtaposed with those who are guided by

---

[18] The Greek text follows Gronewald 1985. For a different reconstruction, see Spinelli 1992, 10. Distribution of the text among speakers is not always clear and differs in various publications.

τὸ καλόν. Consequently, he thought, the author should be placed among the circles of the Socratic or post-Socratic hedonists. He also noted that the hedonistic perspective is associated, somewhat surprisingly, with the conviction that there is nothing in life that a man of reason would deplore were he to die: in preceding sections Socrates and his interlocutor apparently were not able to find a proof "that the life of a reasonable man is pleasant... than more painful" (col. ii.10–14: ὡς ὁ τοῦ νοῦν ἔχοντος βί[ο]ς ἡδίων ἐστὶ [ . . . . . . . . ] ἢ ἐπιλυπότερος).[19] This, Spinelli has observed, recalls the teachings of the post-Epicurean Cyrenaics of the third century BCE, in particular the school of Hegesias of Cyrene nicknamed Πεισιθάνατος, "Death-Persuader," who combined hedonism with the conviction that happiness was impossible (on Hegesias, see Chapter 6.3).[20]

It should be observed, however, that while it is striking that the interlocutor lists himself and Socrates together with people who believe that pleasure is the ultimate life-goal, τέλος, this does not necessarily mean that Socrates and his interlocutor identified as hedonists throughout the dialogue. It is possible, for instance, that Socrates argued that his decision can be justified from different perspectives: not only from a perspective that he and his interlocutor shared (which perhaps has been discussed earlier in the dialogue) but also from the perspective of hedonists as well as from the perspective of the third group of people, that is those who take τὸ καλόν, "the noble," as the life's end. In such case, Socrates would assume the hedonist position merely for the duration of the argument.[21]

### 2.2.4 A Protreptic Dialogue: Nothing Is Useful for a Bad Man (POxy. 53.3699 [MP³ 2592.610])

This fragment, dated to the second century CE, appears to have belonged to a non-Socratic narrated dialogue of a protreptic character. There are two interlocutors of unknown identity; speaker changes are marked by a combination of a *paragraphos* and a *dicolon*. The narrator's interventions are limited to several occurrences of

---

[19] The sentence is damaged and has been interpreted variously. Gronewald 1985, 45: "daß das Leben des Vernünftigen entweder lustvoller ist [als der Tod] oder betrüblicher" ("that the life of a reasonable man is either more pleasant [than death] or more distressing"), which would mean that the interlocutors found arguments neither for life's preferability over death nor vice versa (a skeptical coloring). Spinelli 1992, 10–11 divides the text among two interlocutors and understands that the speakers were not able to find proof that human life is pleasant: "– Dunque fino ad ora secondo nessuno dei (nostri) discorsi possiamo scoprire che la vita dell'uomo assennato è (alquanto) piacevole. – Cosa dici? Forse (è alquanto) penosa? No, di certo, infatti, per Zeus. – Né dunque l'uomo assennato qualora sia sul punto di morire, potrebbe rattristarsi nel lasciare proprio quelle cose, perche sono meno piacevoli" (the intervention of Socrates' interlocutor is unclear to me). I find Lampe's interpretation the most persuasive (Lampe 2015, 137: "So up until now we haven't in any part of our discussion been able to find that the life of a sensible person is more pleasant [*approximately eight characters missing*] than distressing").
[20] Spinelli 1992.     [21] As suggested by Barnes 1987, 365.

ἔφη, used by both interlocutors, which indicates that neither speaker played the role of the narrator. There is a dominant interlocutor, who leads the conversation; his partner follows his argument and agrees with him. Legible sections of the text read (POxy. 53.3699 col. ii.5–iv.12):[22]

...ποιῆσαι ἕ[νε]κεν ἀργυρίου· πάλιν τε ὁ [Ἀλ]κμέων ὡς παρακεκοφώς τις καὶ οἰόμενος χαρ[ι]ε[ῖσ]θαί τι ἢ τῶι πα[τρὶ ἢ τοῖς] θεοῖς, τὴν μητέρ[α] ἀποκτείνας κ[.].εμεν ἐπιθυμεῖν ἀποκτεῖναι· ὕστερον δὲ ποιήσας μεταμέλεσθαι καὶ κακοδαιμονίζειν αὐτὸν καὶ μαίνεσ[θαι] (6 lines lost/damaged)
οὗ ἔφη ὁ βίος ἀλ[υσιτε]λὴς καὶ βλαβερός ἐστ[ι(ν)] ἐ[κε]ίνω ἰ τί λυσιτελε ῖ̓ [[ς]] ὑπάρχειν;
– ἥδιόν τε τοῦ [βίο]υ ἀλυ[σιτ]ελοῦς κα[ὶ βλαβερ]οῦ οὗτος τα(...) (2.5 lines lost/damaged)
– οὗ οὖν ἔφη [ὁ βίος] μοχθηρός ἐστιν, [ἐκεῖνο]υ οὐκ ἀλυσιτελὴς καὶ βλαβερὸς ὁ βίος ἐστίν;
– ἀλυσιτελὴς μὲν οὖν ἔφη.
– οὐκοῦν ἔφη παντὸς τοῦ ἀπαιδεύτου μοχθηρὸς ὁ βίος καὶ αἱ πράξεις εἰσὶν[[ν]] ἢ οὔ;
– καὶ μ[άλα] ἔφη.
– τί ἂν οὖν ἔφη [τ]ῷ̣ι τοιούτωι [[α]]λυσιτ[ελ]ὲ̣ς ὑπ̣ά[ρ]χοι; καὶ γὰρ εἰ καθ᾽ ἕν τις ἔφη ζητοί[η], χρ[ή]μα[τα] δόξα ῥώμη κάλλος [πάντ]α̣ ταῦτά γε εἰ ο̣ἷ̓ ὅν τ᾽ εἰπεῖ̣ν ἀλυσιτελῆ ἐστιν τῶι [τ]ο[ι]ούτωι· σχεδὸν γὰρ ὥσπερ πα[ιδὶ] μά[χ]αιρα γείνεται ἀπαιδ ἐύ̓[τ]ωι ἀνθρώπω[ι] τῶν [τοι]ούτων τι· χρημά[των] μὲν γὰρ ὑπαρξάν[τ]ων ἀφορμὴν ἔχειν [τ]ῆι ἀκρασια ἰ εἰς ἡδυπαθίας κα[ὶ] ἤδη ̓ καὶ μ[ά]λλο(ν)᾽ κύβ[ου]ς καὶ γυναῖκας κα[ὶ] τὰ λοιπ̣[ὰ] τα .[]α [c.7] δοξο[c.8] (7 lines damaged) καὶ ῥώμης τῆς . [. .]μένης ἐνγεινο[μέ]νης, βίαιοι θρα̣ς̣[εῖς] (text damaged)

(a quotation from Euripides' *Autolycus I* follows)
...acted for the sake of money. Alcmaeon in his turn, like a deranged man and thinking that he would do either his [father or the] gods a favour, killed his mother... desired to kill. But later he regretted doing so, cursed himself and went mad.... (4 lines lost)
A man whose [life] is unprofitable and harmful, he said, what is useful for him to possess?
– This man... something more pleasant than the unprofitable and harmful life
....
– So a man whose life is wretched, he said, is his life not unprofitable and harmful?
– Unprofitable indeed, he said.
– So, he said, the life and actions of every uneducated man are wretched, right?
– Yes indeed, he said.

---

[22] The Greek text and translation are based on Verhasselt 2015.

– What then would be profitable for such a man? Indeed, if one examined it one by one, money, reputation, strength and beauty, all these things are, if it is possible to say so,[23] unprofitable for such a man. For surely to an uneducated man any of such things becomes like a knife to a child. For if he has money, his lack of self-control prompts him to luxury, as well as / and even more so to dice games, women, and so on.

The fragment begins with a reference to the myth of Alcmaeon and his mother Eriphyle, according to which she was bribed with a gold necklace to persuade her husband Amphiaraus to take part in the expedition against Thebes, which led to his death; Alcmaeon then avenged his father's death by killing her and was subsequently pursued by Erinyes. ποιῆσαι ἕ[νε]κεν ἀργυρίου must have been somehow connected to Eriphyle having been bribed with a necklace.[24] When speaking of Alcmaeon's matricide, the author hints at two versions of the myth: one which had him kill Eriphyle on instructions of Amphiaraus, the other which had him follow the orders of Apollo's oracle.[25] The passage might have been inspired by a play on the topic—the words ὕστερον δὲ ποιήσας μεταμέλεσθαι καὶ κακοδαιμονίζειν αὑτὸν καὶ μαίνεσ[θαι] ("but later he regretted doing so, cursed himself and went mad") suggest a dramatic representation of Alcmaeon, pronouncing himself κακοδαίμων, like Euripides' Hippolytus.[26]

It is next argued that a bad life (μοχθηρός), which is associated with a lack of education, is unprofitable and harmful (ἀλυσιτελὴς καὶ βλαβερός),[27] and that for people living such a life, wealth, fame, strength, and beauty (χρήματα, δόξα, ῥώμη, κάλλος) are potentially harmful like a sword for a child (a reference to the proverb μὴ παιδὶ μάχαιραν, "do not give a sword to a child"). It seems that subsequently the speaker briefly discussed each of the four possessions—wealth, fame, strength, and beauty—in order to demonstrate their potential harmfulness. He begins by arguing that if an uneducated man happens to be rich, his lack of self-control (ἀκρασία) will lead him to luxury, gambling, and debauchery. Next the text appears to have discussed the harm done by fame (cf. δοξο[] in col. iv.2), and then by strength (ῥώμη, col. iv.10), which is associated with violence (βίαιοι θρασ[εῖς]). The latter argument was supported by a citation of at least six lines

---

[23] I modify Verhasselt's translation who renders the phrase as "so to speak."
[24] The necklace was made of gold; the word ἀργυρίου in the papyrus perhaps occurred in a general statement about people's wickedness activated by greed. Eriphyle's story is used as an example of destructive effect of gold in Plato's *Republic* 590a.
[25] Alcmaeon's matricide is also mentioned by Aristotle, *EN* 1110a27–9.
[26] Euripides, *Hipp.* 1361–3: πρόσφορά μ' αἴρετε, σύντονα δ' ἕλκετε τὸν κακοδαίμονα καὶ κατάρατον πατρὸς ἀμπλακίαις. The phrase οἴμοι κακοδαίμων is a recurrent one in Aristophanes' comedies.
[27] The expression "unprofitable and harmful life" (ἀλυσιτελὴς καὶ βλαβερὸς βίος, repeated three times if the text's reconstruction is correct) strikes one as odd. Is it "unprofitable and harmful" to the person living it, and therefore, a peculiar equivalent for "bad life"?

from Euripides' *Autolycus I*, in which athletes were denigrated as the worst breed in Greece (*TrGF* F 282).

The ideas expressed in the dialogue are rooted in Socratic literature, where the notion recurs that wealth, strength, and beauty—and sometimes also health, fame, and prosperity—are not real goods and may be harmful to a person without proper understanding.[28] Consider, for instance, the conversation between Socrates and Euthydemus in Xenophon's *Memorabilia* 4.2.34–5:

> Κινδυνεύει, ἔφη, ὦ Σώκρατες, ἀναμφιλογώτατον ἀγαθὸν εἶναι τὸ εὐδαιμονεῖν. Εἴ γε μή τις αὐτό, ἔφη, ὦ Εὐθύδημε, ἐξ ἀμφιλόγων ἀγαθῶν συντιθείη. Τί δ' ἄν, ἔφη, τῶν εὐδαιμονικῶν ἀμφίλογον εἴη; Οὐδέν, ἔφη, εἴ γε μὴ προσθήσομεν αὐτῷ κάλλος ἢ ἰσχὺν ἢ πλοῦτον ἢ δόξαν ἢ καί τι ἄλλο τῶν τοιούτων. Ἀλλὰ νὴ Δία προσθήσομεν, ἔφη· πῶς γὰρ ἄν τις ἄνευ τούτων εὐδαιμονοίη; Νὴ Δί', ἔφη, προσθήσομεν ἄρα, ἐξ ὧν πολλὰ καὶ χαλεπὰ συμβαίνει τοῖς ἀνθρώποις· πολλοὶ μὲν γὰρ διὰ τὸ κάλλος ὑπὸ τῶν ἐπὶ τοῖς ὡραίοις παρακεκινηκότων διαφθείρονται, πολλοὶ δὲ διὰ τὴν ἰσχὺν μείζοσιν ἔργοις ἐπιχειροῦντες οὐ μικροῖς κακοῖς περιπίπτουσι, πολλοὶ δὲ διὰ τὸν πλοῦτον διαθρυπτόμενοί τε καὶ ἐπιβουλευόμενοι ἀπόλλυνται, πολλοὶ δὲ διὰ δόξαν καὶ πολιτικὴν δύναμιν μεγάλα κακὰ πεπόνθασιν.

"Happiness seems to be unquestionably a good, Socrates." "It would be so, Euthydemus, were it not made up of goods that are questionable." "But what element in happiness can be called in question?" "None, provided we don't include in it beauty or strength or wealth or glory or anything of the sort." "But of course we shall do that. For how can anyone be happy without them?" "Then of course we shall include the sources of much trouble to mankind. For many are ruined by admirers whose heads are turned at the sight of a pretty face; many are led by their strength to attempt tasks too heavy for them, and meet with serious evils; many by their wealth are corrupted, and fall victims to conspiracies; many through glory and political power have suffered great evils."

(trans. E. C. Marchant)

The speaker in the papyrus fragment develops the concept of what Xenophon's Socrates refers to as ἀμφίλογα ἀγαθά and similarly, though in a more extended form, he presents potential bad outcomes of the supposed goods. The overall scope, however, differs: while Xenophon is preoccupied with the definition of happiness, the intention of the anonymous author is to show the disastrous consequences of the lack of a proper education.

---

[28] They are listed in various constellations, see e.g. Xenophon, *Mem.* 4.2.34: κάλλος, ἰσχύς, πλοῦτος, δόξα, 3.8.2: χρήματα, ὑγίεια, ῥώμη, τόλμα; Plato, *Men.* 87e: ὑγίεια, ἰσχύς, κάλλος, πλοῦτος, *Euthd.* 281a–c πλοῦτος, ὑγίεια, κάλλος; [Plato], *Eryx.* 393b–394a: πλοῦτος, ὑγίεια, εὐδαιμονία, *Alc. II* 147a: χρήματα, ῥώμη.

The fragment bears a striking resemblance to a passage of Aristotle (probably from the *Protrepticus*) preserved in POxy. 4.666.[29] Aristotle argues there that happiness does not rely on possessions, but on the right disposition and training of the soul; the terms he uses, such as πεπαιδευμένη and ἀπαιδευσία, are reminiscent of ἀπαίδευτος ἄνθρωπος in POxy. 53.3699. Then he says (POxy. 4.666 col. iii.139-70):

τοῖς γὰρ διακειμέ[νοις] τὰ περὶ τὴν ψυχὴν κακῶς οὔτε πλοῦτος οὔτ' ἰσχὺς οὔτε κάλλος τῶν ἀγαθῶν ἐστ[ιν]· ἀλλ' ὅσωι περ ἂν α[ὔ]ται μᾶλλον αἱ διαθέσεις καθ' ὑπ[ερ]βολὴν ὑπάρξ[ωσι], τοσούτῳ μείζ[ω] καὶ πλείω τὸν κεκτημένον βλάπτουσιν, <ἐὰν> ἄν[ευ] φρονήσεως [πα]ραγένωντα[ι· τὸ] γὰρ μὴ παιδ[ὶ μά]χαιραν τοῦτ' [ἐστι] τὸ μὴ τοῖς φ[αύ]λοις τὴν ἐξου[σί]αν ἐγχειρίζε[ιν]. Τὴν δὲ φρόν[ησιν] ἅπαντες ἂν ὁ[μολο]γήσειαν εἰς τὸ [μαν]θάνειν γίγνεσθ[αι <καὶ> ζητεῖν ὧν τὰς [δυ]νάμεις φιλοσοφ[ία] περιείληφεν, ὥστε πῶς οὐκ ἀπ[ρο]φασίστως φιλο[σο]φητέον ἐστὶ καὶ....

In a bad state of the soul neither wealth nor strength nor beauty are good things, but the greater the abundance of these qualities, the more they injure their possessor, if they are unaccompanied by reason. "Do not give a child a knife," is as much as to say, "Do not entrust bad men with power." Now reason, as all would admit, exists for the acquisition of knowledge, and seeks ends the means to which are contained in philosophy; why then should philosophy not be pursued without hesitation...?[30]

The concurrences between Aristotle's fragment and POxy. 53.3699—the overall message and the use of the same proverb—can hardly be accidental. Like Aristotle, the author of the dialogue aims to demonstrate that moral training is necessary for people to make proper use of other goods. The nature of the dependence between the two texts, however, is uncertain. Based on the linguistic features of POxy. 53.3699, a late fourth-century date seems possible; but the text cannot be decisively classified as post-Aristotelian on linguistic grounds.[31] It has been argued that the similarity with Aristotle's passage as well as the use of proverbs and poetic

---

[29] The same passage, slightly abbreviated, is quoted by Stobaeus who assigns it to Aristotle (3.3.25). It is included as a fragment of the *Protrepticus* in Düring 1961 (F B 2-5) and Rose³ (F 57).

[30] Greek text and translation Grenfell and Hunt 1904; for a discussion and new edition, see Vendruscolo 1989.

[31] ἀλυσιτελής occurs, though infrequently, in Xenophon (four times), Plato (once), and Isocrates (once); the phrase εἰ οἷόν τ' εἰπεῖν is attested for the first time in Demosthenes; ἡδυπαθία has three occurrences in Xenophon. κακοδαιμονίζειν does not occur in the Classical period and is rare afterwards, but Haslam 1986, 21 rightly observes that it is easily formed from κακοδαίμων. ἀκρασία is not used by Plato, who prefers ἀκράτεια, but recurs eight times in Xenophon's Socratic texts, and is used profusely by Aristotle.

quotations suggest a Peripatetic background (Theophrastus and Clearchus were proposed as potential authors).[32]

## 2.2.5 Dialogue on Ideas (PAï Khanoum inv. Akh IIIB77P.O.154 [MP³ 2563.010])

This fragment of a Greek dialogue was found in the remains of a palace in Aï Khanoum (modern northern Afghanistan). The papyrus itself has decomposed, but the ink has left imprints on clods of earth. It is dated to the first half or middle of the third century BCE; we do not know whether the roll was produced locally or was imported from distant Greece. The text preserves a narrated dialogue between two unidentified characters; six *paragraphoi* mark speaker changes. A dominant speaker guides the discussion and leads his interlocutor, using verbal forms such as μανθάνεις, "you understand"; his partner merely expresses agreement with responses familiar from Plato's dialogues (φαμὲν γάρ, ἀναγκαῖον, δικαίως, πάνυ γε).[33] The narrative bits consist of mere εἶπεν,[34] used exclusively by the responder, never by the main speaker—the dialogue, then, might have been narrated by the main interlocutor, though there may have been a third character acting as a narrator. Here are the most legible sections, which, though damaged, give some sense of the dynamics of the conversation (col. ii.2–iv.7):

col. ii
οὐ μόνον τῶν ἰδεῶν φάμ]εγ [γ/κ τὰ] αἰσθητὰ ἀλλὰ [κ]αὶ τὰς ἰδέας αὐτὰς ἀλ[λ]ήλων.
– φάμεγ γὰρ εἶπεν.
– οὐκοῦν [ὡς] αὐτὸ αἴτιον τῷ[ν α]ὐ[] τῶν ου. [. .] μετίσχει τῶν ὄντων τ[ὰ]ς ἰδέας ὅπερ καὶ τ[ο]ῦ μ ε[τέχ]ειν τἄλλ[α.]ε τ[ο]ύτ[ων] αιτια [. .]ν ο . . . ω . . . [] [αἴ]τιον . . . .
– [We say that not only] the sensible objects [partake of Ideas] . . . but also the Ideas of one another.
– We say so, he said.
– Surely then this cause . . . partakes of beings . . . Ideas . . . and of partaking . . . other . . . cause . . . .

---

[32] Haslam 1986, 16 thinks that the earliest author to consider is Antisthenes, but also finds it probable the work is post-Aristotelian; Verhasselt 2015, 14–15 argues for a Peripatetic background and notes that a passage in Athenaeus suggests that the proverb μὴ παιδὶ μάχαιραν was used by both Aristotle and Theophrastus (*Deipn.* 5.214a).
[33] Hadot in Rapin et al. 1987, 245.
[34] Plato prefers ἔφη to εἶπεν, with the exception of *Prm.* 131–3. εἶπεν appears in [Plato], *Demodocus* 3 and 4 and in a fragment of Aristotle's *On Noble Birth*, preserved in Stobaeus.

## col. iii

ὥ[στ]ε διὰ [τούτων τ]ῶν [αὐ]τῶν αἰτιῷ[ν].[ ]ον ἀναγκαῖον ε[ἶναι] τὸ τῆς μεθ
.έξως αἴ[τι]ον, ἀκίνητον γὰρ ἕκαστον τῶν εἰδῶν διὰ ταῦτά τε καὶ τὸ τὴν γένεσιν
εἶναι καὶ τὴν φθορὰν ἀίδιον τὴν τῶν αἰσθητῶν.
– ἀναγκαῖον εἶπεν.
– ἀλλὰ μὴν καὶ κυριώτατόγ γε καὶ πρῶτον τῶν αἰτίων δόξειεν ἂν τοῦ[το].
– δικαίως [].
– τοῦτο μέγ γὰρ [αἴτι]ον πᾶσι καὶ πάσαις ταῖς ἰδέαις [2–3] ἀ[λλ]ήλων...

– ...so that by [these] causes... necessarily... cause of partaking, each of the Ideas is immobile for these reasons, and the coming into being and corruption of the sensible objects is everlasting.
– Necessarily.
– But then it would seem that this is the principal and first of the causes.
– That's right.
– For this is the cause of everything and of all Ideas... each other....

## col. iv

... μανθάνεις γὰρ [ ]
– πάνυ γε εἶπε[ν ]

– ...for you understand....
– yes, he said....[35]

The fragment reports a discussion of Ideas (referred to as ἰδέαι and εἴδη): it appears to have been argued that not only do sensible objects (τὰ αἰσθητά) participate in Ideas but that Ideas also participate in one another (μετίσχει, με[τέχ]ειν). Sensible objects are characterized as being subject to eternal processes of coming into being and corruption (γένεσις, φθορά), while Ideas are immobile (ἀκίνητος). The cause and principle of this double participation—of the sensibles in the Ideas, and of the Ideas in one another—is discussed next (τὸ τῆς μεθέξεως αἴ[τι]ον) and is characterized as κυριώτατον καὶ πρῶτον τῶν αἰτίων, "the principal and first of the causes."

The terminology and preoccupations of the passage suggest an Academic background: Plato's discussions of the Forms, of the relation between the sensible world and the Forms, as well as the relation between the Forms themselves are in the background, although the passage also contains some philosophical concepts which are not found in Plato, such as the idea of the first and principal cause

---

[35] Greek text after Rougemont 2012, 236–40. My translation is minimal; for translations involving more interpretation, see Isnardi Parente 1992; Lerner 2003a; and, most recently, Rougemont 2012, 239–40.

of participation.[36] But, given that the text was a dialogue, there remains a possibility that the passage relates philosophical ideas which were rejected in a subsequent section. Therefore, Academic origins cannot be taken for granted; in particular, the dialogue may have originated in a Peripatetic milieu and might have rejected the doctrines presented. Among potential authors, there have been listed Speusippus, Xenocrates, Aristotle, Theophrastus, and Heraclides of Pontus.[37]

The fact that a fragment of such an early philosophical text has been found in a location so geographically distant testifies to the proliferation of Greek culture in the East. Interestingly, an inscription was also found in Aï Khanoum with five Greek maxims accompanied by an epigram announcing that they were written down in Delphi by a certain Clearchus. It has been argued that the Clearchus in question may have been Aristotle's student, Clearchus of Soli; if so, he might have also brought the papyrus with the philosophical dialogue.[38]

### 2.2.6 On Animals and their Affinity with Humankind(?) (PPetr. 2.49e (= PLit.Lond. 159a) [MP³ 2593])

The papyrus, dated to the second half or end of the third century BCE, preserves two different philosophical texts, one on the recto and one on the verso.[39] The former seems to have come from a dramatic dialogue, with *paragraphoi* probably marking a change of speakers. Here are two columns which are best preserved (col. ii.1–iii.17):

col. ii
ἀσεβεῖς ἔσεσθαι κα[3] τοὺς κλέπτας ἢ τοὺς λῃστὰς ε.[4–5]π[. .]οντες εν.... .
[traces] γελοίως .[.]ν καὶ ᾧδ' ἐμοὶ δοκεῖ πως ἔπασχεν λεγομένου γὰρ καὶ τοῦτον τὸν [τ]ρόπον ὁμόφυλα εἶναι ὅμπερ καὶ ὁ ποιητὴς λέγει διότι ἐκ τῆς αὐτῆς κράσεως γεγόναμεν καὶ νηδ[ύος] οὕτως ὥσπερ τα ..[1–2]. ἅπαντα τοῖς . [......] ἅπασιν λέγε-

---

[36] For the philosophical contents, see Hadot in Rapin et al. 1987, 245–7; Isnardi Parente 1992, 174–80; Hoffmann 2016, 189–91.

[37] For various hypotheses, see Hadot in Rapin et al. 1987, 248; Isnardi Parente 1992, 174–88; Hoffmann 2016, 192–203.

[38] For identification of Clearchus of the inscription with the Peripatetic philosopher, see Robert 1968, 443–54 and a recent discussion in Hoffmann 2016, 203–27. The identification has been rejected by e.g. Lerner 2003b, 393–4. For arguments for and against the identification, see Rougemont 2012, 203–7.

[39] The text on the verso (MP³ 2862), probably of a protreptic nature, does not appear to be a dialogue. For the dialogue format of the recto text, see Gorteman 1958, 96, who observes that the *paragraphoi* (col. ii.4 and 6, and col. i.10 and 11) are too close to mark an end of one argument and beginning of another, and therefore must mark a change of speakers. His hypothesis is accepted, with some caution, by Funghi and Roselli 1997, 68 ("la posizione delle paragraphoi rende possibile l'ipotesi che il testo del papiro avesse una struttura dialogica") and by Fortenbaugh et al. 1992b, 603 n. 2.

being impious... the thieves or brigands... ridiculous... and so it seems to me to somehow have experienced.... being said to be of the same race in the same way as the poet says, because we have come into being from the same mixture and womb, just as all... all... is said....

col. iii

.[.]. αὐτῷ τὰ τέκνα μὴ ἀποκτείνειν ἵνα μὴ συμβῇ τοῦτον τὸν τρόπο[ν α]ὐτῷ τὰ ὁμόφυλα ἀπ[ε]κτονηκέναι ὅμπερ λέγεται τοὺς ἀποκτείναντάς τινα τῶν ἐγχωρίων [τ]ῶν ὑπὸ τοὺς αὐτο[ὺς] νόμους τεταγμένῳ[ν κ]αὶ μηθὲν ἀδικού[ντ]ων ἐὰν ἀποκτ[είν]ωσιν ἀσεβεῖν καὶ [τοὺ]ς ἐκείνως ἀποσυ[μβο]υλεύοντας μὴ [ἀποκ]τείνειν τὸ ὁμο[φυλο]μ π̣ο.[1–2] . εδ .. [ ] .. [3–4]φυλα.

to him not to kill children, so that he does not happen to have killed beings belonging to the same race in this way, as one says that those who have killed one of the inhabitants living under the same laws, who did no injustice—if they kill such person, they act impiously and those who advise against killing one belonging to the same race....[40]

If the text was a dialogue, the phrase καὶ ὧδ' ἐμοὶ δοκεῖ might have been uttered by an interlocutor agreeing with the main speaker.

While the topic of the text is not immediately clear, it is most probable it discussed proper treatment of animals by people. Plutarch and Porphyry provide evidence that philosophers who argued that animals should not be killed and eaten by men characterized animals as kin to people (συγγενῆ, ὁμόφυλα) and maintained that they should be treated with justice; they also considered the act of killing animals for sacrifice and food as impiety.[41] The fragment appears to have developed the same idea and to have argued that animals belong to the same race as people (are ὁμόφυλα) because they have come "from the same mixture and the same womb" (a paraphrase or quotation of an unknown poetic text), and characterized their killing as impious (ἀσεβεῖν).

The fragment, then, comes from a philosophical text, probably a dialogue, composed in the fourth or third century BCE, influenced by Empedocles and Pythagoreanism. The preoccupation with the relationship between humans and animals recurs in later Platonists, in particular in Plutarch and Porphyry, and the fragment may have come from a text that was among their sources and inspirations. It has been speculated that the fragment might have come from Theophrastus' *On Piety*; other potential authors include Xenocrates and Hermarchus.[42]

---

[40] The Greek text follows Funghi and Roselli 1997.
[41] e.g. Plutarch, *De soll. an.* 964a; Porphyry, *Abst.* 1.5, 1.19, 3.25.
[42] Gorteman 1958, 88–93 argues that the fragment comes from Theophrastus' *On Piety*; it has been included in an Appendix to the recent edition of the philosopher (Fortenbaugh et al. 1992b, 600–3). Funghi and Roselli 1997, 68–9 remain skeptical concerning Theophrastean authorship, believing that there are more potential authors in the fourth and third century BCE.

## 2.3 Dialogues on Literature

While the genre of the dialogue retained its connection with philosophy throughout antiquity, other fragments provide evidence of the concurrent development of dialogues of a non-philosophical character, dissociated from philosophy sensu stricto. The first category, dialogues on literature, is represented by Satyrus of Callatis' *Life of Euripides* (POxy. 9.1176) and fragments of two dialogues on Homeric topics (PGiss.Univ. 4.39 + PLit.Lond. 160; PSchub. 4). While Plato and the Socratics discussed literature, and their work certainly influenced the emergence of ancient philology and literary criticism, they tended to explore them from a philosophical, in particular moral or political, perspective. The preserved fragments of dialogues on literature, on the other hand, do not betray philosophical or moralizing inclinations and focus instead on literary techniques, the history of literature, and textual interpretation. This dialogue category, then, seems to be a new, post-Platonic development, influenced by Peripatetic and Alexandrian literary criticism and an interest in the history of literature, including Homeric studies; Aristotle and his students as well as Heraclides of Pontus seem to have composed a fair number of such works.

What is particularly noteworthy in the case of this group of fragments is that they betray the influence of other Hellenistic period genres: Satyrus' work combines dialogue with biography, while dialogues on Homer incorporate Homeric *zetemata* within a dialogue form. They therefore bear evidence of blending prose types and of the dialogue's potential to encompass other literary formats. As such, the fragments provide a valuable context not only for later dialogues on literature (such as Cicero's *Brutus* and Dio Chrysostom's dialogues on literary subjects, such as *Chryseis, Second Kingship Oration*, or *Nestor or Deianeira*) but also for imperial period hybrid formats, such as Plutarch's *Table-Talks*, which fuses the format of sympotic dialogues with that of *zetemata*.

### 2.3.1 Satyrus' *Life of Euripides* (POxy. 9.1176 [MP³ 1456])

An Oxyrhynchian papyrus, POxy. 9.1176, preserves fragments of Satyrus of Callatis' *Life of Euripides*, which, despite the title suggesting a biography, is a dramatic dialogue. Satyrus, a Peripatetic according to Athenaeus (*Deipn.* 12.541c),[43] was the author of numerous biographies of poets, philosophers, kings, and statesmen which were cited by both Diogenes Laertius and Athenaeus. The *Life of Euripides* belonged to Book 6 of the *Lives* which also included the *bioi* of Aeschylus and Sophocles. We do not know whether these

---

[43] For this identification, see West 1974 and Schorn 2003 with references to earlier scholarship.

other lives were also in a dialogue form. The composition of the *Life of Euripides* has been dated to sometime between 240–170 BCE.[44]

While the dialogue format of the *Life of Euripides* is unquestionable, the condition of the papyrus sometimes makes it impossible to see where speaker changes occur. It is also unclear whether in the extant sections there are two or three interlocutors. There is a dominant speaker whose identity is unknown (henceforth referred to as "A"). It is possible that he is Satyrus himself—in such a case the dialogue would follow the "Aristotelian" model, with the author among the speakers—but he also might have been some other figure, real or fictitious.[45] It is usually presumed that the main character is a man, though there is no direct evidence of this in the text; the thought that "A" might have been a woman has been entertained by Lefkowitz.[46] Two other names appear in the dialogue: Eucleia and Diodor(-). The latter is addressed twice, but in each case the ending of the vocative is lost, and therefore the gender remains uncertain, though the words ascribed to this character suggest that it is a woman. Eucleia and Diodor(-) may be two different characters, or Diodor(-) might have been addressed once playfully as Eucleia.[47] The dramatic time and place are not known.[48]

The conversational dynamics between interlocutors has been interpreted either as a "teacher-student" relation, with the main interlocutor playing the authority figure, or as a "reversed classroom," in which the female participant(s) challenge the position of the main speaker. Neither interpretation seems wholly adequate.[49] While the distribution of the text among characters is not proportional, and "A" seems to be the major speaker, the other character(s) freely object, comment, and express their opinions. There is no evident intellectual disparity between "A" and the other speaker(s) and, as a result, the text does not read like a teacher-student conversation. On the other hand, the female speaker(s) do not appear to be

---

[44] The papyrus is dated to the second century CE; for the time of composition, see Schorn 2004, 6–10. The title is preserved in the papyrus: F 6 Schorn Fr. 39 col. xxiii.1–6: Σατύρου βίων ἀναγ<ρ>αφῆς ϛ' Αἰσχύλου Σοφοκλέους Εὐριπίδου. Besides the editio princeps in vol. 9 of *The Oxyrhynchus Papyri* there are two other commented editions: Arrighetti 1964 and Schorn 2004. For a discussion of the text, see also Arrighetti 1977; Lefkowitz 1979; Lefkowitz 1981, 88–104.

[45] Leo 1912, 276 and Arrighetti 1964, 34 thought that Satyrus himself is the main speaker; it seemed improbable to Lewis 1921, 146–7; Schorn 2004, 32 seems skeptical.

[46] Lefkowitz 1984, 342.

[47] Eucleia is addressed in F 6 Schorn Fr. 39 col. xiv.31, Diodor(-) in F 6 Schorn Fr. 39 col. iii.19–20, xv.13–14. Two interlocutors are assumed by Gerstinger 1916, 61 n. 1 and Arrighetti 1964, 34, 133–4, while Hunt in the editio princeps and Schorn 2004 assume three speakers (with Hunt believing that Diodor(-) is a man).

[48] Schorn 2004, 31 believes that the fact that "A" relates the death of Euripides as having been narrated by οἱ λόγιοί τε καὶ γεραίτατοι...Μακεδ[ό]νων ("the learned and the oldest from among Macedonians") indicates that the dramatic time is no later than the last decades of the fourth century BCE; however, the phrase does not imply that the Macedonian story-tellers witnessed the event themselves.

[49] Teacher-student relationship: Schorn 2004, 32. Knöbl 2010, 44: "not so much the dramatization of an ideal classroom situation, but rather its reversal"; at 45–6 she argues that the main speaker's authority is not accepted by the female interlocutor.

particularly confrontational or challenging; rather, judging from the preserved text, the atmosphere is relaxed and friendly.

The contents of the conversation include a discussion of Euripides' style (its rhetorical and "prosaic" character), his greatness as a poet, the influence on him of Anaxagoras and Socrates, the condemnation of wealth in the poet's works, his political stance, and his influence on New Comedy and rhetoric. In terms of biographical information, we learn that Euripides spent most of his time in a cave on the seashore, meditating and writing; that he was disliked by men because of his unsociability, and by women because he denounced them in his plays (consequently, he was prosecuted by Cleon and attacked by women at the Thesmophoria); Euripides' enmity towards women is explained as being due to his wife's affair with the slave Cephisophon. A discussion follows of Euripides' reasons for leaving Athens for Macedonia and Archelaus' court, in which it is stated that the Athenians recognized the poet's genius later than the Macedonians and Sicilians; finally, there is an account of Euripides' death in Macedonia (he was accidentally killed by Archelaus' hunting dogs). The beginning of the text, in which the poet's birth, origin, education, and dramatic career must have been discussed, has been lost. The information provided in the course of conversation was ordered both chronologically and thematically.[50]

The *Life of Euripides*, then, combined biographical and anecdotal material with a discussion of style and of the development of dramatic genres. Satyrus used numerous, not always exact quotations, mostly from works by Euripides and contemporary comic poets (although there is also a quotation from Plato's *Phaedrus* and Homer's *Odyssey*), from which he extracted biographical information.[51] These citations characterize the interlocutors as a community of educated readers who discuss and interpret literature together. In this respect, Satyrus' choice of the dialogue format for the *Life of Euripides* was ingenious: it allowed him not only to present biographical material but, above all, to represent the reception of Euripides in the here-and-now of the dialogue's dramatic world.[52]

The inclusion of the female interlocutor(s) is among the most remarkable features of the text, as female speakers are very rare in Greek dialogues. Three notable exceptions include Diotima in an inset dialogue in Plato's *Symposion*, Theodote in Xenophon's *Apomnemoneumata*, and probably Aspasia in a number

---

[50] For the disposition of the material, see Leo 1912, 286–7; he distinguishes the discussion of τέχνη, ἦθος, his reasons for leaving Athens and staying in Macedonia, and his death.

[51] Schorn 2004, 37 lists twenty-five quotations, of which thirteen are from Euripides, nine come from comedy, and three are of unknown provenience. See also Leo 1912, 276, who observes that Satyrus "deduced" the life of Euripides from his plays, and notes that he might have used a similar strategy in his life of Empedocles (cf. Diogenes Laertius 8.59). For the use of quotation as a way to characterize interlocutors, see Schorn 2004, 46.

[52] As Knöbl 2010, 39 observes, the text becomes therefore a "commentary...on biographical writing." I am less persuaded by her assertion that Satyrus is criticizing the genre of biography and that the *Life* is intended as its mock version.

of Socratic dialogues,[53] but these ambiguous figures oscillate between the real, the fictional, and the symbolic. When "ordinary" women make an appearance in Socratic dialogues, they are the wives of male characters, revealing at best practical intelligence in household matters and frequently remaining conspicuously anonymous: this includes the short appearance of Socrates' wife Xanthippe in Plato's *Phaedo* 60a, Aeschines of Sphettus' account of Xenophon's (unnamed) wife being questioned by Aspasia (in Cicero, *Inv. rhet.* 1.31.51-2), and (the most elaborate) Ischomachus' account of his conversations with his wife (again unnamed) in Xenophon's *Oeconomicus*. The *Life of Euripides* presents a different type of a female character: an educated woman, a reader and interpreter of literature. This is most unusual, and though educated female characters may have been represented in other Hellenistic dialogues, they could not have appeared frequently—at any rate, an unwillingness to introduce female speakers is still evident in Cicero and Plutarch. Dio Chrysostom's *Chryseis*, a dialogue in which a dominant speaker converses with an unnamed woman on Homer's representation of Chryses' daughter (and argues that she is very smart and intelligent) may be the closest parallel in this respect to Satyrus' work.[54]

The presence of female interlocutor(s) is, of course, particularly pointed in regard to discussion about Euripides' misogyny. The image of Euripides as an enemy of women is rooted in a tradition reaching back to Aristophanes.[55] The *Life* does not take issue with this portrayal, and the main speaker explains the poet's dislike for women biographically, as a result of his wife's infidelity. This is commented on by his interlocutor, probably Diodor(-) (F 6 Schorn Fr. 39 col. xiii.23-38):

νὴ γελοίως γε· τί γὰρ ἄν τις εὐλογώτερο[ν] διὰ τὴν φθαρεῖσαν ψέγοι τὰς γυναίκας ἢ διὰ τὸν φθείραντα τοὺς ἄνδρας; ἐπεὶ τ[άς] γε κακίας καὶ τὰς ἀρετάς, καθάπερ ἔλεγ‹ε›ν ὁ Σω‹κρ›άτης, τὰς αὐτὰς [ἐν] ἀμφοῖν ἔσ[τιν] εὑρεῖν.

This is ridiculous. Why is it more reasonable to blame women on account of a woman having been seduced rather than to blame men on account of a man who seduced? Vices and virtues, as Socrates said, are the same in both genders.[56]

The defense of women in this passage suggests that the speaker is female; if so, Satyrus depicts an educated woman offended by Euripides' misogyny, evoking

---

[53] e.g. in *Aspasia* by Aeschines and by Antisthenes. Cf. also Plutarch, *Per.* 24.3, where it is said that Socrates' friends used to bring their wives to Aspasia to hear her talk.

[54] Both texts discuss literature and touch upon the representation of female characters by Euripides and Homer respectively; both represent female characters who are intelligent, educated, and familiar with literature. Dio's interest in tragedy is well attested, and it is probable that he knew Satyrus' dialogue. For Dio's representation of his interlocutress, see Blomqvist 1995.

[55] Cf. e.g. Aristophanes, *Lys.* 283, 368; *Thesm.* 81-5.

[56] Greek text follows Schorn 2004, 105. For a disposition of speakers in this passage, see Schorn 2004, 303.

Socrates as an ally, and pointing out that one woman's infidelity should not have influenced the poet's opinion on the whole female race.[57] Her words are reminiscent of the speech of Euripidean Melanippe, who in an extant fragment complains (*TrGF* F 494 vv. 23–6):

πῶς οὖν χρὴ γυναικεῖον γένος κακῶς ἀκούειν; οὐχὶ παύσεται ψόγος μάταιος ἀνδρῶν
†οἵ τ' ἄγαν ἡγούμενοι† ψέγειν γυναῖκας, εἰ μί' ηὑρέθη κακή, πάσας ὁμοίως;

Why then should womankind be denigrated? Will the vain censures of men not cease †and those excessively thinking† if just one is found to be bad, to condemn all women alike?[58]

Satyrus, then, has his (probably female) interlocutor criticize Euripides with a paraphrase of the words of Euripides' own character.[59] This is a noteworthy literary strategy, and one reminding the reader that, for all his reputation as a women-hater, Euripides' female characters are outspoken, intelligent, and daring (though also deceptive and dangerous) to an unprecedented degree. Satyrus points in a sly way to a parallel between Euripides' plays and the dramatic reality of his dialogue.[60]

There is no doubt that Satyrus' dialogue departs greatly from the Socratic tradition, both thematically and formally. The dialogue format has been detached from philosophy and moral or political concerns. While we have no information about the setting, the text does not seem to be located in the past, but rather "reports" a contemporary discussion and represents contemporary literary culture. The combined interest in biography and literary criticism affiliates Satyrus' work with Peripatetic texts such as Aristotle's and Praxiphanes' dialogues *On Poets* and, perhaps, also with Heraclides of Pontus' texts on literature.[61] While the text is an important witness to the development of the ancient biography, it is also

---

[57] Probably a reference to *Meno* 71e–73b, where Socrates argues that virtues such as justice and moderation are the same in men and women (for Aristotle's disagreement, see *Pol.* 1260a21-2: καὶ οὐχ ἡ αὐτὴ σωφροσύνη γυναικὸς καὶ ἀνδρός, οὐδ' ἀνδρεία καὶ δικαιοσύνη, καθάπερ ᾤετο Σωκράτης ("neither the temperance of a man and of a woman, nor the courage and justice are the same, as Socrates maintained"). According to Diogenes Laertius 6.12, Antisthenes said that ἀνδρὸς καὶ γυναικὸς ἡ αὐτὴ ἀρετή.
[58] The Greek text and translation after Collard and Cropp (2008). Cf. also Euripides, *Protesil.* F 657 ("Anyone who puts all women together and blames them indiscriminately is foolish and not wise. There are many of them, and you will find one bad while another is of noble character, as this one is (*or* was), trans. Collard and Cropp (2008)."
[59] The allusion to *Melanippe* was noted by Arrighetti 1964, 132, though Schorn 2004, 304 is skeptical. But this hardly can be an accidental resemblance, as earlier in the *Life* we find a direct quotation from Melanippe's speech (F 6 Schorn Fr. 39 col. xi).
[60] Cf. Lefkowitz 1984, 342; Knöbl 2010, 52.
[61] Leo 1912, 274 referred to the text as "der peripatetische Dialog literarischen Inhalts" and saw Cicero's *Brutus* as the closest parallel among extant dialogues; Ruch 1958, 46 notes that the *Life of Euripides* is halfway between Aristotle and Cicero.

remarkable evidence for historians of the ancient dialogue. As Hermann Frey has observed, "Das ist auch für die Geschichte des Dialoges etwas Neues."[62]

### 2.3.2 Dialogues on Homeric Topics (PGiss.Univ. 4.39, PLit.Lond. 160, PSchub. 4 [MP³ 1215, 1214, 1229])

Two different papyri fragments contain remnants of the same anonymous dramatic dialogue, in which a certain Theophanes converses with an unnamed interlocutor on the Homeric epic: PGiss.Univ. 4.39 (dated to the third century BCE)[63] and PLit.Lond. 160 (the first century BCE). The existence of two different papyri with the same dialogue suggests that it enjoyed some popularity. The dialogue format is recognizable thanks to *paragraphoi* and the name of Theophanes in the vocative. In both fragments Theophanes is speaking with another character whose name we do not know; as far as we can tell, their status in the conversation is similar—there is no evidence of one of them being a dominant speaker (in the Giessen fragment, both have a similar amount of speech; in the London papyrus, it is difficult to divide the text among the speakers).[64]

The focus of the Giessen fragment is the Circe-episode. The interlocutors agree that she did not possess prophetic powers (Fr. A ll. 6–7: ἀλλὰ δῆλον ὅτι μαντικὴν μέγ οὐ κεκτη[μένη] ἦν) and believe that this is confirmed by several Homeric passages. The text is damaged, but it seems to have been argued that had Circe possessed *mantike*, she would have been aware that Hermes had given Odysseus *moly*, which prevented him from turning into an animal (Fr. A l. 3: ἔδει δεδ[ιέν]αι τὸ φάρμακ[ο]ν, "she should have feared the drug"); it might have been pointed out that she did not foresee that Odysseus would not want to stay with her (Fr. A ll. 3–6: εἰδυῖαν, ὅτι ἕ[τερον] οὐθέν ἐσ[τιν] δυνατὸν ἢ καταπέμπει[ν,] γειγν[ώσκ]ουσαν, ὅτι μένειν οὐδ' οὕτως θελήσει, "being aware that nothing else is possible than to send [him] down, knowing that he will not want to stay"). The passage might have been inspired by the question of why Circe did not disclose the future to Odysseus herself, but instead sent the hero to Hades to consult Teiresias—this problem was discussed later by a scholiast of Homer and by Eustathius of Thessalonica, who thought, however, unlike the author of the dialogue, that Circe possessed

---

[62] Frey 1919, 51.
[63] Eberhart 1935, 14–19: around 200 BCE, Kuhlmann 1994, 55–60: third century BCE.
[64] For various reconstructions of the division of the text of the London papyrus among the speakers, cf. Körte 1932, 225; Eberhart 1935, 17; Kuhlmann 1994, 59–61. Milne 1927, 129–31 and Kuhlmann 1994, 59 seem to have incorrectly marked *paragraphoi*; judging from the papyrus' photograph, they should be marked at ll. 69, 70, 75, and 76. Eberhart 1935, 16 believes that Theophanes did not have a leading role in the discussion.

prophetic powers but did not disclose the future to Odysseus, for he might not have believed her.[65]

In the London fragment, another Homeric passage is examined, namely one in which Odysseus meets the beggar Irus. The speakers discuss the episode's role within the text: one of them must have suggested that it was included in the poem primarily for humorous effect, while another argues that the episode is not merely playful (PLit.Lond. 160 col. ii.67: ἡ παιγνία), but has an important dramatic function, as it enables the poet to introduce Odysseus into Penelope's household without being questioned about his identity and intentions (col. ii.71–5: μὴ γὰρ προεισαγαγὼν τὸν Ἶρον, ζητεῖσθαι τοῦτον ἐποίει τίς ἐστιν ἢ τί βουλόμενος εἰσελήλυθεν;). Here also the discussed problem resonates with later Homeric scholarship. The playfulness of the encounter between Odysseus and Irus (which amused the suitors in *Odyssey* 18.35-40) was noted by [Demetrius] (*Eloc.* 163):

Διαφέρουσι δὲ τὸ γελοῖον καὶ εὔχαρι πρῶτα μὲν τῇ ὕλῃ· χαρίτων μὲν γὰρ ὕλη νυμφαῖοι κῆποι, ἔρωτες, ἅπερ οὐ γελᾶται· γέλωτος δὲ Ἶρος καὶ Θερσίτης. τοσοῦτον οὖν διοίσουσιν, ὅσον ὁ Θερσίτης τοῦ Ἔρωτος.

Laughter and charm are, however, different. They differ first in their material. Gardens of the nymphs and loves are material for charm (they are not humorous), Irus and Thersites are material for laughter, and the two concepts will be as different as Thersites and Love.   (trans. D. C. Innes)

Eustathius speaks of τὸ γελοιαστικὸν τοῦ Ἴρου καὶ τοῦ ξείνου ἐπεισόδιον and adds that Homer in the *Odyssey*, unlike in the *Iliad*, introduces many joyful elements (μυρίας ἱλαρότητας), including jokes and jests (τὸ σκώπτειν καὶ παίζειν).[66] The phrase τῷ τοῦ Ὀδυσσέως ἐν ὁδῷ ("because of Odysseus on the road") which we find in the papyrus suggests an allusion to the etymology of Odysseus' name, known to us from Byzantine scholars.[67]

---

[65] Cf. *Scholia vet. in Hom. Od.* 10.492: διὰ τί οὖν οὐκ αὐτὴ μαντεύεται; ὅτι οὐκ ἂν ἐπίστευσεν Ὀδυσσεὺς ἐρώσης αὐτῆς. εἶτα κατὰ μὲν Σειρῆνας καὶ τὸν πορθμὸν ὡς γειτνιῶσα μηνύει, περὶ ὧν οὐδ' ὁ Τειρεσίας εἶπεν εἰδὼς ἐροῦσαν τὴν Κίρκην, περὶ δὲ τῶν λοιπῶν ἐπιτρέπει τῷ μάντει; Eustathius, *Od.* 10.491: αὐτὴ μὲν ἡ Κίρκη οὐ προλέγει φασὶ τὰ ἐσόμενα τῷ Ὀδυσσεῖ δυσχερῆ, ἵνα μὴ ἀπιστηθῇ ὡς δι' ἔρωτα τερατευομένη καὶ φοβερὸν πλαττομένη τὸν πλοῦν.

[66] Eustathius, *Od.* 2.166–7: καθάπαξ γὰρ εἰπεῖν, ὁ διὰ πάσης τῆς Ἰλιάδος σκυθρωπὸς ποιητὴς καὶ ὡς οἷον ἄγριος μυρίας ἱλαρότητας ἐν Ὀδυσσείᾳ σοφίζεται οὐ μόνον ἐν ἐκφράσεσι καὶ ξενικαῖς διηγήσεσι καὶ ἀνδρῶν τρυφώντων ἐκθέσει καὶ ἀοιδῶν αἷς οἱ τοιοῦτοι χαίρουσιν ἀλλὰ καὶ ἐν τῷ σκώπτειν καὶ παίζειν, ὃ καὶ ἐνταῦθα ποιεῖ μετὰ καὶ ποιητικῆς χάριτος.

[67] For the etymology of Odysseus from ὁδός, see e.g. Photius, *Bibl.* 190.147a; and Eustathius, *Il.* 1.108 and *Od.* 2.210 (he disagrees with this etymology but notes that some people pronounce the name of Odysseus with *spiritus asper* on its account). Editors prefer reading ἐν ὁδῷ, from οὐδός, "on the threshold," which perhaps makes better sense, but seems grammatically odd (one would expect it to be preceded by preposition ἐπί rather than ἐν).

The dialogue, then, was a discussion of various problems relating to Homer's *Odyssey* (we do not know whether the *Iliad* was discussed). The passage about Circe's prophetic power focuses on a seeming inconsistency in the *Odyssey* (if Circe could see the future, why did she send Odysseus to Teiresias?), while the London papyrus is preoccupied with Homer's literary strategies; in both cases Homeric poetry is treated with respect and subjected to exegesis. The principle of organization of the material remains unknown.

As the Giessen fragment comes from the third century BCE, we may locate the composition of the dialogue in the early Hellenistic period or slightly earlier. The text must have enjoyed popularity if two fragments from different centuries have been preserved.[68] There are visible influences of Homeric philology and of *zetemata* literature: the combination of both was delivered by Aristotle's highly influential *Homeric Problems* (Ἀπορήματα Ὁμηρικά) and, probably, by Heraclides of Pontus, who according to Diogenes Laertius composed *Homeric Solutions* in two books (Λύσεων Ὁμηρικῶν).[69]

A smaller fragment of a dramatic dialogue on Homer seems to have been preserved in PSchub. 4, dated to the first half of the first century BCE, and while the damaged state of the papyrus does not allow us to extract much information, considered alongside the discussed fragments it confirms the development of dialogues on Homeric topics.[70] The dialogue format is suggested by punctuation marks (*dicolon* in col. i.29, large blank spaces in col. i.32, 33, *paragraphoi* in col. ii.42, 46, 52, 60, 67).[71] In col. i.29, the word καλῶς follows a *dicolon*, and probably stands at the beginning of a response. In the second column, which preserves the beginnings of the lines, five *paragraphoi* are visible—if they mark speaker changes, the passage must have been a lively conversation rather than an *oratio continua* of one of the interlocutors.

A Homeric topic is indicated by the presence of particular names and phrases (Achaeans, Achilles, Odysseus' *nostos*). A certain Peisander is mentioned— probably not the Homeric character of the *Iliad*, but rather the epic poet from the archaic period, known to us merely as the author of *Heracleia*. The discussion might have centered on some temporal aspects of the Homeric epic (col. i.2-3: πρεσ[β]υ[τ]έρου καὶ νεω[τ]έρου, l. 6: ἐκ τῶν χρόνων ἐλεγχον[], col. i.19-20: ὑπὲρ τῶν πρότε[ρον], col. i.33: τὰς ἡλικί[]), and contains numerous phrases suggesting

---

[68] Eberhart 1935, 16; Körte 1939, 118.

[69] For Aristotle's *Homeric Problems*, see F 142-79 Rose³ (mostly quotations from Homeric *scholia*; notice recurrent "Aristotle solves...," λύων, λύει). For Heraclides, see Diogenes Laertius 5.88. There is no sign of an allegorical reading of Homer, and therefore a Stoic provenience, considered by Eberhart 1935, 15, seems unlikely.

[70] Schubart, who worked from his own transcriptions of the papyrus, which were subsequently lost, dated the fragment to the third century CE. The papyrus was found after the Cold War and has been re-dated by Colella 2013 to the first half of the first century BCE.

[71] Some of the *paragraphoi* are missing from Schubart's edition but are visible in a photograph of the papyrus.

intellectual scrutiny (col. i.4: ἐκ τῶν ἐπῶν ἐπ[ισκ]οπουμένω[ν], 5–6: τοὺς ὑπ[ὲρ] ἐκείνων ἀποφαινο[μ]ένους, 6: ἐλεγχον[], 11 and 32: [ὑ]ποθέσεις, ὑπόθεσιν, 23: ἐξ[ετ] άζειν, δεῖ δὲ γινώ[σκειν], 24: ὑποκειμε[], 26, 28: εἰδέναι, 28: εἰσόμεσ[θ]α πε[ρ]ὶ τῶν [ἐν τοῖ]ς μύθοις εἰρημένων, 33: ὑπεθέμεθα).

## 2.4 Historical Dialogues

In addition to philosophical dialogues and dialogues on literature, we also find in the papyri dialogues set in the past and reviving historical characters (statesmen, tyrants, kings, orators, etc.) and circumstances other than those of Socrates and the default Socratic milieu. While these texts at times touch on philosophical, and in particular moral or political topics, their most eminent feature is the fictionalization of history. These dialogues develop out of Socratic literature and the Platonic dialogue, which engaged in a creative historical exercise when it depicted Socrates in conversation with figures such as, for instance, Parmenides, Gorgias, or Nicias. Xenophon's *Hiero* is an early surviving example of venturing beyond the default Socratic setting. Cicero and his Roman friends seem to have associated this type of dialogue particularly with Heraclides of Pontus.

Papyri that preserve historical dialogues include POxy. 4.664/50.3544, set in the archaic period and having Peisistratus among its interlocutors—it has been speculated that this may be a dialogue by Heraclides of Pontus—and PBerol. inv. 13045, depicting the trial of the Athenian orator Demades. A comparison of these two works shows the diverse functions and interests of historical dialogue literature. The former work leans towards the philosophical dialogue: it seems to have explored and illuminated moral and political questions by means of, on the one hand, a report of discussions on government and political power and, on the other, by having the speakers live in and react to the historical and political circumstances of their times (the tyranny of Peisistratus and Periander). The "Trial of Demades", on the other hand, does not reveal moral preoccupations; rather, it seems to appropriate the dialogue format for the sake of a rhetorical historical exercise in *ethopoiia*. This fusion of rhetoric and dialogue connects well with a few papyri from the end of the Hellenistic period and the early centuries of the Roman empire which indicate that short dialogized compositions on historical themes were used in schools as exercises in writing and composition.[72] These include remnants of a dialogized text representing Alexander the Great in conversation with an Indian Gymnosophist (PBerol. inv. 13044), which finds parallels

---

[72] How far back this practice goes is difficult to say. In later *progymnasmata*-textbooks, dialogues are included among exercises in composition (e.g. Theon, *Progymn.* 89–90, where a conversation about the battle at Plataea is presented as an example; and 60, where the dialogue is associated with the exercise of *prosopopoeia*). For links between *progymnasmata* and Lucian's miniature dialogues, see Anderson 1993, 188.

in various short dialogized compositions on Alexander and Macedonia from the imperial period (see below, Chapter 2.6.1).

The process of composing a historical dialogue requires the imaginative use of historical information, an interest in developing the characters of the speakers, and in the case of narrated dialogues, decisions regarding the character of the narration—all of these elements make a historical dialogue a particularly creative and bold enterprise, in which history is being reimagined and rewritten. The remains of historical dialogues provide context for kindred compositions from the Roman period, such as Cicero's *Republic*, Plutarch's *Symposion of Seven Sages* or *On the Daimonion of Socrates*, or Dio Chrysostom's *Second* and *Fourth Kingship Orations*.

## 2.4.1 "Peisistratus' Dialogue" (POxy. 4.664/50.3544 [MP³ 2562])

Two Oxyrhynchian papyri preserve the remains of a historical dialogue with an unnamed internal narrator who presents himself as a friend of Solon and Peisistratus.[73] The papyrus has been dated by the editors to the third century CE, but the work itself, written in good Attic, seems to be significantly older, possibly from the end of the fourth or from the third century BCE.[74]

The anonymous dialogue is remarkable for its archaic period setting: the author located it in the distant past and, judging from the remaining fragments, exercised considerable skill in bringing to life historical characters. Three legible columns are preserved: the first one consists of a first-person narration, while the second and the third relate a conversation between several people, including the narrator, Peisistratus, and one Ariphron and Adeimantus. The first column seems to preserve a portion of the text close to the beginning as it contains some information of an introductory nature.[75] We may infer that the action takes place in the mid-sixth century BCE, during the tyranny of Peisistratus, presumably shortly after his first coup in 561/560, as there is no allusion to his subsequent overthrow.[76] The identity of the narrator remains unknown; it must have been disclosed in lost sections of the dialogue. The text might have been either a reported or a mixed dialogue (the narrator's report of the conversation might have been embedded within a frame dialogue—he might have been responding to another character's request to give an account of his encounter with Peisistratus).

---

[73] The two fragments are pieces of the same text: POxy. 50.3544 combines with the last column of POxy. 4.664.
[74] Haslam 1992, 211–14, though some scholars have speculated that the dialogue may be a work of a Roman period Atticist (Wilamowitz-Möllendorff 1904, 666; Edwards 1929, 104–6).
[75] Such narrative passages precede sometimes accounts of proper conversations in narrated or mixed dialogues, see e.g. introductory passages in Plato, *Phd.* 59d–e; Xenophon, *Symp.* 1.1–3; and Plutarch, *Conv. sept. sap.* 146b–e.
[76] Cf. Herodotus 1.59–60.

Here is the first preserved column, which contains vivid narration (POxy. 4.664/50.3544, Fr. A col. i.1-45):

πρότερον ἢ Πισίστρατον λαβεῖν τὴν ἀρχὴν ἀπεδήμησεν, ἐπειδὴ προλέγων
Ἀθηναίοις ὅτι Πισίστρατος ἐπιβουλεύει τυραννίδι πείθειν αὐτοὺς οὐκ ἦν δυνατός·
ἐγὼ δὲ καταμείνας, ἤδη Πισιστράτου τυρανν[ο]ῦντος ἀποδημίαν ἐντεῦθεν
ποιησάμενος ἐν Ἰωνίᾳ μετὰ Σόλωνος διέτριβον· χρόνῳ δέ, τῶν φίλων
σπουδαζόντων ἥκειν με καὶ μάλιστα Πισιστράτου διὰ τὴν οἰκειότητα, Σόλωνος
κελεύοντος ἐπανῆλθον Ἀθήναζε. κατέλ<ε>ιπον μὲν οὖν ἐνταῦθα παῖδα
Θρασύβουλον τὸν Φιλομήλου· κατειλήφειν δὲ μειράκ[ι]ον ἤδη μάλα καλὸν
κἀγαθὸν καὶ τὴν ὄψιν καὶ τὸν τρόπον πολὺ διαφέροντα τῶν ἡλικιωτῶν·
τεταπεινωμένων γὰρ τῶν ἄλλων διὰ τὴν τῶν πραγμάτων κατάστασιν οὐδεὶς
ἐπεδεδώκει πρὸς μεγαλοφυΐαν· πάντας δὲ ὑπερέβα<λ>λεν ἱπποτροφίαις καὶ
κυνηγίαις καὶ ταῖς ἄλλαις δαπάν[αις].[77] δ[ιε]βέβλητο δ' ἐν τῇ πόλ[ε]ι τῆς
νεωτέρας τῶν τοῦ {του} Πισιστράτου θυγατέρων ἐρᾶν ἰδὼν ἀρρηφοροῦσαν.
Ἁγνόθεος οὖν ὁ πάππος αὐτοῦ, παρ' ᾧ καὶ τρεφόμενος ἐτύγχανεν ὁ Θρασύβουλος
διὰ τὸ τοῦ πατρὸς καὶ τῆς μητρὸς ὀρφανὸς καταλειφθῆναι, τραχυνθείς τί μοι δοκε[ῖ]
πρὸς αὐτόν, καλεῖ μ' εἰς οἶκον, συγγενῆ τε αὐτοῖς ὄντα καὶ καταλελειμμένον
ἐπίτροπον ὑπὸ τοῦ Φιλομήλου. κἀγὼ μάλα προθύμως ἐβάδιζον· καὶ γὰρ ἦν ἐν
ἡδονῇ μοι τὸ συνδιατρίβειν Ἁγνο[θέῳ] ....

(Solon) before Peisistratus seized the government went abroad because his warning to the Athenians that Peisistratus was aiming at a tyranny failed to convince them. I, however, stayed on; but when the tyranny of Peisistratus was already established I left the country and lived in Ionia with Solon. After some time my friends were anxious for my return, and particularly Peisistratus, on account of our intimacy; so as Solon urged it I went back to Athens. Now I had left there a boy named Thrasyboulos, the son of Philomelos. I found him grown into a very handsome and virtuous young man, far superior in looks and manners to the others of his age; for in the general debasement due to the political situation no one had advanced to any nobility of character. He surpassed them all in horse-breeding and the chase and other such expensive pursuits; and it was said against him in the city that he was in love with the younger daughter of Peisistratus, whom he had seen carrying the vessels of Athene. His grandfather Hagnotheos in whose house it happened that Thrasybulus, who had been bereft of both father and mother, was being brought up, being, I think, a little annoyed with him, invited me to his house as I was their kinsman and had been left

---

[77] Characterization of the young Thrasyboulus is reminiscent of Thucydides' description of Alcibiades (6.15.3: ὢν γὰρ ἐν ἀξιώματι ὑπὸ τῶν ἀστῶν, ταῖς ἐπιθυμίαις μείζοσιν ἢ κατὰ τὴν ὑπάρχουσαν οὐσίαν ἐχρῆτο ἔς τε τὰς ἱπποτροφίας καὶ τὰς ἄλλας δαπάνας· ὅπερ καὶ καθεῖλεν ὕστερον τὴν τῶν Ἀθηναίων πόλιν οὐχ ἥκιστα).

guardian by Philomelos. I was very ready to go, for Hagnotheos' company was a pleasure to me....[78]

The author carefully works out the character of the narrator. He connects him with various historical figures: he is a friend of both Solon and Peisistratus, though he seems to have protested, together with Solon, against Peisistratus' assumption of power by leaving Athens. He is also the guardian of a youth named Thrasyboulus, who fell in love with a daughter of Peisistratus. We hear about Thrasyboulus from several imperial period authors, who report that after he kissed Peisistratus' daughter, the tyrant agreed to give her to him as a wife.[79] These events are not described in the extant fragments, and we may infer from the first column that the dramatic time of the dialogue predates them. They might have been reported in later sections of the dialogue.

The narrator followed Solon to Ionia after Peisistratus became a tyrant, but later decided to return at the request of his friends and Peisistratus himself, as well as at the urging of Solon. He remains critical of the tyrant's influence on Athens and observes that the situation in the city had led to the deterioration of its people (τεταπεινωμένων γὰρ τῶν ἄλλων), who were unable to acquire nobleness (μεγαλοφυία). This critical appraisal of Peisistratus' rule differs from the generally positive accounts of Aristotle and Herodotus, though it probably reflects the author's general criticism of tyranny as a form of government rather than being a vilification of Peisistratus himself (no particular faults of the tyrant are mentioned in the fragment).

Two remaining legible columns report a conversation (POxy. 4.664/50.3544, Fr. B col. i.1–29, ii.5–45):

"...μὲν οὕτως πιθανῷ ἔοικεν." "εἰ τοίνυν" ἔφην "ἀληθῆ ταῦτ' [ἐ]στίν, οὔτ' ἂν Περιάνδρῳ λυσιτελοίη μᾶλλον ἄρχειν ἢ ὑφ' ἑτέρου ἄ[ρχ]εσθαι οὔτ' ἄλλῳ οὐθενὶ τῷ[ν] φαύλως ἀρχόντων. δοκῶ γὰρ α̣[ὐτ]ὸν" ἔφην "ἐν τοῖς φιλτάτοις [ἐξακ]εῖσθαι τὰς ἁμαρτίας· τί γὰρ [φίλ]τερον ἀνδρὶ γοῦν ἔχο[ντι] πατρίδος καὶ [κ]ατὰ φύσιν [οἰ]κείων ἀνθρώ[π]ων;" ὑπο[λαβ]ὼν οὖν ὁ Ἀρί[φ]ρων "ἀλη[θῆ ν]ὴ Δί'" ἔφη "λέ [γ]εις. καὶ βου[λ]όμεθά σοι μαρ[τ]υρῆσαι ἐγὼ καὶ Ἀδείμαντος [ο]ὑτοσὶ παραγενόμενοι νυνὶ [Πε]ριάνδρῳ διὰ τὴν ὠμότη[τ]α μεγάλῃ πάνυ συμφορᾷ [π]εριπεσόντι." καὶ ὁ Πισίστρα[τ]ος "τίνι ταύτῃ;" ἔφ[η]. "ἐγὼ" εἶπ[ε]ν "φράσω. πρότ[ερον ἢ] Κύ[ψε]λον τὸν Περιάνδρ[ου π]ατέ[ρ]α̣ λαβεῖν τὴν ἀρχὴ[ν ἐκ]ρά[το]υν τῆς πόλεως ο[ἱ καλο]ύ[μ]ενοι Βακχι[άδαι], συ[γγένεια με]γάλη· λαβ[όν]τος [δὲ Κυψέλο]υ τὴν ἀρχὴν το[ύτων τὸ μὲν] πλῆθος ἔφυγε τ[ότε τὴν πόλ]ιν, ὀλίγο[ι] δὲ....

---

[78] The Greek text follows Haslam 1992; a translation of fragment A and B col. i follows Grenfell and Hunt 1904, 78–9 with slight modifications; the translation of B col. ii is mine.

[79] Plutarch, *Reg. imp. apophth.* 189c, *De coh. ira* 457f; Diodorus Siculus 9.37.1; Polyaenus 5.14 (the youth's name is "Thrasymedes"); Valerius Maximus 5.1(ext)2.

"This accordingly seems probable. If then," I said, "this be true, it would be of no more advantage to Periander to rule than be ruled by another nor to any other bad ruler. For I suppose," I said, "that he will reap the reward of his misdeeds among those dearest to him. For what is dearer to a sensible man than his country and his blood-relations?" "Yes, by Zeus," struck in Ariphron, "you speak truly, and I and Adeimantus here wish to bear you out, having just been with Periander when his cruelty plunged him into a terrible disaster." "What disaster?" said Peisistratus. "I will tell you," he said. "Before Cypselos, the father of Periander, obtained the supremacy, the great clan of the Bacchiadae, as they are called, ruled the city. When he became supreme the majority of them fled... a few however...." (*16 corrupted lines follow*)

Fr. B col. ii

(*two lines missing*) αὐτοὺς πρὸς τὸν [...]ογκώσας τὸ πρᾶγ[μα, πρὸς] οἷς ἤκουσεν πλασάμε[νος] τοιαῦτα ἐξ ὧν ἤμελλε [μά]λιστα εἰς ὀργὴν καταστῆ[σαι] τὸν Περίανδρον. ὁ δ' ἀκ[ού]σας ταῦτα καὶ πάλι[ν] μνη[μον]εύσ[α]ς (*three corrupted lines*) ὑπὸ Κυψ[έλο]υ το[ῦ] αὐτοῦ πατρὸς ἀποστ[ε]ρή[σε]σθαι παρετήρει καὶ ἐπεβο[ύ]λευεν, θέλων ἀνελεῖν. ἐν δὲ τῇ [Κ]ορί[νθ]ῳ δύναμιν ἔφασαν ὑπερβάλλουσάν τινα γένεσθαι φαρμάκου το[ι]αύτην οἷον πάντας [.]ρπ[] ἀποκτιννύναι τοὺς ψαύοντας· ἐλέγετο δὲ καὶ χρ[ισθέ]ντων τῷ φαρμάκῳ τῷ[ν βε]λῶν θανάσιμα γίνες[θαι τὰ] τραύματα. περὶ τοῦ φα[ρμ]άκου δὲ τοῦδε καὶ τὸν ['Ό]μηρον [ἔ]φασαν οἱ Κορίνθιοι [μνη]σθῆναι· τοὺς γὰρ μνησ[τῆρ]ας ἀπορουμένους πο[. .]. περὶ τῆς ἀποδημίας [τ]οῦ Τηλεμάχου λέγειν φησὶν α[ὐ]τοὺς "ἠὲ καὶ ἐς Ἐφύρην [ἐ]θέλει πίειραν ἄ[ρ]ου[ρ]αν ἐλθεῖν ὄφρ' ἔνθεν [θ]υμοφθόρα φάρμακ' ἐνείκῃ, ἐ]ν δὲ βάλῃ κ[ρη]τῆρι καὶ ἡ]μέας π[άντας ὀ]λέσσῃ" καὶ πάλ[ιν....]ησεν [εἰς] Ἐφύ[ραν ἐλθ]εῖν τὸν ['Οδυ]σσέα ["φάρμακο]ν ἀνδ[ρ]ο[φό]νον [διζήμενο]ν εἴ ποῳ [ἐφ]εύροι [ἰοὺς χρί]εσθαι χ[αλκή]ρεας."

...in addition to what he heard also making up such things that in particular angered Periander. Having heard this and remembered again (... *three corrupted lines*) to have been robbed by Cypselus, his own father, he began to look for opportunity and to plot against him, planning to kill him. They said that in Corinth there was a poison of such great power that it killed everyone who touched it. It was said that it was enough to dip the arrows in it to make the wounds fatal. According to Corinthians also Homer had mentioned this poison, for he says that when the suitors wondered about Telemachus' journey, they said, "Or he was meaning to go to Ephyre, that rich land, to get deadly poisons from there and put them in the wine-bowl and kill all of us"; and again he stated that Odysseus went to Ephyre "in search of lethal poison, if he could find any to besmear his bronze-tipped arrows."

Narrative interventions are few, brief, and assume a form known from the dialogues of Plato and Xenophon (ἔφην, ἔφη, ὑπολαβὼν... ἔφη, εἶπεν). In addition to the narrator and Peisistratus, two other interlocutors are named: Ariphron and Adeimantus (the latter is not speaking in the fragments but is mentioned as being present). The name "Ariphron" circulated in Pericles' family (it was the name of his paternal grandfather as well as of his brother). As for Adeimantus, we know of a Corinthian commander of this name at the battle of Salamis, and his ancestor might be meant here, though it was also a name circulating in Plato's family, and for an ancient reader, it was certainly reminiscent of Plato's older brother, who was Socrates' interlocutor in the *Republic*.

The topic of this section of the dialogue is the rule and misfortunes of Periander. The narrator counts him among bad rulers (as the phrase οὔτ᾽ ἄλλῳ οὐθενὶ τῷ[ν] φαύλως ἀρχόντων implies) and predicts that his faults will bring unhappiness to his family and country (foreshadowing Periander's murder of Melissa and the exile of his son Lycophron). This premonition is confirmed by Ariphron, who reveals that he and Adeimantus have been at Periander's court at Corinth and have witnessed his misfortunes, which were brought upon him by his cruelty (ὠμότης).[80] There probably followed a longer excursus about the fate of Periander's family by Ariphron, going back to the rule of the tyrant's father, Cypselus, whom Periander apparently attempted to kill. The account is enriched with a digression about a local Corinthian poison which, according to Corinthians, was mentioned by Homer.

As far as the fragments allow us to judge, the dialogue perused historical material to explore political questions concerning good and bad rule. Its version of Athenian history differs in several points from other accounts: both Aristotle and Plutarch state that Solon was the first to realize that Peisistratus aimed at tyranny, and that he was unable to convince his compatriots, yet neither author has him leave Athens as a result; some other writers have Solon travel to Egypt or Corinth,[81] from which we can infer that the relationship between Solon and Peisistratus kindled the imagination of ancient authors and was frequently fictionalized. The appeal of these stories, which sometimes stretch chronology, is easy to comprehend, as Solon enjoyed fame of an adversary of tyranny, and his encounters with Peisistratus might have been reimagined as those between a wise man and a tyrant. The author of the dialogue appears particularly interested in the problem of tyranny and proper rule: this is suggested by the cast of characters both present and discussed (Solon, Peisistratus, and Periander, whose

---

[80] Wilamowitz-Möllendorff 1904, 667 proposes that Ariphron was an exile from Periander's Corinth; see also Haslam 1992, 208. For the chronological difficulty of Periander being contemporary with the tyranny of Peisistratus, see Grenfell and Hunt 1904, 74, 78–9; Haslam 1983, 95–6; for various chronological issues, Lapini 1996.

[81] Aristotle, *Ath.* 14.2 and Plutarch, *Sol.* 29.5: Solon realizes that Peisistratus aims at tyranny; Plutarch, *Sol.* 30.8: Solon's friends suggested that he flee Athens, but he refused. Diogenes Laertius (1.50) has Solon leave Athens for Egypt and Cyprus after Peisistratus became a tyrant. In Favorinus' *Corinthian Oration* ([Dio Chrysostom], 37.5) Solon is said to have left Athens for Corinth after Peisistratus gained power. Cf. also the pseudepigraphic letters of Solon in Diogenes Laertius 1.64–7.

fate served as a cautionary example). In dialogue literature, he had precedents in Xenophon's *Hiero*, featuring the Syracusan tyrant and the poet Simonides, and in Plato's discussion of forms of government in the *Republic*. Plato's encounters with Dionysius the Younger might also have provided some inspiration (the narrator's return to Athens under Peisistratus at the request of his friends and the tyrant himself is reminiscent of Plato's returns to Syracuse).[82]

Friedrich Blass proposed that the fragments may come from Heraclides of Pontus' Περὶ ἀρχῆς (*On Government*, listed by Diogenes Laertius in 5.87 and mentioned in 1.94 in the context of the history of the family of Periander).[83] Heraclides was known for dialogues set in the past with historical characters and for his vivid style and story-telling (see Chapter 3.2). We also know from Plutarch's *Life of Solon* that a work of his discussed Solon and Peisistratus. Plutarch mentions Heraclides four times as a source (*Sol.* 1.3, 22.4, 31.4, 32.3), and two passages are reminiscent of the papyrus fragment: 32.3, where we read that according to Heraclides, Solon lived many years after Peisistratus became a tyrant, and 1.3, where Heraclides is a source of information that Solon's mother was a cousin of the mother of Peisistratus—Plutarch follows with information that the two men were at first friends on account of their kinship and the beauty of Peisistratus, and adds that for this reason Peisistratus and Solon, though they differed in their political views, never became enemies. It is unclear how much of this passage comes from Heraclides;[84] still, it is possible that Plutarch was drawing from the dialogue preserved in the Oxyrhynchian fragments. Consequently, while there is no proof of Heraclides' authorship, Blass's hypothesis seems probable.[85]

### 2.4.2 "Trial of Demades" (PBerol. inv. 13045 [MP³ 2102])

The papyrus has been dated based on the writing to the end of the second century BCE. It preserves fragments of two different texts: in first three columns, A i–iii, there are remnants of a text which compares political constitutions, extols monarchy, and praises Egypt and Alexandria. The scanty fragment makes identification of the genre difficult: it has been proposed that the text might have been an example of Hellenistic oratory, a rhetorical exercise, or a philosophical treatise on kingship; the use of the first- and second-person forms makes a dialogue format also possible.[86] The second text, which spreads over columns B i and G iii, is an

---

[82] Cf. [Plato], *Ep.* 7.327d, 7.339d.   [83] Wilamowitz-Möllendorff 1904, 666.

[84] Heraclides may be merely a source of the information about the mothers of the two men being cousins (only this part is in an accusative-infinitive construction).

[85] Wehrli 1953, 110 rejects Heraclides' authorship on grounds that Plutarch in *Sol.* 31, in Wehrli's view under the influence of Heraclides, has Solon remain in Athens after Peisistratus gained power. Yet, it is not clear whether Plutarch follows Heraclides here. Cf. overview of the discussion in Dorandi 2009, 15–19.

[86] See Amendola 2018 with an overview of earlier scholarship.

anonymous dialogue of a dramatic type relating the trial of Demades. Demades, the famous Athenian orator and demagogue from the fourth century BCE, was known in antiquity for his pro-Macedonian position after the battle of Chaeroneia (he supported Alexander's and then Antipater's interests in Athens), his enmity towards Demosthenes (it was believed that the Athenians passed a death sentence on Demosthenes on Demades' motion), and his natural rhetorical talent for improvisation. Imperial period sources portrayed Demades in a negative light and emphasized his corruption and disrespect for the law. It is debatable to what extent this representation reflects reality and to what extent it has been forged as a counter-image for Demosthenes.[87] Plutarch in the *Life of Demosthenes* considers Demades a traitor to the Athenian state and describes his death as rightful retribution for his crimes: he and his son were murdered by Cassander during a diplomatic mission to Antipater's court (the goal of the mission was to have the Macedonian garrison removed from Munychia in Piraeus), after his letter to Perdiccas, in which he urged him to attack Antipater, was discovered.[88]

It is precisely this event that is the topic of the fragmentary dialogue, which contains a rhetorized exchange between Demades and his prosecutor, the Corinthian Deinarchus, in front of a jury consisting of Athenian envoys. Demades' son seems to be present (he is the νεανίας mentioned in col. C.iii.153). The dramatic date is 319 BCE, and the place—the Macedonian capital Pella. The exchange is hostile and emotional: Demades insults Deinarchus, seems to compare him to notorious tyrants such as Phalaris and Alexander of Pherae (col. C. ii.118-19), and blames him for committing murder without a trial (col. C.iii.144). Deinarchus in turn accuses the orator of conspiring against Antipater and of handing over Athens to Perdiccas in hope of becoming the city's tyrant. The dialogue alludes to several historical events connected with the Lamian War and its aftermath—the battle at Crannon in 322, the stationing of a Macedonian garrison in Munychia, and the loss of Samos by Athens.

The dialogue consists entirely of the direct speech of Demades and Deinarchus, and pretends to be a report of the trial. The presence of other people besides Demades' son is implied, most importantly, that of the Athenian envoys who act as a jury and whom Deinarchus addresses several times. We do not know whether the text contained anything besides the exchange between Demades and Deinarchus (was for instance Cassander introduced at some point?) or whether the author sided decisively with one of them—neither Demades nor Deinarchus

---

[87] On Demades see Brun 2000; Dmitriev 2016a; Dmitriev 2016b, 934-49. Amendola 2017 argues that column B ii in the papyrus contains an account of Demosthenes' suicide (other scholars suspect a reference to Alexander's death).

[88] Plutarch, *Dem.* 31.4-6; for Plutarch's negative representation of Demades, see also *Phoc.* 1.1-2 and 30.2-3. Details of Demades' end in Macedonia differ: in Plutarch's *Phocion* 30.5, the incriminating letter is to Antigonus; in Diodorus Siculus 18.48 it is Antipater (rather than Cassander) who has Demades killed. Photius, *Bibl.* 92.70a, who follows Arrian's lost work, has Demades' son killed in the orator's arms. For sources on Demades' death, see Brun 2000, 123-30.

had good press. There is no doubt that this is not an actual trial protocol, but a work of historical fiction. Two generic inspirations are detectable. As a dramatic dialogue, the text is a descendant of Socratic literature, which included partial representations of trials in the *Apologies of Socrates*. The dialogue format is supplemented with elements characteristic of judicial rhetoric, such as a public reading of written evidence: Deinarchus asks an attendant several times to read Demades' letters to Perdiccas (e.g. col. D.ii.189-90: λέγε δὲ ποιησάμενος ἀπὸ τούτων τὴν ἀρχήν, col. E.i.246: λέγε δέ μοι τὰ λοιπά, col. E.i.253-4: λέγε σύ μὴ διάλειπε, col. F.ii.329-30: εἰ θέλεις, τὴν λοιπὴν ἐπιστολὴν ἄφες). This is an imitation of court proceedings, where documents (testimonies, contracts, laws) were read aloud by a clerk. The full contents of the letters is not included, but Deinarchus recapitulates the most incriminating points of the letters for the audience, whom he addresses in a way reminiscent of courtroom speeches (col. D.ii.190: ἀκούετε, col. E.i. 254-5: τί τούτων ἀκοῦσαι μῖζον ἀδίκημα βούλεσθε).

The dialogue does not touch upon philosophical topics nor does it betray a moralizing agenda. The fragments focus on Athenian politics after the death of Alexander (Lamian War); apart from Demades and Deinarchus, other Athenian statesmen and orators are also mentioned (Hyperides, Phocion, Demosthenes). The text has a certain rhetorical flavor, with word-plays (col. C.iii.142-3: ἐπὶ καταλύσει τῶν νόμων, ἐπὶ καταστροφῇ τῶν δικαίων, col. E.i.235: προδότης παλινπροδότης, κάπη[λο]s παλικάπηλος κακίας, col. F.ii.342: παῦσαι παίζων), emphatic questions and enumerations (col. C.iii.151-2: τί φοβῇ; φυγεῖν οὐ δυνάμεθα. [πῶς;] ποῖ; δορυφόροι θύραι κλεῖδες), antitheseis (col. C.iii.152-3: ἐγὼ γέρων, ο[ὗ]τος δὲ νεανίας), metaphorical language (cf. the recurrent metaphor of the city as a ship, col. B.iii.83-4, col. E.i.247-9,[89] or 249-50: κῦμα προδότου φωνή), and emotional appeals to the jury (col. E.ii.267-9: ἐλεεῖτε τοῦτον εἰ μεταλλάξει τὸν βίον; οὐκ ἐλεε[ῖ] δ' ἕκαστος ὑμῶν αὐτῶν;).

The authorship and the date of the composition remain unknown; the text is certainly of Hellenistic origin, as it must have been composed sometime between the dramatic date (319 BCE) and the writing of the papyrus (end of the second century BCE). As a blend of historical fiction and rhetoric, the dialogue is reminiscent of rhetorical exercises on historical themes we know from later literature, though these are usually put in the form of continuous speech rather than in dialogue format.[90]

---

[89] For Demades' comparing Athens to a shipwreck, see Plutarch, *Phoc.* 1.1 and *Praec. ger.* 803a. The mention of the bronze statue in col. F.ii.327-8, where Deinarchus says to the Athenian jury: τὸν χαλκοῦν ἀνδριάντα κε[ρδ]αίνετε, may be an allusion to Demades' statues being made into chamber pots (Plutarch, *Praec. ger.* 820f).

[90] For the dialogue as a rhetorical school exercise, see De Falco 1954², 68-9; Brun 2000, 32.

## 2.5 Dialogized Anecdotes

In Chapter 1, I discussed the relationship and mutual influence of dialogue and anecdotal and biographic literature. As I observed there, Xenophon's *Apomnemoneumata*, as a collection of short dialogues, anecdotes, and sayings, wielded considerable influence on subsequent authors who composed works similar in character. Three papyri fragments which preserve dialogized stories about philosophers supplement the evidence discussed in Chapter 1: PHibeh 182, with anecdotes about Socrates; PVindob. G 29946, dedicated to Diogenes the Cynic; and POxy. 52.3655, which contains a fragment of a conversation between the Megarian Stilpo and the Cynic Metrocles.

### 2.5.1 Ethical Views of Socrates (PHibeh 182 [MP³ 2084])

The papyrus, which reports the views and sayings of Socrates, is of an early date: it has been dated to *c*.280–250 BCE by Turner in the editio princeps and to the mid-third century BCE by Italo Gallo in the *Corpus dei papiri filosofici greci e latini*.[91] The text is written in a documentary cursive, with interlinear and intercolumnar words and phrases added in the same hand, which suggests an autograph. Linguistic features indicate that the work was composed by a Hellenistic author rather than a fourth-century Socratic.[92]

The chief interest of the fragments is ethical and moralizing rather than anecdotal. It is impossible to determine the overall form of the text based on the fragments, but two passages indicate that the work reported certain sayings of Socrates and short exchanges involving him. The second column preserves an anecdote about Xanthippe worrying about having visitors over to their house. Socrates tells her not to be alarmed (col. ii.7–14):

οὐ δ[υσθυ]μεῖν [ἐ]πὶ οὐθεν[ὶ] δεῖ, ἔφ[η,] ᾧ Ξανθίππη, σὺ δ[ὲ] ἀκή[δε]ι τούτων. εἰ μὲν γά[ρ,] ἔφη, εἰσὶ χαρ[ίεν]τες, οὐθὲν αὐτοῖς διοίσει μετέχε[ιν] τῶν παρόντων· εἰ δὲ μὴ εἰσι χαρίεντες, ἐμοὶ αὐτῶν οὐθὲν μελήσει.

There is no need to worry at all, Xanthippe, he said, do not be troubled by this. For if they are cultured people, he said, it will not be a problem for them to share in what is at hand; and if they are not cultured, I do not care about them.[93]

---

[91] Turner 1955; Gallo 1999.

[92] On the text being an autograph, see Gallo 1999, 722, 740; for Hellenistic linguistic features, Turner 1955, 27–8; Gallo 1980, 183.

[93] The Greek text and the numeration of the columns follows Gallo 1999. The anecdote is also preserved in a slightly different form in Diogenes Laertius 2.34.

Apart from this anecdote, Socrates' words are quoted in other fragments: the word ἔφη is repeated numerous times, suggesting that his utterances played an important part in the text; there is also a reconstrued vocative ὦ μειρ[άκιον] (col. iv.4bis), and in column vi the editors propose to read [ἀπο]φθεγμάτω[ν], "of sayings," which could have introduced a section with Socrates' utterances quoted and scrutinized. The text appears to have been not so much a collection of *chreiai*, but rather a moralizing work with a specific (perhaps Cynic) agenda. The author may have used the figure of Socrates to support his own philosophical position: Socrates' views on wealth and poverty are reported (the point is made that money is useful in disease and old age, though it is not clear whether this opinion was ascribed to Socrates), desires were condemned as evil (μοχθηραί), and it was proposed that habit rather than reason has the power of curbing them; the notion of nature, φύσις, appears several times; insatiable people are condemned.

It is uncertain, whether the author reported Socrates' opinions only as responses to questions referred in indirect speech, or included full conversations as well, with words of both parties in quoted direct speech. Turner hypothesized that the work was "anecdotal dialogue" resembling Xenophon's *Apomnemoneumata*: "[i]n its use of question and answer, and in general development it might be regarded as approximating to the methods of Xenophon's *Apomnemoneumata*, in that Socrates is depicted as meeting associates, questioning or being questioned by them, and developing a philosophical position on a certain topic, but not proceeding to philosophical analysis."[94]

## 2.5.2 Anecdotes about Diogenes the Cynic (PVindob. G 29946 [MP³ 1987])

The papyrus fragment is dated in a recent edition to around the mid-third century BCE, which makes it, next to fragments of Teles, the earliest surviving evidence of Diogenes of Sinope.[95] It contains a series of anecdotes with Diogenes as a protagonist. The name of the philosopher appears only once, in a dialogized exchange in the vocative, and never in narrated parts, which indicates that he was the topic of the work or at least of this section of it. The anecdotes preserved in the fragment are relatively short (6–24 lines), yet still considerably longer and more complex than *chreiai* in the form canonized by later rhetoricians. They consist mostly of a short exchange between Diogenes and another interlocutor, framed by simple narration. In some cases, there occur formulae familiar from later *chreiai* (e.g. col. ii.1–2: ἐρωτώντων δέ τινων ... ἔ[φ]η, col. v.11–13:

---

[94] Turner 1955, 27.
[95] For the numeration of the columns and lines I follow Bastianini 1992. A school context for the text has been rejected by Gallo 1980, 261; Bastianini 1992, 102.

ἐρωτηθείς...ἔφη, col. v.20-3: ἰδών...φησίν). The conversation is sometimes initiated by Diogenes, sometimes by someone else. The sources of the anecdotes are not mentioned, even in the form of general "it is said that..." or "they say that..."[96] One anecdote involves Diogenes' conversation with Dionysius of Syracuse, a retired Sicilian tyrant (col. iv.25-v.10), known to us from other sources.[97] In another, Diogenes starts a conversation with Menander who, he notices, is rich but stingy (col. v.20-5). Only the beginning of the exchange is preserved, but as Diogenes starts with εἰπέ μοι, "tell me," his question must have been followed by Menander's answer. Whether the Menander in the anecdote is the famous comic poet is uncertain.[98]

One of the anecdotes concerns Diogenes' encounter with city officials (col. ii.7-iii.2):

> ἐν πανδοκείῳ δέ ποτε αὐτοῦ κατακειμένου, ἠρώτων οἱ φύλακες τῶν στρατηγῶν τίς εἴη καὶ ποδαπός· "ἐγώ, ἔφη, κύων Μολοττικός." "ποῦ δέ, [ἔ]φασαν, πορεύει;" οὐκ ἀποκρινομένου δὲ αὐτοῦ, κατηγόρουν πρὸς τοὺς στρατηγούς· καὶ μεταπεμψαμένων τῶν στρατηγῶν αὐτὸν καὶ λεγόντων εἰ οὕτω καταφρονεῖ τῆς πόλεως καὶ τῶν νόμων ξένος ὤν, ὥστε οὐδὲ τὰ ἐρωτώμενα ἔτι ἀποκρίνεται, "οὐκ ἔγωγ', εἶπεν, ἀλλὰ πυνθανομένων τίς εἴην καὶ ποδαπός, ἀπεκρινάμην ὅτι κύων Μολοττικός· προσεπερωτώντων δὲ αὐτῶν ποῦ πορευοίμην, μαίνεσθαι ὑπέλαβον αὐτούς, οἳ ὁρῶντές με ἀνακείμενον ἠρώτων ποῦ ποτε πορευοίμην."[99]

> Once, when he stayed in an inn, guards of *strategoi* asked him, who he is and where he comes from. "I am a Molossian dog," he said. "And where are you going?" they asked. He did not answer, so they accused him before the *strategoi*. When they summoned him and asked whether he, being a foreigner, despised the city and the laws to such degree that he does not even answer questions, he replied: "Not at all; but when I was asked who I am and where I come from, I answered that I am a Molossian dog. However, when they asked also where I was going, I assumed that they are mad, because they asked me where I am going even though they saw me sitting at the table!"

The anecdote is reminiscent of a passage from the *Life of Aesop* (65). It exemplifies Diogenes' *parrhesia* and highlights tension between Diogenes' free spirit and the city's rules and institutions. Civic hierarchy is also challenged in another passage, in which Diogenes ridicules some Athenians (col. iv.1-24):

---

[96] Gallo 1980, 262.
[97] Plutarch, *Tim.* 15.8-9; *An seni* 783d. See also pseudepigraphic *Ep.* 8 of Diogenes the Cynic, where Diogenes reports his meeting with the retired tyrant.
[98] Arguments for and against identification of the character with the poet are discussed in Gallo 1980, 305-7; Bastianini 1992, 142-3.
[99] The Greek text follows Bastianini 1992.

κατέβαλεν δέ [ποτέ τις αὐ]τὸν ὀργισθεὶς ἐν τῇ ἀ[γο]ρ[ᾷ]· καὶ δὴ καὶ ὅ[s] ἐβλάβη [κα]τὰ τὸν ἀγκῶνα. πορευόμενος δ' ὡς ἦλθε πρ[ὸ]s τὰ κουρεῖα καὶ εἶδεν συνέδριόν τι ἐνδόξων καθημένων ἐν τῷ κουρείῳ, προσελθὼν [τό]τε [ὦ] ἄνδρες, ἔφη, ὕβρισμαι ὑπ' ἀνθρώπου τινὸς ἐν τῇ ὑμετέ[ρᾳ] ἀγορᾷ τηλικοῦτο[s] ὤν· εἰ μ[ὲ]ν οὖν, ἔφη, ἐν Ἀρείῳ [πάγ]ῳ ἡ βουλὴ ἐκάθητο, πρόσοδ[ο]ν ἂν ἐποιησάμην πρὸς αὐτήν· νῦν δὲ μετ' ἐκείνου τόπου [ῥ]ᾳδίω[s] ὑπολαβὼν ὑμᾶς κρα[τίσ]τους ε[ἶ]ναι Ἀθηναίων ἁπάντων καὶ εὐγενεστ[ά]τους, προσελήλυθα πρὸς ὑμᾶς. οἱ δ' ἐπαινούμενοι ἔχαιρον καὶ ἔχασ[κ]ον πρὸς αὐτόν. [ῥαι]βοὶ ἂν' ἐγκέφαλόν γ', ἔφη, νὴ [τὸν] Δία τὸν Σωτῆρα· ὑπομέ[νετε] ταῦτα ἀκούοντες ὑμεῖς; [ἀβοήθη]τοι, ἔφη γελάσας, ὑμεῖς.

Once someone angry with Diogenes threw him on the ground in the marketplace so that he hurt his elbow. As he walked by a barber's shop, he saw a council of famous citizens sitting there. He approached them and said: "Sirs, I, being in such an age, was insulted by some man in your marketplace. If there were a council gathered on the Areopagus, I would turn there. But now, instead of (going) there, I turn to you, as I suppose you to be the best and most noble of all the Athenians." His praise pleased them and they looked at him with their mouths open. "O crooked minds," he said, "for Zeus the Savior! Can you bear to hear it? You are hopeless," he said with laughter.

Another passage preserves a fragment of a dialogic altercation with some anonymous people, probably young men (col. iii.16–24):

"τί οὖν; γράμματ', [ἔφη, οὐ] πε[παί]δευσθε;" [ἐ]ξωμολο[γοῦντο δ]ή· "τί δέ; περὶ πάλαιστρ[αν οὐκ ἦτε;"] οἱ δὲ καὶ ταῦτα συνε[ῖπαν·] "τί δέ; κιθαρίζειν κ[αὶ αὐλεῖν μὴ ἀ]φεῖσθε;" "καὶ ταῦτ'" ἔφ[ασα]ν· "εἰ τέως πεπαιδευμένοι, ἔφη, πρὸς ἐμὲ ἔρχεσθε θ.[ ...].. [.] τὴν βακτηρί[α]ν....

"What then? Have you not learned the letters?" They confirmed. "What else? Didn't you attend the wrestling school?" They agreed also to that. "What else? Certainly, you did not neglect kithara and aulos-playing?" "This too," they said. "If with such education," he said, "you come to me,.... a staff...."[100]

This is part of a longer anecdote at the core of which is a juxtaposition between a traditional Greek education with the one being offered by Diogenes; it is possible that it was linked to lines above the quoted verses in which Diogenes is said to have walked around with his followers (col. iii.3–4: μετὰ τῶν ὁμιλητῶν πορευόμενος). The sequence of questions and answers makes the passage closely

---

[100] For a different reconstruction of this passage, see Gallo 1980, 270; he connects it to ll. 2–11 in column iii, which Bastianini considers a separate anecdote. For Diogenes' attitude to music, see also Diogenes Laertius 6.27–8 and 6.73.

related to Socratic dialogue.[101] The staff, ἡ βακτηρία, is traditionally associated with Diogenes; here it is probably referred to as a pedagogical "aid" (cf. lines above, where Diogenes was depicted as striking one of his followers with it: col. iii.7-8: λαβὼν τὴν βακτηρίαν, καθικνεῖ[τό] τινος αὐτῶν).[102]

It can be concluded that the preserved fragment contains partially preserved anecdotes referring to relatively short conversations between Diogenes and various people. Their length is sometimes difficult to determine: for instance, Diogenes' encounter with Menander in column v perhaps extended into ll. 13-25 of column vi, in which Diogenes urges his interlocutor to "find some carriage as fast as possible, get wings, and flee from vice (κακία)."[103] The text shares several thematic and stylistic parallels with Xenophon's *Apomnemoneumata* and fragments of Antisthenes, which underlines the Socratic background of Diogenes' cynicism.[104]

In terms of genre, it has been proposed that the work was a biography of Diogenes or a collection of anecdotes about him (though it is also possible that merely this section was devoted to Diogenes, with other characters being the topic of other parts of the text).[105] It may have been a work similar to Xenophon's *Apomnemoneumata*, namely a text protreptic and commemorative in character, in which the philosopher's conversations, sayings, and actions are reported because they are deemed to provide the best encouragement to and model for a virtuous life. As the papyrus is dated to the mid-third century BCE, the writer must have lived merely decades after Diogenes. Metrocles the Cynic has been proposed as the potential author: he wrote a work titled *Chreiai* from which Diogenes Laertius drew an anecdote about Diogenes the Cynic (6.33).[106]

### 2.5.3 Conversation between Stilpo of Megara and Metrocles(?) (POxy. 52.3655 [MP³ 2592.200])

The papyrus (dated second-third century CE) preserves a fragment of a conversation between Stilpo of Megara and another philosopher, perhaps Metrocles the Cynic (ll. 1-16):

τοὺς ὑπολειπομένους τῶν τοῦ Στ]ίλπωνος μαθητῶν, ἐν οἷς κ[αὶ ὁ ῥή]τωρ Ἄλκιμος ἦν ἤδη παρὰ [Στίλπω]νι διατρίβων. "του[τον]; [τί" ἔφη,] "ᾧ ἀναίσθητοι, τὸν [παῖδα τιμᾶ]τε ὡς ὄντα τινά;" κα[ὶ ὁ Στίλπω]ν "ἐμοί," ἔφη, "ὦ Μητρό[κλεις, ἀρκεῖ]

---

[101] Cf. Brancacci 1996, 412: "la sua struttura fa pensare a un vero e proprio frammento di dialogo, successivamente ridotto ad aneddoto."

[102] Cf. also Diogenes' pseudepigraphic *Letter* 38, in which the philosopher beats a diviner with his staff, and Antisthenes' response to one asking why he has so few disciples: "Because I cast them out with a silver rod!" (Diogenes Laertius 6.4).

[103] As proposed by Brancacci 1996, 409-10.

[104] The parallels are discussed at length by Brancacci 1996, 412-22.   [105] Gallo 1980, 263-4.

[106] For this hypothesis and other potential authors, see Bastianini 1992, 106-8.

παιδεύειν ἄνθρωπ[ον." ὁ δέ· "τί βού]λῃ; π[ό]τερα [πα]ῖδας ἐ[γγράψαι] εἰς τοὺς μαθητάς, ἢ [ἄνδρας;" "πα]ῖδα ἔγωγε" ἔφη. "ἆρ' οὖ[ν οἶδε τὰ ἀγ]αθὰ καὶ τὰ κα<κά>, ἢ [ο]ὔ; φή[σαντος δὲ αὐ]τοῦ "πάν[υ,"] "τί οὖν κακόν ἐσ[τι, νεανί]α, διαίρ[ει."] καὶ ὁ Ἄλκιμος .[. . . . . . . . .]τ.[. . . .] καὶ τὸ μοιχ[εύειν . .]. .[. . .]διδάσκεις το[

[He visited] the remaining pupils of Stilpo, among whom was also the rhetor Alcimus, already attending Stilpo's school. "You fools," he said, "why do you respect this child as being really someone?" "For me, Metrocles," replied Stilpo, "it is enough that I should have a human being to educate." "What do you want? To enroll children into your school, or men?" "In my case, a child," he said. "Does he then know what goods and evils are, or not?" "Certainly," said he. "Then define what evil is, boy." (". . . " replied) Alcimus, "and adultery." ". . . you teach . . . ."[107]

Caution is due in interpretating this fragment, as the name of Metrocles is conjectured from a badly damaged end of the line. The mention of "the remaining pupils of Stilpo" suggests that the reported conversation was not isolated, but had some background in the preceding text, now lost (perhaps other students have left the scene, or abandoned Stilpo's school altogether).[108] The extant fragment has the form of a narrated dialogue with three speakers, Stilpo, his student Alcimus (later a celebrated rhetor, mentioned by Diogenes Laertius 2.114), and Stilpo's adversary, probably Metrocles, who assumes the role of the questioner. Alcimus' answer is lost; he appears to have listed τὰ κακά, including adultery among them, in response to the question. His answer must have been followed by a comment by the adversary and possibly by a further exchange between him and Stilpo.

If the passage preserves an encounter between Stilpo and Metrocles, it constitutes an episode in the polemical relations between the Megarians and the Cynics.[109] Diogenes of Sinope is said to have written a dialogue against Ichthyas (Diogenes Laertius 2.112 and 6.80). Stilpo is depicted in a number of encounters with the Cynic Crates (Diogenes Laertius 2.117–19) and is said to have composed a dialogue titled *Metrocles* (2.120). Plutarch in *On Tranquility of the Mind* (468a) reports an exchange between Stilpo and Metrocles, which I discuss in Chapter 1.2. In the Plutarchan passage, the story favors Stilpo, whose argument is "gentle and philosophic" (πράῳ λόγῳ καὶ φιλοσόφῳ), while Metrocles' attitude is "idle yapping" and "slander" (κενὸν . . . ὕλαγμα τὴν τοῦ κυνικοῦ βλασφημίαν). The ending of the conversation in the papyrus fragment is not preserved, and it remains unclear who wins the argument.

---

[107] The reconstruction of the Greek text and translation (the latter with slight modification) after the editio princeps by Sedley 1984. A new edition, with less conjectural supplements in lacunae, has been published by Capuccino and Iovine 2019.
[108] Capuccino and Iovine 2019, 438.   [109] Brancacci 2004, 234–5.

It has been proposed that the papyrus preserves a fragment of Stilpo's *Metrocles* or Metrocles' *Chreiai*.[110] As for the former, one would have to presume that Stilpo's work was a narrated dialogue in which he presented Metrocles and himself in conversation and spoke of himself in the third person. This is not wholly unprecedented in the Socratic literature, though it would still be somewhat unusual in a dialogue with Stilpo as the main interlocutor.[111] In support of this proposition, a passage from *Lexicon Patmense* is quoted, which is believed to preserve a fragment of Stilpo's *Metrocles*. The text reads in Sakkelion's edition as follows:

ἐνεβρίμει· ἀντὶ τοῦ ὠργίζετο· Στίλπωνι Μητροκλῆς· Ἐνεβρίμει τῷ Στίλπωνι Μητροκλῆς.

*enebrimei*: instead of "was angry at." Metrocles at Stilpo: "Metrocles *enebrimei* at Stilpo."[112]

The line was amended by Gomperz to Στίλπων Μητροκλεῖ· Ἐνεβρίμει τῷ Στίλπωνι Μητροκλῆς and interpreted as "Stilpo in *Metrocles*: 'Metrocles was angry at Stilpo'" (though one would expect the preposition ἐν before the title rather than merely the dative). Gomperz concluded that Stilpo's dialogue *Metrocles* was of the Aristotelian type, with the author included among the speakers.[113] This appears to me too speculative to be accepted as evidence concerning the format of Stilpo's *Metrocles* and, consequently, as an aid in determining authorship of the papyrus fragment. There is also no sufficient evidence to postulate that the fragment comes from Metrocles' *Chreiai*.

Putting aside the question of authorship, we can see a similarity between the fragment and dialogic sections of Xenophon's *Apomnemoneumata*. One is especially reminded of Socrates' exchanges with his adversaries. In *Mem.* 1.6, Antiphon comes to Socrates "with the intention of drawing his companions away from him" and challenges him in their presence (ὁ γὰρ Ἀντιφῶν ποτε βουλόμενος τοὺς συνουσιαστὰς αὐτοῦ παρελέσθαι προσελθὼν τῷ Σωκράτει παρόντων αὐτῶν ἔλεξε τάδε); in *Mem.* 3.8, Aristippus attempts to question Socrates publicly, in front of his followers; in *Mem.* 4.4, Hippias confronts Socrates. Similar conversational dynamics emerge from the papyrus fragment. It is not necessary, however, for the fragment to have originated from a work favoring Stilpo. The Cynics were proudly and unapologetically confrontational and refutatory, as stories about Diogenes of Sinope clearly show; it is therefore possible that the fragment comes from a work which approved of Metrocles and his ways.

---

[110] Sedley 1984, 44–5; Brancacci 2004, 234–5; Capuccino and Iovine 2019, 434–6.
[111] Cf. Xenophon, *Mem.* 1.3.9–13. Xenophon's *Anabasis* provides a precedent in another generic tradition.
[112] Sakkelion 1877, 151.   [113] Gomperz 1877, 477–8.

## 2.6 School Compositions

There are a few fragments of what appear to be school exercises from the late Hellenistic and early imperial period, which indicate that brief dialogues on historical themes and dialogized animal fables were used in education.

### 2.6.1 Alexander the Great and Gymnosophists (PBerol. inv. 13044 [MP³ 2099])

The papyrus, dated to the second or first century BCE, depicts a conversation between Alexander and Gymnosophists. The exchange is rendered partially in direct, partially in indirect speech; the amount of narration and indirect speech is considerable, and the text should be situated somewhere between a *diegesis* and a narrated dialogue.[114] Alexander asks the Indian wise men tricky questions: are the living more numerous than the dead? what is the most cunning of all creatures? which came first, day or night? The "riddle contest" and the motif of the confrontation of power with wisdom is reminiscent of the Seven Sages tradition. Besides this text, the papyrus contains various lists—of famous men, seven wonders, largest islands, etc.—which suggests a school context. If so, the papyrus bears valuable evidence of the use of short dialogues on historical themes in education; in this particular case, the text might have been written down by a teacher and intended for copying or dictation.[115] A noteworthy imperial age parallel is PSI 7.743 (MP³ 2100, first or second century CE), which transmits the same conversation between Alexander and Gymnosophists transcribed in Latin letters, probably as an aid for Latin-speakers learning Greek.[116]

Comparable texts of the early imperial period include PGenev. inv. 271 + PDuk. inv. 777 + PKöln inv. 907 (MP³ 2580, second century CE), containing an exchange between Alexander and Dandamis, the Indian wise man, with a third-person narration;[117] and two dialogues on Macedonian themes, set after the death of Alexander: PFreib. 2a and PFreib. 2b (MP³ 2101), dated tentatively to the second century CE. One of them contains a short exchange between two men, named Callistratus and Mnesippus. Callistratus is afraid that a spy or a demagogue might hear him; he complains about the state of affairs in Macedonia after Alexander's death: the laws have no power, the country is ruled by a tyrant, fear is everywhere.

---

[114] The work is sometimes referred to as a diatribe, see e.g. Martin 1959; for the genre, see Szalc 2011, 14–15. The fragment had been labelled "Cynic" in the past, but this affiliation has been rightly refuted by Bosman 2010.
[115] Cribiore 1996, 53, 270.
[116] A new edition and commentary in Ciriello and Stramaglia 1998.
[117] For the papyrus, its character and textual problems, Martin 1959; Willis and Maresch 1988; Nodar 2000.

Mnesippus alludes to Alexander's divinity. At the end of the fragment, Antipater enters; the dialogue breaks in mid-sentence. PFreib. 2b contains a conversation between Cassander and Antipater; Olympias is mentioned as a "mother of god." Both "Macedonian" works show signs of school provenience: they are probably exercises in composition. Both PFreib. 2a and 2b contain indications of speakers (the names of interlocutors are spelled out in the text). This is unusual in ancient dramatic dialogues and is probably due to their school provenience—the animal fables, discussed below, share the same feature.[118]

### 2.6.2 Prose Animal Fables (PMed. inv. 70.01 recto, MPER 3.30 (= PVindob. inv. G 29813–14) [MP³ 2652.100 and 2652])

In an early phase of education, there was some use of dialogized animal fables. We have two papyri fragments preserving fables about a mouse and a weasel put in the form of a dramatic dialogue: PMed. inv. 70.01 recto (end of the first century BCE) and MPER 3.30 (= PVindob. inv. G 29813–14, end of the first century CE). These might have been exercises in prose paraphrase of a versified fable (there are traces of iambic trimeter).[119] In both cases, animals speaking at given moment are clearly marked with the indications μῦς, γαλῆ (sometimes set in separate lines), at times unnecessarily repeated, which may suggest a student's hand.

## 2.7 Other Fragments

Below I provide some brief information about pre-imperial papyri which (1) seem to preserve fragments of dialogues, and (2) were once identified as dialogue fragments, but this identification is no longer upheld.

### 2.7.1 PIen. inv. 660 [MP³ 2584.010]

Papyrus from the third century BCE, probably containing a Socratic dialogue, as suggested by vocative ὦ Σώκρατες in Fr. A col. i.6, and ἔλεγες in the subsequent one. The topic is difficult to determine, but it might have been political (cf. ἡγεμόνες [ἄ]ρχοντ[ες] καὶ βοηθοί in Fr. B, ll. 13–14). A philosophical character is suggested by [δι]ατριβὰς ποιεῖται in Fr. B, l. 11 and [φι]λοσοφοῦσι in Fr. B, l. 17).

---

[118] On speaker indications, see Jażdżewska 2018. Macedonian-themed dialogues might have been somewhat popular; cf. the second part of the *Encomium of Demosthenes*, in which Lucian quotes a conversation between Antipater and Archias, which, he claims, he found in an old book.

[119] So Daris 1972, 91 and Lenaerts 2009, 244. For the Hellenistic mock-epic on the war of mice and weasels preserved in PMich. inv. 6946, see Schibli 1983; Schibli 1984.

## 2.7.2 PBerol. inv. 21256 (= BKT 9.160) [MP³ 2099.010]

Papyrus from the third century BCE. Perhaps a philosophical dialogue, as suggested by partial words: l. 1: γνῳ[], 4: ἐρωτ[ώμενος], 6: [ἀποκ]ρίναιο ταῦτ[α], 8: []αγνωμεν, 9: δεῖ γνῶ[ναι]). The theme is unclear.

## 2.7.3 PKöln 9.360 [MP³ 2103.010]

Papyrus from the first century CE. A small fragment, perhaps of a dialogue, as suggested by vocative ὦ μακά[ριε], verbal forms of the first-person plural (ἐσμεν, ending -ομεν), and second-person possessive pronoun (σῆς). The theme is unclear.

## 2.7.4 PRein.1.5 (= PSorb. inv. 2014) + PBerol. inv. 9869 (= BKT 2.55) [MP³ 2444]

Papyrus from the second century BCE. The format is uncertain; there are no clear indications of a dialogue form. There is one *paragraphos*, which seems to have led the BKT editor to refer to the text as the "Philosophischer Dialog(?)." Blass 1906, 499–500 is skeptical; he thinks that the text discussed Plato's *Laws*; de Giorgi 1995, 251–2 discusses it in her overview of papyri on music.

## 2.7.5 PHeid. G inv. 28 + PGraec.Mon. 21 [MP³ 1389.100, previously 2560 + 2561]

Papyrus from the third century BCE. PGreac.Mon. 21 was identified as a dialogue by Wilcken 1901, 475–9 and Crönert 1903, 367, who observes that "die dialogische Form der Darstellung ist deutlich erkennbar." Currently the fragment is believed to come from a commentary on Plato's *Phaedo*; see Carlini 1995.

## 2.8 Conclusion

The fragments discussed in the first part of this chapter provide important evidence for the use of the dialogue for philosophical inquiry. While some of these texts appear to have been composed in the first half of the fourth century, perhaps by the Socratics, other have been associated by scholars with post-Platonic environments, including the third-century hedonist school of Hegesias, the Old Academy, and the Peripatos. Other fragments testify to innovative employment of the dialogue for literary studies, which developed under the influence of Peripatetic and Alexandrian scholarship; here, as we have seen, the dialogue opened up to influences from Hellenistic period genres of biography and Homeric *zetemata*. The dialogue format allowed for a "staging" of erudition and philological competence, performed by a community of educated readers (among whom sometimes, as in Satyrus' *Life of Euripides*, women were included).

The third category of fragments examined—that is, fragments of historical dialogues—turn the spotlight on a specific moment in the past, sometimes the very distant past, as in "Peisistratus' Dialogue," sometimes more recent, as in the "Trial of Demades." These carefully written works are focused on the figures of high-powered men and combine history with fiction—and in the "Trial of Demades" with rhetorical verve. Fragments of what appear to be a school composition from the late Hellenistic and early imperial period suggest that short dialogues on historical themes were used in education (extant papyri suggest a particular interest in Alexander the Great and the Macedonian court), perhaps as exercises both in writing and in composition. Other uses of the dialogue in education included dialogized animal fables.

Papyri fragments preserving sayings and dialogized anecdotes supplement the examination of mutual influences between the dialogue and anecdote in Chapter 1.2. Fragments preserving exchanges by Diogenes the Cynic and Stilpo's conversation with (probably) Metrocles are reminiscent of Xenophon's *Apomnemoneumata* and constitute the meagre remnants of what appears to have been a very popular literary format that reported the memorable words and actions of philosophers as reflections of their personalities and opinions.

# 3
# Dialogue in the Academy

## 3.1 Introductory Remarks

The period between the mid-fourth century BCE and the mid-first century CE covers several phases of the post-Platonic Academy: the so-called Old Academy of Plato's immediate successors, followed by the skeptical New Academy starting with Arcesilaus c.268/4, and finally the birth of Middle Platonism, associated with Antiochus of Ascalon and his falling out with Philo of Larissa, the last undisputed scholarch of the school.[1] Besides doctrinal fluctuations and changes, the Athenian school witnessed profound social and cultural transformations: Athens became the center for philosophical education, rival schools—the Peripatos, the Epicurean Garden, the Stoa—opened in the latter half of the fourth century and together with the Academy began attracting students from throughout the Greek-speaking world. The Academy became increasingly diverse: starting with Arcesilaus, no Athenian would become a scholarch for the next two hundred years, including the last known head of the school, Philo of Larissa; the community of students was also predominantly non-Athenian.[2] From the mid-second century on, the Academy's contacts with the Romans intensified—Carneades famously traveled to Rome with an Athenian embassy in 155 BCE, Clitomachus dedicated some of his works to Romans, and Philo of Larissa eventually moved to Rome in 88 BCE during the unrest of the Mithridatic War.[3]

The Academy, both during Plato's life and after his death, must have witnessed fervent writing activity as suggested by extensive lists of the titles produced by some of its members; unfortunately only a few are extant. The three centuries witnessed diversification in terms of the literary forms used by philosophers, Platonists included. The systematic treatise, protreptic and paraenetic continuous discourse,[4] the philosophical letter, commentary, and other types of exegetical literature, the consolation—these formats were becoming available at one point or

---

[1] For a periodization of the history of the post-Platonic and Hellenistic Academy, see Dörrie 1987, 33–41; Flashar 1994, 779–81; Dorandi 1999, 31–5.
[2] Habicht 1994, 232; he also notes that among some forty students of Carneades listed in Philodemus' *History of Academy* there are only two Athenians, and among fifteen known students of Arcesilaus—none.
[3] For the Athenian embassy to Rome in 155, see Powell 2013; for the circumstances of Philo's moving to Rome, see Brittain 2001, 58–64.
[4] For the distinction between *paraenesis* and protreptic, see Swancutt 2005; for genres popular among Hellenistic philosophers, White 2010, 370–82.

*Greek Dialogue in Antiquity: Post-Platonic Transformations.* Katarzyna Jażdżewska, Oxford University Press.
© Katarzyna Jażdżewska 2022. DOI: 10.1093/oso/9780192893352.003.0004

another as alternatives to the dialogue. Yet, while the dialogue certainly lost the preeminence it enjoyed in Plato's corpus, there are no reasons to believe that it was abandoned. Plato established it as *the* philosophical genre, providing his successors with an approved model of philosophy that did not eschew the literary dimension as mere embellishment, but celebrated it and used it in ingenious ways. The Academy was a natural place for the dialogue to thrive and transform, and we may assume that it suited the spirit of the school, which fostered doctrinal diversity and internal debates and polemics.[5]

Still, it is one thing to argue that there is neither evidence nor reason to stipulate an abandonment or eclipse of the genre, and another to provide positive confirmation for its continuous use in the post-Platonic and Hellenistic Academy, when writings produced by its members have been almost completely lost. A recent list of Academic philosophers active between the fourth and the first century BCE, based mostly on Philodemus and Diogenes Laertius, includes about one hundred and fifty names: in the vast majority of cases, all that is left is the person's name and information about whose student he (or in exceptional cases, she) was.[6] Even if not all of these people were writers (some might not have been full-fledged philosophers or committed Academics), a comparison of this list with the meagre body of extant texts reveals the extent of this loss and underscores the serious limitations facing any attempt to draw a general picture of the school's literary activity. It may therefore be useful to precede an examination of positive evidence of dialogue composition in the Academy with a brief overview of the preserved remains of the school's writings, which will serve as a reminder of what has been lost.

Extant writings of the Old Academy include the *Epinomis* and probably some dialogues from among the Platonic *dubia* and *spuria* (which are discussed in Chapter 4), which appear to have been composed in the fourth and early third century. Diogenes Laertius preserves catalogues of works of Speusippus and Xenocrates, the first two scholarchs to lead the Academy after Plato's death, which allows for discussion, however speculative, on the nature of their literary output. We have no such lists for the next two heads of the school, Polemo and Crates; Diogenes merely says that the former died "leaving behind a considerable number of works" (4.20: ἱκανὰ συγγράμματα καταλιπών; cf. *Suda* s.v. Πολέμων (π 1887): πολλὰ μὲν συνέγραψε βιβλία), and that the latter left "some philosophical works, some on comedy, and speeches delivered in the assembly or during

---

[5] Cf. e.g. recently El Murr 2018, 343, "Being a member of the Academy, during Plato's lifetime as well as after his death, never meant subscribing to an orthodoxy that would have stymied discussion and debate"; Algra 2018, 411: unlike Stoicism and Epicureanism, "... the schools of Plato and Aristotle had to some extent functioned as research institutes with an open and critical attitude even towards the theories of their founding fathers...."

[6] Dorandi 2018; the list is based, for the most part, on Philodemus' *History of the Academy* and Diogenes Laertius. For need for caution when considering the philosophical affiliation of Hellenistic period thinkers, see Hahm 1990, 3044–5.

embassies" (4.23: ἀπέλιπε βιβλία τὰ μὲν φιλοσοφούμενα, τὰ δὲ περὶ κωμῳδίας, τὰ δὲ λόγους δημηγορικοὺς καὶ πρεσβευτικούς). The only title known to have been written by Polemo is Περὶ τοῦ κατὰ φύσιν βίου, *On Life according to Nature*, which, according to Clement of Alexandria, argued that eating meat was harmful for the soul (*Strom.* 7.6.32.9); we also learn from the *Suda* that Polemo greatly valued Homer and Sophocles. Nothing is known of the formats and literary character of Polemo's and Crates' works. For other students of Plato and the philosophers associated with the Old Academy, we rarely have more than an occasional title, quotation, or anecdote. Crantor of Soli, a student of Xenocrates and Polemo, was said to have been an inventive writer and father of the consolation genre; regrettably, we know close to nothing about the formats of his works—though a dialogized parable depicting a contest between earthly goods was transmitted by Sextus Empiricus, and will be discussed later in this chapter.

Evidence of the writings of members of the skeptical Academy is even scarcer.[7] While the doctrines of the Academics of this period have been partially preserved by subsequent skeptically inclined philosophers, such as Cicero and the Pyrrhonist Sextus Empiricus, we have very little information about specific works. The two key figures, Arcesilaus and Carneades, are said to have left no philosophical texts,[8] though accounts of their teachings, composed by students, appear to have circulated. Of Lacydes, Arcesilaus' successor as a scholarch, we know merely that he wrote φιλόσοφα καὶ Περὶ φύσεως, "philosophical works and *On Nature*" (*Suda* s.v. Λακύδης (λ 72)). Of the literary activity of other scholarchs—Evander and Telecles of Phocaea, Carneades the Younger, and Crates of Tarsus—we have no information. Clitomachus of Carthage, a student of Carneades and a scholarch before Philo of Larissa, was probably the most prolific writer of the New Academy: Cicero speaks of the "*multitudo librorum*" he left (*Acad.* 2.6.16), and according to Diogenes Laertius (4.67) he wrote over four hundred texts. Yet, although his works were crucial for the transmission of Carneades' teaching, only two titles are preserved of his apparently abundant oeuvre: *On Suspending Assents* (Cicero, *Acad.* 2.31.98: *De sustinendis adsensionibus*) and a doxographic work Περὶ αἱρέσεων, *On the Sects* (Diogenes Laertius 2.92). He also wrote a consolation for his fellow Carthaginians after the Romans destroyed the city in 146 (Cicero, *Tusc.* 3.12.54). Two of his works on the epistemology of unknown titles were dedicated to Romans, one to the satirist Lucilius and the other to Lucius Censorinus (Cicero, *Acad.* 2.32.102). Next to

---

[7] For the New Academy, see the general overviews in Long 1986², 88–106; Görler 1994, 775–937; Algra et al. 1999, 323–51; and the contributions in Bett 2010; for fragments with commentary, Mette 1984; Mette 1985. The skeptical phase of the school is treated by Philodemus in *Acad. ind.* col. xvii-xxxiii and in Diogenes Laertius 4.28–67.

[8] This, however, might not have been wholly accurate; for traces of evidence concerning Arcesilaus' writings, see Görler 1994, 786–7. In the case of Carneades, we hear only of his letters to Ariarathes, king of Cappadocia (Diogenes Laertius 4.65).

nothing is also known about the works of Philo of Larissa, notwithstanding the fact that he was Cicero's teacher.[9] The only text that is explicitly referred to in the sources is one that angered Antiochus of Ascalon; it is usually referred to by scholars as "the Roman books" because it was written in Rome in 88-87 BCE; but neither the title nor the form is known. Antiochus' response to Philo was a work titled *Sosus* after a Stoic philosopher; the title suggests that it was a dialogue; of the other works of Antiochus, we know only two other titles, *Canonika* and *On the Gods*, though he seems to have been a productive writer.[10]

The nature of the evidence makes it extremely difficult, if not outright impossible, to draw general conclusions on the use of the dialogue or any other format by Plato's successors in the period covered in the book, and anyone attempting such has to be aware of the fragmentary and distorting nature of our sources. My aim is to gather and carefully assess the available information. I will begin with evidence of the employment of the dialogue format by Plato's students and early successors, including Heraclides of Pontus, Speusippus, Eudoxus of Cnidus, and Xenocrates, and inspect testimonies and fragments of Crantor of Soli. The subsequent section discusses changes in the dialogue format in the New Academy. Chapter 4, focused on Platonic *dubia* and *spuria*, is complementary to this one.

## 3.2 Heraclides of Pontus

Heraclides of Pontus played a substantial role in the development of the dialogue, although the loss of his texts makes it impossible to fully grasp his impact. Dubbed "Theophrastus Paracelsus des Altertums" by Rudolf Hirzel and a "notorious maverick" by John Dillon,[11] Heraclides was an imaginative and daring writer who expanded the boundaries of the genre by moving away from the verisimilitude of the Socratic dialogue and by reaching for fictionalized historical settings and miraculous stories.

Born in the early 380s BCE, Heraclides was a contemporary of Aristotle. Coming from Heraclea on the Black Sea, he must have arrived in Athens in his youth. Diogenes Laertius and Philodemus list him among the students ($\mu\alpha\theta\eta\tau\alpha\iota$) of Plato (3.46; *Acad. ind.* col. v.13-vi.1); Strabo calls him a Platonist ($\Pi\lambda\alpha\tau\omega\nu\iota\kappa\acute{o}s$, 12.3.1), and Cicero considers him "*auditor et discipulus Platonis*" (*Div.* 1.23.46). Heraclides' importance in the Academy and his closeness to Plato is suggested by the *Suda*, where it is said that when Plato was in Sicily, Heraclides was overseeing

---

[9] For Cicero's philosophical affiliation and his possible turn to Philo's skepticism after a period of Antiochus' influence, see Glucker 1988. Görler 1995 argues for Cicero's continuous adherence to the skeptical Academy.

[10] See Rawson 1985, 58 for the suggestion that the *Sosus* might have been set in Italy. For more on Antiochus' writings, see Barnes 1989, 62-4; Görler 1994, 945-7.

[11] Hirzel 1895a, 323; Dillon 2003, 204.

the Academy (s.v. Ἡρακλείδης (η 461)). Proclus reports that Heraclides maintained that Plato preferred the poetry of Antimachus over that of Choerilus, and that Plato sent him to Colophon to gather the poems of the poet (*In Ti.* 1.90 Diehl). He also seems to have remained an influential member of the Academy post-Plato: according to Philodemus, upon Speusippus' death in 339 BCE Heraclides lost his leadership to Xenocrates by just a few votes (*Acad. ind.* col. vii.3–5).[12] Afterwards he returned to Pontus, where he seems to have opened his own school: Dionysius of Heraclea, later called Μεταθέμενος ("the Renegade"), apparently began his philosophical education under him.[13]

While there is clear evidence of Heraclides' association with Plato and the Academy, several ancient authors are reluctant to consider him an Academic. Diogenes Laertius places him among the Peripatetics, and reports that after coming to Athens Heraclides associated himself with Speusippus, but also listened to the Pythagoreans, embraced Plato's instructions, and attended Aristotle's lectures (5.86). Proclus denies that Heraclides was a disciple (ἀκουστής) of Plato (*In Ti.* 3.138 Diehl). Plutarch includes Heraclides, together with Aristotle, Theophrastus, and Dicaearchus, among the philosophers who opposed and fought Plato (*Adv. Col.* 1115a: ὑπεναντιούμενοι, μαχόμενοι) on the most important questions of natural philosophy; elsewhere he lists him with Aristotle and Dicaearchus as authors who wrote in a similar vein about Homer and Euripides (*Non posse* 1095a).

Regardless of this tendency to see Heraclides as being affiliated with the Peripatos, it is clear that he could not have been a member. Aristotle left Athens after Plato's death in 348 BCE, spent years in Assus, Lesbos, and Macedon, and returned to Athens around 335 BCE. Heraclides, on the other hand, was an influential member of the Academy after Speusippus became the head, but by the time Aristotle returned, he seems to have moved back to Heraclea. The inconsistency and ambivalence of sources is due to the fact that Heraclides' case was not a straightforward one, in terms of either institutional affiliation or philosophical views. While he was clearly associated with the Academy in his youth, he apparently disassociated himself from the school after Xenocrates became the scholarch, and as he was active for the next twenty years or so, many of his writings must have been composed after he left Athens. The testimonies of Plutarch and Proclus indicate that he was not a faithful follower of the Academy, and that he explicitly disagreed with Plato's teachings.[14]

---

[12] For Heraclides in Philodemus' *History of the Academy*, see Dorandi 2009, 2–5. For his biography, see Wehrli 1953, 59–64; Gottschalk 1980a, 1–12.

[13] For Dionysius of Heraclea, see Diogenes Laertius 7.37 and 7.166–7 (he was later a student of Zeno, but after becoming severely ill, he left the Stoics and associated himself with the Cyrenaics).

[14] See Sollenberger 1992, 3808–9; Mejer 2009, 38–9. Dillon 2003, 216 considers Heraclides "an original mind produced by the milieu of Plato's Academy." For Heraclides' life in Diogenes Laertius, see Ehrman 2013, 11–14; for his philosophical views, Gottschalk 1980a; Krämer 2004², 72–80; and contributions in Fortenbaugh and Pender 2009.

Heraclides was a prolific and valued writer, with dialogues constituting an important part of his output. Diogenes Laertius praises his works as "writings most beautiful and excellent" (συγγράμματα κάλλιστά τε καὶ ἄριστα) and then refers to them as "dialogues."[15] However, the word διάλογοι is followed by the phrase ὧν ἠθικὰ μέν, "of which ethical are" (5.86), and as ἠθικά is not in grammatical agreement with διάλογοι, the latter word is probably a later addition.[16] Therefore, it should not be assumed that all the texts listed by Diogenes were dialogues; still, even if added later, the term indicates that Heraclides was known as a dialogue-writer.

Most of Heraclides' works listed by Diogenes Laertius are relatively short, one-book compositions on a variety of themes: besides ethical texts (*On Justice, On Self-Control, On Piety, On Courage, On Virtue, On Happiness, On the Good*), the list comprises political works (*On Government, Laws*) and writings on the human condition (*On Mind, On the Soul*), on philosophical topics, including examinations of the doctrines of various philosophers (e.g. *On the Things <in> Heaven, On the Things in the Underworld, Expositions of Heraclitus, Expositions in Reply to Democritus, On the Pythagoreans*), and texts on literature and music (e.g. *On the Age of Homer and Hesiod, On Archilochus and Homer, On Issues in Euripides and Sophocles, On the Three Tragic Poets, On Poetics and the Poets, On Music*). This list is not comprehensive, as it does not include, for instance, works such as *Abaris, Zoroaster*, or *On the Woman not Breathing*, which are mentioned elsewhere.[17] Two things in particular draw attention here: Heraclides' preoccupation with pre-Socratic philosophy and his interest in poetry (the latter he shares with Aristotle and the Peripatetics).

Diogenes relates that Heraclides was an author "varied and lofty in style" (ποικίλος τε καὶ διηρμένος τὴν λέξιν) who was able "to lead the soul" (ψυχαγωγεῖν) (5.89). Since Plato's *Phaedrus*, ψυχαγωγία had been a recurrent term in ancient discussions of oratory, poetry, and historiography, and was associated with making up stories, with pleasure, deception, and relaxation—in other words, with enjoyable fiction—and contrasted with truth, usefulness, and instruction.[18] Diogenes' comment recognizes Heraclides as an author of fiction and possibly reflects a discussion regarding the usefulness of his texts. We find echoes of such a discussion in Cicero's *On the Nature of the Gods*, where

---

[15] The term συγγράμματα ("writings") does not signal any specific generic identification; see Introduction, p. 3.

[16] For this textual problem see Hirzel 1895a, 322 n. 1; Wehrli 1953, 65; Gottschalk 1980a, 6 n. 20.

[17] Though they might have been listed under different titles in Diogenes' catalogue. On the list, see Gottschalk 1980a, 6.

[18] Plato, *Phdr.* 261a, 271c; see Fox 2009, 53. Diodorus Siculus says that historians are blamed for making things up for the sake of ψυχαγωγία (1.69.7); associates ψυχαγωγία with deception (ἀπάτη, 1.76.2); lists two types of authors that should not be trusted: those who believe false reports and those who themselves fabricate things because of ψυχαγωγία (3.11.7); juxtaposes literature aimed at ψυχαγωγία with literature intended to profit (ὠφελεία) the readers (32.12.1). Dionysius of Halicarnassus, *Dem.* 44, distinguishes two styles of an orator: one for public gatherings and crowds,

Heraclides' fondness for made-up stories is ridiculed by the Epicurean Velleius, who derides the philosopher for, among other things, "stuffing his books with childish stories" (*Nat. D.* 1.13.34: *puerilibus fabulis refersit libros*).[19] Plutarch in *Life of Camillus* 22.3 says that Heraclides was μυθώδης καὶ πλασματίας, "a fabulist and a fiction-maker," and therefore that it would not be surprising if he inflated an historical account with fictitious details (Plutarch refers to Heraclides' account of the capture of Rome, where the city was said to have been taken by an army of Hyperboreans). The comment is not necessarily critical of Heraclides: it merely points out his shortcomings as a historical source. In *How a Young Man Should Listen to Poetry* 14e–f [F 130 Schütrumpf], Plutarch finds Heraclides' writing style didactically useful:

ὅτι δὲ τῶν ἐν φιλοσοφίᾳ λεγομένων οἱ σφόδρα νέοι τοῖς μὴ δοκοῦσι φιλοσόφως μηδ' ἀπὸ σπουδῆς λέγεσθαι χαίρουσι μᾶλλον.... δῆλόν ἐστιν ἡμῖν. οὐ γὰρ μόνον τὰ Αἰσώπεια μυθάρια καὶ τὰς ποιητικὰς ὑποθέσεις ἀλλὰ καὶ τὸν Ἄβαριν τὸν Ἡρακλείδου καὶ τὸν Λύκωνα τὸν Ἀρίστωνος διερχόμενοι, τὰ περὶ τῶν ψυχῶν δόγματα μεμιγμένα μυθολογίᾳ, μεθ' ἡδονῆς ἐνθουσιῶσι.

It is clear to us that, as far as philosophical discourses are concerned, the very young enjoy more these that seem not to be uttered philosophically or seriously.... For when they read not only Aesop's fables and summaries of poetic works but also Heraclides' *Abaris* and Aristo's *Lyco*—doctrines about souls mixed with story-telling—they become both pleased and inspired.[20]

Heraclides' *Abaris* did not read like a serious philosophical text—what must be meant by this is that it did not contain protracted philosophical arguments, but instead conveyed a philosophical message by means of story-telling, μυθολογία.

The terms used in reference to Heraclides by later authors—ψυχαγωγία, *pueriles fabulae*, μυθολογία—indicate that he was known for imaginative story-writing and inventiveness. Literary features provide a basis for the classification of his texts related by Diogenes Laertius (5.88): they included works composed in a comic manner, κωμικῶς (for instance *On Pleasure* and *On Self-Control*), in a tragic manner, τραγικῶς (*On the Things in the Underworld*, *On Piety*, and *On Power*), and texts in "a certain middle style of conversation," μεσότης τις

---

which yearn for ἀπάτη and ψυχαγωγία, and one for courts and assemblies, which look for information and help (διδαχή, ὠφελεία). Cf. also Dionysius of Halicarnassus, *Pomp.* 6.4–5; Strabo 1.1.10, 1.2.3; Lucian, *VH* 1.2.

[19] Heraclides' *pueriles fabulae* are in the noble company of Plato's *demiourgos* and Stoic *Pronoia*, also derided by Velleius. According to Plutarch, *Non posse* 1086e, Heraclides was vehemently criticized by Epicurus and Metrodorus; see Dorandi 2009, 5–7 for a fragment of Philodemus, which seems to refer to Epicurus' work against Heraclides (PHerc. 1471 Fr. 20) and Diogenes Laertius (5.92) for an Epicurean criticism of Heraclides' *On Justice*.

[20] The second sentence of the passage is damaged; the edition is Schütrumpf 2008, but I follow Hunter and Russell 2011, 31 (with a note at 72) in adding ἀλλά after ὑποθέσεις.

ὁμιλητική, which depicted philosophers, generals, and statesmen in discussion (φιλοσόφων τε καὶ στρατηγικῶν καὶ πολιτικῶν ἀνδρῶν πρὸς ἀλλήλους διαλεγομένων). It is not immediately clear what Diogenes means in these "confused sentences," as Gottschalk dubs them. The labels "in a tragic manner," "in a comic manner," and in "a middle style of conversation" seem to apply to dialogues; this, in any case, is implied by the characterization of the final category. If we assume that Diogenes presents a coherent threefold distinction (though this does not have to be the case, as he may be fusing several sources), we may take it as referring to the tone and character of dialogues ("humorous," "grand and serious," and "in-between") or to their style and language.[21] Another possibility is to follow the logic of the passage and assume that the differentiating factor is provided in Diogenes' characterization of the "middle style" and that it is a choice of interlocutors. This would fit with Aristotle's distinction between tragedy and comedy based on the characters they represent (*Poet.* 1448a16–18). If Heraclides' "middle-style" dialogues represented known, historical characters—statesmen and philosophers—then, perhaps, "tragic" dialogues featured legendary or mythological figures, and "comic" dialogues contemporary interlocutors. Such a classification would to some extent overlap with the threefold division of narratives which developed out of Aristotle's theory, known to us from Latin rhetoric, which distinguished between *fabula*, *historia*, and *argumentum*, associated with, respectively, tragedy (mythical or legendary events), history (real past events), and comedy (imaginary, but probable events).[22] This interpretation remains speculative; while we know that Heraclides wrote historical dialogues, and the characters of Abaris and Empedotimus may well be considered legendary figures, we have no direct evidence that Heraclides composed dialogues set in the present, depicting contemporary interlocutors.

Diogenes' distinction implies that Heraclides' dialogues were diverse and numerous enough to allow a threefold classification. Owing to Cicero, however, we tend to consider Heraclides above all as an author of historical dialogues. In a letter to his brother Quintus from 54 BCE, Cicero mentions that when his *Republic*

---

[21] Wehrli 1953, 65–6 believes that the distinction between comic and tragic works applies to dialogues and connects it with Plato's *Resp.* 606b and Aristotle's *Poet.* 1448b25. Gottschalk 1980a, 7–8 argues that Diogenes could not have been thinking of three types of dialogue (comic, tragic, and intermediate) because "[a]ncient literary theory did not recognize a third species of dramatic composition," and thinks that it refers to language and diction.

[22] Cicero, *Rhet. Her.* 1.8.13: *Id, quod in negotiorum expositione positum est tres habet partes: fabulam, historiam, argumentum. Fabula est, quae neque veras neque veri similes continet res, ut eae sunt, quae tragoedis traditae sunt. Historia est gesta res, sed ab aetatis nostrae memoria remota. Argumentum est ficta res quae tamen fieri potuit, velut argumenta comoediarum.* Cicero, *Inv. rhet.* 1.19.27: *Ea, quae in negotiorum expositione posita est, tres habet partes: fabulam, historiam, argumentum. Fabula est, in qua nec verae nec veri similes res continentur, cuiusmodi est:* "Angues ingentes alites, iuncti iugo...." *Historia est gesta res, ab aetatis nostrae memoria remota; quod genus:* "Appius indixit Carthaginiensibus bellum." *Argumentum est ficta res, quae tamen fieri potuit. Huiusmodi apud Terentium:* "Nam is postquam excessit ex ephebis, [Sosia]...." Cf. also Asclepiades of Myrleia's division of narratives in Sextus Empiricus, *Adv. math.* 1.252–3, 263–5.

was read, his friend Gnaeus Sallustius suggested that it would have been better if Cicero himself had been a speaker (*si ipse loquerer*); this would have provided the work with "much more authority" (*multo maiore auctoritate*) particularly as Cicero is "not a Heraclides Ponticus, but a former consul, and one who has been involved in the greatest affairs in the state" (*praesertim cum essem non Heraclides Ponticus sed consularis et is qui in maximis versatus in re publica rebus essem*, QFr. 3.5.1). In another letter, sent to Atticus in 45 BCE, Cicero discusses the choice of speakers in the *Academica* and juxtaposes dialogues in which an author does not appear as an interlocutor with dialogues of the Aristotelian kind (*quae... Ἀριστοτέλειον morem habent*) in which an author assumes the *principatus*, "the principal part." Dialogues of the former type feature historical characters (*antiquae personae*) as speakers; to this category belong many works of Heraclides (*ut Heraclides in multis*) and Cicero's own *Republic* (Att. 13.19.3–4).[23]

The letters indicate that Sallustius and Cicero considered the format of the *Republic*, in particular its setting in the past and the absence of the figure of the author, as typically Heraclidean.[24] To be sure, such a setting was not Heraclides' invention, yet he must have used this format skillfully in several of his works. However, the typology in Diogenes Laertius, which lists conversations between "philosophers, generals, and statesmen" as one of three categories of Heraclides' dialogues, suggests that this is a partial image, one which was probably shaped by the Roman authors' particular interest in reviving the past. At the same time, Sallustius' comment reveals certain misgivings regarding this type of dialogue. He argues that Cicero's *Republic* would have more authority if Cicero was a speaker— though not because he had more authority than the interlocutors in the dialogue (prominent statesmen, including Scipio Aemilianus), but because the dialogue would not have been blatantly fictional (*quae tam antiquis hominibus attribuerem, ea visum iri ficta esse*, Cicero, QFr. 3.5.1). Sallustius' comment reflects the same concern about the use of fiction and story-telling in "serious" literature that we have encountered in other authors.

Cicero's debt to Heraclides must have extended beyond the dialogue format. The motif of the Milky Way in the *Dream of Scipio* seems to go back to Heraclides;[25] we also know that Cicero considered Heraclides an important political thinker. In the *Laws*, when discussing philosophical schools that engaged

---

[23] For Heraclides in Cicero, Fox 2007, 87–8, 119–20; Fox 2009, 56–64. For Aristotle's dialogues, see Chapter 5.2.

[24] Cf. also Cicero's correspondence from 44 BCE: Atticus asked Cicero to write "something Heraclidean" (Ἡρακλείδειον *aliquod*) and in several letters sent subsequently Cicero promises to do so (Att. 15.4.3, 15.27.2, 16.2.6, 15.13.3). Two letters (Att. 16.11.3, 16.12) mention Varro's work in the style of Heraclides (neither topic nor title is known; it might have been identical with Varro's διάλογος, mentioned in Att. 15.13.3). The proposition that Varro's "Heraclidean" work was identical with the *Logistorici* was rejected by Hirzel 1895a, 329–30 and Gottschalk 1980b.

[25] Cf. Cicero, Resp. 6.16.16 with Iamblichus, *De anima* 26 and Philoponus, *In Meteor. I* 117.

in discussions of *res publica*, Cicero lists him among the authors who made a significant contribution to political philosophy even though they were not statesmen themselves, and he might have had Heraclides in mind when he wrote an analogous passage in the *Republic*.[26] It is therefore reasonable to assume that the dialogues of Heraclides on which Cicero modeled his *Republic* were works on political themes. Two titles in Diogenes Laertius' catalogue, *On Governance* (Περὶ ἀρχῆς) and *Laws* (Νόμοι), are potential candidates.

It is impossible to say to what extent Cicero's *Republic* was modeled on Heraclides. Cicero's dialogue is narrated, with a lengthy preface of a polemical character written in Cicero's own voice; it was probably addressed to a named person (Quintus?), and although the recorded conversation preceded Cicero's birth by over twenty years, Cicero claimed that he had heard about it in his youth from Publius Rutilius Rufus, a man who knew Scipio personally. We do not know whether Heraclides made use of any of these features. Proclus' criticism of Heraclides and Theophrastus for preceding dialogues with προοίμια "utterly different from what followed" has been sometimes interpreted as proof that Heraclides made use of the type of introductions we know from Cicero; however, Proclus did not mean separate prefaces in the author's own voice, but merely opening chapters of dialogues.[27]

While we know that Heraclides was famous in antiquity for his dialogues, evidence concerning the formats of specific titles is scarce. Ethical texts, which open Diogenes Laertius' list, include: *On Justice, On Self-Control, On Piety, On Courage, On Virtue, On Happiness*, and, in addition, *On Pleasure*, mentioned in 5.88.[28] At least some of these works seem to have been dialogues: *On Piety* is said to have been composed "in a tragic manner," while *On Self-Control* and *On Pleasure*—"in a comic manner." Thanks to Athenaeus, we have quotations from *On Pleasure* which seem to preserve the original text verbatim. They present contradictory perspectives on pleasure, and one way of making sense of them is to assume that the text was a dialogue in which opposing positions were confronted. One passage defends pleasure (*Deipn.* 12.512a–d [F 39 Schütrumpf]):

οἱ τύραννοι καὶ οἱ βασιλεῖς πάντων ἀγαθῶν ὄντες κύριοι καὶ πάντων εἰληφότες πεῖραν τὴν ἡδονὴν προκρίνουσιν, μεγαλοψυχοτέρας ποιούσης τῆς ἡδονῆς τὰς τῶν ἀνθρώπων φύσεις. ἅπαντες γοῦν οἱ τὴν ἡδονὴν τιμῶντες καὶ τρυφᾶν προῃρημένοι μεγαλόψυχοι καὶ μεγαλοπρεπεῖς εἰσιν, ὡς Πέρσαι καὶ Μῆδοι. μάλιστα γὰρ πάντων ἀνθρώπων τὴν

---

[26] Cicero, *Leg.* 3.6.14, *Resp.* 1.7.12. Cicero expands here on Aristotle's *Pol.* 1266a31–2, where it is said that private people, philosophers, and statesmen wrote works on the subject of government.

[27] Proclus, *In Parm.* 1.659 Cousin: τὸ δὲ παντελῶς ἀλλότρια τὰ προοίμια τῶν ἑπομένων εἶναι, καθάπερ τὰ τῶν Ἡρακλείδου τοῦ Ποντικοῦ καὶ Θεοφράστου διαλόγων, πᾶσαν ἀνιᾷ κρίσεως μετέχουσαν ἀκοήν. That Proclus does not think of separate prefaces is clear from a preceding passage, in which he talks of Plato's *prooimia*—that is, opening chapters of dialogues—as being in harmony with the core of his works because, when interpreted allegorically, they announce their key problems.

[28] For *On Pleasure* possibly being identical with *On Self-Control*, see Schütrumpf 2009, 69–70.

ἡδονὴν οὗτοι καὶ τὸ τρυφᾶν τιμῶσιν, ἀνδρειότατοι καὶ μεγαλοψυχότατοι τῶν βαρβάρων ὄντες. ἐστὶ γὰρ τὸ μὲν ἥδεσθαι καὶ τὸ τρυφᾶν ἐλευθέρων, ἀνίησι γὰρ τὰς ψυχὰς καὶ αὔξει, τὸ δὲ πονεῖν δούλων καὶ ταπεινῶν. διὸ καὶ συστέλλονται οὗτοι καὶ τὰς φύσεις. καὶ ἡ Ἀθηναίων πόλις, ἕως ἐτρύφα, μεγίστη τε ἦν καὶ μεγαλοψυχοτάτους ἔτρεφεν ἄνδρας. ἁλουργῆ μὲν γὰρ ἠμπίσχοντο ἱμάτια, ποικίλους δ' ὑπέδυνον χιτῶνας, κορύμβους δ' ἀναδούμενοι τῶν τριχῶν χρυσοῦς τέττιγας περὶ τὸ μέτωπον καὶ τὰς κόρρας ἐφόρουν. ὀκλαδίας τε αὐτοῖς δίφρους ἔφερον οἱ παῖδες, ἵνα μὴ καθίζοιεν ὡς ἔτυχεν. καὶ τοιοῦτοι ἦσαν οἱ τὴν ἐν Μαραθῶνι νικήσαντες μάχην καὶ μόνοι τὴν τῆς Ἀσίας ἁπάσης δύναμιν χειρωσάμενοι. καὶ οἱ φρονιμώτατοι δέ, φησίν, καὶ μεγίστην δόξαν ἐπὶ σοφίᾳ ἔχοντες μέγιστον ἀγαθὸν τὴν ἡδονὴν εἶναι νομίζουσιν.

Tyrants and kings, who have control over all the good things and have tried them all, judge pleasure the foremost good because pleasure makes the nature of humans more magnanimous. In any case, all those who value pleasure and choose to live in luxury are magnanimous and magnificent, such as the Persians and the Medes. For these people most of all human beings value pleasure and living in luxury, and they are the bravest and most magnanimous of the barbarians. For experiencing pleasure and living in luxury are characteristic of free people, because this frees their souls and strengthens them, whereas laboring is characteristic of slaves and the lowly: for this reason such people are actually contracted in their natures. And the city of the Athenians, as long as it enjoyed luxury, was at its greatest and nurtured the most magnanimous men. For they wore purple cloaks, and they put on embroidered tunics, and they bound up their hair in knots on the crown of their head and wore golden cicadas as ornaments on their brow and temples. And their slaves carried folding chairs for them, so that they would not sit down just in any place. Such were those who were victorious at Marathon and single-handedly defeated the power of all Asia. The most sensible men, he says, who have the greatest reputation for wisdom, believe pleasure is the greatest good.     (trans. P. Stork, J. van Ophuijsen, S. Prince)

This excursus is followed by three quotations (Simonides, Pindar, Homer) which support the argument.

Athenaeus ascribes the text to Heraclides (Ἡρακλείδης... τάδε λέγει), which does not mean that Heraclides embraced the views expressed in the passage. The text is carefully composed: the clauses are balanced and symmetrical, with repetitions, antitheseis, and assonances.[29] The clarity of the passage is ensured by the recurrence of key concepts: pleasure, ἡδονή, is tied with luxury, τὸ τρυφᾶν, and

---

[29] e.g. anaphoras: πάντων ἀγαθῶν ὄντες κύριοι καὶ πάντων εἰληφότες πεῖραν; μεγίστην δόξαν ἐπὶ σοφίᾳ ἔχοντες μέγιστον ἀγαθὸν τὴν ἡδονὴν εἶναι νομίζουσιν; symmetrical clauses: ἁλουργῆ μὲν γὰρ ἠμπίσχοντο ἱμάτια, ποικίλους δ' ὑπέδυνον χιτῶνας; τὸ μὲν ἥδεσθαι καὶ τὸ τρυφᾶν ἐλευθέρων... τὸ δὲ πονεῖν δούλων καὶ ταπεινῶν; a word play: ἡ Ἀθηναίων πόλις, ἕως ἐτρύφα... μεγαλοψυχοτάτους ἔτρεφεν ἄνδρας.

contrasted not so much with pain, λύπη (as usual in Plato and Aristotle), but with hard work, τὸ πονεῖν, which is denigrated as fit for slaves and lowly people (an implied opponent is one who values πόνος over pleasure, like Antisthenes and the early Cynics). The speaker believes that pleasure leads to a free and virtuous life— it liberates souls and makes them grow (ἀνίησι τὰς ψυχὰς καὶ αὔξει), it renders people magnanimous and magnificent (μεγαλόψυχοι, μεγαλοπρεπεῖς)—and repeatedly associates it with the growth and expansion of individuals and societies (μεγαλόψυχοι, μεγαλοπρεπεῖς; ἀνίησι ... τὰς ψυχὰς καὶ αὔξει; ἡ Ἀθηναίων πόλις ... μεγίστη τε ἦν καὶ μεγαλοψυχοτάτους ἔτρεφεν ἄνδρας; μεγίστην δόξαν ... μέγιστον ἀγαθόν). Its effects are therefore contrary to those of hard work, which makes things small and lowly (τὸ δὲ πονεῖν ... ταπεινῶν; συστέλλονται).

The position defended in the passage is a "refined" hedonism which justifies the pursuit of pleasure as being conducive to moral growth: the speaker takes issue with the Greek notion that luxury renders people soft and overly delicate, and argues, paradoxically, that it makes them brave and strong. He also associates pleasure with reason, and presents a pleasant life as the choice of a sensible man (οἱ φρονιμώτατοι ... καὶ μεγίστην δόξαν ἐπὶ σοφίᾳ ἔχοντες μέγιστον ἀγαθὸν τὴν ἡδονὴν εἶναι νομίζουσιν). There is something not only paradoxical but also excessive in the passage, both stylistically[30] and in terms of content: Thucydides' restrained description of the appearance of the Athenians of the past,[31] clearly in the background, is supplemented with additional details (embroidered and purple clothing, assistants with folding chairs who prevent the Athenians from sitting in an undignified manner), while the phrase immediately following this description—"such were those who were victorious at Marathon"—is reminiscent of Aristophanes' *Clouds*, where old-style cicada ornaments and Marathon are mentioned together (*Nub.* 984-6).

Other fragments of *On Pleasure* argue for an opposing perspective and might have come from the utterances of other speaker(s). They show the disastrous consequences of pleasure and indulgence: examples of cities destroyed by excessive luxury (Samians, Sybarites) as well as of individuals ruined by wealth (Callias, the descendants of Nicias and Ischomachus, Deinias the perfume-seller, whose life of unbridled indulgence led him to cut off his genitals) are brought up (Athenaeus, *Deipn.* 12.525f-526a; 12.536f-537c; 12.533c; 12.552f). In yet another fragment, Heraclides describes the madness of Thrasyllus of Aexone. Again, Athenaeus appears to quote Heraclides verbatim (*Deipn.* 12.554e-f [F 40 Schütrumpf]):

---

[30] Cf. e.g. the accumulation of superlatives (ἀνδρειότατοι, twice μεγαλοψυχότατοι, φρονιμώτατοι, three times μέγιστος) and the recurrence of forms of πᾶς (five times).

[31] Thucydides 1.6.3. He speaks merely of "linen chitons" (χιτῶνας λινοῦς) and a tie with golden grasshoppers used to fasten a knot of hair (χρυσῶν τεττίγων ἐνέρσει κρωβύλον ἀναδούμενοι τῶν ἐν τῇ κεφαλῇ τριχῶν).

ὁ Αἰξωνεὺς Θράσυλλος ὁ Πυθοδώρου διετέθη ποτὲ ὑπὸ μανίας τοιαύτης ὡς πάντα τὰ πλοῖα τὰ εἰς τὸν Πειραιᾶ καταγόμενα ὑπολαμβάνειν ἑαυτοῦ εἶναι, καὶ ἀπεγράφετο αὐτὰ καὶ ἀπέστελλε καὶ διώκει καὶ καταπλέοντα ἀπεδέχετο μετὰ χαρᾶς τοσαύτης ὅσης περ ἄν τις ἡσθείη τοσούτων χρημάτων κύριος ὤν. καὶ τῶν μὲν ἀπολομένων οὐδὲν ἐπεζήτει, τοῖς δὲ σῳζομένοις ἔχαιρεν καὶ διῆγεν μετὰ πλείστης ἡδονῆς. ἐπεὶ δὲ ὁ ἀδελφὸς αὐτοῦ Κρίτων ἐκ Σικελίας ἐπιδημήσας συλλαβὼν αὐτὸν παρέδωκεν ἰατρῷ καὶ τῆς μανίας ἐπαύσατο, διηγεῖτο <πολλάκις περὶ τῆς ἐν μανίᾳ διατριβῆς> οὐδεπώποτε φάσκων κατὰ τὸν βίον ἡσθῆναι πλείονα. λύπην μὲν γὰρ οὐδ' ἡντινοῦν αὐτῷ παραγίγνεσθαι, τὸ δὲ τῶν ἡδονῶν πλῆθος ὑπερβάλλειν.

Thrasyllus of the deme Aexone, son of Pythodorus, was once afflicted with a madness of such a kind, with the result that he took all the ships landing at the Peiraeus to be his own. He registered them in his accounts, and sent them out and managed them, and when they returned, he received them with such great joy, as one would feel with pleasure in being the owner of so much wealth. He made no search at all for those that were lost, but he rejoiced in those that came back safe, and he lived with the greatest pleasure. But when his brother Crito returned home from Sicily, he (Crito) took hold of him (Thrasyllus) and turned him over to a doctor, and (Thrasyllus) was cured of his madness. Then he <quite often told stories about his life in madness,> saying that he had never once enjoyed life more. For not a single sort of pain had befallen him, and the quantity of his pleasures was far greater.   (trans. P. Stork, J. Ophuijsen, S. Prince)

The narration is clear and well-organized; the style simpler than in the passage arguing in favor of pleasure, which suggests that Heraclides adjusted the language to the personality of a speaker. Thrasyllus' life in insanity is vividly rendered with the polysyndetic phrase καὶ ἀπεγράφετο αὐτὰ καὶ ἀπέστελλε καὶ διώκει καὶ καταπλέοντα ἀπεδέχετο. The purpose of the story appears to be to demonstrate that pleasure is sometimes dissociated from reason.[32]

If *On Pleasure* was a dialogue, as suggested both by Diogenes Laertius' reference to its having been composed "in a comic manner" and by the contrasted views expressed in the fragments, we may cautiously venture some observations. There is no indication of the question-and-answer format; rather, we have remnants of speeches representing opposing positions, which are supported with abundant poetic quotations, historical examples, and anecdotes, including ludicrous and grotesque stories (Thrasyllus' madness, Deinias' self-castration).[33]

---

[32] Perhaps there is some engagement here with Plato's *Philebus* 36c–42c, where false pleasures and pleasures experienced in madness are discussed.
[33] It does not follow that Heraclides' works consisted mostly of anecdotes, but merely that they were of particular interest to later authors, in this case Athenaeus; as Fox 2009 rightly points out, our knowledge of Heraclides' in necessarily skewed by the existing evidence, which reflects his reception.

At the philosophical level, *On Pleasure* probably reflected current debates. It is unlikely that Heraclides sided with the defenders of pleasure;[34] rather, the belief that the pursuit of pleasure is congruent with a virtuous and sensible life most likely reflects a contemporary strand of hedonism. The Cyrenaic school was active throughout the fourth century, with Aristippus the Younger among its prominent figures; but within the Academy itself, the problem of pleasure was also far from settled, as evidenced by the opposing positions of Speusippus, a proponent of strict anti-hedonism, and Eudoxus of Cnidus, who considered pleasure the ultimate good. A fragment of Heraclides' contemporary, Aristoxenus of Tarentum, in which pleasure is defended by Polyarchus, nicknamed Ἡδυπαθής, in front of Archytas and his followers, shows numerous concurrences with Heraclides' arguments for pleasure (Athenaeus, *Deipn.* 12.545a–546c [F 50 Wehrli]).[35]

Heraclides seems to have elaborated on the motif of a meeting between a wise man and a ruler in more than one text, and a work with such a subject is explicitly referred to as a dialogue by Strabo (2.3.4; Strabo's source is Posidonius), who says that Heraclides in a dialogue (ἐν διαλόγῳ) made some Magus come to the Sicilian tyrant Gelon and report that he circumnavigated Libya (ποιεῖν ἀφιγμένον παρὰ Γέλωνι μάγον τινὰ περιπλεῦσαι φάσκοντα).[36] The phrasing suggests that the text directly reported an encounter between the tyrant and a Persian wise man, rather than that the meeting was narrated by someone else. The work, then, could have been a historical dialogue and a variation on the popular theme of "power meets wisdom," perhaps inspired by Xenophon's *Hiero*, a dialogue in which Hiero, the Syracusan tyrant and a brother to Gelon, conversed with Simonides (another encounter of this kind, between Pythagoras and the tyrant Leon, was described by Heraclides in his work *On the Woman Not Breathing*; I will discuss it below).[37] Strabo does not inform us about the title of this work, but it is probable that the conversation was reported in the *Zoroaster*. Zoroaster might have been an interlocutor in a dialogue narrated by the Magus to Gelon or one of the topics of the dialogue. Zoroaster and the Magi were associated with religious expertise, various

---

[34] Though Diogenes Laertius portrays Heraclides as "wearing soft clothes and very corpulent" for which he was called Πομπικός instead of Ποντικός (5.86).

[35] For Aristoxenus and his *Life of Archytas*, see, Chapter 1.4 and Chapter 5.6; for a comparison of Heraclides' passage with that of Aristoxenus, see Huffman 2005, 316; Schütrumpf 2009.

[36] Posidonius rejected Heraclides' story as lacking proof. Heraclides might have been inspired by Herodotus, who described the first circumnavigation of Africa by the Phoenicians, sent by the Egyptian king Neco (4.42). Kingsley 1995, 188 considers the meeting in the context of political relations between Sicily and Persia, and links it to Gelon's attempt to form an alliance with Persia. Wehrli 1953, 83 observes that Heraclides' coming from the Pontian Heraclea might have had more direct knowledge of the Persians.

[37] Heraclides' attention to the figure of a tyrant acquires an additional dimension when considered against the background of the political situation in Heraclea, which became a tyranny in 364 when it was seized by Clearchus (a student of Isocrates and Plato), who is said to have emulated the ways of Dionysius of Syracuse (Diodorus Siculus 15.81.5). Clearchus was assassinated in 352 by Chion of Heraclea, likewise an Academic, and some other conspirators. For Clearchus' rule in Heraclea, see Düring 1951, 9–13; Burstein 1974, 47–66.

forms of divination, and eschatological doctrine, and any of these subjects might have been discussed in the dialogue.

Heraclides' interest in the Magi reflects the contemporary Academic and Peripatetic preoccupation with Eastern wisdom.[38] Zoroaster is mentioned in the *Alcibiades I*, 122a, and philosophers who discussed him or the Magi include Aristotle (who wrote a work titled *Magicus*), Hermodorus of Syracuse (a student of Plato and an author of his biography), and Eudoxus of Cnidus (Diogenes Laertius 1.1-9). In the pseudo-Platonic *Axiochus*, Socrates reports his encounter with a Persian Magus Gobryas (*Ax.* 371a-372a), while Aristotle narrated a meeting of Socrates with a Syrian Magus, and Aristoxenus of Tarentum—with a wise man from India (Diogenes Laertius 2.45; Eusebius, *PE* 11.3.8). In the biographic tradition dating back to the early Academy, a Chaldaean wise man is said to have visited Plato shortly before his death and conversed with him about music (the encounter might have been reported in a dialogue by Philip of Opus).[39] Theophrastus wrote about the Aramean sage Ahiquar in a work titled *Acicharus*, and Clearchus wrote about Aristotle's meeting with a Jewish wise man in his *On Sleep*. While Heraclides' interest in Eastern wisdom was by no means an isolated case, it should be noted that his work probably did not depict an encounter between Greek philosophy and Persian wisdom: the Magus was represented as talking to a tyrant, not to a Greek philosopher.

Heraclides' interest in pre-Socratic and pre-Platonic philosophy is apparent in the curiously titled *(On) The Woman Not Breathing* (Περὶ τῆς ἄπνου or Ἄπνους); the work also seems to have been known as *On Diseases* (Περὶ νόσων). It reported the miraculous story of a woman (sometimes identified as Pantheia of Acragas) who did not breathe for thirty (in some versions seven) days, and was then brought back to life by Empedocles (Diogenes Laertius 8.60-2). The events were apparently narrated by Empedocles to his friend Pausanias (Diogenes Laertius 8.60: Ἡρακλείδης τε ἐν τῷ Περὶ νόσων φησὶ καὶ Παυσανίᾳ ὑφηγήσασθαι αὐτὸν [sc. Empedocles] τὰ περὶ τὴν ἄπνουν), a physician, and probably the addressee of the philosopher's poem (Plutarch, *Quaest. conv.* 728d-f). The work also described a sacrifice offered by Empedocles in the vicinity of Acragas, and a subsequent feast at which Pausanias was a guest, as well as the disappearance of Empedocles on the following morning: one of characters claimed that he heard a voice at night summoning Empedocles, and saw a great light, which led Pausanias to conclude that Empedocles had become a god; Pausanias is also said to have refuted (ἀντέλεγε) other versions of Empedocles' death (Diogenes Laertius 8.67-72).[40]

---

[38] Gottschalk 1980a, 111-12; Kingsley 1995; Horky 2009; West 2015, 442-4.
[39] Philodemus, *Acad. ind.* col. iii.35-v. The papyrus credits the story to ἀστρολόγος ἀναγραφεὺς τοῦ Πλάτωνος καὶ ἀκουστής, which probably refers to Philip of Opus. Horky 2009, 94 observes that the story has elements reminiscent of Plato (e.g. the figure of the "Chaldaean Stranger," ξένος Χαλδαῖος) and proposes that Philodemus is summarizing a dialogue by Philip.
[40] For a detailed discussion and reconstruction, see Gottschalk 1980a, 14-36.

Pausanias clearly must have played an important role in the text; perhaps, then, it was a dialogue in which his character reported the events of Empedocles' last day: the feast and its attendant conversations (in particular Empedocles' account of the case of the woman) and the philosopher's subsequent disappearance.[41] Such a dialogue would be a creative rewriting of Plato's *Phaedo* and *Symposion*, combining an account of a banquet with that of the death of a philosopher, two themes which are recurrently tied together in the ancient dialogue tradition.[42] In fact, Heraclides' representation of the last moments of the feast bears the mark of the influence of the *Symposion*: the guests are said to have departed and fallen asleep in the fields, while Empedocles remained alone at the place where he had reclined; at daybreak, when everyone woke up, he was nowhere to be found (Diogenes Laertius 8.68). The scene rewrites the closing of the *Symposion*, where all banqueters fall asleep apart from Socrates (and half-asleep Aristodemus), who leaves the company and heads off to the Lyceum—a noteworthy case of the literary technique of *oppositio in imitando* (in Plato, Socrates departs and leaves others sleeping at Agathon's house; in Heraclides, everyone departs and falls asleep outside, and Empedocles is staying alone). Heraclides also appears to have been influenced by the emergent Peripatetic interest in biography, in particular if one assumes that *On Diseases* was another title for *On the Woman Not Breathing*: in such case, apart from describing Empedocles' healing of the woman and his death, the work also included information about his family (he came from a distinguished family and his grandfather was a breeder of horses, Diogenes Laertius 8.51) and gave his age at the time of death (he was 60, 8.52).[43] The philosophical contents of the work is not clear; the main theme might have been the soul's immortality and independence from the body—the recovered woman's story could have exemplified such a doctrine.[44] Galen's interest in the text and the alternative title *On Diseases* suggest that themes of a medical nature were discussed as well,[45] which is all the more likely given that both Empedocles and his friend Pausanias were physicians.

*On the Woman Not Breathing* also contained an account of the famous conversation between Pythagoras and tyrant Leon during which the word "philosopher" was to be used for the first time. According to Cicero, Heraclides reported that Pythagoras went to Phlius and discussed certain themes "learnedly and at length" (*docte et copiose*) with its tyrant Leon. Asked by Leon what is his art, Pythagoras called himself a philosopher, and explained what he meant by this

---

[41] Wehrli 1953, 86; Gottschalk 1980a, 12ff.
[42] See Hirzel 1895a, 326; Gottschalk 1980a, 17 calls the work "essentially a fusion...of the Platonic *Phaedo* and *Symposium*." For combination of sympotic and death themes in ancient dialogues, see Jażdżewska 2013. For Speusippus' *Funeral Feast of Plato*, see below, the section on Speusippus.
[43] Mejer 2009, 33 thinks that the work was "an early example of the Peripatetic biographico-literary tradition."
[44] Gottschalk 1980a, 18–19.   [45] Gottschalk 1980a, 19–20.

with an elaborate analogy: he likened human life to a festival which people attend either in pursuit of glory, or looking for profit, or for the sake of the spectacle. Similarly in life: some seek fame, others money; but there are also those who call themselves lovers of wisdom, that is, philosophers (*hos se appellare sapientiae studiosos, id est enim philosophos*), who spend their lives in contemplation of the nature of things (*Tusc.* 5.3.8–9). This famous story has several variants in ancient sources, with Heraclides being the earliest.[46] It is not clear how it was incorporated in *On the Woman Not Breathing* and whether it was dialogized or diegetic, as in Cicero. It is built around the familiar motif of a sage coming to the court of a ruler, and in this respect is reminiscent of the meeting between Gelon and the Magus. While this account in combination with other sources has been conventionally used both in antiquity and in modern times as evidence for Pythagoras' invention of the term "philosophy," one should be cautious in accepting the story's historicity, especially in the context of Heraclides' fame as an inventive story-teller.

Heraclides' particular interest in Pythagoras is confirmed by another passage from Diogenes Laertius (8.4–5), which describes the philosopher's reincarnations (Heraclides appears to be the first extant author to have discussed Pythagoras' previous reincarnations in detail).[47] According to Heraclides, Pythagoras claimed that he had been granted by Hermes (whose son he was believed to be) the wish to retain a memory of what happened to him both during life and after death.[48] He was first born as Aethalides, then as Euphorbus (who remembered his previous life as Aethalides as well as what had happened after his death, including wanderings of his soul), next as Hermotimus, then as a Delian fisherman named Pyrrhus, and then as Pythagoras. This seems to have been a complex and rich narrative which probably included an account of the afterlife in Hades. Heraclides apparently claimed to be relating Pythagoras' own words (περὶ αὐτοῦ τάδε λέγειν)— whether this was in direct speech or not is unclear. The divine element was emphasized: Pythagoras was a presented as a descendant of Hermes and linked

---

[46] Burkert 1960; Gottschalk 1980a, 23–33. Cf. also Diogenes Laertius 8.8 (where Sosicrates' *Succession of Philosophers* is quoted as a source) and Iamblichus, *VP* 58. For Jaeger 1948², 98, Heraclides "has obviously been stimulated by the *Protrepticus*" of Aristotle, as in Iamblichus' *Protrepticus*, which is believed to have drawn directly from Aristotle; when asked about the purpose of human life, Pythagoras replied that it was "to observe the heavens"; next, contemplation of the universe is compared to watching spectacles (F B 18, 20, 44 Düring). On the link between *Protrepticus* and Heraclides' passage, see Düring 1961, 212; Gottschalk 1980a, 33–5, rightly as I believe, remains skeptical.

[47] Though Aethalides, one of Pythagoras' reincarnations, seems to have been mentioned by Pherecydes of Athens, according to whom Hermes granted him that his soul spent some time on earth, and some time in Hades (*Schol. in Apoll. Rhod.* I 645). Heraclides' slightly younger contemporaries, Peripatetics Clearchus and Dicaearchus, also wrote on the subject, though in a less reverent manner (perhaps parodying Heraclides?), as they listed the courtesan Alco among Pythagoras' reincarnations (Gellius, *NA* 4.13). Gottschalk 1980a, 116 n. 94 suggests that these versions were parodies; likewise Burkert 1972, 139: "the 'beautiful prostitute' may be a sarcastic addition of Dicaearchus."

[48] The passage is included by editors among the probable fragments of *On the Woman Not Breathing*, but there is little ground for this attribution; see Gottschalk 1980a, 115 n. 93. For a thorough discussion of the fragment, see Gottschalk 1980a, 121–6.

with Apollo by several elements of the story.[49] As in the story of Empedocles' apotheosis in *On the Woman Not Breathing*, Heraclides here was also interested in the marvelous and in the exploitation of religious motifs.

Pythagoras might also have featured in Heraclides' *Abaris*. In the passage from *How a Young Man Should Listen to Poetry* which has been quoted above, Plutarch listed this text along with Aristo's *Lyco* as examples of works that bore little resemblance to serious philosophical texts, and therefore appeared to have been aimed at young readers; we also learn that it contained "doctrines about souls mixed with story-telling" (*De aud. poet.* 14e).[50] The name-title suggests that it could have been a dialogue. Abaris was a Hyperborean legendary sage and healer, mentioned by both Herodotus (4.36: he traveled with an arrow around the world and did not eat anything) and Plato (*Charm.* 158b: enchantments of Abaris). Our knowledge of him is based mostly on Pythagorean works by Porphyry (*VP* 28–9) and Iamblichus (*VP* 19, 28, 32), from which we learn that he was a priest of Apollo and traveled with an arrow which he received from the god; as an older man he went to Pythagoras, who instructed him in his doctrines. In a version narrated by Iamblichus, Abaris visited Pythagoras when the philosopher was detained by the tyrant Phalaris; angered by their discussion, Phalaris wanted to kill them both but was murdered beforehand (*VP* 32). Iamblichus' account certainly reads like a paraphrase of a dialogue: we learn what questions Abaris asked Pythagoras, what the contents were of Pythagoras' instructions, and how Phalaris reacted at various points (he was angered, uttered blasphemies against the gods, argued against prophecies, and was later refuted by Pythagoras). It is therefore very probable that Iamblichus' sources included a dialogue reporting such an encounter; however, as Iamblichus' account contains terms and concepts of later philosophical provenance, he cannot merely be paraphrasing Heraclides' work.[51] Perhaps the *Abaris* contained a conversation between the Hyperborean sage and Pythagoras in the presence of Phalaris, which was subsequently reworked by a later Hellenistic period philosopher.

Several ancient authors quote Heraclides as the source of information concerning the Syracusan Empedotimus. The character might have been invented by

---

[49] On the connection of Euphorbus, Hermotimus, and the Delian fisherman with Apollo, see Casadesús Bordoy 2013, 165–8.

[50] For Aristo and his *Lyco*, see Chapter 5.9. There are two probable quotations of the *Abaris* in a grammatical work on syntax (F 131–2 Schütrumpf), but the passages, chosen for their syntactical features, remain enigmatic; see Wehrli 1953, 84–6; Gottschalk 1980a, 118–21. As the *Abaris* does not appear in Diogenes Laertius' catalogue, it might have been identical with one of the works included there. Heraclides referred to Abaris in *On Justice*, where he mentioned the arrow of Apollo by which the sage traveled (F 24B Schütrumpf), but Gottschalk 1980a, 122 rightly points out that other fragments of *On Justice* do not seem to fit the character of the *Abaris*.

[51] Boyancé 1934 argues that Heraclides' *Abaris* is Iamblichus' model. Festugière 1937, 474–6 points out similarities with Hermetic literature, above all with *CH* XII. See also the discussion in de Vogel 1965; Gottschalk 1980a, 125–7. According to Dillon and Hershbell 1991, 215 n. 2 "[m]uch of the terminology is certainly Hellenistic, chiefly Stoic, and so Heraclides could only be an ultimate, and not a proximate source."

Heraclides—later authors unanimously cite him as the source of the story, and there is no evidence of a parallel tradition.[52] According to Proclus, Empedotimus, while hunting at noon, experienced the epiphany of Pluto and Persephone and saw the whole truth about souls (πᾶσαν τὴν περὶ ψυχῶν ἀλήθειαν) (*In Remp.* 2.119.18–27 Kroll). From other fragments we learn that Empedotimus was granted by a *daimon* a "rise" or a "lifting up" (μετεωρισμός), through which he was initiated into the immortality of the souls (δι' οὗ τὴν τῶν ψυχῶν μυεῖται ἀθανασίαν). He learned that the Milky Way was the path of souls traveling through Hades, and he saw three gates and three paths—one at the sign of Scorpio, the other between Leo and Cancer, and the third one between Aquarius and Pisces—and learnt of the division of the heavens into three realms, belonging to Zeus, Poseidon, and Pluto (F 52, 54B, 57, 58 Schütrumpf). Heraclides' work thus contained several elements: a divine epiphany, instruction about the soul's nature and immortality, a discussion of the afterlife, and an account of the structure of the universe with some astrological details.[53] We do not know the text's title; it might have been *On the Soul*, listed among Heraclides' works by Diogenes Laertius (5.87).[54] It is probable that in the same text Heraclides developed his concept of the "light-like," φωτοειδής, soul, i.e. consisting of some luminous substance rather than being immaterial as in Plato. No ancient author refers to the text as a dialogue, but it is a justified assumption that it was. Empedotimus must have been vividly rendered, and some later authors considered him a historical figure and ascribed to him certain philosophical views;[55] it is therefore most probable that Heraclides made him narrate his vision.

A few titles in Diogenes Laertius' catalogue suggest that Heraclides might have also composed Socratic dialogues: these would include *Cleinias* and *On Public Speaking or Protagoras* (Περὶ τοῦ ῥητορεύειν ἢ Πρωταγόρας). Both Protagoras and Cleinias appear in Socratic literature, and we know that Plato's students wrote Socratic dialogues.[56]

---

[52] "Empedotimus" may be a fusion of "Empedocles" and "Hermotimus" (Hermotimus of Cladzomenae, associated with Pythagoras, was a subject of miraculous stories) or a semantic equivalent to Empedocles. See Gottschalk 1980a, 111 n. 79.

[53] There are numerous parallels with Plato, including the eschatological vision of Er in the *Republic*, the myths of the afterlife in *Phaedo* 107c–115a and *Gorgias* 523a–527e, and the discussion of the soul in *Phaedrus* 245c–249c. Heraclides' timing of the vision of Empedotimus precisely to "still noon" (μεσημβρία σταθερά) appears to allude to *Phaedrus* 242a (see Jażdżewska 2020, 65–7).

[54] For an attempt to reconstruct the contents of Heraclides' work on Empedotimus, see Gottschalk 1980a, 98–105; Kupreeva 2009.

[55] Philoponus, *In Meteor. I* 117 speaks of "Empedotimus' [instructions] about the Milky Way" (τὴν Ἐμπεδοτίμου περὶ τοῦ γάλακτος) which were appropriated by Damascius. Julian the Apostate referred to teachings which Heraclides took from Empedotimus and Pythagoras (Suda s.v. Ἐμπεδότιμος (ε 1007)).

[56] Cf. Πρωταγόρας ἢ Πολιτικός listed as a work of Crito (Diogenes Laertius 2.121) and Plato's *Protagoras* referred to as Πρωταγόρας ἢ σοφισταί (Diogenes Laertius 3.59). Diogenes Laertius lists *Eroticus and Cleinias* as if it was one work; perhaps the title was *Eroticus or Cleinias*, in which case the Cleinias referred to was probably the beautiful son of Axiochus, cousin of Alcibiades, known from

Dio Chrysostom says that Aristotle discussed Homer "in many dialogues" (*Or.* 53.1: ἐν πολλοῖς διαλόγοις), "and so does Heraclides of Pontus" (ἔτι δὲ Ἡρακλείδης ὁ Ποντικός). We do not know whether he means dialogues dedicated to Homer, or discussions of the Homeric epic interwoven into works on other subjects—as, for instance, in Dio's own *Second Kingship Oration*, a dialogue between Alexander the Great and Philip, in which a discussion of Homer takes up the majority of the text. Three of Heraclides' works listed by Diogenes Laertius bear the name of Homer (*On the Age of Homer and Hesiod, On Archilochus and Homer*, and *Solutions to Homeric Problems*) and an anonymous commentator on Aristotle's *Nicomachean Ethics* mentions Heraclides' *On Homer* (in which the story of Aeschylus, almost killed on stage for revealing the secrets of the mysteries, was told, *Comm. in Arist. EN* 145). The title *Solutions to Homeric Problems* suggests *problemata*-format rather than a dialogue, but it should be noted that papyri fragment provide evidence for fusion of Homeric *zetemata* with dialogue.[57]

Finally, two titles on Diogenes' list suggesting political topics—*On Governance* (Περὶ ἀρχῆς) and *Laws* (Νόμοι)—might have been among the dialogues written in "the middle style," with philosophers conversing with statesmen and generals on political questions (a type of dialogue which seems to have been particularly popular in Cicero's milieu). In the *Laws* Heraclides mentioned or discussed Protagoras of Abdera and his laws for the citizens of Thurii; in *On Governance*—Periander (Diogenes Laertius 1.94, 9.50). It has been proposed that two Oxyrhynchian papyri, POxy. 4.664 and 50.3544, may preserve fragments of the latter text: they come from a narrated dialogue set in the archaic period and reported by someone who presents himself as an eye-witness and a friend of Solon and Peisistratus (I have discussed these in detail in Chapter 2.4.1).

While evidence for Heraclides' dialogues is limited and necessarily skewed on account of the interests of his ancient readers, to whom we owe existing fragments and testimonies, we may conclude with confidence that Heraclides was a skillful writer with a knack for entertaining stories, while at the same time being capable of communicating philosophical messages through his works. Inspired by Plato's dramatic settings and myths, he unabashedly developed the literary side of the dialogue, though his free use of imagination accompanied by unconcern for verisimilitude did not appeal to all ancient readers. His dialogues were diverse enough to allow for a threefold typology. He was drawn to pre-Socratic philosophy, in particular, it seems, to Pythagoras and Empedocles, as well as to figures of foreign sages, and invented marvelous stories—he might even have written about

---

Plato's *Euthydemus*, Xenophon's *Symposion*, and the pseudo-Platonic *Axiochus* (see Nails 2002, 100–1 s.v. Clinias III). For Plato's students writing Socratic dialogues, cf. e.g. titles of works by Speusippus in Diogenes Laertius 4.4–5.

[57] See Chapter 2.3.2. For Heraclides' works on Homer, see Heath 2009. Krämer 2004[2], 71 characterizes Heraclides, on account of his works on literature, as "von der Sophistik beeinflusster Wegbereiter der Alexandriner."

a man who fell from the moon (Diogenes Laertius 8.72, quoting Timaeus: ἐκ τῆς σελήνης πεπτωκέναι ἄνθρωπον λέγων). His interest in poetry—Homeric epic and tragedy in particular—as well as in historical anecdotes and legends concurs with the interests of the Peripatetics.

Several stories widely known in antiquity—for instance Pythagoras' reincarnations, his explanation of the term "philosopher" to the tyrant Leon, and the vision of Empedotimus—seem ultimately to go back to Heraclides, who either invented them or popularized them through his vivid renditions, which might have taken a dialogue form. In all probability, later dialogue authors interacted with Heraclides' works, though proving specific occurrences of such intertextual relations is speculative.[58] We may imagine that Heraclides especially appealed to authors who were likewise interested in the literary and the imaginative, such as Dio Chrysostom and Lucian. In fact, in at least two instances Lucian seems to rework Heraclides' stories: first, in *Lover of Lies* 22-4, where Eucrates' parodic narration of his midday encounter with Hecate may be a rewriting of the vision of Empedotimus[59] and in the *Cock*, where the cobbler's talking rooster is reincarnated Pythagoras.[60]

### 3.3 Speusippus

Speusippus, Plato's nephew, who succeeded him and remained the head of the Academy until 339 BCE, was an original thinker with a variety of interests, which included metaphysics, ethics, epistemology, logic, and perhaps even biology.[61] None of his philosophical works survived; his only extant texts are, if authentic, a letter to Philip of Macedon and one or two epigrams.[62] While there is no doubt that Speusippus was the author of several dialogues, our knowledge of them is severely limited and relies for the most part on the list of his works in Diogenes Laertius (4.4-5 [T 1 Tarán]):

Καταλέλοιπε δὲ πάμπλειστα ὑπομνήματα καὶ διαλόγους πλείονας, ἐν οἷς καὶ Ἀρίστιππον τὸν Κυρηναῖον· Περὶ πλούτου α΄, Περὶ ἡδονῆς α΄, Περὶ δικαιοσύνης α΄, Περὶ φιλοσοφίας α΄, Περὶ φιλίας α΄, Περὶ θεῶν α΄, Φιλόσοφος α΄, Πρὸς Κέφαλον α΄, Κέφαλος α΄, Κλεινόμαχος ἢ Λυσίας α΄, Πολίτης α΄, Περὶ ψυχῆς α΄,

---

[58] For a possible link between Heraclides and the pseudo-Platonic *Axiochus*, see Nilsson 1950, 229-30; Wallace 2015, 95.
[59] Radermacher 1902, 203-4.
[60] Diogenes Laertius says that Heraclides talked about Pythagoras' reincarnations in various plants and animals (8.4). For Pythagoras' reincarnations in other dialogues, see also Lucian, *DMort*. 6.3; Philostratus, *Her*. 42.
[61] For an overview of biographical material concerning Speusippus as well as a reconstruction of his philosophy, see Isnardi Parente 1980; Tarán 1981; Dillon 2003, 30-88. Speusippus' dialogues are briefly discussed in Hirzel 1895a, 313-15.
[62] For the letter, see Natoli 2004, 23-31. For the epigrams, see F 86-7 Tarán with commentary.

Πρὸς Γρύλλον α', Ἀρίστιππος α', Τεχνῶν ἔλεγχος α', Ὑπομνηματικοὶ διάλογοι, Τεχνικὸν α', †Διάλογοι† τῆς περὶ τὰ ὅμοια πραγματείας ὁμοίων α' β' γ' δ' ε' ς' ζ' η' θ' ι', Διαιρέσεις καὶ πρὸς τὰ ὅμοια ὑποθέσεις, Περὶ γενῶν καὶ εἰδῶν παραδειγμάτων, Πρὸς τὸν Ἀμάρτυρον, Πλάτωνος ἐγκώμιον, Ἐπιστολαὶ πρὸς Δίωνα, Διονύσιον, Φίλιππον, Περὶ νομοθεσίας, Μαθηματικός, Μανδρόβολος, Λυσίας, Ὅροι, Τάξεις ὑπομνημάτων.

...left numerous *hypomnemata* and many dialogues, among which there are *Aristippus the Cyrenaic*; *On Wealth*, one book; *On Pleasure*, one book; *On Justice*, one book; *On Philosophy*, one book; *On Friendship*, one book; *On the Gods*, one book; *The Philosopher*, one book; *To Cephalus*, one book; *Cephalus*, one book; *Cleinomachus or Lysias*, one book; *The Citizen*, one book; *On the Soul*, one book; *To Gryllus*, one book; *Aristippus*, one book; *Examination of Arts*, one book; *Hypomnematic Dialogues*; *Technikon*, one book; *Dialogues on Similar Things*, ten books; *Divisions and Hypotheses concerning Similarities*; *On Examples of Genera and Species*; *To the Unwitnessed*; *Encomium of Plato*; *Letters to Dion, Dionysius, Philip*; *On Legislation*; *The Mathematician*; *Mandrobolos*; *Lysias*; *Definitions*; *Taxeis Hypomnematon*.[63]

Diogenes begins by noting that the philosopher left many ὑπομνήματα and dialogues, suggesting that these are two distinct types of writings. The term ὑπομνήματα is notoriously ambiguous; its meaning probably shifted in antiquity and oscillated between "notes, reminders, instructions," "commentary," and "treatise."[64] Whatever the exact meaning of the term, Diogenes' distinction between the dialogues and ὑπομνήματα suggests that the latter were works in a non-dialogic format.

The format of the works with *peri*-titles on Diogenes' list (*On Wealth, On Pleasure, On Justice, On Philosophy, On Friendship, On the Gods, On the Soul*) is not known, as this kind of title does not indicate the genre. We may presume, however, that works bearing name-titles were dialogues. To these belong *Aristippus the Cyrenaic* (probably identical with *Aristippus*), *Cephalus*, and *Cleinomachus or Lysias* (*Lysias* may be a duplicate).[65] Lysias and Cephalus are probably the logographer and his father, represented in Plato's *Phaedrus* and the *Republic*.[66] The identity of Cleinomachus is not certain: he may have been the student of Euclides

---

[63] I leave obscure titles in transliteration. The list is not comprehensive and similarities between certain titles (e.g. *Aristippus the Cyrenaic* and *Aristippus*, or *Cleinomachus or Lysias* and *Lysias*) suggest that it conflates a few sources. For a discussion on this, see Bywater 1869, 27–8; Tarán 1981, 188–99; Dillon 2003, 34–40.

[64] See Bömer 1953, 215–26 and Introduction, p. 3. In *Epinomis* 980d, a written account of a conversation carried on in Plato's *Laws* is referred to as ὑπομνήματα; see Chapter 4.2.1 p. 131.

[65] For the combination of two names in *Cleinomachus or Lysias*, cf. parallels in Diogenes Laertius 2.120 (Stilpo's *Aristippus or Callias*) and 3.62 (*Eryxias or Erasistratus*; cf. Lang 1911, 44 n. 2 for manuscript evidence of two titles of the *Eryxias*).

[66] Though there is another Cephalus in the Platonic corpus, one of Clazomenae, who is the reporter of a conversation in the *Parmenides*. Cf. also Diogenes Laertius 2.124, where a dialogue entitled *Cephalus* is ascribed to a Glaucon of Athens.

of Megara who, Diogenes Laertius says, was the first one to write "on propositions and predicates" (2.112). His field, then, would likely have been dialectics: are we, then, to imagine *Cleinomachus or Lysias* as a dialogue between the young dialectician and the old orator, with a dramatic date years after the death of Socrates? The title *Aristippus* suggests a dialogue arguing against Cyrenaic hedonism, though possibly also reflecting the internal polemics within the Academy, as Speusippus' strictly anti-hedonistic position was opposed to that of a fellow student of Plato, Eudoxus of Cnidus.[67] The eponymous Aristippus may have been Aristippus the Older—if he were an interlocutor, we would be dealing with a Socratic dialogue used as a guise for contemporary polemics—but Aristippus the Younger is also a viable option. At any rate, it is probable that at least some of Speusippus' dialogues were Socratic dialogues with fifth-century Athens as their setting. This is not surprising: Speusippus was probably born around 410–408 BCE and as a young man witnessed the extraordinary bloom of *Sokratikoi logoi*.

*Philosopher, Citizen*, and *Mathematician* (unless we are to understand Μαθηματικός as Ὁ μαθηματικὸς λόγος) were also probably dialogues. Plato did not write the *Philosopher*, although he mentions it in the *Sophist* and *Statesman* as the third part of a trilogy (*Sph.* 216c–217a, 253e–254b; *Plt.* 257a–c), and Speusippus' *Philosopher* may have been a follow-up to Plato's project. If so, the dialogue probably departed from the format of the Socratic dialogue, with Socrates as the dominant figure, like in Plato's *Sophist* and *Statesman*. The title *Mathematician* fits with Speusippus' interest in mathematical entities and Pythagorean doctrines (he was also the author of a work titled *On Pythagorean Numbers*). The meaning of the title *Hypomnematic Dialogues* (Ὑπομνηματικοὶ διάλογοι) is elusive. ὑπομνηματικός is a rare adjective and most of its attestations come from the imperial and Byzantine period; Aristotle's commentators distinguish between the philosopher's comprehensive and systematic works, which they call τὰ συνταγματικά, and works which merely sketch the main points of a discussed topic τὰ ὑπομνηματικά; perhaps something similar is meant here.[68] In the case of *Dialogues on Similar Things* in ten books (Διάλογοι τῆς περὶ τὰ ὅμοια πραγματείας),[69] scholars bracket the word διάλογοι on the grounds that the work focused on the classification of and similarities between plants and animals, and as

---

[67] Eudoxus' argument that pleasure is the ultimate good is discussed by Aristotle, *EN* 1172b9–25; Speusippus' criticism of Eudoxus may be referred to in *EN* 1153b4–6; see Warren 2009. For Speusippus' view that both pain and pleasure are evil, see F 80a–81b Tarán with commentary; Dillon 2003, 64–77 (who believes that Speusippus' ethical position is targeted by Plato in *Philebus* 44a–d). Athenaeus' claim that Speusippus was φιλήδονος (*Deipn.* 12.546d) probably relies on a hostile biographical tradition rather than reflecting the philosopher's theoretical position.

[68] e.g. Ammonius, *In Cat.* 4.5. Cf. also Dionysius of Halicarnassus, *Dem.* 46, who says that he will not go over every example, for his work would assume τοὺς σχολικοὺς...χαρακτῆρας ἐκ τῶν ὑπομνηματικῶν. Other interpretations of the title include "Memoirs in dialogue form" and "Dialogues for mnemonic purpose," see Tarán 1981, 195.

[69] The title is reconstructed; the manuscripts have Διάλογοι τῶν περὶ τὴν πραγματείαν ὁμοίων.

such is difficult to imagine having been written in a dialogue format.[70] It is not impossible, though, that the books had dialogue frames.

We have more information on two of Speusippus' texts. Diogenes Laertius lists the title *Mandrobolos*, and Aristotle probably refers to this text in *Sophistic Refutations* 174b23-7 [F 5a Tarán]:

ὥσπερ τε καὶ ἀποκρινόμενοι πολλάκις, ὅταν ἐλέγχωνται, ποιοῦσι διττόν, ἂν μέλλῃ συμβαίνειν ἐλεγχθήσεσθαι, καὶ ἐρωτῶντας χρηστέον ποτὲ τούτῳ πρὸς τοὺς ἐνισταμένους—ἂν ὡδὶ μὲν συμβαίνῃ ὡδὶ δὲ μή, ὅτι οὕτως εἴληφεν, οἷον ὁ Κλεοφῶν ποιεῖ ἐν τῷ Μανδροβούλῳ.

just as answerers, too, often, when they are in process of being refuted draw a distinction, if their refutation is just about to take place, so questioners also should resort to this from time to time to counter objectors, pointing out, supposing that against one sense of the words the objection holds, but not against the other, that they have taken it in the latter sense, as e.g. Cleophon does in the *Mandroboulus*. (trans. W. A. Pickard-Cambridge)

Although Speusippus' name does not appear, it is reasonable to assume that Aristotle refers to his work. Who was Cleophon? A scholiast on this passage explains that the *Mandroboulus* was "a Platonic dialogue" (F 5b Tarán: ὁ Πλατωνικὸς διάλογος, presumably meaning "a dialogue in Plato's style," and not "Plato's dialogue"); if so, then the text may have been a dialogue (at least partly) elenchic in character, with Cleophon among the interlocutors.[71] The title is enigmatic. Mandroboulus was the hero of an aetiological story: Aelian relates that, according to Aristotle, the people of Samos pay honor to sheep because a sheep once discovered a treasure. Mandroboulus, apparently the owner, dedicated a sheep to Hera on this occasion (*NA* 12.40). From other authors we learn that Mandroboulus, after finding the treasure, offered to Hera a golden sheep in the first year, a silver one in the second, and a bronze one in the third, whence the proverb ἐπὶ τὰ Μανδροβόλου χωρεῖ τὰ πρᾶγμα, "it's going Mandroboulus' way," spoken when things are getting worse.[72] Mandroboulus, then, was probably not a speaker, and his story was merely related in the dialogue, like the stories of Minos and Hipparchus in the pseudo-Platonic *Minos* and *Hipparchus*.

---

[70] Lang 1911, 16-17; Tarán 1981, 196. The fragments of the work come mostly from Athenaeus, who refers to the text as *Homoia*. Cf. Plato, *Plt.* 264a-267c for some divisions between types of animals.

[71] Bywater 1883, 21-30; Tarán 1981, 242-3. There were two known Cleophons, a politician and demagogue of the fifth century BCE (mentioned inter alia by Aristophanes in the *Frogs*; another comedian, Plato, wrote a play titled after him) and a poet of the fourth century BCE, mentioned by Aristotle. Hirzel 1895a, 314 speculated that the Cleophon mentioned was the Athenian demagogue, and that he was portrayed in Speusippus' dialogue in a manner parallel to Callicles in Plato's *Gorgias*.

[72] Cf. e.g. Lucian, *Merc. cond.* 21. The saying was to appear in a comic play by Plato *comicus* (F 53 K–A).

Speusippus was also the author of Πλάτωνος περίδειπνον, *Plato's Funeral Feast*, in which he related the story of Ariston, Plato's father, attempting unsuccessfully to consummate his marriage with Perictione. Afterwards, Apollo appeared to him in a vision; Ariston therefore left Perictione in peace until she gave birth to a child (Diogenes Laertius 3.2). The story implied, then, that Plato's real father was Apollo, not Ariston. Philodemus in the *History of the Academy* appears to refer to *Plato's Funeral Feast* as the source of information that Timolaus of Cyzicus, Calligenes, and Timolaus the Athenian were among Plato's students (*Acad. ind.* col. vi.1a–12a; the papyrus is damaged, and several letters are unclear). The format of the work is nowhere specified, but a dialogue, with speeches in honor of Plato (and Plato's particular connection with Apollo discussed), is a reasonable supposition.[73] If so, Plato's students listed by Philodemus may have been present among the guests.[74] Such a work, commemorating the death of the philosopher, i.e. Plato, would belong to the same sub-category of dialogues as Plato's *Phaedo*, Aristotle's *Eudemus*, and Heraclides of Pontus' *On the Woman Not Breathing*. Speusippus' text might have been parodied a century later by Timon of Phlius, a Pyrrhonist who wrote *Arcesilaus' Funeral Feast* (on Timon, see Chapter 6.7). Plutarch in *Table Talk* 612d-e lists Speusippus among the philosophers who "considered it worthy of effort to record conversations held in a drinking party" (ἄξιόν τινος σπουδῆς πεποιημένους ἔργον ἀναγράψασθαι λόγους παρὰ πότον γενομένους). It is not impossible that he is referring to *Plato's Funeral Feast*; at any rate this is the only extant title by Speusippus that bears any relation to sympotic literature, and while we know very little about the Greek *perideipnon*, it seems to have included a drinking event.[75]

### 3.4 Eudoxus of Cnidus

Eudoxus of Cnidus, a student of Plato known mostly for his interest in mathematics, astronomy, and geography as well as a hedonistic position in ethics, is said to have written *Dialogues of Dogs*, Κυνῶν διάλογοι (Diogenes Laertius 8.89, who

---

[73] Hirzel 1895a, 345–6, n. 5 proposed that it was a dialogue and that the *perideipnon* ("Totenmahl") constituted a new category of the sympotic dialogue; Martin 1931, 165 argued that there are no similarities between a *symposion* and a *perideipnon*, and that Speusippus' work must have been a speech in praise of the deceased. Yet, it would be odd if Speusippus' encomiastic speech would have been referred to as a "funeral feast." For criticism of Martin's argument, see Tarán 1981, 231 n. 15. On Plato's connection with Apollo, see Riginos 1976, 9–32.

[74] Dillon 2003, 37–8, n. 19 writes that Speusippus made Timolaus the host of the feast; however, the word ἑστιάσας makes no appearance in the text, but is an addition by Crönert 1906, 184. It would be odd if the *perideipnon*, customarily held at the house of the closest relative of the dead (Demosthenes, *De cor.* 288), would have been hosted by the otherwise unknown Timolaus.

[75] Drinking at *perideipnon* seems to be alluded to in Anaxandrides, where "drinking from left to right and speaking" is associated with a funerary ritual (Athenaeus, *Deipn.* 11.464a [F 1 K-A]: τὸν ἐπιδέξια λέγειν, Ἄπολλον, ὥσπερεὶ τεθνηκότι;); cf. Wecowski 2014, 97–8.

claims that this information comes from Eratosthenes). This is the only title of Eudoxus' work besides *Octaëteris* that Diogenes mentions, though he adds that Eudoxus κατέλιπε... ὑπομνήματα κάλλιστα, "left beautiful writings." Some ancient authors maintained that the *Dialogues of Dogs* was a translation of an Egyptian text, which perhaps suggests some Egyptian coloring in the work, but other than that we know nothing else about the text.[76] Whether speaking animals in a fable-like world were featured, as is usually assumed, is difficult to say.

## 3.5 Xenocrates

Xenocrates succeeded Speusippus in 339 BCE and remained the head of the Academy for twenty-five years, until his death in 314 BCE. He was famously advised by Plato to make a sacrifice to the Graces on account of his seriousness (Diogenes Laertius 5.6: Ξενόκρατες, θῦε ταῖς Χάρισι), which suggests that he may not have been the most imaginative and pleasant writer. All his works have been lost. Diogenes Laertius lists over seventy titles, the majority of which bear straightforward *peri*-titles (4.11–14). Most of them focus on ethics (e.g. *On Wealth, On Freedom, On Friendship, On Happiness, On Justice, On the Emotions, On Death*), while some suggest more technical philosophical or scientific works (e.g. *On Ideas, On the One, On Knowledge, On Numbers, On Geometers*).[77] While the *peri*-titles do not permit a definite genre affiliation, a few titles suggest a dialogue form, namely *The Arcadian, Callicles, The Statesman*, and *Archedemus or On Justice*. No fragments survive, and it is difficult to speculate about their contents. The *Callicles* is reminiscent of Socrates' formidable opponent in Plato's *Gorgias*. The *Statesman*—if this is the right interpretation of the title Πολιτικός—mirrors the title of Plato's dialogue. *Archedemus or On Justice* might have featured Archedemus of Syracuse, mentioned in the Platonic *Seventh Epistle* as an associate of Archytas and the man valued most by Plato of all the Sicilians (*Ep.* 7.339a).[78] Dionysius is said to have sent a trireme for Plato with Archedemus, among others, on board; later, when Dionysius asked Plato temporarily to leave the citadel, the philosopher lived in Archedemus' house (*Ep.* 7.349d). According

---

[76] Hirzel 1895a, 339–40 discusses them under the category "phantastische Dialoge" and believes that they were not bereft of a moralizing layer. There was much speculation regarding the character and content of these dialogues, as well as suggestions that κυνῶν is an error and should be amended; see the discussion in Griffiths 1965; Lasserre 1966, 268–9.

[77] From other sources we learn also of Xenocrates' *On the Life of Plato* (F 264–6 Isnardi Parente) and *On the Food Derived from Animals* (F 267 Isnardi Parente).

[78] Rather than the Archedemus known from Xenophon's *Apomnemoneumata*, characterized there as a good speaker, but a poor man (*Mem.* 2.9.4), as Dillon 2003, 97 n. 29 proposes. That Xenocrates' Archedemus may have been Plato's associate from Syracuse is suggested by Huffman 2005, 8 n. 2. Archedemus appears also in other pseudo-Platonic letters (*Ep.* 2.310b, 2.312d, 2.313d, 2.313e, 3.319a). In *Letters of Chion of Heraclea*, an epistolographic novel, which probably drew loosely from the Platonic epistles, some Archedemus, an astronomer, is mentioned; see Düring 1951, 88.

to Plutarch, Archedemus was sent for Plato by the Pythagoreans associated with Archytas (*Dion* 18.6). The choice of Archedemus as a speaker would have fitted with Xenocrates' attested interest in Pythagoreanism.

Finally, the *Oeconomicus* on Diogenes' list might have been a dialogue on household management, like Xenophon's work by the same name, though a continuous format is not excluded, as there is a homonymous pseudo-Aristotelian treatise in two books, the first of which appears to have come from the early Peripatos.

## 3.6 Crantor

Crantor belongs to the next generation of Platonists; he was born probably around 340 in Soli in Cilicia and might have lived until 275 BCE. According to sources he was first a student of Xenocrates and later of Polemo, and anecdotes describe him as having been responsible for Arcesilaus' joining the Academy.[79] We have no catalogue of his works. According to Diogenes Laertius, he left thirty-thousand lines of *hypomnemata* (4.24), which suggests a corpus of modest size, slightly exceeding the *Iliad* and the *Odyssey* combined.[80] Contrary to Xenocrates, he enjoyed a reputation as a skillful author; he was fond of poetry and is characterized by Diogenes Laertius as a man of verbal inventiveness (4.27: δεινὸς ὀνοματοποιῆσαι). Homer and Euripides were his favorite poets; he also wrote poetry himself and was called "pleasing to the Muses" by the poet Theaetetus (4.25), perhaps Theaetetus of Cyrene, a friend of Callimachus. He is also connected, though in a not wholly clear way, with the poet Antagoras of Rhodes, whose hymn *To Eros* was somehow associated with Crantor (Diogenes Laertius 4.26–7; perhaps Crantor was the poetic "I" of the poem).[81]

Although our knowledge of Crantor's work is extremely scanty, he was not inconsequential to the history of the dialogue. In antiquity he was known principally as the author of the famous *On Grief* (Περὶ πένθους), "not a large work, but a golden little book" (Cicero, *Acad.* 2.44.135: *non magnus, verum aureolus libellus*), which gave rise to consolatory literature and influenced later writers, including those composing dialogues. The text was written for some Hippocles to comfort him after the death of his children, and was probably written in a letter format,

---

[79] According to Diogenes Laertius, Arcesilaus was a lover of Crantor and the two lived together (4.30); see also Philodemus, *Acad. ind.* col. xvi. For stories of philosophical conversion in Diogenes Laertius, including the one of Arcesilaus, see Warren 2009 esp. 144–5; Eshleman 2007, esp. 136.

[80] The *Iliad* and *Odyssey* together count 27,793 lines. The approximate length of a hexameter line was also used in counting prose texts, see Ohly 1928; Obbink 1997, 62 n. 1.

[81] So Cuypers 2004, 99–101. For other connections of Antagoras with the Academy, see Diogenes Laertius 4.21.

with a specified recipient addressed in the second person.[82] This *libellus* was certainly influenced by Academic and Peripatetic dialogues on death: above all, Plato's *Phaedo*, but possibly also Aristotle's *Eudemus* and Theophrastus' *Callisthenes* or *On Grief*. Influences from the *Eudemus* are particularly likely: Aristotle's dialogue contained the famous account of Midas' capture of Silenus, and the latter's revelation that the best thing for a human being is not to be born, and second after that—to die as quickly as possible. Crantor's *On Grief*, on the other hand, reported that after some Euthynous died suddenly, the father of the youth, suspecting that he might have been poisoned, went to the place where the spirits of dead may be consulted (ψυχομαντεῖον) and had a vision: his father (i.e. grandfather of the deceased) appeared and showed him the ghost of his son, who handed him a text consisting of three lines, set in elegiac meter, saying that people are ignorant and that Euthynous' death was destined—and that it would not be good if he had lived, neither for himself nor for his parents.[83] Crantor might have developed this story with Aristotle's myth in mind.

Crantor's *On Grief* not only developed out of the tradition of philosophical dialogues on death but also greatly impacted later dialogue authors by providing an impetus for the development of "consolatory dialogues," works merging a dialogue format with consolatory preoccupations, such as the pseudo-Platonic *Axiochus* (see Chapter 4.3.6) and Dio Chrysostom's *Charidemus*. Like non-dialogic consolations, they focus on soothing pain or fear, and therefore on practical efficacy rather than on the search for truth; hence their frequent eclectic character and employment of arguments of various philosophical provenance.

The popularity of *On Grief* must have been due both to its usefulness as an assortment of consolatory arguments and to its pleasing style, for which Crantor was praised by Diogenes Laertius. Crantor's literary temperament can be gleaned from a passage of Sextus Empiricus, which appears to be either a direct quotation from Crantor's unknown text or a close paraphrase.[84] The passage preserves a dialogized contest between personifications of goods and as a unique piece of evidence of Crantor's style merits to be quoted in full (*Adv. math.* 11.51–8 [F 7a Mette]):

ἔνθεν καὶ ὁ Κράντωρ εἰς ἔμφασιν τοῦ λεγομένου βουλόμενος ἡμᾶς ἄγειν πάνυ χαρίεντι συνεχρήσατο παραδείγματι. εἰ γὰρ νοήσαιμεν φησί κοινόν τι τῶν Πανελλήνων θέατρον, εἰς τοῦτό τε ἕκαστον τῶν ἀγαθῶν παριὸν καὶ τῶν

---

[82] For such a format, cf. Plutarch, *Consolation to his Wife*, pseudo-Plutarch, *Consolation to Apollonius*; Seneca's consolations to Marcia, Helvia, and Polybius. For Crantor's *On Grief*, see Hirzel 1895a, 349–50; Kassel 1958, 35–6; Mette 1984, 34–6.

[83] Pseudo-Plutarch, *Cons. ad Apoll.* 109b-d; a shorter version in Cicero, *Tusc.* 1.48.115. Some scholars hypothesize that Crantor might have quoted Aristotle's story of Midas and Silenus; see e.g. Mette 1984, 35; Dillon 2003, 228 and n. 126; arguments contra, Kassel 1958, 78–9.

[84] Bett 1997, 90–1. For stylistic features of the text, see Kuiper 1901, 343–6.

πρωτείων ἀντιποιούμενον ἥκειν, εὐθὺς καὶ εἰς ἔννοιαν ἀναχθησόμεθα τῆς ἐν τοῖς ἀγαθοῖς διαφορᾶς. πρῶτον μὲν γὰρ ὁ Πλοῦτος παραπηδήσας ἐρεῖ· "ἐγώ, ἄνδρες Πανέλληνες, κόσμον παρέχων πᾶσιν ἀνθρώποις καὶ τὰς ἐσθῆτας καὶ τὰς ὑποδέσεις καὶ τὴν ἄλλην ἀπόλαυσιν χρειώδης ‹τ'› εἰμὶ νοσοῦσι καὶ ὑγιαίνουσι, καὶ ἐν μὲν εἰρήνῃ παρέχω τὰ τερπνά, ἐν δὲ πολέμοις νεῦρα τῶν πράξεων γίνομαι." τούτων γὰρ δὴ τῶν λόγων ἀκούσαντες οἱ Πανέλληνες ὁμοθυμαδὸν κελεύ‹σ›ουσιν ἀποδοῦναι τὰ πρωτεῖα τῷ Πλούτῳ. ἀλλ' ἐὰν τούτου ἤδη ἀνακηρυττομένου ἐπιστᾶσα ἡ Ἡδονή, "τῇ ἔνι μὲν φιλότης, ἔνι δ' ἵμερος, ἐν δ' ὀαριστύς, πάρφασις, ἥ τ' ἔκλεψε νόον πύκα περ φρονεόντων," λέγῃ ‹δ'› εἰς μέσον καταστᾶσα, ὅτι αὐτὴν δίκαιόν ἐστιν ἀναγορεύειν, 'ὁ δ' ὄλβος οὐ βέβαιος, ἀλλ' ἐφήμερος ἐξέπτατ' οἴκων, μικρὸν ἀνθήσας χρόνον," διώκεταί τε πρὸς τῶν ἀνθρώπων οὐ δι' ἑαυτόν, ἀλλὰ τὴν ἐξ αὐτοῦ περιγι‹γ›νομένην ἀπόλαυσιν καὶ ἡδονήν, πάντως οἱ Πανέλληνες, οὐκ ἄλλως ἔχειν τὸ πρᾶγμα ἢ οὕτως ὑπολαβόντες, κεκράξονται δεῖν τὴν Ἡδονὴν στεφανοῦν. ἀλλὰ καὶ ταύτης τὸ βραβεῖον φέρεσθαι μελλούσης, ἐπὴν εἰσβάλλῃ ἡ Ὑγεία μετὰ τῶν συνέδρων αὐτῇ θεῶν, καὶ διδάσκῃ, ὡς οὔτε ἡδονῆς οὔτε πλούτου ὄφελός τι ἐστὶν ἀπούσης αὐτῆς—"τί γάρ με πλοῦτος ὠφελεῖ ‹x-› νόσον; μίκρ' ἂν θέλοιμι καὶ καθ' ἡμέραν {ἄλυπον} ἔχων ‹ἄλυπον› οἰκεῖν βίοτον ἢ πλουτῶν νοσεῖν"—ἀκούσαντες πάλιν οἱ Πανέλληνες καὶ μεταμαθόντες, ὡς οὐκ ἔνεστι κλινοπετῇ καὶ νοσοῦσαν ὑποστῆναι τὴν εὐδαιμονίαν, φήσουσι νικᾶν τὴν Ὑγείαν. ἀλλὰ καὶ τῆς Ὑγείας ἤδη νικώσης, ἐπὰν εἰσέλθῃ ἡ Ἀνδρεία πολὺ στῖφος ἀριστέων καὶ ἡρώων ἔχουσα περὶ ἑαυτήν, καταστᾶσά τε λέγῃ· "ἐμοῦ μὴ παρούσης, ἄνδρες Ἕλληνες, ἀλλοτρία γί‹γ›νεται ἡ κτῆσις τῶν παρ' ὑμῖν ἀγαθῶν εὔξαιντό τε ‹ἂν› οἱ πολέμιοι περιουσιάζειν ὑμᾶς πᾶσι τοῖς ἀγαθοῖς ὡς μελλήσοντες ὑμῶν κρατεῖν," καὶ τούτων οὖν ἀκούσαντες οἱ Ἕλληνες τὰ μὲν πρωτεῖα τῇ Ἀρετῇ ἀποδώσουσι, τὰ δὲ δευτερεῖα τῇ Ὑγείᾳ, τὰ δὲ τρίτα τῇ Ἡδονῇ, τελευταῖον δὲ τάξουσι τὸν Πλοῦτον.

Hence Crantor, wishing to give us a clear picture of the matter being discussed, employed a most elegant parable. If we conceive, he says, a theatre common to all the Greeks, and that each of the goods is present at this place, and is coming forward and competing for the first prize, we will be led straight away to a conception of the difference among the goods. For first wealth will leap up and say, "I, men of all Greece, providing ornament to all people and clothes and shoes and every other enjoyment, am needed by the sick and the healthy, and in peace I provide delights, while in war I become the sinews of action." Then of course all the Greeks, hearing these words, will unanimously order that the first prize be given to wealth. But if, while wealth is already being proclaimed the winner, pleasure appears, "In whom is love, is desire, is intimacy, allurement, which steals the sense even of shrewd thinkers,"[85] and taking a position in the middle says that it is just to declare *her* the winner—"For wealth is not steady, but lasts just a day; It blooms a short time and then flies away,"[86] and it is pursued by people not for

---

[85] Homer, *Il.* 14.216–17.   [86] Euripides, *Ph.* 558 and *El.* 944.

its own sake, but for the sake of the enjoyment and pleasure which result from it—then surely all the Greeks, supposing that this is exactly how the matter stands, will shout that pleasure must be crowned. But as she too is about to carry off the prize, once health enters with her companion gods, and teaches that pleasure and wealth are no use in her absence—"For what benefit is wealth to me when I am sick? I would rather live a painless life, from day to day and having little, Than to be wealthy but diseased"[87]—then again all the Greeks, having heard her and having been informed that it is not possible for happiness to exist when bedridden and sick, will say that health wins. But though health is already victorious, once courage enters, with a great throng of warriors and heroes around her, and taking her position says "If I am not present, men of Greece, the possession of your goods passes to others, and your enemies would pray for you to have abundant supplies of all goods, presuming that they are going to conquer you"; then, having heard this, the Greeks will award the first prize to virtue, the second to health, the third to pleasure, and they will rank wealth last.

(trans. R. Bett)[88]

Crantor's *paradeigma*, as Sextus calls it, in which personified goods argue with each other over their superiority, is reminiscent of Xenophon's personification of Virtue and Vice in the "Choice of Heracles" (*Mem.* 2.1.21–34). Other earlier or contemporary parallels in philosophical literature include the personification of the Laws in Plato's *Crito* (50a–54d) and the Stoic Cleanthes' depiction of a dialogue between Anger and Reason (Galen, *Hipp. et Plat. plac.* 5.6.35 CMG; see Chapter 6.5). Crantor, then, works within a certain tradition present in philosophical literature; at the same time, he also draws from the Greek drama: the contest takes place in a theater, the text is studded with poetic quotations (five lines of Euripides are cited), and there is some theatric quality to Courage being accompanied by a "throng of warriors and heroes" (στῖφος ἀριστέων καὶ ἡρώων), and Health by her "companion gods" (σύνεδροι θεοί).[89]

We do not know what text this piece comes from and how much it has been abridged or altered by Sextus.[90] It may have appeared in a longer text discussing the nature of the goods. Discussions on what to include among the goods were a

[87] Euripides, *TrGF* F 714 (ll. 2 and 3 are also quoted by Stobaeus, 4.31c.64 and 4.33.11, under headings *Blame of Wealth* and *Comparison of Poverty and Wealth*). To Crantor himself are attributed two iambic passages apparently praising wealth and condemning poverty in Stobaeus 4.32b.33 and 4.33.6 [F 12–13 Mette].

[88] The Greek text follows Mette's edition (1984).

[89] For personifications of abstract concepts in comedy and tragedy cf. e.g. Kratos and Bia in Aeschylus' *Prometh. desm.*; Ambition in Euripides' *Phoenician women* (531–5) and Holiness in his *Bacchae* (370–3). Wealth and Poverty are famously personified in Aristophanes' *Ploutos*.

[90] White 2010, 374 implies that the story was a part of Crantor's famous *On Grief*, but there is no evidence for that. The passage has sometimes been referred to as diatribe; cf. Kuiper 1901, who observes certain stylistic negligence, which he interprets as "non imprudentiae peccata sed quaesitae simplicitatis indicia, quibus multo magis diatribe accredit ad colorem sermonis cottidiani . . . ."

staple among post-Platonic and Hellenistic philosophers: Speusippus and Xenocrates seem to have included wealth and health among them, while the Stoics conceived them as *adiaphora*.[91] Crantor's text, however, is rather simplistic for a serious philosophical attempt to rank the goods, and the arguments made by the personifications do not make for a coherent philosophical position.[92] Yet, it is perhaps unfair to consider the narrative as being reflective of Crantor's philosophical potential, as the plot of the story suggests its humorous character. The repeated give-and-take-back of the prize, the assembly of the Hellenes changing their mind (μεταμαθόντες) at a whim, the mixture of prose and poetry, repetitions on a structural and verbal level (ἀκούσαντες οἱ Πανέλληνες—ἀκούσαντες πάλιν οἱ Πανέλληνες—τοῦτον οὖν ἀκούσαντες οἱ Ἕλληνες), vivid vocabulary (παραπηδήσας, ἐπιστᾶσα, εἰσβάλλῃ, κεκράξονται)—all these elements suggest that the passage is not a serious philosophical investigation but rather a satire on the Greeks who lead an unexamined and unphilosophical life.

As we consider Crantor's contribution to the dialogue, it should be recorded that Proclus called him ὁ πρῶτος τοῦ Πλάτωνος ἐξηγητής, "the first interpreter of Plato" (*In Ti.* 1.76 Diehl), which might have meant that he authored the first extensive commentary on a dialogue by Plato, probably on the *Timaeus*.[93] He discussed there Plato's account of the generation of the cosmos in the *Timaeus*, which he interpreted figuratively, and of the composition of the soul. He also commented on the Atlantis-story.[94] Proclus' discussion of three commenting strategies on the Platonic proems—(1) the proems are irrelevant and do not require a commentary; (2) they model appropriate moral attitudes; (3) they prefigure and announce themes at the core of the dialogue—may have originally come from Crantor.[95]

## 3.7 The New Academy

Although no works by skeptical philosophers associated with the New Academy before Cicero are preserved, we can assume that the skeptical turn influenced and

---

[91] According to Plutarch, *Comm. not.* 1065a, Speusippus and Xenocrates did not hold health as indifferent (ἀδιάφορον), nor wealth as useless (ἀνωφελές). For wealth, health, and pleasure as *adiaphora* in Stoicism, see e.g. Zeno (*SVF* 1.47 F 190); Diogenes Laertius 7.102 (on Zeno); Arrian, *Epict. Diss.* 2.19.13. See also Plato, *Lg.* 661a, where it is observed that it is commonly believed that health comes first, beauty second, and wealth third and the pseudo-Platonic *Eryxias* where Socrates discusses the relationship between different goods (wealth, health, prosperity, and wisdom) and argues that wisdom is the most valuable (*Eryx.* 393b-394a). See also Chapter 2.2.4, p. 55.

[92] Bett 1997, 90-1, concluding that the story "does not provide a particularly flattering picture of Crantor as philosopher." It is not clear why courage, ἀνδρεία, becomes virtue, ἀρετή, at the end of the passage (for a half-hearted attempt to explain this, see Dillon 2003, 230-1).

[93] Cf. Sedley 1999, 143-4; Dillon 2003, 218.

[94] Proclus, *In Ti.* 1.76 Diehl says that Crantor considered the Atlantis story ἱστορία ψιλή, "a simple story"; for discussions of this passage see Tarán 2001, 615-18; Tarrant 2007, 63-5.

[95] Proclus, *In Parm.* 1.659 Cousin. See Sedley 1999, 140-8, with whom Tarrant disagrees 2007, 70 n. 107.

transformed the oral and written formats of Academic discourse. Some representatives of the skeptical Academy appear to have privileged oral instruction over the dissemination of their philosophy via writing: Arcesilaus and Carneades, two key figures, though remembered as formidable speakers and disputants, probably left no philosophical writings.[96] While not all ancient skeptics refused to leave written records—hundreds of Clitomachus' lost texts as well as extant works by Cicero and Sextus Empiricus provide ample evidence—one can see how an unwillingness to write and focus on oral philosophizing is consistent with an undogmatic position.[97]

Still, accounts of Arcesilaus' and Carneades' teachings, composed by students, appear to have circulated. Philodemus reports that Pythodorus wrote down σχολαί, "instructions, teachings," originating from Arcesilaus;[98] Lacydes, Arcesilaus' successor as a scholarch, also might have recorded them. Zeno of Alexandria and Hagnon of Tarsus are said to have written down σχολαί of Carneades (though the work of the former did not meet with Carneades' approval).[99] Clitomachus, the

---

[96] For the verbal and argumentative mastery of Arcesilaus and Carneades cf. e.g. Cicero, *Acad.* 2.6.16: *floruit* [sc. Arcesilaus] *cum acumine ingeni tum admirabili quodam lepore dicendi*; *Acad.* 2.18.60: *tanta in Arcesila, multo etiam maior in Carneade et copia rerum et dicendi vis.* Diogenes Laertius calls Arcesilaus εὑρεσιλογώτατος and πειστικός (4.37). For Carneades' excellence in oral expression, see Usher 2006; Powell 2013, 224–5. For the claim that Arcesilaus left no philosophical writings, see Plutarch, *Alex. fort.* 328a; Diogenes Laertius 4.32. Philodemus (*Acad. ind.* col. xviii.34–40) and Diogenes Laertius (4.32) say that Arcesilaus was found "correcting works of Crantor"; the meaning is uncertain. Diogenes Laertius preserves two epigrams by Arcesilaus (4.30–1) and perhaps hints at Arcesilaus' work about the poet Ion of Chios (4.32); he also cites Arcesilaus' letter concerning his will (4.44); see Görler 1994, 786–7. Carneades, Diogenes Laertius claims (4.65), wrote no philosophical texts (though letters to King Ariarathes, ascribed to him, were in circulation).

[97] Diogenes Laertius explicitly ties Arcesilaus' reluctance to write to his *epoche*: διὰ δὲ τὸ περὶ πάντων ἐπέχειν οὐδὲ βιβλίον, φασί τινες, συνέγραψεν (4.32). The connection between skepticism and a preference for oral teaching is also manifest in the fact that Pyrrho of Elis, the founder of the skeptical school, left no writings (Diogenes Laertius 9.102).

[98] For various meanings of σχολή, see Glucker 1978, 160–2. Here the term refers to school instructions, probably both in continuous and conversational formats, and their written accounts. It recurs also in the titles of works by philosophers of other than an Academic affiliation, e.g. Diogenes Laertius 5.47: Theophrastus' Ἠθικαὶ σχολαί, 7.28: the Stoic Persaeus wrote about Zeno's death ἐν ταῖς Ἠθικαῖς σχολαῖς, 7.163: Aristo of Chios wrote Σχολαί in six books, 7.41: Phaenias, a pupil of Posidonius, wrote down Ποσειδωνεῖαι σχολαί, "Scholai of Posidonius," 10.26: Diogenes of Tarsus, Epicurus' student, wrote Ἐπίλεκτοι σχολαί, "Selected scholai" (presumably of Epicurus) in at least twenty books (cf. 10.138). The term σχολαί used for written texts emphasizes their school provenance—they are presumed to be records of oral instruction carried in a philosophical school, their shape and character informed by a teacher–student relation. This is confirmed by the recurrent notion of σχολαί of a philosopher written down by a student. The conventional plural form σχολαί suggests an assortment of relatively short texts on various subjects (as confirmed by Cicero, *Tusc.* 3.34.81: the Greeks deal with various subjects *in singulas scholas et in singulos libros*). There is, however, no evidence for σχολαί being a philosophical genre with a well-defined form and structure throughout the Hellenistic period. Cicero considers *scholae* as a typical Greek philosophical discourse, and while in *On Moral Ends* he dissociates himself from it (*Fin.* 2.1.1), in the *Tusculan Disputations* he tries his hand at it (*Tusc.* 1.4.7–8) (for Cicero's attitude to *scholae*, see Gorman 2005, 65–73; Gildenhard 2007, 12–14).

[99] Pythodorus: Philodemus, *Acad. ind.* col. xx.42–4; Zeno of Alexandria and Hagnon: col. xxii.35–xxiii.6. On Lacydes, cf. Diogenes Laertius 5.41: τοῦτο λέγειν Ἕρμιππον παρατιθέμενον ἱστορεῖν Ἀρκεσίλαον τὸν Πιταναῖον ἐν οἷς ἔφασκε πρὸς Λακύδην τὸν Κυρηναῖον; Görler 1994, 786 notes that Hermippus could have referred to "durch Arkesilaos autorisierte Aufzeichnungen des Lakydes."

most prominent of Carneades' students, a prolific writer, and a scholarch of the Academy, preserved his teacher's legacy in numerous writings. We may assume that like *Sokratikoi logoi* reporting Socrates' conversations and Arrian's records of Epictetus' discourses, such accounts of the New Academy philosophers' instructions favored the informal, colloquial, and spontaneous over a polished and carefully structured text.

Cicero in several passages emphasizes that the skeptical Academy developed distinct forms of discourse. In *On Moral Ends*, he provides a concise overview of evolution of philosophical formats in the Academy (*Fin.* 2.1.2–3):

> is [i.e. Socrates] enim percontando atque interrogando elicere solebat eorum opiniones, quibuscum disserebat, ut ad ea, quae ii respondissent, si quid videretur, diceret. qui mos cum a posterioribus non esset retentus, Arcesilas eum revocavit instituitque ut ii, qui se audire vellent, non de se quaererent, sed ipsi dicerent, quid sentirent; quod cum dixissent, ille contra. sed eum qui audiebant, quoad poterant, defendebant sententiam suam. apud ceteros autem philosophos, qui quaesivit aliquid, tacet; quod quidem iam fit etiam in Academia. ubi enim is, qui audire vult, ita dixit: 'Voluptas mihi videtur esse summum bonum', perpetua oratione contra disputatur, ut facile intellegi possit eos, qui aliquid sibi videri dicant, non ipsos in ea sententia esse, sed audire velle contraria.

> He [i.e. Socrates] used to elicit views of interlocutors by means of questions and cross-examination, so that he might express his views in reply to their answers. This habit was not kept by his successors; but Arcesilaus revived it and established that those who wanted to hear him, should not ask him questions, but should state their own views; when they had done so, he argued against them. Those who listened to him would defend their opinions as well as they could. But with other philosophers, the one who has asked the question remains then silent—this indeed happens nowadays in the Academy. When the person who wants to listen says, for example, "It is my opinion that pleasure is chief good," then it is argued against this view in continuous speech, so that it is easily seen that those who say that they held certain opinion, do not themselves believe it, but want to hear arguments against it.

In this diachronic account, Cicero distinguishes four phases of development of philosophical discourse in the Academy, of which the last two stages are of interest here: Arcesilaus' revival of the Socratic dialectic and the practice of Cicero's contemporary Academics which evolved from it.[100] The form of discourse

---

[100] Cf. also Cicero, *De or.* 3.18.67, about Arcesilaus: *primumque instituisse... non quid ipse sentiret ostendere, sed contra id, quod quisque se sentire dixisset, disputare*; 3.21.80: *...hoc Arcesilae modo et Carneadi contra omne quod propositum sit disserat...*; *Nat. D.* 1.5.11: *ratio contra omnia disserendi nullamque rem aperte iudicandi*. For a discussion of the Socratic background of Arcesilaus' skeptical

developed by Arcesilaus and that used by contemporary Academics share a key feature: they open with a thesis which provides a starting point for refutation.[101] They differ in two important aspects: Arcesilaus argued against the personal opinions of his interlocutors, who were actively defending them, while Cicero's contemporaries argued against a thesis proposed by someone who did not subsequently engage in discussion. Arcesilean discourse, then, was a dialogue involving two interlocutors engaged in a cooperative disputation, with unambiguous discursive roles assigned, that of a philosopher-teacher and a student-*hetairos*; later Academic development was a simplification of this model.

The passage, unfortunately, lacks precision, as Cicero does not specify who the "other philosophers" who simplified the Arcesilean discourse were; consequently, it is unclear when the simplified form—a thesis followed by a continuous refutation—developed. Clitomachus may have reported Carneades' instruction in this format. In the *Tusculan Disputations* Cicero says that after the destruction of Carthage in 146 BCE Clitomachus sent to his fellow citizens a consolation[102] which included a discourse by Carneades, still alive at the time (*Tusc.* 3.22.54):

> in eo est disputatio scripta Carneadis, quam se ait in commentarium rettulisse. Cum ita positum esset, videri fore in aegritudine sapientem patria capta, quae Carneades contra dixerit, scripta sunt.
>
> It contains a disputation by Carneades which Clitomachus took down in his notes. The opinion stated as the thesis is that the wise person would be grieved if his homeland were to be conquered in war. Then are recorded Carneades' arguments in the negative.   (trans. M. Graver)

The form of Carneades' discourse as presented by Cicero conforms with the simplified Academic discourse, in which a thesis is followed by a refutation in continuous speech. Admittedly, Cicero may not be precise, and Clitomachus' account might have included additional interventions of the person who proposed the thesis.

To return to Arcesilaus: the type of discourse which he developed appears to have been a lively discussion in which refutation was interspersed with utterances of his interlocutors. This is confirmed by Cicero's claim that Arcesilaus revived the Socratic dialectic and by Diogenes Laertius' statement that Arcesilaus was "the

---

turn, see Annas 1994; Shields 1994; for Cicero's Socrates, conceived primarily as the initiator of the dialectic method of the skeptical Academy, see Long 1995, 44; and a thorough discussion in Gorman 2005.

[101] For the *thesis*-argument format, cf. also Cicero's *Paradoxa Stoicorum*, where Stoic philosophical theses are stated and next defended (rather than refuted, as in the *Tusculan Disputations*).

[102] For the consolation to the Carthaginians and the complex identity of figures such as Clitomachus (a Carthaginian living in Athens and being on good terms with several Romans), see Momigliano 1975, 5. For Cicero's use in the *Tusculan Disputations* of Carneades' discourse quoted by Clitomachus, see Ioppolo 1980.

first one who changed the traditional Platonic discourse and made it, by means of question and answer, more combative/eristic" (4.28: πρῶτος τὸν λόγον ἐκίνησε τὸν ὑπὸ Πλάτωνος παραδεδομένον καὶ ἐποίησε δι' ἐρωτήσεως καὶ ἀποκρίσεως ἐριστικώτερον). These accounts of Arcesilaus' transformation of Academic discourse allow us to presume that at least some records of his σχολαί, and perhaps of other Academic skeptics, were in the form of a dialogue between a philosopher and his students.

Cicero's own *Tusculan Disputations*, known for their unusual dialogue form, may be the closest parallel to these lost texts of the New Academy. Cicero introduces there two figures: a dominant *persona* of a philosopher—from prefaces we know that he is Cicero himself—and a cooperative student-companion.[103] The latter proposes a thesis, which is next argued against by the philosopher. The text consists partially of dialectical exchanges, and partially of Cicero's continuous expositions. Cicero himself announces that this structure is informed by the discourse forms of the skeptical Academy when in a preface to *Book* 1 he describes the format of the *Tusculan Disputations* in a manner reminiscent of *On Moral Ends* 2.1.2–3, quoted above (*Tusc.* 1.4.8):

> Fiebat autem ita ut, cum is qui audire vellet dixisset, quid sibi videretur, tum ego contra dicerem. Haec est enim, ut scis, vetus et Socratica ratio contra alterius opinionem disserendi. Nam ita facillime quid veri simillimum esse inveniri posse Socrates arbitrabatur.

> The procedure was that, after the would-be listener had expressed his view, I opposed it. This, as you know, is the old Socratic method of arguing against your adversary's position; for Socrates thought that in this way the probable truth was most readily discovered.[104]   (trans. J. E. King)

The Academic provenance of the format of the *Tusculan Disputations* is also mentioned in *On Fate* 4 by Cicero's friend Hirtius, who observes that the dialogue follows *Academicorum contra propositum disputandi consuetudinem*. The fact that Cicero's interlocutor in the *Tusculan Disputations* does not disappear after stating the theses and appears to believe in them—or at least to be troubled by them—affiliates the dialogue with the Arcesilean type of discourse, as do dialectical exchanges between Cicero and his conversation partner.[105]

---

[103] For Cicero's characterization of himself and the interlocutor, see Gildenhard 2007, 64–78.

[104] *Fin.* 2.1.2: <u>qui se audire vellent</u>, non de se quaererent, sed ipsi <u>dicerent, quid sentirent</u>; quod cum dixissent, ille <u>contra</u> ~ *Tusc.* 1.4.8: *fiebat autem ita ut, cum* <u>qui audire vellet dixisset, quid sibi videretur</u>, *tum ego* <u>contra</u> *dicerem*. Cf. also *Tusc.* 5.4.11, where Cicero draws a link between the *Tusculan Disputations* and Carneadean discourse; 1.4.7–1.4.8 where discussions reported there are characterized as Greek-style *scholae* (*scholas Graecorum more habere auderemus... quinque scholas, ut Graeci appellant, in totidem libros contuli*).

[105] Gildenhard 2007, 18–19 believes that in the *Tusculan Disputations* Cicero follows a simplified Academic format, but alters it in one detail by making his interlocutor believe in what he proposes and

Another of Cicero's dialogues written in the fashion of the New Academy is *On Fate*, in which Cicero converses with Hirtius. In the dialogue (unfortunately, only fragmentarily preserved), Hirtius expresses a wish to provide a thesis in order to hear Cicero talk (4: *ponere aliquid ad quod audiam... volo*); the phrasing suggests that he does not intend to express his own view, but, as in post-Arcesilean Academic discourse, to stimulate Cicero to discuss a problem at length. The thesis is lost; the extant text contains Cicero's refutation of the Stoic concept of fate and the Epicurean attempt to save free-will by introducing the notion of the "swerve" of atoms. Hirtius does not interrupt Cicero in the extant passages, which likewise implies an affinity between *On Fate* and the post-Arcesilean, simplified Academic form.

A striking feature of the *Tusculan Disputations* missing from *On Fate* and other Cicero's dialogues is the anonymity of the speakers accompanied by a modest elaboration of the setting (information on the circumstances of the reported conversations is placed mostly in the preface). Anonymous speakers appear in some dialogues of the *Appendix Platonica*, such as *On Justice* and *On Virtue* (where Socrates converses with an unidentified interlocutor) and *Demodocus* 2–4 (where neither part is identified). Cicero's recurrent insistence on the distinctly Academic format of the *Tusculan Disputations* makes one wonder whether the speakers' anonymity could have been popular in the skeptical Academy.

## 3.8 Conclusion

Dialogues of all sorts were composed by Plato's early successors and philosophers associated with the Old Academy. Preserved titles of works by Heraclides of Pontus, Speusippus, and Xenocrates suggest that they might have composed Socratic dialogues. At the same time, novel non-Socratic formats were also developed. Heraclides of Pontus played a particularly important role in pushing the dialogue in new directions, drawing from pre-Socratic philosophy (he was fascinated with the figures of Pythagoras and Empedocles), inventing marvelous stories, and experimenting with a variety of historical settings. Although we tend to consider him above all as an author of historical dialogues, his dialogues were diverse and allow for a threefold typology (comic, tragic, in the middle style); he was also interested in poetry and probably discussed Homer in a few of his dialogues.

---

utter "deeply felt personal credos"; as a result, the *Tusculan Disputations* are "much closer to the Socratic elenchus: a testing of a person... and his system of beliefs"; in his view Cicero combines the *oratio perpetua* "with elements of Socratic inquisition... and the sort of follow-up debate that is the hallmark of Arcesilaus." On the form of the *Tusculan Disputations* see also Douglas 1995; Gorman 2005, 64–84; see also Wynne 2020, who argues for a skeptical character of the dialogue and thinks that Cicero might have modeled it after Clitomachus' consolation to Carthaginians.

We know very little about the works written by Crantor (there is no catalogue of his writings), but he was also apparently interested in developing the literary layer. Whether he composed self-standing dialogues is unknown, but his contest between personifications of goods provides an example of the use of dialogized stories in ethical discourse. His *On Grief*, which gave rise to the genre of consolation, while itself not a dialogue, developed out of the tradition of Academic and Peripatetic dialogues on death, and inspired in turn later dialogue writers, such as the author of the pseudo-Platonic *Axiochus*.

The New Academy of Arcesilaus and his successors introduced new forms of oral and written discourse, suitable for skeptical reasoning. A thesis was proposed by a student, followed by a refutation by a philosopher-teacher, either with or without the former's interventions. Cicero's *Tusculan Disputations* and *On Fate* were composed in the fashion of the New Academy and provide the closest extant parallels to the formats developed in it.

The dialogue format was not abandoned in the Middle Platonism. We know very little about the works of Antiochus of Ascalon, the philosopher responsible for the dogmatic turn, but his *Sosus*, responding to Philo of Larissa, was probably a dialogue. The departure from the skepticism of the New Academy yet again caused a change in discursive strategies and, as a result, presumably also in literary forms. The dialogues of Plutarch, which lie beyond the chronological boundaries of the book, illustrate these potentialities.

# 4
# Platonic *Dubia* and the *Appendix Platonica*

## 4.1 Introductory Remarks

Unlike other parts of the book, this chapter examines a body of extant dialogues rather than fragmentary evidence and testimonia left by later writers. For this reason, Platonic *dubia* and *spuria* are of particular interest to a scholar of post-Platonic dialogue, even though when approaching them one faces fundamental difficulties attempting to establish their authorship, dating, and intellectual background.

Two types of dialogues will be discussed in this chapter: dubious works that were included in antiquity in the so-called "Thrasyllan canon" (= *dubia*) and texts which were not accepted in the canon, sometimes referred to as the *Appendix Platonica* (= *spuria*). This distinction is based on information given by Diogenes Laertius who, quoting as a source Tiberius' court astrologer Thrasyllus, provides a catalogue of thirty-six of Plato's works (thirty-four dialogues, the *Apology*, and the *Epistles*), organized in tetralogies and provided with double titles, usually consisting of a name and a topic (3.57–61). Apart from the dialogues organized in the tetralogies, he also gives a list of dialogues not included in them, which he calls "bastard" dialogues (3.62: νοθεύονται).[1]

While Thrasyllus apparently claimed that Plato himself published his works in tetralogies, the arrangement must date to a later time, though it is not clear to when.[2] The authenticity of some dialogues from the Thrasyllan catalogue was doubted already in antiquity (*Epinomis*, *Hipparchus*, *Alcibiades II*, and *Rival Lovers*), and most scholars agree today that inclusion of a dialogue in the tetralogies does not prove Plato's authorship. Many dialogues from the Thrasyllan canon were athetized by scholars at some time or another in an attempt to maintain the coherence of the Platonic corpus or because they were deemed too unsophisticated to have been written by Plato.[3] In past decades, a more inclusive

---

[1] For a recent discussion of the possible meaning of the verb, see Joyal 2014.
[2] Cf. Diogenes Laertius 3.56: Θράσυλος δέ φησι καὶ κατὰ τὴν τραγικὴν τετραλογίαν ἐκδοῦναι αὐτὸν [sc. Plato] τοὺς διαλόγους. Scholars disagree whether Thrasyllus' organization of the dialogues goes back to the early Academy or not, and whether it precedes or postdates the division of the dialogues into trilogies, attributed by Diogenes Laertius to Aristophanes of Byzantium (3.61–2); for discussion, see e.g. Philip 1970; Müller 1975, 22–41; Solmsen 1981; Pangle 1987a, 1–20; Tarrant 1993, 85–107; Mansfeld 1994, 58–107.
[3] As Tigerstedt 1977, 19 notes, the problem is that "there is no agreement among scholars as to the real nature of Platonic philosophy." On the "atheticist attacks" on Plato's corpus, see Bowen 1988, 52; on the "fluidity of the Platonic canon," Charalabopoulos 2012, 12–16.

approach prevailed, and efforts were made to re-integrate some of the dubious dialogues back into the corpus of Plato's works, with scholars arguing, with varying success, for Plato's authorship of *Greater Hippias, Alcibiades I, Rival Lovers, Hipparchus, Minos, Epinomis,* and *Cleitophon*.[4] Selection of the dialogues to be discussed in this chapter was therefore not straightforward; I decided to include seven dialogues (*Epinomis, Hipparchus, Minos, Theages, Cleitophon, Alcibiades II,* and *Rival Lovers*) which the majority of scholars consider unauthentic, but which provide interesting material for studying the development of the dialogue format.

Diogenes' list of "bastard dialogues" includes *Midon, Horsebreeder, Eryxias or Erasistratus, Halcyon, Acephali or Sisyphus, Axiochus, Phaeacians, Demodocus, Chelidon, The Seventh Day,* and *Epimenides*. Of these, five works are preserved: *Eryxias, Halcyon, Sisyphus, Axiochus,* and *Demodocus* (if the text—or, strictly speaking, four separate compositions preserved under this title—is identical with the work listed by Diogenes). In addition, medieval manuscripts contain two brief dialogues, *On Justice* and *On Virtue*, which appear neither in the Thrasyllan tetralogies nor on the list of Diogenes' "bastard" works. These seven dialogues, now almost unanimously considered spurious, constitute the *Appendix Platonica*.

Examination of the Platonic *dubia* and dialogues of the *Appendix Platonica* poses serious challenges. It is a diverse group of texts whose authorship, dating, and philosophical environment remain debatable, and scholars working on them frequently come to strikingly different conclusions. In several cases, it is impossible to rule out the possibility of Plato's authorship based on firm, objective evidence. Some scholars question the very polarity of the labels "genuine" and "spurious," arguing that there is a wide range of possibilities between them: for instance, some dialogues might have been Plato's unfinished drafts, perhaps later elaborated, revised, and made "publishable" by his students. Categories of shared and collective authorship, semi-authenticity and semi-spuriousness have also been proposed, complicating the issue.[5] In many cases, disagreement regarding dating leads to conflicting interpretations: where some discern allusions to Hellenistic period philosophical schools or veiled references to Alexander the Great, others see concepts that could have easily originated in Socratic milieus. Moreover, while numerous verbal parallels have been noted between the pseudo-Platonica and Plato (and occasionally Xenophon and Aristotle), in some cases it is debatable whether these parallels reflect a direct influence between the texts and, if so, which work alludes to which. This chapter has no ambitions to solve these

---

[4] For the *Greater Hippias*, see Woodruff 1982, 93–104; *Alcibiades I*: Denyer 2001; *Rival Lovers*: Annas 1985; *Hipparchus* and *Minos*: Bloom 1987; Cobb 1988; Mulroy 2007; *Epinomis*: Altman 2012; *Cleitophon*: Slings 1999; and contributions in Kremer 2004a.

[5] See e.g. Gigon 1955, 15; Thesleff 1967, 12–13 (who speaks of "semi-spurious material" and asks: "how much is authentic material in the spurious works, and how much is interpolation in the authentic ones?"); Tarrant 2018, 390–3.

problems; nor does it offer comprehensive analysis of the texts discussed, which would demand far more space than is available. Its aim is to provide an overview of the *dubia* and *spuria* with focus on their recurrent features, such as frequent use of anonymous speakers, brevity accompanied by conciseness and certain abruptness, and concentration on one problem, clearly stated in the opening. A crucial feature of the *dubia* and *spuria* is an extensive intellectual and literary interaction with Plato, which can take a variety of forms—mirroring dramatic settings, employing Plato's interlocutors, reusing and modifying his themes and motifs, sewing in phrases originating from one or many Platonic dialogues. Such elements taken from Platonic dialogues are sometimes incorporated in works which develop strikingly un-Platonic concepts and arguments, and can coexist with references to and interaction with other authors and intellectual traditions. Extensive conceptual and intertextual engagement with Plato is a constitutive feature of the pseudo-Platonica, and it is useful to consider their practices within the broader context of Hellenistic period's literary trends, in particular its hallmark employment of mimetic techniques by which authors evoke subtext and at the same time signal their departure from it (*variatio* and *oppositio in imitando*).

## 4.2 Selected *Dubia* in the Thrasyllan Canon

### 4.2.1 The *Epinomis*

According to Diogenes Laertius (3.62), Aristophanes of Byzantium made the *Epinomis* part of a trilogy with the *Minos* and the *Laws*; this implies that the dialogue was included in the Platonic corpus from an early date, around the end of the third century BCE. Scholars today tend to consider the *Epinomis* as spurious, largely under the influence of Tarán (though arguments for Plato's authorship are occasionally raised).[6] The dialogue's authenticity was also occasionally questioned in antiquity. Diogenes Laertius reports that some claimed that the author was Philip of Opus, who also copied out the *Laws* (3.37). According to the anonymous *Prolegomena to Platonic Philosophy*, Proclus argued against Plato's authorship on two grounds: first, tradition held the *Laws* to be Plato's last, unfinished text, and therefore the philosopher could not have composed the *Epinomis*; second, there are some conceptual differences between the dialogue and Plato's other works.[7]

---

[6] For arguments against Plato's authorship, see above all Tarán 1975, and more recently, Brisson 2005; the authenticity of the dialogue was defended by e.g. Des Places 1931; Des Places 1942; Des Places 1952; Festugière 1973; and recently Altman 2012. See also the overview of the discussion in Krämer 2004², 84.

[7] Cf. *Proleg. in Plat. phil.* 25.2–10 which relates that Proclus proved that the *Epinomis* is spurious by two arguments: "the first of which is this: since death prevented Plato from revising the *Laws*, he cannot

In the early imperial period, Nicomachus of Gerasa referred to the *Epinomis* as the "thirteenth book of the *Laws*."[8]

According to Diogenes Laertius (3.60), the *Epinomis* had two additional titles: Νυκτερινὸς σύλλογος (*Nocturnal Council*) and Φιλόσοφος (*The Philosopher*). The latter derives from the main focus of the dialogue, namely the problem of wisdom and a proper educatory program (*Epin.* 973a: τὸ τῆς φρονήσεως, 973b: τί ποτε μαθὼν θνητὸς ἄνθρωπος σοφὸς ἂν εἴη), which to some degree overlaps with the philosophers' education proposed in Book 7 of the *Republic*.[9] The titles *Epinomis* and *Nocturnal Council* emphasize the connection between the dialogue and Plato's *Laws*: the former title pronounces it an appendix or sequel to them,[10] the latter connects it thematically by referring to the institution of the Nocturnal Council discussed by the Athenian in the *Laws*. The Council was conceived there as a body consisting of, among others, the ten eldest Guardians, a supervisor of education, and some chosen younger men. It was to gather every day at dawn and proceed until the sun was up in the sky; its aim was to discuss the laws of the city, foreign laws, and teachings that illuminated legal matters (*Lg.* 951d–952a, 961a–b).[11] At the end of the *Laws*, the Athenian refuses to legislate regarding the activities of the council and its education (*Lg.* 968d: ἃ δεῖ μανθάνειν), arguing that these issues should be left to the council itself and decided after it has been established. The *Epinomis* picks up from there, purporting to fill in this resolutely unfilled gap. At the beginning of the dialogue, it is revealed that the characters of the *Laws* have agreed to meet again to discuss the unexplored question of wisdom and the means to achieve it; after going over the curriculum required, the dialogue concludes by deeming it suitable for the members of the Nocturnal Council.

The *Epinomis* draws on the *Laws* distinctly and presupposes the readers' familiarity with it. The main speaker is never identified as an Athenian (he is addressed merely as ὦ ξένε), and the reader is expected to identify the conversation participants from the opening sentence, spoken by Cleinias: "We have come to do what we agreed, my friend—the three of us, I, you, and Megillus here" (*Epin.* 973a). The figures of Cleinias and Megillus (who remains silent throughout the dialogue) bring little to the conversation, acting rather as an extension of the dialogic setting of the *Laws*. While the *Laws–Epinomis* pair has parallels in other

---

possible have written the *Epinomis* after it; the second is: in his other dialogues he says that the planets move from right to left, in the *Epinomis*, on the contrary, from left to right" (trans. Westerink 2011²). For Proclus' arguments, see Tarán 1975, 8–11; Brisson 2005, 22.

[8] Asclepius, *In Nicomachi intr. arithm.* 1.24: ...ἐν τῷ τρισκαιδεκάτῳ τῶν νόμων τῷ καλουμένῳ φιλοσόφῳ....

[9] Brisson 2005, 15–16.

[10] The title used most frequently is ἡ Ἐπινομίς, though Theon of Smyrna in the early imperial period and the *Prolegomena to Platonic Philosophy* used the form τὸ Ἐπινόμιον. For a discussion of the title ("the little supplement to the *Laws*") and its formation, see Brisson 2005, 12–13.

[11] Despite the importance of the institution for the city of Magnesia (it is referred to as "the anchor of the whole city" and the "salvation of the government and the laws") its role remains obscure; see discussion in Morrow 1993², 500–15.

dialogue sequences in the Platonic corpus—such as the pairings *Timaeus-Critias* and *Sophist-Statesman*—its peculiarity is that the *Epinomis* reopens an exploration that had been explicitly pronounced closed in the *Laws*. This incompatibility is one of the grounds for rejecting Plato's authorship of the sequel.[12]

The purpose of the *Epinomis* is to decide on the education essential for acquiring wisdom, and at its core the dialogue discusses various types of knowledge. Ultimately, the Athenian decides that real wisdom should be identified with the science of numbers, which is a gift to humankind bestowed by the supreme divinity, referred to as Ouranos. There follows a discussion of the constitution and categories of living beings, and then, an explanation of the true nature of the gods: the highest divinities are identified with celestial bodies; they are followed in the hierarchy by *daimones* and other imperceptible beings who fill the heavens. The ultimate virtue is identified with piety, while the highest form of wisdom—with knowledge about the supreme gods, that is, with astronomy. Preliminary studies include arithmetic, geometry, stereometry, and harmonics.[13] At the end of the dialogue, the Athenian states—and pronounces his statement legally binding (*Epin*. 992d: ἰδίᾳ λέγομεν καὶ δημοσίᾳ κατὰ νόμον τίθεμεν)—that the highest offices should be bestowed upon those who have mastered these studies, and that the Nocturnal Council should be urged to pursue them. The dialogue, then, begins and ends with a reminiscence of the *Laws*.

The philosophical theology of the *Epinomis* develops the themes of Book 10 of the *Laws*, in which the Athenian introduces a law against impiety and argues for the existence of the gods and their care for human beings.[14] The *Epinomis* refers to this section of the *Laws* explicitly and proclaims itself its continuation (*Epin*. 980c–d):

θεογονίαν τοίνυν καὶ ζῳογονίαν ἀναγκαῖον, ὡς ἔοικεν, πρῶτόν μοι, κακῶς ἀπεικασάντων τῶν ἔμπροσθεν, βέλτιον ἀπεικάσαι κατὰ τὸν ἔμπροσθεν λόγον, ἀναλαβόντα ὃν πρὸς τοὺς ἀσεβεῖς ἐπικεχείρηκα λέγων, φράζων ὡς εἰσὶν θεοὶ ἐπιμελούμενοι πάντων, σμικρῶν καὶ μειζόνων, καὶ σχεδὸν ἀπαραμύθητοι τῶν περὶ τὰ δίκαιά εἰσιν πράγματα—εἰ δὴ μέμνησθέ γε, ὦ Κλεινία· ἐλάβετε μὲν γὰρ δὴ καὶ ὑπομνήματα—καὶ γὰρ ἦν τὰ ῥηθέντα τότε καὶ μάλα ἀληθῆ· τόδε δὲ αὐτῶν ἦν τὸ μέγιστον, ὅτι πρεσβύτερον εἴη ψυχὴ σώματος ἅπασα παντός—ἆρα μέμνησθε; ἢ πάντως που τοῦτό γε;

Since people in the past have failed badly in describing the generation of gods and living things, it appears that I must begin by constructing an account based on

---

[12] Tarán 1975, 22–4.
[13] For a discussion of the philosophical content of the *Epinomis*, see Tarán 1975; Dillon 2003, 183–97; Krämer 2004², 86–92.
[14] For Book 10 of the *Laws* and its context, see Morrow 1993², 470–96; Mayhew 2008 provides a thorough commentary.

my previous one, taking up again my attack on impious accounts, and declaring that there are gods who care for all things, great and small, who are inexorable in matters of justice. I suppose you remember, Cleinias, since you have even received a written record. What we said then was quite true. The most important point was that as a whole, soul is older than anybody. Do you recall? You surely must remember. (trans. R. D. McKirahan, Jr.)

The passage contains a succinct summary of the Athenian's argument in Book 10 of *Laws*, where three conceptions are identified as being at the root of impiety: that the gods do not exist, that they exist but do not care about people, and that they care but can be influenced with sacrifices and prayers.[15] Remarkably, the Athenian expects his companions not only to remember the discussion but to possess a written account (ὑπομνήματα) of it.[16] The author may have been inspired by two self-referential passages of the *Laws* in which the Athenian alludes to a conversation he is carrying on with Cleinias and Megillus as a written text (*Lg.* 811b–e, 817b). But while in the *Laws* the written account is seen as being useful for civic education of the young, in the *Epinomis* it is to serve Cleinias and Megillus as a reminder of the Athenian's arguments and expositions; as a result, the two elderly men are somewhat oddly cast as diligent students, expected to have been re-reading and memorizing the previous discussion. The author seems to conflate, perhaps playfully, the dramatic world with the extratextual experience of his audience, readers of Plato's *Laws*—and he invites them to read the *Epinomis* with particular passages of Plato's dialogue in mind. In this respect the *Epinomis* conveys the atmosphere of a philosophical school, in which arguments are written down, disseminated, read, discussed, supplemented, and expanded.[17]

Within the dramatic frame of the *Epinomis*, the ostensible purpose of the Athenian's discussion is to sketch out a model of proper education for the people ruling the imaginary Magnesia; but what message does the text carry for its readers? The *Epinomis* shares certain preoccupations and themes with protreptic texts, such as Plato's *Euthydemus*, Book 1 of Aristotle's *Metaphysics*, and

---

[15] Cf. Plato, *Lg.* 885b: Θεοὺς ἡγούμενος εἶναι κατὰ νόμους οὐδεὶς πώποτε οὔτε ἔργον ἀσεβὲς ἠργάσατο ἑκὼν οὔτε λόγον ἀφῆκεν ἄνομον, ἀλλὰ ἓν δή τι τῶν τριῶν πάσχων, ἢ τοῦτο, ὅπερ εἶπον, οὐχ ἡγούμενος, ἢ τὸ δεύτερον ὄντας οὐ φροντίζειν ἀνθρώπων, ἢ τρίτον εὐπαραμυθήτους εἶναι θυσίαις τε καὶ εὐχαῖς παραγομένους. The three parts of the argument begin at, respectively, *Lg.* 893b, 899d, 901d.

[16] Tarán 1975, 259–60 and Brisson 2005, 19–20 note that ἐλάβετε ὑπομνήματα has two potential meanings: (1) "you have taken notes"; (2) "you have received notes." But there is no evidence of the former idiom in the Classical or Hellenistic period; in Plato we find more specific expression ὑπομνήματα γράφειν (*Tht.* 143a, *Plt.* 295c) used for "writing down notes, recollections, reminders." For the second meaning ("to receive notes"), cf. [Plato,] *Ep.* 12.359c: ὑπομνήματα... ἐλάβομεν. Cf. also *Phdr.* 276d, where the knowledgeable author is said to write in order to store ὑπομνήματα, "reminders," for himself.

[17] Brisson 2005, 17–21 speaks of "scholastic background" of the dialogue.

his *Protrepticus*;[18] it is an exhortation to pursue wisdom and engage in scientific study: happiness, the Athenian says, depends on wisdom and a knowledge of mathematics and astronomy. Such recommendations are directed not so much at a general audience as at a limited group of people interested in and capable of pursuing philosophical studies. The author's clear expectation that his readers are familiar with the *Laws* implies that the intended audience consists of fellow philosophers, and the dialogue's purpose is to present the author's philosophical theology and to outline the proper course of a philosophical education.

While it is perhaps not impossible to imagine Plato himself writing an addendum to his own dialogue, it appears more probable that the *Epinomis* is an "exercise in pseudepigraphy,"[19] evocative of the spirit of the Old Academy, where Plato's dialogues served as a point of reference and elaboration, but also provided a hypotextual stratum recalled and evoked by a variety of literary techniques. Since antiquity it has been proposed that the author of the *Epinomis* was Philip of Opus, who is also reported to have arranged for the publication of the *Laws*, left unfinished by Plato. He is referred to by Philodemus as ἀστρολόγος and ἀναγραφεύς ("secretary"?) of Plato (*Acad. ind.* col. iii.35-9).[20] The *Suda* ascribes to him several works dealing with ethics, astronomy, and mathematics (s.v. φιλόσοφος (φ 418); Philip's name is lost, but the contents of the entry points to him). Philip might also have written a work reporting an encounter between Plato and a Chaldaean wise man.[21] His authorship would help explain stylistic similarities between the *Epinomis* and the *Laws*, but as Tarán emphasizes, we are dealing here with "the realm of what is merely possible and at best probable but not certain."

### 4.2.2 *Hipparchus or The Lover of Gain*

Doubts regarding the authenticity of the dialogue were first raised in antiquity. While various dates have been proposed, the tendency is to situate the composition of the work in the first half of the fourth century BCE.[22] It is a dramatic

---

[18] For protreptic character of the *Epinomis*, see Einarson 1936; Festugière 1973 (who takes the *Epinomis* as Plato's own work and calls it "un Protreptique à la Sagesse, et... le dernier Protreptique de Platon" (9); Tarán 1975, 66-9 ("undeniably a protreptic to the purer and happy life"). For similarities between the *Epinomis* and Aristotle, see Einarson 1936; Tarán 1975, 140-50.

[19] Dillon 2003, 188.

[20] Philip's name is not preserved in the papyrus, but it is inferred from the context that the passage refers to him. The term ἀναγραφεύς is rare; Lysias, *In Nic.* 2 and 25, uses it in the context of transcribing laws. Testimonies which seem to refer to Philip of Opus have been collected and discussed by Tarán 1975, 115-39, but the evidence is difficult to interpret as the texts may not refer to one person.

[21] See Chapter 3.3, n. 39.

[22] For ancient doubts, see Aelian, *VH* 8.2. Friedländer 1930, 117-27 considered it is one of the earliest dialogues of Plato, while recent scholars who accept Plato's authorship include Bloom 1987 and Mulroy 2007. Souilhé 1930a, 51-8 thinks that it was composed by a Socratic author in the first half of the fourth century, before Thucydides wrote his work; Schorn 2005 and Aronadio 2008, 50-3 reject

dialogue reporting a conversation between Socrates and an interlocutor whose identity remains undisclosed. The time and place are unspecified, but nothing suggests that the conversation takes place outside of Athens, the usual setting of a Socratic dialogue. Socrates is an older man (*Hipparch.* 225e–226a: με... ἄνδρα πρεσβύτερον) and a dominant figure, initiating and leading the conversation by asking questions. His interlocutor is a young Athenian (*Hipparch.* 226a, 228b); he answers Socrates willingly and, though frustrated and confused at times, does not question the usefulness of the inquiry. He is not a completely colorless figure: when asked to define profit-lovers, he resorts to disapproving moral vocabulary (*Hipparch.* 225a–b); elsewhere he gets annoyed and accuses Socrates of deceiving him (*Hipparch.* 228a); and at the end, he remains unwilling to whole-heartedly agree with Socrates (*Hipparch.* 232b).

The dialogue opens with a straightforward question posed by Socrates: what is greed (τὸ φιλοκερδές) and who are greedy people (οἱ φιλοκερδεῖς).[23] As is frequently the case in *dubia* and *spuria*, the question is not triggered by a specific event or situation, which provides the conversation with an air of academic discussion. Socrates' companion condemns greed as morally reprehensible, but Socrates notes that τὸ φιλοκερδές literally means "love of profit," and that profit, as the opposite of loss, must be always good; consequently, everyone is a lover of profit. The conclusion at the end of the dialogue is that one cannot censure someone for being φιλοκερδής, because this term can be used to describe everyone, including the accuser.

In the middle of the discussion of greed, Socrates digresses and discusses the figure of Hipparchus whom he considers the eldest son of Peisistratus and a tyrant after the latter's death. It is not clear how this digression connects with the discussion of greed, though the figure of a tyrant was closely associated with greed in the ancient imagination, and in Plato's *Republic* the part of the soul characterized as φιλοκερδές is associated with the tyrannical disposition of the soul.[24] In Socrates' account, however, Hipparchus is a lover of wisdom and a zealous educator who brought Homer's poems to Athens, introduced rhapsodes' recitation at Panathenaia, and invited the poets Simonides and Anacreon to the city. After he thought that the people in the city were sufficiently educated, he turned his attention to the countryfolk: he put herms at roads between the city and demes and engraved on them his own sayings in elegiacs as evidence of his

---

Plato's authorship and propose the 380s as the date. Thesleff 1982, 229, who rejects Plato's authorship on account of, among others, the dialogue's linguistic oddities, stipulates that there may be a connection between the digression about Hipparchus and the murder of Dion of Syracuse.

[23] τὸ φιλοκερδές or φιλοκερδεία are not typical Classical prose terms for greed, which is referred to as πλεονεξία (Weber 1967). It was used by poets (Theognis, *Eleg.* 1.198; Pindar, *Isthm.* 2.6; Aristophanes, *Plut.* 591); and Plato in Book 9 of the *Republic* (581c) in reference to one of three parts of the soul (φιλόσοφον, φιλόνικον, and φιλοκερδές). Cf. also distinction between ἀνὴρ φιλότιμος and ἀνὴρ φιλοκερδής in Xenophon's *Oec.* 14.10.3. See also Massaro and Massaro 1997, 117–18.

[24] Massaro 1997, 31. For an attempt to connect the story of Hipparchus with the general theme of the dialogue, see also Tipton 1999; Mulroy 2007.

wisdom (ἐπιδείγματα τῆς σοφίας). He wanted people to consider his words wiser (μᾶλλον σοφά) than Delphic pronouncements, and hoped some people would be inspired to move from the country to the city to obtain more education. Socrates claims that Hipparchus was murdered by Harmodius and Aristogeiton because of his wisdom and educative mission: the two were jealous that a certain youth, Harmodius' former lover, had begun to associate with Hipparchus and favored his wisdom over theirs (*Hipparch.* 229b-d).

In Socrates' account, Hipparchus is an Athenian cultural hero, an image strikingly different from his representation in Thucydides and other sources,[25] though the author appears to have drawn from an alternative historical tradition rather than having fabricated the story.[26] However, although Socrates in the dialogue appears to applaud and rehabilitate Hipparchus (and the tyrant's death, which is presented as a direct result of his educative activity, is somewhat reminiscent of Socrates' fate),[27] this positive appraisal of the tyrant's actions is destabilized by some aspects of the story. The tyrant's desire to compete with the Delphic oracle is anything but prudent and commendable, while the installation of the herms with his own poetry suggests that his chief motivation was self-promotion and self-aggrandizement. These various dimensions of the account undermine each other, suggesting a certain irony underpinning the dialogue.[28]

### 4.2.3 *Minos or On Law*

The *Minos* is sometimes called a "twin dialogue" of the *Hipparchus* and shares with it several features.[29] Like the *Hipparchus*, it is a dramatic dialogue,

---

[25] Herodotus (5.55) and Thucydides (1.20.2, 6.54.2-55) consider Hippias, Hipparchus' brother, as the eldest son of Peisistratus and a tyrant, though Thucydides is aware of an alternative tradition. Aristotle, *Ath.* 18.1, writes that both Hippias and Hipparchus were rulers of Athens, but Hippias did the actual governing. For ancient accounts about Hipparchus and comparison with the version in the dialogue, see Schorn 2005, 230-47.

[26] The existence of Hipparchus' herms is attested: *IG* I³ 1023, the so-called "Fourmont herm," found in the eighteenth century, now lost; see Peek 1935; Lavelle 1985; Osborne 1985, 47-57. Hipparchus' rivalry with the Delphic oracle fits in with Peisistratids' strained relations with Delphi (Shapiro 1989, 49-50; Larson 2000, 210-11). Aristotle calls Hipparchus φιλόμουσος and claims, like the author of the dialogue, that he invited Simonides and Anacreon to Athens (*Ath.* 18.1), though the direct influence of Aristotle on *Hipparchus* or vice versa is considered unlikely by Osborne 1985, 50 and Schorn 2005, 236 n. 38. The claim that Hipparchus brought Homeric epics to Athens and introduced their recitations at Panathenaia has parallels in analogous stories about Peisistratus; on the so-called "Peisistratean recension" of Homer, see Janko 1992, 29-32; Nagy 1996, 65-112; Graziosi 2002, 203-34; Schorn 2005, 242-7. The Athenians introduced a law forbidding defamation of Harmodius and Aristogeiton (Hyperides, *In Philippid.* 3) which indicates that versions of events unfavorable to them circulated there. Schorn (2005, 248 n. 97) suggests that the law provides terminus ante quem for the dialogue.

[27] Bloom 1987, 47 thinks that the story of Hipparchus "is nothing but a description of Socrates"; similarly, Tipton 1999, 203 says it is a "mirror" of "Socrates' own situation."

[28] On irony in the story of Hipparchus, see Schorn 2005; Mulroy 2007, 127, 129.

[29] e.g. Pavlu 1910: "Zwillingsdialoge"; Massaro and Massaro 1997, 115: "l'*Ipparco* e il suo gemello *Minosse*."

presumably set in Athens, which opens with Socrates inquiring about the meaning of a term (in this case "law," νόμος), though in this case both Socrates and his anonymous interlocutor are advanced in age (*Min.* 321d: τῆς ἡλικίας). A question-and-answer exchange is combined with an excursus rehabilitating the character from whom the title derives. Upon closer inspection, however, key differences between the dialogues, both in tone and in conversational dynamics, become apparent.

In the opening section Socrates, after asking his interlocutor what law is, refutes his attempts at a definition and proposes that the law "wishes to be a discovery of reality" (*Min.* 315a: βούλεται τοῦ ὄντος εἶναι ἐξεύρεσις). When his companion points out that the diversity of laws undermines this definition, Socrates states that discovery of reality is the law's goal, even though it may be unattainable. It is then agreed that true experts do not differ in their judgments; in the domain of law, such experts are politicians and kings (*Min.* 317a). This inquiry is followed by a search for good laws and lawgivers in human history. Socrates suggests that the Cretan laws, established by the mythical kings Minos and Rhadamanthus, are the best and most divine. He argues that, despite popular opinion, Minos was not cruel and unjust, as evidenced by the testimonies of Homer and Hesiod, who praised Minos (*Min.* 318e): Homer in the *Odyssey*, when he stated that Minos ruled as a king in Cnossus "in the ninth season, being a friend with great Zeus" (*Od.* 19.179: ἐννέωρος βασίλευε Διὸς μεγάλου ὀαριστής), and Hesiod in a line in which he depicted Minos as "having the scepter of Zeus" (*Min.* 320d [F 144 Merkelbach and West]: Ζηνὸς ἔχων σκῆπτρον). These phrases, Socrates claims, are evidence that Minos was educated by Zeus and gave Crete divinely inspired laws.[30] The work ends rather abruptly when Socrates' interlocutor admits that he cannot answer a question about how a good lawgiver helps make the soul better: Socrates says that it is a disgrace not to know what is good and bad for the soul, and the dialogue breaks off.

This brief dialogue asks important questions, enquiring about the origins and authority of the law and its influence on the human soul. The latter problem is left unsolved, but the problem of the origins of the law is resolved: the issue goes back to divinely inspired legislators. This is a key difference between the *Minos* and the *Hipparchus*: unlike the latter, the *Minos* moves beyond refutation and reaches a positive outcome. The inset account of the eponymous figure, loosely connected with the rest of the dialogue in the *Hipparchus*, is well integrated in the *Minos*; and

---

[30] Socrates explains that the meaning of the Homeric passage is that Minos met with Zeus every ninth year in order to be educated by the god. The exact meaning of the words ἐννέωρος and ὀαριστής was debated in antiquity (Poland 1932, 1902–3). According to Strabo, Ephorus, Plato's younger contemporary, said that Minos went to the cave of Zeus every ninth year and then returned with precepts written down that he said had come from Zeus (10.4.8; Morrow 1993², 24–5 thinks that Ephorus is probably influenced here by Plato's *Laws* and by *Minos*). For other accounts of Minos, see Souilhé 1930a, 77–81; Poland 1932.

while the *Hipparchus* is an ambivalent work in which various layers undermine each other; there are no clear indications of dissimulation or irony in the *Minos*.

There are numerous parallels between the *Minos* and Plato's *Laws*; in particular, the author appears to allude to the opening of the *Laws*, in which Minos and the Cretan laws are mentioned (*Lg.* 624a–b).[31] There are also verbal similarities with other dialogues by Plato, including *Protagoras, Phaedrus, Symposion,* and *Statesman*.[32] Other probable influences include Antisthenes, Cynics and Stoics, as well as Hellenistic kingship-theories.[33] There is no agreement about the dating of the dialogue, but there is tendency to consider it a product of the early Academy.[34]

### 4.2.4 Theages or On Philosophy

Plato's authorship of the *Theages* (with the subtitle *On Philosophy*, though the concept of philosophy is not explicitly discussed) appears to have been accepted in antiquity.[35] It is a dramatic dialogue between Socrates and two interlocutors, Demodocus and his son Theages. The two men are historical figures, but ones with a modest presence in the Platonic corpus.[36] The dialogue begins with Demodocus asking Socrates for advice about the education of his son, who desires to become wise and insists that his father finds him teachers. Such an opening resonates with Plato's *Laches*, in which Lysimachus and Melesias seek advice—initially from Laches and Nicias, and then from Socrates—about the proper training for their sons. In the *Theages*, Socrates' young interlocutor sincerely declares that his aim is political power, though not tyrannical rule by means of

---

[31] For other parallels, see Morrow 1993², 36. Müller 1995, 252 n. 25 thinks that the similarities are by no means a proof of the dependence of the author of the *Minos* on the *Laws*.

[32] Souilhé 1930a, 82 n. 2; Manuwald 2005, 139–43.

[33] On influence of Antisthenes, see Müller 1975, 174–87; Müller 1995; Manuwald 2005. Stoic and Cynic elements are postulated by Pavlu 1910, 9; Rowe 2000, 304, 308 sees influences of the Hellenistic theories of kingship.

[34] Souilhé 1930a, 75–85 believes that it was written by a member of the Academy or a Socratic who made use of Plato's late dialogues. Müller 1995 thinks that it originated within the Academy and might have been influenced by Antisthenes. Rowe 2000, 307 notes that in form, *Minos* resembles early Socratic dialogues, but its subject is affiliated with Plato's late dialogues, the *Laws* and the *Statesman*. Cobb 1988 and Mulroy 2007 believe the dialogue was composed by Plato, and Morrow 1993², 35-9 that it might have been written by Plato, but left unfinished.

[35] Plutarch perhaps wrote a work on *Theages*, as the Lamprias catalogue preserves the title Ὑπὲρ τοῦ Πλάτωνος Θεάγους, *In Defence of Plato's Theages* (see Joyal 1993). Aelian quotes *Theages* as a work by Plato (*VH* 4.15) and Albinus in *Prologus* 4 says that some people advise to start reading Plato with *Theages*. In the past two decades, three detailed commentaries on the dialogue have been published (Joyal 2000; Bailly 2004; Döring 2004), with none of the scholars arguing for Plato's authorship. For reading of *Theages* as Plato's genuine work, see Pangle 1987b.

[36] Both are named in Plato's *Apology* 33e–34a. Theages is also mentioned by Socrates in the *Republic*, where he is said to have been kept from politics by an illness (*Resp.* 496b). Immediately afterwards, Socrates mentions his daimonic sign (*Resp.* 496c); it is probable that the author of *Theages* (in which the *daimonion* of Socrates is discussed at length), had the *Republic* passage in mind when composing his dialogue (Carlini 1962, 43). Demodocus is an addressee of Socrates' speech in *Demodocus I* discussed later in this chapter.

violence, but a rule voluntarily accepted by the people (*Thg.* 126a). Theages admits that he has heard that people who spent even a short time with Socrates made impressive progress and would like to have Socrates as a teacher. Socrates reveals that it is his *daimonion* that exerts such influence on his associates, and he relates a string of anecdotes that showcase its workings (*Thg.* 128e–131e). They reveal the *daimonion*'s prophetic faculty and its power to bring about improvement in Socrates' followers. The influence of the *daimonion*, however, is peculiar as it depends on physical closeness to Socrates: as the anecdote about Aristides shows, one may lose the abilities one has gained when associating with Socrates after leaving him. Aristides also claimed that his abilities increased when he was close to Socrates, particularly when he touched him (*Thg.* 130d–e). The educational influence of Socrates is thus presented as being exercised through close association, συνουσία.[37] Such an understanding of Socrates' *daimonion*, though peculiar and unparalleled in Plato, appears to have been influenced by a passage in the *Theaetetus* in which Socrates tells of his art of midwifery and of how some of his companions, if god allowed, experienced great progress thanks to their association with him; he also mentions Aristides as one of those who left him earlier than they should have and therefore suffered a "miscarriage" or lost the "offspring" which resulted from their association with Socrates (*Tht.* 150b–151a; note that Socrates' *daimonion* is referred to in *Tht.* 151a).[38] The author clearly rewrites the Platonic passage, manipulating and reorganizing its elements in a way that fundamentally changes its meaning.

The anecdotes reported by Socrates consist of direct speech exchanges between himself and other characters (Charmides, Timarchus, and Aristides). The lengthiest one, describing an encounter with Aristides, is a miniature narrated dialogue, preceded by a short introduction outlining the circumstances of their conversation, and is reminiscent of exchanges between Socrates and his companions in Xenophon's *Apomnemoneumata*. The author of the *Theages*, however, decided to have Socrates himself relate and thus "authorize" the anecdotes.[39] A similar literary device is used by the author of the spurious *Halcyon*, who makes Socrates in *propria voce* "confirm" the rumors of having two wives, Myrto and Xanthippe (see below, in section on the *Halcyon*).

The dialogue might have been composed in the fourth century BCE, either during Plato's lifetime or after his death; the composition of the *Theaetetus*

---

[37] On importance of the motif of συνουσία and its erotic implications, see Tarrant 2005; Joyal 2016, 126–31.

[38] Joyal 2000, 82–9 thinks that the author of the *Theages*, while inspired by *Theaetetus* 150b–151a, either misunderstood the passage or disregarded Plato's intentions; in a recent article, he finds the latter more probable rather than being mistaken, as the figure of Socrates is deliberately reshaped (Joyal 2016, 146 n. 78).

[39] On the anecdotes in the *Theages*, see Joyal 2000, 77, 100–1, 144–6, 265, who thinks that the author's interest in the biographical and anecdotal material is suggestive of the environment of the post-Platonic Academy.

(369 BCE) provides a terminus post quem.[40] Numerous resonances between *Theages* and the dubious *Alcibiades I* suggest the influence of one dialogue on the other.[41] The dialogue might have originated in the Old Academy, in which there was some interest in *daimones* (Xenocrates, Heraclides of Pontus, the author of the *Epinomis*).[42]

### 4.2.5 Cleitophon or Exhortation

Plato's authorship of this short dramatic dialogue, representing a conversation between Socrates and Cleitophon, has been both accepted and rejected by scholars in recent decades.[43] There are clear ties with Book 1 of the *Republic*, manifest both in the theme (justice) and choice of characters (the three people mentioned by Socrates in the opening—Cleitophon, Thrasymachus, and Lysias—appear in the first book of Plato's dialogue), but the dramatic chronology of the two dialogues remains unclear.[44] In the *Republic*, Cleitophon is a minor figure who sides with Socrates' opponent Thrasymachus (*Resp.* 328b, 340a–b); in the *Cleitophon* he is given a fuller life. The dialogue starts with Socrates saying that he has heard that Cleitophon criticized his teaching and praised Thrasymachus (*Clit.* 406). Cleitophon confirms and admits that he was disappointed with Socrates. When he hears the latter praise justice, he becomes enthusiastic and desires to take care of his soul, but Socrates fails to take the next step, namely to explain what justice is. In what appears to be a reworking of Plato's *Apology* 21b–e, where Socrates describes how he went from one expert to another only to discover their ignorance,[45] Cleitophon describes how he went to Socrates' companions and examined them one after another in order to gain an understanding of justice, but these men were unable to provide him with a satisfactory answer (*Clit.* 408c–409e). Eventually he turned to Socrates himself, but received two contradictory answers: one, that justice consisted of harming enemies and benefitting

---

[40] There are no references to the Hellenistic period philosophical schools, hence Döring 2004, 81 thinks that the dialogue must have originated in the fourth century BCE. Some scholars see a reference to *Theages* 125e–126a in Aristotle's *Eudemian Ethics* 1225b32–5 and consider the writing of the latter work as a terminus ante quem (Müller 1969).

[41] For an overview of parallels between *Theages* and *Alcibiades I*, see Bailly 2004, 272–84 (he concludes that while the connection between the dialogues is unquestionable, it is impossible to determine whether the author of *Theages* responds to Plato or vice versa); Tarrant 2012, 154–8 (who entertains the possibility that *Alcibiades I* is later than *Theages*). Cf. also a parallel between description of Socrates' *daimonion* in *Theages* 128d and Plato's *Apology* 31c–d.

[42] Joyal 2000, 141–5. Tarrant 2005, 142–5 and Tarrant 2012, 158–60 argues for a link between the author's disinterest in dialectic and the emphasis on συνουσία and close companionship and the Academy of Polemo and Crates.

[43] Slings 1999, contributors in Kremer 2004a, and Bryan 2012, 22 believe that the dialogue is Plato's work; for a contrary view, see e.g. Rowe 2000, 159–63; Rowe 2005; for an overview of different arguments, Demetriou 2000; Bowe 2007.

[44] Bowe 2007, 253.   [45] Rowe 2000, 305.

friends, and a second, that a just man never harms anyone (*Clit.* 410a–b). Cleitophon concludes that Socrates either does not have the knowledge or does not want to share it; at any rate, while he is of help to people who have not yet been converted to the pursuit to virtue, he is an obstacle to those seeking it.

The dialogue ends without Socrates having answered or rebutted Cleitophon's accusations; read at face value, then, it is a criticism of Socrates and his pedagogy. Such an interpretation has been problematic for many readers, both ancient and modern, who found it disconcerting that the *Cleitophon* uses the format of the Socratic dialogue as a platform to accuse and challenge Socrates. No wonder, therefore, that readers have embarked on an interpretative quest. According to Proclus, some thought that Cleitophon was simply not worthy of Socrates' answer (*In Ti.* 1.20 Diehl), and such reading is not unparalleled among modern scholars.[46] The works has been also interpreted as criticism not of the real Socrates, but of certain representations of the philosopher and of a specific branch of Socratic literature (namely one that employed explicit protreptic),[47] or as a gentle parody of the *Republic* and Plato's Socrates.[48] Whatever the intentions, the transformation of the motifs from the *Republic* and *Apology* and the provocative use of the Socratic dialogue against the grain of the genre can be read as a play with the Platonic legacy along the lines of the Hellenistic poetics of the *oppositio in imitando*.[49]

An important backdrop for the *Cleitophon* appears to be the development of the philosophical protreptic, and it has been suggested that the dialogue may be a pastiche of lost protreptic works.[50] Xenophon in the *Apomnemoneumata* mentions people who say that Socrates was great at exhorting people to virtue but unable to lead them to it (*Mem.* 1.4.1: προτρέψασθαι μὲν ἀνθρώπους ἐπ' ἀρετὴν κράτιστον γεγονέναι, προαγαγεῖν δ'ἐπ'αὐτὴν οὐχ ἱκανόν); he may be thinking here of the *Cleitophon*, but it is also possible that both writers are referring to and elaborating on an opinion expressed in another text.[51] The figures of Socrates' companions being questioned by Cleitophon suggest an intellectual landscape in which Socrates' pupils have gained some independent authority; as Rowe observes, they are referred to as Socrates' ἡλικιῶται (*Clit.* 408c), which should be understood not so much as "men equal in age" (Socrates' companions were usually much younger than he), but rather as "contemporaries" of Socrates, a term suggesting that the author is looking at the days of Socrates from a chronological distance.[52]

---

[46] Cf. e.g. Kremer 2004b, 28: Socrates' silence signifies that there is an "unbridgeable chasm between himself and Cleitophon."
[47] Slings 1999, 18, 93.   [48] Rowe 2005, 219–20.   [49] Erler 2008.
[50] Gigon 1953, 119 considers it "ein Cento aus Texten Platons und anderer Sokratiker"; Slings 1999, 124 thinks that Socrates' protreptic speech in the dialogue is a cento of protreptic texts. For fourth-century protreptics, see Slings 1999, 59–93.
[51] Slings 1999, 77–82.   [52] Rowe 2005, 219.

### 4.2.6 *Alcibiades II* or *On Prayer*

The dialogue was also referred to in antiquity as the *Lesser Alcibiades* to distinguish it from another work with the same title in the Platonic corpus.[53] This is one of the numerous works titled after the Athenian politician and notorious friend of Socrates, while the work *On Prayer* was composed by Aristotle (Diogenes Laertius 5.22). Plato's authorship of the *Alcibiades II* was not unchallenged in antiquity: Athenaeus says that it was sometimes ascribed to Xenophon (*Deipn.* 11.506b). The language of the dialogue, however, displays features which do not appear in Plato and Xenophon, such as the Hellenistic use of οὐθέν and μηθέν instead of οὐδέν and μηδέν. The dialogue was probably composed in the environment of the Academy, and some scholars discern in it a polemic against the Stoics and Cynics.[54]

Like the *Alcibiades I*, with which the author appears to have been familiar, *Alcibiades II* is a dramatic dialogue, reporting a conversation between Socrates and Alcibiades. The dramatic date is impossible to determine due to chronological inconsistencies. The conversation takes place when Alcibiades is a youth and Pericles is still alive (*Alc. II* 143e–144a), that is, no later than 429 BCE; on the other hand, Socrates speaks of the death of the Macedonian king Archelaus who died in 399 BCE, and quotes from Euripides' *Antiope*, which was probably performed around 410 BCE. These temporal inconsistencies may be a playful imitation of Plato's well-known anachronisms in the *Gorgias*, the dialogue with which the *Alcibiades II* shares a quotation from Euripides' *Antiope* (cf. *Grg.* 484e; *Alc. II* 146a) and a reference to Archelaus (*Grg.* 470d–471d; *Alc. II* 141d).[55]

The dialogue opens with Socrates meeting Alcibiades, who is on his way to say prayers. He observes that in order to pray for something, one has to possess knowledge of what is good and what is harmful; otherwise one risks praying for things which may turn bad for oneself. That's why the Spartans used to pray simply that the gods would give them good and noble rather than for specific things. The dialogue ends with Alcibiades postponing his prayers until he attains a proper level of understanding under Socrates' guidance. Apart from the parallels with the *Gorgias*, there are reminiscences of the *Alcibiades I*, but also similarities

---

[53] Diogenes Laertius refers to it as *The Second Alcibiades or On Prayer* (3.59: Ἀλκιβιάδης δεύτερος ἢ περὶ εὐχῆς) and to the *Alcibiades I* as *The Greater Alcibiades* (3.62: Ἀλκιβιάδης ὁ μείζων). Olympiodorus speaks of *Alcibiades II* as *The Lesser Alcibiades* (*In Alc.* 3: Ἀλκιβιάδης ὁ ἐλάττων).

[54] Bickel 1904 and Carlini 1962, 46–8 consider the dialogue a product of the Academy of Arcesilaus; Magris 1992 of the Old Academy, perhaps of Crantor. On probable criticism of the Cynics and Stoics, in particular in passages in which Socrates pronounces a negative judgment on μεγαλοψυχία, "high-mindedness" (*Alc. II* 140c, 150c), see Souilhé 1930a, 10–11.

[55] Renaud and Tarrant 2015, 103–4. On irreconcilable chronological discrepancies in the *Gorgias*, see Dodds 1959, 17–18.

with Xenophon's *Apomnemoneumata*.⁵⁶ If the work was composed towards the end of the fourth century BCE or later, some passages may have been intended as allusions to Alexander the Great (*Alc. II* 148e–149b: a mention to the oracle of Ammon; *Alc. II* 141c: the notion of "a tyranny of all the land of the Greeks and of the barbarians," τὴν πάντων Ἑλλήνων τε καὶ βαρβάρων χώραν τε καὶ τυραννίδα), but they are not inconceivable pre-Alexander.⁵⁷

One of the peculiarities of the dialogue is the author's fondness of poetry. He makes Socrates quote several times from Homer's *Iliad* and *Odyssey*, Euripides' *Antiope* and *Phoenician Women*, *Margites*, and an *adespoton* epigram. In some cases, a short poetic phrase is integrated into Socrates' speech without explicit acknowledgment of the source, lending poetic color to it.⁵⁸ At one point, Socrates weaves into his utterance a passage of Euripides' *Antiope* which in the *Gorgias* is used by Socrates' opponent Callicles (*Alc. II* 146a; *Grg.* 484e [*TrGF* F 184]). Elsewhere he engages in the exegesis of poetry, as when he quotes Zeus' complaint that mortals blame the gods instead of their own wickedness for their sufferings (*Od.* 1.33–34) and explains that the "wickedness" should be understood as "foolishness" (*Alc. II* 142d–e). In *Alc. II* 149d–e, he quotes five lines from Homer which are not preserved in the extant poems and may be either a pastiche or a fragment of a lost epic work.⁵⁹ When quoting from the *Margites*, Socrates observes that poetry is riddling by nature (*Alc. II* 147b: ἔστιν τε γὰρ φύσει ποιητικὴ ἡ σύμπασα αἰνιγματώδης), therefore not everyone can understand it; and Homer in particular liked to conceal his wisdom (*Alc. II* 147c: ἀποκρύπτεσθαι ὅτι μάλιστα τὴν αὑτοῦ σοφίαν). The passage is certainly inspired by interpretations of poetry in Plato, such as Socrates' explanation of the "real" meaning of verses by Simonides in *Protagoras* 339e–347a, and his statement in the *Republic* that Simonides "spoke in riddles, in a poetic manner" (*Resp.* 332b: ᾐνίξατο ἄρα... ὡς ἔοικεν, ὁ Σιμωνίδης

---

⁵⁶ Cf. e.g. *Alc. II* 141a–b with *Alc. I* 105a–c; *Alc. II* 144d–146d with *Alc. I* 117d–118b; Sharpe 2011, 136–7 and Renaud and Tarrant 2015, 107 read *Alcibiades II* as a sequel to *Alcibiades I*: in this reading, the dialogue reports Alcibiades' education by Socrates after the meeting described in *Alcibiades I*. Xenophon's Socrates, like Socrates in *Alcibiades II*, discussed the concept of madness as the opposite of wisdom and its relationship to stupidity (cf. *Alc. II* 138c–140c with *Mem.* 3.9.6–7) and advised praying for "good things" in general rather than for specific, named things, for the gods know what is good and bad (*Mem.* 1.3.2, cf. with *Alc. II* 143a).

⁵⁷ Thesleff 1982, 232 notes that the image of the world-tyrant is immediately followed by a reference to the Macedonian Archelaus; though cf. also the motif of the world-ruler in *Alc. I* 105a–c and *Thg.* 125e–126a. The oracle of Ammon was visited by the Greeks before Alexander: according to Plutarch, Alcibiades consulted it before the Sicilian expedition (*Nic.* 13.1). Other Athenians consulting the oracle included Cimon, while the Spartan Lysander was accused of trying to bribe its priests (Plutarch, *Cim.* 18.6, *Lys.* 25.3).

⁵⁸ *Alc. II* 141d: χθιζά τε καὶ πρωϊζά; cf. Homer, *Il.* 2.303; *Alc. II* 140a: σύν τε δύο σκεπτομένω is a playful modification of Homer, *Il.* 10.224: σύν τε δύ' ἐρχομένω (quoted in Plato, *Symp.* 174d, *Prt.* 348d).

⁵⁹ *Alc. II* 149d–e; cf. Hom. *Il.* 2.306, 1.315, 8.549, 24.27, 4.47, 4.165, 6.449. The lines quoted in *Alcibiades II* were incorporated by Barnes in his 1711 edition of the *Iliad* in Book 8 as verses 548, 550–2. Wilamowitz-Möllendorff 1916, 30 n. 1 proposed that the author of *Alcibiades II* excerpted them from the *Little Iliad*.

ποιητικῶς). Unlike in Plato's dialogues, however, Socrates in the *Alcibiades II* is not ironic, but sincere and serious in his appreciation of poetry.[60]

### 4.2.7 Rival Lovers or On Philosophy

Plato's authorship of the *Rival Lovers* (or *Lovers*) was doubted already in antiquity.[61] The work is a reported dialogue with an internal narration familiar to readers of Plato: Socrates relates to an unknown audience his visit to a grammarian's school where he found two boys discussing astronomical problems.[62] He meets there two *erastai* of one of the boys: one of them an athlete committed to training and wrestling, the other—a man dedicated to philosophy and intellectual pursuits (*Amat.* 132c–d). The conversation is spurred by the athlete's disparaging remark that the boys' discussion is philosophical nonsense and babbling (he therefore essentially reiterates what was said by an anonymous character in Plato's *Euthydemus* 304e–305a). "The intellectual" enthusiastically jumps to the defense of philosophy, which he associates with learning and polymathy (*Amat.* 133c: πολυμαθία). This leads Socrates to scrutinize the value of erudition and demonstrate that moderate learning is better than extensive education. A polymath is compared to a pentathlon athlete: he is always second best to experts in a given field and of less use compared with them (*Amat.* 135e–137a). This refutatory part of the conversation is followed by Socrates' attempt to establish what philosophy really is (*Amat.* 137b–139a). Far from being encyclopedic knowledge, it has to do with ethical and political skills, with justice, prudence, and self-knowledge (*Amat.* 138c).[63] The dialogue ends with the intellectual ashamed and silent, while the athlete agrees with Socrates.

The author of the dialogue decided to keep Socrates' interlocutors anonymous even though it would have been easier to have Socrates refer to them by names rather than to resort to circumlocutory phrases such as "the one considering himself wiser," "the wiser one" (*Amat.* 132d: ὁ σοφώτερος προσποιούμενος, 135b: ὁ σοφώτερος), "the other one" (132c, 133a: ὁ ἕτερος), "the rival lover" (132c, 133b: ὁ ἀντεραστής), "the lover of athletics (134a: φιλογυμναστής), "the wise one ... the unlearned one..." (139a: ὁ σοφὸς ... ὁ ἀμαθής ... ). The anonymity of the *erastai* underscores that their role in the dialogue is to represent disparate ways of life and embody conflicting attitudes towards learning. This opposition, a sort of

---

[60] On the recurrence of tragic themes and motifs, see Sharpe 2011, 137–8.

[61] A passage in Diogenes Laertius indicates that Thrasyllus had doubts (or was responding to someone having doubts) concerning the dialogue's authenticity (9.37: εἴπερ οἱ Ἀντερασταὶ Πλάτωνός εἰσι, φησὶ Θράσυλλος ... ). While most scholars today reject Plato's authorship, Annas 1985 finds it plausible that it is an early work of Plato; Bruell 1987 and Peterson 2011, 196 n. 1 see no reasons to reject Plato's authorship.

[62] Later authors considered Dionysius, the grammarian mentioned in the dialogue, a teacher of Plato (Apuleius, *De Plat.* 1.2; Diogenes Laertius 3.4); see Riginos 1976, 40, n. 8.

[63] On self-knowledge in the dialogue, see Annas 1985; Moore 2015, 236–9.

reenactment of the Amphion and Zethus debate,[64] is underscored by the lovers' mutual contempt for each other: "the intellectual" derides the athlete for spending his life "wrestling, stuffing himself, and sleeping" (*Amat.* 132c: τραχηλιζόμενος καὶ ἐμπιμπλάμενος καὶ καθεύδων), while the athlete mocks him for not sleeping and eating, and being emaciated from all the thinking he does (*Amat.* 134b: ἄγρυπνόν τε καὶ ἄσιτον καὶ ἀτριβῆ τὸν τράχηλον ἔχοντα καὶ λεπτὸν ὑπὸ μεριμνῶν). While the intellectual considers Socrates to be his natural ally, the philosopher, somewhat surprisingly, sides with the athlete. This does not mean, to be sure, that Socrates embraced the wrestler's life, but it underscores the extent of dissonance between his and the intellectual's understanding of philosophy.

The *Rival Lovers* contains many reminiscences from Plato's works, in particular from *Charmides*, *Lysis*, and *Euthydemus*. Dating of the dialogue remains unclear, with some scholars seeing it as a product of Polemo's Academy, while others believed it was produced in Arcesilaus' times.[65] Though polymathy is critically assessed by Socrates in Plato's *Laws* (*Lg.* 811a-b; 819a) and Xenophon's *Apomnemoneumata* (*Mem.* 4.4.6; cf. also Xenophon's portrayal of Euthydemus at *Mem.* 4.2), the notion of extensive learning creates associations with Peripatetic scholarship and erudite Hellenistic culture, and if the dialogue originated in late fourth or early third century BCE, it might have reflected a reaction against these trends. It is not impossible that the comparison of a polymath to a pentathlon athlete might have given origin to Eratosthenes' nickname; according to *Suda* (s.v. Ἐρατοσθένης (ε 2898)), he was called a Pentathlete (Πένταθλος) because he was second best one in every branch of knowledge (διὰ τὸ δευτερεύειν ἐν παντὶ εἴδει παιδείας τοῖς ἄκροις ἐγγίσασι).[66]

## 4.3 Dialogues from the *Appendix Platonica*

### 4.3.1 *Sisyphus*

This is a short dramatic dialogue containing a conversation between Sisyphus of the Thessalian Pharsalus and a dominant interlocutor whose name is not disclosed. The Sisyphus of the dialogue is probably to be identified with a historical figure, a son of Daochos I and a father of Daochos II. The latter was an ally of Philip II and the dedicator of the famous Daochos Group at Delphi, representing

---

[64] Souilhé 1930a, 106. The debate between Amphion and Zethus, famously represented in Euripides' *Antiope*, is referred to by Callicles in Plato's *Gorgias*.

[65] Souilhé 1930a, 105–12 proposes that the dialogue was written by an imitator of Plato's *Charmides* and *Euthydemus* around the time of Polemo; Carlini 1962, 58–9 thinks the period of Arcesilaus is more probable. Männlein-Robert 2005, 120 considers it an early Hellenistic work of the late fourth or early third century BCE.

[66] For the same reason, he was called "Beta" (βῆτα, *Suda* s.v. Ἐρατοσθένης (ε 2898); τὰ βήματα in the original text is a mistake). Hirzel 1895a, 407–8 thinks that the author of the *Rival Lovers* was aware of Eratosthenes' nickname and was targeting him.

the family's eight male members from several generations, including Sisyphus. If this identification is correct, the Sisyphus of the dialogue was an influential figure, belonging to a powerful Thessalian family.[67]

The unnamed interlocutor of Sisyphus is not a Pharsalian (in *Sis.* 387c, Sisyphus explains to him the customs of Pharsalus) and reveals certain Socratic features: he starts with an ironic praise of Sisyphus on account of his expertise in deliberation (τὸ βουλεύεσθαι) and then proceeds to question and perplex him about the very nature of this skill. Why, then, did the author not identify this character explicitly as Socrates? After all, there was nothing simpler than to have Sisyphus address him at least once by name, a conventional way of revealing speakers' identities in dramatic dialogues. The reason, perhaps, was the chronology. There are some indications that the dramatic date of the dialogue is around mid-fourth century BCE, decades after Socrates' death. The Stratonicus whose show is mentioned (*Sis.* 387b) is probably Stratonicus of Athens, a famous kitharist, teacher, and theorist of music, active in the first half of the fourth century BCE.[68] In *Sis.* 388c–d the unnamed speaker mentions Callistratus and his unknown whereabouts, probably referring to Callistratus of Aphidnae, who was condemned to death in 362 and fled Athens.

The setting of the conversation is unidentified. While conventions of the Socratic dialogue suggest Athens as the default place, other details make this unlikely. We learn from the opening that on the day before the conversation Sisyphus was in Pharsalus, where he participated in the deliberations of the city's politicians. As Pharsalus is located some 280 km from Athens, it would be impossible for him to reach Athens the next day, a fact which could have hardly been missed by ancient readers. One should assume, then, that the dialogue takes place in the vicinity of Pharsalus. Such a non-Athenian setting provides an additional argument against identifying the unnamed speaker with Socrates, who rarely left Athens.[69] The dominant speaker is thus a Socrates-like figure, freed from the temporal and chronological confines of the real Socrates.

---

[67] The epigram inscribed on Daochos I's statue says that he ruled over Thessaly for twenty-seven years (probably *c.*440–413). The monument is dated to between 336–332 BCE (*Carmina epigraphica graeca* 2.795; *Fouilles de Delphes* III.4.460; see Ridgway 1990, 46–50; Edwards 1996, 135–7; Jacquemin and Laroche 2001; Keesling 2017, 108–11). For the political organization of Thessaly at the time, see Hornblower 2011[4], 101–4; Bouchon and Helly 2015. Sisyphus was mentioned in Theopompus' *Hellenica*; Athenaeus refers to the Pharsalian in a passage discussing relationships between flatterers and powerful men (e.g. Philip of Macedon, the tyrants Dionysius I and II, Hiero, Alexander the Great) (*Deipn.* 6.252f).

[68] On Stratonicus, see Barker 2007, 75–6, 86–7; Creese 2010, 142–6. According to Athenaeus, Stratonicus was killed (forced to drink poison) by the Cyprian king Nicocles (*Deipn.* 8.352d), who ruled from 373 BCE till late 360s.

[69] Müller 1975, 48–50 assumes an Athenian setting and thinks that the author did not care about the exact chronology. He also takes Sisyphus' interlocutor to be Socrates and, consequently, thinks that the dialogue takes place before the latter's death in 399 BCE. A non-Athenian setting is therefore unlikely in his view, as Socrates tended not to leave Athens.

The chief topic of the *Sisyphus* is the nature of deliberation. The theme also appears in the *Alcibiades I* (*Alc. I* 106c, 125e–126a) and is discussed at length by Aristotle (*EN* 1112a18–1113a14, 1142a31–b33; *EE* 1226a21–1127a30).[70] In the *Sisyphus*, the main speaker asks his interlocutor to explain to him the nature of deliberation. After it is agreed that it consists of trying to find the best way to act, he asks whether people deliberate about things they know, or about things they do not know. He then proceeds to demonstrate that in the first case there is no need for deliberation as one does not search for something one already knows, while in the second it is impossible to deliberate, as one cannot search for something when one does not know what it is. This conundrum is reminiscent of the paradox in Plato's *Meno*, where it is observed that one cannot try to find out neither what one already knows nor what one does not know (*Men.* 80d–e). The anonymous speaker then observes that it is impossible to deliberate about future because it does not exist, and notes that it is unclear what the difference is between people deemed good or bad at deliberating. The dialogue ends with him suggesting that perhaps he and Sisyphus can return to this question some other time.

The Pharsalian context creates a link between the dialogue and Plato's *Meno*, in which Socrates converses with Meno of Pharsalus, a youth from a prominent Thessalian family, who came to Athens. However, unlike Meno, Sisyphus is a mature man, perhaps even elderly, if the dialogue takes place in late 360s BCE.[71] This is not the only link between the *Sisyphus* and the *Meno*: there are other parallels with Plato's dialogue, which suggest that the author had it in mind when composing the piece.[72] The dating of the text is uncertain; most scholars suggest the middle or second half of the fourth century BCE.[73]

### 4.3.2 *Eryxias*

In Diogenes Laertius, the title is *Eryxias or Erasistratus* (3.62). Stobaeus (4.31b.51, 4.31d.117, 4.33.33) quotes passages from it under the heading "from Plato's *Eryxias*" (Πλάτωνος ἐκ τοῦ Ἐρυξίου). Suda lists *Eryxias* and, separately, *Erasistratoi* as works by Aeschines of Sphettus (s.v. Αἰσχίνης (αι 346)), but

---

[70] See Müller 1975, 86–94 for a comparison of the *Sisyphus* and Aristotle's treatment of deliberation, and the possibility that Aristotle had read the *Sisyphus*.

[71] Meno is identified as a Pharsalian by Diogenes Laertius 2.50. Diodorus Siculus 14.19.8 seems to be mistaken when he says that Meno came from Larissa (Socrates in *Meno* 70b speaks to Meno of οἱ τοῦ σοῦ ἑταίρου Ἀριστίππου πολῖται Λαρισαῖοι, which suggests that Meno himself did not come from Larissa). On Plato's portrayal of Meno, who is described as a black character in Xenophon's *Anabasis*, see below, n. 88.

[72] For a discussion of the *Sisyphus*-argument in the context of the *Meno*, see Fine 2013.

[73] Souilhé 1930b, 61, 65 dates the dialogue to the second half of the fourth century BCE (times of Aristotle or slightly later), and suggests that it might have originated in sophistic circles. Müller 1975, 94–104 and Aronadio 2008, 59 argue for the 50s of the fourth century BCE.

Aeschines' authorship is unlikely, and there is general agreement that the dialogue comes from the last decades of the fourth century at the earliest.[74]

The *Eryxias* is a narrated dialogue in which Socrates reports to an unidentified audience how he, while walking with Eryxias, encountered Critias and Erasistratus. Critias is a familiar figure to readers of Plato and Xenophon; Eryxias and Erasistratus, on other hand, do not appear in the extant Socratic literature. In the dialogue, Eryxias is said to be a relative of Critias (*Eryx.* 396d) and Erasistratus is identified as a nephew of Phaeax (*Eryx.* 392a), probably the man who led an embassy to Sicily in 422 BCE (Thucydides 5.4–5). The conversation takes place in the Stoa of Zeus Eleutherios in the Athenian agora, not long before the Sicilian expedition in 415 BCE. We learn from the opening that Erasistratus has just returned from Sicily, convinced that it is necessary for Athens to attack Syracuse. Erasistratus compares the Syracusans to wasps (*Eryx.* 392b: οἱόνπερ οἱ σφῆκες), and thinks that they must be destroyed for otherwise they will become more and more difficult to handle. The image of wasps suggests a few potential intertexts, such as Homer's *Iliad* (*Il.* 12.167–79, 16.259–65), Aristophanes' *Wasps* (cf. especially *Vesp.* 223–7, where the irritability and belligerent character of the insects is emphasized), and Xenophon's *Hellenica* (*Hell.* 4.2.11–12: Timolaus of Corinth compares Lacedemonians to wasps).[75]

The topic of Socrates' conversation is wealth. This is spurred by the sight of Syracusan envoys passing by, one of whom, Erasistratus says, is extremely rich, but also has a reputation of being a bad man. Socrates starts by discussing the relationship between different goods (wealth, health, prosperity, and wisdom—πλοῦτος, ὑγίεια, εὐδαιμονία, σοφία) and argues that wisdom is the most valuable (*Eryx.* 393b–394a). The passage is reminiscent of the exploration of the goods in Plato's *Euthydemus* (279a–282e) and of Crantor's contest between Wealth, Pleasure, Health, and Courage, discussed in Chapter 3.6. The discussion then turns to the question of whether wealth is good or bad, with Critias refuting Eryxias and demonstrating that wealth can harm people possessing it, and therefore cannot be considered good (*Eryx.* 395e–397b). Socrates reports a conversation on a similar topic he heard recently, between the sophist Prodicus and an unnamed young man (*Eryx.* 397c–399a); this inset dialogue is followed by Socrates' suggestion that they turn to the question of what wealth really is (*Eryx.* 399d). The speakers agree that wealth consists of things which are useful for taking care of the body; this, however, means that people who possess the most have the greatest bodily needs, and, therefore, are in worse condition than people who need fewer resources.

---

[74] The office of a gymnasiarch as the supervisor of a gymnasium (*Eryx.* 399a) was established after 338/7 BCE; see Schrohl 1901, 42–3; Eichholz 1935, 141–2; Döring 2005, 76.
[75] Donato 2017.

Despite its brevity, the dialogue was carefully crafted. The references to Sicily and foreshadowing of the Sicilian expedition at the beginning of the dialogue are not unconnected with the main theme: the figure of the rich Syracusan ambassador reminds the reader that the Athenians' desire for private enrichment from the Sicilians' wealth played a crucial role in their decision to launch their ill-fated expedition.[76] This adds a political dimension to the discussion of wealth. The inset conversation between Prodicus and a young man, in which the sophist is refuted by a youth and then expelled from a gymnasium by its supervisor, adds some flourish and opens up additional interpretative possibilities. There is, however, little sense of philosophical progress due to the fact that Socrates tends to drop a line of argument when he senses that his interlocutors have become flustered (*Eryx.* 395c–d, 397c, 405b).[77]

The opening of the dialogue is reminiscent of the *Charmides*, where Socrates as a narrator reports how he met with his acquaintances after he returned from war in Thrace. In the *Eryxias*, it is Erasistratus who has returned from abroad and is asked about the state of things there. In both dialogues, a discussion is prompted by the sight of a specific person who passes by: in Plato, it is the beautiful Charmides, in the *Eryxias*, a Syracusan ambassador.[78] The comparison of a discussion to a board game (*Eryx.* 395a–b) is reminiscent of a passage in the *Republic* (487b–c). There are also parallels between *Eryxias* and Xenophon's *Oeconomicus* (a discussion of wealth and its usefulness occupies paragraphs 1.7–14 of the *Oeconomicus*; the Stoa of Zeus, in which the conversation in *Eryxias* takes place, provides a setting for a conversation between Socrates and Ischomachus in *Oec.* 7.1). Stoic and Cynic influences are also possible: the idea that the wisest men are also the most prosperous, happy, and wealthy (*Eryx.* 394a) perhaps alludes to the Stoic doctrine, while the notion that one who possesses the largest number of material goods is in the worst moral condition (*Eryx.* 406a) may reflect a Cynic influence.[79]

### 4.3.3 *On Justice*

In this dramatic dialogue, Socrates converses with an anonymous interlocutor. As in the *Hipparchus* and the *Minos*, he starts by asking about the meaning of a term: "Can you tell us what justice (τὸ δίκαιον) is?" This theme dominates the first part of the dialogue (*De iust.* 372a–373e). Socrates questions and tries to guide his interlocutor, approaching the problem of justice from various angles (by offering a

---

[76] On the importance of the desire for profit in the Sicilian episode, see Kallet 2001; as she notes, "...Thucydides cites money as a chief factor for the common soldiery and throng.... Love of money—greed, then—impelled the majority toward Sicily" (45).
[77] Döring 2005, 77.   [78] Schrohl 1901, 10–12.   [79] Eichholz 1935, 142–8.

definition, identifying the use of justice, recognizing skills and methods related to it, identifying people who have expertise in it), but his companion confesses, again and again, that he is confused and unable to proceed. As a result, the outcome of this section is extremely modest: the only thing agreed upon is that judges make their decisions by speaking. Socrates then turns abruptly to another question, namely whether people act unjustly willingly or unwillingly (*De iust.* 373e: ἑκόντας... ἢ ἄκοντας). His companion thinks that they act willingly out of wickedness. Socrates quotes a poet who said that nobody is bad willingly, nor blessed unwillingly (*De iust.* 374a), which makes his companion remind him that poets tell many lies.[80] Socrates disagrees and guides him towards accepting that just people act justly because of knowledge, while unjust people act unjustly because of ignorance (and therefore unwillingly).

There are several parallels with Xenophon's and Plato's dialogues.[81] It is difficult to determine when, in what environment, and with what intention the dialogue was written. It may have been a school exercise.[82]

### 4.3.4 On Virtue

Like *On Justice*, *On Virtue* is a brief dramatic dialogue in which Socrates talks with an anonymous interlocutor.[83] The reader, however, is provided with more information about Socrates' companion: he is an Athenian (cf. *De virt.* 376c where he refers to Thucydides, Themistocles, Aristides, and Pericles as the "good men among us"); in the past, he associated with Lysimachus, the son of Aristides (*De virt.* 377d) and was in love with one of Pericles' sons (*De virt.* 377d-e). Socrates' opening question introduces three separate problems which will be discussed in

---

[80] The verse quoted by Socrates is also referred to by Aristotle, *EN* 1113b14–15, who disagrees with it. The sentiment of the first part of the verse echoes in a line ascribed to Epicharmus (F 66 K–A: οἴομαι δ' οὐδεὶς ἑκὼν πονηρὸς οὐδ' ἄταν ἔχων). For possible connections between these texts, see Müller 1975, 169–70; Aronadio 2008, 302 n. 5. The answer of Socrates' interlocutor ("poets tell many lies"), appears also in Aristotle, *Metaph.* 983a3–4.

[81] For instance, the examination of lying, deceiving, and harming in *De iust.* 374b–d resembles Socrates' conversation with Euthydemus in Xenophon, *Mem.* 4.2.12–19, and the discussion of willing vs. unwilling injustice is reminiscent of Plato's Book 1 of the *Republic*, *Protagoras* (345d–e) and *Laws* (861d–862a). For other parallels, see Pavlu 1913, 8–19; Müller 1975, 134–62.

[82] Pavlu 1913, 6: "eine Schulübung"; Souilhé 1930b, 10: "probablement un exercice d'école." Müller 1975, 129–91 considers the dialogue to reflect the ideas of the early Socratics, in particular Antisthenes, whose work might have been a model for the dialogue's author. Aronadio 2008, 60–2 thinks that parallels between *On Justice* and Plato's dialogues suggest that it originated in the context of the Old Academy, not long after Plato's death.

[83] In some manuscripts, the companion is referred to as "Meno" or as "Hippotrophus" ("a horse-breeder"). These attempts to identify Socrates' interlocutor are probably guess-work of some Byzantine critic (the identification with Meno is due to the fact that *On Virtue* freely adapts several passages from Plato's dialogue *Meno*; as for "Hippotrophus," Diogenes Laertius mentions a dialogue titled *Midon or Horse-Breeder* among the Platonic *spuria* (3.62), which might have influenced the Byzantine scholar who proposed this identification; see Müller 1975, 192–4. There is nothing, however, within the dialogue that would allow us to identify the speaker, which suggests that his anonymity is resolute.

the dialogue: whether virtue is teachable, whether one becomes virtuous by nature, and if not—in what manner (*De virt.* 376a: ἆρα διδακτόν ἐστιν ἡ ἀρετή; ἢ οὐ διδακτόν, ἀλλὰ φύσει οἱ ἀγαθοὶ γίγνονται ἄνδρες, ἢ ἄλλῳ τινὶ τρόπῳ;).[84] His interlocutor is not able to answer the question (*De virt.* 376b: Οὐκ ἔχω εἰπεῖν ἐν τῷ παρόντι); Socrates guides him with questions towards the conclusion that virtue is not teachable (virtuous Athenians—Thucydides, Themistocles, Aristides, and Pericles—did not have teachers of virtue, and did not manage to instruct their sons in virtue). He then demonstrates that one does not become virtuous by nature. His companion becomes curious: how do men, then, become good? Socrates' guess is that virtue is a divine possession (*De virt.* 379c: θεῖόν τι... τὸ κτῆμα) and is received through divine allotment (*De virt.* 379d: θείᾳ μοίρᾳ): good men are inspired by the gods, like prophets and diviners: if gods wish the city well, they provide it with virtuous men; if they intend for the city to fail, they remove them.

*On Virtue* is a reworking of Plato's *Meno* (which bore the subtitle *On Virtue*), with some elements originating from other Platonic dialogues.[85] Socrates' opening question is reminiscent of the one asked by Meno at the beginning the Platonic model: he asks Socrates whether virtue is teachable, whether it can result from practice, and whether it comes by nature, or in some other way (*Men.* 70a: ἆρα διδακτὸν ἡ ἀρετή; ἢ οὐ διδακτὸν ἀλλ' ἀσκητόν; ἢ οὔτε ἀσκητὸν οὔτε μαθητόν, ἀλλὰ φύσει παραγίγνεται τοῖς ἀνθρώποις ἢ ἄλλῳ τινὶ τρόπῳ;).[86] The author of *On Virtue* also modeled Socrates' arguments and examples on the *Meno* (e.g. the example of Themistocles, Aristides, Pericles, and Thucydides who were unable to teach virtue to their sons, comes from *Meno* 93c–94e), and numerous passages repeat *Meno* word-for-word, amounting to about half of the text.[87] Socrates' conclusion in *On Virtue*—that virtue does not come from teaching or nature—mirrors his statements in the *Meno*, and his closing verdict that virtue is a gift from the gods likewise derives from Plato's dialogue.

This reworking of the Platonic model, however, produces a strikingly different text. In the *Meno*, the identities of interlocutors add to the dialogue's ambiguity: Meno was a Thessalian aristocrat, who would die in 400 BCE, about two years after the dramatic date of the dialogue, as described in Xenophon's *Anabasis*, in which

---

[84] The issue of whether virtue can be taught is a recurrent one in Greek thought. It is discussed in *Dissoi logoi*, and several Socratics, including Crito and Simon the cobbler, are ascribed texts arguing that virtue cannot be taught (Diogenes Laertius 2.121, 2.122). It is also a recurrent topic in Plato, whose *Meno* was the main model for the author of *On Virtue*. Xenocrates was ascribed a work titled *That Virtue Can Be Taught* (Diogenes Laertius 4.12).

[85] For possible echoes of other Platonic dialogues, including *Gorgias*, *Protagoras*, and *Apology*, see Müller 1975, 197–220.

[86] Practice, included in the opening question in the *Meno* as a potential means of acquiring virtue (but absent in *On Virtue*), is not discussed later in Plato's dialogue. Scott 2006, 16–17 thinks that it might have been an interpolation.

[87] For a comparison of passages from *On Virtue* with *Meno*, see Müller 1975, 197–220; Müller 2005, 158.

he is portrayed as a villain;[88] Anytus, his Athenian host, also a speaker in the *Meno*, would become one of Socrates' accusers in 399 BCE. They are not Socrates' friends or companions, and the fact that it is Meno who accosts Socrates and inquires about the teachability of virtue at the beginning of the dialogue raises questions regarding his intentions and Socrates' sincerity. In *On Virtue*, the same question is posed by Socrates to a *hetairos*, who substitutes for Meno and Anytus, in an attempt to engage his companion in an ethical examination. The ambiguity of the *Meno*, resulting from the choice of speakers, disappears. In addition, while in Plato the examination of the origins of virtue is marked as provisional by Socrates, who emphasizes that it should have been preceded by scrutiny of what virtue really is (*Men.* 86c-d), in *On Virtue* the problem of defining virtue is never mentioned and the results of the discussion are phrased as definite and final. Using Plato's own phrases, the author reaches an un-Platonic result, creating "a new Plato with Plato's words" in a manner reminiscent of the Hellenistic strategies of the reception of Classical predecessors.[89]

The date and purpose of *On Virtue* remain unclear. It may have originated within the context of Academic skepticism in the first half of the third century BCE as a polemic against proponents of the teachability of virtue, in particular Xenocrates and the Stoics, who are refuted with Plato's own words taken from the *Meno*.[90] Other scholars think it might have originated in a didactic setting, perhaps as a student exercise, or as a school text intended to introduce students to philosophical questions and stimulate discussion.[91]

### 4.3.5 *Demodocus*

Four separate compositions are transmitted in manuscripts under the title *Demodocus*. The first one (I will refer to it as *Demodocus 1*) is a monologue by an unidentified speaker, addressed to Demodocus; the following three (I will call them *Demodocus 2-4*, though Demodocus makes no appearance there) are short narrated dialogues. The Demodocus who is the addressee of the first piece is, presumably, the father of Theages mentioned by Socrates in Plato's *Apology*

---

[88] For Meno in Xenophon and Plato, see Nails 2002, 204-5. The question of how to reconcile Plato's representation of Meno with Xenophon's depiction was pondered in antiquity (in Athenaeus, *Deipn.* 11.505a-b, it is proposed that Plato's dialogue is an *encomium* of Meno, and that Plato praises him out of spite and rivalry against Xenophon). Modern scholars variously approach this problem (e.g. Klein 1965 assumes that there are layers of irony in the *Meno*; Holzhausen 1994 thinks that familiarity with Xenophon's image of Meno is necessary to properly understand Plato's dialogue, and that Plato's Meno is a prototype for people who do not understand the Platonic model of teaching and learning).

[89] Müller 2005, 163.

[90] According to Müller 1975, 249-61 and Müller 2005, 160-3, the dialogue was written against the position of Xenocrates and the Stoics, who considered virtue to be teachable, probably around the time of Arcesilaus; similarly Aronadio 2008, 83-5.

[91] Souilhé 1930b, 26; Brisson 2014, 374.

(*Ap.* 33e), and who is Socrates' interlocutor in the opening chapters of the dialogue *Theages* (*Thg.* 121a–d).

The speaker in *Demodocus 1* is not explicitly identified, but the fact that he addresses Demodocus—Socrates' interlocutor in *Theages*—may suggest that he is Socrates.[92] He says that he was approached by Demodocus and asked for advice on an undisclosed political matter, which was to be discussed in an assembly. Rather than providing advice, he challenges the very process of political decision-making, which involves listening to advice offered by a number of people and then reaching a decision by vote. He argues that this process is absurd because one either knows what the right decision is, or not: in the first case, one does not need advice, and in the latter, one is unable to distinguish between good and bad advice. The theme is similar to that of another Platonic *spurium*, namely the *Sisyphus*, discussed earlier in this chapter.

The three short dialogues that follow differ from *Demodocus 1* in format, but are similarly intent on questioning common-sense, popular opinions and customs. All three are reported by an internal, first-person narrator who provides an account of an overheard conversation. In *Demodocus 2*, he relates how he heard a man reproach his friend for having believed an accuser without hearing the defendant, arguing that one should listen to both sides. The friend retorts that it would be absurd if it were impossible to determine whether someone was speaking truly or falsely after listening to him, but possible after listening to two people. *Demodocus 3* contains an account of a discussion carried on by several men, one of whom disparages another for not wanting to lend him money. A third man interrupts and argues that he should blame himself since he apparently failed to persuade the friend. *Demodocus 4* reports a discussion about trust. One man is criticizing another one for naivety and trusting people too easily. As in *Demodocus 3*, a third man joins in and challenges the idea that one should not be quick to trust other people, and strangers in particular, arguing that all one should do is to determine whether someone is telling the truth or not.

The format of the three dialogues is exceptional. They all feature a first-person narrator who reports exchanges in which one of the interlocutors questions a common-sense opinion. The speakers are unnamed, and the time and place of the conversation are unspecified. The narrator does not take part in the conversations, remaining a silent listener. He is sometimes identified by scholars with Socrates, but his name does not appear in the dialogues, and he does not betray any familiar Socratic features. At the end of *Demodocus 2* and *4*, he expresses puzzlement and addresses directly his audience:

---

[92] Byzantine manuscripts identify Socrates and Demodocus as characters at the beginning of *Demodocus 1*, but this notation is a later addition. It is not clear why the figure of Demodocus has been chosen as the addressee (in *Theages*, he plays the part of a concerned father rather than a politician).

Ἐγὼ γοῦν ἀκούων αὐτῶν ἠπόρουν καὶ κρίνειν οὐχ οἷός τ' ἦν· οἱ μὲν γὰρ ἄλλοι ἔφασαν οἱ παρόντες τὸν πρῶτον λέγειν ἀληθῆ. εἰ οὖν τι ἔχεις συμβάλλεσθαί μοι περὶ τούτων, πότερόν ἐστιν ἑνὸς λέγοντος γνῶναι τί λέγει, ἢ προσδεῖται τοῦ ἀντεροῦντος, εἰ μέλλει τις γνώσεσθαι πότερον ὀρθῶς λέγει· ἢ οὐκ ἀναγκαῖόν ἐστιν ἀμφοτέρων ἀκούειν. ἢ πῶς νομίζεις;

When I heard them I myself was perplexed and could not come to a judgment—though the others who were present said that the first man spoke the truth. So help me with the matter if you can: when one man speaks can you assess what he says, or do you need his opponent too if you are to know whether he is telling the truth? Or is it unnecessary to hear both sides? What do you think?
(*Dem. 2*, 384a–b, trans. J. Barnes)

Ταῦτ' οὖν λεγόντων αὐτῶν ἠπόρουν τίσιν ποτὲ δεῖ πιστεύειν καὶ τίσιν οὔ, καὶ πότερον τοῖς πιστοῖς καὶ τοῖς εἰδόσι περὶ ὧν λέγουσιν ἢ τοῖς οἰκείοις καὶ τοῖς γνωρίμοις. περὶ τούτων οὖν πῶς σὺ νομίζεις;

While they argued in this way I was perplexed as to who on earth I should and shouldn't trust, and whether I should trust the trustworthy and people who know what they're talking about, or rather relations and acquaintances. What do you think about this? (*Dem. 4*, 386c, trans. J. Barnes)

These endings aim to engage the reader, to invite him to critically assess the argument and examine the problem further. While scholars tend to disparage *Demodocus 2–4* as shows of futile eristic,[93] one can imagine the effective employment of such texts as exercises in a school setting.

The relationship between *Demodocus 1* and *Demodocus 2–4* is unclear. They betray a similar interest in counter-intuitive arguments which challenge general opinions. Perhaps they circulated together as a collection of *aporiai* like *Dissoi logoi* or later compilations of *problemata*, and were used for didactic purposes in the Academy (which would explain their inclusion in the Platonic corpus).[94] Souilhé associated them with Megarian eristic and considered them a product of the fourth century BCE.[95] Müller and Aronadio thought that they originated in the Academy, though in different phases: *Demodocus 1* in the Old Academy, before the school took the sceptic turn, and *Demodocus 2–4* in the New Academy of Arcesilaus.[96]

---

[93] See e.g. Souilhé 1930b, 40; Taylor 1949[6], 547: the author must have been "a person of low intelligence, with no power of expression and a taste for futile eristic."
[94] Souilhé 1930b, 40; Thesleff 1982, 230.   [95] Souilhé 1930b, 41–2; similarly Brisson 2014, 122.
[96] Müller 1975, 126–8, 268–71; Aronadio 2008, 62–5, 81–3.

### 4.3.6 *Axiochus*

The *Axiochus* is a reported dialogue with Socrates as the narrator, relating a conversation to an undisclosed audience in a manner reminiscent of several of Plato's dialogues. The narrative format is retained only in the first section of the dialogue (*Ax.* 364a–365a); the remaining part is entirely in dramatic form.[97] Socrates' interlocutor in the opening of the dialogue is Cleinias (a speaker in Plato's *Euthydemus*), and in the main part—his father Axiochus. Damon and Charmides, both familiar to readers of Plato, are silent characters.[98]

Socrates narrates how he was asked by Cleinias to pay a visit to his father who, seriously ill, became overwhelmed by a fear of death. He hurried to Axiochus' house and found him "strong in body, but weak in soul" (*Ax.* 365a: τῷ σώματι ῥωμαλέον, ἀσθενῆ δὲ τὴν ψυχήν), weeping, groaning, and in great need of consolation (πάνυ ἐνδεᾶ παραμυθίας). Socrates goes over a variety of arguments, drawn from different philosophical traditions—including Epicurean, Platonic, Stoic, and Orphic-Pythagorean—in order to persuade Axiochus that death is not an evil. He starts with the Epicurean argument that there is no reason to fear death as it means deprivation of sensation (*Ax.* 365d: ἀναισθησία).[99] Then he argues that life is full of suffering and therefore its end is welcome, and relates a speech by Prodicus deploring human life and its hardships (*Ax.* 366a–369a).[100] He then adds the argument that death is nothing to us, as it concerns the dead, not the living (*Ax.* 369b–c), another Epicurean axiom.[101] These do not persuade Axiochus, who bluntly declares that he is pained at the prospect of losing earthly goods (ἡ στέρησις τῶν ἀγαθῶν τοῦ ζῆν). Socrates changes his strategy and argues that the soul is immortal, and that death does not deprive one of good things, but brings greater and purer pleasures (*Ax.* 370c–d). Axiochus is immediately

---

[97] Chevalier 1915, 15. One is reminded of Plato's *Theatetus*, where Euclides says that he will discard narrative bits between speakers' utterances (*Tht.* 143b–c).

[98] Cleinias is also talked about in Xenophon's *Symposion* (4.12–26). Charmides is the speaker in Plato's *Charmides* and is mentioned in several other works by Plato and Xenophon; Damon, a musical teacher, is mentioned inter alia in Plato's *Laches* and *Republic*. On characters, including Axiochus and his bad reputation, see Irwin 2015, 65–70.

[99] On deprivation of sensation after death, see Epicurus in Diogenes Laertius 10.81 (*Ep. Hdt.*): τὴν ἀναισθησίαν τὴν ἐν τῷ τεθνάναι; 10.125 (*Ep. Men.*): στέρησις δέ ἐστιν αἰσθήσεως ὁ θάνατος; 10.139 (*RS 2*): ὁ θάνατος οὐδὲν πρὸς ἡμᾶς· τὸ γὰρ διαλυθὲν ἀναισθητεῖ· τὸ δ' ἀναισθητοῦν οὐδὲν πρὸς ἡμᾶς; also Philodemus, *Mort.* col. i.5, i.9, i.18, xxviii.15–16, xxxix.22–3. Warren 2021 argues that the concept of the absence of sensation is not per se incompatible with the Platonic doctrine of the soul's immortality.

[100] Prodicus is frequently mentioned by Plato's Socrates and is a speaker in the *Protagoras*, while his myth of Heracles is reported in Xenophon's *Apomnemoneumata* (*Mem.* 2.1.21–34). His conversation with an unnamed youth is reported by Socrates in the pseudo-Platonic *Eryxias* (*Eryx.* 397c–399c).

[101] Cf. Diogenes Laertius 10.125 (*Ep. Men.*): ὁ θάνατος οὐδὲν πρὸς ἡμᾶς, ἐπειδή περ ὅταν μὲν ἡμεῖς ὦμεν, ὁ θάνατος οὐ πάρεστιν; 10.139 (*RS 2*); cf. also Philodemus, *Mort.* col. i.6–7, xxvi.8–9. For a comparative reading of the Epicurean arguments in the *Axiochus* and in Lucretius, see Furley 1986, 77–81.

convinced, and his fear of death is replaced with a longing and desire for it. Socrates reinforces Axiochus' newly found tranquility with a myth he once heard from Gobryas, a Persian Magus. Gobryas learnt it from his grandfather, also named Gobryas, who had once discovered bronze tablets on Delos, which were brought there from the Hyperboreans, the legendary people of the far north.[102] It said on them that people who were guided in life by a good *daimon* (*Ax.* 371c: δαίμων ἀγαθός) will reside in a beautiful and pleasant place, while the wicked men will be taken to Erebos and Chaos and subjected to eternal punishments. This vision further calms and comforts Axiochus.

The *Axiochus* belongs to the tradition of dialogues centered on death, initiated by Plato's *Phaedo* (to which there are numerous allusions)[103] and continued by later authors (Aristotle, Theophrastus, Heraclides of Pontus). It ingeniously combines the format of the Socratic dialogue with the tropes and conventions of a consolation, a Hellenistic genre the origins of which were associated with Crantor of Soli (Chapter 3.6). Unlike in typical specimens of this type of literature, however, in the *Axiochus* it is the person about to die who needs comforting, not the relatives or friends of a deceased, and the emotion which needs to be addressed is fear, not grief.[104] The consolatory character of the dialogue required adaptation of the figure of Socrates, who has been placed in the role of a wise man and psychical therapist, displaying his "widely known wisdom" (*Ax.* 364b).[105] The metaphor of philosophy as medicine, and of a philosopher as a physician of the soul, immensely popular in the Hellenistic schools, is dramatized: Axiochus is physically ill, though it transpires that it is an illness of the soul that torments him most, and Socrates is there to heal him with his wisdom.[106] The opening scene redefines Socratic activity on another level as well. Socrates reports to his undisclosed listeners that he was on his way to the *gymnasion* at Cynosarges when he was redirected by Cleinias to Axiochus' house. As a public place frequented by young people, a *gymnasion* would be a typical setting for a Socratic dialogue (though the author's choice of Cynosarges in particular, which could be used by boys and men who were not born from two Athenian parents, is remarkable); but

---

[102] The author perhaps wished the reader to identify Gobryas the grandfather with the military leader in Herodotus 7.72. Diogenes Laertius mentions a certain Gobryas in a list of Magi (1.2), but it is possible that he was influenced by *Axiochus* (he claims that the list, which goes down to Alexander's conquest of Persia, originated from Xanthus of Lydia, which is impossible, as Xanthus lived in the fifth century BCE).

[103] For some reminiscences from the *Phaedo*, see Chevalier 1915, 68–70.

[104] On consolatory elements in the *Axiochus*, see Chevalier 1915, 77–81; Souilhé 1930b, 119–23, 130–1; Kassel 1958, 37–8.

[105] On Socrates as a wise man in the *Axiochus*, see Joyal 2005; Erler 2012, 102–5.

[106] Joyal 2005, 105–10; Erler 2012, 104–5. While the metaphor of philosophy as medicine goes back to the Socratics, in the Hellenistic period it became fundamental for understanding the essence of philosophical activity. For extensive treatment of the medical analogy in Hellenistic philosophy, see Nussbaum 1994.

instead of practicing his philosophy there, Socrates performs his philosophical *therapeia* in a private, domestic space.[107]

The myth revealing the fate of the soul in the afterlife makes use of many familiar motifs. The Persian Gobryas represents the figure of an Eastern wise man, time and again deployed in dialogic literature.[108] The transmission of the story from Gobryas the grandfather to Gobryas the Magus is reminiscent of how the Atlantis story in Plato's *Timaeus* and *Critias* was received by Critias from his grandfather (*Ti.* 20d–e; *Criti.*113a–b). It is noteworthy, however, that in the *Axiochus*, the Persian Magus is not the ultimate source of wisdom but merely a reporter of what he discovered on the Hyperborean tablets. Socrates says that they were brought to Delos by Opis and Hecaerge, alluding to Herodotus' story of the Hyperborean maidens who came to Delos with offerings (Callimachus is the first extant author to name the girls Opis and Hecaerge).[109] The association of the Hyperboreans with knowledge regarding the afterlife perhaps comes from another tradition, namely, the one about the Hyperborean sage Abaris. Mentioned briefly in Herodotus (4.36) and Plato's *Charmides* (158b), he was featured in Heraclides of Pontus' *Abaris*, in all probability a dialogue, which, according to Plutarch, contained "doctrines about souls mixed with story-telling" (*De aud. poet.* 14e).

Further possible literary contexts emerge. Axiochus' complete change of heart and his desire for death is reminiscent of Callimachus' famous epigram about Cleombrotus, who committed suicide after reading Plato's *Phaedo*, a story, as Stephen White notes, "bizarre, even shocking" as it shows that it took just one book to convince Cleombrotus to end his life.[110] One is also reminded of the Cyrenaic philosopher Hegesias, nicknamed Πεισιθάνατος, "Death-Persuader," who, according to Cicero, was banned by the king Ptolemy from lecturing because many people killed themselves after listening to him (*Tusc.* 1.34.83–4). It is probable that the author had either Hegesias or Callimachus (or both) in mind when composing his piece.[111]

In spite of the solemn theme, the *Axiochus* does not strike one as grave and serious, with some scholars suspecting that it might have been intended as a

---

[107] On the setting, see Joyal 2005, 99–100; on Cynosarges, Irwin 2015, 82–3. Antisthenes was supposed to teach at Cynosarges (Diogenes Laertius 6.13), while according to the *Suda*, the place gave rise to the name of the Cynic school (s.v. Ἀντισθένης (α 2723)); perhaps the author's intention was to allude to the Cynics.

[108] See Chapter 3.2, p. 103.

[109] Herodotus 4.33–5: he mentions maidens named Hyperoche, Laodice, Arge, and Opis; Callimachus, *Del.* 292: Upis (instead of Opis), Loxo, and Hecaerge. For various versions of the story, see Sandin 2014a, 208–13.

[110] White 1994, 135. The author of the *Axiochus* amplifies the bizarre, as both Socrates and Axiochus at some point confess that they desire death: Socrates became a death-lover after listening to Prodicus (*Ax.* 366c), and Axiochus after listening to Socrates.

[111] On Hegesias, see Chapter 6.3, p. 200–2. For the suggestion that Callimachus' epigram alludes to Hegesias, see White 1994.

parody.[112] The representation of Axiochus—groaning, sobbing, beating himself in distress (*Ax.* 365a: πολλάκις δὲ ἀναφερόμενον καὶ στεναγμοὺς ἱέντα σὺν δακρύοις καὶ κροτήσεσι χειρῶν)—smacks of caricature in a philosophical dialogue. Axiochus not only does not live up to the philosophical ideal of death-bed serenity immortalized in the figure of the dying Socrates, but he also vividly reminds the reader of the representation of Xanthippe in the *Phaedo*: shouting in sorrow, crying aloud, and beating herself in grief (*Phd.* 60a–b; her lamenting is considered womanish, and she is quickly removed from the scene after Socrates asks Crito to have her taken home). One also cannot help but notice that—unlike Cephalus in Book 1 of Plato's *Republic*—Axiochus never stops to ask himself whether the eternal bliss which, as Socrates emphasizes, is reserved for the pious, will become his experience (and that despite his involvement in the profanation of mysteries and his bad reputation). Furthermore, the reader is struck by the speed with which conflicting arguments are produced by Socrates and the ease with which they are discarded or accepted, depending on whether they are considered to be psychologically effective. Although drawing from a wide philosophical repertoire, not restricted to one intellectual tradition, is a recurrent feature in consolatory texts which offer a hodgepodge of arguments as a provisional remedy in a period of acute grief,[113] in the *Axiochus* Socrates applies such a half-measure treatment to a person nearing death, which gives his arguments a sense of finality. Generic expectations of the reader add to the sense of discomfort with the dialogue: while the argumentative mode prioritizing psychological effectiveness over truth fits a consolatory letter, it seems disingenuous, even alarming in a philosophical dialogue, a genre intimately associated with the pursuit of truth.

Many features of the *Axiochus*—its language, philosophical ideas evocative of the Hellenistic school, engagement with the consolation—indicate that the work postdates the fourth century BCE, though its precise dating is uncertain; most scholars consider it a late Hellenistic work, perhaps from the first century BCE.[114] As the author remodels the figure of Socrates, transplants the consolatory argumentative mode into a philosophical dialogue, and engages with post-Platonic intellectual traditions, the Socratic dialogue is reshaped in a manner reminiscent of Hellenistic literary aesthetics and its poetics of *variatio in imitando*.[115]

---

[112] Cf. Nesselrath 2012, 126.     [113] As argued by O'Keefe 2006.
[114] Souilhé 1930b, 135; Hershbell 1981, 20–1; Männlein-Robert 2012, 6–7. For a discussion of the language, see Chevalier 1915, 43–66; Männlein-Robert 2012, 10–13. Diogenes Laertius ascribes a work titled *Axiochus* to Aeschines of Sphettus (2.61), but the dialogue certainly postdates the Socratic. Clement of Alexandria ascribes the dialogue to Plato (*Strom.* 6.2.17.5), and so does Stobaeus (1.49.47, 4.34.75, 4.52b.54, 4.53.38).
[115] See Erler 2012, 114–15 who discusses the employment of *oppositio in imitando* in the dialogue.

### 4.3.7 Halcyon

POxy 52.3683, a papyrus fragment from the late second century CE, ascribes the dialogue to Plato, while Nicias of Nicaea and Favorinus name certain Leon as the author (Athenaeus, *Deipn.* 11.506c; Diogenes Laertius 3.62).[116] At some point, it was assigned to Lucian and transmitted among his works. As a result, the dialogue was not included in Stephanus' 1578 edition of Plato, is frequently omitted from editions of the Platonic *spuria*, and has remained understudied by scholars, which is regrettable, as it creatively enriches the format of the Socratic dialogue with post-Classical themes and motifs.

The work is a miniature dramatic dialogue of less than one thousand words. Socrates converses with his friend Chaerephon on a beach stroll in Phaleron. They hear a bird call; Socrates identifies the bird as a kingfisher and narrates the myth of Alcyone who was in such grief after death of her husband Ceyx that gods turned her into the bird.[117] The metamorphosis myth is supplemented with zoological information about the bird's habitat, voice, size, and nesting period. Socrates also talks about the so-called halcyon days, that is days of calm weather in the middle of winter, occurring around the time of kingfishers' breeding, which, he explains, are the honor the gods bestowed on the kingfisher for wifely devotion.[118] Chaerephon voices his doubts concerning veracity of such improbable metamorphosis myths. Socrates responds that people are "dim-sighted judges of what is possible and what is impossible" (*Halc.* 3: τῶν δυνατῶν τε καὶ ἀδυνάτων ἀμβλυωποί τινες εἶναι κριταί), their perception of what is easy and difficult, attainable and unattainable is faulty (δυνατά—ἀδύνατα, εὔπορα—ἄπορα, ἐφικτά—ἀνέφικτα), and they are incapable of understanding the powers of gods and nature (τὰς τῶν θεῶν καὶ δαιμονίων δυνάμεις ἢ τὰς τῆς ὅλης φύσεως). He reiterates his position the end of the dialogue, where he notes that people are unable to discern things which are great and things which are small (*Halc.* 8: τὰ μεγάλα, τὰ σμικρά), and are ignorant concerning most of the things that happen to them (τὰ πλείω ... τῶν περὶ ἡμᾶς συμβαινόντων παθῶν). There is a tinge of skepticism here; at the same time, Socrates' image of the world betrays a Stoic influence: the universe is imagined as being filled with the divine element, and nature as a demiurgic and purposeful power creating animals with help of "sacred

---

[116] Athenaeus calls him "Leon the Academic"; perhaps Leon of Byzantium is meant, a contemporary of Philip of Macedon and, according to the *Suda*, a pupil of Plato or Aristotle (s.v. Λέων (λ 265)). The dialogue, however, appears to have been composed later, perhaps in the third or second century BCE (Brinkmann 1891, 7–14; Müller 1975, 285–97).

[117] The *Halcyon* is probably the first extant account of the Alcyone myth, which goes back to the archaic period (see Hesiod, F 10d Merkelbach and West). The myth is narrated in Ovid's *Metamorphoses* 11.410–748; Fantham 1979, 332 finds it plausible that both Ovid and the author of the *Halcyon* drew from Nicander of Colophon. For an overview of the kingfisher stories in antiquity, see Jażdżewska 2015c, 426–7.

[118] Cf. e.g. Aristotle, *HA* 593b8–10: kingfisher's habitat and song; 616a14–34: its size, appearance, and nest; 542b1–17: nesting and halcyon days.

arts of the great aether" (τέχναις ἱεραῖς αἰθέρος μεγάλου προσχρωμένη).[119] The dialogue ends with Socrates lavishly praising the kingfisher and intending to hymn its pious and husband-loving affection (τὸν εὐσεβῆ καὶ φίλανδρον ἔρωτα) to his two (!) wives, Xanthippe and Myrto, and Chaerephon's observation that the story offers "a double exhortation to the bond between wives and husbands" (Halc. 8: διπλασίαν ἔχει τὴν παράκλησιν πρὸς γυναικῶν τε καὶ ἀνδρῶν ὁμιλίαν).

The Halcyon interacts with several generic and intellectual traditions. It is a Socratic dialogue, composed in a stylized and poetic diction,[120] which engages with Plato, in particular with the Phaedrus of which it is a playful, miniature re-enactment. There are parallels in the setting: in both cases, characters take a walk outside the city and next to a body of water (Ilissus in the Phaedrus, the sea in the Halcyon). The conversations unfold at a special, "divine" time: in the Phaedrus it is midday, a time of divine epiphany, while in the Halcyon it is a short period of calm weather in the middle of winter, sent by the gods to honor Alcyone and facilitate the breeding of the kingfisher. Both dialogues end with interlocutors going back to the city: at the end of the Phaedrus, Socrates promises to deliver a message to Isocrates from the gods of the place and prays to Pan and other local divinities; at the end of Halcyon, he addresses the kingfisher, which has been honored by the gods, and departs with the intention to share its story with his wives. There are also thematic parallels. Chaerephon's doubts concerning the veracity of metamorphosis stories evoke two passages from the Phaedrus: one in which the problem of the truthfulness of myths is posed (Phdr. 229c: Phaedrus asks Socrates whether he thinks the myth of Boreas' kidnapping of Oreithyia tells the truth) and the story of the cicadas and their transformation (Phdr. 259b–c: they were once humans and loved singing so much that they forgot to eat and drink; as a result, they died and were reborn as cicadas; note that the theme of music is central to both the kingfisher and cicadas tale). However, in the Halcyon Socrates assumes a different position on the value of myths and metamorphosis narratives than in the Phaedrus, as he emphasizes the analogy between miraculous metamorphoses in myths and astounding transformations occurring in the physical world when the demiurgic nature creates living beings and brings them to maturity.[121]

The combination of zoological and mythical material in the Halcyon and the author's interest in the miraculous is reminiscent of paradoxographical literature, while Socrates' appreciation of the didactic potential of the kingfisher *exemplum* fits in with paradeigmatic and paraenetic use of animals we encounter in the early imperial period (Philo of Alexandria, Plutarch, Aelian), and which certainly continues a Hellenistic tradition. The motif of Myrto, Socrates' second wife, on

---

[119] On the skeptic coloring of the dialogue and its links with the New Academy, see Müller 1975, 304–7 and Müller 2005, 165–9; for Stoic parallels, Brinkmann 1891, 16–27.

[120] Müller 1975, 276–8, 291–5 discusses the poetic language and rhythmic patterns in the dialogue.

[121] On the striking similarities between this passage and Ovid's *Metamorphoses* 15.382–8, see Müller 1975, 312–15.

the other hand, points towards engagement with the Peripatetic biographic tradition. Aristotle is said to have mentioned her in his *On Noble Birth*, though presumably not with the intention of attacking Socrates' morals.[122] He was followed by Demetrius of Phaleron, Callisthenes, Aristoxenus of Tarentum, Hieronymus of Rhodes, and Satyrus of Callatis (Plutarch, *Arist.* 27.2; Athenaeus, *Deipn.* 13.555d–556a; Diogenes Laertius 2.26). Aristoxenus discussed Socrates' relationship with Myrto and Xanthippe in a passage describing the philosopher's strong sexual drive, and depicted his family life as turbulent, with the women fighting against one another and attacking Socrates.[123] His account was read as malicious by later authors, who defended Socrates against accusations of bigamy and sexual licentiousness: we know that in the second century BCE, the Stoic Panaetius wrote against people who claimed that Socrates had lived with Myrto (Plutarch, *Arist.* 27.2 and Athenaeus, *Deipn.* 13.556b). The author of the *Halcyon* humorously settles the controversy by making Socrates himself in *propria voce* refer to his two wives (*Halc.* 8: γυναιξὶ ταῖς ἐμαῖς). The serene family picture the reader is to envisage—with Socrates hymning the wifely virtues of the kingfisher to his two wives—replaces the image of turbulent relations in his household painted by Aristoxenus.

Chaerephon's comment at the end of the dialogue that Socrates has offered "a double exhortation to the bond between wives and husbands" (*Halc.* 8: διπλασίαν ἔχει τὴν παράκλησιν πρὸς γυναικῶν τε καὶ ἀνδρῶν ὁμιλίαν) evokes yet another context, namely the philosophical controversy about the value of marriage. Hellenistic and imperial era Stoics were particularly interested in this issue and produced treatises insisting that marriage was good and in accordance with nature and the rules of the universe; members of other schools assumed various positions in this matter.[124] Chaerephon draws the reader's attention to the fact that Socrates has provided "a double" exhortation to marriage—as it consisted both of the myth of the faithful Alcyone turned into the kingfisher, and of the exemplum of Socrates' own life, happily shared with Myrto and Xanthippe. At the same time, the adjective διπλασία humorously alludes to Socrates' double marriage and

---

[122] The story of Myrto and Xanthippe appears not to have been present in any Socratic writings, but only in a later tradition; interestingly, though, in Plato's *Phaedo* we read about women (plural) from Socrates' household who came to prison shortly before his death (*Phd.* 116b).

[123] Haake 2013, 100–7 argues that Aristoxenus intended to discredit Socrates; Huffman 2012, 269–79 thinks that he wished to paint a non-idealized image of Socrates, revealing the complexity of his character (for the rehabilitation of Aristoxenus as a biographer, see also Schorn 2012, with the *Life of Socrates* discussed at 199–217).

[124] For an overview of the philosophical debate on marriage in the Hellenistic period, see Deming 2004², 47–72. Stobaeus preserves fragments of *On Marriage* (Περὶ γάμου) and *On Living with a Woman* (Περὶ γυναικὸς συμβιώσεως) by the Stoic Antipater (perhaps Antipater of Tarsus, second century BCE, though it is also possible that Antipater of Tyre of the first century BCE is meant), which praise marriage (4.22a.25, 4.22d.103); the early imperial period Stoics Musonius Rufus and Hierocles demonstrate a similar appreciation. The idea of the "exhortation to marriage" appears in Hierocles the Stoic who says that nature seems to "exhort us to marriage" (Stobaeus 4.67.22: παρακαλεῖν ἡμᾶς... ἐπὶ τὸν γάμον).

results in a humorous take on the marriage controversy: apparently, Socrates is such an advocate of the married life that he has two wives!

The dialogue's post-Classical character is evident from its engagement with Hellenistic philosophic and generic traditions, though exact dating is debatable; proposed dates range from the third to the first century BCE.[125] The author has confidently remodeled the Socratic dialogue and woven into his miniature a playful imitation of the Platonic *Phaedrus* and a variety of contemporary motifs and philosophical ideas.

## 4.4 Conclusion

The dialogues discussed in this chapter, written by different authors in different times and circumstances, vary in form and in philosophical intent and seriousness. Most of them belong to the category of Socratic dialogue and feature Socrates as the main character.[126] The *Epinomis*, with the same set of characters as Plato's *Laws*, is an exception. Other works which to some extent deviate from the Socratic format are *Demodocus 2–4*, where all characters are unnamed and the narrator does not betray typical Socratic features; the *Sisyphus* in which the dominant figure is never named even though his behavior is reminiscent of Socrates; and the *Cleitophon*, in which Socrates' speaking role is radically limited. Socrates' interlocutors are frequently anonymous (*Hipparchus*, *Minos*, *Rival Lovers*, *On Justice*, *On Virtue*).[127] In some cases, suppression of speakers' names is accompanied by erasure of any individualizing marks. As they become generic companions of Socrates, their personalities and life-stories do not resonate or interfere with the philosophical argument. In other works, speakers' anonymity is used to transform them into embodiments of certain attitudes, as in the *Rival Lovers*, where Socrates converses with "the intellectual" and "the athlete." In dialogues with named interlocutors, there is an interest in characters who are merely mentioned or make a brief appearance in Plato such as Demodocus and Theages in the *Theages*, Cleitophon, and Axiochus; these characters are provided in the *dubia* and *spuria* with distinct personalities and communicate their worries and

---

[125] Brinkmann 1891, 25 proposes third or second century BCE; Müller 1975, 315–16 and Müller 2005, 164 argue for the second half of the second century BCE. Hutchinson in Cooper and Hutchinson 1997, 1714 finds the range of 150–50 BCE most likely.

[126] On the Socrates of the pseudo-Platonica and the recurrent features which set him apart from the Platonic Socrates, see Joyal 2019; Donato 2021.

[127] The speakers' anonymity is not unparalleled in Plato and Xenophon. Plato plays with a variety of anonymous figures, for instance, in the openings of the *Protagoras* and the *Symposion*; in the *Sophist*, the *Statesman*, and the *Laws*, in which he introduces mysterious unnamed strangers characterized solely by the city they come from (Elea or Athens); or in the *Phaedo*, where Phaedo refers to an intervention by someone whose name Phaedo forgot (*Phd.* 103a) (for discussion of anonymous speakers in Plato, see Desclos 2001; Blondell 2002, 318–26). In Xenophon's *Apomnemoneumata*, Socrates' conversational partner sometimes remains anonymous (e.g. *Mem.* 3.1, 3.3, 3.14.2–3).

concerns. Well-known companions and acquaintances of Socrates are only occasionally his main partners in conversation (as Alcibiades in the *Alcibiades II* and Chaerephon in the *Halcyon*), although they sometimes make a short appearance at the beginning of a dialogue (Cleinias in *Axiochus*, Critias in *Eryxias*). Rare are speakers unknown from extant Socratic literature, such as Eryxias and Erasistratus in the *Eryxias* and Sisyphus in the *Sisyphus*. While the conversation between Socrates and his interlocutor typically follows a familiar script in which the former plays the dominant figure, the *Cleitophon* challenges this model by making Cleitophon the main speaker and assigning Socrates a reduced speaking role.

Most of the dialogues assume a dramatic format, with only a few making use of the first-person narration by Socrates (*Rival Lovers, Eryxias, Axiochus*). No dialogue employs non-Platonic third-person narration. The *Axiochus* offers an interesting formal variation as narrative interventions occur only in the opening of the dialogue and are omitted altogether afterwards; as a result, the dialogue combines the reported and dramatic formats. The three dialogues of *Demodocus 2–4* are the most striking outliers as they employ the figure of an unnamed and un-Socratic narrator who does not partake of the conversation but remains a silent listener. Two of these pieces, *Demodocus 2* and *4*, are also noteworthy for directly engaging the audience, which is addressed at the end of the dialogues and asked about their opinions concerning the problem discussed.

Another typical feature of the *dubia* and *spuria* is their relative brevity. Only three dialogues (*Epinomis, Eryxias*, and *Alcibiades II*) exceed four thousand words and are longer than Plato's shortest dialogue, *Ion*, with the remaining works ranging from around three thousand six hundred words (*Theages*) to under five hundred (*Demodocus 2–4*). Carl Müller observed that in several dialogues of the *Appendix Platonica* (*On Justice, On Virtue, Sisyphus, Demodocus 2–4*, and the *Halcyon*) the brevity is accompanied by other characteristics, such as anonymity and limited intellectual independence in Socrates' interlocutor, lack of a dramatic setting, a certain schematism in the flow of conversation, clearly marked and frequently abrupt transitions in the argument, clear formulation of the problem about to be discussed in the opening question, and explicitly stated results at the end (Müller proposed to consider these works as belonging to a sub-genre of the dialogue which he referred to as *Kurzdialog*).[128] These features recur also in some of the Platonic *dubia*, for instance in the *Cleitophon*, as Slings argued,[129] but also in the *Hipparchus* and the *Minos* (anonymous speakers, introducing the topic in the first sentence, in the *Hipparchus* also ending the dialogue with a clear formulation of the result reached in the discussion).

---

[128] Müller 1975, 322–4. Müller 1975, 324 considers the format of the *Kurzdialog* to be a post-Platonic development, while Slings 1999, 21–6 thinks that some of the Socratics wrote dialogues with these characteristics.
[129] Slings 1999, 26–34.

The main characteristic the examined dialogues share is close interaction with Plato, both on the conceptual and literary level (the only exception are the three pieces in *Demodocus 2–4* which do not engage closely with Plato's dialogues). The modes of literary engagement with Plato differ radically. In some cases, the audience's familiarity with Plato is necessary for understanding a dialogue even on a very elementary level: the reader of the *Epinomis* must have read the *Laws* in order to know who the speakers are. The *Cleitophon* presupposes the reader's familiarity with the first book of the *Republic* and with the character of Thrasymachus. Some dialogues reorganize, abridge, and condense Platonic material, as for example, *On Virtue*, which reworks and modifies the *Meno*; some contain a mosaic of thoughts and phrases deriving from multiple works of Plato. In certain cases, a knowledge of Platonic texts, even if not necessary, opens additional venues for interpretation, for example, by allowing the reader to discern the author's departure from or polemic with Plato, as in the *Halcyon*, which deviates from the *Phaedrus* in its appraisal of myths, or in the *Theages* which, by means of transposition and manipulation of material from *Theaetetus*, produces a very un-Platonic conception of Socrates' *daimonion*.

When considering literary and dramatic imitation of Plato in the *dubia* and *spuria*, the concepts of *variatio* and *oppositio in imitando*, which entail a creative alteration (*variatio*) or inversion (*oppositio*) of the hypotext. These concepts are closely associated with (though not limited to) Hellenistic aesthetics, which relied on the reader's literary competence and familiarity with earlier literature. They prove useful when thinking about the pseudo-Platonica which, as Michael Erler has observed, are characterized by "*palintonos harmonia* of closeness and distance" to Plato's works.[130] The *Halcyon*, which offers a miniature version of the *Phaedrus*, provides a great example. The miniaturization itself is one of the components of the *variatio*; other elements include transformed Platonic motifs and themes (for instance, substitution of Ilissus' bank by the beach at Phaleron, or of the story of the cicadas' transformation by the myth of Alcyone). The author of the *Cleitophon* reuses and reverses motifs of the *Republic* and the *Apology* and assigns Cleitophon the discursive role conventionally belonging to Socrates. In the *Sisyphus*, which draws significantly from the *Meno*, the Pharsalian youth Meno has been substituted with Sisyphus, another Pharsalian, but one older and experienced in politics; the dialogue also moves beyond the usual Socratic topography as the course of events described in the opening makes it impossible that the speakers are in Athens. *On Virtue*, on the other hand, substitutes *Meno*'s characters with an unnamed *hetairos* and by skillful stitching of *Meno*'s passages conveys a very different message to the one the reader finds in Plato, while the

---

[130] Erler 2008, 226: "Emerge però una forma di *palintonos harmonia* di vicinanza e distanza dagli originali. Si pone l'accento da una parte sulla stretta dipendenza da Platone, ma si constata ad un tempo anche l'impiego di dottrine o motivi lettarari di Platone in aperta opposizione a Platone."

author of the *Theages* cleverly rewrites a passage from the *Theaetetus* to create a fundamentally different concept of Socrates' *daimonion*.

While Plato is the main point of reference for the authors of *dubia* and *spuria*, they also engaged with other intellectual traditions, including (apart from the Socratics) Hellenistic period philosophical schools and their doctrines. Such interactions are most evident in the *Axiochus* (with the Epicureanism) and the *Halcyon* (with the Stoicism), the authors of which transport Socrates into the Hellenistic intellectual landscape, imbuing the dialogues with an anachronistic, playful feel. In the case of other dialogues, the traces of the Hellenistic philosophy are less obvious and often generate scholarly disagreement, as what one scholar perceives as, for instance, a trace of Cynic teachings or an anti-Stoic polemic another finds perfectly conceivable within the Socratic milieu. Platonic dialogue is also occasionally enriched with other generic elements and components such as consolation (*Axiochus*), paradoxography (*Halcyon*), and Socratic anecdote (*Theages*). Such blending was encouraged by Hellenistic aesthetics, with growing multiplicity of Hellenistic prose providing fecund ground for it.

# 5
# Aristotle and Peripatetics

## 5.1 Introductory Remarks

As Bernays observed in his 1863 book on Aristotle's dialogues, our knowledge of the philosopher is extremely one-sided: we know his treatises, but his dialogues have been lost.[1] The difference between these two groups of works was not limited to a difference in format. The dialogues, ancient authors repeatedly say, belonged to so-called "exoteric" writings, that is, works intended for a wider audience and written in a way that was easy to follow for non-philosophers. In his influential *Aristoteles: Grundlegung einer Geschichte seiner Entwicklung*, Werner Jaeger proposed that Aristotle's dialogues were the fruit of the philosopher's youth and were written when he was a member of the Academy and still under Plato's influence.[2] Jaeger's developmentalist theory has been for the most part dismissed today, and scholars accept the possibility that Aristotle composed his dialogues at the same time as he wrote his treatises.

The loss of Aristotle's dialogues makes it difficult to assess their place in the history of the genre. There is a recurrent notion in scholarship that they marked the genre's decline. For Hirzel, it was in Aristotle's dialogues that the first symptoms of *Verfall* became clear.[3] Jaeger thought that the transformation of the genre after Plato was unavoidable: Aristotle and other members of the Academy initially wrote dialogues in imitation of Plato because "they had not yet realized that Plato's dialogue in its classical perfection was something absolutely inimitable." When Aristotle comprehended that Plato's greatness was unattainable, he developed a new dialogic format in which questions and answers were replaced with long speeches and in which he represented himself as a leading speaker (Jaeger, however, explicitly refused to consider this development as a "decline").[4] Ingemar Düring believed that the development and systematization of Aristotle's scientific reasoning was "a turning point in the history of the dialogue" because this is when the genre lost its purpose and soon degenerated.[5] Some

---

[1] Bernays 1863, 1.
[2] Jaeger 1923; I use a second edition of an English translation below (Jaeger 1948[2]). On developmentalist narrative in the Aristotelian scholarship, see Witt 1996. For arguments against Jaeger's model, see e.g. Gigon 1973, 181–3; Bos 1989, 97–101.
[3] Hirzel 1895a, 272.
[4] Jaeger 1948[2], 27–9; Leo 1912, 275 also reacted against the putative "decline" of the dialogue in the hands of Aristotle.
[5] Düring 1961, 31.

scholars positively assessed the shift towards philosophical exposition and away from the emphasis on question-and-answer, which, they thought, characterized Aristotle's dialogues (and which is noticeable also in the late works of Plato): Anton-Hermann Chroust calls the Aristotelian format "a dialogue of discussion" in which "the scientific or systematic element gradually and inexorably asserted itself."[6] All of these pronouncements imagine Aristotle's dialogues as methodological and technical, and thus similar to his extant treatises—a view unwarranted, as I will argue, in light of ancient testimonies.

I will start this chapter with a careful reexamination of the evidence on Aristotle and discussion of fragments of his dialogues, in particular, of *On Noble Birth* and *Eudemus or On the Soul*, which allow us to get a glimpse of Aristotle as a dialogue writer. I will then discuss the employment of the format by his students (Theophrastus, Clearchus, Dicaearchus, Aristoxenus, Demetrius of Phaleron, and Chamaeleon), and by the next generations of Peripatetics (Praxiphanes, Prytanis, Hieronymus of Rhodes, Aristo of Ceos).

## 5.2 Aristotle

Although no dialogues by Aristotle are extant, there is abundant evidence from antiquity that they were an important part of his legacy. They were still available to authors of the Roman period, who valued them highly and regarded them with interest.[7] Cicero appears to have known Aristotle chiefly from his dialogues rather than his treatises.[8] Dio Chrysostom notes that Aristotle in his "many dialogues" (ἐν πολλοῖς διαλόγοις) admired and honored Homer (*Or.* 53.1). Plutarch mentions Aristotle's "exoteric dialogues" (ἐξωτερικοὶ διάλογοι) alongside his treatises on ethics and natural philosophy (τὰ ἠθικὰ ὑπομνήματα and τὰ φυσικὰ ὑπομνήματα) (*Adv. Col.* 1115c). This notion of "exoteric" works, that is, works intended for a non-specialist audience, goes back to Aristotle himself.[9] However, while Aristotle never comments on the format of these writings, Plutarch appears to differentiate between dialogues, which were exoteric, and treatises, which, implicitly, were not. Cicero also implies that there was a difference in format between Aristotle's

---

[6] Chroust 1973, 115.
[7] On the reception of Aristotle's works in antiquity and the gradual shift of interest from exoteric works towards more technical, acroamatic ones, see Gottschalk 1987; Chiaradonna 2011; Hatzimichali 2016.
[8] Dillon 2016; on Cicero's knowledge of acroamatic works, see Barnes 1997, 48–59.
[9] e.g. Aristotle, *EE* 1217b22: a distinction is made between exoteric writings and strictly philosophical texts (ἐν τοῖς ἐξωτερικοῖς λόγοις καὶ ἐν τοῖς κατὰ φιλοσοφίαν) (for other references and discussion, see Gigon 1987, 232–6). In Lucian, *Vit. auct.* 26, a Peripatetic is called "two-fold" (διπλοῦς) because he appears differently from the outside (ἔκτοσθεν) than from the inside (ἔντοσθεν); depending on his appearance he should be called either *exoterikos* or *esoterikos*; and in Gellius, *NA* 20.5, we read that Aristotle held serious philosophical lectures in the morning and exoteric instructions in the evening. For other authors speaking of Aristotle's *exoterica*, see Düring 1957, 426–43.

exoteric writings and philosophical works for specialized readers. In *On Moral Ends*, he makes a distinction between two types (*duo genera*) of Aristotle's writings: the exoteric type "written in a popular style, which is called exoteric" (*populariter scriptum quod ἐξωτερικόν appellabant*) and more rigorous texts written in treatise form (*in commentariis*) (*Fin.* 5.5.12).

Aristotle's late antique commentators are unequivocal in identifying his exoteric writings with dialogues and distinguishing them from his "lecture-style" works (τὰ ἀκροαματικά, they are referred to as αὐτοπρόσωπα, that is, written in Aristotle's own voice rather than mediated through interlocutors).[10] Ammonius characterizes Aristotle's dialogues as works in a dramatic format with questions and answers by multiple speakers (*In Cat.* 4.15–16: δραματικῶς διεσκεύασται κατὰ πεῦσιν καὶ ἀπόκρισιν πλειόνων προσώπων), and says that they are called exoteric because Aristotle (*In Cat.* 4.23–5):

> πρὸς τοὺς ἐπιπολαίως συνιέντας γέγραπται ἐπιτηδεύσαντος τοῦ φιλοσόφου ἐν αὐτοῖς φράσιν τε σαφεστέραν καὶ τὰς ἀποδείξεις οὐκ ἀποδεικτικὰς ἀλλὰ μᾶλλον πιθανὰς ἐξ ἐνδόξων.
>
> ...wrote <them> for those who understand superficially. The philosopher deliberately used a clearer style in these works and his proofs are not so much demonstrative as they are plausible, <deriving> from received opinions.
>
> (trans. S. M. Cohen, G. B. Matthews)

As such, Aristotle's dialogues differed from his acroamatic works, which should be studied by an earnest student (τὸν σπουδαῖον) and a real lover of philosophy (τῷ ὄντι γνήσιον ἐραστὴν τῆς φιλοσοφίας) (*In Cat.* 4.26–7). Similar pronouncements appear in other commentators who tend to dismiss the philosophical significance of the dialogic-exoteric works and consider them as composed for the benefit of a general audience and adjusted to its capabilities.[11] We do not know whether all of exoteric works were in the dialogue format, but there must have been at least a substantial overlap between his dialogues and his works written in a popular style.[12]

---

[10] Cf. e.g. Ammonius, *In Cat.* 4.18–19: καλεῖται δὲ τὰ μὲν διαλογικὰ καὶ ἐξωτερικά, τὰ δὲ αὐτοπρόσωπα καὶ ἀξιωματικὰ ἤτοι ἀκροαματικά; Simplicius, *In Phys.* 8.16: διχῇ δὲ διῃρημένων αὐτοῦ τῶν συγγραμμάτων εἴς τε τὰ ἐξωτερικὰ οἷα τὰ ἱστορικὰ καὶ τὰ διαλογικά...καὶ εἰς τὰ ἀκροαματικά; Olympiodorus, *Proleg.* 7.6–7: τὰ διαλογικὰ καὶ ἐξωτερικὰ ὀνομάζεται τὰ δὲ αὐτοπρόσωπα καὶ ἀκροαματικά.

[11] e.g. Simplicius, *In Phys.* 8.17: the dialogic-exoteric works did not investigate philosophical problems with great precision (ὅλως τὰ μὴ ἄκρας ἀκριβείας φροντίζοντα); Elias, *In Cat.* 114.23: they were written for people who were "unfit for philosophy" (πρὸς τοὺς ἀνεπιτηδείους πρὸς φιλοσοφίαν); Philoponus, *In Cat.* 4.15: Aristotle's dialogues were called exoteric because they were written for the benefit of the many (διὰ τὸ πρὸς τὴν τῶν πολλῶν γεγράφθαι ὠφέλειαν).

[12] For the identification of exoteric works with dialogues, see Bernays 1863, 29–93; Laurenti 1987a, 74–88. Düring 1957, 442 thought that *exoterica* were not identical with the dialogues, and that ancient commentators' distinctions should be approached with caution.

Ancient readers of Aristotle noted that there were inconsistencies between the things said by Aristotle in his exoteric works and his acroamatic texts. Cicero was clearly aware of discussions about inconsistencies between these two groups of Aristotle's works when he remarked that Aristotle and Theophrastus in their exoteric writings seem to have expressed views different from those they pronounced in their treatises (*non semper idem dicere videntur*), but thought that there was no real difference when it came to the most important points (*summa*) (*Fin.* 5.5.12). We find echoes of these discussions in late antique commentators. Elias writes that according to Alexander of Aphrodisias the difference between Aristotle's acroamatic and dialogic works was that in the former he expressed ideas that were his and true (τὰ δοκοῦντα αὐτῷ λέγει καὶ τὰ ἀληθῆ), while in the latter, the opinions are those of other people and false (τὰ ἄλλοις δοκοῦντα, τὰ ψευδῆ) (*In Cat.* 115.3–5). Elias emphatically disagrees: this would be unbecoming of a philosopher (οὐκ ἔστιν τοῦτο φιλοσόφου), as it would not be right to choose falsehood and conceal the truth (τὸ γὰρ ψεῦδος μὲν ἑλέσθαι, ἀφανίσαι δὲ τὸ ἀληθές, οὐχὶ θεμιτόν).[13] Elias may be overstating Alexander's position, but the idea that Aristotle's exoteric works did not contain his real philosophy circulated at least from the second century CE, and may have contributed to the disappearance of the dialogues.[14]

The evidence, then, suggests that Aristotle's dialogues belonged to his exoteric works, which significantly differed from his acroamatic texts; in particular, his philosophical arguments were simpler and easier to follow. For more specifics we need to turn to Cicero. In a letter to Atticus he writes that in the *Republic* he will follow the example of Aristotle and put prefaces at the beginning of each book (*Att.* 4.16.2: *in singulis libris utor prooemiis, ut Aristoteles in eis quos* ἐξωτερικοὺς *vocat*). This indicates that Aristotle used prefaces in his dialogues, and in the case of dialogues consisting of several books—he may have preceded each of them with a preface.[15]

In another letter to Atticus, Cicero comments on his recent dialogues which, unlike the *Republic* and *On Orator*, were set in the present and depicted contemporary people as interlocutors. Cicero thought that it would be inappropriate if he had no speaking part in such dialogues and comments that they were composed "in the Aristotelian pattern in which the speeches by others are introduced in such a way that the authority is with the author" (*Att.* 13.19.4: Ἀριστοτέλειον morem

---

[13] Cf. also Ammonius, *In Cat.* 4.20–2; Olympiodorus, *Proleg.* 7.8–15.
[14] Düring 1957, 438–9 thinks that Elias mistakenly attributes to Alexander the opinion that the exoteric works contained false doctrines; Melzer 2014, 39–44 thinks that Elias may be correct and that Alexander's position was associated with the idea of Aristotle's esotericism. For Aristotle's esoteric (secret) doctrines, see Plutarch, *Alex.* 7.5; Gellius, *NA* 20.5.
[15] For possible contents of Aristotle's prefaces, see Gigon 1987, 248–9.

*habent in quo ita sermo inducitur ceterorum ut penes ipsum sit principatus*).[16] Elsewhere, he writes that Sallustius encouraged him to include himself as a speaker in the *Republic* after the model of Aristotle who "speaks himself" (*Aristotelem... ipsum loqui*) in some of his political works (*QFr.* 3.5.1). He associated, then, the Aristotelian dialogue with a contemporary setting and the author's presence as a leading speaker (fragments of Aristotle's *On Noble Birth*, discussed below, give us an idea of how Aristotle might have represented himself). It should be noted, however, that these features did not necessarily recur in each and every dialogue by Aristotle, as Jaeger has rightly pointed out.[17]

A passage from Cicero's *On Orator* is frequently cited as evidence that Aristotle's dialogues consisted of contradictory speeches. It says that it is "Aristotelian" (*Aristotelio more*) to be able to speak on both sides of a question (*in utramque sententiam*) about every topic and to make two opposite speeches in every case (*in omni causa duas contrarias orationes*), and that such an ability comes from a familiarity with Aristotle's rules (*De or.* 3.21.80). There is a similar statement in *Tusculan Disputations*, where Cicero says that Aristotle was the first to argue on opposite sides (*in contrarias partes*) of all questions (*Tusc.* 2.3.9). However, neither remark refers to Aristotle's dialogues specifically; for all we know, Cicero may be referring to Aristotle's advice expressed in one of his lost works, or to an oral tradition. Consequently, the passages should not be taken as evidence of the format of the dialogues.[18]

Aristotle's dialogues are also referred to by Basil of Caesarea. He mentions Aristotle and Theophrastus as dialogue-writers in one of his letters and observes that they "went directly to the problem itself for they were aware that they lacked the Platonic graces" (*Ep.* 135: εὐθὺς αὐτῶν ἥψαντο τῶν πραγμάτων, διὰ τὸ συνειδέναι ἑαυτοῖς τῶν Πλατωνικῶν χαρίτων τὴν ἔνδειαν). We do not know whether Basil had first-hand knowledge of Aristotle's and Theophrastus' dialogues; from the context we can infer that he means that Aristotle and Theophrastus did not elaborate on characters and their personalities, but rather focused on arguments, unlike Plato, who introduced the colorful and memorable figures of Thrasymachus, Hippias, and Protagoras.[19] Basil presents Aristotle and Theophrastus as a model to Diodorus, his addressee (who sent Basil his works and expected his opinion), whom he wants to dissuade from writing elaborate

---

[16] Though in *Fam.* 1.9.23 Cicero says that his *On Orator*, a dialogue set in the past, was written *Aristotelio more*; what he means remains unclear. Ruch 1958, 40 thinks that it implies diversity in Aristotle's dialogues, in some of which the philosopher did not appear as a speaker. Fantham 2004, 161-2 proposes that Cicero thinks of longer speeches (as opposed to Platonic interrogation and refutation) as "Aristotelian." Schofield 2008, 76 suggests that Cicero has in mind the presence of a preface.

[17] Jaeger 1948², 28-9; also Ruch 1958, 40-1.

[18] Gigon 1959, 150-1. Long 2006, 301 thinks that Cicero refers to a rhetorical handbook on Aristotle's *Topica* and *Rhetoric*.

[19] Ruch 1958, 42.

dialogues in a flowery style and rich in characterization: he tells Diodorus that he should not try to write like Plato, who could at the same time produce a philosophical argument and vividly render the personalities of his interlocutors, but rather follow Aristotle and Theophrastus, who focused on the philosophical component. Basil, then, refers to the two philosophers to sweeten his criticism of the addressee's dialogues (he is not a new Plato, but he can still be an Aristotle or Theophrastus).

Basil's comment that Aristotle "lacked the Platonic graces" is contradicted by Cicero's enthusiasm about the philosopher's style: he speaks of the "golden stream of speech" (*Acad.* 2.38.119: *flumen orationis aureum*) and a combination of wisdom with rhetorical fluency (*Tusc.* 1.4.7: *prudentiam cum eloquentia iungere*). We may assume that he is referring here to exoteric works, with which he was most familiar, in which Aristotle adopted, apparently with success, a polished, literary style.[20] Ammonius says that Aristotle in his dialogues "deliberately employs a certain volume and overelaboration of speech and metaphor; moreover, he changes the form of speech depending on the personalities of the speakers, and, in a word, knows how to embellish any type of discourse" (*In Cat.* 7.3: καὶ ὄγκου φροντίζει τινὸς καὶ περιεργίας λέξεων καὶ μεταφορᾶς, καὶ πρὸς τὰ τῶν λεγόντων πρόσωπα μετασχηματίζει τὸ εἶδος τῆς λέξεως, καὶ ἁπλῶς ὅσα λόγου καλλωπίζειν οἶδεν ἰδέαν; trans. S. M. Cohen, G. B. Matthews), likewise testifying to the philosopher's rhetorical and stylistic aptitude.

I will now turn to evidence concerning individual dialogues. Diogenes Laertius provides an incomplete catalogue of Aristotle's works. It has been assumed since Brandis and Rose that the list opens with dialogues; Bernays proposed that the first nineteen texts were written in the dialogue format.[21] The catalogue opens with longer works: *On Justice* (four books), *On Poets* (three books), *On Philosophy* (three books), *On Statesman* (two books). There follow writings consisting of one book: *On Rhetoric or Grylus, Nerinthus, Sophist, Menexenus, Eroticus, Symposion, On Wealth, Protrepticus, On the Soul, On Prayer, On Noble Birth, On Pleasure, Alexander or On Colonies, On Kingship,* and *On Education* (Diogenes Laertius 5.22). Whether all these nineteen titles were dialogues as Bernays thought we do not know; in only a few cases do we know for sure.[22] As noted, the catalogue is incomplete: for instance, several sources mention Aristotle's *Magicus*, perhaps a dialogue, that does not appear in the list.

We can be certain about the dialogue format of *On Noble Birth*, three substantial fragments of which are preserved by Stobaeus. Nobility by birth (εὐγένεια) was

[20] Hatzimichali 2016, 81; Dillon 2016, 184.
[21] Brandis 1853, 82–3; Rose 1854, 47; Bernays 1863, 131–2.
[22] Moraux 1951, 27–8 considered some to have been paraenetic exhortations in a continuous form. Gigon 1987, 219–22 thought that for most of them it was possible to stipulate the dialogue format based on the title, contents, or an extant fragment. Laurenti 2003, 382 refers to the nineteen texts as "dialogues" for the sake of convenience, thinking that it is probable that some of them were not.

a frequent motif in Greek literature and philosophy and recurs in extant works by Aristotle, where it is generally appreciated and considered a good thing.[23] The verdict is also positive in what remains of the dialogue. The first passage in Stobaeus reads as follows (4.29a.24 [F 91 Rose³]):

"ὅλως περὶ εὐγενείας ἐγὼ ἀπορῶ τίνας χρὴ καλεῖν τοὺς εὐγενεῖς." "Εἰκότως γε," ἔφην, "τοῦτο σὺ διαπορῶν· καὶ γὰρ παρὰ τῶν πολλῶν καὶ μᾶλλον παρὰ τῶν σοφῶν τὰ μὲν ἀμφισβητεῖται τὰ δ' οὐ λέγεται σαφῶς, εὐθὺς τὰ περὶ τῆς δυνάμεως. λέγω δὲ τοῦτο, πότερον τῶν τιμίων ἐστὶ καὶ σπουδαίων ἤ, καθάπερ Λυκόφρων ἔγραψε, κενόν τι πάμπαν. ἐκεῖνος γὰρ ἀντιπαραβάλλων ἑτέροις ἀγαθοῖς αὐτήν, εὐγενείας μὲν οὖν φησὶν ἀφανὲς τὸ κάλλος, ἐν λόγῳ δὲ τὸ σεμνόν· ὡς πρὸς δόξαν οὖσαν τὴν αἵρεσιν αὐτῆς, κατὰ δ' ἀλήθειαν οὐθὲν διαφέροντας τοὺς ἀγεννεῖς τῶν εὐγενῶν."

"In short, with regard to good birth, I for my part am at a loss to say whom one should call well-born." "Your difficulty," I said, "is quite reasonable; for among the many and even more among the wise there is division of opinion and obscurity of statement, for instance about its value. What I mean is this: is it a valuable and good thing, or, as Lycophron the sophist wrote, something altogether empty? For, comparing it with other goods, he says the beauty of good birth is obscure, and its dignity a matter of words—the preference for it is a matter of opinion, and in truth there is no difference between the low-born and the well-born." (trans. J. Barnes and G. Lawrence, modified)

The text is a reported dialogue with a first-person narrator, perhaps Aristotle himself. The narration is limited to ἔφην, "I said" (similarly in two other fragments in Stobaeus, where narratorial interventions include εἶπεν, ἔφη, and ἔφην ἐγώ). The conversational roles are asymmetrical: the narrator is the mentor and teacher, coming to aid his interlocutor, who admits confusion (ἐγὼ ἀπορῶ) regarding the question of noble birth. It is possible that we are in the middle of the dialogue, after some (unsuccessful) attempts to tackle the problem have already been made—if so, the opening sentence would acknowledge the failure of the discussion thus far[24]—though one cannot exclude that this is an (abrupt) opening. Abrupt beginnings are not unprecedented in ancient dialogues (and abruptness could have been mitigated if the dialogue had a preface), while a notice of general disagreement concerning the value of noble birth could serve as a good starting point for discussion.

---

[23] Laurenti 1987b, 767–81. Stobaeus in the section dedicated to noble birth (4.29a) cites passages from, among others, Euripides, Menander, Sophocles, Bion of Borysthenes, Democritus, Diogenes the Cynic, and *Alcibiades I*. For the importance of noble birth for moral development in Aristotle, see Leunissen 2017, 90–2.

[24] Laurenti 1987b, 750.

The next fragment in Stobaeus focuses on the question of who can rightly be called well-born. The argument is carried by the dominant speaker, while his interlocutor's responses are limited to voicing agreement. The main speaker quotes views on noble birth held by Socrates,[25] Simonides, and Theognis. He discards them and proceeds to formulate a definition of noble birth, ensuring that his partner follows him (4.29a.25 [F 92 Rose³]):

"Τὸ εὖ σημαίνει τι δήπου τῶν ἐπαινετῶν καὶ σπουδαίων, οἷον τὸ 'εὐπρόσωπον' καὶ τὸ 'εὐόφθαλμον'· ἀγαθὸν γάρ τι ἢ καλὸν σημαίνει κατὰ τοῦτον τὸν λόγον." "Πάνυ γ'," εἶπεν. "Οὐκοῦν εὐπρόσωπον μέν ἐστι τὸ ἔχον ἀρετὴν προσώπου, εὐόφθαλμον δὲ τὸ ὀφθαλμοῦ ἀρετήν;" "Οὕτως," εἶπεν. "Ἀλλὰ μὴν ἔστι γένος τὸ μὲν σπουδαῖον, τὸ δὲ φαῦλον ἀλλ' οὐ σπουδαῖον." "Πάνυ γ', εἶπεν." "Σπουδαῖον δέ γέ φαμεν ἕκαστον κατὰ τὴν αὐτοῦ ἀρετὴν εἶναι, ὥστε καὶ γένος σπουδαῖον ὡσαύτως." "Οὕτως," εἶπε. "Δῆλον ἄρ'," ἔφην, "ὅτι ἔστιν ἡ εὐγένεια ἀρετὴ γένους."

"'Good' means, I suppose, something praiseworthy and excellent; e.g. having a good face or good eyes means, on this showing, something good or fine." "Certainly," he said. "Well then, having a good face is having the excellence proper to a face, and having good eyes is having the excellence proper to eyes, is it not?" "Yes," he said. "But one family (*genos*) is good, another bad and not good." "Certainly," he said. "And we say each thing is good in virtue of the excellence proper to it, so that a family is good in the same way." "Yes," he said. "Clearly, then," I said, "good birth (*eugeneia*) is excellence of family (*genos*)."

(trans. J. Barnes and G. Lawrence)

This exchange shows that even if Aristotle's dialogues had a large proportion of speeches, they need not have been bereft of exchanges consisting of short utterances, in which the dominant speaker guided his interlocutor through argument, proceeding step-by-step and ensuring his acceptance.

The third fragment in Stobaeus (4.29c.52 [F 94 Rose³]) preserves extended excursus by the main speaker, who argues that good families are ones in which many good men are born (though not all family members have to be good); the family's ability to produce good men is dependent on its origin and founder (ὁ ἀρχηγὸς τοῦ γένους); and people born into such families are correctly called well-born. Euripides' opinion that well-born simply means a man who is good and not those whose ancestors were good, is discarded.

The three fragments show that conversational dynamics fluctuated throughout the dialogue: in some passages, the main speaker proceeds slowly, making sure at every step that his companion is following and paying attention; in others, he goes

---

[25] He is said to have considered Myrto, Aristides' daughter, well-born. Ancient sources make her the second wife of Socrates; Aristotle appears to have been familiar with this tradition (Laurenti 1987b, 781–804). The mention of Socrates excludes the possibility that he was a speaker in the dialogue.

through a few argumentative steps without a pause. These dynamics are familiar from many Socratic dialogues, in which the pace of the conversation and length of utterances likewise change over the course of the conversation.

Another Aristotelian dialogue of which we are relatively well informed is *Eudemus or On the Soul*.[26] This was a dialogue commemorating Eudemus of Cyprus, a friend of Aristotle and member of the Academy (Plutarch, *Dion* 22.5), which contained a discussion of the immortality of the soul. Ancient authors disagreed about whether Aristotle's position in the *Eudemus* was consistent with the one professed in his acroamatic works, in particular, in the treatise *On the Soul*, where Aristotle held the intellect to be indestructible and immortal, but not the soul as a whole (*De an.* 408b18–19, 430a22–3); some late antique commentators believed that in the *Eudemus*, Aristotle accepted the immortality of the whole soul.[27]

From Cicero's *On Divination* we know that in this dialogue, Aristotle described a journey of Eudemus to Macedonia (*Div.* 1.25.53 [F 37 Rose³]). Eudemus, it was reported, stopped at Pherae, which was ruled at the time by the tyrant Alexander. While there, he fell seriously ill and had a prophetic dream: he saw a handsome youth who told him that Alexander would die within a few days, while Eudemus would soon recover and return home in five years. The first two things happened as predicted. Five years later, while in Sicily, Eudemus hoped for a safe return to Cyprus, as prophesized in the dream. Instead, he died in battle at Syracuse. The "return home," then, should have been interpreted as the soul's departure from the body, Cicero remarks (*ita illud somnium esse interpretatum, ut, cum animus Eudemi e corpore excesserit, tum domum revertisse videatur*).

As Gigon observed, the conceptualization of death as a return home "is not so common in the literature of the time as might be expected."[28] It is therefore worthwhile considering its origins. We may presume that Aristotle fashioned the prophecy of Eudemus' death with Plato's *Crito* 44a–b in mind. In the Platonic passage, Socrates, shortly before his death, relates his dream to Crito: a beautiful woman told him that on the third day he would arrive in fertile Phthia (ἤματί κεν τριτάτῳ Φθίην ἐρίβωλον ἵκοιο); Socrates interprets this as a prophecy of his death. When foretelling Socrates' "arrival in fertile Phthia," the woman quotes from Homer's *Iliad*, from a passage in which Achilles considers returning home to Phthia and living a long, but undistinguished life—rather than dying in battle and

---

[26] The double title, combining a name with a topic, appears in pseudo-Plutarchan *Consolation to Apollonius* 115b. *Eudemus or On the Soul* should be identified with *On the Soul*, consisting of one book, in Diogenes Laertius' catalogue of Aristotle's writings (Aristotle's extant treatise *On the Soul* was in three books).

[27] Elias, *In Cat.* 114.32–115.12. See Chroust 1966a, 22–6; Bos 2003, 289–306; Laurenti 2003, 447–51; Gerson 2005, 52–9.

[28] Gigon 1960, 23.

attaining everlasting glory (*Il.* 9.363).²⁹ Plato's Socrates questions the validity of Achilles' choice—to die or to go home—and implies that death is the real return to Phthia, the real homecoming.

Aristotle in the *Eudemus* was thus not using a common metaphor, but rather alluding to and building creatively on Plato, who was already engaged intertextually with Homer. This is one of the few moments in which we catch a glimpse of Aristotle writing literature. It is certainly noteworthy that Eudemus, unlike Plato's Socrates, did not understand the prediction and hoped that it foretold his return to Cyprus—a clear indication that Aristotle did not depict him as a larger-than-life figure like Socrates, but as man with all the usual limitations of human nature: homesick, incapable of comprehending the prophecy, and nourishing vain hopes for the future.

Another important testimony for the *Eudemus* comes from the pseudo-Plutarchan *Consolation to Apollonius*. The author quotes directly from Aristotle's work, retaining the dialogue format (*Cons. ad Apoll.* 115b–e [F 44 Rose³]):

"διόπερ, ὦ κράτιστε πάντων καὶ μακαριστότατε, πρὸς τῷ μακαρίους καὶ εὐδαίμονας εἶναι τοὺς τετελευτηκότας νομίζειν καὶ τὸ ψεύσασθαί τι κατ' αὐτῶν καὶ τὸ βλασφημεῖν οὐχ ὅσιον ὡς κατὰ βελτιόνων ἡγούμεθα καὶ κρειττόνων ἤδη γεγονότων. καὶ ταῦθ' οὕτως ἀρχαῖα καὶ παλαιὰ παρ' ἡμῖν, ὥστε τὸ παράπαν οὐδεὶς οἶδεν οὔτε τοῦ χρόνου τὴν ἀρχὴν οὔτε τὸν θέντα πρῶτον, ἀλλὰ τὸν ἄπειρον αἰῶνα διατελεῖ νενομισμένα. πρὸς δὲ δὴ τούτοις τὸ διὰ στόματος ὂν τοῖς ἀνθρώποις ὁρᾷς ὡς ἐκ πολλῶν ἐτῶν περιφέρεται θρυλούμενον." "τί τοῦτ';" ἔφη. κἀκεῖνος ὑπολαβὼν "ὡς ἄρα μὴ γενέσθαι μέν," ἔφη, "ἄριστον πάντων, τὸ δὲ τεθνάναι τοῦ ζῆν ἐστι κρεῖττον. καὶ πολλοῖς οὕτω παρὰ τοῦ δαιμονίου μεμαρτύρηται. τοῦτο μὲν ἐκείνῳ τῷ Μίδᾳ λέγουσι δήπου μετὰ τὴν θήραν ὡς ἔλαβε τὸν Σειληνὸν διερωτῶντι καὶ πυνθανομένῳ τί ποτ' ἐστὶ τὸ βέλτιστον τοῖς ἀνθρώποις καὶ τί τὸ πάντων αἱρετώτατον, τὸ μὲν πρῶτον οὐδὲν ἐθέλειν εἰπεῖν ἀλλὰ σιωπᾶν ἀρρήτως· ἐπειδὴ δέ ποτε μόγις πᾶσαν μηχανὴν μηχανώμενος προσηγάγετο φθέγξασθαί τι πρὸς αὐτόν, οὕτως ἀναγκαζόμενον εἰπεῖν, 'δαίμονος ἐπιπόνου καὶ τύχης χαλεπῆς ἐφήμερον σπέρμα, τί με βιάζεσθε λέγειν ἃ ὑμῖν ἄρειον μὴ γνῶναι; μετ' ἀγνοίας γὰρ τῶν οἰκείων κακῶν ἀλυπότατος ὁ βίος. ἀνθρώποις δὲ πάμπαν οὐκ ἔστι γενέσθαι τὸ πάντων ἄριστον οὐδὲ μετασχεῖν τῆς τοῦ βελτίστου φύσεως (ἄριστον γὰρ πᾶσι καὶ πάσαις τὸ μὴ γενέσθαι)· τὸ μέντοι μετὰ τοῦτο καὶ πρῶτον τῶν ἀνθρώπῳ ἀνυστῶν, δεύτερον δέ, τὸ γενομένους ἀποθανεῖν ὡς τάχιστα.' δῆλον οὖν ὡς οὔσης κρείττονος τῆς ἐν τῷ τεθνάναι διαγωγῆς ἢ τῆς ἐν τῷ ζῆν, οὕτως ἀπεφήνατο."

"For that reason, best and most blessed of all men, in addition to thinking that the dead are blessed and happy, we hold it impious to speak any falsehood about them or to slander them, since they have now become better and greater. And

---

²⁹ The connection between the dreams of Socrates and Eudemus was apparent to Cicero, who mentions them one after another in *On Divination* (1.25.52–3).

these customs are so ancient and long-established among us that no one at all knows when they began or who first established them, but they have been continuously acknowledged for an indefinite age. In addition to that, you observe the saying which has been on men's lips for many years." "What is that?" he said. He said in reply: "That not to be born is best of all, and to be dead better than to be alive. Heaven has given this testimony to many men. They say that when Midas had caught Silenus he interrogated him after the hunt and asked him what was the best thing for men and what the most desirable of all. Silenus at first would not say anything but maintained an unbroken silence; but when, after using every device, Midas with difficulty induced him to address him, he said under compulsion: 'Short lived seed of a toiling spirit and a harsh fortune, why do you force me to say what is better for you not to know? For a life lived in ignorance of its own ills is most painless. It is quite impossible for the best thing of all to befall men, nor can they share in the nature of what is better. For it is best, for all men and women, not to be born; and second after that the first of things open to men is, once born, to die as quickly as possible.' It is clear that he meant that time spent dead is better than time spent alive."

(trans. J. Barnes and G. Lawrence)

The fragment preserves the format of a narrated dialogue (ἔφη, "he said," and κἀκεῖνος ὑπολαβών...ἔφη, "and he, taking up...said") with a third-person narrator. Who the interlocutors are remains a puzzle. The first speaker addresses the other with ὦ κράτιστε πάντων καὶ μακαριστότατε, "best and most blessed of all men," which indicates that he is not talking to a common man. Gigon thought that the person being addressed was a divine being, depicted in conversation with a man who is providing information about human beliefs and customs. This divine being lived somewhere "remote and separated from the human world," Gigon hypothesized; and, perhaps, after listening to his human interlocutor, he revealed the true fate of the soul after death.[30] Gaiser, however, pointed out that it is unlikely that a god other than Zeus would be called κράτιστος πάντων, and considered it improbable that a divine being would need to be informed about human affairs. He proposed instead that it was a powerful ruler who was addressed as the "best of all and most blessed"—addressed with conventional exaggeration, though not without irony, as it becomes clear soon enough that it is the deceased who should be considered blessed. Noting that according to Cicero Eudemus stopped at Pherae on his way to Macedonia, Gaiser proposed that the ruler was Philip II. Philip would have been a young king at the time, having recently come to power, while the person addressing him—Eudemus, who would

---

[30] Gigon 1960, 26; similarly Flashar 2004², 281. See also Gigon 1973, 202–3 for the hypothesis that the *Eudemus* contained a myth describing a trip to the far north-west and to the island of Cronus, where the traveler received instructions about the nature and fate of the soul.

remind the ruler that his earthly power and happiness are, like everything in human life, imperfect and passing. It is thus an encounter between wisdom and power, mirrored by the insert story of Midas and Silenus, who likewise represent power and wisdom.[31] If Eudemus spoke with Philip at the Macedonian court, the story of Midas and Silenus would resonate with the setting since, according to ancient tradition, Silenus was captured by Midas in Macedonia (Herodotus 8.138). We may note that the circumstances of Eudemus' death—in battle at Syracuse, fighting on the side of Dion against Dionysius II (Cicero, *Div.* 1.25.53; Plutarch, *Dion* 22.5)—would offer another opportunity to underline the problem of autocracy.

While Gaiser's reconstruction is unavoidably speculative, the tone of the conversation is reminiscent of the famous encounter between Solon, the sage, and the king Croesus (Herodotus 1.30-3). In Herodotus, like in Aristotle, the problem of human happiness is in the spotlight. Solon argues that nobody can be pronounced happy before death because as long as one lives, misfortunes can happen—this position is modified by Aristotle's Silenus, who maintains that there is no such thing as a happy human life.[32] It is therefore probable that the character addressed as the "best and most blessed of all men" is a ruler; and the Macedonian motifs in the narration (Eudemus' travel to Macedonia, the Macedonian setting of the story of Midas and Silenus) suggest that he may have been Philip II. Whether the other speaker was Eudemus, as Gaiser thought, we do not know. There is no evidence of Aristotle being an interlocutor, though nothing precludes that he appeared in some part of the dialogue (for instance, in a frame conversation).[33]

The *Eudemus* engaged with Plato on several levels. As we have seen, the prophetic dream of Eudemus mirrored Socrates' vision in the *Crito*. The *Phaedo* was certainly another important subtext: both works were known in antiquity as dialogues "on the soul" (περὶ ψυχῆς), both commemorated a deceased friend and discussed the immortality of the soul and its fate after death. It is also probable that the comparison of human life to prison, φρουρά, which is developed in the *Phaedo*, also played an important role in the *Eudemus*.[34]

---

[31] Gaiser 1985, 460-4 points out to a fragment of Philodemus' *On Rhetoric* where Aristotle is said to have tried to induce Philip to give up the monarchical rule (Sudhaus II 61, col. lvi.16-18: σχεδὸν ἐ[κ] βασιλείας παρεκάλει [Φ]ίλιππο[ν]); he believes that Philodemus is thinking of Aristotle's dialogue and Eudemus' attempt to persuade Philip.

[32] For Aristotle's disagreement with Solon's pronouncement that nobody can be declared happy before death, see *EN* 1100a10–1101b9.

[33] Aristotle's involvement as a speaker is assumed by e.g. Gigon 1960, 22, probably under the influence of Cicero's characterization of Aristotle's dialogues as ones in which the figure of the author played an essential part. As noted above, however, we do not know whether Aristotle depicted himself as a speaker in all of his dialogues.

[34] Hirzel 1895a, 285; Gigon 1960, 29–30; Chroust 1966b; Bos 1989, 103–5. On the prison-motif, see Jażdżewska 2015b.

Composed after the death of a friend, the Eudemus had a consolatory undertone.[35] Silenus' pessimistic view on human life fits into such a consolatory context (if life is miserable, there is no reason to lament its end). It must have influenced the nascent development of the genre of consolation: Theophrastus' *Callisthenes or On Grief* (possibly a dialogue) and Crantor's famous *On Grief*.[36]

Apart from the fragments of *On Noble Birth* and *Eudemus or On the Soul*, we also have an interesting testimony concerning a work by Aristotle titled *Corinthian Dialogue*. It comes from a passage in Themistius, where instances of people turning to philosophy after reading a philosophical work are discussed (*Or.* 23.295 [F 64 Rose³]):

ὁ δὲ γεωργὸς ὁ Κορίνθιος τῷ Γοργίᾳ ξυγγενόμενος—οὐκ αὐτῷ ἐκείνῳ Γοργίᾳ, ἀλλὰ τῷ λόγῳ ὃν Πλάτων ἔγραψεν ἐπ' ἐλέγχῳ τοῦ σοφιστοῦ—αὐτίκα ἀφεὶς τὸν ἀγρὸν καὶ τὰς ἀμπέλους Πλάτωνι ὑπέθηκε τὴν ψυχὴν καὶ τὰ ἐκείνου ἐσπείρετο καὶ ἐφυτεύετο. καὶ οὗτός ἐστιν ὃν τιμᾷ ὁ Ἀριστοτέλης τῷ διαλόγῳ τῷ Κορινθίῳ.

When the Corinthian farmer became acquainted with *Gorgias*—I do not mean the famous person of that name, but the work of that title that Plato wrote to refute the sophist—he immediately left his field and his vines and submitted his soul to Plato, becoming a sower and planter of Platonic teachings. (This farmer is the person Aristotle honors in his Corinthian dialogue). (trans. R. J. Penella)

The figure of the Corinthian farmer must have played a prominent role. Themistius says that he was "honored" by Aristotle, and the title, *Corinthian Dialogue*, derives from his city, which may have served as a setting. Whether the dialogue contained a conversation between Plato and the farmer, as some scholars propose,[37] we do not know. It must have emphasized the universal appeal of Plato's philosophy and persuasiveness of his writings, which made a simple farmer abandon his life and become a philosopher.[38] The farmer is said to have turned to the "sowing and planting" (ἐσπείρετο καὶ ἐφυτεύετο) of Platonic instructions: the parallel between agriculture and philosophy, between cultivation of the land and cultivation of the soul, perhaps comes from Aristotle's text rather than being Themistius' addition. If so, this could be an allusion to Plato's *Phaedrus*, where Socrates says that a dialectician "chooses a fitting soul and plants and sows in it words accompanied with knowledge" (*Phdr.* 276e: λαβὼν ψυχὴν προσήκουσαν, φυτεύῃ τε καὶ σπείρῃ μετ' ἐπιστήμης λόγους).[39] Remarkably, the passage appears in the famous section of the dialogue in which Socrates denounces the written word

---

[35] Jaeger 1948², 40; Chroust 1966a, 21.   [36] Gigon 1960, 31.
[37] Rose 1863, 73–4. Laurenti 1987a, 467–8 considers this as a possibility.
[38] Riginos 1976, 185 considers it possible that the dialogue was critical of Plato and "belittle[ed] the *Gorgias*' defense of philosophy by implying that only a country farmer would be won over by the dialogue." I find this unlikely as Aristotle is said to have "honored" the farmer.
[39] I thank an anonymous reviewer for this point.

for, among others, its inability to choose the right recipient and to defend itself. The story of the Corinthian farmer converted to philosophy after *reading* Plato's dialogue probably should be read against this background.

The title *Corinthian Dialogue* does not appear on Diogenes Laertius' list or anywhere else, which has led some scholars to identify it with *Nerinthus* in Diogenes' catalogue: the presumption is that the word Κορίνθιος was corrupted into Νήρινθος.[40] However, as Gigon observed, the corruption of a well-known Κορίνθιος into unclear and unattested elsewhere Νήρινθος appears unlikely.[41] As Themistius is our only source for the existence of the dialogue, it is of course not impossible that the work was pseudo-Aristotelian.

Other works by Aristotle that can be safely identified as dialogues include *On Poets*, which is explicitly referred to as a dialogue in *Vita Marciana* (4: ὁ περὶ ποιητῶν διάλογος; a fragment in Athenaeus contains a first-person verbal form, *Deipn.* 11.505c [F 72 Rose³]: μὴ φῶμεν). *On Justice* probably also had a dialogue format: [Demetrius] refers to words spoken there by "the one who is lamenting the city of the Athenians" (*Eloc.* 28 [F 82 Rose³]: ὁ τὴν Ἀθηναίων πόλιν ὀδυρόμενος), presumably referring to one of the dialogue's characters. The *Statesman* is referred to by Cicero, who in a letter to Quintus says that Aristotle "speaks himself" the things he wrote there about the state and preeminent man (*QFr.* 3.5.1 [F 78 Rose³]: *Aristotelem denique quae de re publica et praestanti viro scribat ipsum loqui*), which indicates that Aristotle was a speaker in the dialogue.

In other cases, the dialogue format is sometimes suggested by titles—as in the case, for instance, of *Grylus or On Rhetoric* (composed to commemorate the son of Xenophon, who died in 362 BCE), *Alexander or On Colonies*, *Symposion* (perhaps to be identified with *On Drunkenness*, not on Diogenes Laertius' list, but mentioned by several other authors),[42] *Sophist*, and *Menexenus*. There is nothing to prevent *Eroticus* or works with *peri*-titles, such as *On Philosophy*, *On Wealth*, *On Prayer*, *On Pleasure*, *On Kingship*, and *On Education*, from being dialogues, but we lack positive evidence. Unclear also is the format of Aristotle's *Protrepticus*: although we know much of its contents thanks to the Neoplatonist Iamblichus, who used it extensively in his own work under the same title, no fragment retains the dialogue form.[43] Also the format of Aristotle's *Magicus*, mentioned twice by Diogenes Laertius (1.1, 1.8), is unknown.[44]

---

[40] Rose in his edition (=Rose³) prints this fragment of Themistius under the title *Nerinthus* (F 64), similarly Laurenti 1987. See also Rose 1863, 73–4, Laurenti 1987a, 465–8, Laurenti 2003, 418–21.
[41] Gigon 1987, 220 and 275; see also Bernays 1863, 90–1; Moraux 1951, 32; Penella 2000, 123 n. 26.
[42] Laurenti 1987b, 611.
[43] The *Protrepticus* was considered a dialogue by e.g. Bywater 1869; Diels 1888. Arguments against the dialogue format were raised by Hirzel 1876 and Düring 1961, 29–32. Recently, the discussion was revived by Hutchinson and Johnson 2018, who propose that the work was a dialogue containing both protreptic and apotreptic speeches, and that the speakers included Isocrates, Aristotle, and Heraclides of Pontus.
[44] Rose 1863, 50 thought that *Magicus* was a Socratic dialogue. *Suda*, s.v. Ἀντισθένης (α 2723), mentions *Magicus* as a work by Antisthenes, but adds that some people ascribed it to Aristotle. Rose

We may conclude that the evidence indicates that Aristotle's dialogues belonged to exoteric works intended for a non-specialist audience; they were written in an attractive, polished style (which appealed to Cicero), with arguments relatively easy to follow. As can be inferred from preserved titles and fragments, there was some overlap of topics with acroamatic works (e.g. *On Poets—Poetics, Eudemus or On the Soul—On the Soul*, perhaps *Grylus or On Rhetoric—Rhetoric*). At least some of the dialogues were preceded by prefaces, and in the case of dialogues in multiple books, individual books might have had their own prefaces. Apart from speaking directly in the prefaces, Aristotle also represented himself in his dialogues—though not necessarily in all of them—and took a leading role in developing arguments. The dialogues probably did not have elaborate settings, and while Basil's testimony suggests that Aristotle did not engage in extensive *ethopoiia*, that is, careful crafting of the personalities of the characters, Ammonius' remark that he changed the speech depending on interlocutors suggests that there was certain diversity in speech-styles among the speakers. There is, however, no strong evidence that Aristotle's dialogues contained speeches on opposite sides of the problem: as we have seen when speaking of arguments *in utramque sententiam*, Cicero does not refer specifically to Aristotle's dialogues.

Aristotle's dialogues, as far as extant fragments allow us to judge, were narrated, sometimes with a first-person narration. In some cases, the dialogic exchanges consisted of a series of short utterances; sometimes speakers were producing longer statements. In fragments of *On Noble Birth* we find a dialogue with asymmetrical conversational roles: there is the main speaker (perhaps Aristotle himself), who guides his interlocutor and construes the argument. We can also note that the speaker recurrently refers to poetic passages and judgments expressed in them (Simonides, Theognis, Euripides) and rejects them as inadequate. This strategy, which acknowledges the importance of poetry for shaping common ethical concepts and judgments, is reminiscent of Plato's Socrates; another Socratic legacy is working towards a definition of the thing discussed.

The fragments of the *Eudemus or On the Soul* provide a remarkable testimony to Aristotle's extensive engagement with Plato, an engagement not restricted to philosophical ideas, but also emergent on the literary level. As Aristotle employs the concept of death as a homecoming by developing a motif from the *Crito* and its subtext, Homer's *Iliad*, we get a glimpse here of the philosopher as a reader of

---

concluded that in order to have been ascribed to Antisthenes, *Magicus* must have been a Socratic dialogue; he proposed that it reported a conversation between Socrates and a Magus who visited Athens. Rives 2004 rightly points out that Antisthenes did not write exclusively Socratic dialogues; and that the passage in Diogenes Laertius which reports the meeting of Socrates with Magus, names Aristotle, but not *Magicus* specifically, as the source. I am not convinced, however, by Rives's argument that the title *Magicus* indicates that the work was not a dialogue as titles ending in -ικος were chiefly used for speeches. As Rives himself notes, Xenophon's *Oeconomicus* and *Tyrannicus* (i.e. *Hiero*) provide examples against his thesis, and some works titled *Eroticus* were also dialogues (we have an extant specimen, composed by Plutarch).

Plato and a confident writer of literature. We can assume that engagement with Plato was also present in the *Corinthian Dialogue*, in which the Platonic *Gorgias* (and perhaps the *Phaedrus*) must have been given the prominent place.

## 5.3 Theophrastus

Aristotle's student Theophrastus was widely popular as a teacher and philosopher. He was a man of varied interests and the author of over two hundred and twenty works, of which only a few are extant, including the humorous *Characters*, two botanical works (*Research on Plants* and *Plant Explanations*), several short works on natural science (such as *On Fire, On Winds, On Stones, On Dizziness*), a work on sense perception, and another on metaphysics.[45] There are no dialogues among the extant works, but we know that Theophrastus did compose some. Plutarch mentions a sympotic dialogue by Theophrastus in which music was discussed (*Non posse* 1095e: ἐν δὲ συμποσίῳ Θεοφράστου περὶ συμφωνιῶν διαλεγομένου). Basil of Caesarea, in the passage discussed in the preceding section, refers to Aristotle and Theophrastus as "authors who composed dialogues" (*Ep.* 135: οἱ τοὺς διαλόγους συγγράψαντες). Proclus speaks of "dialogues by Heraclides of Pontus and Theophrastus" (*In Parm.* 1.659 Cousin). Cicero and Galen provide evidence that Theophrastus' works, like Aristotle's, encompassed exoteric texts composed for a wider audience as well as specialized lectures for his associates,[46] and it is reasonable to suppose that Theophrastus' dialogues belonged to his exoteric writings.

As for the character of Theophrastus' dialogues, we have only a couple of references in later authors, which do not provide us with much information. As we saw in the previous section, Basil of Caesarea said that, unlike Plato, both Aristotle and Theophrastus "went directly to the problem itself" (*Ep.* 135: εὐθὺς αὐτῶν ἥψαντο τῶν πραγμάτων, διὰ τὸ συνειδέναι ἑαυτοῖς τῶν Πλατωνικῶν χαρίτων τὴν ἔνδειαν), that is, they did not elaborate on the speakers and their personalities, but instead focused on their arguments. According to Proclus, Heraclides of Pontus and Theophrastus preceded dialogues with openings (προοίμια) that were "utterly different from what followed" (*In Parm.* 1.659 Cousin: παντελῶς ἀλλότρια τὰ προοίμια τῶν ἑπομένων εἶναι); what he means here is that their openings did not offer hints at the key problems to be discussed in the course of their dialogues. Such statements, however, should not lead us to imagine Theophrastus' dialogues as being dry and technical. Ancient authors appreciated

---

[45] On the catalogue of Theophrastus' works in Diogenes Laertius, which consists of several lists, see White 2002.
[46] Cicero, *Fin.* 5.5.12 (discussed in the preceding section); Galen, *De subst. nat. fac.* 4.758 Kühn (Aristotle and Theophrastus intended some works for a general audience, τὰ μὲν τοῖς πολλοῖς, but also wrote lectures for their associates, τὰς δὲ ἀκροάσεις τοῖς ἑταίροις).

Theophrastus as a writer and as a stylist. Strabo considered him the most eloquent (λογιώτατος) of Aristotle's students and related that his real name was "Tyrtamus," but that he was renamed "Theophrastus" ("divinely speaking") by Aristotle because of "the zeal of his speech" (13.2.4: τὸν τῆς φράσεως αὐτοῦ ζῆλον),[47] while Cicero considered the philosopher's style "sweet" (*Brut.* 31.121: *quis... Theophrasto dulcior?*).

There are no fragments of Theophrastus that retain the dialogue format. It is therefore necessary to make hypotheses based on titles. In Diogenes' catalogue of Theophrastean works (5.42–50), there are only three name-titles: *Acicharus, Megacles*, and *Callisthenes or On Grief*. Acicharus can be identified with the Aramean wise man Ahiqar (sometimes assimilated with Aesop by the Greeks): the story of his life and proverbs were widely popular in the Near East.[48] We do not know the contents and format of Theophrastus' work, but it fits in with interest in non-Greek wisdom attested in both the Academy and Peripatos. The title *Megacles* perhaps referred to the son of Alcmaeon, a rival to Peisistratus; if so, the work could have been a dialogue on a political topic, perhaps set in the archaic past like the "Peisistratus' Dialogue" in POxy. 4.664/50.3544, discussed in Chapter 2.4.1. *Callisthenes or On Grief*—sometimes called simply *Callisthenes*[49]— centered on death and followed on Plato's *Phaedo* and Aristotle's *Eudemus or On the Soul*. The work was a commemoration of a friend, Callisthenes of Olynthus, a relative of Aristotle, who took part in Alexander the Great's expedition and wrote about it. He was accused of conspiring against Alexander in 327 BCE and died, either by execution or in prison.[50] Cicero says that Theophrastus deplored his death and the fact that his path crossed that of Alexander, "a man with the greatest power and the most favorable fortune, who, however, did not know how to make use of his prosperity properly" (*Tusc.* 3.10.21: *incidisse in hominem summa potentia summaque fortuna, sed ignarum quem ad modum rebus secundis uti conveniret*); although he does not explicitly refer to *Callisthenes*, it is a reasonable assumption that he has this text in mind. If so, Theophrastus in *Callisthenes* referred to Callisthenes' conflict with Alexander as well as to the king's character and its shortcomings.[51] The subtitle *On Grief* suggests a slightly different angle than those in Plato's *Phaedo* and Aristotle's *Eudemus*, both of which had the subtitle *On the Soul* and, fittingly, examined questions concerning the nature of the soul and immortality. It is reminiscent of the famous *On Grief* (Περὶ πένθους) by Theophrastus' younger contemporary Crantor, which it might have influenced—unless Theophrastus was responding to a work by a younger colleague.

---

[47] Similarly, Cicero, *Or.* 19.62 and Diogenes Laertius 5.39.
[48] Wilsdorf 1991; Fortenbaugh 2014, 119–24. For various versions of the story of Ahiquar circulating in antiquity, see Lindenberger 1983; for the assimilation of the sage with Aesop, Kurke 2011, 176–85.
[49] Cicero, *Tusc.* 5.9.25; Alexander of Aphrodisias, *De anima libri mantissa* 25.
[50] On Callisthenes, see Pearson 1960, 22–49.    [51] Fortenbaugh 2011, 171-2.

Other titles that suggest the dialogue format include *Eroticus*, *Megaricus*, and *Homileticus*.[52] Some works with *peri*-titles on themes that are appropriate for a general audience—such as *On Happiness*, *On Wealth*, *On Piety*, *On Old Age*—were perhaps also exoteric dialogues. A fragment of *On Drunkenness* quoted in Athenaeus appears to preserve a dialogic utterance (*Deipn.* 10.424e–f): πυνθάνομαι δ' ἔγωγε καὶ Εὐριπίδην τὸν ποιητὴν οἰνοχοεῖν Ἀθήνῃσι τοῖς ὀρχησταῖς καλουμένοις ("I have learned that the poet Euripides poured wine for those who are called dancers"). The words πυνθάνομαι δ' ἔγωγε suggest that the fragment comes from a dialogue, probably from an utterance spoken by Theophrastus himself, as suggested by the preceding words Θεόφραστος γοῦν ἐν τῷ περὶ μέθης φησί.[53] While we have little information concerning the format of Theophrastus' dialogues, we may suppose that he followed Aristotle and included himself among the speakers.

Finally, in Chapter 2.2.6, I discussed a papyrus fragment (PPetr. 2.49e = PLit. Lond. 159a) preserving a fragment of a text, probably a dialogue, which discussed the concept of the kinship between people and animals. We know that this topic was discussed in Theophrastus' *On Piety*, and this work has been proposed as a possible source of the fragment.

## 5.4 Clearchus of Soli

Josephus, Plutarch, and Athenaeus agree that Clearchus of Soli in Cyprus was a student and associate of Aristotle; this suggests a date of birth in 340 or earlier.[54] We know nothing of his life. It is possible that he is named in an inscription from Aï Khanoum (first half or middle of the third century BCE) which contains five Greek maxims accompanied by an epigram announcing that they were written down in Delphi by a certain Clearchus.[55]

Although Diogenes Laertius mentions Clearchus a few times, he does not devote a separate section to him. Consequently, we have no catalogue of his works. He appears to have had an interest in Plato—we know that he authored *Encomium of Plato* and a work on mathematical sections in the *Republic*. He also wrote on ethical and psychological topics (e.g. *On Education*, *On Friendship*, *On Panic*, *On Sleep*), on love (*Erotica*), and on various topics concerning natural philosophy (*On Water Animals*, *On Skeletons*). We know that *On Sleep* was a dialogue thanks to a lengthy fragment preserved by Josephus, which I discuss in

---

[52] They are translated as *(Dialogue) Concerning Love*, *Megarian (Dialogue)*, and *(Dialogue) Concerning Social Interaction* in Fortenbaugh et al. 1992a, 29, 31, 37. Hirzel 1876, 317 speculates that in the *Megaricus* Theophrastus introduced Diogenes the Cynic as a speaker, but there is no evidence supporting this.
[53] Fortenbaugh 2011, 725.
[54] Josephus, *Ap.* 1.22.176; Plutarch, *De facie* 920e–f; Athenaeus, *Deipn.* 6.234f, 7.275d, 15.701c.
[55] See also Chapter 2.2.5.

detail below; for other works with *peri*-titles, we lack information. His *Arcesilaus* may have been a dialogue with Arcesilaus, the Academic philosopher, as a speaker; this would have been a late work, as Arcesilaus, born in 316/5, was considerably younger than Clearchus. A work titled *Gergithius* after a courtier of Alexander the Great discussed flattery and likewise might have been a dialogue.[56]

Clearchus also authored *On Lives*, a lengthy work in at least eight books, from which Athenaeus quotes several times. From extant fragments we can infer that it was not a biographical work; rather, it discussed the lifestyles of political communities and individuals, and demonstrated the negative consequences of luxury and extravagance (τρυφή). Wehrli and Tsitsirides consider a dialogue format likely. They propose that Euxitheus, a Pythagorean mentioned in one of the fragments, might have been a speaker (cf. Athenaeus, *Deipn.* 4.157c [F 38 Wehrli]: "Euxitheus the Pythagorean... as Clearchus the Peripatetic says in the second book of *Lives*, used to say," Εὐξίθεος ὁ Πυθαγορικός ... ὥς φησι Κλέαρχος ὁ Περιπατητικὸς ἐν δευτέρῳ βίων, ἔλεγεν). They also think that some other fragments preserve words spoken by a dialogue speaker who acted as an advocate of pleasure.[57] It is not impossible, though the evidence here is inconclusive.

One work by Clearchus which was unquestionably a dialogue is *On Sleep*. We owe the longest extant fragment to Flavius Josephus, who in his *Against Apion* argued that the Greeks of old knew the Jews and their culture. He finds confirmation in Clearchus (*Ap.* 1.22.176–82 [F 6 Wehrli]):

Κλέαρχος ... ἐν τῷ πρώτῳ περὶ ὕπνου βιβλίῳ φησὶν Ἀριστοτέλην τὸν διδάσκαλον αὐτοῦ περί τινος ἀνδρὸς Ἰουδαίου ταῦτα ἱστορεῖν, αὐτῷ τε τὸν λόγον Ἀριστοτέλει παρατιθείς· ἔστι δὲ οὕτω γεγραμμένον· "ἀλλὰ τὰ μὲν πολλὰ μακρὸν ἂν εἴη λέγειν, ὅσα δ' ἔχει τῶν ἐκείνου θαυμασιότητά τινα καὶ φιλοσοφίαν ὁμοίως διελθεῖν οὐ χεῖρον. σαφῶς δ' ἴσθι, εἶπεν, Ὑπεροχίδη, θαυμαστὸν ὀνείροις ἴσα σοι δόξω λέγειν. καὶ ὁ Ὑπεροχίδης εὐλαβούμενος, δι' αὐτὸ γάρ, ἔφη, τοῦτο καὶ ζητοῦμεν ἀκοῦσαι πάντες. οὐκοῦν, εἶπεν ὁ Ἀριστοτέλης, κατὰ τὸ τῶν ῥητορικῶν παράγγελμα τὸ γένος αὐτοῦ πρῶτον διέλθωμεν, ἵνα μὴ ἀπειθῶμεν τοῖς τῶν ἀπαγγελιῶν διδασκάλοις. λέγε, εἶπεν ὁ Ὑπεροχίδης, εἴ τί σοι δοκεῖ. κἀκεῖνος τοίνυν τὸ μὲν γένος ἦν Ἰουδαῖος ἐκ τῆς κοίλης Συρίας. οὗτοι δέ εἰσιν ἀπόγονοι τῶν ἐν Ἰνδοῖς φιλοσόφων, καλοῦνται δέ, ὥς φασιν, οἱ φιλόσοφοι παρὰ μὲν Ἰνδοῖς Καλανοί, παρὰ δὲ Σύροις Ἰουδαῖοι τοὔνομα λαβόντες ἀπὸ τοῦ τόπου· προσαγορεύεται γὰρ ὃν κατοικοῦσι τόπον Ἰουδαία. τὸ δὲ τῆς πόλεως αὐτῶν ὄνομα πάνυ σκολιόν ἐστιν· Ἱερουσαλήμην γὰρ αὐτὴν καλοῦσιν. οὗτος οὖν ὁ ἄνθρωπος ἐπιξενούμενός τε πολλοῖς κἀκ τῶν ἄνω τόπων εἰς τοὺς ἐπιθαλαττίους ὑποκαταβαίνων Ἑλληνικὸς ἦν οὐ τῇ διαλέκτῳ μόνον,

---

[56] We can infer from a fragment preserved in Athenaeus that Clearchus in *Gergithius* spoke in the first person (*Deipn.* 6.256c [F 19 Wehrli]: παρ' ἡμῖν, that is among inhabitants of Cyprus), but whether as a dialogue character or as the author, we do not know.

[57] F 50, 51, 56 Wehrli. See Wehrli 1968², 58, 64–5; Tsitsiridis 2013, 160–1.

ἀλλὰ καὶ τῇ ψυχῇ. καὶ τότε διατριβόντων ἡμῶν περὶ τὴν Ἀσίαν παραβαλὼν εἰς τοὺς αὐτοὺς τόπους ἄνθρωπος ἐντυγχάνει ἡμῖν τε καί τισιν ἑτέροις τῶν σχολαστικῶν πειρώμενος αὐτῶν τῆς σοφίας. ὡς δὲ πολλοῖς τῶν ἐν παιδείᾳ συνῳκείωτο, παρεδίδου τι μᾶλλον ὧν εἶχεν." ταῦτ' εἴρηκεν ὁ Ἀριστοτέλης παρὰ τῷ Κλεάρχῳ καὶ προσέτι πολλὴν καὶ θαυμάσιον καρτερίαν τοῦ Ἰουδαίου ἀνδρὸς ἐν τῇ διαίτῃ καὶ σωφροσύνην διεξιών.

For Clearchus... says in the first book *On Sleep* that his teacher Aristotle recounted the following about a certain Judean man (he attributes the words to Aristotle himself). The text goes like this: "Yet, it would take a long time to recount the full details, but it would not be amiss to describe those aspects of the man which indicate something extraordinary, and likewise philosophical. Be fully aware, Hyperochides," he said, "that I will give you the impression of saying something equivalent to dreams." Hyperochides replied modestly, "It is for this very reason that we all want to hear it." "Well then," said Aristotle, "in accordance with the rules of rhetoric, let us first describe his ancestry, so we don't disobey the teachers of narrative-technique." "Tell us," said Hyperochides, "if you wish." "This man, then, was a Judean by descent from Coele-Syria. These people are descendants of the philosophers in India. Among the Indians, they say, the philosophers are called Calanoi, and among the Syrians, Judeans, taking their name from the place; for the place they inhabit is called Judea. The name of their city is extremely contorted: they call it Hierousaleme. Now this man, both because he was welcomed as a guest by many and because he was in the habit of coming down from the highlands to the coast, was Greek, not only in his speech but also in his soul. At that time we were staying in Asia, and this man visited the same places and encountered us and some other scholars, testing our wisdom; but as he had been in the company of many educated people, it was he, rather, who conveyed some of what he had." Such were Aristotle's words, as found in Clearchus, and he further relates in detail the immense and extraordinary endurance of the Judean man in his mode of life, and his moderation.[58]

(trans. J. M. G. Barclay)

We can infer from the fragment that *On Sleep* consisted of at least two books and was a dialogue in which Aristotle reported to a certain Hyperochides and other people (whose presence is indicated by the phrase ζητοῦμεν ἀκοῦσαι πάντες) an encounter with an unnamed Judean man, whom he met during his stay in Asia.[59] Clearchus' Aristotle precedes his account with a remark that he will follow the rules of rhetoric and instructions by "teachers of narrative" (τοῖς τῶν ἀπαγγελιῶν

---

[58] The fragment is also quoted in Eusebius of Caesarea, *PE* 9.5.2–7. For textual difficulties, see Barclay 2007, lxi–lxiv; for different variants of the text, see notes in Barclay 2007, 103–5.
[59] The encounter of Aristotle and the Jew is probably Clearchus' invention. Jews, at any rate, are never mentioned in extant writings by Aristotle; see Bar-Kochva 2010, 47–8.

διδασκάλοις). This comment is self-referential as it draws the reader's attention to Clearchus' composition of a story narrated by Aristotle; it is also humorous considering Aristotle's authorship of the *Rhetoric*.[60]

The figure of the Jewish sage is reminiscent of other representatives of non-Greek wisdom in the Academy and Peripatos (see Chapter 3.2, p. 103). Clearchus depicted the Judeans, with whom his readers were little familiar, as a tribe of philosophers and compared them with the Indian "Calanoi." The latter term was coined—perhaps by Clearchus—from the name of Calanus, a Gymnosophist described by Onesicritus, a Cynic philosopher who accompanied Alexander the Great during his expedition to India.[61] Josephus says that Clearchus described "the immense and extraordinary endurance" (πολλὴν καὶ θαυμάσιον καρτερίαν) and "moderation" (σωφροσύνην) of the Jew, traits regularly associated in Greek literature (perhaps under influence of Onesicritus) with the Indian Gymnosophists. It is unclear whether the miraculous, "dream-like" story announced by Aristotle at the beginning of the fragment concerned these traits.

Another fragment of *On Sleep* comes from a passage by Proclus, in which the Neoplatonic philosopher argues that it is possible for the soul to exit and enter the body. This, Proclus says, was demonstrated by Clearchus, whose *On Sleep* described a man who, in the presence of Aristotle, drew the soul from a sleeping youth with a soul-drawing wand (τῇ ψυχουλκῷ ῥάβδῳ) and then led it back. The soul next reported all that had happened to it (ἀπαγγέλλειν ἕκαστα) when it was outside the body. The miracle-worker showed, Proclus says, that the soul uses the body as an inn (οἷον καταγωγίῳ), and that the body deprived of the soul does not move or feel. His demonstration persuaded Aristotle that the soul was separable from the body (*In Remp.* 2.122.22–123.12 Kroll [F 7 Wehrli]).

There were attempts to identify Josephus' Jew with Proclus' wonder-maker,[62] but such an identification is uncertain. While drawing the soul from out of the body with a wand would certainly qualify as a marvelous story, Bar-Kochva rightly advises caution. It is clear from Josephus that the story of the Jewish sage was not the centerpiece of the dialogue: Josephus says that Clearchus spoke about the Judean man "in a digression because his main interest was elsewhere" (*Ap.* 1.22.183: ἐν παρεκβάσει ταῦτ' εἴρηκεν, τὸ γὰρ προκείμενον αὐτῷ ἦν [καθ'] ἕτερον). Clearchus' dialogue in all probability contained a whole host of miraculous stories, for collecting examples was a usual Peripatetic practice for supporting

---

[60] On the "ironic" reference to the rules of rhetoric, see Lewy 1938, 213 n. 38; Barclay 2007, 104 n. 589; Bar-Kochva 2010, 45 n. 19; Tsitsiridis 2013, 56–7. ἡ ἀπαγγελία, "a report, description" was a technical term in literary criticism and rhetoric, cf. Plato, *Resp.* 394b–c; Aristotle, *Poet.* 1449b11, 26.

[61] On Onesicritus, see Chapter 6.4. Bar-Kochva 2010, 67–74 suggests that Clearchus might have responded to the Gymnosophists episode in Onesicritus.

[62] The Jew is identified with Proclus' miracle-worker by von Gutschmid 1893, 587–8 and Lewy 1938, 209–10. Wehrli 1969²a and Tsitsiridis 2013, 64 find it unlikely.

an argument.[63] We know, for instance, that Clearchus wrote about people who lived without any food and got the warmth their bodies needed from the sun.[64] The story about Cleonymus the Athenian reported by Proclus, probably also derived from *On Sleep* (*In Remp.* 2.113.19–115.7 Kroll [F 8 Wehrli]; Proclus mentions Clearchus as a source, but does not provide a title). Cleonymus, Proclus writes, died from grief after the death of a friend, but later was restored to life and reported what his soul saw and heard during its separation from the body. It rose above the earth as if freed from its bonds and saw rivers and places in different shapes and colors below; then it arrived in a place run by divine powers in female forms and was ordered to remain silent and observe; it witnessed there punishments, judgments, and purifications of souls. It also met the soul of a certain Lysias of Syracuse, and some time afterwards, after Cleonymus had returned to normal life, he met Lysias in Athens and the two men recognized each other.

There are clear Platonic subtexts in the Cleonymus-story: the myth of Er at the end of the *Republic* (614b–621b), which relates Er's apparent death, his soul's experiences, and subsequent return to life; and the description of the Earth in the *Phaedo* (109b, 110b–c). Aristotle's words in Josephus' passage "it would take a long time to recount the full details" (ἀλλὰ τὰ μὲν πολλὰ μακρὸν ἂν εἴη λέγειν) may be intended to remind the reader of Socrates' "there is a lot to tell, Glaucon, and it would require much time" (*Resp.* 615a: τὰ μὲν οὖν πολλά, ὦ Γλαύκων, πολλοῦ χρόνου διηγήσασθαι), which appears in the account of what the soul of Er saw during its travel.[65] Clearchus' interest in miraculous stories concerning the separation of the soul from the body and its separate existence has parallels in Heraclides of Pontus, in particular, in the dialogue about a woman brought to life by Empedocles after many days of not breathing, and in the story about Empedotimus, who encountered the epiphany of Pluto and Persephone and was instructed about the nature of the soul and the afterlife.

## 5.5 Dicaearchus of Messana

Cicero also mentions dialogues by Aristotle's student Dicaearchus of Messana in Sicily; from his letters to Atticus we know that he had access to several works by the philosopher and took pleasure in reading them. Dicaearchus was particularly

---

[63] Bar-Kochva 2010, 55–6. He proposes that the miraculous things Aristotle reported about the Jew had to do with his endurance and moderation (58–67).

[64] We owe this information to the Syriac philosopher Probus; the fragment appears in English translation in Brock 2011, 200 and is discussed in Tsitsiridis 2013, 63. Probus' fragment confirms that two passages in Damascius (*In Phd.* 1.530, 2.138) in which Aristotle is said to have maintained that there are people who do not eat, but are nourished by the rays of the sun, draw from Clearchus' *On Sleep* (and concerning Aristotle as a dialogue character).

[65] Lewy 1938, 213 n. 39; Tsitsiridis 2013, 71.

interested in ethics, literature (Plutarch, *Non posse* 1095a, refers with approval to what he wrote about Homer and Euripides), and human societies and customs. In the *Tusculan Disputations*, Cicero mentions his dialogue set in Corinth, consisting of three books. In the first book, Dicaearchus represented "many of the learned men in discussion" (*doctorum hominum disputantium... multos loquentes*), and in Books 2 and 3, he introduced Pherecrates, an old man from Phthia and descendant of Deucalion, who argued that there was no such thing as a "mind" (*animus*) or "soul" (*anima*) which could be separated from the body; rather, the force enabling people to act and feel is spread throughout the body (*Tusc.* 1.10.21). "There is nothing except the body, single and simple, so fashioned, that it lives and feels thanks to natural constitution" (*nec sit quicquam nisi corpus unum et simplex, ita figuratum, ut temperatione naturae vigeat et sentiat*).

Cicero mentions also three books by Dicaearchus which were called "Lesbian" because the conversation took place at Mytilene (*Tusc.* 1.31.77: *tres libros scripsit, qui Lesbiaci vocantur quod Mytilenis sermo habetur*); we can infer, therefore, that this was a dialogue with a Lesbian setting. Cicero says that Dicaearchus argued there that "minds are mortal" (*animos esse mortales*). As the topic is similar to the one discussed in the Corinthian dialogue, it is probable that the Corinthian and Lesbian books constituted two parts of a single work titled *On the Soul*, which Cicero mentions in a letter to Atticus: he speaks there of *Dicaearchi Περὶ ψυχῆς utros*, "both (books? parts?) of Dicaearchus' *On the Soul*," perhaps referring to its two components, the Lesbian and the Corinthian dialogues (*Att.* 13.32.2).[66]

In another letter to Atticus, Cicero mentions a work by Dicaearchus on a political topic set in Olympia, also likely a dialogue (*Att.* 13.30.2; he refers to it as πολιτικὸν σύλλογον), and perhaps identical with a text which Athenaeus calls *The Olympian* (*Deipn.* 14.620d: Ὀλυμπικός). Scholars also propose that other works, such as *Tripoliticus*, *Panathenaicus*, and the *Sacrifice at Ilium* were dialogues, but there are no fragments or testimonies that would confirm this.

Athenaeus mentions Dicaearchus' *The Descent into (the Cave of) Trophonius*, which consisted of at least two books (*Deipn.* 14.641e: Εἰς Τροφωνίου κατάβασις; cf. 13.594e). Cicero calls it simply Κατάβασις (*Att.* 13.32.2, 13.33.2) and refers to it as *Trophoniana Chaeronis narratio*, "The Trophonian Story of Chaeron" (*Att.* 6.2.3). The identity of Chaeron, probably a speaker in a dialogue, is unclear. It was proposed that he is a mythical figure, the son of Apollo and Thero, who founded the city of Chaeroneia. This would certainly fit with the Boeotian setting of the work, as the oracle of Trophonius was located at Lebadeia, less than fifteen kilometers south of Chaeroneia.[67] In Plutarch's dialogue *On the Daimonion of*

---

[66] Dicaearchus' *On the Soul* is also mentioned by Plutarch, *Adv. Col.* 1115a. Identification of the Lesbian and Corinthian dialogues with *On the Soul* was proposed by Schmidt 1867, 40 and Wehrli 1967², 44. Hirzel 1895a, 319, n. 1 argues against it.

[67] Wehrli 1967², 47.

*Socrates*, the descent into the cave of Trophonius by a certain Timarchus is described: Timarchus spent there two nights and a day, and after his return, reported miraculous visions he had had there and instructions he had obtained about the soul; he also received a prophecy of his death, which was soon fulfilled (*De genio* 590a–592e). Plutarch certainly knew of Dicaearchus' account of the descent into the Trophonian cave (as a Boeotian, he must have been particularly interested in Boeotian-themed works), and we may suppose that he elaborated some of Dicaearchan motifs.

## 5.6 Aristoxenus of Tarentum

Aristoxenus' father was a musician, and it is to him that the philosopher owed his musical education and interests. He is said to have studied philosophy, first with Pythagoreans and then with Aristotle. According to the *Suda*, he left more than four hundred and fifty works, including writings on Pythagorean philosophy, biographies (of Pythagoras, Socrates, Plato, the Pythagorean philosopher Archytas), works on education and music, and several miscellanies. Only his treatises on music—*Elementa harmonica* and *Elementa rhythmica*—are partially preserved, providing testimony to the sophistication and ingenuity of his musical theory.[68]

Some of Aristoxenus' works were probably dialogues. Athenaeus quotes a passage from his sympotic miscellany titled Σύμμικτα συμποτικά, where someone, perhaps a dialogue character, complains about the degeneration of contemporary music (*Deipn.* 14.632a–b). Plutarch may be referring to this work when he notes in his polemic with Epicurus that Aristoxenus found it appropriate to discuss music at a *symposion* (*Non posse* 1095e). Several authors also quote from Aristoxenus' work or works titled *Hypomnemata*, which may have included some dialogized passages.[69]

Aristoxenus was known in antiquity as one of the early biographers: he is the first author to whom works titled βίοι, "lives" (of Pythagoras, Socrates, Plato, Archytas, and a poet Telestes) were ascribed.[70] We do not know whether these titles originated with Aristoxenus or to what extent the lives he composed resembled the biographies we know from later periods, when the conventions of the genre had already crystallized. His *Life of Archytas*, a biography of the

---

[68] On Aristoxenus' musical treatises, see Barker 1989, 119–25.

[69] Diogenes Laertius refers to Aristoxenus' *Historical Hypomnemata* (9.40: τὰ ἱστορικὰ ὑπομνήματα) and Athenaeus to his *Brief Hypomnemata* (*Deipn.* 14.619e: τὰ κατὰ βραχὺ ὑπομνήματα); Porphyry (*In Ptol. Harm.* 1.4.80) and Photius (*Bibl.* 161.103b) to *Miscellaneous Hypomnemata* (σύμμικτα ὑπομνήματα). For *hypomnemata* literature, see Chapter 1.2, p. 17.

[70] Schorn 2014a, 705. On Aristoxenus as the first biographer in the Peripatos, see Momigliano 1971, 73–6; for a discussion of fragments of his biographies, Schorn 2012.

Pythagorean philosopher, appears to have included an inset dialogue between Archytas and Polyarchus, an ambassador of Dionysius the Younger, nicknamed Ἡδυπαθής, "Voluptary," on account of his hedonism. Athenaeus quotes a speech in defense of pleasure delivered by Polyarchus (*Deipn.* 12.545a–546c; see Chapter 1.4), which was probably followed by a counter speech by Archytas. The figure of Polyarchus revives Plato's Callicles or Thrasymachus, while the association of Polyarchus with the tyrant Dionysius suggests that the episode was a re-enactment of an encounter between wisdom and political rule.

## 5.7 Demetrius of Phaleron and Chamaeleon of Heraclea

In Diogenes Laertius' catalogue of writings by Demetrius of Phaleron there is a cluster of ten titles suggesting the dialogue format (*Ptolemy, Eroticus, Phaedonidas, Maedon, Cleon, Socrates, Artoxerxes, Homericus, Aristides, Aristomachus*), further in the catalogue, the title *Dionysius* is listed (5.81).[71] Some ethical works on problems of general interest—such as *On Fate, On Marriage, On Old Age*—might also have been dialogues. Demetrius himself is a character in Aristeas' *Letter to Philocrates* (discussed in Chapter 1.3), where he is in charge of Ptolemy II Philadelphus' library. At the beginning of the work, he is represented in conversation with Ptolemy: he informs the king about Jewish Law and recommends acquiring it for the library. The text also ends with an exchange between Demetrius and Ptolemy.

Dialogues were probably also written by Chamaeleon of Heraclea, who wrote *On Pleasure* and *On Drunkenness*; it is likely that these works were dialogues, like works with the same titles authored by other philosophers of this period.[72]

## 5.8 Praxiphanes of Mytilene

Praxiphanes, a student of Theophrastus, represents a younger generation of Peripatetics. He was born in the last quarter of the fourth century BCE (*c.*320/310) and became particularly renowned for his work in the field of grammar and literary criticism. His importance in these fields is confirmed by Clement of Alexandria's remark that he was the first one who was called "a grammarian in our sense," which means that he was among the first people to develop the field of

---

[71] Wehrli 1968², 66; Sollenberger 2000, 327.
[72] Fortenbaugh 2012. In all probability Heraclides of Pontus' *On Pleasure* and Theophrastus' *On Drunkenness* were dialogues.

literary criticism.⁷³ Callimachus appears to have reacted to his work in a text titled *To (or Against) Praxiphanes*.

At least one of Praxiphanes' works on literature was a dialogue. It was probably titled *On Poets* (like one of Aristotle's dialogues) and depicted a conversation between Plato and Isocrates (διατριβήν τινα περὶ ποιητῶν γενομένην) which took place when Isocrates visited Plato's place in the country (ἐν ἀγρῷ παρὰ Πλάτωνι ἐπιξενωθέντος τοῦ Ἰσοκράτους, Diogenes Laertius 3.8 [F 11 Wehrli]).⁷⁴ As he made Plato converse with Isocrates, Praxiphanes was probably inspired by the Platonic *Phaedrus*, where Isocrates is mentioned as a young friend of Socrates and praised (perhaps ironically) for his philosophical and noble character. In Praxiphanes, the conversation was certainly friendly, as Diogenes Laertius refers to Praxiphanes' dialogue to support the opinion that Plato was a friend with Isocrates (3.8: ὁ δ' οὖν φιλόσοφος καὶ Ἰσοκράτει φίλος ἦν). If Praxiphanes was inspired by the *Phaedrus* in his choice of Isocrates and Plato's interlocutor, it is very likely, as Maddalena Vallozza argued recently, that the rural setting of Plato's and Isocrates' conversation in *On Poets* was a conscious allusion to the suburban walk that Socrates and Phaedrus take in Plato.⁷⁵ We do not have evidence concerning the content of the dialogue, but we may assume that Praxiphanes, known for his innovative work in the field of literary criticism, channeled some of his concepts through the figures of Plato and Isocrates.

Praxiphanes also wrote a work on friendship, with which the Epicurean Carneiscus polemized in his *Philistas*. It might have been a dialogue, as suggested by the phrase ἀλλοῖον ἑαυτὸν εἰσάγει ϙῦν ἐν τῶι ϙ[υ]γγράμματι Πραξιφάνης (PHerc. 1027 col. xviii.6-9: "Praxiphanes introduces himself in a different way in this work").⁷⁶

Hirzel's reconstruction of Praxiphanes' Περὶ ἱστορίας (either *On History* or *On Inquiry*) as a dialogue set in the court of the Macedonian king Archelaus—with Thucydides and the poets Plato, Agathon, Niceratus, Choerilus, and Melanippides as speakers—is highly speculative and goes beyond available evidence.⁷⁷

---

⁷³ [Achilles Tatius], *Arat.* 9. For overview of Praxiphanes' interests and writings, see Matelli 2012.

⁷⁴ The work might have been identical with *On Poems* (Περὶ ποιημάτων) attested in Philodemus, *Poem.* 5 col. xii.30-1, though existence of two different works is plausible.

⁷⁵ Vallozza 2011; Vallozza 2012. As she observes, in a passage directly preceding the information on Praxiphanes' dialogue, Diogenes quotes Eupolis and Timon of Phlius, who describe the Academy as a nice and shady place, with Timon making a parallel between Plato's educational activity in his school and Socrates' conversation with Phaedrus. She proposed that the quotations from Eupolis and Timon likewise come from Praxiphanes.

⁷⁶ Crönert 1906, 72; Wehrli 1969²b, 107. Capasso 1988, 252-4 considers the evidence insufficient to stipulate the dialogue format.

⁷⁷ Hirzel 1895a, 311; he bases his reconstruction on a passage in Marcellinus saying that Praxiphanes wrote that Thucydides lived at the same time as the five other poets; and that he was little known in the time of Archelaus, but was admired greatly later. The passage presents many difficulties (e.g. it is not clear whether Marcellinus refers to Thucydides the historian or the poet); see notes in Martano et al. 2012, 96-9 and discussion in Matelli 2012, 545-9. The dialogue format is assumed by Corradi 2012.

## 5.9 Prytanis and Hieronymus of Rhodes, Aristo of Ceos, Satyrus of Callatis

Prytanis and Hieronymus, two third-century Peripatetics, are mentioned by Plutarch in the opening chapters of *Table Talk* as authors who wrote sympotic dialogues (*Quaest. conv.* 612d–e). Hieronymus is elsewhere ascribed the work *On Drunkenness* (Περὶ μέθης), perhaps identical with the sympotic work referred to by Plutarch.

We know more about Aristo of Ceos, born in the mid-third century BCE, a student of Lyco of Troas. Unfortunately, our knowledge of him is complicated by the fact that there was another Hellenistic philosopher of the same name, the Stoic Aristo of Chios; therefore, unless ancient authors specify which Aristo they quote or refer to, it is frequently difficult to decide between them. Moreover, ancient writers also debated which works were authored by which philosopher (for instance, Diogenes Laertius in 7.163 writes that Panaetius ascribed works by Aristo of Chios to Aristo of Ceos); consequently, even when a specific Aristo is named in a source, we cannot be certain that the attribution is correct. The only text that can be attributed without doubt to Aristo the Peripatetic is *Lyco*, titled after his teacher Lyco of Troas, probably a dialogue based on the title. It is mentioned by Plutarch in *On Listening to Poetry*, where it is listed, together with Heraclides' *Abaris*, as a work from which young readers drew both inspiration and pleasure (*De aud. poet.* 14e–f: μεθ' ἡδονῆς ἐνθουσιῶσι). It must have been written, therefore, in a popular and enjoyable style, suitable for a younger audience.

Cicero in *On Moral Ends* characterizes Aristo of Ceos as lacking gravity becoming of a great philosopher (*quae desideratur a magno philosopho gravitas in eo non fuit*), and notes that his many works, though polished, lacked authority (*auctoritatem oratio non habet*) (*Fin.* 5.5.13). This criticism resonates with a passage in Cicero's *Cato Maior, On Old Age*, where he mentions a dialogue by Aristo on old age:[78] he says that Aristo introduced Tithonus, the mythological figure, as a speaker; Cicero, however, thought that there was "too little authority in a fable" (*parum enim esset auctoritatis in fabula*)—a comment reminiscent of the criticism expressed in *On Moral Ends*—and chose the stately Cato as an interlocutor.[79]

Satyrus of Callatis, considered a Peripatetic according to some ancient sources, authored numerous biographies of poets, philosophers, kings, and statesmen, cited by both Diogenes Laertius and Athenaeus. An Oxyrhynchian papyrus

---

[78] While identification of the Aristo in this passage is confused in medieval manuscripts, some of which refer to him as *Chius* and some as *Ceus*, it is most probable that it is the Peripatetic philosopher who is meant.

[79] Hahm 1990, 180–1, 201–2.

(POxy. 9.1176) preserves fragments of the *Life of Euripides* which is in the format of a dramatic dialogue; I discuss it in Chapter 2.3.1.

## 5.10 Conclusion

The material discussed in this chapter demonstrates the vitality of the dialogue in the Peripatos in the fourth and third centuries BCE. As we have seen, the dialogue format was employed by Aristotle and his immediate students. Both Aristotle and Theophrastus appear to have used the dialogue format for writings aimed at a wider audience, composed in a literary style: the arguments were easier to follow and the topics relevant to people who were not professional philosophers. Cicero, who had a great interest in rhetoric and eloquence, valued the style of both Aristotle and Theophrastus, in all probability basing his high opinion on their dialogues. This should caution us against imagining their dialogues as technical, dry, and scientific. There is also evidence of the Peripatetics' intertextual engagement with Plato's dialogues—for instance, in Aristotle's *Eudemus*, in Clearchus, and in Praxiphanes. Although Cicero associated Aristotle mostly with contemporary settings, other Peripatetics composed dialogues set in the past (perhaps Theophrastus' *Megacles*, and almost certainly Praxiphanes' *On Poets*, with Plato and Isocrates as speakers) or in mythological scenery (Tithonus as a speaker in Aristo of Ceos). We may also notice a shift in title-conventions: there are less name-titles and more *peri*-titles, and there are dialogues labeled after the place in which the conversation took place (Dicaearchus' Corinthian and Lesbian dialogues).

There is no ancient evidence supporting the idea that Aristotle wrote his dialogues in his youth, when he was still under Plato's spell. If we accept the ancient authors' insistence that Aristotle's dialogues were exoteric, there is no reason to assume that the desire to reach a wider audience was limited to the early period of his philosophical activity. Gellius' wonderful image of Aristotle having serious lectures in the morning and popular talks in the evening (*NA* 20.5), though of little historical value, nevertheless shows clearly that ancient readers saw no essential contradiction between the exoteric and acroamatic parts of Aristotle's corpus. It is also noteworthy that Cicero considers inclusion of the author as the authoritative speaker and authorial prefaces to be two characteristic traits of the Aristotelian dialogue. Such an assertive authorial presence suggests an established philosophical voice and supports the supposition that at least some of the dialogues were composed by the mature Aristotle. It is probable that other Peripatetics followed the model of Aristotle and used the dialogue format to treat subjects which had the potential to engage a non-philosophical audience. The evidence confirms that they wrote sympotic dialogues, as well as dialogues that treated ethical and psychological problems of general interest. The nature of the soul and the problem of death and the afterlife are recurrent dialogue-subjects: the spotlight on the impermanence of human life and intransparency of human nature could well serve as an initiation into philosophy. We also observe the emergence of dialogues dedicated to poetry and literary criticism, interests well attested in the Peripatos, but also common outside the philosophic schools.

The Peripatos played an important role in the development of the biography as a genre. It is therefore noteworthy that some Peripatetic biographies incorporated sections influenced by the tradition of the dialogue (Aristoxenus' *Life of Archytas*), and some were written in the dialogue format (Satyrus of Callatis' *Life of Euripides*).

# 6
# Other Schools and Authors

## 6.1 Introductory Remarks

The Academy and the Peripatos constitute the two main philosophical environments in which dialogues were composed. However, the genre was also employed by other schools as well as by authors who do not easily fit into any specific philosophical tradition. The dialogue was certainly in use in the so-called Minor Socratic schools, that is, those that originated from Socrates' followers other than Plato.[1] While a comprehensive discussion of dialogues by Socrates' immediate students is beyond the scope of this book, I will devote the first two sections to the Megarians and the Cyrenaics (who originated from Euclides of Megara and Aristippus of Cyrene, respectively) because we have evidence that the dialogue was also used in these traditions by the founders' successors, such as Stilpo of Megara and Hegesias of Cyrene.

The next section examines the Cynics and demonstrates that philosophers associated with Cynicism engaged with the dialogue in a variety of ways: they used it to bring to life the figure of Diogenes, incorporated dialogized passages into paraenetic discourse, and wrote parodic dialogues. There is less evidence about the Stoics' engagement with the dialogue, which is the subject of the next part of the chapter; the Epicurean tradition, on the other hand, offers relatively ample material for analysis.

The next two sections discuss two individuals from the third century BCE, an early representative of Pyrrhonism, Timon of Phlius, who interacted with the genre of dialogue in prose and in parodic poetry, and the renowned scholar and poet Eratosthenes of Cyrene. With the extant anonymous *Tablet of Cebes* (first century BCE or first century CE) we enter the Roman period, to which also belongs Philo of Alexandria, among whose fragments we find the remains of two philosophical dialogues—important evidence for the enduring vitality of the genre in the mid-first century CE.

---

[1] For more on the term and a general overview of the Minor Socratic schools, see Zilioli 2015, xiii–xx.

## 6.2 Megarians

The Megarians were identified as a separate philosophical group already by Aristotle (*Metaph.* 1046b29). Diogenes Laertius traces the school's roots to one of Socrates' students, Euclides of Megara, who was also inspired by Parmenides (2.106).[2] According to Diogenes, Euclides' followers were initially called "Megarians," later *eristikoi*, and then *dialektikoi* (the latter name was given to them by Dionysius of Chalcedon on account of the school's custom to "put their arguments into the form of question and answer").[3] The Megarians appear to have been a diverse group of philosophers who shared methods of argument and an interest in dialectic and eristic rather than a body of specific dogmatic assertions.[4] They were engaged in polemics with other Hellenistic philosophical schools, in particular with the Stoics and Epicureans.[5]

Euclides, the founder of the school, appears as a character in Plato's *Theaetetus* and *Phaedo*. While in the latter dialogue he remains silent, in the *Theaetetus* he plays an important role: not only does the work open with his exchange with Terpsion, but the reported conversation between Socrates, Theodorus, and Theaetetus that constitutes the core of the dialogue is said to have been written down by him after he heard it related by Socrates. Plato's Euclides says that he made notes immediately after the conversation and afterwards consulted Socrates several times in order to get it straight (*Tht.* 142c–143a). He also emphasizes that he decided to write the conversation in a dramatic format, without the narrative bits that were present in Socrates' report (*Tht.* 143b–c), perhaps an indication that Euclides' own dialogues were dramatic rather than reported.

According to Diogenes Laertius (2.108) and *Suda* (s.v. Εὐκλείδης (ε 3539)), Euclides wrote six dialogues, titled *Lamprias*, *Aeschines*, *Phoenix*, *Crito*, *Alcibiades*, and *Eroticus*; there is no evidence of other works composed by him. Diogenes Laertius informs us that these were Socratic dialogues and that their authenticity had been doubted by Panaetius (2.64). The titles *Aeschines*, *Crito*, and *Alcibiades* refer to figures known from the Socratic circle; the *Eroticus* was centered on love, a recurrent topic in Socratic literature. The identities of Lamprias and Phoenix

---

[2] On the controversial topic of the extent of the Eleatic influence upon Euclides and the Megarians, see Brancacci 2018.

[3] Sedley 1977, 75 believes that the three names refer to different groups of philosophers who were Euclides' followers, but had different philosophical views.

[4] On the Megarian school and the scholarly controversies around it, see von Fritz 1931; Giannantoni 1990c, 41–50; on their contributions to dialectic and logic, and role as precursors of the Stoics, see Allen 2019. Fragments and testimonies have been collected and discussed by Döring 1972; Giannantoni 1990a, 375–483; Giannantoni 1990c, 33–113.

[5] Alexinus of Elis disagreed with Zeno (Diogenes Laertius 2.109 and Sextus Empiricus, *Adv. math.* 9.108) and was the object of an attack by the Epicurean Hermarchus (Philodemus, *Rhet.* 2, col. xliv.19–27); Stilpo was attacked by Epicurus and his follower Colotes (Seneca, *Ep.* 9.1; Plutarch, *Adv. Col.* 1119c–1120b); on the list of Epicurus' works there is one titled *Against the Megarians* (Diogenes Laertius 10.27).

remain unclear (the latter may have been the Homeric character or a historical figure known from Plato's *Symposion* 172b and 173b).

Stobaeus preserves a passage attributed to Euclides which appears to be a direct quotation from one of his works (3.6.63 [F 19 Döring; SSR II A 11]). It shows no signs of the dialogue format; perhaps it comes from a longer utterance by an unknown interlocutor.[6] In the passage, a distinction is made between two types of dreams which are imagined as *daimones*. One is young, persuadable, and prone to take flight. The other is old and gray, visits mostly older people, and is impossible to persuade on account of being deaf and blind. Dream and death were imagined as brothers by Homer and Hesiod, and Euclides' image interacts with this tradition, though the philosopher emphasizes the differences between them rather than the similarities.[7] It has been hypothesized that the passage originates from the dialogue *Crito*, perhaps from a speech by the imprisoned Socrates, comforting his friend.[8] Euclides' interest in the theme of human mortality and his employment of evocative imagery for ethical purposes fit in with the preoccupations and character of Socratic literature.

Ancient sources list several pupils of Euclides, including Ichthyas, Eubulides, Cleinomachus, and Stilpo. We know very little of their writings. According to the *Suda*, after Euclides' death, the leadership of the Megarian school was assumed by Ichthyas (s.v. Εὐκλείδης (ε 3539)). Diogenes Laertius writes that Diogenes the Cynic wrote a dialogue against him (2.112: πρὸς ὃν καὶ Διογένης ὁ κυνικὸς διάλογον πεποίηται; cf. also the title *Ichthyas* on a list of Diogenes' writings at 6.80). Cleinomachus may have featured in a dialogue authored by Speusippus titled *Cleinomachus or Lysias* (Diogenes Laertius 4.4). Eubulides' student Alexinus of Elis composed *Apomnemoneumata*, in which he included a conversation between Alexander the Great as a boy and his father Philip, and in which Alexander expressed contempt for Aristotle's teachings and spoke approvingly of Nicagoras, the tyrant of Zeleia (see Chapter 1.2, p. 16–17).

We know more of Stilpo of Megara, one of the most prominent and famous Megarian thinkers. He is called by Diogenes Laertius "a most distinguished philosopher" (2.123: διασημότατος φιλόσοφος) and, apart from Euclides, is the only Megarian whose life Diogenes includes in his work (remarkably, Stilpo's biography is longer than Euclides'). Stilpo's life is tentatively dated to about 360–280 BCE, which makes it improbable that he studied under Euclides. Diogenes Laertius depicts him as a celebrity and claims that under his influence the whole of Greece wanted to join the Megarians—students abandoned other philosophical schools and flocked to him, and whenever he visited Athens, people

---

[6] See Döring 1972, 80–1; Giannantoni 1990c, 38–9.
[7] Cf. Homer, *Il.* 14.231, 16.682; Hesiod, *Th.* 212, 756–66. For a comparison of death to sleep, see also Plato, *Ap.* 40c–d.
[8] Brancacci 2005.

left their workshops and ran to see him. Both Ptolemy I Soter and Demetrius Poliorcetes are said to have respected him, and the former invited him to come with him to Egypt (Diogenes Laertius 2.113-15). Stilpo is sometimes named as a teacher to Crates the Cynic and Zeno of Citium, founder of the Stoic school (Diogenes Laertius 2.114, 7.2, 7.24).

According to Diogenes Laertius, Stilpo wrote nine dialogues: *Moschus, Aristippus* or *Callias, Ptolemy, Chaerecrates, Metrocles, Anaximenes, Epigenes, To his Daughter*, and *Aristotle* (2.120).[9] In the *Suda* (s.v. Στίλπων (σ 1114)) we read that he left over twenty dialogues (no titles are listed). Diogenes Laertius refers to Stilpo's dialogues as "cold," ψυχροί, which might have meant that later critics found his style and language extravagant and excessively attracted to the unusual and novel. But it is also possible that the term referred to the contents of the dialogues, for instance to their technical character and lack of literary charm.[10] Some of the titles suggest that Stilpo may have composed dialogues with Socrates as a speaker (Chaerecrates and Epigenes are probably to be identified with lesser-known followers of Socrates,[11] while Aristippus and Callias—with the founder of the Cyrenaic school and the speaker in Plato's *Protagoras*, respectively). Some may have been polemics with other schools and philosophers: Moschus may have been a student of Phaedo of Elis (Diogenes Laertius 2.126); Aristotle—either the Stagirite or a Cyrenaic philosopher from whom two students deserted to Stilpo (2.113); Anaximenes—the rhetorician and historian from Lampsacus, the probable author of the *Rhetoric to Alexander*. Metrocles was a Cynic philosopher and a student of Crates; he appears as Stilpo's opponents in a few anecdotes. The title *Ptolemy* refers in all probability to Ptolemy I Soter; perhaps from this work comes the story of Stilpo's refusal to go to Egypt with the king. This dialogue might have been a source of the anecdote about Diodorus Cronus who, when staying with Ptolemy (παρὰ Πτολεμαίῳ τῷ Σωτῆρι διατρίβων), was questioned dialectically by Stilpo (λόγους τινὰς διαλεκτικοὺς ἠρωτήθη) at a banquet. He was not able to solve the problems proposed; as a result, he was rebuked by Ptolemy and given the nickname "Cronus" (Diogenes Laertius 2.111). The title *To his Daughter* is reminiscent of a *Letter to his Daughter Arete* attributed to Aristippus of Cyrene, mentioned elsewhere by Diogenes Laertius (2.84). In both cases, works of a seemingly epistolographic format appear in lists of dialogues. This may be due to error or negligence, though it is not impossible that an epistolographic frame contained a dialogue (I discuss blending of epistolography and dialogue in

---

[9] Though elsewhere Diogenes Laertius says that some people asserted that Stilpo did not write anything (1.16).

[10] On the meaning of ψυχρός in ancient literary criticism, see van Hook 1917. See also Plato, *Lg.* 802d, where ψυχρός has a meaning similar to ἀηδής, "unpleasant."

[11] Chaerecrates (the younger brother of Chaerephon): Xenophon, *Mem.* 1.2.48, 2.3.1-19; Plato, *Ap.* 21a (unnamed, mentioned as Chaerephon's brother); Epigenes: Plato, *Ap.* 33e, *Phd.* 59b; Xenophon, *Mem.* 3.12.1-8.

Chapter 1.3). According to ancient sources, Stilpo's daughter led an immoral life, and the philosopher's attitude to her profligacy is a recurrent theme in anecdotes.

As noted in Chapter 1.2, Athenaeus says that sympotic dialogues (συμποτικοὺς διαλόγους) by the Stoic Persaeus were "compiled from the *apomnemoneumata* of Stilpo and Zeno" (*Deipn.* 4.162b-c: συντεθέντας ἐκ τῶν Στίλπωνος καὶ Ζήνωνος ἀπομνημονευμάτων). This is a reference probably not to works actually entitled *Apomnemoneumata* and authored by Stilpo and Zeno, but to written reminiscences about them composed by others, perhaps by Persaeus himself. Stilpo was the protagonist of numerous dialogized anecdotes that may have originated from dialogues or *apomnemoneumata*-type texts featuring him. To these belong the conversation between Stilpo and (probably) Metrocles in POxy. 52.3655; between Stilpo and Metrocles in Plutarch's *On Tranquility of Mind* (468a); and between Stilpo and the *hetaira* Glycera in Athenaeus (*Deipn.* 13.584a) (see Chapter 2.5.3 and Chapter 1.2).

While Stilpo was known as a master of dialectic and paradoxical arguments, his legacy was wider. Plutarch distinguishes the "little word games" and "dialectic exercises" (λογάρια, γύμνασμα διαλεκτικόν) with which Stilpo occupied himself without serious intentions, from his "real teachings" (ἀληθινὰ δόγματα), by which he clearly means Stilpo's ethical instructions, for which he was greatly respected (*Adv. Col.* 1119c-d). In his ethical positions, he seems to have been close to the Cynics (in fact, in some accounts, he is claimed to have been a student of Diogenes the Cynic and a teacher of Crates, though his relationship with Metrocles the Cynic is depicted as strained). A Cynic moralist Teles quotes approvingly Stilpo's views on exile and the proper attitude towards death of close ones, and in one passage appears to quote Stilpo directly (Stobaeus 3.40.8 [F 3 Fuentes González]):

πρὸς δὲ τὸν κατ' ἄλλο τι ἡγούμενον τὴν φυγὴν βλαβερὸν εἶναι, μὴ οὐδὲν λέγηται πρὸς τὸ τοῦ Στίλπωνος, ὃ καὶ πρώην εἶπον· τί λέγεις, φησί, καὶ τίνων ἡ φυγή, ποίων ἀγαθῶν στερίσκει; τῶν περὶ ψυχὴν ἢ τῶν περὶ τὸ σῶμα ἢ τῶν ἐκτός; εὐλογιστίας, ὀρθοπραγίας, εὐπραγίας ἡ φυγὴ στερίσκει; οὐ δή. ἀλλὰ μὴ ἀνδρείας ἢ δικαιοσύνης ἢ ἄλλης τινὸς ἀρετῆς; οὐδὲ τοῦτο. ἀλλὰ μὴ τῶν περὶ τὸ σῶμά τινος ἀγαθῶν; ἢ οὐχ ὁμοίως ἔστιν ἐπὶ ξένης ὄντα ὑγιαίνειν καὶ ἰσχύειν καὶ ὀξὺ ὁρᾶν καὶ ὀξὺ ἀκούειν, ἐνίοτε δὲ μᾶλλον <ἢ> ἐν τῇ ἰδίᾳ μένοντα; καὶ μάλα. ἀλλὰ μὴ τῶν ἐκτὸς στερίσκει ἡ φυγή; ἢ οὐ πολλοῖς ὤφθη τὰ πράγματα κατὰ τὴν τῶν τοιούτων ὕπαρξιν ἐπιφανέστερα γεγονότα φυγάδων γενομένων; ἢ οὐ Φοῖνιξ ἐκ Δολοπίας ἐκπεσὼν ὑπὸ Ἀμύντορος εἰς Θετταλίαν φεύγει;... Θεμιστοκλῆς ἐκεῖνος "ὦ παῖ" φησίν "ἀπωλόμεθ' ἂν εἰ μὴ ἀπωλόμεθα". νῦν δὲ πολλὴ τῶν τοιούτων ἀφθονία. ποίων οὖν ἀγαθῶν ἡ φυγὴ στερίσκει, ἢ τίνος κακοῦ παραιτία ἐστίν; ἐγὼ μὲν γὰρ οὐχ ὁρῶ. ἀλλ' ἡμεῖς πολλαχοῦ αὐτοὺς κατορύττομεν καὶ φυγάδες γενόμενοι καὶ ἐν τῇ ἰδίᾳ μένοντες.

And in answer to someone who thinks that exile is harmful, there is nothing else to say except the argument of Stilpo, which I have quoted before. – What do you say? – he asks – Of which goods and of what sort of them does exile deprive a person? The ones that have to do with the soul, the ones that have to do with the body, or the external ones? Does exile deprive one of prudence, right conduct, proper action? – Certainly not. – But also not of courage, justice, or any other virtue? – Also not. – But also not of any of the bodily goods? Is it not that while abroad, one is also healthy, strong, sees well and hears well, and sometimes even better than when staying in his own country? – Yes, indeed. – But isn't it that exile does not deprive one of external goods? Is it not the case that for many people, their affairs, as far as their possessions are concerned, gained prominence after they became exiles? Didn't Phoenix, exiled from Dolopia by Amyntor, flee to Thessaly? ... And the famous Themistocles said: "O child, we would have been destroyed, if we had not been destroyed already." Nowadays there is a great abundance of these.[12] Of what kind of goods, then, does exile deprive one, or what harm does it cause? For I do not see any. In fact, we frequently ruin ourselves, whether we are in exile or stay in our own country.[13]

Caution is needed when interpreting this passage: Stobaeus appears to have taken fragments of Teles from an epitome by some Theodorus, and the extent of the epitomator's interventions is difficult to assess. Even if Theodorus preserves the text faithfully, it remains unclear whether the text quotes or merely paraphrases Stilpo, and where the quotation or paraphrase ends.[14] With these caveats in mind, we can make a few observations. The fragment preserves a dialogue between a dominant speaker and an interlocutor with whose opinion (that exile is harmful) he disagrees. It is possible to consider the passage as a pseudo-dialogue of sorts, in which both positions are channeled by one speaker imagining on the spot someone's answers; however, as Stilpo was known as a writer of dialogues, it is probable that there was a figure of a second speaker of some distinctness. The dominant speaker appears to be reacting to his interlocutor's statement that exile deprives a man of goods. He then refutes this position by asking a series of questions which lead his partner towards proper understanding. He controls the flow of the exchange by asking leading questions and delimiting potential answers. In particular, there is an abundance of polar (yes/no) questions with negative particles (recurrent ἀλλὰ μή and ἦ οὔ), which impart on the recipient the assumptions of the questioner and compel agreement with him.[15] The dominant speaker asks two open-ended questions ("of which goods and of what sort of them does exile

---

[12] Perhaps external goods are meant here.   [13] The Greek text follows Fuentes González 1998.
[14] See Giannantoni 1990c, 102–3; Fuentes González 1998, 28–9. The passage appears as a fragment of Stilpo in Döring 1972 (F 192) and *SSR* (II O 31). On Teles, see the section on the Cynics in Chapter 6.4.
[15] On negative polar questions, see Estes 2013, 153–4.

deprive a person?" and "of what kind of goods, then, does exile deprive one, or what harm does it cause?"); however, he does not wait for the interlocutor's response, but either follows with additional leading questions or states his own position. A similar asymmetrical conversational pattern in which the dominant speaker closely controls the conversation and guides his interlocutor has parallels in Socratic literature, in particular, in Xenophon's *Apomnemoneumata*, where it is a recurrent format in Socrates' exchanges with his companions.

Diodorus Cronus, the philosopher who was to be questioned by Stilpo at Ptolemy's court, was an important philosopher and dialectician. He appears to have left no writings; however, Clement of Alexandria says that one of his students, Philo the Dialectician, wrote a work titled *Menexenus*. The title, reminiscent of one of Plato's works, suggests a dialogue-format, though it remains unclear whether the similarity was an intentional allusion on Philo's part and who the eponymous Menexenus was. Clement writes (*Strom.* 4.19.121.5-6 [F 101 Döring]):

αἱ γὰρ Διοδώρου τοῦ Κρόνου ἐπικληθέντος θυγατέρες πᾶσαι διαλεκτικαὶ γεγόνασιν, ὥς φησι Φίλων ὁ διαλεκτικὸς ἐν τῷ Μενεξένῳ, ὧν τὰ ὀνόματα παρατίθεται τάδε· Μενεξένη, Ἀργεία, Θεογνίς, Ἀρτεμισία, Παντάκλεια.

The daughters of Diodorus, nicknamed Cronus, all became dialecticians, as Philo the Dialectician says in the *Menexenus*. Their names are as follows: Menexene, Argeia, Theognis, Artemisia, Pantacleia.[16]

Unfortunately, we do not know whether Diodorus' five daughters were merely mentioned in the *Menexenus* or played a more substantial role. In Plato's *Menexenus*, the core of the dialogue is constituted by a funeral speech delivered by Socrates, who claims to have heard it from Aspasia, whom he playfully calls his teacher of rhetoric. The motif of educated women in Philo may indicate his interaction with the Platonic precedent.

## 6.3 Cyrenaics

According to ancient sources, the school was founded in Libyan Cyrene by Aristippus. He was a follower of Socrates and must have lived for some time in Athens, but he apparently originated a philosophical tradition in his homeland (after him, the school is said to have been led by his daughter Arete and a student, Antipater). There is controversy over whether the Cyrenaics should be considered a philosophical school with a consistent body of doctrines.[17] It is also unclear

---

[16] I follow Döring 1972 for the Greek text.
[17] See e.g. Giannantoni 1990c, 169–71; Zilioli 2012, 3–16.

whether Aristippus laid the theoretical foundations for Cyrenaic hedonism. His life in Diogenes Laertius consists for the most part of anecdotes and sayings exemplifying his *parrhesia*, his unabashed affinity for a luxurious and extravagant life, and his quick wit; he is also frequently presented interacting with the Sicilian tyrant Dionysius, Diogenes the Cynic, and Plato. These anecdotes might have originated from Aristippus' own texts[18] or from the works of his followers and associates. Aristippus was represented as a speaker in Xenophon's *Apomnemoneumata* and, perhaps, in dialogues by Speusippus and Stilpo (Diogenes Laertius 4.4 and 2.120).

There is lack of clarity about Aristippus' writings. The information in Diogenes Laertius 2.83–5 comes from different, sometimes contradictory sources. He quotes Sosicrates who maintained that Aristippus left no writings, but this claim should probably be rejected.[19] According to another source, Aristippus wrote a history of Libya and twenty-five dialogues, some in Attic, some in Doric, which were placed together in one book (ἕν, sc. βιβλίον). Doric Greek was spoken in Cyrene, and it is probable that at some point Aristippus began writing in his native dialect. Diogenes lists twenty-three (rather than twenty-five) titles of these works. Only a few are name-titles: *Artabazus* (either the Persian general of Xerxes or the satrap of Phrygia of the fourth century BCE),[20] *Hermias* (probably the tyrant of Atarneus in Mysia and Aristotle's friend), and *Philomelus*. None of the titles refers to characters known from the Socratic circle which suggests that Aristippus composed dialogues that did not feature Socrates.[21] The titles *Questioning* and *Another Questioning* (Ἐρώτησις, Ἄλλη ἐρώτησις) suggest an erotapocritic format. The list also includes *Letter to his Daughter Arete* and several titles starting with πρός, "to" (such as *To the Exiles* or *To Lais*), which suggest an epistolary format. If the more than twenty works listed by Diogenes were collected in one volume, they must have been very short compositions. Other sources credited Aristippus with writing, among other works, six books of *Diatribai*, three books of *Chreiai*, a work *To Socrates*, and several texts on moral topics (*On Education, On Virtue, On Fortune*).

We know exceedingly little about later Cyrenaics and their writings, but there is evidence that dialogues were composed by Hegesias of Cyrene, nicknamed Πεισιθάνατος, "Death-Persuader" (Diogenes Laertius 2.86; cf. Plutarch, *De am. prol.* 497d: Ἡγησίας <δὲ> διαλεγόμενος πολλοὺς ἔπεισεν ἀποκαρτερῆσαι τῶν ἀκροωμένων). He combined hedonism with a conviction that happiness is impossible:

---

[18] Mannebach 1961, 79; Giannantoni 1990c, 159.   [19] Mannebach 1961, 77–8.
[20] Giannantoni 1990c, 159–60.
[21] Hirzel 1895a, 109; Mannebach 1961, 77; Giannantoni 1990c, 158.

τὸ μὲν γὰρ σῶμα πολλῶν ἀναπεπλῆσθαι παθημάτων, τὴν δὲ ψυχὴν συμπαθεῖν τῷ σώματι καὶ ταράττεσθαι, τὴν δὲ τύχην πολλὰ τῶν κατ' ἐλπίδα κωλύειν, ὥστε διὰ ταῦτα ἀνύπαρκτον τὴν εὐδαιμονίαν εἶναι.

...for the body is infected with much suffering, while the soul shares in the sufferings of the body and is a prey to disturbance, and fortune often disappoints. From all this it follows that happiness cannot be realized.

(Diogenes Laertius 2.94, trans. R. D. Hicks)

Hegesias also maintained that while life is advantageous to a fool, it is indifferent to a sensible man (Diogenes Laertius 2.95).[22] According to Cicero, Hegesias wrote a book with the curious title Ἀποκαρτερῶν, that is *The Man Starving Himself to Death*. Cicero reports (*Tusc.* 1.34.83-4 [*SSR* IV.F 3-4]):

A malis igitur mors abducit, non a bonis, verum si quaerimus. Et quidem hoc a Cyrenaico Hegesia sic copiose disputatur, ut is a rege Ptolemaeo prohibitus esse dicatur illa in scholis dicere, quod multi is auditis mortem sibi ipsi consciscerent... eius autem, quem dixi, Hegesiae liber est, Ἀποκαρτερῶν, quo a vita quidem per inediam discedens revocatur ab amicis; quibus respondens vitae humanae enumerat incommoda.

Death, then, removes us from bad things, not from good ones, if we aim at truth. In fact, this idea was so amply discussed by Hegesias the Cyrenaic that they say that he was banned by King Ptolemy from lecturing in schools on the topic, for many after listening to his words killed themselves.... There is a book by the above-mentioned Hegesias, titled *The Man Starving Himself to Death*, in which a man departing from life by starvation is being dissuaded by friends; he answers them by listing the misfortunes of human life.

Hegesias' work appears to have been a dialogue with the starving man conversing with friends and justifying his decision to commit suicide. The circumstances of the conversation—a man about to die talking about death with friends—are reminiscent of the Platonic *Phaedo*, as is the topic of suicide; in Plato, Socrates acknowledges misfortunes inherent in human life and advises Evenus (via Cebes) to follow him—that is, to die—as soon as possible if he considers himself wise (*Phd.* 61b). Socrates' statement spurs a discussion on suicide and leads to the conclusion that death is desirable for a philosopher; however, one has to wait for it to come as it is not right (θεμιτόν) to kill oneself (*Phd.* 61c). It has been proposed by Stephen White that Callimachus' famous epigram about Cleombrotus, who committed suicide after reading Plato's *Phaedo*, may allude to Hegesias (he was

---

[22] Ancient reports about Hegesias' teachings are at times contradictory; for a discussion, see Lampe 2015, 120-46.

Callimachus' compatriot and older contemporary). If Ptolemy really banned Hegesias from lecturing, perhaps Callimachus targeted the absurdity of his decision by pointing out that reading Plato also posed a grave danger.[23]

The motif of suicide by starvation is a recurrent one in anecdotes about ancient philosophers.[24] In the imperial period, Arrian's Epictetus relates his visit to a friend who decided, for no apparent reason, to starve himself to death (*Epict. Diss.* 2.15.4: ἐξ οὐδεμιᾶς αἰτίας ἔκρινεν ἀποκαρτερεῖν) and who had already abstained from food for three days. Epictetus reports a short conversation he had with the starving friend: he asked him about the reasons behind his decision and, though not without difficulty, managed to change his mind.

In Chapter 2.2.3, I discussed PKöln 5.205, which preserves a fragment of a Socratic dialogue which may have been composed either by Hegesias or by someone from his circle. It combines hedonism with a pessimistic conviction that there is nothing in life a man of reason would regret losing if he were to die.

## 6.4 Cynics

Diogenes Laertius considers Socrates' student Antisthenes to be the founder of Cynicism and Diogenes of Sinope's mentor (6.19, 6.21). The connection between one of the more influential Socratics and Diogenes remains debatable, with some scholars accepting the ancient tradition and other considering Antisthenes as a forerunner rather than the founding father.[25] Antisthenes' writings are largely lost (apart from two speeches, *Odysseus* and *Ajax*), but he was certainly a prolific and inventive writer, and like other Socratics he used the dialogue format. Diogenes Laertius includes several name-titles in the catalogue of Antisthenes' writings (6.15-18), of which some clearly belong to the Socratic tradition (e.g. *Aspasia* or *Alcibiades*). Works such as *Archelaus or On Kingship* or *Cyrus* probably did not involve Socrates; still other dialogues may have depicted mythological figures such as Heracles as speakers.[26] Some titles—such as *On Questions and Answers* (Περὶ ἐρωτήσεως καὶ ἀποκρίσεως) or *On Discussion, a Work on Disputation* (Περὶ τοῦ

---

[23] White (1994); see also Williams 1995, 165-6.

[24] Philosophers who are said to have starved themselves to death include Menedemus (Diogenes Laertius 2.143), Zeno and Cleanthes (Lucian, *Macr.* 19), and Dionysius "the Renegade" (Diogenes Laertius 7.167). Crates is said to have persuaded Metrocles to abandon a plan to starve himself (Diogenes Laertius 6.94) and Plotinus did the same with Porphyry (Eunapius, *VS* 4.1.8). The verb ἀποκαρτερεῖν appears in Philodemus' *On Death* (col. vi.10). For starvation as a method of suicide, see van Hooff 1990, 41-7.

[25] For a discussion, see Giannantoni 1990c, 223-33; Giannantoni 1993; Goulet-Cazé 1996; Fuentes González 2013. For a thorough examination of evidence concerning Antisthenes, see Prince 2015; Meijer 2017.

[26] Cf. Plutarch, *De vit. pud.* 536b where we read that ὁ Ἀντισθένειος Ἡρακλῆς παρῄνει and Proclus, *In Alc.* I. 98.14-15 Westerink: λέγει ... ὁ Ἀντισθένους Ἡρακλῆς.

διαλέγεσθαι ἀντιλογικός)—suggest that Antisthenes was interested in dialectics and the art of argumentation, both closely related to the dialogue format.

Diogenes of Sinope, the first uncontested Cynic and a vastly influential figure, in all probability left some writings, but they must have been lost relatively early. Diogenes Laertius (6.80) says that according to Sosicrates and Satyrus he did not write anything, but other authors have ascribed to him letters, tragedies, and thirteen dialogues, titled *Cephalion, Ichthyas, Jackdaw, Pordalus, The Athenian Demos, Republic, The Art of Ethic, On Wealth, Eroticus, Theodorus, Hypsias, Aristarchus*, and *On Death*. Sotion, on the other hand, maintained that genuine works of his include the following titles: *On Virtue, On Good, Eroticus, A Beggar, Tolmaeus, Pordalus, Casandrus, Cephalion, Philiscus, Aristarchus, Sisyphus, Ganymedes, Chreiai*, and *Letters*.[27] Some of the works labeled by Diogenes Laertius as dialogues are attested elsewhere. *Cephalion* is mentioned by Athenaeus (*Deipn*. 4.164a; the context suggests that it may have touched on the issue of eating and feasting). *Ichthyas*, according Diogenes Laertius, was written against the Megarian philosopher Ichthyas (2.112). In *Pordalus* (the meaning of the title remains unclear; it may be corrupted), Diogenes confessed to have adulterated coinage (Diogenes Laertius 6.20). Diogenes' authorship of the *Republic* was questioned already in antiquity, but Philodemus in *On the Stoics* argues for its authenticity and notes that Cleanthes, Chrysippus, and Antipater knew and discussed it (*Sto.* col. xv.21–xvii.10).[28] The work was considered scandalous: Diogenes is said to have recommended replacing coins with dice (probably a derisive comment on the monetary system) and the consumption of human flesh (*Sto.* col. xvi.4–9 and xvi.21).

Lack of evidence makes it impossible to say anything precise about the form of Diogenes' writings. There is no reason to reject Diogenes Laertius' claim that some of them were dialogues, particularly since name-titles appearing on the list suggest such a format. If Diogenes admitted in the *Pordalus* that he adulterated the coinage, then his works included autobiographical material and were perhaps a source of dialogized anecdotes about the philosopher which circulated in antiquity and constitute a large part of his biography in Diogenes Laertius.

Dialogue and dialogized anecdotes provided an apt medium for bringing to life the rebellious and parrhesiastic figure of Diogenes. The earliest evidence of the dialogized biographic-anecdotal tradition comes from PVindob. G 29946, which I have discussed in Chapter 2.5.2. The papyrus is dated to around the mid-third century BCE and contains partially preserved reports of short conversations between Diogenes and other people. The fragment may have come from a protreptic and commemorative work, similar in character to Xenophon's

---

[27] For a discussion of individual titles, see von Fritz 1926, 54–60; Giannantoni 1990c, 461–84.
[28] Here and elsewhere numeration of columns after Dorandi 1982. For more on the content of Diogenes' *Republic*, see Dorandi 1993; Goulet-Cazé 2003, 33–8.

*Apomnemoneumata*. Later offshoots of this tradition include the pseudepigraphic letters of Diogenes, probably the product of an early imperial period, among which we find pieces that merge an epistolographic frame with a dialogue (I discuss them briefly in Chapter 1.3). Diogenes is also the protagonist of several dialogues and semi-dialogized works by Dio Chrysostom (*Or.* 4, 8, 9, 10) and a character in several conversations in Lucian's *Dialogues of the Dead*. We may suppose that these imperial works follow an earlier tradition of presenting Diogenes as an interlocutor, a tradition in which anecdotes were stretched into self-standing dialogues or, conversely, fragments of dialogues were turned into pithy anecdotes in the manner described in Chapter 1.2.

Several Cynics were associated with Alexander the Great. According to the *Suda* (s.v. Φιλίσκος (φ 359)), Philiscus of Aegina, a student of either Diogenes the Cynic or Stilpo, was Alexander's teacher, and a writer of some dialogues (the only title provided is *Codrus*). While Philiscus remains an elusive figure, more is known about Onesicritus of Astypalaea, a member of Alexander's expedition to India and a helmsman on Alexander's ship.[29] The sources consistently present him as a student of Diogenes, though this does not necessarily mean that he was a full-fledged philosopher.[30] He is said to have composed a work entitled Πῶς Ἀλέξανδρος ἤχθη—the title perhaps means *How Alexander Was Educated*— which Diogenes Laertius calls an *encomium* of Alexander and compares with Xenophon's *Cyropaedia* (6.84).[31] This must have been a narrative work about Alexander's expedition to India (perhaps with a section dedicated to Alexander's childhood and education), most certainly presenting Alexander favorably and containing geographical and ethnographical inserts. Onesicritus' work was a source for later authors writing about Alexander in India, though it earned him the reputation of being an untruthful witness and one with an affinity for the marvelous (Strabo called him "the chief helmsman of the incredible," τῶν παραδόξων ἀρχικυβερνήτην (15.1.28)).

Onesicritus' Cynic identity is not prominent in the preserved fragments of his work apart from an account about his conversation with Indian naked sages, whom Greek authors called Gymnosophists.[32] Strabo (15.1.63–5) provides the most extensive version, which probably retains some of Onesicritus' wording.[33] In it Onesicritus reported that he was sent to the Indian sages in order to talk to them (διαλεξόμενος) because Alexander heard about their nakedness, endurance, and

---

[29] On Onesicritus, see Brown 1949; Pearson 1960, 83–111; Whitby 2011.
[30] e.g. Strabo 15.1.65; Plutarch, *Alex. fort.* 331e, *Alex.* 65.2; Diogenes Laertius 6.84, 6.75–6 (if Onesicritus of Aegina, mentioned there, is identical with Onesicritus of Astypalaea).
[31] Diogenes seems to conflate Xenophon's *Cyropaedia* and *Anabasis*, the former focusing on the education of Cyrus the Elder, the latter reporting Xenophon's participation in an expedition by Cyrus the Younger. On difficulties with the title, see Pearson 1960, 87–90; on the possibility that Onesicritus consciously modeled his work on Xenophon, Pearson 1960, 90–2.
[32] On Onesicritus as a Cynic, see Brown 1949, 24–53; Pearson 1960, 88–9; Powers 1998, 74–7.
[33] For a shorter report of Onesicritus' account, see Plutarch, *Alex.* 65.1–4.

renown. Onesicritus found the Gymnosophists some distance from the city, motionless in the scorching sun, and asked them to share their wisdom so that he could report it to the king. The first man he talked to, named Calanus, laughed at him and repudiated contemporary people as unbridled and dissolute, warning that Zeus would punish humankind and destroy everything; then he demanded that Onesicritus strip and lie down on the hot rocks if he wanted to listen to the Indian wisdom. Mandanis (named Dandamis in other versions), the eldest and wisest, intervened and praised Alexander who, though a great ruler, desired wisdom. He then explained to Onesicritus the teachings of the Gymnosophists, which were strikingly similar to Cynic philosophy in their endorsement of hardship and self-restraint as well as in their valorization of nature. Asked whether there were similar teachings among the Greeks, Onesicritus pointed to Pythagoras, Socrates, and Diogenes the Cynic "to whom he had listened himself."

Strabo's account preserves only Calanus' words in direct speech, but it is probable that Onesicritus' exchange with Mandanis was also reported directly. The conversations of philosophers with non-Greek sages were a recurrent feature in ancient dialogues, and Onesicritus might have had this tradition in mind when composing his account.[34] The story gained popularity and, as Bosman observes, "proved to be fertile ground for moral elaboration."[35] In PGenev. inv. 271 + PDuk. inv. 777 + PKöln inv. 907 (second century CE) we find fragments of a dialogue between Dandamis and Alexander in which the Indian sage admonishes the king. Even though Alexander does not follow Dandamis' advice, he is presented rather positively: he praises the Gymnosophist and wishes to honor him with gifts (which are not accepted). The unknown author seems to have drawn inspiration from several sources, including, probably, Onesicritus, as the Cynic undertone to Dandamis' teachings suggests.

It is possible that with Onesicritus also originated the ancient tradition about the meeting between Alexander and Diogenes the Cynic known from both ancient *chreiai* and dialogues (e.g. Dio Chrysostom, *Or.* 4 and *Ep.* 33 from the pseudepigraphic letters of Diogenes).[36] While Dio Chrysostom favors Diogenes in his reworking of the encounter in the *Fourth Kingship Oration*, at the beginning of his work he alludes to earlier versions which contained flattery of the king. He says that many past authors produced accounts of the meeting which praised

---

[34] The extent of the fictionalization of Onesicritus' account is uncertain. Mandanis' remark that his conversation with the Gymnosophists was mediated through three interpreters has been interpreted as a hint that the episode was fabricated (see Stoneman 1995, 103–4, with an overview of previous scholarship). For more on the encounters of Greek philosophers with "barbarian" wisdom, see Chapter 3.2, p. 103.

[35] Bosman 2010, 178; he argues that PBerol. inv. 13044 (discussed in Chapter 2.6.1), reporting a "riddle contest" in which Alexander questioned Indian philosophers and threatened them with death belongs to a different tradition that probably did not originate with Onesicritus.

[36] Pearson 1960, 92 (who thinks that in Onesicritus' work, the meeting of Alexander and Diogenes paralleled Xenophon's encounter with Socrates before joining the expedition of Cyrus the Younger); Bosman 2007.

Alexander, who, though the greatest ruler, did not look down on a poor man who was excelling in reason and endurance (*Or.* 4.1). The passage is reminiscent of the words of Onesicritus' Mandanis who called Alexander "a philosopher in arms" (ἐν ὅπλοις φιλοσοφοῦντα) and praised him for his interest in philosophy even though he was a king (Strabo 15.1.64). It is probable that in earlier sections of his work Onesicritus described Alexander's conversation with Diogenes before the expedition to India, in which the king was likewise praised for his appreciation of philosophy.

Apart from the dialogue's employment in the Cynic anecdotal-biographic tradition, interaction with the dialogue is also traceable in Teles, a Hellenistic Cynic who incorporated dialogized material into his moralizing popular discourse. He might have been inspired by Bion of Borysthenes. They are both associated with the so-called "Cynic diatribe." I will, however refrain from using this category, as it is notoriously problematic: as several scholars have demonstrated, the Greek term διατριβή did not refer in antiquity to a specific form of writing.[37]

According to Diogenes Laertius (4.51), Bion of Borysthenes (c.335–245 BCE) started off in the Academy. He then adopted a Cynic life under the influence of Crates, later joined Theodorus the Atheist, and subsequently Theophrastus.[38] His philosophical biography suggests a variety of philosophic influences, and one may suspect that he followed Cynics in his interest in practical ethics combined with a rejection of theoretical philosophy and traditional education, and in allotting prime importance to the concepts of freedom and self-sufficiency—as well as in his theatricality, biting sense of humor, and taste for parody. His negative attitude to religious practices and beliefs might have been a Cyrenaic legacy.[39]

We know that he wrote much, in a style considered theatrical and showy, and interspersed his works with witticisms, vulgar words, and memorable sayings.[40] A passage in Diogenes Laertius preserves his conversation with Antigonus Gonatas (Diogenes Laertius 4.46 [F 1A Kindstrand]):

ἐρομένου γὰρ αὐτὸν τίς πόθεν εἰς ἀνδρῶν; πόθι τοι πόλις ἠδὲ τοκῆες; αἰσθόμενος ὅτι προδιαβέβληται, φησὶ πρὸς αὐτόν· "ἐμοὶ ὁ πατὴρ μὲν ἦν ἀπελεύθερος, τῷ ἀγκῶνι

---

[37] Halbauer 1911, 8 proposes that the term διατριβή indicated a didactic set-up rather than a specific format. On the elusiveness of the term, see Kindstrand 1976, 23–5; Huffman 2005, 228–32; on "diatribe" as a scholarly creation rather than an ancient concept, see Fuentes González 1998, 44–50. Cf. also a spirited discussion between Jocelyn and Gottschalk in *Liverpool Classical Monthly*: Gottschalk 1982; Jocelyn 1982; Gottschalk 1983; Jocelyn 1983.

[38] Bion's life in Diogenes Laertius is found in the book on the Academics; on his connection with the Academy, see Kindstrand 1976, 56–8.

[39] For Bion's links with the Cynics and Cyrenaics (and some overlap between the two schools), see Kindstrand 1976, 62–70.

[40] Cf. Diogenes Laertius 4.47: he wrote many ὑπομνήματα and ἀποφθέγματα χρειώδη πραγματείαν περιέχοντα (perhaps "sayings of useful application" as Hicks in the Loeb translates; on possible meaning, see Kindstrand 1976, 150). On his style, see Diogenes Laertius 4.52.

ἀπομυσσόμενος—διεδήλου δὲ τὸν ταριχέμπορον—γένος Βορυσθενίτης, ἔχων οὐ
πρόσωπον, ἀλλὰ συγγραφὴν ἐπὶ τοῦ προσώπου, τῆς τοῦ δεσπότου πικρίας
σύμβολον· μήτηρ δὲ οἵαν ὁ τοιοῦτος ἂν γήμαι, ἀπ' οἰκήματος. ἔπειτα ὁ πατὴρ
παρατελωνησάμενός τι πανοίκιος ἐπράθη μεθ' ἡμῶν. καί με ἀγοράζει τις ῥήτωρ
νεώτερον ὄντα καὶ εὔχαριν· ὃς καὶ ἀποθνῄσκων κατέλιπέ μοι πάντα. κἀγὼ
κατακαύσας αὐτοῦ τὰ συγγράμματα καὶ πάντα συγξύσας Ἀθήναζε ἦλθον καὶ
ἐφιλοσόφησα. ταύτης τοι γενεῆς τε καὶ αἵματος εὔχομαι εἶναι. ταῦτά ἐστι τὰ κατ'
ἐμέ. ὥστε παυσάσθωσαν Περσαῖός τε καὶ Φιλωνίδης ἱστοροῦντες αὐτά· σκόπει δέ
με ἐξ ἐμαυτοῦ."

For, when Antigonus inquired: "Who among men, and whence, are you? What is your city and your parents?", he, knowing that he had already been maligned to the king, replied, "My father was a freedman, who wiped his nose on his sleeve"— meaning that he was a dealer in salt fish—"a native of Borysthenes, with no face to show, but only the writing on his face, a token of his master's severity. My mother was such as a man like my father would marry, from a brothel. Afterwards my father, who had cheated the revenue in some way, was sold with all his family. And I, then a not ungraceful youngster, was bought by a certain rhetorician, who on his death left me all he had. And I burnt his books, scraped everything together, came to Athens and turned philosopher. This is the stock and this the blood from which I boast to have sprung. Such is my story. It is high time, then, that Persaeus and Philonides left off recounting it. Judge me by myself."[41]   (trans. R. D. Hicks)

We do not know whether the passage and Bion's bitter self-presentation ("inverted boasting," as Jan Kindstrand calls it)[42] originated with Bion himself or with another author. It certainly appears to be an extract from a longer text— one should assume that Persaeus' and Philonides' animosity towards Bion and their slandering of the philosopher before Antigonus was mentioned in an earlier section. That this is not a simple *chreia* is also indicated by the length, complexity, and detailed nature of Bion's response, as well as, on a linguistic level, by the use of *hapax legomena* and unusual words.[43] Stobaeus (4.29a.13 [F 2 Kindstrand]) preserves a passage in which Bion provides a different answer to the same question by Antigonus: he remarks that one should choose one's friends like archers, not by asking about their ancestors, but by putting up a target and choosing the best ones. It is possible that both fragments originate from the same work.

Antigonus' question consists of a Homeric quotation, and Bion aptly concludes his response also with a Homeric line ("This is the stock and this the blood from

---

[41] Hense 1909², lxxxvii thought that the passage derives from Bion's letter; this is rightly rejected by Hirzel 1895a, 368 n. 1 and Kindstrand 1976, 177.
[42] Kindstrand 1976, 183.   [43] Hirzel 1895a, 368 n. 1; commentary in Kindstrand 1976, 176–83.

which I boast to have sprung").[44] Bion's liking for Homeric quotations and parodies is apparent in Diogenes Laertius 4.52 [F 7 Kindstrand], where he wittily twists Homeric lines when addressing Archytas. Bion shares this liking for transposition and transformation of epic verses with Greek comedy and the serio-comic Cynic tradition associated predominantly with Menippus, his younger contemporary, whom I discuss later in this section.[45] This is not the only connection between Bion's response to Antigonus and Menippean satire: other shared elements include the serio-comic tone, self-deprecatory humor, and unashamed frankness, interweaving dialogic exchanges with poetic quotations and merging high and low linguistic registers.

Some fragments of Bion originate from Stobaeus' excerpts from Teles, a Cynic moralist living probably in the mid-third century BCE (I have discussed one of his fragments above, in the section on Megarians). Dialogization is a recurrent feature in these extracts. There are eight passages preserved by Stobaeus, who introduces them with the following headings:

F 1 (Stobaeus 2.15.47): Ἐκ τοῦ Θεοδώρου τῶν Τέλητος ἐπιτομῆς, Περὶ τοῦ δοκεῖν καὶ τοῦ εἶναι (From Theodorus' *epitome* of the writings of Teles, on seeming and being).

F 2 (Stobaeus 3.1.98): Ἐκ τοῦ Τέλητος περὶ αὐταρκείας (From Teles, on self-sufficiency).

F 3 (Stobaeus 3.40.8): Τέλητος περὶ φυγῆς (Teles' on exile).

F 4a–4b (Stobaeus 4.32a.21, 4.33.31): Ἐκ τῶν Τέλητος ἐπιτομή (From an epitome of the writings of Teles).

F 5 (Stobaeus 4.34.72): Ἐκ τῶν Τέλητος Περὶ τοῦ μὴ εἶναι τέλος ἡδονήν (From the writings of Teles, that pleasure is not the end).

F 6 (Stobaeus 4.44.82): Ἐκ τῶν Τέλητος Περὶ περιστάσεων (From the writings of Teles, on circumstances).

F 7 (Stobaeus 4.44.83): Ἐκ τῶν Τέλητος Περὶ ἀπαθείας (From the writings of Teles, on freedom from emotions).[46]

---

[44] The line quoted by Antigonus appears six times in the *Odyssey* (1.170, 10.325, 14.187, 15.264, 19.105, 24.298); the verse used by Bion—twice in the *Iliad* (6.211, 20.241).

[45] For more on the association of Bion with comedy, see Diogenes Laertius 4.10 where Xenocrates identifies himself with tragedy, and Bion—with comedy. Interestingly, the Homeric verse quoted by Antigonus became a staple in later satirical literature: it appears in Seneca's *Apocolocyntosis* 5.4 (Hercules to Claudius) and Lucian's *Icaromenippus* 23 (Zeus to Menippus).

[46] All quotations from Teles come from Fuentes González 1998. It is uncertain whether all fragments come from the same epitome by the otherwise unknown Theodorus mentioned in the first heading, and if so, as scholars tend to assume, whether they originate from one work by Teles or from separate texts. It is also unclear whether Stobaeus' headings are based on Teles' (or the epitomator's) titles or indicate the contents of the passage selected for inclusion by the anthologist.

Bion's name appears seven times in these excerpts, almost as frequently as the names of Diogenes of Sinope and Crates, an unmistakable sign of his significance for Teles.[47] In F 2, Teles refers to Bion's discourse, in which the philosopher imagined a personification of Poverty defending herself against accusations hurled at her by humankind.[48] She addresses directly a man complaining about her, and by asking a series of rhetorical questions, points out that a good and pleasant life is possible even for a pauper. The personification of Poverty is reminiscent of Penia in Aristophanes' *Ploutos*,[49] but personifications of abstract concepts conversing with human beings are also a recurrent feature in philosophical prose from the time of Plato and Xenophon. In some texts we find a pair of opposites arguing against each other (as in Xenophon's *Apomnemoneumata* 2.1.21–34, where Virtue and Vice approach Heracles, or in Cleanthes' dialogue between Anger and Reason), or even multiple personifications in conversation, as in Crantor's contest of goods, in which Wealth, Pleasure, Health, and Courage take part.[50] Less known—and therefore worth being quoted—is an excerpt in Stobaeus deriving from a certain Demetrius, whom scholars tentatively identify with Demetrius the Cynic, a first-century CE philosopher of some prominence, who lived in Rome and was friends with Seneca the Younger and Thrasea Paetus (3.8.20):[51]

*Αὐτίκα γὰρ εἰ τῷ πολεμοῦντι καὶ παρατεταγμένῳ παρασταῖεν ἥ τε Ἀνδρεία καὶ ἡ Δειλία, πόσον ἂν οἴεσθε διαφόρους εἰπεῖν λόγους; ἆρ' οὐχ ἡ μὲν Ἀνδρεία μένειν <ἂν> κελεύοι καὶ τὴν τάξιν διαφυλάττειν; "Ἀλλὰ βάλλουσιν"· "Ὑπόμενε." "Ἀλλὰ τρωθήσομαι"· "Καρτέρει." "Ἀλλ' ἀποθανοῦμαι"· "Ἀπόθανε μᾶλλον ἢ λίπῃς τὴν τάξιν." Ἀτενὴς οὗτος ὁ λόγος καὶ σκληρός. ἀλλ' ὁ τῆς Δειλίας νὴ Δία φιλάνθρωπος καὶ μαλακός· ὑπάγειν γὰρ δῆτα κελεύει τὸν φοβούμενον. "Ἀλλ' ἡ ἀσπὶς ἐνοχλεῖ"· "Ῥῖψον." "Ἀλλὰ καὶ ὁ θώραξ"· "Παράλυσον." Παντὶ δήπου πραΰτερα ταῦτ' ἐκείνων. ὁμοίως δὲ καὶ ἐπὶ τῶν ἄλλων. "μὴ λάβῃς" φησὶν ἡ Ἐγκράτεια "ὅθεν οὐ δεῖ· μὴ φάγῃς, μὴ πίῃς, ἀνέχου, καρτέρει· τὸ τελευταῖον, ἀπόθανε πρότερον ἢ πράξῃς ὅπερ οὐ δεῖ." ἡ δ' Ἀκρασία "πῖθι, ὅτε βούλει, φάγε, ὅ τι ἂν ἥδιστα φάγοις. ἡ τοῦ γείτονος ἀρέσκει σοι γυνή· πέραινε. χρημάτων ἀπορεῖς·*

---

[47] Four times in F 2, one time in F 3, and two times in F 4a. This does not mean, though, that Teles was a simple reproducer of Bion, as Hense 1909[2] thought. Hirzel 1895a, 367–9 considered Teles to be a more independent writer; similarly Kindstrand 1976, 82–5; Fuentes González 1998, 23–32.

[48] It is unclear how much of the text originates from Bion and how much is Teles' own elaboration. Fuentes González 1998, 181–2 argues against considering the whole section in which Poverty speaks as a quotation from Bion. Kindstrand 1976, 213 thinks that originally in Bion's text there might have been two personifications of abstract concepts (presumably Poverty and Wealth), each pleading its case.

[49] On the parallels with Aristophanes and other authors, see Fuentes González 1998, 185–6.

[50] For other examples, see Kindstrand 1976, 212–13.

[51] On the fragment's authorship, see Billerbeck 1979, 57–60; Kindstrand 1980, 93. Seneca is the main source of information about Demetrius, but he is mentioned also by Suetonius, and probably by Lucian, Philostratus, Dio Cassius, and Eunapius. According to Tacitus, Demetrius accompanied Thrasea Paetus on the day of the latter's death and discussed with him the nature of the soul and the separation of the spirit and the body (*Ann.* 16.34).

δάνεισαι. δανεισάμενος ἀδυναμεῖς· μὴ ἀποδῷς. οὐ πιστεύουσιν ἔτι δανείζειν· ἅρπασον." πολύ γε κἀνταῦθα τὸ μεταξύ. ἀλλὰ τίς οὐκ οἶδεν ὅτι ἡ μὲν τοιαύτη χάρις ὀλέθριος γίνεται τοῖς προσδεξαμένοις, ἡ δ' ἐκ τῶν ἐναντίων σωτήριος;

For if Bravery and Cowardice were to stand next to a soldier put in the battle order, how different do you think would be the words they would say? Wouldn't Bravery command him to hold the post? "But they are shooting." "Stay." "But I'll get wounded." "Endure." "But I'll die." "Better to die than leave the post." These words are stern and harsh. Those of Cowardice, by Zeus, are kind and lenient, for she orders the fearful to withdraw. "But the shield overburdens me." "Throw it away." "And the corslet." "Take it off." These words are much milder than the others. It is the same with other things. "Do not take from where it is not allowed", says Restraint, "do not eat, do not drink, hold on, endure. In the end, sooner die than do something you should not do." And Incontinence: "Drink whenever you want, eat whatever brings you the most pleasure. You find the neighbor's wife pretty—proceed! You need money—borrow! You have borrowed but cannot pay back—do not return the money! They don't trust you and will not lend you anymore—steal!" Certainly, there is also much in between. But who does not know that such goodwill is destructive to those who accept it, while its opposite—salvatory?

Returning to Teles' writings, we may note that in other fragments the moral argument is frequently written for two voices: the dominant voice of the philosopher leading the discourse and the voice of an unspecified interlocutor. The sense that we are overhearing a conversation is enhanced by the main speaker's frequent use of second-person pronouns and verb forms. I have discussed above, in the section on the Megarians, Teles' quotation or paraphrase of Stilpo, which takes the form of a short dialogue and is devoted to the issue of exile: the dominant speaker argues against the opinion ascribed to his interlocutor that exile deprives people of good things, and his partner follows his lead. In the second part of F 3, which seems to originate from Teles himself rather than from Stilpo, the secondary interlocutor voices a number of objections (usually starting with ἀλλά, "but") which point to difficulties with which exiles meet: "But the exiles cannot rule in their countries" (Ἀλλ' ἔν γε τῇ ἰδίᾳ οὐκ ἄρχουσιν οἱ φυγάδες), "But you will not be able to enter your country" (Ἀλλ' οὐδὲ ἐξουσίαν ἕξεις εἰσελθεῖν εἰς τὴν ἰδίαν), "How about that: is it not an insult to be exiled by base people?" (Τί οὖν; ὑπὸ χειρόνων φυγαδεύεσθαι οὐ παροινία;), "Is it not a disgrace to be discredited by such people voting by a show of hands or pebbles?" (Παρευδοκιμεῖσθαι οὖν ὑπὸ τῶν τοιούτων καὶ χειροτονίᾳ καὶ ψήφῳ οὐκ ὄνειδος;), "But how is it not a misfortune to find the homeland, for which one toiled so much, so base and ungrateful?" (Ἀλλὰ τοῦτό γε, εὑρεθῆναι τὴν πατρίδα μοχθηρὰν καὶ ἀχάριστον οὖσαν, εἰς ἣν πολλά τις ἐπόνησε, πῶς οὐκ ἀκλήρημα;), "But still, it seems to me a great thing to live there where one was born and raised" (Ἀλλ' ὅμως μέγα μοι δοκεῖ τὸ ἐν ᾗ ἐγένετό τις καὶ ἐτράφη, ἐν ταύτῃ καταγενέσθαι), "But people reproach you for being a metic" (Ἀλλὰ καὶ ὅτι μέτοικος ὀνειδίζουσι δὲ πολλοί), "But how is it not a disgrace not to be allowed to be buried in one's country" (Ἀλλὰ τό γε ἐν τῇ ἰδίᾳ μὴ ἐξεῖναι ταφῆναι πῶς οὐκ ὄνειδος;). Each question is answered by the leading speaker, who explains that none of these have to be painful to an exiled person.

Also F 1 is dialogized. This is how it starts in Stobaeus:

"Κρεῖττόν φασι τὸ δοκεῖν δίκαιον εἶναι τοῦ εἶναι· μὴ καὶ τὸ δοκεῖν ἀγαθὸν εἶναι τοῦ εἶναι κρεῖττόν ἐστιν;" "Ἀμέλει." "Πότερον οὖν διὰ τὸ δοκεῖν ἀγαθοὶ ὑποκριταὶ εἶναι <εὖ> ὑποκρίνονται ἢ διὰ τὸ εἶναι; κιθαρίζουσι δὲ <εὖ> πότερον διὰ τὸ δοκεῖν ἀγαθοὶ κιθαρισταὶ ἢ διὰ τὸ εἶναι;" "Διὰ τὸ εἶναι." "Τὰ δ' ἄλλα πάντα ἁπλῶς διὰ τὸ δοκεῖν ἀγαθοὶ εὖ πράττουσιν ἢ διὰ τὸ εἶναι;" "Διὰ τὸ εἶναι."

"People say that it is better to appear to be just than to be such. Is it not better also to appear to be good than to be?" "Indeed." "Well, do actors act well because they are believed to be good or because they are good? And do people play kithara well because they appear to be good kithara players, or because they are such?" "Because they are." "How about all other things, in general: do people do things well because they appear to be good at them, or because they are good?" "Because they are."

The dominant speaker starts by quoting what he claims to be a popular opinion (it is better to appear just than to be just) and maneuvers his interlocutor into agreeing with a more generalized version of this statement (it is better to appear good than to be good). In the next step, he proceeds to refute the thesis he made his interlocutor agree with by asking a series of questions to demonstrate that it is usually better to have certain qualities than to seem to have them. His partner tends to agree with him, though he objects at one moment, saying: "But I would prefer to appear to be brave rather than to be" (Ἀλλὰ καὶ ἀνδρεῖος ἂν μᾶλλον βουλοίμην δοκεῖν ἢ εἶναι); asked why, he answers that he would be honored by people (Τιμήσουσί με). In response, the main speaker points out that it is not advantageous for a coward to appear courageous as he may be chosen then to fight in a single combat or treated as a highly dangerous enemy when taken prisoner.

In both F 1 and F 3 the secondary speaker is presented as being rather inexperienced in philosophical discussion and as upholding a position congruent with popular opinion. He is then guided by the dominant interlocutor towards a better understanding. He is a cooperative partner: he tends to agree with the other speaker, and answers his leading questions, though he sometimes also raises objections, either by voicing his own feelings or by referring to a popular sentiment.[52]

---

[52] For an analysis of the dialogic dynamics in Teles' fragments, see Tsekourakis 1980, 65–7.

The dynamics is one of a simplified dialogue in which the individuality and personality of the secondary speaker is obliterated: he becomes a voice easy to identify with, articulating doubts and reservations of a potential listener.

F 4a and F 4b offer a further simplification of this pattern. Both open straightforwardly with a thesis:

F 4a: Δοκεῖ μοι ἡ τῶν χρημάτων κτῆσις σπάνεως καὶ ἐνδείας ἀπολύειν.
It seems to me that possession of wealth frees one from poverty and deprivation.
F 4b: Ἡ πενία κωλύει πρὸς τὸ φιλοσοφεῖν, ὁ δὲ πλοῦτος εἰς ταῦτα χρήσιμον.
Poverty stands in the way of philosophizing, while wealth is useful in this respect.

The thesis is then refuted in a continuous discourse, with a single objection being raised in each case (in F 4a: καὶ πῶς σπανίζουσιν οὗτοι τούτων ἃ ἔχουσι; "How can people lack what they possess?," and in F 4b: φασὶ δὲ καὶ ἐν ταῖς πόλεσιν ἐντιμοτέρους εἶναι μᾶλλον τοὺς πλουσίους τῶν πενήτων, "but some say that rich people are more respected than poor ones in the cities"). It is possible that the simplification is due to the epitomator's interventions. On the other hand, one can notice that fragments 4a and 4b are reminiscent of the form of discourse which, according to Cicero, was developed in the New Academy (*Fin.* 2.1.2-3). According to Cicero, Arcesilaus "established that those who wanted to hear him, should not ask him questions, but should state their own views; when they had done so, he argued against them." Arcesilaus argued against the personal opinions of his interlocutors, who were actively defending them. Later Academic philosophers however, Cicero says, simplified the Arcesilean discourse, which took the form of a thesis proposed by someone followed by a continuous refutation (I discuss Cicero's testimony in Chapter 3.7). In fragments of Teles we find a similar pattern, which suggests that the formats associated by Cicero with the New Academy were not limited to this philosophical school, but were used by other philosophers around the mid-third century BCE.

A different type of engagement with the dialogue is exemplified by Menippus of Gadara, a third-century BCE Cynic philosopher and satirist, called by Strabo Μένιππος ὁ σπουδογέλοιος, 'the serio-comic Menippus' (16.2.29). According to Diogenes Laertius (6.99), he was a slave in Pontus; after gaining freedom, he settled in Thebes. His writings influenced Varro's *Menippean Satires*, Seneca's *Apocolocyntosis*, and Lucian, who made the philosopher a protagonist in several dialogues (*Necyomantia, Icaromenippus,* and *Dialogues of the Dead*).[53] There is exceedingly little evidence about Menippus' writings, and it is unavoidably

---

[53] For more on Menippus and his ancient reception, see Dudley 1937, 69-74; Relihan 1993, 39-48; Relihan 1996; Desmond 2008, 36-9; Baldwin 2014, 159-79; for an in-depth examination of the ancient 'genre' of the Menippean satire and its specimens, Relihan 1993. The few fragments have been collected by Riese 1865, 245-6.

speculative to reconstruct their character from the testimonies of later authors (whose works are sometimes, as in Varro's case, preserved only in fragments). Diogenes Laertius mentions his *Sale of Diogenes* and quotes some of the Sinopean's utterances from this text (6.29-30). He also provides an incomplete list of Menippus' works (6.101), among which he includes Νέκυια, *Necromancy*. In *Suda* (s.v. Φαιός (φ 180)), we read that Menippus walked around disguised as a Fury, "saying that he had come from Hades as an observer of sins and that, after returning down again, he would report them to gods."[54] It is probable, then, that Menippus in the *Necromancy* presented himself as a character who went to the underworld, and that the text served as a model for Lucian's *Necyomantia* and *Dialogues of the Dead* (in both works, the character of Menippus plays a central role).[55]

Lucian characterized Menippus as "one of the old dogs with a loud bark and saw-like teeth," whose bite comes unexpected because he laughs when he bites (*Bis acc.* 33). We may presume that biting mockery pervaded works such as *The Birth of Epicurus* and *On their Observation of the Twentieth Day*, which must have derided Epicureans' customary celebrations of their founder's birthday and of the twentieth day of each month, prescribed in Epicurus' will. The format of these works is unknown. Athenaeus mentions two other works by Menippus, the *Symposion* (*Deipn.* 14.629e) and *Arcesilaus* (*Deipn.* 14.664e). The *Symposion* was probably a parody of a philosophical dialogue. Menippus is said to have mentioned there a dance called the "cosmic conflagration," κόσμου ἐκπύρωσις, clearly a mocking allusion to the Stoic concept of periodic destruction of the world by conflagration.

The *Arcesilaus* also probably had a sympotic setting, as suggested by a fragment Athenaeus quotes (*Deipn.* 14.664e):

ὁ δὲ κυνικὸς Μένιππος ἐν τῷ ἐπιγραφομένῳ Ἀρκεσιλάῳ γράφει οὕτως· πότος ἦν ἐπικωμασάντων τινῶν καὶ ματτύην ἐκέλευσεν εἰσφέρειν Λάκαινάν τις· καὶ εὐθέως περιεφέρετο περδίκεια ὀλίγα καὶ χήνεια ὀπτὰ καὶ τρύφη πλακούντων.

There was a party that included some people who had barged in already drunk, and someone called for a Spartan *mattue* to be served. Immediately a few small partridges were brought around, along with roasted geese and some fancy cakes.

(trans. S. D. Olson)

The Arcesilaus of the title is probably the scholarch of the Academy, who was Menippus' contemporary. Perhaps this work was also a parody of the philosophical *symposion*: the satirical intention of the passage is suggested by the mention of

---

[54] Diogenes Laertius perhaps erroneously tells the story about Menedemus rather than Menippus (6.102).
[55] On the centrality of the figure of Menippus in the *Dialogues of the Dead*, see Relihan 1987, 191.

drunk symposiasts and the description of the food served, a motif frequent in comedy and parody.[56]

While direct evidence on Menippus' works is scanty, his extensive engagement with the dialogue is indicated by their ancient reception. Seneca's *Apocolocyntosis* and Lucian's dialogues featuring Menippus are certainly influenced by the Cynic's texts.[57] Hirzel considers Menippus to be the originator of a new type of dialogue ("neue Gattung des Dialogs")—one that aimed at amusement rather than instruction and was affiliated with the Old Comedy; and Dudley proposes that the chief contribution of Menippus to literature was "the adaptation of the dialogue for comic and satiric purposes."[58]

There is also evidence that Menippus' dialogues interweaved prose with poetic passages. This is suggested by a Vergilian scholar who remarks that the Cynic "embellished his satires with verses of all sorts" (*omnigeno carmine satiras suas expoliverat*), as well as by the fact that Varro's *Menippean Satires* and Seneca's *Apocolocyntosis* were prosimetric.[59] Lucian also appears to have considered the mixture of prose and poetry a Menippean legacy. The first five utterances of Menippus in Lucian's *Necyomantia* consist wholly of quotations of poetry, which annoys his interlocutor (*Nec.* 1); and in the *Dialogues of the Dead*, Croesus complains that he, Midas, and Sardanapalus cannot bear Menippus because he abuses them and sometimes "disrupts our lamentations by singing" (*DMort.* 3(2).1: ᾄδων ἐπιταράττει ἡμῶν τὰς οἰμωγάς), that is, by chanting poetry lines.

Menippus had a follower in the poet Meleager of Gadara, born c.135 BCE. In his poems, Meleager twice boasts that he wrote *Menippean Graces* (*Anth. Gr.* 7.417 and 418: Μενιππείοις... Χάρισιν),[60] and the title *Graces* is attested by Athenaeus (*Deipn.* 4.157b). Athenaeus mentions also his *Symposion* (*Deipn.* 11.502c). Meleager is also evoked in the parodic *Cynics' Symposium* by Parmeniscus, whose work is dated tentatively to the late first century BCE and has the form of a letter reporting on a banquet; our knowledge of it comes from Athenaeus, who quotes a lengthy fragment (discussed in Chapter 1.3, p. 33-6). Here, one of Parmeniscus' characters, a courtesan called Nicion, refers to "Meleager the Gadarian" as the ancestor (πρόγονος) of Cynic banqueters, and says that in Meleager's *Graces* it was argued that Homer represented the Achaeans as abstaining from eating fish because he was a

---

[56] On Menippus' parodical *symposion*, see Martin 1931, 211-12; Relihan 1993, 41.

[57] The form of fragmentarily preserved *Menippean Satires* by Varro is less clear; for a suggestion that dialogue was an important component, see Riese 1865, 29-30, although, as Bompaire 1958, 552 notes, the appearance of phrases such as *inquam, inquit, non vides* should not be taken as a certain indication of the dialogue.

[58] Hirzel 1895a, 380; Dudley 1937, 70.

[59] Cf. Probus, *Comm. ad Verg. Ecl.* 6.31. On the mixture of prose and verse as a characteristic feature of the Menippean satire, see Relihan 1993, 17-21; Ziolkowski 1997, 48-53.

[60] See also Strabo 16.2.29, where Menippus and Meleager are listed together among famous people coming from Gadara, and Diogenes Laertius 6.99, where works of both Menippus and Meleager (erroneously considered the former's contemporary) are said to be filled with laughter. For more on the double identity of Meleager as a poet and a Cynic and as Menippus' imitator, see Gutzwiller 1998.

Syrian and followed his country's customs (Athenaeus, *Deipn.* 4.157b).[61] She also refers to another work by Meleager which contained a comparison of bean soup to lentil soup; perhaps the reference is to the *Symposion*, as such a theme would certainly be at home in a parodic sympotic dialogue.

The parodic *Cynics' Symposion* by Parmeniscus is noteworthy per se as an offshoot and continuation of the literary tradition represented by Menippus and Meleager. Parmeniscus' work is parodic in character and infused with a sense of the absurd. The discussion of the symposiasts, consisting of seven Cynics, two courtesans, and a narrator, fuses high and low register as it goes from a discussion of lentil dishes to quotations from philosophers on the matter of suicide. Noteworthy in this context is also Parmeniscus' use of poetic quotations. Both the narrator and the Cynic symposiasts occasionally speak in verse, usually parodying tragic lines (Athenaeus, *Deipn.* 4.156e–f). Verse parodies are a "weapon in the arsenal of Menippean satire," and making characters speak poetry "is itself a parody of conventions of rational and civilized discourse," as Relihan notes.[62]

In this context, Nicion's reference to Meleager as the ancestor of the Cynic banqueters, mentioned above, may be interpreted as a meta-reference. The courtesan derides the Cynics on account of their meal (no fish, but instead a variety of lentil dishes) and wonders whether they had been influenced by reading Meleager: on the meta-level, this translates to the author drawing attention to his engagement with his predecessor's works.

## 6.5 Stoics

The engagement of the Cynics with the dialogue was varied and extensive. Evidence concerning the Stoics in this regard, however, is much more limited. David Sedley has observed that there is no evidence that Zeno of Citium, the school's founder, composed any of his works, including the *Republic*, in the dialogue format. The same is true, he remarks, of the most influential Stoics after him such as Cleanthes, Chrysippus, Antipater, Panaetius, and Posidonius. He notes:

> The only exceptions known to me are dialogues written by Zeno's own contemporaries, Stoics whose philosophical careers at least overlapped with his own: Ariston, Persaeus, Herillus, and Sphaerus. All this probably reflects the fact that

---

[61] Calling Meleager the "ancestor" of the Cynics is somewhat puzzling as he was neither far removed in time nor, it seems, particularly influential as a Cynic philosopher. Sandin 2014b, 109 n. 97 proposed that it is a mistake, and that the text originally referred to Menippus rather than to Meleager; the problem with his proposal is that the title *Graces* is clearly associated with Meleager rather than Menippus.

[62] Relihan 1993, 18–19.

the founder of a school was not normally credited with complete authority during his own lifetime, but that his thought was standardly canonized by his followers after his death. The later Stoic avoidance of the dialogue form strongly suggests that Zeno had condemned it, so that after his death it was semi-officially outlawed.[63]

The reason for Zeno's dismissal of the dialogue format, Sedley proposes, was his rejection of instruction on practical ethics by means of exemplification: the paradigmatic figure for him was the idealized sage rather than an earthly individual.[64]

While arguments ex silentio are by necessity speculative, lack of evidence of Zeno's use of the dialogue format is noteworthy. There are no name-titles in Diogenes Laertius' catalogue of Zeno's writings (7.4); the only title that suggest some engagement with the dialogue tradition is *Apomnemoneumata of Crates*.[65]

As Sedley notes, however, Zeno's immediate students, in particular the ones that Diogenes Laertius considers "heterodox" (7.167), composed dialogues. To this group belongs Aristo of Chios, a follower of Zeno with ties to the Cynics.[66] According to Diogenes Laertius, he was credited with authorship of several works, including *Dialogues* (Διάλογοι), *Erotic Discourses* (Ἐρωτικαὶ διατριβαί), and *Apomnemoneumata*.[67] He also may have been represented as a character in a dialogue: his students Eratosthenes of Cyrene and Apollophanes are said to have authored works, titled *Aristo*, in which among the topics discussed was Aristo's hedonism (Athenaeus, *Deipn.* 7.281c–d).

Persaeus of Citium was a close associate of Zeno, sent by him to the court of Antigonus Gonatas, where he appears to have been a significant figure. Among the titles related by Diogenes Laertius (7.36) are *Thyestes*, *Diatribai*, *Chreiai*, and *Apomnemoneuata*, all of which may have included dialogized passages. Athenaeus mentions his *Dialogues to Zeno* (Διάλογοι πρὸς Ζήνωνα), in which an argument was made that the wise man would also be a good general (*Deipn.* 4.162d). In Chapter 1.2, I have discussed testimony concerning Persaeus' sympotic

---

[63] Sedley 1999, 149.

[64] Sedley 1999, 150; as he notes, the Stoics' attitude towards moral exemplarity changed later, perhaps under the influence of the Roman moral tradition. Note, however, that Diogenes Laertius ascribed to Zeno the authorship of *Chreiai* and *Apomnemoneumata of Crates* (6.91, 7.4); both titles suggest engagement with the tradition of moral instruction by example.

[65] On *apomnemoneumata* literature, see Chapter 1.2, p. 13–17.

[66] On the connection between Aristo of Chios and the Cynics, see e.g. Porter 1996.

[67] Cf., however, Diogenes Laertius 7.163, 1.16: Panaetius and Sosicrates believed that these works were by Aristo of Ceos, while the Stoic Aristo wrote nothing except *Letters*. Steinmetz 1994, 559 thinks that Aristo limited himself to oral teaching and that the titles in Diogenes Laertius are either to be ascribed to Aristo the Peripatetic or are reports of the Stoic's teachings written by his students. Hahm 2006, 191–9 argues that Panaetius' judgment was not a scholarly but a philosophical opinion: as a committed Stoic, he reassigned to the Peripatetic Aristo the works authored by the Stoic Aristo in order to purge the Stoic tradition from Cynic elements present in the Chian's philosophy.

dialogues (συμποτικοὺς διαλόγους), probably a collection of sympotic conversations with Zeno and Stilpo of Megara as protagonists. Topics discussed included wine, food, love, and their proper place at a *symposion* (*Deipn.* 4.162b-c). This work may have been identical with the *Sympotic Hypomnemata*, mentioned by Athenaeus elsewhere (*Deipn.* 13.607a), in which proper sympotic themes and behaviors appear to have been discussed and in which it was argued that sex, τὰ ἀφροδίσια, was an appropriate sympotic topic. The work is also mentioned by Diogenes Laertius (7.1), who says that Persaeus related there that Zeno declined most invitations to dinner parties. In Chapter 1.2, I examined a fragment of the *Sympotic Hypomnemata* quoted by Athenaeus (*Deipn.* 13.607a-e), in which Persaeus described a visit by Arcadian delegates to the court of Antigonus Gonatas. As I noted there, the phrases ὃ καὶ πρώην ἐγένετο ("this happened the other day") and οὐχ ... ἡμῶν τινα προσβλέποντες ("not looking at any of us," of the Arcadian envoys) suggest that the narrator claimed to have witnessed the events himself and that he was relating them to other people—it is to be assumed, therefore, that the work was a dialogue.

According to the *Suda* (s.v. Ἑρμαγόρας (ε 3023)), Persaeus' student Hermagoras of Amphipolis wrote dialogues with the following titles: *The Dog-Hater* (Μισοκύων; it could be an anti-Cynic work, but also could represent a figure of an anti-Cynic interlocutor who was then argued against), *On Misfortunes* (Περὶ ἀτυχημάτων), *Ekchyton* (Ἔκχυτον, "poured forth"(?), a dialogue on egg-divination), and *On Sophistry against the Academics* (Περὶ σοφιστείας πρὸς τοὺς Ἀκαδημαϊκούς).

Dialogues are also ascribed to Sphaerus and Herillus, students of Zeno. The former, linked in our sources with Ptolemy Philopator and Cleomenes of Sparta, is said to have composed *Erotic Dialogues* (Diogenes Laertius 7.178). We read about Herillus, whose main tenet was that knowledge is the chief good, in Cicero that despite being a student of Zeno, he was closer to Plato (*Acad.* 2.42.129). Diogenes Laertius (7.165) says that his works were short but full of power, and contained statements contradicting Zeno. Among the titles we find *Dialogoi*; suggestive of the dialogue format are the titles *The Lawmaker* (Νομοθέτης) and *The Teacher* (Διδάσκαλος), as well as ones that consist of a masculine participle: *The Opponent* (Ἀντιφέρων), *The Arranger* (Διασκευάζων), *The Chastiser* (Εὐθύνων). The title Μαιευτικός, clearly gesturing toward Socratic maieutics, may refer to a person skilled in philosophical midwifery, unless it is to be understood as μαιευτικὸς λόγος, "a work of maieutic character."[68] The genres of *Hermes* and *Medea* are unclear.

Among the works of Zeno's successor Cleanthes we find the *Statesman* (Πολιτικός; Diogenes Laertius 7.175), the title of which mirrors one of Plato's

---

[68] On the adjective μαιευτικός being used in reference to people, cf. Plato, *Tht.* 151c.

dialogues. Cicero reports that when refuting hedonism, Cleanthes had the audience imagine a painting showing a personification of Pleasure being served by the Virtue (Fin. 2.21.69). His liking of personifications and vivid imagery is apparent in a short, versified dialogue between Reason and Anger, quoted by Galen (Hipp. et Plat. plac. 5.6.35 CMG [SVF 1.129 F 570]):

> τί ποτ' ἔσθ' ὃ βούλει, θυμέ; τοῦτό μοι φράσον. | Ἐγώ, λογισμέ; πᾶν ὃ βούλομαι ποιεῖν. | <Νὴ> βασιλικόν γε· πλὴν ὅμως εἶπον πάλιν. | Ὡς ἂν ἐπιθυμῶ, ταῦθ' ὅπως γενήσεται.

> "What, Anger, is it that you want? Tell me that." "I, Reason? To do everything I wish." "Why that is royal; but still, say it once again." "In whatever way I desire, that this will come about."[69]

I have discussed elsewhere in the book examples of debates between personifications of abstract concepts such as virtues and external goods; Cleanthes makes a different use of personifications as he employs them in order to render an internal conflict between reason and affections.

Chrysippus, who was Cleanthes' student and successor, was one of the most productive writers: according to Diogenes Laertius, he authored over 705 works (7.180; see also the extensive catalogue in 7.189–202). Later authors were in general critical of his style (Dionysius of Halicarnassus, Comp. 4; Cicero, De or. 1.11.50; Diogenes Laertius 7.180). Fronto, however, in the second letter on eloquence sent to Marcus Aurelius points to Chrysippus as a model and praises his rhetorical skill (SVF 2.11 F 27):

> Evigila et attende, quid cupiat ipse Chrysippus. Num contentus est docere, rem ostendere, definire, explanare? Non est contentus: verum auget in quantum potest, exaggerat, praemunit, iterat, differt, recurrit, interrogat, describit, dividit, personas fingit, orationem suam alii accommodat: ταῦτα δ' ἐστὶν αὔξειν, διασκευάζειν, ἐξεργάζεσθαι, πάλιν λέγειν, ἐπαναφέρειν, παράπτειν, προσωποποιεῖν.

> Wake up and hear what Chrysippus himself prefers. Is he content to teach, to disclose the subject, to define, to explain? He is not content: but he amplifies as much as he can, he exaggerates, he forestalls objections, he repeats, he postpones, he harks back, he asks questions, describes, divides, introduces fictitious characters, puts his own words in another's mouth: those are the meanings of αὔξειν, διασκευάζειν, ἐξεργάζεσθαι, πάλιν λέγειν, ἐπαναφέρειν, παράπτειν, προσωποποιεῖν.
>
> (trans. C. R. Haines)

---

[69] I quote Greek text and translation after Tieleman 2003, 264, who also discusses this fragment in the context of Cleanthes' philosophy. Cleanthes was committed to using poetry for philosophical purposes as his *Hymn to Zeus* demonstrates (for a thorough discussion of this poem, see Thom 2005).

Fronto's remark that Chrysippus *personas fingit, orationem suam alii accommodat* was noted by Hirzel.[70] This does not mean that Chrysippus wrote full-fledged dialogues, but rather indicates that he used various techniques of dialogization, introduced the figures of other speakers, and put some statements and utterances in direct speech for the sake of persuasion.

There is little evidence of the use of the dialogue format in the Middle Stoa. The writings of Panaetius and Posidonius, the two most influential Stoics of the late second and the first century BCE, have been lost, while extant titles, fragments, and references show no indications of the dialogue format having been employed. Also lost are the works of Antipater of Tarsus, a student of Diogenes of Babylon and a teacher of Posidonius; substantial fragments from his work discussing marriage, preserved in Stobaeus, bear no trace of the dialogue format. A passage in Athenaeus (*Deipn.* 5.186c [*SVF* 3.246 F 14]) in which we read that Antipater "once arranged a banquet and made the guests discuss sophistic arguments" (συμπόσιόν ποτε συνάγων συνέταξε τοῖς ἐρχομένοις ὡς περὶ σοφισμάτων ἐροῦσιν) may refer to a sympotic dialogue, or derive from the biographical tradition.[71] Cicero in *On Duties* depicts in the form of a dialogue a disagreement between Antipater of Tarsus and his teacher Diogenes of Babylon on the conflict between morality and advantage, and on whether a seller had the moral responsibility to disclose the whole truth to a buyer (*Off.* 3.12.51–3.13.55 and 3.23.91 [*SVF* 3.253–4 F 61; 3.219–20 F 49]). Cicero has them dispute with one another in direct speech, preceding their utterances with *inquit*. The idea of a dialogue between the two Stoics may have been Cicero's own invention, or may have been inspired by an earlier author who represented them as interlocutors (perhaps, as some scholars propose, Hecato of Rhodes, a student of Panaetius, whom Cicero quotes in *Off.* 3.15.63 and 3.23.89).[72]

## 6.6 Epicureans

From Epicurus' voluminous writings only three philosophical letters are extant in their entirety;[73] Epicureans' liking for the epistolary form as a philosophical

---

[70] Hirzel 1895a, 371 n. 1, who proposes that Chrysippus quoted his adversaries in direct speech rather than relating their views. *Personas fingit* and *orationem suam alii accommodat* are Fronto's translations of παράπτειν and προσωποποιεῖν. On προσωποποιία, sometimes distinguished from διάλογος, see Quintilian, *Inst.* 9.2.29.

[71] Cf. Plutarch, *Quaest. conv.* 614d, who argues against discussing dialectical topics at symposia (Εἶναι δὲ δεῖ καὶ αὐτὰς τὰς ζητήσεις ὑγροτέρας καὶ γνώριμα τὰ προβλήματα καὶ τὰς πεύσεις ἐπιεικεῖς καὶ μὴ γλίσχρας; 614f: εἰς λεπτὰ καὶ διαλεκτικὰ προβλήματα).

[72] Hecato was proposed as a source by Hirzel 1882, 726, 733; this hypothesis is considered probable by Dyck 1996, 557–8 and Schofield 1999, 143 (with n. 21); Annas 1989, 154 thinks that the debate was made up by Cicero.

[73] *The Letter to Herodotus*, *The Letter to Pythocles*, and *The Letter to Menoeceus*, preserved in Diogenes Laertius 10.34–117 and 10.121–35.

medium is confirmed by the titles of lost works originating from the school. Noting this, Hirzel proposed that the letter played for the Epicureans a role analogous to that of the dialogue for the Socratics and associated the school's adherence to the epistolographic rather than dialogic format with the fact that the Epicureans were more removed from the Socratic tradition than other philosophical schools.[74]

Nevertheless, Epicurus' use of the letter for instruction and the dissemination of philosophical doctrines should not obfuscate the fact that he occasionally also reached for the dialogue. His *Symposion* was known to Plutarch and Athenaeus, who are the main source of information about the dialogue.[75] In a prologue to *Table Talk*, Plutarch lists Epicurus among the philosophers who recorded sympotic conversations carried over a cup of wine (*Quaest. conv.* 612e: λόγους παρὰ πότον γενομένους). According to Athenaeus, Epicurus, unlike Xenophon and Plato, did not specify the time and place of the banquet (οὐ τόπον, οὐ χρόνον ἀφορίζει), nor preceded it with an introduction (οὐ προλέγει οὐδέν), "so that one is forced to divine for oneself how it is that someone is suddenly holding a cup and advancing topics for conversation as if he were speaking in a philosophical school" (δεῖ οὖν μαντεύσασθαι πῶς ποτ' ἄνθρωπος ἐξαπίνης ἔχων κύλικα προβάλλει ζητήματα καθάπερ ἐν διατριβῇ λέγων) (*Deipn.* 5.186e [F 251 Arrighetti]; trans. S. D. Olson). We can infer from this passage that Epicurus suppressed circumstantial detail and eschewed literary elaboration. This does not necessarily mean that the *Symposion* was a dramatic dialogue, though we should assume that if it had a narrative frame, it must have been a simple one.

The expression καθάπερ ἐν διατριβῇ, "as if in a (philosophical) school," points to a certain tension between the sympotic setting and the serious-minded philosophical lecturing which fills the dialogue. Concurrent with this strict philosophical character of the dialogue is Epicurus' decision to break with the dialogic tradition of including a variety of symposiasts, with different backgrounds, occupations, and views. Epicurus, Athenaeus says, depicted only "atom-prophets" (ἅπαντας εἰσήγαγε προφήτας ἀτόμων), even though he had as models (παραδείγματα) "the variety of the poet's (i.e. Homer's) *symposia* and the charm of Plato and Xenophon" (*Deipn.* 5.187b: τήν τε τοῦ ποιητοῦ τῶν συμποσίων ποικιλίαν καὶ τὴν Πλάτωνός τε καὶ Ξενοφῶντος χάριν). Elsewhere we read that in the *Symposion*, Epicurus depicted "a symposion attended by philosophers only" (*Deipn.* 5.177b: συμπόσιον φιλοσόφων μόνων) and "a gathering of flatterers praising one another" (*Deipn.* 5.182a: κολάκων ἄγυρις ἀλλήλους ἐπαινούντων). With the homogeneity of the interlocutors and the philosophical tenor, Epicurus'

---

[74] Hirzel 1895a, 355–7. For more on Epicurus' letters, see the overview in Erler 1994a, 75–80 (extant letters) and 103–18 (fragments of lost epistles).

[75] For a general discussion of Epicurus' *Symposion*, see Hirzel 1895a, 363–4; Martin 1931, 208–11; Bignone 1973², 189–217 (who compares the dialogue with Aristotle's *Symposion*); and recently Hobden 2013, 230–1.

*Symposion* provided an alternate model of feasting, perhaps one intended as a blueprint for Epicurean communities. Communal conviviality was an important part of their life. Seneca described the Epicureans as a "voluptuous and shade-loving crowd who philosophize at their banquets" (*Ben.* 4.2.1: *delicata et umbratica turba in convivio suo philosophantium*; the pronoun *suo* emphasizes the homogeneity of the participants) and who pass life "among banquets and songs" (*Ep.* 88.5: *inter convivia cantusque*); the passages could allude to written Epicurean *symposia*.[76] Athenaeus also tells us that there was no libation or offering to the gods in Epicurus' *Symposion* (*Deipn.* 5.179d: οὐ σπονδή, οὐκ ἀπαρχὴ θεοῖς).[77] This may have been a consequence of Epicurus' decision to suppress circumstantial detail in his *Symposion* rather than a demonstration of disregard for traditional religious rites, as we have evidence that Epicurus did not abjure conventional religious practices.[78]

As far as it is possible to judge from references to the dialogue in later authors, the topics discussed in Epicurus' *Symposion* were fairly conventional. From Athenaeus we learn that there was a discussion of divination from indigestion, followed by a conversation about fevers (*Deipn.* 5.187b: περὶ δυσπεψίας ὥστ' οἰωνίσασθαι... περὶ πυρετῶν). Medical topics are a recurrent feature in sympotic dialogues, which frequently, after the fashion of Plato's *Symposion*, include physicians among the guests.[79] Another theme discussed was wine. According to Diogenes Laertius, Epicurus in the *Symposion* said that the wise man will not speak nonsense when drunk (10.119). Plutarch informs us that Epicurus and Polyaenus (a close friend and follower of Epicurus) deliberated on the heating properties of wine (*Adv. Col.* 1109e–f [F 21.1 Arrighetti]):

Ὅρα δὴ ἃ περὶ τοῦ οἴνου τῆς θερμότητος ἐν τῷ Συμποσίῳ Πολύαινον αὐτῷ διαλεγόμενον Ἐπίκουρος πεποίηκε. λέγοντος γάρ "οὐ φῄς εἶναι, ὦ Ἐπίκουρε, τὰς ὑπὸ τοῦ οἴνου διαθερμασίας;" ὑπέλαβε "τί δεῖ τὸ καθόλου θερμαντικὸν ἀποφαίνεσθαι τὸν οἶνον εἶναι;" καὶ μετὰ σμικρόν, "φαίνεται μὲν γὰρ δὴ τὸ καθόλου οὐκ εἶναι θερμαντικὸς ὁ οἶνος, τοῦδε δέ τινος ὁ τοσοῦτος εἶναι θερμαντικὸς ἂν ῥηθείη."

---

[76] Cf. a passage in Philodemus' *On Epicurus* (PHerc. 1232 Fr. 8 col. i.7–12), where Philodemus says that Epicurus invited to a banquet members of his household and people well disposed to him and his friends. Plutarch, *De lat. viv.* 1129a, speaks of Epicurean "common meals" and "gatherings of associates and noble people" (αἱ κοιναὶ τράπεζαι... αἱ τῶν ἐπιτηδείων καὶ καλῶν σύνοδοι). Communal meals were a fixed feature of the Epicurean calendar and included a celebration of Epicurus' birthday on the tenth of Gamelion and festivities on the twentieth of every month; see Clay 1998, 71–2, 78–100.

[77] The libation was an element of Plato's and Xenophon's *Symposia* (Plato, *Symp.* 176a; Xenophon, *Symp.* 2.1).

[78] Cf. Philodemus, *Piet. 1*, col. xxvi–xxxi. Epicurus' opponents were quick to point to a discrepancy between his theology and the acceptance of conventional religious rites and accused him of insincerity and fear of the public (Plutarch, *Non posse* 1102b; cf. also Cicero, *Nat. D.* 1.44.123 and 3.1.3; Origen, *Cels.* 7.66; Eusebius, *PE* 14.27.11 and 15.5.12).

[79] For more on the figure of the physician in the sympotic dialogue, see Martin 1931, 79–92.

Consider the discussion that Epicurus in his *Symposium* presents Polyaenus as holding with him about the heat in wine. When Polyaenus asks, "Do you deny, Epicurus, the great heating effect of wine?", he replies, "What need is there to generalize that wine is heating?" A little later he says, "For it appears that it is not a general fact that wine may be said to be heating for a given person."

(trans. B. Einarson, P. D. De Lacy)

Plutarch next relates Epicurus' atomistic explanation of the effects of wine, paraphrasing and quoting Epicurus' utterances in the dialogue. The topic fits well with sympotic literature, and Plutarch himself in *Table Talk* dedicates one *problema* to discussion about whether wine has cooling properties (*Quaest. conv.* 651f; Epicurus' *Symposion* is mentioned in 652a).

From Plutarch we know that Epicurus in the *Symposion* also discussed the proper time for sex. Although erotic themes were not alien to sympotic dialogue,[80] Epicurus' treatment offended some of Plutarch's young acquaintances, who considered it most licentious (ἐσχάτης ἀκολασίας εἶναι) for an older man to ponder at dinner in presence of young people whether one should make love before or after a meal (*Quaest. conv.* 653b). Another of Plutarch's interlocutors, the physician Zopyros, defended Epicurus and observed that it was not the main topic of discussion, but that Epicurus (*Quaest. conv.* 653c-d):

τοὺς νέους ἀνιστάντα μετὰ δεῖπνον εἰς περίπατον ἐπὶ σωφρονισμῷ διαλέγεσθαι καὶ ἀνακρούειν ἀπὸ τῶν ἐπιθυμιῶν, ὡς ἀεὶ μὲν ἐπισφαλοῦς εἰς βλάβην τοῦ πράγματος ὄντος, κάκιστα δὲ τοὺς περὶ πότον καὶ ἐδωδὴν χρωμένους αὐτῷ διατιθέντος.

...took the youths for a walk after dinner and talked with them to teach them moderation and check their desires, showing that sex always brings risk of harm, but it affects worst the people who engage in it after eating and drinking.

We can infer from this passage that Epicurus' *Symposion* consisted of a dinner, δεῖπνον, which was followed by a walk, περίπατος (perhaps followed by wine-drinking, that is, a *symposion* proper).[81] Plutarch's phrasing (τοὺς νέους ἀνιστάντα μετὰ δεῖπνον εἰς περίπατον, "took the youths for a walk after dinner") suggests that

---

[80] As one of Plutarch's company notes, at the end of Xenophon's *Symposium* the speakers hurry home to make love to their wives (*Quaest. conv.* 653c). Still, the propriety of such themes was questioned, as implied by Athenaeus, *Deipn.* 13.607a-b, where we read that the Stoic Persaeus of Citium in his *Sympotic Hypomnemata* said that "speaking of sex while drinking is appropriate" (περὶ ἀφροδισίων ἁρμοστὸν εἶναι ἐν τῷ οἴνῳ μνείαν ποιεῖσθαι); it is then argued that such discussions provide opportunity to commend and urge moderation.

[81] Peripatetic conversations are not a *novum* in a sympotic dialogue: in Plato's *Symposion*, Aristodemus opens his narration with a report of his talk with Socrates on the way to Agathon's house (walks appear also in non-sympotic dialogues such as the *Protagoras* and *Phaedrus*). They also frequently appear in Plutarch (*Symposion of the Seven Sages*, *Amatorius*, *De facie in orbe lunae*, *Non posse*). See also Hirzel 1895a, 364 n. 2.

the peripatetic conversation did not involve all the symposiasts, but only Epicurus and the young men. The occurrence of the walk implies that the *Symposion* was not utterly bereft of dramatization, contrary to the impression one gets from the remarks in Athenaeus.

Epicurus' *Symposion* is also mentioned in Philodemus' *On Rhetoric*. Philodemus defends there the position of his teacher Zeno of Sidon, who maintained that Epicurus and the other founders of Epicureanism did not deny the name of art to rhetoric as a whole, but only to its political and forensic branches; at the same time, they considered sophistic (that is, epideictic) rhetoric a *techne*. Philodemus argues against contemporary Epicurean schools which claimed that the founders of Epicureanism deprived all rhetoric of the name of art. He polemicizes with a work produced by one of the Rhodian Epicureans, who maintained that some students of Zeno, while supporting their teacher's view, referred to a passage from Epicurus' *Symposion* as confirming Zeno's position. Philodemus, however, denies that rhetoric was discussed in extenso in the *Symposion* and suggests that in order to understand Epicurus' position on rhetoric one should look elsewhere.[82]

Slightly later in *On Rhetoric*, Philodemus takes issue with the Rhodian's interpretation of a passage from a work by Epicurus. The fragment does not preserve the title of the text; what we learn is that the work discussed a variety of topics and was about three thousand lines long (ἐπῶν ... σχεδὸν τ[ρ]ισχιλίων).[83] Philodemus summarizes the contents of the passage in the following manner (*Rhet.* 2, col. x.21–xi.1 [F 21.4 Arrighetti]):

κ[αὶ] δὲ παρίστησιν ἐλεγχομένους ⌜ὁ⌝ Ἐπίκουρος τὸ[ν νέ]ον [ἐ]⌜κ⌝εῖνον᾽ [ἐκ μ]ε[λ]έτης ῥητορικῆ[ς] μ[ία]ν δύ[ναμ]ιν ⌜ἐπ⌝αγγε[λλόμε]νον τ[οῦ σο]φισ[τ]⌜εύ⌝ειν τὴν [π]ανη[γυρι]κὴν κα[ὶ] τὴν πολ[ε]ιτικ⌜ή⌝[ν]· <καὶ> [π]οιεῖ τὸν Ἰδομε[νέα] μετὰ τὸ "πα<ρ>ρησιάζ[θω]" μετὰ τῶν "ΕΓΑCΤΟ ὑμεῖν" [ἐξ]αιτούμενον συγγνώ[μ]ην, εἰ νέος ὢν θρασύνετ[α]ι κα[ὶ σ]υνάπτοντά τιν᾽ α⌜ὑτῶ⌝ν τοιαῦτα κατὰ λέξιν "θαυμαστὸν [δὴ εἰ σὺ μὲν οὐδὲν ἐξε[ίργ]ου διὰ τὴν ἡλικίαν, ⌜ὡς⌝ α[ὐ]τός ἂν φήσαις, τῶν κατὰ σεα[υτ]ὸν ἁπάντων νέος ὢν π[ρε]σβυτ⌜ῶ⌝ν ἀνδρῶν καὶ ἐ⌜ν⌝δόξων πολὺ ἐ[ν τῆι ῥη]τορικ⌜ῆ⌝ι δυ⌜νά⌝μει ὑπερέχειν."

And Epicurus represents some people refuted [like] this youth who declares that panegyric and political rhetoric belong to a single faculty of sophistic which originates from rhetorical practice. And after the words "Let him speak openly"

---

[82] Philodemus, *Rhet.* 2, col. lii–lvii (numeration of columns follows Longo Auricchio 1977). Philodemus implies that the Rhodian author misrepresented Zeno's students' argument in order to easily refute it.

[83] On ἔπη as an equivalent to στίχοι ("lines"), see Ohly 1928, 4–9. A length of three thousand lines would situate the dialogue between Plato's *Protagoras* and *Gorgias* (Kennedy 2010, 10 estimates the length of the *Protagoras* to be two thousand four hundred lines, and the *Gorgias* three thousand six hundred).

he portrays Idomeneus with "...to you" ask to forgive him if, on account of his youth, he is arrogant. And he then depicts one of them as saying the following: "It is amazing that you have not been at all hindered by your age, as you would yourself say, from exceeding in rhetorical faculty all your contemporaries, even though you are young and they old and of great repute."[84]

As we can see, in the contested passage (derived from a dialogue by Epicurus), someone (perhaps Idomeneus of Lampsacus, Epicurus' student) is refuting a youth who is boasting of his rhetorical capability. The title of the dialogue does not appear in the fragment, though scholars tend to assume that the passage comes from the *Symposion* of which Philodemus spoke previously (even though Philodemus denies that this work contained an extensive treatment of rhetoric, it nevertheless must have included a passage in which the question was raised).[85]

Traces of the dialogue format are also discernable in what is believed to be a fragment of Epicurus' *On Nature*, preserved in PHerc. 1413 [F 37 Arrighetti].[86] The passage focuses on the nature of time and complements other reports of Epicurean theories of time.[87] Col. xii.3–5 reads:

καὶ μά[λ]α εὖ, ἔφη, μοὶ δο[κ]εῖς ἅπαντα τὰ προ[ειρη]μένα διειλέχθαι....

And very well, he said, you seem to me to have discussed everything so far....

The form ἔφη, which appears also in col. xv.10, suggests a narrated dialogue. Other phrases suggestive of the dialogue format include col.v.2–3: ὦ πρὸς θε[ῶν, ὅ]τι ταῦθ' ὁρᾶις, col. xx.2–5: εἰ ἄρα σοι [περὶ] τα[ῦτα] ἐκ τῆς ἐκκειμ[ένης] λέξεως ὁ λόγος ᾖ, οὐδ' ἂν ὀκνήσα[ι]μι οὐ χρόνον εἶναι τὰς ἡμέρας φῆσαι καὶ τὰς νύ[κτας], and col. xxxv.9–10: [ἱκα]ναῖς λέξεσιν ὀκνεῖς χρῆσ[θ]αι).[88] If, as scholarly consensus has it, PHerc. 1413 has preserved a fragment of Epicurus' *On Nature*, this implies, as Sedley notes, a certain "stylistic heterogeneity" in the Epicurean *opus magnum*, which in some parts was set as a continuous discourse, and in others as a dialogue.[89] Such a heterogeneity is also suggested by PHerc. 1479 and PHerc. 1417 [F 31 Arrighetti]. The two papyri are parts of a single roll and, as stated in the colophon, derive from Book 28 of *On Nature*; they discuss epistemological problems related to language and the use of ordinary words for philosophizing. The papyrus ends as follows (Fr. 13 col. xii.inf.i–xiii.10):

---

[84] I follow the Greek text as printed in Longo Auricchio 1977.

[85] Scholars who ascribe this fragment to the *Symposion* include von Arnim 1893, 8–14; Sudhaus 1895, 85–8; Arrighetti 1973², 576; Chandler 2006, 129–34. Sedley 1989, 114 n. 40 considers it unlikely.

[86] I follow Arrighetti's edition for the Greek text. Arrighetti marks it as belonging to an *incertus liber* of *On Nature*; Sedley 1998, 118 proposes assigning it to Book 10.

[87] On Epicurean theories of time, see Warren 2006; Zinn 2016.

[88] The dialogue format is accepted by Crönert 1906, 104 n. 501; Arrighetti 1973², 650; Sedley 1998, 118; Del Mastro 2011, 32. Barigazzi 1959, 30–1 is skeptical.

[89] Sedley 1998, 118.

ἧι δ' ἔτι τοιοῦ[το ἡμ]ῖν ἐστίν, οὐκ ὀκνήσ[ω, σ]οί τε κα[ὶ] τοῖσδε πολλάκις προφέρειν καὶ τὰ λοιπᾷ δέ, τὰ μὴ ἧι τοιαῦτα, δόξαντα δ' ἂν διημαρτῆ[σθ]ᾳι. ἀλλ' οὐ βούλομαι ἐπὶ τοῦ παρόντος προφέρεσθαι αὐτά, μὴ ἀρχὴμ ποιησώμεθα μῆκος ἐχόντων ἱκανὸν λόγων. [ἱκ]ανῶ[ς] οὖν ἡμῖν ἠδολεσχήσθω ἐπὶ τοῦ παρόντος. καὶ ὑμεῖς [μ]υ[ρι]άκι[ς μνημο]νεύε[ι]μ π[ειρᾶ]σθε τὰ ἐμοί τε καὶ Μητρ[ο]δώρωι τῶιδε ν[εωστὶ εἰ]ρημένα. οἶμαι δ' ὑμῖν ὄ[γδο]ον καὶ εἰκοστὸν εἶδος ἀκ[ρο]άσεως τῆ[ς] ἑξῆς περαιν[ο]μένης τουτὶ ν[ῦ]ν [ἠ]δολε[σ]χῆσθαι.

Nor shall I hesitate to cite repeatedly, to you and to these others, cases where there is still error of this kind among us; and so too all other cases which are not of this kind, but which we would nevertheless consider to involve error. For the present, however, I do not wish to cite them, to avoid making a new start in a discussion which has already reached sufficient length. So let the words which we have prattled suffice for the present. And you others, try ten thousand times over to commit to memory what I and Metrodorus here have just said. And now I think I have finished prattling to you this twenty-eighth instalment of our consecutive lecture series.[90]

The pronoun σοί in the first sentence refers to Metrodorus, whom Epicurus explicitly identifies as his interlocutor towards the end of the passage. Their discussion is said to have taken place before other students of Epicurus and with an eye to their instruction. Metrodorus' name appears in the vocative several times in earlier sections of the papyrus, confirming that Epicurus treats him as a conversational partner. Other places suggesting a dialogic format include:

Fr. K col. i.4-6: ἔμοιγε δὴ [δοκε]ῖ καὶ πάλαι καὶ νῦν [.....] ἔχειν ὡ[ς] λέγεις.
it seems to me, both in the past and now, to be as you say.

Fr. 13 col. ii.sup.4-5: [ὡς] λέγεις, Μητρόδ[ω]ρε.
as you say, Metrodorus.

Fr. 13 col. iv.inf.9-col.v.sup.8: ἀλλὰ γὰρ ἴσως οὐκ εὐκαιρόν ἐστ[ι ταῦ]τ[α] προφέροντα μηκύνει[ν]· [κ]αὶ μαλ' ὀρθῶς [γε, ὦ] Μητρόδωρε· πάνυ γὰρ οἶμαί σε πολλὰ ἂν ἔχειμ προε[ν]έγκασθαι ἃ ἐθεώρεις γελοίως [π]ῶ[ς] τι[να]ς ἐγδεξαμένους καὶ π[άν]τ[α] μᾶλλον ἢ τὸ νοούμενον κατὰ τὰς λέξεις.

Perhaps, though, you might say that it is inappropriate to lengthen the discussion by citing these cases. Quite so, Metrodorus. For I do not doubt that you could cite many cases, from your own past observations, of certain people taking words in various ridiculous senses, and indeed in every sense in preference to their actual linguistic meanings.

---

[90] Here and below I follow the edition and translation of Sedley 1973.

Sedley refers to the text as a "pseudo-dialogue" and notes that "[t]o judge from the surviving portions of the text, Metrodorus has no speaking part, but his views and comments are relayed to us by Epicurus."[91] In such a case, we would have a dialogue in which the figure of the secondary interlocutor has been radically suppressed. Yet, it is also possible (and in my opinion, more probable) that Metrodorus did speak in some parts of the text, though his words were either in the lost sections or are impossible to be identified as his due to the damaged state of the papyrus. It would be extravagant if Epicurus spoke of "things said by me and Metrodorus," τὰ ἐμοί καὶ Μητροδώρῳ εἰρημένα, while keeping Metrodorus silent the whole time.[92]

Based on the discussed evidence it is clear that the dialogue-format was not utterly shunned by Epicurus. He certainly assumed the role of a mentoring, dominant speaker, which must have resulted in conversational asymmetry, congruent with the school's emphasis on the founder's authority. It is therefore not improbable that Epicurus also made some use of the dialogue format in other works, as well. It is noteworthy in this context that several of them bear name-titles, common in dialogic literature. Here belong, for instance, *Chairedemus*, *Hegesianax*, *Neocles to Themista*, *Eurylochus to Metrodorus*, *Aristobulus*, *Polymedes*, *Timocrates* (in three books), *Metrodorus* (in five books), *Antidorus* (in two books), *Callistolas*, and *Anaximenes* (Diogenes Laertius 10.27–8). Several names refer to people close to Epicurus: Neocles, Chairedemus, and Aristobulus were Epicurus' brothers, who, Diogenes Laertius says, studied philosophy upon Epicurus' encouragement (10.3); Metrodorus was his close associate and Timocrates—Metrodorus' brother who later left the school; Themista was Epicurus' student.[93] These works were probably not a homogenous group: some of them were considerably longer than others (five books of *Metrodorus*), while others were probably polemics (*Timocrates* and *Antidorus*).

The possibility that these works were at least in some part dialogized is rarely contemplated.[94] Usener acknowledged that the name-titles recall dialogues (such as Cicero's *Laelius* or *Cato*), but argued that a fragment of Carneiscus' *Philistas*, preserved in PHerc. 1027, provides a better *comparandum* and, consequently

---

[91] Sedley 1973, 13; cf. also Sedley 1998, 104: "Epicurus is... conducting a one-way conversation with his colleague Metrodorus"; Erler 1994b, 217: "Scheindialog mit Metrodor in Anwesenheit anderer Schüler."

[92] I concur with Clay 2009, 21 who remarks that *Book* 28 "is cast as a dialogue between Epicurus and Metrodorus."

[93] Timocrates appears to have been attacked by Epicurus on account of a conflict with Metrodorus (Cicero, *Nat. D.* 1.33.93; Plutarch, *Adv. Col.* 1126c). Antidorus is mentioned as an Epicurean in Diogenes Laertius 5.92 (though in 10.8 he is said to have been insulted by Epicurus, who twisted his name to Sannidorus). We know nothing of Polymedes and Callistolas; the identity of Anaximenes is uncertain. Hegesianax is mentioned by Plutarch (*Non posse* 1101b: Epicurus wrote about his death to his father Dositheus and brother Pyrson). Eurylochus was, according to Diogenes Laertius, an addressee of one of Epicurus' letters (10.13).

[94] De Sanctis 2011, 219 n. 16 appears to entertain such a possibility.

considered these works as commemorative literature and *laudes amicorum*. Bignone thought that some of these works were funerary *encomia*, while Clay referred to them as "memorial pamphlets" and observed that in some of them Epicurus spoke of ill or dying friends.[95]

There is no doubt that celebrating the memory of individuals was a characteristic trait of the early Epicurean community; ample evidence confirms this. However, a commemorative character does not prevent a text from being a dialogue or containing dialogized sections; after all, much of Socratic literature was commemorative.[96] Depicting people engaged in discourse and remembering them communally in conversation was an inherently philosophical practice for honoring and commemorating them.[97] A passage from Plutarch's *Non posse* is worth recalling in this context. Plutarch seems to talk about Epicurus who (1097e–f):

νοσῶν νόσον ἀσκίτην τινὰς ἑστιάσεις φίλων συνῆγε καὶ οὐκ ἐφθόνει τῆς προσαγωγῆς τοῦ ὑγροῦ τῷ ὕδρωπι καὶ τῶν ἐσχάτων Νεοκλέους λόγων μεμνημένος ἐτήκετο τῇ μετὰ δακρύων ἰδιοτρόπῳ ἡδονῇ.

... when suffering from the dropsy invited friends to a number of common meals and in spite of the disease did not refuse to take liquid, and was softened, recalling Neocles' last words, by the curious pleasure that is mingled with tears.

(trans. B. Einarson and P. D. De Lacy)[98]

The passage appears to preserve some of the original wording of the work to which Plutarch refers,[99] in which Epicurus, in presence of his friends, recalled Neocles'

---

[95] Usener 1887, 93; Bignone 1973², 542; Clay 1998, 63–6. On the commemorative intention of Epicurus' works on his family and friends, see Plutarch, *De lat. viv.* 1129a; for Epicurus "constantly tending in illness or mourning in death" his friends and family members, Plutarch, *Non posse* 1103a. Carneiscus' *Philistas* was edited (and preceded by an extensive introduction and commentary) by Capasso 1988, who discusses it in the context of Epicurean commemorative literature (37–53).

[96] Cf. also Geus 2002, 59–60 on fluidity of prose genres in the Hellenistic period: "Die Grenzen der Biographie zu den verwandten Genera der Laudatio funebris, des Enkomions, des literarischen Portraits, der Gerichtsrede, des philosophischen Dialogs, der grammatischen Dichtervita, der Panegyrik, der Hagiographie und der Memoirenliteratur sind fließend und sicherlich nicht terminologisch scharf gewesen."

[97] Cf. Plato, *Phd.* 58d, where Phaedo considers his recalling of Socrates' last conversation as an act of remembering Socrates (τὸ μεμνῆσθαι Σωκράτους). Diogenes Laertius quotes Epicurus' letter to Idomeneus, in which Epicurus, near the end of his life, wrote that he draws solace in his illness and suffering from "memories of our past *dialogismoi*" (10.22: ἐπὶ τῇ τῶν γεγονότων ἡμῖν διαλογισμῶν μνήμῃ). While it may be tempting to understand διαλογισμοί as "conversations," one should note that in the epistles to Herodotus and Pythocles Epicurus uses the term in reference to his continuous expositions (10.68 and 10.84, 10.85); the phrase in the letter to Idomeneus should be understood analogously as "memories of our arguments/reasonings."

[98] It is not explicitly said in the text who is the subject; Usener 1887 (F 186 and 190) and Clay 1998, 66, 72, 92, 99 take him to be Epicurus, while Körte 1890—Metrodorus (F 46). Arrighetti does not include the passage in his edition of Epicurus.

[99] Armstrong 2008, 96; the rare adjective ἰδιότροπος occurs also in Epicurus' *Letter to Herodotus* (Diogenes Laertius 10.52) (and nowhere else in Plutarch). On the Homeric image of "melting with tears," cf. Plutarch, *Non posse* 1101a, about Epicureans' grieving: λιπαίνειν τοὺς ὀφθαλμοὺς καὶ τήκεσθαι, literary "to glisten and melt in the eyes."

last words. The notion of a mixture of pleasure and tears is reminiscent of Plato's *Phaedo* (58e–59a). This suggests Epicurus' interaction with the tradition of dialogues on death, which was initiated by the *Phaedo*, and, consequently, the possibility of at least some dialogization. We are, to be sure, in the realm of speculation here; but imagining these works as *laudes amicorum*, funerary *encomia*, or "memorial pamphlets" is likewise speculative.

We know little of the works of other Hellenistic Epicureans, and there is no evidence of the dialogue format being used by them. Diogenes Laertius mentions that some people ascribed a dialogue titled *Medios* to Polyaenus (2.105). It seems that Carneiscus' *Philistas* was not a dialogue; Zopyrus, who is addressed in the vocative at one place, should probably be considered the text's addressee (col. xv.2). There is no evidence of the employment of the dialogue format in the papyri fragments of Philodemus. We do have, however, fragments of an Epicurean dialogue from the early imperial period, and although it is beyond the time frame of this book, I will briefly discuss it as it remains little known. The monumental inscription by Diogenes of Oenoanda, engraved in a public stoa and dated tentatively to the second century CE, contains among other Epicurean writings Diogenes' letter to his friend Antipater, in which he reports to his addressee his conversation with a certain Theodoridas of Lindus on the infinite number of worlds. Diogenes writes from Rhodes; Antipater probably is in Athens (Fr. 63 M. F. Smith, col. ii.4–iv.14):

> ἐπεὶ δ' ἀβέβαιον τοῦτό ἐστιν διά τε τὸ ἐν τοῖς πράγμασι ποικίλως ἄστατον καὶ τὸ ἐμὸν ἔξωθε γῆρας, τὰ περὶ ἀπειρίας κόζμων, ὡς ἠξίωσας, ἀπέστειλά σοι. συντυχίᾳ δὲ τοῦ πράγματος ἀγαθῇ κέχρησαι· πρὶν ἢ γὰρ ἐλθεῖν σου τὴν ἐπιστολήν, Θεοδωρίδας ὁ Λίνδιος, ἑταῖρος ἡμῶν, ὃν οὐκ ἀγνοεῖς, ἀρχόμενος ἔτι τοῦ φιλοσοφεῖν, τὸν αὐτὸν ἔπραττεν λόγον. ἐναρθρότερος δ' οὗτος ἐγ[ε]ίνετο, διὰ τὸ ἐν ἀμφοῖν ἡμεῖν παροῦσι στρέφεσθαι· αἱ γὰρ ἐξ ἀλλήλων συνκαταθ[έσ]εις τε καὶ ἀντιφά[σει]s, ἔτι δ' ἐρωτήσεις, ἀκριβεστέραν ἐπ[οιο]ῦντο τοῦ ζητο[υ]μένου τὴν ἔρε[υν]αν. διὰ τοῦτο οὖν, Ἀντίπατρε, τὴν διάλε[ξ]ιν ἐκείνην ἀπέστειλά σοι, ἵν[α] δὴ τὸ ἴσον γένηται τῷ κἂν παρὼν αὐτός, ὁμοίως Θεοδωρίδᾳ, τὰ μὲν ὡμολόγεις, οἷς δ' ἐπηπόρεις καὶ προσεπυνθάνου. ἔστιν δὲ αὕτη τοιαυτηνεί τινα τὴν ἀρχὴν ἔχουσα· "ὦ Διόγενες," ὁ Θεοδωρίδας εἶπεν, "ὅτι μὲν ἀληθές ἐστιν τὸ Ἐπικούρῳ περὶ ἀπειρίας κόσμων...."

But, since this is uncertain, both on account of the changeability and inconstancy of our fortunes and on account of my old age besides, I am sending you, in accordance with your request, the arguments concerning an infinite number of worlds. And you have enjoyed good fortune in the matter; for, before your letter arrived, Theodoridas of Lindus, a member of our school not unknown to you, who is still a novice in philosophy, was dealing with the same doctrine. And this doctrine came to be better articulated as a result of being turned over between the two of us face to face; for our agreements and disagreements with one another, and also our questionings, rendered the inquiry into the object of our search more precise. I am therefore sending you that discourse, Antipater, so that you may be in the same position as if you yourself were present, like Theodoridas, agreeing about some matters and making further inquiries in cases where you had doubts. It began something like this: "Diogenes," said Theodoridas, "that the [doctrine laid down] by Epicurus on an infinite number of worlds is true...."[100]

Not much is left from the dialogue itself, yet this introductory passage is most instructive. We learn that the dialogue reported a conversation between Diogenes—an elderly, seasoned Epicurean—and a budding philosopher whom he had met in Rhodes. Theodoridas approached Diogenes as an authority and initiated the conversation, asking the philosopher to explain some aspects of the Epicurean doctrine of an infinite number of worlds. This communicative frame is mirrored by the relationship between Diogenes and Antipater, who likewise requested the former to clarify for him the same subject.

We do not know whether Diogenes' conversation with Theodoridas really took place—as Smith rightly observes, it may be an invention[101]—but even if there was such an event in the background, it provided inspiration and raw material rather than a ready blueprint. In other words, the dialogue is a literary composition. Diogenes remarks that thanks to the conversation with Theodoridas, thanks to their "agreements and disagreements" (συνκαταθ[έσ]εις τε καὶ ἀντιφά[σει]s) and "questions" (ἐρωτήσεις), the problem they discussed gained clarity. His considerate phrasing tactfully mitigates the asymmetry inherent in the figures of the speakers: the conversation is presented as a joint exploration rather than Diogenes' authoritative clarification of Theodoridas' confusions. On a metaliterary level, Diogenes' remark provides a rationale for discussing the problem of infinite worlds in a dialogue rather than in a work written in continuous discourse. Diogenes believes that by reading the dialogue, Antipater will feel as if he were present during the discussion (παρὼν αὐτός) and could have voiced his own agreement or doubt (ὁμοίως Θεοδωρίδᾳ τὰ μὲν ὡμολόγεις, οἷς δ' ἐπηπόρεις καὶ προσεπυνθάνου). Antipater, then, and by extension the reader of the inscription, is welcome to identify with Theodoridas and engage in the imaginary conversation with Diogenes.

---

[100] Greek text and English translation follows Smith 1993, modified. For more on Diogenes of Oenoanda, see Smith 1993, 35–48; Gordon 1996; Clay 1998, 189–255. Gordon 1996, 24–5 believes that other sections of the inscription also contain passages in the dialogue form, specifically, Diogenes' *On Old Age* (Fr. 138 M. F. Smith) which, she writes, "clearly takes the form of a dialogue between an old man (Diogenes himself) and a group of young men" and Fr. 154 M. F. Smith; however, neither passage shows clear signs of deriving from a dialogue.

[101] Smith 1993, 36.

Clay proposed that in combining the philosophical letter with dialogue, Diogenes imitates on one hand Epicurus' *Letter to Pythocles*, and on the other— Epicurus' *Symposion*.[102] The evidence discussed above, however, indicates that the *Symposion* was not the only work in which Epicurus made use of dialogue, even though the extent of his use of the dialogue remains uncertain.

## 6.7 Timon of Phlius

Timon of Phlius (c.320–230) was a student of Pyrrho of Elis, considered the originator of the skeptical tradition.[103] He was a prolific and versatile writer of prose and poetry, best known for his hexameter *Silloi* (*Lampoons*), which were written in the language of Homer and Hesiod and parodied dogmatic philosophers from the perspective of a skeptic. It opened with the line "Speak to me now, you meddlesome sophists!" (ἔσπετε νῦν μοι ὅσοι πολυπράγμονές ἐστε σοφισταί), an imitation of epic invocations to the Muses.[104] According to Diogenes Laertius (9.111), the work consisted of three parts: the first book was a narrative with Timon as the narrator (τὸ μὲν πρῶτον αὐτοδιήγητον ἔχει τὴν ἑρμηνείαν; cf. also 9.112 where it is called μονοπρόσωπος), while the second and the third were in the form of a dialogue (ἐν διαλόγου σχήματι):

> φαίνεται γοῦν ἀνακρίνων Ξενοφάνην τὸν Κολοφώνιον περὶ ἑκάστων, ὁ δ' αὐτῷ διηγούμενός ἐστι· καὶ ἐν μὲν τῷ δευτέρῳ περὶ τῶν ἀρχαιοτέρων, ἐν δὲ τῷ τρίτῳ περὶ τῶν ὑστέρων· ὅθεν δὴ αὐτῷ τινες καὶ Ἐπίλογον ἐπέγραψαν.
>
> for he represents himself as questioning Xenophanes of Colophon about each philosopher in turn, while Xenophanes answers him; in the second he speaks of the more ancient philosophers, in the third of the later, which is why some have entitled it the Epilogue. (trans. R. D. Hicks)

The conversational structure and the alternating questions and answers create a clear link between the mock-epic *Silloi* and the philosophical dialogue. The choice of Xenophanes as interlocutor must have been due to the fact that he was known for his iambic poetry, which, among other things, attacked Hesiod's and Homer's

---

[102] Clay 1998, 241. It is not inconceivable that works by Epicurus such as *Neocles to Themista* or *Eurylochus to Metrodorus* combined an epistolary format with a dialogue.

[103] Diogenes Laertius (9.109–10) provides a colorful biography of Timon: he started as a dancer, then studied with Stilpo of Megara, then married, then joined Pyrrho—but only for a short time, as he had to make money in order to sustain his family, and became a sophist. For Timon's biography, see Clayman 2009, 6–21. All poetic fragments of Timon are included in the *Supplementum Hellenisticum* (*SH*) (Lloyd-Jones and Parsons 1983, 368–95).

[104] Diogenes Laertius 9.112 (*SH* 775); cf. Homer, *Il.* 2.484, 11.218, 14.508; Hesiod, *Th.* 114. On the relationship between the *Silloi* and Greek parody and comedy, see Clayman 2009, 117–30; for more on Cynic influences, Long 2006, 82–5; Clayman 2009, 133–6.

beliefs about the gods.¹⁰⁵ Timon's Xenophanes confessed that his philosophy was mistaken because he was not familiar with the skeptical method (Sextus Empiricus, *Pyr.* 1.224 [*SH* 833]):

ὡς καὶ ἐγὼν ὄφελον πυκινοῦ νόου ἀντιβολῆσαι | ἀμφοτερόβλεπτος. δολίῃ δ' ὁδῷ ἐξαπατήθην | πρεσβυγενὴς ἔτ' ἐὼν καὶ ἀμενθήριστος ἁπάσης | σκεπτοσύνης. ὅππῃ γὰρ ἐμὸν νόον εἰρύσαιμι | εἰς ἕν ταὐτό τε πᾶν ἀνελύετο· πᾶν δ' ἐὸν αἰεὶ | πάντῃ ἀνελκόμενον μίαν εἰς φύσιν ἵσταθ' ὁμοίην.

If only I had had a share of shrewd thought and looked in both directions! But I was deceived by the treacherous path, being a man of the past and having no care for any inquiry. For wherever I turned my thought, everything resolved into one and the same; and everything, existing always, was drawn back all about and came to a stand in one homogenous nature.    (trans. J. Annas and J. Barnes)

Apparently, Timon transported Xenophanes to his own times and made him a convert to skepticism. Timon and Xenophanes discussed a variety of thinkers, including pre-Socratic philosophers like Thales, Pythagoras, and Parmenides, Socrates and the Socratics, Plato and the Academy (in particular Arcesilaus), Aristotle, Zeno of Citium and other Stoics, and Epicurus and a few of his followers. At least a part of the *Silloi* was set in the underworld and had the form of a mock-epic *nekyia*, perhaps with Xenophanes serving as a guide.¹⁰⁶ There was also a mock-heroic battle of philosophers fighting in arguments and a market-scene with philosophical ideas on auction, perhaps even a fishing scene.¹⁰⁷ There is little doubt that Timon exerted substantial influence on Lucian's comic dialogues.

Another of Timon's poetic works, the *Indalmoi* (*Images* or *Appearances*, written in elegiac couplets) appears to also have had a dialogic format, with Timon talking to his master Pyrrho: one fragment preserves Timon's question to Pyrrho about how the philosopher achieved his wondrous tranquility.¹⁰⁸

The *Pytho*, on the other hand, appears to have been a prose dialogue. According to Eusebius of Caesarea (who quotes Aristocles of Messene) Timon described there in an extended report (διηγεῖται, μακρόν τινα κατατείνας λόγον) how he chanced upon Pyrrho besides the shrine of Amphiaraus (we learn that Pyrrho was

---

¹⁰⁵ Diogenes Laertius 9.18; cf. also Athenaeus, *Deipn.* 2.54e where Xenophanes' *Parodiai* are mentioned. It is possible that Xenophanes' work was titled *Silloi*—the title is ascribed in the first century BCE to Xenophanes by Strabo (14.1.28) and in POxy. 8.1087 (scholia to Homer's *Iliad*), col. ii.41, though this might have happened under influence of Timon's text.
¹⁰⁶ Ax 1991; Clayman 2009, 81–3.
¹⁰⁷ Clayman 2009, 95–112. While fish-related imagery clearly was present in the *Silloi*, a self-standing fishing scene is not accepted unanimously by scholars.
¹⁰⁸ *SH* 841 (Diogenes Laertius 9.65; Sextus Empiricus *Adv. math.* 11.1 and 1.305). For more on the proposition that the *Indalmoi* presented "images of Pyrrho," see Brunschwig 2004, 221; Clayman 2009, 73–4 suggests a connection between Timon's work and the literary tradition of *apomnemoneumata* and *chreia*.

on his way to Delphi) and what they discussed (τίνα διαλεχθεῖεν ἀλλήλοις) (PE 14.18.14). From Aristocles' attack on Timon we can infer that in the course of the conversation Pyrrho criticized philosophers for their ignorance (PE 14.18.15: ἡνίκα δ' ἤρξατο κατηγορεῖν τῶν ἀνθρώπων καὶ τῆς ἀγνοίας αὐτῶν). The dialogue probably contained a detailed exposition of Pyrrho's philosophy.[109] The opening motif of a chance encounter is reminiscent of the Socratic dialogue, while the mention of the oracles of Amphiaraus and Delphi perhaps served to depict Pyrrho as a god-like figure. It is probable that the *Pytho* was a fictionalized account of Timon's initiation into Pyrrhonism.

Timon was also the author of *Funeral Feast of Arcesilaus* (Ἀρκεσιλάου περίδειπνον). Diogenes Laertius tells that, unlike in the *Silloi*, Timon praised the philosopher in this work (9.115). Based on what we know about Timon's works, it is possible that the text was a mock-dialogue, perhaps a parody of Plato's *Funeral Feast* by Speusippus (for more on parodies of sympotic dialogues, see Chapter 1.2).

## 6.8 Eratosthenes of Cyrene

The *Suda*'s entry on Eratosthenes of Cyrene tells us that the renowned Hellenistic scholar, poet, and polymath wrote "philosophical works, poems and histories; *Astronomy*, or *Catasterisms*; *On the Philosophical Sects*; *On Freedom from Pain*; many dialogues (διαλόγους πολλούς); and numerous grammatical works." Unfortunately, we know extremely little of Eratosthenes' "many dialogues," though we may assume that his employment of the format was a result of his philosophical education (he studied in Athens under the Stoic philosopher Aristo of Chios, and perhaps was also associated with the Academic Arcesilaus). *Suda* also informs us that Eratosthenes was nicknamed "the second Plato" or "the new Plato" (δεύτερος ἢ νέος Πλάτων); this might have been due to his compositions in the dialogue format or to his authorship of a work titled *Platonicus*. There may also be a connection between Eratosthenes' nickname *Pentathlete* and the pseudo-Platonic dialogue *Rival Lovers*, where a polymath is compared to a pentathlon athlete, that is, a person who is always second best to people specializing in a given discipline.

We do not possess a catalogue of Eratosthenes' writings and have to rely on interspersed testimonies by various later authors. One of the works which may have been a dialogue is titled *Arsinoe*, a fragment of which is preserved in Athenaeus (*Deipn.* 7.276a–c [*BNJ* 241 F 16]). In the fragment, Arsinoe is said to

---

[109] Diogenes Laertius 9.67: Timon shows clearly Pyrrho's disposition (τὴν διάθεσιν) in the *Pytho* (the Greek says πρὸς Πύθωνα, "to Pytho," which probably is a mistake).

have asked a passer-by what festival he was celebrating at the moment, to which he responded:

"καλεῖται μὲν Λαγυνοφόρια, καὶ τὰ κομισθέντα αὐτοῖς δειπνοῦσι κατακλιθέντες ἐπὶ στιβάδων καὶ ἐξ ἰδίας ἕκαστος λαγύνου παρ' αὐτῶν φέροντες πίνουσιν." ὡς δ' οὗτος ἀπεχώρησεν, ἐμβλέψασα πρὸς ἡμᾶς "συνοικιά γ'," ἔφη, "ταῦτα ῥυπαρά· ἀνάγκη γὰρ τὴν σύνοδον γίνεσθαι παμμιγοῦς ὄχλου, θοίνην ἕωλον καὶ οὐδαμῶς εὐπρεπῆ παρατιθεμένων. εἰ δὲ τὸ γένος τῆς ἑορτῆς ἤρεσκεν, οὐκ ἂν ἐκοπίασε δήπου τὰ αὐτὰ ταῦτα παρασκευάζων καθάπερ ἐν τοῖς Χουσίν· εὐωχοῦνται μὲν γὰρ κατ' ἰδίαν, παρέχει δὲ ταῦτα ὁ καλέσας ἐπὶ τὴν ἑστίασιν."

"It's called the Lagynophoria. They lie down on camp-beds and eat the food they've brought for themselves, and everyone drinks from a personal wine-flask (*lagynos*) he's brought (*pherontes*) from home." He went on his way, and she looked at us and said: "This is a filthy celebration. It's inevitable that the crowd will include people of every kind, who'll serve themselves a meal consisting of nasty leftovers. If this was the sort of festival he wanted, he wouldn't have had any difficulties making the same arrangements as at the Choes festival; they eat individually there, but the host supplies the material for the feast."

(trans. S. D. Olson)[110]

The passage, as argued by Geus, appears to derive from a dialogue. This is suggested not only by direct quotations of the words of the anonymous man and Arsinoe but, above all, by the phrase "she looked at us and said" (ἐμβλέψασα πρὸς ἡμᾶς... ἔφη), which indicates that the event was related by a first-person narrator (who, if the text were a dialogue, did not have to be Eratosthenes himself).[111]

Another work by Eratosthenes which may have been a dialogue is *Aristo*, titled after Aristo of Chios, his Stoic mentor. The name-title is the only indication of the potential dialogue format. From Athenaeus we learn that in this text, Eratosthenes "alludes obliquely to his master's eventual movement toward a life of luxury, saying the following: I have caught him before this digging through the wall that separates the houses of Pleasure and Virtue, and appearing in Pleasure's company" (*Deipn.* 7.281c–d: παρεμφαίνει τὸν διδάσκαλον ὡς ὕστερον ὁρμήσαντα ἐπὶ τρυφήν, λέγων ὧδε· ἤδη δέ ποτε καὶ τοῦτον πεφώρακα τὸν τῆς Ἡδονῆς καὶ Ἀρετῆς

---

[110] παρασκευάζων is Olson's conjecture for παρασκευάζουσα ἡ βασίλεια; if one accepts the manuscript version, one has to take it as being spoken by the narrator rather than by Arsinoe. Cf. also Geus 2002, 63 who acknowledges that it is not certain how far Eratosthenes' text extends, and proposes that it ends either before εἰ δὲ τὸ γένος or even before ἀνάγκη γὰρ (in the latter case, the words spoken by Arsinoe would be limited to "This is a filthy celebration"). The Ptolemy and Arsinoe mentioned are probably to be identified with Ptolemy IV Philopator and Arsinoe III Philopator.
[111] Geus 2002, 66–8. Hirzel 1895a, 404 thinks that the work (like *Aristo*, discussed below) was a biography.

μεσότοιχον διορύττοντα καὶ ἀναφαινόμενον παρὰ τῇ Ἡδονῇ).[112] If the work was a dialogue, the accusation of Aristo did not have to derive from Eratosthenes himself, but could have come from one of the characters (merging the author of a dialogue with the dialogue's interlocutors occurs frequently in ancient sources). Strabo says that in one of his works Eratosthenes boasted of his association with many great men (1.2.2: πλείστοις ἐντυχών, ὡς εἴρηκεν αὐτός, ἀγαθοῖς ἀνδράσιν) and specifically listed Aristo and Arcesilaus as the most prominent philosophers of the time; he also spoke highly of Bion of Borysthenes. While we do not know whether Strabo draws here from the *Aristo*, as Geus hypothesizes,[113] his testimony demonstrates that some of Eratosthenes' works reflected on his philosophical education and time spent in Athens.

Eratosthenes was also the author of a work titled *Platonicus*, which discussed mathematical problems and was inspired by Plato's *Timaeus*. Hirzel thought that the work was a dialogue, but there is no confirming evidence.[114] The same is true of lost works on ethical subjects—for instance, *On Wealth and Poverty*, *On Relief from Pain*, *On Good and Bad*, *On Schools of Philosophers*.[115]

## 6.9 The *Tablet of Cebes*

I wish to devote the last two sections of this chapter to two works that originated towards the end of the Hellenistic or in the early imperial period: the *Tablet of Cebes* and dialogues by Philo of Alexandria. These works precede better-known dialogues by Plutarch, Dio Chrysostom, or Lucian, and bear evidence to the vitality of the dialogue before them.

The *Tablet of Cebes* is an anonymous dialogue dated to either the first century BCE or first century CE.[116] The title may refer to the Cebes of Thebes known from Plato, but the language and contents of the text exclude the possibility that it was written in the fourth century BCE.[117] The work was certainly known in the early imperial period: Lucian alludes to it twice and refers to the author as ὁ Κέβης

---

[112] Greek text and translation from Olson 2008. There is an allusion to this Eratosthenes' passage in Athenaeus, *Deipn.* 13.588a.

[113] Geus 2002, 22.

[114] Hirzel 1895a, 405–7 thought that the title is to be understood as Πλατωνικὸς λόγος on analogy with Σωκρατικὸς λόγος and speculated that it was a dialogue with Plato as a speaker; Fraser 1970, 181 also considered the work a dialogue. Solmsen 1942, 193 n. 3 observes that there is no way to decide on the format, while Geus 2002, 192–3 finds the dialogue format unlikely. For more on attempts to reconstruct the work, see Hiller 1870; Geus 2002, 141–94.

[115] They are discussed in a chapter dedicated to Eratosthenes' dialogues in Geus 2002, 59–97.

[116] This dating is speculative; for an overview of the scholarship, see Fitzgerald and White 1983, 1–4; the conclusion is that "the vast majority of scholars would prefer to assign the work to the period of the early Empire, that is, sometime in the period from Augustus to Domitian."

[117] For various attempts to explain the appearance of Cebes' name in the title, see Fitzgerald and White 1983, 5–7.

ἐκεῖνος, "the famous Cebes," Tertullian mentions a relative who turned the *Tablet* into a Virgilian *cento*, and Diogenes Laertius lists the *Tablet* under the works of Cebes of Thebes.[118] There are numerous parallels between the dialogue and early imperial period texts (most notably Dio Chrysostom's works and the *Shepherd of Hermas*), which indicate either a common source or a direct influence.[119] The work is a "piece of moral preaching"[120] and has been variously identified as Socratic, Stoic, Cynic, or neo-Pythagorean in nature, but it is more appropriate to consider it a moralizing discourse transgressing doctrinal boundaries.[121]

The *Tablet* is a dialogue with an internal narrator, whose identity remains undisclosed. He and his friends were visiting a temple of Cronus, where they saw an image of obscure meaning. It depicted an area surrounded by a wall, within which there were two other walled enclosures, one larger and one smaller. There was also a larger crowd and numerous female figures painted, as well as an elderly man who looked as if he was giving orders. An older unnamed man approached the narrator and his company and offered to explain the picture, whose meaning he learned from a philosopher who dedicated the painting to Cronus. He warns them, however, that there is some risk entailed in listening to the explanation: if one understands it, he will become wise and happy, if not—he will end up miserable and foolish. After this opening, the older man explains in detail the meaning of the painting and of the characters depicted. The picture turns out to be an intricate moral allegory, with the walled enclosure representing Life, the old man—Daimon, who prescribes to people entering life what they have to do, and the other human figures—abstract concepts, virtues, and vices. In this regard, the author of the dialogue interacts with the dialogic, paraenetic tradition of representing the personifications of abstract concepts in conversation—though here, the personifications are mute figures represented in the painting, and it is left to the elderly exegete to explain to his audience what they are saying to the crowd depicted on the picture.

What is remarkable in the *Tablet of Cebes*, it is that the dialogue format has been enriched with elements of other provenance. The opening is reminiscent of periegetic literature, which developed in the Hellenistic period, when "tourism" and sight-seeing became an elite cultural activity;[122] more specifically, it resonates with what has been recently called "sightseeing with a religious dimension," or "sacred tourism," combining "vision and intellectual inquiry."[123] The dialogue also interacts with the ancient tradition of *ekphraseis*, descriptions and

---

[118] Lucian, *Merc. cond.* 42, *Rhet. pr.* 6; Tertullian, *De praescr. haeret.* 39.4.
[119] For a discussion of parallels, see Joly 1963, 79–86; Fitzgerald and White 1983, 7–8, 16–20. I am inclined to interpret Dio's remark in *Or.* 10.31-2 as an allusion to the *Tablet*.
[120] Trapp 1997, 162.
[121] I agree here with Trapp 1997, 168–71. For an overview of discussion concerning the text's philosophical affiliations, see Fitzgerald and White 1983, 20–6.
[122] For more on the Hellenistic roots of periegetic literature and ancient tourism, see Cohen 2001.
[123] Rutherford 2001, 43.

interpretations of works of art, and resonates in this respect with extant imperial period novels (two of them, Achilles Tatius' *Leucippe and Cleitophon* and Longus' *Daphnis and Chloe*, open with a description of a painting). Moreover, it has been pointed out that the interplay between text and image, verbalization and visualization, is reminiscent of *Tabulae Iliacae*, marble tablets visualizing Greek epic poems, dating from the late Hellenistic or early imperial period.[124]

## 6.10 Philo of Alexandria

Philo, an Alexandrian Jew from the first century CE, is well known to us: many of his works are preserved thanks to the interest they elicited among adherents of Christianity. None of the works surviving in entirety is written in a dialogue format. However, thanks to Armenian translators we know that Philo authored at least two dialogues: *On Animals*, which is extant only in an Armenian translation, and *On Providence*, preserved in Armenian and in lengthy quotations by Eusebius.[125] While the dialogic format of *On Providence* is lost in Eusebius, the Armenian version, consisting of two books, retained the dialogue form of the second book.[126] Both *On Animals* and *On Providence II* are dramatic dialogues in which Philo presents himself as an interlocutor and argues against the views of a certain Alexander, identified by scholars with Tiberius Julius Alexander, Philo's apostate nephew. The two dialogues were once ascribed to Philo's youth, but more recently it has been argued that they were composed by an older Philo, possibly in the late 40s CE.[127] They belong to Philo's philosophical writings and are firmly rooted in the Greek philosophical tradition: they uphold certain Stoic doctrines, which are consistent with Philo's religious worldview (divine providence in *On Providence II* and the irrationality of animals in *On Animals*).

In *On Providence II*, Philo meets Alexander early at dawn. Alexander could not sleep, his mind occupied by a discussion he had had with Philo the day before. This is a familiar dialogue *topos*: dialogues reporting conversations which pick up themes discussed earlier by the characters outside the frame of the dialogue are well known (among them Plato's *Timaeus* and Plutarch's *On the Intelligence of Animals*). In the discussion that ensues, Alexander presents arguments against divine providence (e.g. bad people enjoy wealth and fame), while Philo argues that

---

[124] Squire 2011, 122–6.

[125] For a discussion of the two dialogues, see Terian 1981, 1–63; Terian 1984. The Armenian versions of *On Animals* and *On Providence* were edited and translated into Latin by Aucher 1822; the fragments of the latter work from Eusebius are also in Colson 1941. An English translation of *On Animals* is in Terian 1981.

[126] Book 1 of *On Providence* may be an abridgment of the original, which has lost its dialogic format in transmission (so Wendland 1892, 38).

[127] Terian 1984, 289–90. *On Providence* might be earlier than *On Animals*, as it represents a less critical image of Alexander.

god is a good king governing the whole world with justice, while the prosperity of the bad is merely apparent, for no bad man can be happy. Philo also critically assesses opinions concerning divinities pronounced by poets, and discusses the creation and structure of the world. Much like Plutarch's dialogues, the text is interwoven with poetic quotations (e.g. Aechylus, Homer, Hesiod, Pindar), references to Plato and other philosophers (Zeno of Elea, Democritus, Empedocles, Parmenides, Xenophanes, Cleanthes, etc.), and to various historical figures. The conversation is friendly and cooperative; Philo is the dominant figure, the philosopher who disperses Alexander's doubts and difficulties with the concept of divine providence.

Works on divine providence were popular among the Stoics, though we do not know whether Philo follows any of the known figures by making his work a dialogue. We know of Chrysippus' lost Περὶ προνοίας, we have Seneca's *On Providence*, and several sections of Arrian's *Epictetus' Discourses* are dedicated to the subject (*Epict. Diss.* 1.6, 1.16, 3.17). The doctrine of divine providence was also embraced by Middle Platonists, and while Philo's views owe much to Stoicism, Plato's dialogues (*Phaedrus*, *Timaeus*) are a frequent point of reference.[128] The doctrine of providence was treated in dialogue format in Cicero's *On the Nature of the Gods*, where it was criticized by the Epicurean Velleius (*Nat. D.* 1.8.18, 1.8.20–1.9.23) and then defended by the Stoic Balbus (2.29.73–2.67.168), and in Plutarch's *On the Delays of the Divine Vengeance*, whose interlocutors defended the concept of providence after it was attacked by an Epicurean philosopher. It is clear that Philo is working within an extensive tradition, which allows him to convey the religious message of the Pentateuch in philosophical language, but his immediate inspirations—also in terms of the genre—are difficult to pin down.

In the second dialogue, *On Animals*, Philo again assumes the role of a knowledgeable, authoritative speaker. He debates there with his young relative Lysimachus. Alexander, who was Philo's interlocutor in *On Providence*, is absent; nevertheless, he plays a crucial role because Lysimachus was inspired by his speech arguing that animals possess reason. In the course of the conversation, Alexander's speech is read aloud and then refuted by Philo, who represents the Stoic position on the question of animal rationality and holds that animals are bereft of reason.[129]

A particularly interesting feature of *On Animals* is that it is a creative imitation of Plato's *Phaedrus*. As I have demonstrated at length in another publication, there are numerous references and allusions to Plato's dialogue; moreover, Philo

---

[128] On divine providence in Stoicism and Middle Platonism, see Dragona-Monachou 1994; Boys-Stones 2016; for more on Philo's concept of providence, Frick 1999.

[129] For the philosophical arguments presented in Philo's *On Animals* and striking parallels between Philo's *On Animals*, Porphyry's *On Abstinence from Killing Animals*, and Sextus Empiricus, see Tappe 1912. For a detailed examination of the debate on the rationality of animals in antiquity and beyond, see Sorabji 1993.

imitates the structure of the first part of the *Phaedrus* (the reading of a speech by an absent character, followed by a refutation) and intimates that Alexander is the new Lysias, while Lysimachus takes the place of Phaedrus and Philo steps into the shoes of Socrates.[130] Philo skillfully makes use of mimetic strategies familiar to scholars of imperial period prose, and resembles in this regard authors such as Plutarch (*On the Daimonion of Socrates, Symposion of the Seven Sages, Amatorius*), Dio Chrysostom (*Charidemus*), and Athenaeus (*Deipnosophists*), who emulate Plato by evoking his dialogues in structure, imagery, and language. It is noteworthy that Philo's use of these mimetic strategies precedes Plutarch, which suggests that by that time, Platonic imitation was part of the established repertoire of the philosophical dialogue—and a Hellenistic legacy rather than fruit of a revival of interest in Plato at the turn of the first and the second century CE.

## 6.11 Conclusion

As we venture to draw some general conclusions from the material discussed in the chapter, we should bear in mind that the evidence that has reached us is extremely limited. The tendencies observable in the examined material, which constitutes just a small fraction of Hellenistic compositions, do not necessarily mirror trends that we would discover if we had access to lost works.

I will start with the representation of historical persons in dialogues and dialogized anecdotes. I have discussed the connection between dialogue and biography and biographical anecdote at length in Chapter 1. In the material examined in this chapter, we saw additional evidence for works aiming at preserving (and shaping) the memory of philosophers and depicting them in conversations with, for instance, kings, philosophical rivals, or friends. Such works contributed to the formation of the colorful figures of, for instance, Diogenes the Cynic and Stilpo of Megara. The Cynics and early Stoics (such as Persaeus) appear to have had a particular liking for representations of their mentors and associates in conversation. Such conversations did not have to be reported in self-standing dialogues, but may have been depicted in inset dialogized sections in narrative works, or in *apomnemoneuamata*-type literature. An interesting Hellenistic development is the inclusion of the figures of monarchs as speakers—Alexander the Great (sometimes depicted in conversation with his father Philip, as in Alexinus of Elis' *Apomnemoneumata*), the diadochi and their successors (think, for instance, of the work titled *Ptolemy* by Stilpo of Megara probably depicting Ptolemy I Soter, of the conversation between Antigonus Gonatas and Bion of Borysthenes, or of Eratosthenes' *Arsinoe*).

---

[130] For a detailed discussion of Philo's imitation of Plato and the dialogue format of *On Animals*, see Jażdżewska 2015a.

Like the Academy and Peripatos, other schools also used the dialogue for disseminating and explaining philosophical ideas: such employment of the format is suggested by testimonies and fragments from Epicurus, and there is some evidence for such use among the early students of Zeno of Citium. Timon of Phlius used the dialogue format to have his teacher Pyrrho explain his skeptical philosophy and refute dogmatic philosophers. In the first century CE, Philo of Alexandria explored in dialogues the issues of divine providence and animal rationality. In the second century CE, this format was assumed by the Epicurean Diogenes of Oenoanda, who perhaps modeled his conversation with Theodoridas after the example of Epicurus. The titles of works by Hellenistic philosophers indicate that dialogues of a polemical character, frequently directed against a specific representative of a rival school, were also composed, but our knowledge of them is limited.

The subversive element in Cynicism led to the formation of a parodic and comic dialogue which ancient authors have associated above all with Menippus of Gadara. His later followers include Meleager of Gadara and Parmeniscus. A parodic character is also found in skeptical works by Timon of Phlius, which seem to share a few other traits with Menippus' compositions: both philosophers appear to have depicted themselves in their works, and enjoyed the fantastical and otherworldly; both also seem to have experimented with merging philosophical dialogue with poetry: Menippus by employing a mixture of prose and poetry, and Timon by writing the *Silloi* and *Indalmoi* in verse.

In the fragments of the Cynic Teles we saw the incorporation of the dialogue into a paraenetic discourse. The argument is written there for two voices, in a sort of simplified, asymmetrical dialogue, with the identity of the secondary interlocutor suppressed and unobtrusive. Teles may have had a predecessor in Bion of Borysthenes. There is suggestive evidence, however, that the Cynics were not the only ones who turned to this format: there are similarities between the dialogization we find in Teles and the type of discourse which Cicero associated with Arcesilaus and the New Academy; Fronto's observation that Chrysippus *personas fingit, orationem suam alii accommodat* perhaps indicates that the Stoic philosopher also made use of this technique.

In their paraenetic works, philosophers also made use of personifications of abstract concepts, moral virtues and vices, human affections, etc.—and had them converse with and argue against one another. We encountered Bion of Borysthenes' personification of Poverty and a whole array of personified opposites in a fragment of Demetrius (the Cynic?), as well as in Cleanthes' versified exchange between Reason and Anger. The *Tablet of Cebes* makes use of a more complex literary technique: instead of depicting personifications directly engaged in conversation, its author has one of the characters explain an image depicting them and report what they are doing and saying.

The ever-actual topic of death was treated in Hegesias of Cyrene's *The Man Starving Himself to Death*; but also probably by Epicurus—who, according to Plutarch, recalled the last words of his brother Neocles. The sympotic dialogue never lost its appeal. I have discussed the dialogue's relationship with sympotic literature in Chapter 1.2; in this chapter, I have added an examination of the format and themes of Epicurus' *Symposion*. Erotic desire was also among the topics of interest in sympotic works, with both Epicurus and the Stoic Persaeus discussing it. Philosophical *symposia* were parodied by the Cynics (Menippus, Meleager, Parmeniscus) and probably by Timon of Phlius (*Funeral Feast of Arcesilaus*).

# Epilogue

The preceding chapters have provided the reader with a glimpse of only a tiny part of the dialogues produced after Plato. We possess mere scraps of ancient literature, and Hellenistic prose has suffered particularly badly. The notion of "gaps in evidence" does not do justice to the losses; a better fit is the image of a huge (and frustrating) jigsaw puzzle of which only a few pieces, most of them damaged, survive. In these six chapters, my main goal has been to collect and examine these pieces. In this section, I will assume more of a bird's-eye perspective and identify some emergent trends and lines of development in the post-Platonic dialogue.

In the Introduction, I emphasized the Protean character of the Socratic and Platonic dialogue, which bequeathed a rich variety of dialogic formats to later authors. This diversity was embraced and increased over the following centuries. Dialogues continued to stage philosophical inquiries and to depict sympotic conversations; they promulgated philosophical doctrines and explained their intricacies, modeled methods and types of reasoning, exhorted to virtue and commemorated teachers, polemicized, and ridiculed.

At the same time, they were increasingly used by non-philosophers for other than philosophical or moral purposes. One of these developments was the employment of the dialogue to represent learned discussions about poetry, as exemplified by the papyri fragments discussed in Chapter 2.3. Influenced by the genres of *zetemata* and biography, these works stage conversations in which speakers ponder philological problems, interpret difficult or unclear passages, and discuss a literary text alongside a poet's biography. They negotiate and transmit philological knowledge, while representing a community of educated, inquisitive readers engaged in erudite inquiry.

Another type of non-philosophical employment of the dialogue is exemplified by fragments of historical dialogues which discard a moralizing agenda, focusing instead on a vivid depiction of known historical actors and their *ethopoiia*. While moral and political reflection may be integrated, as in the "Peisistratus' Dialogue" and in lost dialogues by Heraclides of Pontus, historical dialogues could also become displays of rhetorical flourish, as in the "Trial of Demades." In a simplified form, short dialogues between well-known historical characters could have been used in school settings as writing exercises, and—here our evidence comes from the early imperial period—for composition practice and language learning (fragments discussed in Chapter 2.6.1).

Humorous and satirical dialogues, which parodied the philosophical dialogue, were also composed, frequently with sympotic settings. The Cynic Menippus, in whose works derision of other philosophers was blended with fantastic elements and a sense of the absurd, appears to have been the key figure in the development of this category of dialogue. Parodies of philosophical dialogues could interweave prose with poetic passages, and sometimes, as in the case of Timon of Phlius' *Silloi* and *Indalmoi*, be written in a poetic meter throughout.

A multiplicity of settings were used. Some dialogues revived the figure of Socrates, at times freely remodeled: we find him expressing views incompatible with the Socratic tradition (for instance, in the *Theages* and in PKöln 5.205), using the philosophical idiom of the Hellenistic schools (*Axiochus* and *Halcyon*), and even sacrificing truth for psychological efficacy (*Axiochus*). A variety of other settings were used, with the cast of speakers including philosophers, rulers, orators, and politicians. Heraclides of Pontus brought Empedocles to life, Praxiphanes made Plato converse with Isocrates, the author of the Pseudo-Hippocratic *Letter* 17 reported an encounter of Hippocrates with Democritus, and Alexinus the Megarian had Alexander the Great criticize Aristotle's teachings in a conversation with his father Philip. The realm of the marvelous, legendary, and mythological was by no means out of bounds (the mythological Tithonus was speaking about old age in Aristo of Ceos, Timon of Phlius had Xenophanes return from the dead and become a convert to skepticism), and personifications of abstract concepts talked and polemicized, as in Crantor's short *paradeigma* about the contest of goods, Bion's discourse on poverty, and Demetrius the Cynic's fragment on Bravery and Cowardice.

Another category, the contemporary dialogue set roughly in the present rather than in some distant past, allowed for the inclusion of the author and his friends or antagonists as speakers and reflected current intellectual life and its disputes and preoccupations. It also provided an opportunity to commemorate teachers and colleagues, either during their lives or after death, but also, in the case of Hellenistic philosophical schools, to showcase them to the outside world. It was certainly popular with Aristotle and the Peripatetics, but it was also used by authors from other milieus, including the Epicureans. Eratosthenes of Cyrene's *Arsinoe* was probably a dialogue set in the Alexandria of his time; Alexandria was also presumably the setting of Philo of Alexandria's two dialogues, in which he depicted himself in discussion with his relatives. The commemorative impulse, together with a moralizing agenda, shaped *apomnemoneumata* literature, which, as we saw in Chapter 1.2, included students' memoires of influential philosophers, and appear to have been given the form of collections of anecdotes, sayings, and short dialogues. Some of the most memorable and colorful figures, such as Diogenes the Cynic, sparked great interest among authors who were not directly acquainted with them and were considerably removed from them temporally (the earliest evidence concerning dialogized anecdotes about Diogenes comes from the mid-third century BCE, but he was still inspiring authors in the early imperial period, as short dialogues in pseudepigraphic epistles and several dialogues by Dio Chrysostom demonstrate).

Speakers' identities were also sometimes effaced, as in dialogues in which one or more characters remain nameless. This happened frequently in pseudo-Platonica, where Socrates' interlocutors are recurrently bereft of names; in some dialogues all the speakers are anonymous (*Demodocus* 2–4). The extent of suppression of personal information varied and led to very different outcomes. Some anonymous speakers are indistinct and almost featureless, even if one can deduce one or two things about them (for instance their age or city) as one reads the text. Such suppression of names accompanied by erasing of individualized traits turns the spotlight on the argument. In other cases, this anonymity serves to underscore specific traits of the speakers, as in *Rival Lovers*, where the anonymity of the *erastai* leads to them being wholly defined by their attitude to learning. In the remains of the Cynic Teles, a dialogue appears to be slipping into one speaker's engagement with an imaginary interlocutor voicing doubts and disagreement.

When one considers the evidence concerning the post-Platonic dialogue against the backdrop of trends that shaped Hellenistic literature and its aesthetics, two traits appear particularly significant, namely the inclination of dialogue to interact and blend with other genres, and the employment of a broad range of mimetic practices. As to the first point, I started my examination by discussing a variety of interplays between dialogues and anecdotal, epistolary, and biographic literature (Chapter 1): dialogues could be embedded in other formats (in a letter, perhaps in a biography), they could originate from protracted *chreiai* and get condensed into them—or, as in the pseudo-Platonic *Theages*, host anecdotes within itself. Satyrus' *Life of Euripides* combines the Dialogue form with thematic conventions characteristic of biography. In other sections, we encountered dialogues infringing on the realm of history and rhetoric ("Peisistratus' Dialogue" and "Trial of Demades" in Chapter 2.4), but also engaging with prose-types emerging in the Hellenistic period such as consolation (*Axiochus*), zetemata-literature (dialogues on Homer in papyri in Chapter 2.3.2), paradoxography (*Halcyon*), and *periegesis* (*Tablet of Cebes*). Hellenistic aesthetics encouraged such blending, while the multiplicity of Hellenistic prose provided fecund ground for generic experimentation. The effects of such blending may go well beyond aesthetics. Due to its Socratic origins, the dialogue is intimately associated with the quest for truth, and when it is merged with a format shaped by other priorities, mutual tensions may destabilize the outcome, as in the *Axiochus*, in which the merger of a philosophical dialogue with the argumentative modes characteristic of consolatory writings alert the reader and make them question Socrates' sincerity.

Throughout the chapters we witnessed recurrent employment of mimetic practices in the dialogues examined, most frequently in the form of the adaptation and transformation of Platonic scenes, themes, and motifs. Such acknowledgment of the Platonic legacy anchored dialogues in the generic tradition, but also allowed authors to accentuate their deviations from philosophical positions expressed in Plato. Here the concepts of *variatio* or *oppositio in imitando* (or *Kontrastimitation* in German) from the toolbox of scholars of Hellenistic literature prove useful, as they allow for appreciation of the dynamics of closeness to and distance from Platonic subtexts. As we saw in Chapter 4, the pseudo-Platonica exemplify a wide range of strategies of imitation of and variation on Plato's dialogues: for instance, the *Halcyon* is a miniature version of the *Phaedrus*, the *Cleitophon* reuses and reverses Platonic motifs and assigns Cleitophon the discursive role conventionally assigned to Socrates, and the author of the *Theages* rewrites a passage from the *Theaetetus* to create an un-Platonic concept of Socrates' *daimonion*. But literary imitation of Plato was not restricted to the *dubia* and *spuria*. We can assume it played a large role in the Academy and Peripatos, especially with philosophers writing with a literary verve. In Chapters 3 and 5, we saw several instances of rewriting of and alluding to Plato. For instance, Heraclides of Pontus' *On the Woman Not Breathing* appears to have combined motifs from Plato's *Phaedo* and *Symposion* (and the scene of the last moments of Empedocles' feast appears to rewrite the closing of the *Symposion*). Aristotle's *Eudemus* certainly extensively engaged intertextually with the *Phaedo*, but also—as examination of the motif of the homecoming demonstrated—with the *Crito*. Praxiphanes, who depicted a conversation between Plato and Isocrates in one of his dialogues, was probably inspired by the *Phaedrus* both in choice of interlocutors and of the rural setting. Intertextual engagement with the *Phaedrus* is also apparent in the pseudo-Hippocratic *Letter* 17 and in Philo of Alexandria's *On Animals*. The myth of Er in the *Republic* inspired later authors to report the near-death revelatory experiences of various characters (for instance, Heraclides of Pontus' Empedotimus and Clearchus' Cleonymus). We may suppose that there was also a rich web of intertextual connections within post-Platonic dialogue literature (for instance, one would imagine that Theophrastus' *Callisthenes* referred to both Plato's *Phaedo* and Aristotle's *Eudemus*), but they are, regrettably, irrevocably lost to us.

Post-Platonic and Hellenistic dialogues were not composed in isolation from larger trends of the period—a highly literate era of books, poetic experimentation, philological research, and scholarly debate. It is unsurprising that we witness the expansion of literary strategies involving genre-blending and intertextual engagement with predecessors, strategies which emphasize the dependence of the process of writing on that of reading. At the same time, philosophical schools continued to be places of oral teaching and debate, and now and again efforts were made to put orality at the center of philosophical practice, as in the New Academy, the two most influential leaders of which, Arcesilaus and Carneades, focused on oral philosophizing and probably left no writings. The tension between the orality of the New Academy and literacy is captured vividly in an anecdote reported by Numenius, who is quoted by Eusebius of Caesarea. Numenius says that Carneades was a powerful speaker who always prevailed over other philosophers. His contemporary the Stoic Antipater intended to *write* something as a polemic against him (ἔμελλε μὲν καὶ ἀγωνιᾶν τι γράφειν), but did not engage in a face-to-face exchange: "he said nothing, uttered nothing, not a syllable did anyone hear from him" (οὐδὲ εἶπεν οὐδὲ ἐφθέγξατο οὐδ' ἤκουσέ τις αὐτοῦ... οὐδὲ γρῦ). Instead, he hid in a corner and wrote books with an eye on posterity (γωνίαν λαβὼν βιβλία κατέλιπε γράψας τοῖς ὕστερον)—books, Numenius comments, with little power today, but even more powerless at the time (οὔτε νῦν δυνάμενα καὶ τότε ἦν ἀδυνατώτερα) (*PE* 14.8.11).[1] Interestingly, the new format of oral discourse introduced in the New Academy (a thesis followed by a refutation) influenced the development of a novel dialogue-type, which Cicero used as a template for his *Tusculan Disputations* and *On Fate*. The Philosopher mosaic from the Villa of T. Siminius Stephanus in Pompeii, depicting a group of seven philosophers, some of them with scrolls in hand, nicely captures the combination of oral and literary practices that shaped Hellenistic philosophy.[2]

The book leaves the reader on the threshold of the imperial era. More prose literature of this period survived, including a fair number of dialogues. Sixteen dialogues by Plutarch (with the nine-book long *Table Talk*) and some twenty by Dio Chrysostom are extant; we have around forty dialogues and thematic dialogue collections by Lucian, the massive *Deipnosophists* by Athenaeus, the Philostratean *Heroicus* and *Nero*, Julian's *Caesars*, Christian dialogues by Justin the Martyr, Methodius of Olympus, and Gregory of Nyssa, as well as anonymous dialogues, dialogue fragments, and Syriac translations of original Greek works (the list is not comprehensive).[3] The remains of the multifarious post-Platonic, Hellenistic dialogues provide a crucial backdrop for reading them: although the presence of Plato is pervasive in the imperial dialogue and manifests itself in recurrent allusions and rewritings of Platonic scenes, it should not obfuscate the fact that their authors' perception of the dialogue was formed not exclusively by Plato, but also to a large degree by the heterogenous post-Classical literature that preceded them.

---

[1] Usher 2006, 205–6.
[2] Interpretation of the figures of the seven philosophers varies. While their number suggests the influence of the Seven Sages tradition, they are frequently interpreted as Plato and other philosophers associated with the Academy (see Rashed 2013 for discussion with an overview of different interpretations).
[3] For an overview of Christian dialogues, see now Rigolio 2019.

# References

Algra, K. 2018. "Hellenistic Philosophy." In L. Perilli and D. P. Taormina (eds.), *Ancient Philosophy. Textual Paths and Historical Explorations*, 409–94. London and New York: Routledge.
Algra, K., J. Barnes, J. Mansfeld, and M. Schofield, eds. 1999. *The Cambridge History of Hellenistic Philosophy*. Cambridge: Cambridge University Press.
Allen, J. 2019. "Megara and Dialectic." In T. Bénatouïl and K. Ierodiakonou (eds.), *Dialectic after Plato and Aristotle*, 17–46. Cambridge: Cambridge University Press.
Allen, M. 2013. "Against 'Hybridity' in Genre Studies: Blending as an Alternative Approach to Generic Experimentation." *Trespassing Journal* 2: 3–21.
Altman, W. H. F. 2012. "Why Plato Wrote *Epinomis*: Leonardo Tarán and the Thirteenth Book of Plato's *Laws*." *Polis* 29: 83–107.
Amendola, D. 2017. "The Account of Demosthenes' Suicide in P.Berol. inv. 13045, B II." *ZPE* 204: 16–21.
Amendola, D. 2018. "A Ptolemaic 'Speculum Principis' in P.Berol. inv. 13045, A I–III?" In G. Roskam and S. Schorn (eds.), *Concepts of Ideal Rulership from Antiquity to the Renaissance*, 123–54. Turnhout: Brepols Publishers.
Anderson, G. 1993. *The Second Sophistic*. London: Routledge.
Annas, J. 1985. "Self-Knowledge in Early Plato." In D. J. O'Meara (ed.), *Platonic Investigations*, 111–38. Washington, D.C.: Catholic University of America Press.
Annas, J. 1989. "Cicero on Stoic Moral Philosophy and Private Property." In M. Griffin and J. Barnes (eds.), *Philosophia Togata I: Essays on Philosophy and Roman Society*, 151–73. Oxford: Clarendon Press.
Annas, J. 1994. "Plato the Skeptic." In P. A. Vander Waerdt (ed.), *The Socratic Movement*, 307–40. Ithaca and London: Cornell University Press.
Armstrong, D. 2008. "'Be Angry and Sin Not': Philodemus versus the Stoics on Natural Bites and Natural Emotions." In J. T. Fitzgerald (ed.), *Passions and Moral Progress in Greco-Roman Thought*, 79–121. London and New York: Routledge.
Armstrong, R. H. 2016. "A Wound, Not a World. Textual Survival and Transmission." In M. Hose and D. Schenker (eds.), *A Companion to Greek Literature*, 27–40. Malden and Oxford: Wiley-Blackwell.
Arnim, H. von, 1893. *De restituendo Philodemi de Rhetorica Lib. II*. Rostock: Typis Academicis Adleranis.
Aronadio, F. 2008. *Platone. Dialoghi spuri: Alcibiade primo, Alcibiade secondo, Ipparco, Amanti rivali, Teage, Definizioni, Sul giusto, Sulla virtù, Demodoco, Sisifo, Erissia, Assioco*. Turin: Unione Tipografico–Editrice Torinese.
Arrighetti, G., ed. 1964. *Satiro. Vita di Euripide*. Pisa: Libreria Goliardica Editrice.
Arrighetti, G., ed. 1973² [1960]. *Epicuro. Opere. Nuova edizione riveduta e ampliata*. Turin: Giulio Eindaudi.
Arrighetti, G. 1977. "Fra erudizione e biografia." *SCO* 26: 13–67.
Aucher, J.-B. 1822. *Philonis Judaei sermones tres hactenus inediti: I et II De Providentia et III De animalibus*. Venice: Typis Coenobii PP. Armenorum in insula S. Lazari.

Averintsev, S. 2001. "Genre as Abstraction and Genres as Reality: The Dialectics of Closure and Openness." *Arion* 9: 13–43.
Ax, W. 1991. "Timons Gang in die Unterwelt: Ein Beitrag zur Geschichte der antiken Literaturparodie." *Hermes* 119: 177–93.
Aygon, J.-P. 2002. "Le dialogue comme genre dans la rhetorique antique." *Pallas* 59: 197–208.
Bailly, J. 2004. *The Socratic Theages. Introduction, English Translation, Greek Text and Commentary*. Zürich: Georg Olms Verlag.
Baldwin, B. 2014. "Hell-Bent, Heaven-Sent. From Skyman to Pumpkin." In E. P. Cueva and S. N. Byrne (eds.), *A Companion to the Ancient Novel*, 159–79. Malden: Wiley-Blackwell.
Bandini, M. and L.-A. Dorion, eds. 2000a. *Xénophon Mémorables. Tome I–II*. Paris: Les Belles Lettres.
Bandini, M. and L.-A. Dorion, eds. 2000b. *Xénophon Mémorables. Tome I*. Paris: Les Belles Lettres.
Barclay, J. M. G. 2007. *Flavius Josephus, Against Apion. Translation and Commentary*. Leiden and Boston: Brill.
Barigazzi, A. 1959. "Il concetto del tempo nelle fisica atomistica." In *Epicurea in memoriam Hectoris Bignone. Miscellanea philologica*, 29–59. Genoa: Istituto di filologia classica.
Barker, A. 1989. *Greek Musical Writings. Vol. II: Harmonic and Acoustic Theory*. Cambridge: Cambridge University Press.
Barker, A. 2007. *The Science of Harmonics in Classical Greece*. Cambridge: Cambridge University Press.
Bar-Kochva, B. 2010. *The Image of the Jews in Greek Literature: The Hellenistic Period*. Berkeley and Los Angeles: University of California Press.
Barnes, J. 1987. "Editor's Notes." *Phronesis* 32: 360–6.
Barnes, J. 1989. "Antiochus of Ascalon." In M. T. Griffin and J. Barnes (eds.), *Philosophia Togata: Essays on Philosophy and Roman Society*, 51–96. Oxford: Clarendon Press.
Barnes, J. 1997. "Roman Aristotle." In J. Barnes and M. Griffin (eds.), *Philosophia Togata II: Plato and Aristotle in Rome*, 1–69. Oxford: Clarendon Press.
Bartol, K. 2007a. "Die Schwarzpappeln im Pseudohippokratischen Brief 17,2. Ein Versuch ihrer Deutung." *Eos* 94: 163–8.
Bartol, K. 2007b. *Pseudo-Hippokrates. O śmiechu Demokryta*. Gdańsk: słowo/obraz terytoria.
Bartoletti, V. 1959. "Un frammento di dialogo socratico." *SIFC* 31: 100–3.
Bastianini, G. 1992. "Diogenes Cynicus 8T." In *Corpus dei papiri filosofici greci e latini. Testi e lessico nei papiri di cultura greca e latina. Parte I: Autori noti. Vol. 1\*\**, 99–143. Florence: Leo S. Olschi.
Baumbach, M. and P. von Möllendorf. 2017. *Ein literarischer Prometheus. Lukian aus Samosata und die Zweite Sophistik*. Heidelberg: Universitätsverlag Winter.
Bernays, J. 1863. *Die Dialoge des Aristoteles im Verhältniss zu seinen übrigen Werken*. Berlin: Wilhelm Hertz.
Bett, R. 1997. *Sextus Empiricus. Against the Ethicists (Adversus Methematicos XI)*. Oxford: Clarendon Press.
Bett, R., ed. 2010. *The Cambridge Companion to Ancient Scepticism*. Cambridge: Cambridge University Press.
Bickel, E. 1904. "Ein Dialog aus der Akademie des Arkesilas." *AGPh* 17: 460–79.
Bignone, E. 1973² [1936]. *L'Aristotele perduto e la formazione filosofica di Epicuro. Vol. 1*. Florence: La Nuova Italia.
Billerbeck, M. 1979. *Der Kyniker Demetrius. Ein Beitrag zur Geschichte der Frühkaiserzeitlichen Popularphilosophie*. Leiden: Brill.

Blass, F. 1906. "Literarische Texte mit Ausschluss der christlichen." *APF* 3: 473–502.
Blomqvist, K. 1995. "Chryseis and Clea, Eumetis and the Interlocutress. Plutarch of Chaeronea and Dio Chrysostom on Women's Education." *Svensk exegetisk årsbok* 60: 173–90.
Blondell, R. 2002. *The Play of Character in Plato's Dialogues*. Cambridge: Cambridge University Press.
Bloom, A. 1987. "The Political Philosopher in Democratic Society: The Socratic View." In T. L. Pangle (ed.), *The Roots of Political Philosophy: Ten Forgotten Socratic Dialogues*, 32–52. Ithaca, NY: Agora Editions.
Bömer, F. 1953. "Der Commentarius: Zur Vorgeschichte und literarischen Form der Schriften Caesars." *Hermes* 81: 210–50.
Bompaire, J. 1958. *Lucien écrivain. Imitation et creation*. Paris: De Boccard.
Bos, A. P. 1989. *Cosmic and Meta-Cosmic Theology in Aristotle's Lost Dialogues*. Leiden and New York: Brill.
Bos, A. P. 2003. "Aristotle on the Etruscan Robbers: A Core Text of 'Aristotelian Dualism'." *JHPh* 41: 289–306.
Bosman, P. R. 2007. "King Meets Dog: The Origin of the Meeting between Alexander and Diogenes." *AClass.* 50: 51–63.
Bosman, P. R. 2010. "The Gymnosophists Riddle Contest (Berol. P. 13044): A Cynic Text?" *GRBS* 50: 175–92.
Bouchon, R. and B. Helly. 2015. "The Thessalian League." In H. Beck and P. Funke (eds.), *Federalism in Greek Antiquity*, 231–49. Cambridge: Cambridge University Press.
Bowe, G. S. 2007. "In Defense of Clitophon." *CPh* 102: 245–64.
Bowen, A. C. 1988. "On Interpreting Plato." In C. L. Griswold (ed.), *Platonic Writings/Platonic Readings*, 49–65, 275–7. London: Routledge and Kegan Paul.
Boyancé, P. 1934. "Sur l'*Abaris* d'Héraclide le Pontique." *REA* 36: 321–52.
Boys-Stones, G. R. 2016. "Providence and Religion in Middle Platonism." In E. Eidinow, J. Kindt, and R. Osborne (eds.), *Theologies of Ancient Religion*, 317–38. Cambridge: Cambridge University Press.
Brancacci, A. 1996. "Pericopi diogeniche in PVindob G 29946." *Elenchos* 17: 407–22.
Brancacci, A. 2004. "Il contributo dei papiri alla gnomica di tradizione cinica." In M. S. Funghi (ed.), *Aspetti di letteratura gnomica nel mondo antico. Vol. II*, 221–48. Florence: Leo S. Olschi.
Brancacci, A. 2005. "The Double Daimon in Euclides the Socratic." *Apeiron* 38: 143–54.
Brancacci, A. 2018. "Socratism and Eleaticism in Euclides of Megara." In A. Stavru and C. Moore (eds.), *Socrates and the Socratic Dialogue*, 161–78. Leiden and Boston: Brill.
Brandis, C. A. 1853. *Aristoteles: seine akademischen Zeitgenossen und nächsten Nachfolger*. Berlin: G. Reimer.
Brinkmann, A. 1891. *Quaestionum de dialogis Platoni falso addictis specimen*. Bonn: Typis Caroli Georgi Univ. Typogr.
Brisson, L. 2005. "*Epinomis*: Authenticity and Authorship." In K. Döring, M. Erler, and S. Schorn (eds.), *Pseudoplatonica. Akten des Kongresses zu den Pseudoplatonica vom 6.–9. Juli 2003 im Bamberg*, 9–24. Stuttgart: Franz Steiner Verlag.
Brisson, L. 2014. *Écrits attribués à Platon. Traduction et présentation par Luc Brisson*. Paris: Flammarion.
Brittain, C. 2001. *Philo of Larissa: The Last of the Academic Sceptics*. Oxford: Oxford University Press.
Brock, S. 2011. "The Commentator Probus: Problems of Date and Identity." In J. Lössl and J. W. Watt (eds.), *Interpreting the Bible and Aristotle in Antiquity. The Alexandrian Commentary Tradition between Rome and Baghdad*, 195–206. Farnham and Burlington: Ashgate.

Brodersen, K. 1994. "Hippokrates und Artaxerxes: Zu P.Oxy. 1184v, P. Berol.inv. 7094v und 21137v + 6934v." *ZPE* 102: 100–10.
Brown, T. S. 1949. *Onesicritus. A Study in Hellenistic Historiography*. Berkeley and Los Angeles: University of California Press.
Bruell, C. 1987. "On the Original Meaning of Political Philosophy: An Interpretation of Plato's *Lovers*." In T. L. Pangle (ed.), *The Roots of Political Philosophy: Ten Forgotten Socratic Dialogues*, 91–110. Ithaca, NY: Agora Editions.
Brun, P. 2000. *L'orateur Démade. Essai d'histoire et d'historiographie*. Bordeaux: Ausonius Éditions.
Brunschwig, J. 2004. *Papers in Hellenistic Philosophy*. Translated by Janet Lloyd. Cambridge: Cambridge University Press.
Bryan, J. 2012. "Pseudo-Dialogue in Plato's *Clitophon*." *Cambridge Classical Journal* 58: 1–22.
Burkert, W. 1960. "Platon oder Pythagoras? Zum Ursprung des Wortes 'Philosophie'." *Hermes* 88: 159–77.
Burkert, W. 1972. *Lore and Science in Ancient Pythagoreanism*, trans. E. L. Minar, Jr. Cambridge, MA: Harvard University Press.
Burstein, S. M. 1974. *Outpost of Hellenism: The Emergence of Heraclea on the Black Sea*. Berkeley: University of California Press.
Busine, A. 2002. *Les Sept Sages de la Grèce antique. Transmission et utilisation d'un patrimoine légendaire d'Hérodote à Plutarque*. Paris: De Boccard.
Bywater, I. 1869. "On a Lost Dialogue of Aristotle." *Journal of Philology* 2: 55–69.
Bywater, I. 1883. "The Cleophons in Aristotle." *Journal of Philology* 12: 17–30.
Capasso, M. 1988. *Carneisco. Il secondo libro del Filista (PHerc 1027)*. Naples: Bibliopolis.
Capelle, W. 1896. *De Cynicorum epistulis*. Göttingen: Jaenecke fratres Hannoverae.
Capuccino, C. and G. Iovine. 2019. "1137. Anonymous, *On Stilpon*." In J. H. Brusuelas, D. Obbink, and S. Schorn (eds.), *Die Fragmente der griechischen Historiker. IVA: Biography. Fascicle 8: Anonymous Papyri*, 429–45. Leiden: Brill.
Carlini, A. 1962. "Alcuni dialoghi pseudoplatonici e l'Accademia di Arcesilao." *ASNP* 31: 33–63.
Carlini, A. 1989. "PErlangen 7: Aeschines, Alcibiades (?)." In *Corpus dei papiri filosofici greci e latini. Testi e lessico nei papiri di cultura greca e latina. Parte I: Autori noti. Vol. 1\**, 147–8. Florence: Leo S. Olschi.
Carlini, A. 1995. "Commentarium in Platonis 'Phaedonem' (?)." In *Corpus dei papiri filosofici greci e latini. Testi e lessico nei papiri di cultura greca e latina. Parte III: Commentari*, 203–20. Florence: Leo S. Olschi.
Casadesús Bordoy, F. 2013. "On the Origin of the Orphic-Pythagorean Notion of the Immortality of the Soul." In G. Cornelli, R. McKirahan, and C. Macris (eds.), *On Pythagoreanism*, 153–76. Berlin and Boston: De Gruyter.
Cazzato, V. and E. E. Prodi. 2016. "Introduction. Continuity in the Sympotic Tradition." In V. Cazzato, D. Obbink, and E. E. Prodi (eds.), *The Cup of Song. Studies on Poetry and the Symposion*, 1–16. Oxford: Oxford University Press.
Chandler, C. 2006. *Philodemus, On Rhetoric. Books 1 and 2. Translation and Exegetical Essays*. New York and London: Routledge.
Charalabopoulos, N. G. 2012. *Platonic Drama and its Ancient Reception*. Cambridge: Cambridge University Press.
Chevalier, J. 1915. *Étude critique du dialogue pseudo-platonicien l'Axiochos sur la mort et sur l'immortalité de l'ame*. Paris: Librairie Félix Alcan.
Chiaradonna, R. 2011. "Interpretazione filosofica e ricezione del *corpus*. Il caso di Aristotele (100 a.C.–250 d.C.)." *Quaestio* 11: 82–114.

Chroust, A.-H. 1966a. "*Eudemus or On the Soul*: A Lost Dialogue of Aristotle on the Immortality of the Soul." *Mnemosyne* 19: 17–30.
Chroust, A.-H. 1966b. "The Psychology in Aristotle's Lost Dialogue *Eudemus or On the Soul*." *AClass*. 9: 49–62.
Chroust, A.-H. 1973. *Aristotle: New Light on his Life and on Some of his Lost Works. Vol. 1: Some Novel Interpretations of the Man and his Life*. London: Routledge and Kegan Paul.
Ciriello, S. and A. Stramaglia. 1998. "PSI VII 743 recto (Pack² 2100). Dialogo di Alessandro con i Ginnosofisti e testo giuridico romano non identificato." *APF* 44: 219–27.
Clauss, J. J. and M. Cuypers. 2010a. "Introduction." In J. J. Clauss and M. Cuypers (eds.), *A Companion to Hellenistic Literature*, 1–14. Malden and Oxford: Wiley-Blackwell.
Clauss, J. J. and M. Cuypers, eds. 2010b. *A Companion to Hellenistic Literature*. Malden and Oxford: Wiley-Blackwell.
Clay, D. 1998. *Paradosis and Survival. Three Chapters in the History of Epicurean Philosophy*. Ann Arbor: University of Michigan Press.
Clay, D. 2009. "The Athenian Garden." In J. Warren (ed.), *The Cambridge Companion to Epicureanism*, 9–28. Cambridge: Cambridge University Press.
Clayman, D. L. 2009. *Timon of Phlius. Pyrrhonism into Poetry*. Berlin and New York: De Gruyter.
Cobb, W. S. 1988. "Plato's *Minos*." *AncPhil* 8: 187–207.
Cohen, A. 2001. "Art, Myth, and Travel in the Hellenistic World." In S. E. Alcock, J. F. Cherry, and J. Elsner (eds.), *Pausanias: Travel and Memory in Roman Greece*, 93–126. Oxford: Oxford University Press.
Colella, L. C. 2013. "P.Schubart 4: ricontestualizzazione e nuova proposta di datazione." *Aegyptus* 93: 51–63.
Collard, C. and M. Cropp, eds. 2008. *Euripides: Fragments. Aegeus-Meleager*. Cambridge, MA: Harvard University Press.
Colson, F. H. 1941. *Philo. Volume IX*. Cambridge, MA and London: Harvard University Press.
Cooper, J. M. and D. S. Hutchinson (eds.) 1997. *Plato. Complete Works*. Indianapolis and Cambridge: Hackett Publishing Company.
Corradi, M. 2012. "Thucydides *adoxos* and Praxiphanes." In A. Martano, E. Matelli, and D. Mirhady (eds.), *Praxiphanes of Mytilene and Chamaeleon of Heraclea*, 495–523. New Brunswick and London: Transactions Publishers.
Cox, V. 1992. *The Renaissance Dialogue: Literary Dialogue in its Social and Political Contexts, Castiglione to Galileo*. Cambridge: Cambridge University Press.
Creese, D. 2010. *The Monochord in Ancient Greek Harmonic Science*. Cambridge: Cambridge University Press.
Cribiore, R. 1996. *Writing, Teachers, and Students in Graeco-Roman Egypt*. Atlanta: Scholars Press.
Crönert, W. 1903. "Literarische Texte mit Ausschluss der christlichen." *APF* 2: 337–81.
Crönert, W. 1906. *Kolotes und Menedemos. Texte und Untersuchungen zur Philosophen- und Literaturgeschichte*. Leipzig: Avenarius.
Cuypers, M. 2004. "Prince and Principle: The Philosophy of Callimachus' *Hymn to Zeus*." In M. A. Harder, R. F. Regtuit, and G. C. Wakker (eds.), *Callimachus II*, 95–115. Leuven and Paris: Peeters.
Cuypers, M. 2010. "Historiography, Rhetoric, and Science: Rethinking a Few Assumption on Hellenistic Prose." In J. J. Clauss and M. Cuypers (eds.), *A Companion to Hellenistic Literature*, 317–36. Malden and Oxford: Wiley-Blackwell.
Dalby, A. 1988. "The Wedding Feast of Caranus the Macedonian by Hippolochus." *Petits Propos Culinaires* 29: 37–45.

Dalby, A. 2000. "Lynceus and the Anecdotists.'" In D. Braund and J. Wilkins (eds.), *Athenaeus and his World: Reading Greek Culture in the Roman Empire*, 372-94. Exeter: University of Exeter Press.

Daris, S. 1972. "Papiri letterari dell' Università Cattolica di Milano." *Aegyptus* 52: 67-118.

Davidson, J. N. 1997. *Courtesans and Fishcakes. The Consuming Passions of Classical Athens*. London: Fontana Press.

De Falco, V. 1954² [1932]. *Demade oratore. Testimonianze e frammenti*. Naples: Libreria scientifica editrice.

De Giorgio, J.-P. 2015. "Auditeurs et personnages muets dans le dialogue: quelques remarques sur la définition d'un genre réinvesti à Rome." In S. Dubel and S. Gotteland (eds.), *Formes et genres du dialogue antique*, 107-26. Bordeaux: Ausonius Éditions.

Del Mastro, G. 2011. "PHerc. 1416, cr 5: tre pezzi del papiro Sul tempo (PHerc. 1413)." *CE* 41: 27-32.

Demetriou, K. 2000. "Reconsidering the Platonic *Cleitophon*." *Polis* 17: 133-60.

Deming, W. 2004² [1995]. *Paul on Marriage and Celibacy. The Hellenistic Background of 1 Corinthians 7*. Grand Rapids and Cambridge: William B. Eerdmans.

Denyer, N. ed. 2001. *Plato: Alcibiades*. Cambridge: Cambridge University Press.

De Sanctis, D. 2011. "ὦ φίλτατε: il destinario nelle opere del Giardino." *CE* 41: 217-30.

Desclos, M.-L. 2001. "L'interlocuteur anonyme dans les dialogues de Platon." In F. Cossuta and M. Narcy (eds.), *La forme dialogue chez Platon*, 69-97. Grenoble: Jérôme Millon.

Desmond, W. 2008. *Cynics*. Stocksfield: Acumen.

Des Places, É. 1931. "Sur l'authenticité de *l'Épinomis*." *REG* 44: 153-66.

Des Places, É. 1942. "Une nouvelle défense de *l'Épinomis*." *AC* 11: 97-102.

Des Places, É. 1952. "L'authenticité des *Lois* et de *l'Épinomis*." *AC* 21: 376-83.

Diels, H. 1888. "Zu Aristoteles' *Protreptikos* und Cicero's *Hortensius*." *AGPh* 1: 477-97.

Dihle, A. 1956. *Studien zur griechischen Biographie*. Göttingen: Vandenhoeck und Ruprecht.

Dillon, J. 1996² [1977]. *The Middle Platonists: 80 B.C. to A.D. 220. Revised Edition with a New Afterword*. Ithaca, NY: Cornell University Press.

Dillon, J. 2016. "The Reception of Aristotle in Antiochus and Cicero." In A. Falcon (ed.), *Brill's Companion to the Reception of Aristotle in Antiquity*, 183-201. Leiden and Boston: Brill.

Dillon, J. 2003. *The Heirs of Plato: A Study of the Old Academy (347-274 BC)*. Oxford: Oxford University Press.

Dillon, J. and J. Hershbell. 1991. *Iamblichus. On the Pythagorean Way of Life. Text, Translation, and Notes*. Atlanta: Scholars Press.

Dmitriev, S. 2016a. "Demades of Athens (227)." In I. Worthington (ed.), *Brill's New Jacoby*. Consulted online on September 1, 2020 <http://dx.doi.org/10.1163/1873-5363_bnj_a227>.

Dmitriev, S. 2016b. "Killing in Style. Demosthenes, Demades, and Phocion in Later Rhetorical Tradition." *Mnemosyne* 69: 931-54.

Dodds, E. R. 1959. *Plato: Gorgias. A Revised Text with Introduction and Commentary*. Oxford: Clarendon Press.

Donato, M. 2017. "Socrate e le vespe siracusane: epos e commedia nel proemio dell'*Erissia*." In M. Tulli (ed.), *Poesia e prosa di età ellenistica. In ricordo di Roberto Pretagostini*, 35-49. Pisa: Fabrizio Serra.

Donato, M. 2021. "Reshaping Socrates' Authority in the *Pseudoplatonica*." In R. Berardi, M. Filosa, and D. Massimo (eds.), *Defining Authorship, Debating Authenticity. Problems of Authority from Classical Antiquity to the Renaissance*, 205-21. Berlin and Boston: De Gruyter.

Dorandi, T. 1982. "Filodemo. Gli Stoici (PHerc. 155 e 339)." *CE* 12: 91–133.
Dorandi, T. 1991. *Storia dei filosofi. Platone e l'Academia (PHerc. 1021 e 164)*. Naples: Bibliopolis.
Dorandi, T. 1993. "La *Politeia* de Diogène de Sinope et quelques remarques sur sa pensée politique." In M.-O. Goulet-Cazé and R. Goulet (eds.), *Le cynisme ancien et ses prolongements. Actes du colloque international du CNRS (Paris, 22–25 juillet 1991)*, 57–68. Paris: Presses universitaires de France.
Dorandi, T. 1999. "Chronology." In K. Algra, J. Barnes, J. Mansfeld, and M. Schofield (eds.), *The Cambridge History of Hellenistic Philosophy*, 31–54. Cambridge: Cambridge University Press.
Dorandi, T. 2009. "La tradizione papirologica de Eraclide Pontico." In W. W. Fortenbaugh and E. Pender (eds.), *Heraclides of Pontus: A Discussion*, 1–25. New Brunswick: Transaction Publishers.
Dorandi, T. 2018. "Academic Philosophers (Fourth-First Century BCE)." In L. Perilli and D. P. Taormina (eds.), *Ancient Philosophy. Textual Paths and Historical Explorations*, 355–9. London and New York: Routledge.
Döring, K., ed. 1972. *Die Megariker. Kommentierte Sammlung der Testimonien*. Amsterdam: Verlag B. R. Grüner.
Döring, K. 2004. *Platon, Theages. Übersetzung und Kommentar*. Göttingen: Vandenhoeck & Ruprecht.
Döring, K. 2005. "Die Prodikos-Episode im pseudoplatonischen *Eryxias*." In K. Döring, M. Erler, and S. Schorn (eds.), *Pseudoplatonica. Akten des Kongresses zu den Pseudoplatonica vom 6.-9. Juli 2003 im Bamberg*, 69–79. Stuttgart: Franz Steiner Verlag.
Dörrie, H. 1987. *Der Platonismus in der Antike. Grundlagen–System–Entwicklung. Bd. 1: Die geschichtlichen Wurzeln des Platonismus*. Stuttgart-Bad Cannstatt: Frommann-Holzboog.
Douglas, A. E. 1995. "Form and Content in the *Tusculan Disputations*." In J. G. F. Powell (ed.), *Cicero the Philosopher. Twelve Papers*, 197–218. Oxford: Clarendon Press.
Dover, K. J. 1986. "Ion of Chios: His Place in the History of Greek Literature." In J. Boardman and C. E. Vaphopoulou-Richardson (eds.), *Chios: A Conference at the Homereion in Chios 1984*, 27–37. Oxford: Clarendon Press.
Dragona-Monachou, M. 1994. "Divine Providence in the Philosophy of the Empire." *ANRW* II 36.7: 4418–90.
Dubel, S. 2015. "Avant-propos: théories et pratiques du dialogue dans l'Antiquité." In S. Dubel and S. Gotteland (eds.), *Formes et genres du dialogue antique*, 11–23. Bordeaux: Ausonius Éditions.
Dubel, S. and S. Gotteland, eds. 2015. *Formes et genres du dialogue antique*. Bordeaux: Ausonius Éditions.
Dudley, D. R. 1937. *A History of Cynicism from Diogenes to the 6th Century A.D.* London: Methuen & Co.
Düring, I. 1951. *Chion of Heraclea. A Novel in Letters. Edited with Introduction and Commentary*. Göteborg: Wettergren & Kerbens.
Düring, I. 1957. *Aristotle in the Ancient Biographical Tradition*. Göteborg: Almqvist & Wiksell.
Düring, I. 1961. *Aristotle's Protrepticus. An Attempt at Reconstruction*. Göteborg.
Dyck, A. R. 1996. *A Commentary on Cicero, De Officiis*. Ann Arbor: University of Michigan Press.
Eberhart, H. 1935. *Mitteilungen aus der Papyrussammlung der Giessener Universitätsbibliothek. IV: Literarische Stücke*. Giessen: von Münchow.
Edwards, C. M. 1996. "Lysippos." In O. Palagia and J. J. Pollitt (eds.), *Personal Styles in Greek Sculpture. Yale Classical Studies 30*, 130–53. Cambridge: Cambridge University Press.

Edwards, W. M. 1929. "*ΔΙΑΛΟΓΟΣ, ΔΙΑΤΡΙΒΗ, ΜΕΛΕΤΗ*." In J. U. Powell and E. A. Barber (eds.), *New Chapters in the History of Greek Literature. Second Series. Some Recent Discoveries in Greek Poetry and Prose, Chiefly of the Fourth Century BC and Later Times*, 88–124. Oxford: Clarendon Press.

Ehrman, B. D. 2013. *Forgery and Counterforgery. The Use of Literary Deceit in Early Christian Polemics*. New York: Oxford University Press.

Eichholz, D. E. 1935. "The Pseudo-Platonic Dialogue *Eryxias*." *CQ* 29: 129–49.

Einarson, B. 1936. "Aristotle's *Protrepticus* and the Structure of the *Epinomis*." *TAPhA* 67: 261–85.

El Murr, D. 2018. "The Academy from Plato to Polemo." In L. Perilli and D. P. Taormina (eds.), *Ancient Philosophy. Textual Paths and Historical Explorations*, 337–54. London and New York: Routledge.

Emeljanow, V. E. 1967. *The Letters of Diogenes* (Diss.). Stanford.

Erler, M. 1994a. "Epikur." In H. Flashar (ed.), *Grundriss der Geschichte der Philosophie. Die Philosophie der Antike. Bd. 4: Die hellenistische Philosophie*, 29–202. Basel: Schwabe.

Erler, M. 1994b. "Die Schule Epikurs." In H. Flashar (ed.), *Grundriss der Geschichte der Philosophie. Die Philosophie der Antike. Bd. 4: Die hellenistische Philosophie*, 203–380. Basel: Schwabe.

Erler, M. 2008. "Dire il nuovo in modo vecchio e il vecchio in modo nuovo: gli spuria del *Corpus Platonicum* fra poetica e retorica ellenistica." In *Filologia, papirologia, storia dei testi. Giornate di studio in onore di Antonio Carlini, Udine 9–10 dicembre 2005*, 225–41. Pisa and Rome: Fabrizio Serra.

Erler, M. 2012. "Zur literarisch-philosophischen Einordnung des Dialogs." In *Ps.-Platon. Über den Tod*, 99–115. Tübingen: Mohr Siebeck.

Eshleman, K. 2007. "Affection and Affiliation: Social Networks and Conversion to Philosophy." *CJ* 103: 129–40.

Estes, D. 2013. *The Questions of Jesus in John: Logic, Rhetoric and Persuasive Discourse*. Leiden and Boston: Brill.

Fantham, E. 1979. "Ovid's Ceyx and Alcyone: The Metamorphosis of a Myth." *Phoenix* 33: 330–45.

Fantham, E. 2004. *The Roman World of Cicero's De Oratore*. Oxford: Oxford University Press.

Festugière, A.-J. 1937. "Sur une nouvelle édition du *De Vita Pythagorica* de Jamblique." *REG* 50(238): 470–94.

Festugière, A.-J. 1973. *Les trois "protreptiques" de Platon: Euthydème, Phédon, Epinomis*. Paris: J. Vrin.

Fine, G. 2013. "Meno's Paradox and the *Sisyphus*." *Proceedings of the Boston Area Colloquium in Ancient Philosophy* 28: 113–46.

Finkelberg, M. 2018. *The Gatekeeper: Narrative Voice in Plato's Dialogues*. Leiden and Boston.

Fitzgerald, J. T. and M. L. White. 1983. *The Tabula of Cebes*. Chico, CA: Scholars Press.

Flacelière, R. 1987. "Plutarque dans ses 'Oeuvres morales'." In *Plutarque. Oeuvres morales. Traités 1 et 2. Introduction générale* I.1, VII–CCXXV. Paris: Les Belles Lettres.

Flashar, H., ed. 1994. *Grundriss der Geschichte der Philosophie. Die Philosophie der Antike. Bd. 4: Die hellenistische Philosophie*. Basel: Schwabe.

Flashar, H. 2004² [1983]. "Aristoteles." In H. Flashar (ed.), *Grundriss der Geschichte der Philosophie. Die Philosophie der Antike. Bd. 3: Ältere Akademie, Aristoteles, Peripatos*, 175–457. Basel: Schwabe.

Föllinger, S. and G. M. Müller, eds. 2013. *Der Dialog in der Antike. Formen und Funktionen einer literarischen Gattung zwischen Philosophie, Wissensvermittlung und dramatischer Inszenierung*. Berlin and Boston: De Gruyter.
Ford, A. 2008. "The Beginnings of Dialogue. Socratic Discourses and Fourth-Century Prose." In S. Goldhill (ed.), *The End of Dialogue in Antiquity*, 29–44. Cambridge: Cambridge University Press.
Ford, A. 2010. "*ΣΩΚΡΑΤΙΚΟΙ ΛΟΓΟΙ* in Aristotle and Fourth-Century Theories of Genre." *CP* 105: 221–35.
Fortenbaugh, W. W. 1984. *Quellen zur Ethik Theophrasts*. Amsterdam: Verlag B. R. Grüner.
Fortenbaugh, W. W. 2011. *Theophrastus of Eresus: Commentary. Vol. 6.1: Sources on Ethics*. Leiden and Boston: Brill.
Fortenbaugh, W. W. 2012. "Chamaeleon on Pleasure and Drunkenness." In A. Martano, E. Matelli, and D. Mirhady (eds.), *Praxiphanes of Mytilene and Chamaeleon of Heraclea*, 359–86. New Brunswick and London: Transaction Publishers.
Fortenbaugh, W. W. 2014. *Theophrastus of Eresus: Commentary. Vol. 9.2: Sources on Discoveries and Beginnings, Proverbs et al. (Texts 727–741)*. Leiden and Boston: Brill.
Fortenbaugh, W. W., P. M. Huby, R. W. Sharples, and D. Gutas. 1992a. *Theophrastus of Eresus. Sources for his Life, Writings, Thought and Influence. Part One: Life, Writings, Various Reports, Logic, Physics, Metaphysics, Theology, Mathematics*. Leiden and New York: Brill.
Fortenbaugh, W. W., P. M. Huby, R. W. Sharples, and D. Gutas. 1992b. *Theophrastus of Eresus. Sources for his Life, Writings, Thought and Influence. Part Two: Psychology, Human Physiology, Living Creatures, Botany, Ethics, Religion, Politics, Rhetoric and Poetics, Music, Miscellanea*. Leiden and New York: Brill.
Fortenbaugh, W. W. and E. Pender, eds. 2009. *Heraclides of Pontus: A Discussion*. New Brunswick: Transaction Publishers.
Fowler, A. 1982. *Kinds of Literature. An Introduction to the Theory of Genres and Modes*. Cambridge, MA: Harvard University Press.
Fox, M. 2007. *Cicero's Philosophy of History*. New York: Oxford University Press.
Fox, M. 2009. "Heraclides of Pontus and the Philosophical Dialogue." In W. W. Fortenbaugh and E. Pender (eds.), *Heraclides of Pontus: A Discussion*, 41–68. New Brunswick: Transaction Publishers.
Fraser, P. M. 1970. "Eratosthenes of Cyrene." *PBA* 56: 175–207.
Frey, H. 1919. *Der ΒΙΟΣ ΕΥΡΙΠΙΔΟΥ des Satyros und seine literaturgeschichtliche Bedeutung* (Diss.). Gotha.
Frick, P. 1999. *Divine Providence in Philo of Alexandria*. Tübingen: Mohr Siebeck.
Friedländer, P. 1930. *Platon II: Die platonischen Schriften*. Berlin: De Gruyter.
Fritz, K. von, 1926. *Quellenuntersuchungen zu Leben und Philosophie des Diogenes von Sinope*. Leipzig: Dieteriech'sche Verlagsbuchhandlung.
Fritz, K. von, 1931. "Megariker." In *RE*, Suppl. 5: 707–24.
Fuentes González, P. P. 1998. *Les diatribes de Télès*. Paris: Vrin.
Fuentes González, P. P. 2013. "En defensa del encuentro entre dos Perros, Antístenes y Diógenes: historia de una tensa Amistad." *Estudios griegos e indoeuropeos* 23: 225–67.
Funghi, M. S. and A. Roselli. 1997. "Sul papiro Petrie 49e attribuito al 'De pietate' di Teofrasto. Riedizione di PLitLond 159a–b." In *Papiri filosofici. Miscellanea di studi I*, 49–69. Florence: Leo S. Olschi.
Furley, D. 1986. "Nothing to Us?" In M. Schofield and G. Striker (eds.), *The Norms of Nature. Studies in Hellenistic Ethics*, 75–91. Cambridge: Cambridge University Press.

Gaiser, K. 1985. "Ein Gespräch mit König Philipp: Zum 'Eudemos' des Aristoteles." In J. Wiesner (ed.), *Aristoteles—Werk und Wirkung. Paul Moraux gewidmet. Vol. 1*, 457–84. Berlin and New York: De Gruyter.

Gaiser, K. 1988. *Philodems Academica. Die Berichte über Platon und die Alte Akademie in zwei herkulanischen Papyri.* Stuttgart-Bad Cannstatt: Frommann-Holzboog.

Gallo, I. 1980. *Frammenti biografici da papiri. Volume secondo: La biografia dei filosofi.* Rome: Edizioni dell' Ateneo et Bizzarri.

Gallo, I. 1998. "Forma letteraria nei 'Moralia' di Plutarco: Aspetti e problemi." *ANRW* II.34.4: 3511–40.

Gallo, I. 1999. "Socrates 3T." In *Corpus dei papiri filosofici greci e latini. Testi e lessico nei papiri di cultura greca e latina. Parte I: Autori noti. Vol. 1\*\*\**, 720–53. Florence: Leo S. Olschi.

Gerson, L. P. 2005. *Aristotle and Other Platonists.* Ithaca and London: Cornell University Press.

Gerstinger, H. 1916. "Satyros' ΒΙΟΣ ΕΥΡΙΠΙΔΟΥ." *WS* 38: 54–71.

Geus, K. 2002. *Eratosthenes von Kyrene. Studien zur hellenistischen Kultur- und Wissenschaftsgeschichte.* Munich: C. H. Beck.

Giannantoni, G. 1990a. *Socratis et Socraticorum Reliquiae. Volumen I.* Naples: Bibliopolis.

Giannantoni, G. 1990b. *Socratis et Socraticorum Reliquiae. Volumen II.* Naples: Bibliopolis.

Giannantoni, G. 1990c. *Socratis et Socraticorum Reliquiae. Volumen IV.* Naples: Bibliopolis.

Giannantoni, G. 1993. "Antistene fondatore della scuola cinica?" In M.-O. Goulet-Cazé and R. Goulet (eds.), *Le cynisme ancien et ses prolongements. Actes du colloque international du CNRS (Paris, 22–25 juillet 1991)*, 15–35. Paris: Presses universitaires de France.

Gigante, M. 1948. "Il frammento fiorentino di un dialogo politico." *Aegyptus* 28: 195–8.

Gigante, M. 1949. "Ancora sul frammento fiorentino di un dialogo politico." *Aegyptus* 29: 51–5.

Gigon, O. 1953. *Kommentar zum ersten Buch von Xenophons Memorabilien.* Basel: Verlag Friedrich Reinhardt.

Gigon, O. 1955. review: "Marion Soreth, Der platonische Dialog *Hippias maior*." Munich, Beck 1953." *Gnomon* 27: 14–20.

Gigon, O. 1959. "Cicero und Aristoteles." *Hermes* 87: 143–62.

Gigon, O. 1960. "Prolegomena to an Edition of the *Eudemus*." In I. Düring and G. E. L. Owen (eds.), *Aristotle and Plato in the Mid-Fourth Century. Papers of the Symposium Aristotelicum held at Oxford in August 1957*, 19–33. Göteborg: Elanders.

Gigon, O. 1973. "Die Dialoge des Aristoteles." *EEAth* 24: 178–205.

Gigon, O. ed. 1987. *Aristotelis Opera. Vol. III: Librorum deperditorum fragmenta.* Berlin and New York: De Gruyter.

Gildenhard, I. 2007. *Paideia Romana. Cicero's Tusculan Disputations.* Cambridge: Cambridge Philological Society.

Giorgi, M. C. de, 1995. "Papiri greci di argomento musicale: status e prospettive di ricerca." In M. Capasso (ed.), *Atti del V seminario internazionale di papirologia. Lecce 27–29 giugno 1994*, 247–54. Lecce: Congedo Editore.

Glucker, J. 1978. *Antiochus and the Late Academy.* Göttingen: Vandenhoeck & Ruprecht.

Glucker, J. 1988. "Cicero's Philosophical Affiliations." In J. M. Dillon and A. A. Long (eds.), *The Question of "Eclecticism". Studies in Later Greek Philosophy*, 34–69. Berkeley and Los Angeles: University of California Press.

Goldhill, S., ed. 2008. *The End of Dialogue in Antiquity.* Cambridge: Cambridge University Press.

Gomperz, T. 1877. "Marginalien." *RhM* 32: 475–8.

Gordon, P. 1996. *Epicurus in Lycia. The Second-Century World of Diogenes of Oenoanda.* Ann Arbor: The University of Michigan Press.

Görgemanns, H. 1997. "Dialog." In H. Cancik, H. Schneider, and M. Landfester (eds.), *Der Neue Pauly. Enzyklopädie der Antike. Bd. 3*, 517–21. Stuttgart and Weimar: Metzler Verlag.

Görler, W. 1994. "Älterer Pyrrhonismus. Jüngere Akademie. Antiochos aus Askalon." In H. Flashar (ed.), *Grundriss der Geschichte der Philosophie. Die Philosophie der Antike. Bd. 4: Die hellenistische Philosophie*, 717–989. Basel: Schwabe.

Görler, W. 1995. "Silencing the Troublemaker: *De Legibus* I 39 and the Continuity of Cicero's Scepticism." In J. G. F. Powell (ed.), *Cicero the Philosopher. Twelve Papers*, 85–113. Oxford: Clarendon Press.

Gorman, R. 2005. *The Socratic Method in the Dialogues of Cicero.* Stuttgart: Franz Steiner Verlag.

Gorteman, C. 1958. "Un fragment du Περὶ εὐσεβείας de Théophraste dans le P.Petrie II 49e?" *CE* 33: 79–101.

Gottschalk, H. B. 1980a. *Heraclides of Pontus.* Oxford: Clarendon Press.

Gottschalk, H. B. 1980b. "Varro and Ariston of Chios." *Mnemosyne* 33: 359–62.

Gottschalk, H. B. 1982. "Diatribe Again." *LCM* 7.6: 91–2.

Gottschalk, H. B. 1983. "More on ΔΙΑΤΡΙΒΑΙ." *LCM* 8.6: 91–2.

Gottschalk, H. B. 1987. "Aristotelian Philosophy in the Roman World from the Time of Cicero to the End of the Second Century AD." *ANRW* II 36.2: 1079–1174.

Goulet-Cazé, M.-O. 1996. "Who Was the First Dog?" In R. B. Branham and M.-O. Goulet-Cazé (eds.), *The Cynics: The Cynic Movement in Antiquity and its Legacy*, 414–15. Berkeley and Los Angeles: University of California Press.

Goulet-Cazé, M.-O. 2003. *Les kynica du stoïcisme.* Stuttgart: Franz Steiner Verlag.

Gow, A. S. F., ed. 1965. *Machon. The Fragments. Edited with an Introduction and Commentary.* Cambridge: Cambridge University Press.

Grafton, A., G. W. Most, and S. Settis, eds. 2010. *The Classical Tradition.* Cambridge, MA: Harvard University Press.

Graver, M. 2002. *Cicero on the Emotions. Tusculan Disputations 3 and 4.* Chicago and London: The University of Chicago Press.

Gray, V. J. 1998. *The Framing of Socrates: The Literary Interpretation of Xenophon's Memorabilia.* Stuttgart: Franz Steiner Verlag.

Graziosi, B. 2002. *Inventing Homer. The Early Reception of Epic.* Cambridge: Cambridge University Press.

Greatrex, G. and H. Elton, eds. 2015. *Shifting Genres in Late Antiquity.* Farnham: Ashgate.

Grenfell, B. P. and A. S. Hunt. 1904. *The Oxyrhynchus Papyri. Part IV.* London: Egypt Exploration Society.

Griffiths, J. G. 1965. "A Translation from the Egyptian by Eudoxus." *CQ* 15: 75–8.

Gronewald, M. 1985. "205. Sokratischer Dialog." In M. Gronewald, K. Maresch, and W. Schäfer (eds.), *Kölner Papyri (P.Köln). Bd. 5*, 33–53. Wiesbaden: Springer Fachmedien.

Gruen, E. 2008. "The Letter of Aristeas and the Cultural Context of the Septuagint." In M. Karrer and W. Kraus (eds.), *Die Septuaginta—Texte, Kontexte, Lebenswelten: Internationale Fachtagung veranstaltet von Septuaginta Deutsch (LXX.D), Wuppertal 20.–23. Juli 2006*, 134–56. Tübingen: Mohr Siebeck.

Guardasole, A., ed. 1997. *Eraclide di Taranto. Frammenti. Testo critico, introduzione, traduzione e commentario.* Naples: D'Auria.

Gutschmid, A. von, 1893. "Vorlesungen über Josephos' Bücher gegen Apion." In A. von Gutschmid, *Kleine Schriften. Vol. IV*, 336–589. Leipzig: Teubner.

Gutzwiller, K. 1998. "Meleager: From Menippean to Epigrammatist." In M. A. Harder, R. F. Regtuit, and G. C. Wakker (eds.), *Genre in Hellenistic Poetry*, 81–93. Groningen: Egbert Forsten.

Gutzwiller, K. 2007. *A Guide to Hellenistic Literature*. Malden and Oxford: Blackwell.

Haake, M. 2013. "Illustrating, Documenting, Making-Believe: The Use of Psephismata in Hellenistic Biographies of Philosophers." In P. Liddel and P. Low (eds.), *Inscriptions and their Uses in Greek and Latin Literature*, 79–124. Oxford: Oxford University Press.

Habicht, C. 1994. "Hellenistic Athens and her Philosophers." In *Athen in hellenistischer Zeit. Gesammelte Aufsätze*, 231–47. Munich: C. H. Beck.

Hahn, D. 1990. "The Ethical Doxography of Arius Didymus." *ANRW* II 36.4: 2935–3055.

Hahn, D. 2006. "In Search of Aristo of Ceos." In W. W. Fortenbaugh and S. A. White (eds.), *Aristo of Ceos. Text, Translation, and Discussion*, 179–215. New Brunswick and London: Transaction Publishers.

Halbauer, O. 1911. *De diatribis Epicteti*. Leipzig: Robert Noske.

Hankinson, R. J. 2019. "The Laughing Philosopher and the Physician: Laughter, Diagnosis, and Therapy in Greek Medicine." In P. Destrée and F. V. Trivigno (eds.), *Laughter, Humor, and Comedy in Ancient Philosophy*, 52–79. Oxford: Oxford University Press.

Haslam, M. W. 1983. "3544. Philosophical Dialogue (Heraclides Ponticus, περὶ ἀρχῆς?)." In *The Oxyrhynchus Papyri*. Vol. L, 93–9. London: Egypt Exploration Society.

Haslam, M. W. 1986. "3699. Philosophical Dialogue." In *The Oxyrhynchus Papyri*. Vol. LIII, 15–23. London: Egypt Exploration Society.

Haslam, M. W. 1992. "Heraclides Ponticus. 1: de imperio (?)." In *Corpus dei papiri filosofici greci e latini. Testi e lessico nei papiri di cultura greca e latina. Parte I: Autori noti*. Vol. 1\*\*, 199–214. Florence: Leo S. Olschi.

Hatzimichali, M. 2016. "Andronicus of Rhodes and the Construction of the Aristotelian Corpus." In A. Falcon (ed.), *Brill's Companion to the Reception of Aristotle in Antiquity*, 81–100. Leiden and Boston: Brill.

Heath, M. 2009. "Heraclides of Pontus on Homer." In W. W. Fortenbaugh and E. Pender (eds.), *Heraclides of Pontus: Discussion*, 251–72. New Brunswick: Transaction Publishers.

Heldmann, K. 1982. *Antike Theorien über Entwicklung und Verfall der Redekunst*. Munich: C. H. Beck.

Hense, O. 1909² [1889]. *Teletis reliquiae*. Tübingen: I. C. B. Mohr (P. Siebeck).

Hersant, Y. 1989. *Hippocrate. Sur le rire et la folie*. Paris: Éditions Rivages.

Hershbell, J. P., ed. 1981. *Pseudo-Plato, Axiochus*. Chico, CA: Scholars Press.

Hiller, E. 1870. "Der Πλατωνικός des Eratosthenes." *Philologus* 30: 60–72.

Hirzel, R. 1876. "Über den *Protreptikos* des Aristoteles." *Hermes* 10: 61–100.

Hirzel, R. 1882. *Untersuchungen zu Cicero's philosophischen Schriften. Zweiter Theil: De finibus, De officiis*. Leipzig: Verlag von S. Hirzel.

Hirzel, R. 1895a. *Der Dialog. Ein Literarhistorischer Versuch. Erster Theil*. Leipzig: Verlag von S. Hirzel.

Hirzel, R. 1895b. *Der Dialog. Ein Literarhistorischer Versuch. Zweiter Theil*. Leipzig: Verlag von S. Hirzel.

Hobden, F. 2013. *The Symposion in Ancient Greek Society and Thought*. Cambridge: Cambridge University Press.

Hoffmann, P. 2016. "La philosophie grecque sur les bords de l'Oxus: un réexamen du papyrus d'Aï Khanoum." In J. Jouanna, V. Schiltz, and M. Zink (eds.), *La Grèce dans les profondeurs de l'Asie. Actes du XXVIe colloque de la Villa Kérylos, 9 et 10 octobre 2015*, 165–232. Paris: Académie des Inscriptions et Belles-Lettres.

Holzberg, N. 1994. "Der griechische Briefroman: Versuch einer Gattungstypologie." In N. Holzberg (ed.), *Der griechische Briefroman: Gattungstypologie und Textanalyse*, 1–52. Tübingen: Gunter Narr Verlag.
Holzhausen, J. 1994. "Menon in Platons *Menon*." *WJA* 20: 129–49.
Honigman, S. 2003. *The Septuagint and Homeric Scholarship in Alexandria. A Study in the Narrative of the Letter of Aristeas*. London and New York: Routledge.
Hooff, A. J. L. van, 1990. *From Autothanasia to Suicide. Self-Killing in Classical Antiquity*. London: Routledge.
Hook, L. van, 1917. "Ψυχρότης ἢ τὸ ψυχρόν." *CP* 12: 68–76.
Horky, P. S. 2009. "Persian Cosmos and Greek Philosophy: Plato's Associates and the Zoroastrian Magoi." *OSAP* 37: 47–103.
Hornblower, S. 2011⁴ [1983]. *The Greek World 479–323*. London and New York: Routledge.
Hösle, V. 2006. *Der philosophische Dialog. Eine Poetik und Hermeneutik*. Munich: C. H. Beck.
Huffman, C. A. 2005. *Archytas of Tarentum, Pythagorean, Philosopher and Mathematician King*. New York: Cambridge University Press.
Huffman, C. A. 2012. "Aristoxenus' *Life of Socrates*." In C. A. Huffman (ed.), *Aristoxenus of Tarentum. Discussion*, 251–81. New Brunswick and London: Transaction Publishers.
Hunter, R. and D. A. Russell. 2011. *Plutarch: How to Study Poetry*. Cambridge: Cambridge University Press.
Hutchinson, D. S. and M. R. Johnson, 2018. "Protreptic and Apotreptic: Aristotle's Dialogue *Protrepticus*." In O. Alieva, A. Kotzé, and S. Van der Meeren (eds.), *When Wisdom Calls. Philosophical Protreptic in Antiquity*, 111–54. Turnhout: Brepols.
Hutchinson, G. O. 2014. "Hellenistic Poetry and Hellenistic Prose." In R. Hunter, A. Rengakos, and E. Sistakou (eds.), *Hellenistic Studies at a Crossroads. Exploring Texts, Contexts and Metatexts*, 31–51. Berlin and Boston: De Gruyter.
Ioppolo, A. M. 1980. "Carneade e il terzo libro delle 'Tusculanae'." *Elenchos* 1: 76–91.
Irwin, E. 2015. "The Platonic *Axiochus*: The Politics of Not Fearing Death in 406." In S. Dubel and S. Gotteland (eds.), *Formes et genres du dialogue antique*, 63–85. Bordeaux: Ausonius Éditions.
Isnardi Parente, M. ed. 1980. *Speusippo. Frammenti*. Naples: Bibliopolis.
Isnardi Parente, M. ed. 1982. *Senocrate-Ermodoro. Frammenti*. Naples: Bibliopolis.
Isnardi Parente, M. 1992. "Il papiro filosofico di Aï Khanoum." In *Studi su codici e papiri filosofici. Platone, Aristotele, Ierocle*, 169–88. Florence: Leo S. Olschi.
Jacquemin, A. and D. Laroche. 2001. "Le monument de Daochos ou le trésor des Thessaliens." *BCH* 125: 305–32.
Jaeger, W. 1923. *Aristoteles. Grundlegung einer Geschichte seiner Entwicklung*. Berlin: Weidmannsche Buchhandlung.
Jaeger, W. 1948² [1934]. *Aristotle. Fundamentals of the History of his Development*. Oxford: Clarendon Press.
Janko, R. 1992. *The Iliad: A Commentary. Vol. IV: Books 13–16*. Cambridge: Cambridge University Press.
Jażdżewska, K. 2013. "A Skeleton at a Banquet: Death in Plutarch's *Convivium Septem Sapientium*." *Phoenix* 67: 301–19.
Jażdżewska, K. 2014. "From *Dialogos* to Dialogue: The Use of the Term from Plato to the Second Century CE." *GRBS* 54: 17–36.
Jażdżewska, K. 2015a. "Dialogic Format of Philo of Alexandria's *De animalibus*." *Eos* 102: 45–56.

Jażdżewska, K. 2015b. "Dio Chrysostom's *Charidemus* and Aristotle's *Eudemus*." *GRBS* 55: 679–87.
Jażdżewska, K. 2015c. "Like a Married Woman". The Kingfisher in Plutarch's *De sollertia animalium* and in the Ps.-Platonic *Halcyon*." *Mnemosyne* 68: 424–36.
Jażdżewska, K. 2018. "Indications of Speakers in Ancient Dialogue: A Reappraisal." *JHS* 138: 249–60.
Jażdżewska, K. 2020. "Still Noon in Plato's *Phaedrus* (and in Heraclides of Pontus)." *GRBS* 60: 61–7.
Jennings, V. and A. Katsaros, 2007. "Introduction." In V. Jennings and A. Katsaros (eds.), *The World of Ion of Chios*, 1–14. Leiden and Boston: Brill.
Jocelyn, H. D. 1982. "Diatribes and Sermons." *LCM* 7.1: 3–7.
Jocelyn, H. D. 1983. "'Diatribes' and the Greek Book-Title Διατριβαί." *LCM* 8.6: 89–91.
Joly, R. 1963. *Le Tableau de Cébès et la philosophie religieuse*. Brussels-Berchem: Latomus.
Jong, I. J. F. de, 2004. "Introduction. Narratological Theory on Narrators, Narratees, and Narratives." In I. de Jong, R. Nünlist, and A. M. Bowie (eds.), *Narrators, Narratees, and Narratives in Ancient Greek Literature: Studies in Ancient Greek Narrative*, 1–10. Leiden and Boston: Brill.
Jonge, C. C. de, 2014. "The Attic Muse and the Asian Harlot: Classicizing Allegories in Dionysius and Longinus." In J. Ker and C. Pieper (eds.), *Valuing the Past in the Greco-Roman World. Proceedings from the Penn-Leiden Colloquia on Ancient Values VII*, 388–409. Leiden and Boston: Brill.
Joyal, M. 1993. "A Lost Plutarchean Philosophical Work." *Philologus* 137: 92–103.
Joyal, M. 2000. *The Platonic Theages: An Introduction, Commentary and Critical Edition*. Stuttgart: Franz Steiner Verlag.
Joyal, M. 2005. "Socrates as σοφὸς ἀνήρ in the *Axiochus*." In K. Döring, M. Erler, and S. Schorn (eds.), *Pseudoplatonica. Akten des Kongresses zu den Pseudoplatonica vom 6.-9. Juli 2003 im Bamberg*, 97–117. Stuttgart: Franz Steiner Verlag.
Joyal, M. 2014. "'Genuine' and 'Bastard' Dialogues in the Platonic Corpus: An Inquiry into the Origins and Meaning of a Concept." In J. Martinez (ed.), *Fakes and Forgers of Classical Literature. Ergo Decipiatur!*, 73–93. Leiden and Boston: Brill.
Joyal, M. 2016. "Problems and Interpretation in the Platonic *Theages*." *WS* 129, 93–154.
Joyal, M. 2019. "What Is Socratic about the Pseudo-Platonica?" In C. Moore (ed.), *Brill's Companion to the Reception of Socrates*, 211–36. Leiden and Boston: Brill.
Kallet, L. 2001. *Money and the Corrosion of Power in Thucydides: The Sicilian Expedition and its Aftermath*. Berkeley: University of California Press.
Kassel, R. 1958. *Untersuchungen zur griechischen und römischen Konsolationsliteratur*. Munich: C. H. Beck.
Kassel, R. 1987. *Die Abgrenzung des Hellenismus in der griechischen Literaturgeschichte*. Berlin: De Gruyter.
Keesling, C. M. 2017. *Early Greek Portraiture. Monuments and Histories*. Cambridge: Cambridge University Press.
Kennedy, J. B. 2010. "Plato's Forms, Pythagorean Mathematics, and Stichometry." *Apeiron* 43: 1–31.
Kim, L. 2014. "Archaizing and Classicism in the Literary Historical Thinking of Dionysius of Halicarnassus." In J. Ker and C. Pieper (eds.), *Valuing the Past in the Greco-Roman World. Proceedings from the Penn-Leiden Colloquia on Ancient Values VII*, 357–87. Leiden and Boston: Brill.
Kindstrand, J. F. 1976. *Bion of Borysthenes. A Collection of the Fragments with Introduction and Commentary*. Uppsala: Almqvist & Wiksell.

Kindstrand, J. F. 1980. "Demetrius the Cynic." *Philologus* 124: 83-98.
Kingsley, P. 1995. "Meeting with Magi: Iranian Themes among the Greeks, from Xanthus of Lydia to Plato's Academy." *Journal of the Royal Asiatic Society* 5: 173-209.
Klein, J. 1965. *A Commentary on Plato's Meno*. Chapel Hill: The University of North Carolina Press.
Knöbl, R. 2010. "Talking about Euripides: Paramimesis and Satyrus' *Bios Euripidou*." *Phrasis* 51: 37-58.
Koester, H. 1989. "From the Kerygma-Gospel to Written Gospels." *New Testament Studies* 35: 361-81.
König, J. 2012. *Saints and Symposiasts. The Literature of Food and the Symposium in Greco-Roman and Early Christian Culture*. Cambridge: Cambridge University Press.
Körte, A. 1890. *Metrodori Epicurei fragmenta*. Leipzig: Teubner.
Körte, A. 1932. "Literarische Texte mit Ausschluss der christlichen." *APF* 10: 217-37.
Körte, A. 1939. "Literarische Texte mit Ausschluss der christlichen." *APF* 13: 78-132.
Krämer, H. 2004² [1983]. "Die Ältere Akademie." In H. Flashar (ed.), *Grundriss der Geschichte der Philosophie. Die Philosophie der Antike. Bd. 3: Ältere Akademie, Aristoteles, Peripatos*, 1-165. Basel: Schwabe.
Kremer, M. ed. 2004a. *Plato's Cleitophon. On Socrates and the Modern Mind*. Lanham: Lexington Books.
Kremer, M. 2004b. "Interpretive Essay: Socratic Philosophy and the *Cleitophon*." In M. Kremer (ed.), *Plato's Cleitophon. On Socrates and the Modern Mind*, 17-40. Lanham: Lexington Books.
Krevans, N. and A. Sens. 2006. "Language and Literature." In G. R. Bugh (ed.), *The Cambridge Companion to the Hellenistic World*, 186-207. Cambridge: Cambridge University Press.
Kuhlmann, P. A. 1994. *Die Giessener Literarischen Papyri und die Caracalla-Erlasse. Edition, Übersetzung und Kommentar*. Giessen: Universitätsbibliothek.
Kuiper, K. 1901. "De Crantoris fragmentis moralibus." *Mnemosyne* 29: 341-62.
Kupreeva, I. 2009. "Heraclides' *On Soul* (?) and its Ancient Readers." In W. W. Fortenbaugh and E. Pender (eds.), *Heraclides of Pontus: Discussion*, 93-138. New Brunswick: Transaction Publishers.
Kurke, L. 2002. "Gender, Politics and Subversion in the *Chreiai* of Machon." *PCPhS* 48: 20-65.
Kurke, L. 2011. *Aesopic Conversations: Popular Tradition, Cultural Dialogue, and the Invention of Greek Prose*. Princeton and Oxford: Princeton University Press.
Lampe, K. 2015. *The Birth of Hedonism. The Cyrenaic Philosophers and Pleasure as a Way of Life*. Princeton: Princeton University Press.
Lang, P. 1911. *De Speusippi Academici scriptis. Accedunt fragmenta*. Bonn: Typis C. Georgi.
Lapini, W. 1996. *Il POxy. 664 di Eraclide Pontico e la cronologia dei Cipselidi*. Florence: Leo S. Olschi.
Larson, S. 2000. "Boiotia, Athens, and Peisistratids, and the *Odyssey*'s Catalogue of Heroines." *GRBS* 41: 193-222.
Lasserre, F. 1966. *Eudoxos von Knidos. Die Fragmente*. Berlin.
Laurenti, R. 1987a. *Aristotele. I frammenti dei dialoghi. Vol. 1*. Naples: Luigi Loffredo.
Laurenti, R. 1987b. *Aristotele. I frammenti dei dialoghi. Vol. 2*. Naples: Luigi Loffredo.
Laurenti, R. 2003. "Aristote de Stagire. Les 'dialogues'." In R. Goulet (ed.), *Dictionnaire des philosophes antiques. Supplément*, 379-471. Paris: CNRS Éditions.
Lavelle, B. M. 1985. "Hipparchos' Herms." *EMC* 29: 411-20.
Lefkowitz, M. R. 1979. "The Euripides Vita." *GRBS* 20: 187-210.

Lefkowitz, M. R. 1981. *The Life of the Greek Poets*. London: Duckworth.
Lefkowitz, M. R. 1984. "Satyrus the Historian." In *Atti del XVII Congresso Internazionale di Papirologia, 19-26 maggio 1983. Vol. 2*, 339-43. Naples: Centro Internazionale per lo Studio dei Papiri Ercolanesi.
Lenaerts, J. 2009. "La souris et la belette d'après le P.Vindob. G 29813 + 29814." *CE* 84: 239-46.
Leo, F. 1912. "Satyros βίος Εὐριπίδου." *NAWG*: 273-90.
Lerner, J. D. 2003a. "The Aï Khanoum Philosophical Papyrus." *ZPE* 142: 45-51.
Lerner, J. D. 2003b. "Correcting the Early History of Āy Kānom." *Archäologische Mitteilungen aus Iran und Turan* 35-6: 373-410.
Leunissen, M. 2017. *From Natural Character to Moral Virtue in Aristotle*. Oxford: Oxford University Press.
LeVen, P. A. 2014. *The Many-Headed Muse: Tradition and Innovation in Late Classical Greek Lyric Poetry*. Cambridge: Cambridge University Press.
Lewis, L. C. St. A. 1921. "Satyrus's *Life of Euripides*." In J. U. Powell and E. A. Barber (eds.), *New Chapters in the History of Greek Literature. Recent Discoveries in Greek Poetry and Prose of the Fourth and Following Centuries B.C.* Oxford: Clarendon Press.
Lewy, H. 1938. "Aristotle and the Jewish Sage according to Clearchus of Soli." *HThR* 31: 205-35.
Lindenberger, J. 1983. *The Aramaic Proverbs of Ahiqar*. Baltimore and London: Johns Hopkins University Press.
Lloyd-Jones, H. and P. J. Parsons. 1983. *Supplementum Hellenisticum*. Berlin and New York: De Gruyter.
Long, A. A. $1986^2$ [1974]. *Hellenistic Philosophy: Stoics, Epicureans, Sceptics*. Berkeley and Los Angeles: University of California Press.
Long, A. A. 1995. "Cicero's Plato and Aristotle." In J. G. F. Powell (ed.), *Cicero the Philosopher. Twelve Papers*, 37-61. Oxford: Clarendon Press.
Long, A. A. 2006. *From Epicurus to Epictetus. Studies in Hellenistic and Roman Philosophy*. Oxford: Oxford University Press.
Longo Auricchio, F. 1977. Φιλοδήμου Περὶ ῥητορικῆς. *Libri primum et secundum*. Naples: Giannini.
Luz, M. 2014. "The Erlangen Papyrus 4 and its Socratic Origins," *International Journal of the Platonic Tradition* 8: 161-91.
Magris, A. 1992. "Der 'Zweite Alkibiades.' Ein Wendepunkt in der Geschichte der Akademie." *GB* 18: 47-64.
Maisonneuve, C. 2007. "Les 'fragments' de Xénophon dans les *Deipnosophistes*." In D. Lenfant (ed.), *Athénée et les fragments d'historiens. Actes du colloque de Strasbourg (16-18 juin 2005)*, 73-106. Paris: De Boccard.
Malherbe, A. J. 1977. *The Cynic Epistles. A Study Edition*. Atlanta: SBL.
Mannebach, E. 1961. *Aristippi et Cyrenaicorum fragmenta*. Leiden: Brill.
Männlein-Robert, I. 2005. "Zur literarischen Inszenierung eines Philosophiekonzeptes in den pseudoplatonischen *Anterastai*." In K. Döring, M. Erler, and S. Schorn (eds.), *Pseudoplatonica. Akten des Kongresses zu den Pseudoplatonica vom 6.-9. Juli 2003 im Bamberg*, 119-33. Stuttgart: Franz Steiner Verlag.
Männlein-Robert, I. 2012. "Einführung in die Schrift." In *Ps.-Platon. Über den Tod*, 3-41. Tübingen: Mohr Siebeck.
Mansfeld, J. 1994. *Prolegomena. Questions to be Settled before the Study of an Author, or a Text*. Leiden and New York: Brill.

Manuwald, B. 2005. "Zum pseudoplatonischen Charakter des *Minos*. Beobachtungen zur Dialog- und Argumentationsstruktur." In K. Döring, M. Erler, and S. Schorn (eds.), *Pseudoplatonica. Akten des Kongresses zu den Pseudoplatonica vom 6.-9. Juli 2003 im Bamberg*, 135–53. Stuttgart: Franz Steiner Verlag.

Martano, A., E. Matelli, and D. Mirhady, eds. 2012. *Praxiphanes of Mytilene and Chamaeleon of Heraclea*. New Brunswick and London: Transaction Publishers.

Martin, J. 1931. *Symposion. Die Geschichte einer literarischen Form*. Paderborn: Verlag Ferdinand Schöningh.

Martin, R. P. 1993. "The Seven Sages as Performers of Wisdom." In C. Dougherty and L. Kurke (eds.), *Cultural Poetics of Archaic Greece. Cult, Performance, Politics*, 108–28. Cambridge: Cambridge University Press.

Martin, V. 1959. "Un recueil de diatribes cyniques. Pap. Genev. inv. 271." *MH* 16: 77–115.

Massaro, D. 1997. "Introduzione." In D. Massaro and L. T. Massaro, *Platone: Ipparco*, 7–49. Milan: Rusconi.

Massaro, D. and L. T. Massaro. 1997. *Platone: Ipparco*. Milan: Rusconi.

Matelli, E. 2012. "Praxiphanes, Who Is He?" In A. Martano, E. Matelli, and D. Mirhady (eds.), *Praxiphanes of Mytilene and Chamaeleon of Heraclea*, 525–78. New Brunswick and London: Transaction Publishers.

Mayhew, R. 2008. *Plato: Laws 10*. Oxford: Oxford University Press.

McClure, L. 2003a. *Courtesans at Table. Gender and Greek Literature in Athenaeus*. New York and London: Routledge.

McClure, L. 2003b. "Subversive Laughter: The Sayings of Courtesans in Book 13 of Athenaeus' *Deipnosophistae*." *AJPh* 124: 259–94.

Meijer, P. A. 2017. *A New Perspective on Antisthenes. Logos, Predicate and Ethics in his Philosophy*. Amsterdam: Amsterdam University Press.

Mejer, J. 2009. "Heraclides' Intellectual Context." In W. W. Fortenbaugh and E. Pender (eds.), *Heraclides of Pontus: Discussion*, 27–40. New Brunswick: Transaction Publishers.

Melzer, A. M. 2014. *Philosophy Between the Lines. The Lost History of Esoteric Writing*. Chicago and London: University of Chicago Press.

Mensching, E., ed. 1963. *Favorin von Arelate. Der erste Teil der Fragmente: Memorabilien und Omnigena Historia*. Berlin: De Gruyter.

Merkelbach, R. 1958. "Literarische Texte unter Ausschluss der christlichen." *APF* 16: 82–129.

Mette, H. J. 1984. "Zwei Akademiker heute: Krantor von Soloi und Arkesilaos von Pitane." *Lustrum* 26: 7–94.

Mette, H. J. 1985. "Weitere Akademiker heute (Fortsetzung von Lustr. 26.7–94): Von Lakydes bis zu Kleitomachos." *Lustrum* 27: 39–148.

Milne, H. J. M. 1927. *Catalogue of the Literary Papyri in the British Museum*. London: Trustees of the British Museum.

Momigliano, A. 1970. "J. G. Droysen between Greeks and Jews." *History and Theory* 9: 139–53.

Momigliano, A. 1971. *The Development of Greek Biography*. Cambridge, MA: Harvard University Press.

Momigliano, A. 1975. *Alien Wisdom. The Limits of Hellenization*. Cambridge: Cambridge University Press.

Moore, C. 2015. *Socrates and Self-Knowledge*. Cambridge: Cambridge University Press.

Moraux, P. 1951. *Les listes anciennes des ouvrages d'Aristote*. Louvain: Éditions Universitaires.

Morgan, K. A. 2004. "Plato." In I. de Jong, R. Nünlist, and A. M. Bowie (eds.), *Narrators, Narratees, and Narratives in Ancient Greek Literature: Studies in Ancient Greek Narrative*, 357–76. Leiden and Boston: Brill.

Morgan, T. 2011. "The Miscellany and Plutarch." In F. Klotz and K. Oikonomopoulou (eds.), *The Philosopher's Banquet. Plutarch's Table Talk in the Intellectual Culture of the Roman Empire*, 49–73. Oxford: Oxford University Press.

Morrow, G. R. 1993² [1960]. *Plato's Cretan City. A Historical Interpretation of the Laws.* Princeton: Princeton University Press.

Müller, C. W. 1969. "Weltherrschaft und Unsterblichkeit im pseudoplatonischen *Theages* und in der *Eudemischen Ethik*." In P. Steinmetz (ed.), *Politeia und Res publica: Beiträge zum Verständnis von Politik, Recht und Staat in der Antike*, 135–47. Wiesbaden: Franz Steiner Verlag.

Müller, C. W. 1975. *Die Kurzdialoge der Appendix Platonica. Philologische Beiträge zur nachplatonischen Sokratik.* Munich: Wilhelm Fink Verlag.

Müller, C. W. 1995. "Cicero, Antisthenes und der pseudo-platonisches 'Minos' über das Gesetz." *RhM* 138: 247–65.

Müller, C. W. 2005. "Appendix Platonica und Neue Akademie. Die pseudoplatonischen Dialoge *Über die Tugend* und *Alkyon*." In K. Döring, M. Erler, and S. Schorn (eds.), *Pseudoplatonica. Akten des Kongresses zu den Pseudoplatonica vom 6.-9. Juli 2003 im Bamberg*, 155–74. Stuttgart: Franz Steiner Verlag.

Mulroy, D. 2007. "The Subtle Artistry of the 'Minos' and the 'Hipparchus'." *TAPhA* 137: 115–31.

Murray, O. 1967. "Aristeas and Ptolemaic Kingship." *JThS* 18: 337–71.

Murray, O. 1996. "Hellenistic Royal Symposia." In P. Bilde, T. Engberg-Pedersen, L. Hannestad, and J. Zahle (eds.), *Aspects of Hellenistic Kingship*, 15–27. Aarhus: Aarhus University Press.

Nachmanson, E. 1941. *Der griechische Buchtitel. Einige Beobachtungen.* Göteborg: Elanders Boktryckeri Aktiebolag.

Nagy, G. 1996. *Homeric Questions.* Austin: University of Texas Press.

Nails, D. 2002. *The People of Plato: A Prosopography of Plato and Other Socratics.* Indianapolis: Hackett Publishing.

Natoli, A. F. 2004. *The Letter of Speusippus to Philip II: Introduction, Text, Translation and Commentary.* Stuttgart: Franz Steiner Verlag.

Nesselrath, H.-G. 2012. "*Axiochos* und das Lob des Todes in griechischer Rhetoric, Philosophie und Dichtung." In *Ps.-Platon. Über den Tod*, 117–26. Tübingen: Mohr Siebeck.

Nightingale, A. W. 1995. *Genres in Dialogue: Plato and the Construct of Philosophy.* Cambridge: Cambridge University Press.

Nilsson, M. P. 1950. *Geschichte der griechischen Religion. Bd. II: Die Hellenistische und Römische Zeit.* Munich: C. H. Beck.

Nodar, A. 2000. "The Encounter between Alexander and the Brahmans as in PGen inv. 271: Problems of Interpretation and Edition." In *Papiri filosofici. Miscellanea di studi III*, 141–70. Florence: Leo S. Olschi.

Nussbaum, M. C. 1994. *The Therapy of Desire. Theory and Practice in Hellenistic Ethics.* Princeton: Princeton University Press.

Nüsser, O. 1991. *Albins Prolog und die Dialogtheorie des Platonismus.* Stuttgart: B. G. Teubner.

Obbink, D. 1997. *Philodemus: On Piety. Part 1. Critical Text with Commentary.* Oxford: Clarendon Press.

Obsieger, H. 2007. "Bemerkungen zu der Liebesprosa auf P. Erl. 4 = Nr. 7 Schubart." *ZPE* 162: 85–6.

Ohly, K. 1928. *Stichometrische Untersuchungen.* Leipzig: Harrassowitz.

O'Keefe, T. 2006. "Socrates' Therapeutic Use of Inconsistency in the *Axiochus*." *Phronesis* 51: 388–407.

Olson, S. D. ed. 2006. *Athenaeus. The Learned Banqueters. Books 1–3.106e.* Cambridge, MA: Harvard University Press.

Olson, S. D. ed. 2008. *Athenaeus. The Learned Banqueters. Books 6–7.* Cambridge, MA: Harvard University Press.

Osborne, R. 1985. "The Erection and Mutilation of the Hermai." *Cambridge Classical Journal* 31: 47–73.

Pade, M. 2007. *The Reception of Plutarch's Lives in Fifteenth-Century Italy. Volume 1.* Copenhagen: Museum Tusculanum Press.

Pangle, T. L. ed. 1987a. *The Roots of Political Philosophy: Ten Forgotten Socratic Dialogues.* Ithaca, NY: Agora Editions.

Pangle, T. L. 1987b. "On the *Theages*." In T. L. Pangle (ed.), *The Roots of Political Philosophy: Ten Forgotten Socratic Dialogues*, 147–74. Ithaca, NY: Agora Editions.

Papanghelis, T. D., S. J. Harrison, and S. Frangoulidis, eds. 2013. *Generic Interfaces in Latin Literature. Encounters, Interactions and Transformations.* Berlin and Boston: De Gruyter.

Pavlu, J. 1910. *Die pseudoplatonischen Zwillingsdialoge Minos und Hipparch.* Vienna.

Pavlu, J. 1913. *Die pseudoplatonischen Gespräche über Gerechtigkeit und Tugend.* Vienna.

Pearson, L. 1960. *The Lost Histories of Alexander the Great.* New York: American Philological Association.

Peek, W. 1935. "Eine Herme des Hipparch." *Hermes* 70: 461–3.

Penella, R. J. 2000. *The Private Orations of Themistius.* Berkeley and Los Angeles: University of California Press.

Peterson, S. 2011. *Socrates and Philosophy in the Dialogues of Plato.* Cambridge: Cambridge University Press.

Philip, J. A. 1970; "The Platonic Corpus." *Phoenix* 24: 296–308.

Pohlenz, M. 1980[5] [1948]. *Die Stoa. Geschichte einer geistigen Bewegung. Bd. 2: Erläterungen.* Göttingen: Vandenhoeck und Ruprecht.

Poland, F. 1932. "Minos." *RE* 15.2: 1890–1927.

Porter, J. I. 1996. "The Philosophy of Aristo of Chios." In R. B. Branham and M.-O. Goulet-Cazé (eds.), *The Cynics: The Cynic Movement in Antiquity and its Legacy*, 156–89. Berkeley and Los Angeles: University of California Press.

Powell, J. G. F. 2013. "The Embassy of the Three Philosophers to Rome in 155 BC." In C. Kremmydas and K. Tempest (eds.), *Hellenistic Oratory. Continuity and Change*, 219–48. Oxford: Oxford University Press.

Powers, N. 1998. "Onesicritus, Naked Wise Men, and the Cynics' Alexander." *SyllClass.* 9: 70–85.

Prince, S. 2015. *Antisthenes of Athens. Texts, Translations, and Commentary.* Ann Arbor: University of Michigan Press.

Radermacher, L. 1902. "Aus Lucians *Lügenfreund*." In M. Schwind (ed.), *Festschrift Theodor Gomperz dargebracht zum siebzigsten Geburtstag*, 197–207. Vienna: A. Hölder.

Radicke, J. 1999. "Archetimus of Syracuse, *On the Seven Sages* (?) (1098)." In *Die Fragmente der Griechischen Historiker Continued. Part IV: Biography and Antiquarian Literature. IVA: Biography. Fascicle 7: Imperial and Undated Authors*, 376–9. Leiden and Boston: Brill.

Rajak, T. 2009. *Translation & Survival: The Greek Bible of the Ancient Jewish Diaspora*. Oxford: Oxford University Press.

Rapin, C., P. Hadot, and G. Cavallo. 1987. "Les textes littéraires grecs de la Trésorerie d'Aï Khanoum." *BCH* 111: 225–66.

Rashed, M. 2013. "La mosaïque des philosophes de Naples: une représentation de l'académie platonicienne et son commanditaire." In C. Noirot and N. Ordine (eds.), *Omnia in uno. Hommage à Alain-Philippe Segonds*, 27–49. Paris: Les Belles Lettres.

Rawson, E. 1985. *Intellectual Life in the Late Roman Republic*. London: Duckworth.

Relihan, J. C. 1987. "Vainglorious Menippus in Lucian's *Dialogues of the Dead*." *ICS* 12: 185–206.

Relihan, J. C. 1993. *Ancient Menippean Satire*. Baltimore and London: The Johns Hopkins University Press.

Relihan, J. C. 1996. "Menippus in Antiquity and the Renaissance." In R. B. Branham and M.-O. Goulet-Cazé (eds.), *The Cynics: The Cynic Movement in Antiquity and its Legacy*, 265–93. Berkeley and Los Angeles: University of California Press.

Renaud, F. and H. Tarrant. 2015. *The Platonic Alcibiades I. The Dialogue and its Ancient Reception*. Cambridge: Cambridge University Press.

Rengakos, A. 2017. "The Literary Histories of the Hellenistic Age." In J. Grethlein and A. Rengakos (eds.), *Griechische Literaturgeschichtsschreibung: Traditionen, Probleme und Konzepte*, 71–82. Berlin and Boston: De Gruyter.

Ridgway, B. S. 1990. *Hellenistic Sculpture I. The Styles of ca. 331–200 B.C.* Bristol: Bristol Classical Press.

Riese, A. 1865. *M. Terenti Varronis Saturarum Menippearum reliquiae*. Leipzig: Teubner.

Riginos, A. S. 1976. *Platonica: The Anecdotes Concerning the Life and Writings of Plato*. Leiden: Brill.

Rigolio, A. 2019. *Christians in Conversation. A Guide to Late Antique Dialogues in Greek and Syriac*. Oxford: Oxford University Press.

Rives, J. B. 2004. "Aristotle, Antisthenes of Rhodes, and the *Magikos*." *RhM* 147: 35–54.

Robert, L. 1968. "De Delphes à l'Oxus. Inscriptions grecques nouvelles de la Bactriane." *CRAI* 112: 416–57.

Robinson, C. 1979. *Lucian and his Influence in Europe*. London: Duckworth.

Rose, V. 1854. *De Aristotelis librorum ordine et auctoritate commentatio*. Berlin: G. Reimer.

Rose, V. 1863. *Aristoteles pseudepigraphus. Pars prima continens fragmenta Aristotelis philosophica*. Leipzig: B. G. Teubner.

Rougemont, G. 2012. *Corpus Inscriptionum Iranicarum. Part II: Inscriptions of the Seleucid and Parthian Periods of Eastern Iran and Central Asia. Vol. 1: Inscriptions in non-Iranian languages. Inscriptions grecques d'Iran et d'Asie centrale*. London: School of Oriental and African Studies.

Rowe, C. 2000. "*Cleitophon* and *Minos*." In C. Rowe and M. Schofield (eds.), *Cambridge History of Greek and Roman Political Thought*, 303–9. Cambridge: Cambridge University Press.

Rowe, C. 2005. "What Might We Learn from the *Clitophon* about the Nature of Academy?" In K. Döring, M. Erler, and S. Schorn (eds.), *Pseudoplatonica. Akten des Kongresses zu den Pseudoplatonica vom 6.-9. Juli 2003 im Bamberg*, 213–24. Stuttgart: Franz Steiner Verlag.

Ruch, M. 1958. *Le préambule dans les oeuvres philosophique de Cicéron. Essai sur la genèse et l'art du dialogue*. Paris: Les Belles Lettres.

Rutherford, I. 2001. "Tourism and the Sacred. Pausanias and the Traditions of Greek Pilgrimage." In S. E. Alcock, J. F. Cherry, and J. Elsner (eds.), *Pausanias: Travel and Memory in Roman Greece*, 40–52. Oxford: Oxford University Press.

Rütten, T. 1992. *Demokrit—lachender Philosoph und sanguinischer Melancholiker. Eine pseudohippokratische Geschichte.* Leiden and New York: Brill.
Sakalis, D. 1989. *Ιπποκρατους επιστολαι. Ἔκδοση κριτική και ερμηνευτική.* Ioannina: Πανεπιστήμιο 'Ιωαννίνων.
Sakkelion, I. 1877. "Ἐκ των ανεκδότων της Πατμιακῆς Βιβλιοθήκης. Λέξεις μεθ' ἱστοριῶν ἐκ τῶν Δημοσθένους καὶ Αἰσχίνου λόγων." *BCH* 1: 10–16, 137–55.
Sandin, P. 2014a. "Famous Hyperboreans." *Nordlit* 33: 205–21.
Sandin, P. 2014b. "The Emblems of Excellence in Pindar's First and Third Olympian Odes and Bacchylides' Third Epinician." *Lexis. Poetica, retorica e comunicazione nella tradizione classica* 32: 90–113.
Sawada, N. 2010. "Social Customs and Institutions: Aspects of Macedonian Elite Society." In J. Roisman and I. Worthington (eds.), *A Companion to Ancient Macedonia*, 392–408. Malden: Wiley-Blackwell.
Schibli, H. S. 1983. "Fragments of a Weasel and Mouse War." *ZPE* 53: 1–25.
Schibli, H. S. 1984. "Addendum to 'Fragments of a Weasel and Mouse War'." *ZPE* 54: 14.
Schmidt, F. 1867. *De Heraclidae Pontici et Dicaearchi Messenii dialogis deperditis.* Vratislaviae: A. Neumann.
Schofield, M. 1999. *Saving the City. Philosopher-Kings and Other Classical Paradigms.* London and New York: Routledge.
Schofield, M. 2008. "Ciceronian Dialogue." In S. Goldhill (ed.), *The End of Dialogue in Antiquity*, 63–84. Cambridge: Cambridge University Press.
Schorn, S. 2003. "Wer wurde in der Antike als Peripatetiker bezeichnet?" *WJA* 27: 39–69.
Schorn, S. 2004. *Satyros aus Kallatis. Sammlung der Fragmente mit Kommentar.* Basel: Schwabe Verlag.
Schorn, S. 2005. "Der historische Mittelteil des pseudoplatonischen 'Hipparchos'." In K. Döring, M. Erler, and S. Schorn (eds.), *Pseudoplatonica. Akten des Kongresses zu den Pseudoplatonica vom 6.-9. Juli 2003 im Bamberg*, 225–54. Stuttgart: Franz Steiner Verlag.
Schorn, S. 2012. "Aristoxenus' Biographical Method." In C. A. Huffman (ed.), *Aristoxenus of Tarentum. Discussion*, 177–221. New Brunswick and London: Transaction Publishers.
Schorn, S. 2014a. "Biographie und Autobiographie." In B. Zimmermann and A. Rengakos (eds.), *Handbuch der griechischen Literatur der Antike. Bd. 2: Die Literatur der klassischen und hellenistischen Zeit*, 678–733. Munich: C. H. Beck.
Schorn, S. 2014b. "Nikagoras von Zeleia." *Hermes* 142: 78–93.
Schrohl, O. 1901. *De Eryxia qui fertur Platonis.* Göttingen: L. Hofer.
Schubart, W. 1942. *Die Papyri der Universitätsbibliothek Erlangen.* Leipzig: Harrassowitz.
Schütrumpf, E., ed. 2008. *Heraclides of Pontus: Texts and Translation.* New Brunswick: Transaction Publishers.
Schütrumpf, E. 2009. "Heraclides, On Pleasure." In W. W. Fortenbaugh and E. Pender (eds.), *Heraclides of Pontus: A Discussion*, 69–91. New Brunswick: Transaction Publishers.
Scott, D. 2006. *Plato's Meno.* Cambridge: Cambridge University Press.
Searby, D. M. 2019. "The Fossilized Meaning of Chreia as Anecdote." *Mnemosyne* 72: 197–228.
Sedley, D. 1973. "Epicurus, On Nature. Book XXVIII." *CE* 3: 5–83.
Sedley, D. 1977. "Diodorus Cronus and Hellenistic Philosophy." *PCPhS* 23(203): 74–120.
Sedley, D. 1984. "3655. Philosophical Anecdote." In H. M. Cockle (ed.), *The Oxyrhynchus Papyri. Vol. LII*, 44–6. London: Egypt Exploration Society.
Sedley, D. 1989. "Philosophical Allegiance in the Greco-Roman World." In M. Griffin and J. Barnes (eds.), *Philosophia Togata I: Essays on Philosophy and Roman Society*, 97–119. Oxford: Clarendon Press.

Sedley, D. 1998. *Lucretius and the Transformation of Greek Wisdom*. Cambridge: Cambridge University Press.
Sedley, D. 1999. "The Stoic-Platonist Debate on *kathekonta*." In K. Ierodiakonou (ed.), *Topics in Stoic Philosophy*, 128–52. Oxford: Clarendon Press.
Segoloni, L. M. 2012. "Un genere letterario privo di leggi scritte, legge a se stesso: il dialogo." *Seminari romani di cultura greca* n.s. 1: 339–50.
Shackleton Bailey, D. R. 1966. *Cicero's Letters to Atticus. Vol. V: 48–45 B.C. 211–354 (Books XI to XIII)*. Cambridge: Cambridge University Press.
Shapiro, H. A. 1989. *Art and Cult under the Tyrants in Athens*. Mainz: Von Zabern.
Sharpe, M. 2011. "Revaluing Megalopsuchia: Reflections on the *Alcibiades II*." In M. Johnson and H. Tarrant (eds.), *Alcibiades and the Socratic Lover-Educator*, 134–46. London: Bristol Classical Press.
Shields, C. J. 1994. "Socrates among the Skeptics." In P. A. Vander Waerdt (ed.), *The Socratic Movement*, 341–66. Ithaca, NY: Cornell University Press.
Slings, S. R. 1999. *Plato: Clitophon*. Cambridge: Cambridge University Press.
Smith, M. F., ed. 1993. *The Epicurean Inscription*. Naples: Bibliopolis.
Smith, W. D. 1990. *Hippocrates. Pseudepigraphic Writings. Letters. Embassy. Speech from the Altar. Decree*. Leiden: Brill.
Sollenberger, M. G. 1992. "The Lives of the Peripatetics: An Analysis of the Contents and Structure of Diogenes Laertius' *Vitae philosophorum* Book 5." *ANRW* II 36.6: 3793–879.
Sollenberger, M. G. 2000. "Diogenes Laertius' Life of Demetrius of Phalerum." In W. W. Fortenbaugh and E. Schütrumpf (eds.), *Demetrius of Phalerum. Text, Translation and Discussion*, 311–29. New Brunswick and London: Transaction Publishers.
Solmsen, F. 1942. "Eratosthenes as Platonist and Poet." *TAPhA* 73: 192–213.
Solmsen, F. 1981. "The Academic and Alexandrian Editions of Plato's Works." *ICS* 6: 102–11.
Sorabji, R. 1993. *Animal Minds and Human Morals. The Origins of the Western Debate*. Ithaca, NY: Cornell University Press.
Souilhé, J. ed. 1930a. *Platon. Oeuvres complètes. Tome XIII, 2e partie: Dialogues suspects*. Paris: Les Belles Lettres.
Souilhé, J. ed. 1930b. *Platon. Oeuvres complètes. Tome XIII, 3e partie: Dialogues apocryphes*. Paris: Les Belles Lettres.
Spinelli, E. 1992. "P.Köln 205: Il 'Socrate' di Egesia?" *ZPE* 91: 10–14.
Squire, M. 2011. *The Iliad in a Nutshell: Visualizing Epic on the Tabulae Iliacae*. Oxford: Oxford University Press.
Staden, H. von, 1999. "Rupture and Continuity: Hellenistic Reflections on the History of Medicine." In P. J. van der Eijk (ed.), *Ancient Histories of Medicine. Essays in Medical Doxography and Historiography in Classical Antiquity*, 143–88. Leiden: Brill.
Steinmetz, P. 1994. "Die Stoa." In H. Flashar (ed.), *Grundriss der Geschichte der Philosophie. Die Philosophie der Antike. Bd. 4: Die hellenistische Philosophie*, 491–716, Basel: Schwabe.
Stewart, Z. 1958. "Democritus and the Cynics." *HSCPh* 63: 179–91.
Stoneman, R. 1995. "Naked Philosophers: The Brahmans in the Alexander Historians and the Alexander Romance." *JHS* 115: 99–114.
Sudhaus, S. 1895. "Exkurse zu Philodem." *Philologus* 54: 80–92.
Swancutt, D. M. 2005. "Paraenesis in Light of Protrepsis. Troubling the Typical Dichotomy." In J. Starr and T. Engberg-Pedersen (eds.), *Early Christian Paraenesis in Context*, 113–53. Berlin and New York: De Gruyter.

Szalc, A. 2011. "Alexander's Dialogue with Indian Philosophers: Riddle in Greek and Indian Tradition." *Eos* 98: 7–25.
Tappe, G. 1912. *De Philonis libro qui inscribitur Ἀλέξανδρος ἢ περὶ τοῦ λόγου ἔχειν τὰ ἄλογα ζῷα quaestiones selectae*. Göttingen: Officina Academica Dieterichiana.
Tarán, L. 1975. *Academica: Plato, Philip of Opus, and the Pseudo-Platonic Epinomis*. Philadelphia: American Philosophical Society.
Tarán, L. 1981. *Speusippus of Athens. A Critical Study with a Collection of the Related Texts and Commentary*. Leiden: Brill.
Tarán, L. 2001. *Collected Papers (1962–1999)*. Leiden and Boston: Brill.
Tarrant, H. 1993 *Thrasyllan Platonism*. Ithaca, NY and London: Cornell University Press.
Tarrant, H. 2005. "Socratic Synousia: A Post-Platonic Myth?" *JHPh* 43: 131–55.
Tarrant, H., ed. 2007. *Proclus: Commentary on Plato's Timaeus. Book 1: Proclus on the Socratic State and Atlantis*. Cambridge: Cambridge University Press.
Tarrant, H. 2012. "Improvement by Love: From Aeschines to the Old Academy." In M. Johnson and H. Tarrant (eds.), *Alcibiades and the Socratic Lover-Educator*, 147–63. London: Bristol Classical Press.
Tarrant, H. 2018. "The Socratic Dubia." In A. Stavru and Ch. Moore (eds.), *Socrates and the Socratic Dialogue*, 386–411. Leiden and Boston: Brill.
Taylor, A. E. 1949[6] [1926]. *Plato. The Man and his Work*. London: Routledge.
Temkin, O. 1991. *Hippocrates in a World of Pagans and Christians*. Baltimore and London: Johns Hopkins University Press.
Terian, A. 1981. *Philonis Alexandrini De animalibus: The Armenian Text with an Introduction, Translation, and Commentary*. Chico, CA: Scholars Press.
Terian, A. 1984. "A Critical Introduction to Philo's Dialogues." *ANRW* II 21.1: 272–94.
Thesleff, H. 1967. *Studies in the Styles of Plato*. Helsinki: Society philosophica Fennica.
Thesleff, H. 1982. *Studies in Platonic Chronology*. Helsinki: Society scientiarum Fennica.
Thom, J. C. 2005. *Cleanthes' Hymn to Zeus: Text, Translation, and Commentary*. Tübingen: Mohr Siebeck.
Tieleman, T. 2003. *Chrysippus' On Affections. Reconstruction and Interpretation*. Leiden and Boston: Brill.
Tigerstedt, E. N. 1977. *Interpreting Plato*. Stockholm: Almqvist & Wiksell.
Tipton, J. A. 1999. "Love of Gain, Philosophy and Tyranny: A Commentary on Plato's *Hipparchus*." *Interpretation* 26: 201–16.
Trapp, M. B. 1997. "On the *Tablet of Cebes*." In R. Sorabji (ed.), *Aristotle and After*, 159–78. London: Institute of Classical Studies.
Tsekourakis, D. 1980. "*Τὸ στοιχεῖο τοῦ διαλόγου στὴν κυνικοστωικὴ 'διατριβή'*." *Hellenica* 32: 61–78.
Tsitsiridis, S. 2013. *Beiträge zu den Fragmenten des Klearchos von Soloi*. Berlin and Boston: De Gruyter.
Tuozzo, T. M. 2011. *Plato's Charmides. Positive Elenchus in a "Socratic" Dialogue*. Cambridge: Cambridge University Press.
Turner, E. G. 1955. "182. Life and Apophthegms of Socrates." In E. G. Turner (ed.), *The Hibeh Papyri. Part II*, 26–39. London: Egypt Exploration Society.
Untersteiner, M. 1980. *Problemi di filologia filosofica*. Milan: Istituto Editoriale Cisalpino-La Goliardica.
Usener, H. 1887. *Epicurea*. Leipzig: Teubner.
Usher, M. D. 2006. "Carneades' Quip: Orality, Philosophy, Wit, and the Poetics of Impromptu Quotation." *Oral Tradition* 21.1: 190–209.

Vallozza, M. 2011. "Isocrate ospite di Platone nel dialogo sui poeti di Prassifane." *SCO* 57: 119–36.

Vallozza, M. 2012. "The διατριβὴ περὶ ποιητῶν of Praxiphanes in the Testimony of Diogenes Laertius." In A. Martano, E. Matelli, and D. Mirhady (eds.), *Praxiphanes of Mytilene and Chamaeleon of Heraclea*, 477–94. New Brunswick and London: Transaction Publishers.

Van der Stockt, L. 2000. "Aspects of the Ethics and Politics of the Dialogue in the *Corpus Plutarcheum*." In I. Gallo and Moreschini (eds.), *I generi letterari in Plutarco. Atti del VIII Convegno plutarcheo, Pisa 2–4 giugno 1999*, 93–116. Naples: D'Auria.

Vassallo, C. 2014. "Il ruolo della retorica tra democrazia e oligarchia. Un'ipotesi di attribuzione di un supposto frammento socratico (PSI XI 1215)." *Elenchos* 35: 195–231.

Vendruscolo, F. 1989. "Protrepticus." In *Corpus dei papiri filosofici greci e latini. Testi e lessico nei papiri di cultura greca e latina. Parte I: Autori noti*. Vol. 1*, 269–79. Florence: Leo S. Olschi.

Verhasselt, G. 2015. "A Peripatetic Dialogue in P.Oxy. LIII 3699: A New Edition Based on New Joins." *APF* 61: 5–31.

Vogel, C. J. de, 1965. "On Iamblichus V.P. 215–219." *Mnemosyne* 18: 388–96.

Wallace, R. W. 2015. *Reconstructing Damon: Music, Wisdom Teaching, and Politics in Perikles' Athens*. Oxford: Oxford University Press.

Warren, J. 2006. "Epicureans and the Present Past." *Phronesis* 51: 362–87.

Warren, J. 2009. "Aristotle on Speusippus on Eudoxus on Pleasure." *OSAP* 36: 249–81.

Warren, J. 2021. "Socrates and the Symmetry Argument." In A. G. Long (ed.), *Immortality in the Ancient Philosophy*, 143–60. Cambridge: Cambridge University Press.

Weber, H.-O. 1967. *Die Bedeutung und Bewertung der Pleonexie*. Bonn: Rheinische Friedrich-Wilhelms-Universität.

Wecowski, M. 2014. *The Rise of the Greek Aristocratic Banquet*. Oxford: Oxford University Press.

Wehrli, F. 1953. *Die Schule des Aristoteles. Text und Kommentar. VII: Herakleides Pontikos*. Basel: Schwabe.

Wehrli, F. 1967². *Die Schule des Aristoteles. Texte und Kommentar. I: Dikaiarchos*. Basel: Schwabe.

Wehrli, F. 1968². *Die Schule des Aristoteles. Texte und Kommentar. IV: Demetrios von Phaleron*. Basel: Schwabe.

Wehrli, F. 1969²a. *Die Schule des Aristoteles. Texte und Kommentar. III: Klearchos*. Basel: Schwabe.

Wehrli, F. 1969²b. *Die Schule des Aristoteles. Texte und Kommentar. IX: Phainias von Eresos, Chamaileon, Praxiphanes*. Basel: Schwabe.

Wehrli, F. 1973. "Gnome, Anekdote und Biographie." *MH* 30: 193–208.

Wendland, P. 1892. *Philos Schrift über die Vorsehung. Ein Beitrag zur Geschichte der nacharistotelischen Philosophie*. Berlin: R. Gaertners Verlagsbuchhandlung.

West, M. L. 1985. "Ion of Chios." *BICS* 32: 71–8.

West, M. L. 2015. "The Classical World." In M. Stausberg and Y. S.-D. Vevaina (eds.), *The Wiley Blackwell Companion to Zoroastrianism*, 437–50. Malden: Wiley-Blackwell.

West, S. 1974. "Satyrus: Peripatetic or Alexandrian?" *GRBS* 15: 279–87.

Westerink, L. G. 2011² [1962]. *Anonymous Prolegomena to Platonic Philosophy*. Westbury: The Prometheus Trust.

Whitby, M. 2011. "Onesikritos (134)." In I. Worthington (ed.), *Brill's New Jacoby*. Consulted online on September 5, 2020 <http://dx.doi.org/10.1163/1873-5363_bnj_a134>.

White, S. A. 1994. "Callimachus on Plato and Cleombrotus." *TAPhA* 124: 135-61.
White, S. A. 2002. "Opuscula and Opera in the Catalogue of Theophrastus' Works." In W. W. Fortenbaugh and G. Wöhrle (eds.), *On the Opuscula of Theophrastus. Akten der 3. Tagung der Karl-und-Gertrud-Abel-Stiftung vom 19.-23. Juli 1999 in Trier*, 9-37. Stuttgart: Franz Steiner Verlag.
White, S. A. 2010. "Philosophy after Aristotle." In J. J. Clauss and M. Cuypers (eds.), *A Companion to Hellenistic Literature*, 366-83. Malden and Oxford: Wiley-Blackwell.
Whitmarsh, T. 2004. "Lucian." In I. de Jong, R. Nünlist, and A. M. Bowie (eds.), *Narrators, Narratees, and Narratives in Ancient Greek Literature: Studies in Ancient Greek Narrative*, 465-76. Leiden and Boston: Brill.
Wilamowitz-Möllendorff, U. von, 1904. review: "Egypt Exploration Fund Graeco-Roman Branch. The Oxyrynchos Papyri part. IV edited by B. P. Grenfell and A. S. Hunt. London 1904". *GGA* 166: 659-78.
Wilamowitz-Möllendorff, U. von, 1916. *Die Ilias und Homer*. Berlin: Weidmannsche Buchhandlung.
Wilcken, U. 1901. "Zu den griechischen Papyri der königlich bayerischen Hof- und Staatsbibliothek zu München." *APF* 1: 468-91.
Wilkins, J. 2000. *The Boastful Chef. The Discourse of Food in Ancient Greek Comedy*. Oxford: Oxford University Press.
Williams, G. D. 1995. "Cleombrotus of Ambracia: Interpretations of a Suicide from Callimachus to Agathias." *CQ* 45: 154-69.
Willis, W. H. and K. Maresch. 1988. "The Encounter of Alexander with the Brahmans: New Fragments of the Cynic Diatribe P.Genev. inv. 271." *ZPE* 74: 59-83.
Wilsdorf, H. 1991. "Der weise Achikaros bei Demokrit und Theophrast." *Philologus* 135: 191-206.
Witt, C. 1996. "The Evolution of Developmental Interpretations." In W. R. Wians (ed.), *Aristotle's Philosophical Development: Problems and Prospects*, 67-82. Lanham: Rowman & Littlefield.
Woodruff, P. 1982. *Plato, Hippias Major. Translated with Commentary and Essay*. Oxford: Blackwell.
Wright, B. G. 2015. *The Letter of Aristeas. "Aristeas to Philocrates" or "On the Translation of the Law of the Jews."* Berlin and Boston: De Gruyter.
Wynne, J. P. F. 2019. *Cicero on the Philosophy of Religion. On the Nature of the Gods and On Divination*. Cambridge: Cambridge University Press.
Wynne, J. P. F. 2020. "Cicero's *Tusculan Disputations*: a Sceptical Reading." *OSAP* 58: 205-38.
Zilioli, U. 2012. *The Cyrenaics*. Durham: Acumen.
Zilioli, U., ed. 2015. *From the Socratics to the Socratic Schools. Classical Ethics, Metaphysics and Epistemology*. New York and London: Routledge.
Zinn, P. 2016 "Lucretius On Time and Its Perception." *Kriterion* 30: 125-51.
Ziolkowski, J. 1997. "The Prosimetrum in the Classical Tradition." In J. Harris and K. Reichl (eds.), *Prosimetrum: Crosscultural Perspectives on Narrative in Prose and Verse*, 45-65. Cambridge: D. S. Brewer.
Zuntz, G. 1959a. "Aristeas Studies I: 'The Seven Banquets'." *Journal of Semitic Studies* 4: 21-36.
Zuntz, G. 1959b. "Zu Alexanders Gespräch mit den Gymnosophisten." *Hermes* 87: 436-40.

# Index Locorum

Achilles Tatius
  6.2.3  47n.7
[Achilles Tatius]
  *Arat.*
    9  189n.73
Aelian
  *NA*
    12.40  112
  *VH*
    4.15  136n.35
    8.2  132n.22
Albinus
  *Intr.*
    1  7n.17
    4  136n.35
Alexander of Aphrodisias
  *De anima libri mantissa*
    25  180n.49
Alexinus (ed. Döring)
  F 90  16
Ammonius
  *In Cat.*
    4.5  111n.68
    4.15–16  166
    4.18–19  166n.10
    4.20–2  167n.13
    4.23–5  166
    4.26–7  166
    7.3  169
Anaxandrides (ed. K–A)
  F 1  113n.75
Antipater of Tarsus
  *SVF* 3.246 F 14  219
  *SVF* 3.253–4 F 61  219
Apuleius
  *De Plat.*
    1.2  142n.62
[Aristeas]
  *Ep. Arist.*
    1  29
    9–11  29
    130–69  31
    187–300  31

    200  31, 32n.48
    235  31, 32n.48
    296  31, 32n.48
    312–13  30
Aristophanes
  *Lys.*
    283  64n.55
    368  64n.55
  *Nub.*
    984–6  100
  *Plut.*
    591  133n.23
  *Thesm.*
    81–5  64n.55
  *Vesp.*
    223–7  146
Aristotle
  *Ath.*
    14.2  74n.81
    18.1  134n.25, 134n.26
  *De an.*
    408b18–19  172
    430a22–3  172
  *EE*
    1217b22  165n.9
    1225b32–5  138n.40
    1226a21–1127a30  145
  *EN*
    1100a10–1101b9  175n.32
    1110a27–9  54n.25
    1112a18–1113a14  145
    1113b14–15  148n.80
    1142a31–b33  145
    1153b4–6  111n.67
    1172b9–25  111n.67
  *Fragments* (ed. Rose³)
    F 37  172
    F 44  173–4
    F 57  56n.29
    F 64  176, 177n.40
    F 72  177
    F 78  177
    F 82  177

Aristotle (*cont.*)
    F 91  170
    F 92  171
    F 94  171
    F 142–79  68n.69
  *HA*
    542b1–17  157n.118
    593b8–10  157n.118
    616a14–34  157n.118
  *Metaph.*
    983a3–4  148n.80
    1046b29  194
  *Poet.*
    1448a16–18  96
    1448b25  96n.21
    1449b11  184n.60
    1449b26  184n.60
  *Pol.*
    1260a21–2  65n.57
    1266a31–2  98n.26
  *Protrepticus* (ed. Düring)
    F B 2–5  56n.29
    F B 18  105n.46
    F B 20  105n.46
    F B 44  105n.46
  *Protrepticus*(?)
    POxy.4.666 col. iii.139–70  56
  *SE*
    174b23–7  112
Aristoxenus (ed. Wehrli)
    F 50  41, 102
Arrian
  *Epict. Diss.*
    1.6  237
    1.16  237
    2.15.4  202
    2.19.13  119n.91
    3.17  237
Asclepius
  *In Nicomachi intr. arithm.*
    1.24  129n.8
Athenaeus
  *Deipn.*
    1.5b–d  33n.53
    1.34b  23n.27
    2.54e  231n.105
    3.104b  33n.53
    4.128a–b  32n.50
    4.129a  33
    4.129f  33
    4.130c  33, 33n.51
    4.134e–137c  33n.53

    4.156d–158a  34
    4.156e–f  215
    4.157a–d  34
    4.157b  214, 215
    4.157c  182
    4.157d–f  35
    4.162b–c  25, 197, 217
    4.162d  216
    4.164a  203
    5.177b  220
    5.179d  221
    5.182a  220
    5.186b  24n.29
    5.186c  23, 219
    5.186d  21
    5.186e  220
    5.187b  220, 221
    5.214a  57n.32
    6.234f  181n.54
    6.248d  16n.10
    6.252f  144n.67
    6.256c  182n.56
    7.275d  181n.54
    7.276a–c  232–3
    7.278e–f  33n.53
    7.281c–d  216, 233–4
    8.335b  33n.53
    8.335d–336a  33n.53
    8.341b–d  18
    8.341e  19n.21
    8.348e  18n.19
    8.352d  144n.68
    9.370c  16n.10
    10.418e  16n.13
    10.420c–d  26
    10.424e–f  181
    10.457c–e  33n.53
    11.464a  113n.75
    11.477e  23n.27
    11.502c  23, 214
    11.505a–b  150n.88
    11.505c  177
    11.506b  140
    11.506c  157
    11.507d  16n.10
    12.512a–d  98–9
    12.525f–526a  100
    12.533c  100
    12.536f–537c  100
    12.541c  61
    12.545a–546c  41, 102, 188
    12.546d  111n.67
    12.552f  100
    12.554e–f  100–1
    13.555d–556a  159

# INDEX LOCORUM 275

13.556b 159
13.579d 18n.19
13.584a 27, 197
13.585b 24n.29
13.588a 234n.112
13.588d 21
13.588e–f 20n.22
13.594e 186
13.603f–604d 15
13.607a 25, 217
13.607a–b 222n.80
13.607a–e 17, 217
13.607b 26
14.619e 187n.69
14.620d 186
14.629e 213
14.629e–f 23
14.632a–b 24, 187
14.641e 186
14.664e 23, 213
15.696e 16n.13
15.701c 181n.54

Basil of Caesarea
 *Ep.*
  135 168, 179

Bion of Borysthenes (ed. Kindstrand)
 F 1A 206–7
 F 2 207
 F 7 208

Callimachus
 *Del.*
  292 155n.109

Carneiscus
 *Philistas* (PHerc. 1027)
  col. xv.2 228
  col. xviii.6–9 189

Chariton
 *Callirh.*
  6.3.7 47n.7

Chrysippus
 *SVF* 2.11 F 27 218

Cicero
 *Acad.*
  2.6.16 91, 120n.96
  2.18.60 120n.96
  2.31.98 91
  2.32.102 91
  2.38.119 169
  2.42.129 217
  2.44.135 115
 *Att.*
  4.16.2 167

6.2.3 186
13.19.3–4 97
13.19.4 167
13.30.2 186
13.32.2 186
13.33.2 186
13.42.1 28
15.4.3 97n.24
15.13.3 97n.24
15.27.2 97n.24
16.2.6 97n.24
16.11.3 97n.24
16.12 97n.24

*Brut.*
 31.121 180

*De fato*
 4 123, 124

*De or.*
 1.11.50 218
 2.58.235 36n.60
 3.18.67 121n.100
 3.21.80 121n.100, 168

*Div.*
 1.23.46 92
 1.25.52–3 173n.29
 1.25.53 172, 175

*Fam.*
 1.9.23 168n.16

*Fin.*
 2.1.1 120n.98
 2.1.2 123n.104
 2.1.2–3 121, 123, 212
 2.21.69 218
 5.5.12 166, 167, 179
 5.5.13 190

*Inv. rhet.*
 1.19.27 96n.22
 1.31.51–2 64

*Leg.*
 3.6.14 98n.26

*Nat. D.*
 1.5.11 121n.100
 1.8.18 237
 1.8.20–1.9.23 237
 1.13.34 95
 1.33.93 226n.93
 1.44.123 221n.78
 2.29.73–2.67.168 237
 3.1.3 221n.78

*Off.*
 3.12.51–3.13.55 219
 3.15.63 219

Cicero (cont.)
    3.23.89  219
    3.23.91  219
  Or.
    19.62  180n.47
  QFr
    3.5.1  97, 168, 177
  Resp.
    1.7.12  98n.26
    6.16.16  97n.25
  Rhet. Her.
    1.8.13  96n.22
  Sen.
    12.39–41  41
  Tusc.
    1.4.7  169
    1.4.7–8  120n.98, 123n.104
    1.4.8  123, 123n.104
    1.10.21  186
    1.31.77  186
    1.34.83–4  155, 201
    1.48.115  116n.83
    2.3.9  168
    3.10.21  180
    3.12.54  91
    3.22.54  122
    3.34.81  120n.98
    5.3.8–9  105
    5.4.11  123n.104
    5.9.25  180n.49
Cleanthes
  SVF 1.129 F 570  218
Clearchus (ed. Wehrli)
  F 6  182
  F 7  184
  F 8  185
  F 19  182n.56
  F 38  182
  F 50  182n.57
  F 51  182n.57
  F 56  182n.57
Clement of Alexandria
  Strom.
    4.19.121.5–6  199
    6.2.17.5  156n.114
    7.6.32.9  91
Commentaria in Arist. EN
    145  108
Crantor (ed. Mette)
  F 7a  116–7
  F 12–13  118n.87

Damascius
  In Phd.
    1.530  185n.64
    2.138  185n.64
[Demetrius]
  Eloc.
    28  177
    163  67
    223  29
Demosthenes
  De cor.
    288  113n.74
Dio Chrysostom
  Or.
    4.1  206
    10.31–2  235n.119
    53.1  108, 165
[Dio Chrysostom]
  Or. 37
  see Favorinus
Diodorus Siculus
    1.69.7  94n.18
    1.76.2  94n.18
    3.11.1  94n.18
    9.37.1  72n.79
    14.19.8  145n.71
    15.81.5  102n.37
    18.48  76n.88
    32.12.1  94n.18
Diogenes of Babylon
  SVF 3.219–20 F 49  219
Diogenes Laertius
    1.1  177
    1.1–9  103
    1.2  154n.102
    1.8  177
    1.16  3n.5, 196n.9
    1.40–1  24
    1.50  74n.81
    1.63  16n.10
    1.64–7  74n.81
    1.94  75, 108
    2.23  15n.7
    2.26  159
    2.34  78n.93
    2.45  103
    2.48  14
    2.50  145n.71
    2.61  156n.114
    2.64  194
    2.74  20n.22
    2.83–5  3n.5, 200

2.84  17n.17, 196
2.85  17n.17
2.86  200
2.92  91
2.94  200–1
2.95  201
2.105  228
2.106  194
2.108  194
2.109  16n.13, 194n.5
2.111  195
2.112  111, 195, 203
2.113  196
2.113–15  196
2.114  20, 83, 196
2.117–19  83
2.120  83, 110n.65, 196, 200
2.121  107n.56, 149n.84
2.122  149n.84
2.123  195
2.124  110n.66
2.126  196
2.143  202n.24
3.2  113
3.4  142n.62
3.8  4, 189
3.37  3n.5, 10n.28, 128
3.46  92
3.48  7n.17
3.50  9n.26
3.56  126
3.57–61  126
3.59  107n.56, 140n.53
3.60  129
3.61–2  126
3.62  110n.65, 126, 128, 140n.53,
       145, 148n.83
3.80  3n.5
4.2  15
4.4  109n.60, 195, 200
4.4–5  4n.5, 108n.56, 109
4.10  208n.45
4.11–12  4n.5
4.11–14  114
4.12  149n.84
4.20  90
4.21  115n.81
4.23  91
4.24  115
4.25  115
4.26–7  115
4.27  115
4.28  123
4.28–67  91
4.30  115n.79

4.30–1  120n.96
4.32  120n.96, 120n.97
4.37  120n.96
4.41–2  23n.27
4.42  27, 102n.36
4.44  120n.96
4.46  206
4.47  206n.40
4.51  206
4.52  206n.40, 208
4.65  91, 120n.96
4.67  91
5.6  114
5.22  140, 169
5.39  180n.47
5.41  120n.99
5.42–50  180
5.47  120n.98
5.81  17n.17, 188
5.86  93, 94, 102
5.87  75, 107
5.88  68n.69, 95, 98
5.89  94
5.92  95n.19, 226n.93
6.4  17n.17, 82
6.12  65n.57
6.13  155n.107
6.15–18  202
6.19  202
6.20  203
6.21  202
6.27–8  81n.100
6.29–30  213
6.32  17n.17
6.33  17n.17
6.51–2  21n.23
6.73  81n.100
6.75–6  204n.30
6.76  19n.21
6.80  17n.17, 83, 195, 203
6.84  204, 204n.30
6.91  17n.17, 216n.64
6.94  202n.24
6.95  17n.17
6.99  212, 214n.60
6.101  213
6.102  213n.54
7.1  15, 217
7.2  196
7.4  15, 216, 216n.64
7.24  196
7.26  17n.17
7.28  120n.98
7.36  15n.9, 17n.16, 17n.17, 216
7.37  93n.13

Diogenes Laertius (cont.)
  7.41  120n.98
  7.102  119n.91
  7.163  15n.9, 17n.17, 120n.98, 190
  7.165  217
  7.166–7  93n.13
  7.167  202n.24, 216
  7.172  17n.17
  7.175  24n.29, 217
  7.178  217
  7.180  218
  7.189–202  218
  8.4  109n.60
  8.4–5  105
  8.8  105n.46
  8.51  104
  8.52  104
  8.53  17n.16
  8.59  63n.51
  8.60  103
  8.60–2  103
  8.67–72  103
  8.68  104
  8.72  109
  8.89  113
  9.18  231n.105
  9.37  142n.61
  9.40  187n.69
  9.50  108
  9.65  231n.108
  9.67  232n.109
  9.102  120n.97
  9.109–10  230n.103
  9.111  230
  9.112  230, 230n.104
  9.115  232
  10.3  226
  10.8  226n.93
  10.13  226n.93
  10.22  227n.97
  10.26  120n.98
  10.27  194n.5
  10.27–8  226
  10.52  227n.99
  10.68  227n.97
  10.81  153n.99
  10.84  227n.97
  10.85  227n.97
  10.119  221
  10.125  153n.99, 153n.101
  10.138  120n.98
  10.139  153n.99
Diogenes of Oenoanda (ed. M. F. Smith)
  Fr. 63 col. ii.4–iv.14  228–9

Fr. 138  229n.100
Fr. 154  229n.100
Dionysius of Halicarnassus
  Comp.
    4  218
  Dem.
    44  94n.18
    46  111n.68
  Orat. vett.
    1  4n.8
  Pomp.
    6.4–5  95n.18
Elias
  In Cat.
    114.23  166n.11
    114.32–115.12  172n.27
    115.3–5  167
Epicharmus (ed. K–A)
  F 66  148n.80
Epictetus see Arrian
Epicurus
  Ep. Hdt.
    81  153n.99
  Ep. Men.
    125  153n.99, 153n.101
  Fragments (ed. Arrighetti)
    F 21.1  221–2
    F 21.4  223–4
    F 31  224–5
    F 37  224
    F 251  220
  RS
    139(2)  153n.99, 153n.101
Eratosthenes of Cyrene
  BNJ 241 F 16  232–4
Euclides of Megara (ed. Döring)
  F 19  195
Eunapius
  VS
    4.1.8  202n.24
Euripides
  Ba.
    370–3  118n.89
  El.
    944  117n.86
  Fragments (TrGF)
    F 184 (Antiope)  141
    F 282 (Autolycus I)  55
    F 494 vv. 23–6 (Melanipp. Capt.)  65

## INDEX LOCORUM 279

F 657 (*Protesil.*) 65n.58
F 714 118n.87
*Hipp.*
   1361–3 54n.26
*Med.*
   332 34n.55
*Ph.*
   531–5 118n.89
   558 117n.86
Eusebius of Caesarea
*PE*
   9.5.2–7 183n.58
   11.3.8 103
   14.8.11 245
   14.18.14 232
   14.18.15 232
   14.27.11 221n.78
   15.2.4 15n.9, 16
   15.5.12 221n.78
Eustathius
*Il.*
   1.108 67n.67
   6.211 208n.44
   20.241 208n.44
*Od.*
   1.170 208n.44
   2.166–7 67n.66
   2.210 67n.67
   10.325 208n.44
   10.491 67n.65
   14.187 208n.44
   15.264 208n.44
   19.105 208n.44
   24.298 208n.44
Favorinus
   *Corinth.* ([Dio Chrysostom], *Or.* 37)
      5 74n.81
Galen
   *De subst. nat. fac.* (ed. Kühn)
      4.758 179n.46
   *Hipp. et Plat. plac.* (*CMG* 5.4.1.2)
      5.6.35 118, 218
   *In Hipp. Epid. VI* (*CMG* 5.10.2.2)
      4.10.145 16n.11
Gellius
   *NA*
      4.13 105n.47
      20.5 165n.9, 167n.14
*Greek Anthology*
   7.417 214
   7.418 214

Hegesias of Cyrene
   *SSR* IV.F 3–4 201
Heraclides of Pontus (ed. Schütrumpf)
   F 24B 106n.50
   F 39 98–9
   F 40 100–1
   F 52 107
   F 54B 107
   F 57 107
   F 58 107
   F 130 95
   F 131–2 106n.50
[Hermogenes]
   *Meth.*
      36.455 9n.26
Herodotus
   1.30–3 175
   1.59–60 70n.76
   4.33–5 155n.109
   4.36 106, 155
   4.42 102n.36
   5.55 134n.25
   7.72 154n.102
   8.138 175
Hesiod
   *Fragments* (ed. Merkelbach and West)
      F 10d 157n.117
      F 144 135
   *Th.*
      114 230n.104
      212 195n.7
      756–66 195n.7
Hesychius
   s.v. αἰγείρου θέα (α 1695) 39n.67
   s.v. θέα παρ' αἰγείρῳ (θ 166) 39n.67
   s.v. παρ' αἴγειρον θέα (π 513) 39n.67
[Hippocrates]
   *Ep.*
      15 [68.22–6 Smith] 39
      17.2 [74.15–16 Smith] 37
      17.2 [74.22–6 Smith] 37
      17.3 [76.5–6 Smith] 39
      17.4 [78.18–19 Smith] 39
      17.4 [78.21–80.1 Smith] 37
      17.10 [92.4–6 Smith] 38
      17.10 [92.8 Smith] 39
      17.10 [92.10 Smith] 38
Homer
   *Il.*
      1.315 141n.59
      2.303 141n.58
      2.306 141n.59
      2.484 230n.104

Homer (cont.)
    4.47 141n.59
    4.165 141n.59
    6.211 208n.44
    6.449 141n.59
    8.548 141n.59
    8.549 141n.59
    8.550–2 141n.59
    9.363 173
    10.224 141n.58
    11.218 230n.104
    12.167–79 146
    14.216–17 117n.85
    14.231 195n.7
    14.508 230n.104
    16.259–65 146
    16.682 195n.7
    20.241 208n.44
    24.27 141n.59

  *Od.*
    1.33–4 141
    18.35–40 67
    19.179 135

Horace
  *Epist.*
    2.1.194 36n.60

Hyperides
  *In Philippid.*
    3 134n.26

Iamblichus
  *De anima*
    26 97n.25

  *VP*
    19 106
    28 106
    32 106
    58 105n.46

Ion of Chius
  *Epidemiai*
    BNJ 392 F 6 15
    BNJ 392 F 13 15
    BNJ 392 F 14 15n.6

Josephus
  *Ap.*
    1.22.176 181n.54
    1.22.176–82 182–3
    1.22.183 184

Julian
  *Or.*
    6.181a 19n.21

*Lexicon Patmense*
  s.v. ἐνεβρίμει (151) 84

[Longinus]
  *Subl.*
    44 4n.8, 6n.12

Lucian
  *Bis acc.*
    33 213
    34 7n.17

  *DMort.*
    3(2).1 214
    6.3 109n.60

  *Icar.*
    23 208n.45

  *Macr.*
    19 202n.24

  *Merc. cond.*
    21 112n.72
    42 235n.118

  *Nec.*
    1 214

  *Nigr.*
    38 47n.7

  *Philops.*
    22–4 109

  *Rhet. pr.*
    6 235n.118

  *VH*
    1.2 95n.18

  *Vit. auct.*
    10 19n.21
    26 165n.9

Lysias
  *In Nic.*
    2 132n.20
    25 132n.20

Machon (ed. Gow)
  F 9 18

Metrodorus (ed. Körte)
  F 46 227n.98

Olympiodorus
  *In Alc.*
    3 140n.53

  *Proleg.*
    7.6–7 166n.10
    7.8–15 167n.13

Origen
  *Cels.*
    7.66 221n.78

INDEX LOCORUM 281

Ovid
   *Met.*
      11.410–748  157n.117
      15.382–8  158n.121

Papyri

PAï Khanoum inv. Akh IIIB77P.O.154
   col. ii.2–iv.7  57–8

PBerol. inv. 13045  76–7

PBerol. inv. 21256  87

PBour. 1
   fol. 6–7, ll. 141–68  21n.23

PErl. 4
   col. ii.33–57  46

PGiss. 4.39
   Fr. A  66

PHerc. 1027
   see Carneiscus, *Philistas*

PHibeh 182
   col. ii.7–14  78

PIen.inv. 660
   Fr. A, B  86

PKöln. 5.205
   col. i.30–iii.36  50–2

PLitLond. 160
   col. ii.67, 71–5  67

POxy. 4.664/50.3544
   Fr. A col. i.1–45  71–2
   Fr. B col. i.1–29  72–3
   Fr. B col. ii.5–45  72–3

POxy. 8.1087
   col. ii.41  231n.105

POxy. 52.3655
   ll. 1–16  82–3

POxy. 53.3699
   col. ii.5–iv.12  53–4

PPetr. 2.49e (=PLit.Lond. 159a)
   col. ii.1–iii.17  59–60

PSchub. 4
   col. i.  68–9

PSI XI 1215
   col. i.36–ii.36  48–9

PVindob. G 29946
   col. ii.7–iii.2  80
   col. iii.3–4  81
   col. iii.7–8  82
   col. iii.16–24  81
   col. iv.1–24  80–1
   col. iv.25–v.10  80
   col. v.11–13  79–80

   col. v.20–5  80
   col. vi.13–25  82
   col. xx.42–4  120n.99
   col. xxii.35–xxiii.6  120n.99

Parmenides (ed. Coxon)
   F 1 ll. 22–3  40

Persaeus
   *SVF* 1.100 F 451  17
   *SVF* 1.101 F 452  25

Philodemus
   *Acad. ind.* (PHerc. 1021
      and 164)
      col. iii.35–9  132
      col. iii.35–v  103n.39
      col. v.13–vi.1  92
      col. vi.1a–12a  113
      col. vi.10  15
      col. vii.3–5  93
      col. xvi  115n.79
      col. xvii–xxxiii  91n.7
      col. xviii.34–40  120n.96
      col. xx.7  27n.34
      col. xx.42–4  120n.99
      col. xxii.35–xxiii.6  120n.99
   *De Epic.* (PHerc. 1232)
      Fr. 8 col. i.7–12  221n.76
   *Lib.* (PHerc. 1471)
      Fr. 20  95n.19
   *Mort.* (PHerc. 1050)
      col. i.5  153n.99
      col. i.6–7  153n.101
      col. i.9  153n.99
      col. i.18  153n.99
      col. vi.10  202n.24
      col. xxvi.8–9  153n.101
      col. xxviii.15–16  153n.99
      col. xxxix.22–3  153n.99
   *Piet. 1* (PHerc. 1077/1098)
      col. xxvi–xxxi  221n.78
   *Poem. 5* (PHerc. 1425 and 1538)
      col. xii.30–1  189n.74
   *Rhet.*
      Sudhaus II 61, col. lvi.16–18
         175n.31
   *Rhet. 2* (PHerc. 1674)
      col. x.21–xi.1  223–4
      col. xliv.19–27  194n.5
      col. lii–lvii  223n.82
   *Sto.* (PHerc. 155 and 339)
      col. xv.21–xvii.10  203
      col. xvi.4–9  203
      col. xvi.21  203

Philo the Dialectitian (ed. Döring)
F 101 199
Philoponus
In Cat.
4.15 166n.11
In Meteor. I
117 97n.25, 107n.55
Philostratus
Her.
42 109n.60
VS
511 4n.8
Photius
Bibl.
92.70a 76n.88
161.103b 187n.69
190.147a 67n.67
Lex.
s.v. αἰγείρου θέα καὶ ἡ παρ' αἴγειρον θέα (α 505) 39n.67
s.v. θέαν παρ' αἴγειρον (θ 47) 39n.67
Pindar
Isthm.
2.6 133n.23
Plato (comic poet) (ed. K–A)
F 54 112n.72
Plato
Ap.
21a 196n.11
21b–e 138
31c–d 138n.41
33e 151, 196n.11
33e–34a 136n.36
40c–d 195n.7
Charm.
154d–e 47
158b 106, 155
Crit.
44a–b 172
50a–54d 118
Criti.
113a–b 155
Euthd.
279a–282e 146
281a–c 55n.28
304e–305a 142
Grg.
447b 47n.7
470d–471d 140
484e 140, 141
523a–527e 107n.53

Lg.
624a–b 136
661a 119n.91
802d 196n.10
811a–b 143
811b–e 131
817b 131
819a 143
861e–862a 148n.81
885b 131n.15
893b 131n.15
899d 131n.15
901d 131n.15
951d–952a 129
961a–b 129
968d 129

Men.
70a 149
70b 145n.71
71e–73b 65n.57
80d–e 145
86c–d 150
87e 55n.28
93c–94e 149

Phd.
58d 227n.97
58e–59a 228
59b 196n.11
59d–e 70n.75
60a 64
60a–b 156
61b 201
61c 201
61c–62c 35
103a 160n.127
107c–115a 107n.53
109b 185
110b–c 185
116b 159n.122
118a 19

Phdr.
229c 158
230b 37
242a 107n.53
245c–249c 107n.53
259b–c 158
261a 94n.18
271c 94n.18
276d 131n.16
276e 176

Phlb.
36c–42c 101n.32
44a–d 111n.67

INDEX LOCORUM   283

*Plt.*
  257a–c 111
  264a–267c 112n.70
  284b 141n.58
  295c 131n.16

*Prm.*
  131–3 57n.34
  137c 44

*Prt.*
  339e–347a 141
  345d–e 148n.81
  348d 141n.58

*Resp.*
  328b 138
  332b 141–2
  340a–b 138
  394b–c 184n.60
  487b–c 147
  496b 136n.36
  496c 136n.36
  581c 133n.23
  590a 54n.24
  606b 96n.21
  614b–621b 185
  615a 185

*Sph.*
  216c–217a 111
  253e–254b 111

*Symp.*
  172b 195
  173b 195
  174d 141n.58
  176a 221n.77
  215a 48
  216d 48

*Tht.*
  142c–143a 194
  143a 131n.16
  143b–c 153n.97, 194
  150b–151a 137, 137n.38
  151c 217n.68

*Ti.*
  20d–e 155

[Plato]
  *Alc. I*
    103b 48
    105a–c 141n.56, 141n.57
    106c 145
    117d–118b 141n.56
    122a 103
    125e–126a 145

  *Alc. II*
    138c–140c 141n.56
    140a 141n.58
    140c 140n.54
    141a–b 141n.56
    141c 141
    141d 140, 141n.58
    142d–e 141
    143a 141n.56
    143e–144a 140
    144d–146d 141n.56
    146a 140, 141
    147a 55n.28
    147b 141
    147c 141
    148e–149b 141
    149d–e 141, 141n.59
    150c 140n.54

  *Amat.*
    132c 143
    132c–d 142
    132d 142
    133a 142
    133b 142
    133c 142
    134a 142
    134b 143
    135b 142
    135e–137a 142
    137b–139a 142
    138c 142
    139a 142

  *Ax.*
    364a–365a 153
    364b 154
    365a 153, 156
    365d 153
    366a–369a 153
    366c 155n.110
    369b–c 153
    370c–d 153
    371a–372a 103
    371c 154

  *Clit.*
    406 138
    408c 139
    408c–409e 138
    410a–b 139

  *De iust.*
    372a–373e 147
    373e 148

[Plato] (cont.)
   374a 148
   374b–d 148n.81

*De virt.*
   376a 149
   376b 149
   376c 148
   377d 148
   377d–e 148
   379c 149
   379d 149

*Dem. 2*
   384a–b 152

*Dem. 4*
   386c 152

*Ep.*
   2.310b 114n.78
   2.312d 114n.78
   2.313d 114n.78
   2.313e 114n.78
   3.319a 114n.78
   7.327d 75n.82
   7.339a 114
   7.339d 75n.82
   7.346b–d 29n.39
   7.347b–c 29n.39
   7.348c–e 29n.39
   7.348e–349b 29n.39
   7.349d 114
   7.350c–d 29n.39
   12.359c 131n.16
   13.360b 29n.39

*Epin.*
   973a 129
   973b 129
   980c–d 130–1
   980d 110n.64
   992d 130

*Eryx.*
   392a 146
   392b 146
   393b–394a 55n.28, 119n.91, 146
   394a 147
   395a–b 147
   395c–d 147
   395e–397b 146
   396d 146
   397c 147
   397c–399a 146, 153n.100
   399a 146
   399d 146
   405b 147
   406a 147

*Halc.*
   3 157
   8 157, 158, 159

*Hipparch.*
   225a–b 133
   225e–226a 133
   226a 133
   228a 133
   228b 133
   229b–d 134
   232b 133

*Min.*
   315a 135
   317a 135
   318e 135
   320d 135
   321d 135

*Sis.*
   387b 144
   387c 144
   388c–d 144

*Thg.*
   121a–d 151
   125e–126a 138n.40, 141n.57
   126a 137
   128d 138n.41
   128e–131e 137
   130d–e 137

Plutarch
  *Adv. Col.*
   1109e–f 16n.12, 221–2
   1115a 93, 186n.66
   1115c 165
   1119c–d 197
   1119c–1120b 194n.5
   1126c 226n.93

  *Alex.*
   7.5 167n.14
   65.1–4
   65.2 204n.30

  *Alex. fort.*
   328a 120n.96
   331e 204n.30

  *An seni*
   783d 80n.97

  *Arist.*
   27.2 159

  *Cam.*
   22.3 95

INDEX LOCORUM    285

*Cim.*
  9.1-6  15
  16.10  15n.6
  18.6  141n.57

*Comm. not.*
  1065a  119n.91

*Conv. sept. sap.*
  146b-e  70n.75
  152a-155d  32

*De am. prol.*
  497d  200

*De aud.*
  47a  47n.7

*De aud. poet.*
  14e  106, 155
  14e-f  95, 190

*De coh. ira*
  457f  72n.79

*De esu I*
  995c-d  19n.21

*De facie*
  920e-f  181n.54

*De genio*
  590a-592e  187

*De lat. viv.*
  1129a  221n.76, 227n.95

*Dem.*
  31.4-6  76n.88

*De soll. an.*
  964a  60n.41

*De tranq. anim.*
  468a  19, 83, 197

*De vit. pud.*
  536b  202n.26

*Dion*
  18.6  115
  22.5  172, 175

*Lys.*
  25.3  141n.57

*Nic.*
  13.1  141n.57

*Non posse*
  1086e  95n.19
  1095a  93, 186
  1095e  23, 24, 179, 187
  1097e-f  227
  1101a  227n.99
  1101b  226n.93
  1102b  221n.78
  1103a  227n.95

*Per.*
  24.3  64n.53

*Phoc.*
  1.1  77n.89
  1.1-2  76n.88
  30.2-3  76n.88
  30.5  76n.88

*Praec. ger.*
  803a  77n.89
  820f  77n.89

*Quaest. conv.*
  612d-e  2, 23, 113, 190
  612e  220
  614d  219n.71
  614f  219n.71
  634c  27
  651f  222
  652a  222
  653b  222
  653c  222n.80
  653c-d  222
  711b-c  9n.26
  728d-f  103

*Quomodo adul.*
  63d-e  27n.34

*Reg. imp. apophth.*
  189c  72n.79

*Sol.*
  1.3  75
  22.4  75
  29.5  74n.81
  30.8  74n.81
  31.4  75
  32.3  75

*Tim.*
  15.8-9  80n.97

[Plutarch]
  *Cons. ad Apoll.*
    109b-d  116n.83
    115b  172n.26
    115b-e  173-4

Polyaenus
  5.14  72n.79

Polyzelus (ed. K-A)
  F 3  35n.58

Porphyry
  *Abst.*
    1.5  60n.41
    1.19  60n.41
    3.25  60n.41
  *In Ptol. Harm.*
    1.4.80  187n.69

Porphyry (*cont.*)
*VP*
   28–9  106

Praxiphanes (ed. Wehrli)
   F 11 Wehrli  189

Probus
*Comm. ad Verg. Ecl.*
   6.31  214n.59

Proclus
*In Alc. I* (ed. Westerink)
   98.14–15  202n.26
   274.3–4  7n.17

*In Parm.* (ed. Cousin)
   1.659  98n.27, 119n.95, 179

*In Remp.* (ed. Kroll)
   2.113.19–115.7  185
   2.119.18–27  107
   2.122.22–123.12  184

*In Ti.* (ed. Diehl)
   1.20  139
   1.76  119, 119n.94
   1.90  93
   3.138  93

*Prolegomena in Platonic Philosophy*
(ed. Westerink)
   14.3–4  7n.17
   15.31–32  7n.17
   25.2–10  128n.7

Quintilian
*Inst.*
   9.2.29  219n.70
   10.5.15  10.28

Satyrus (ed. Schorn)
   F 6 Fr. 39 col. iii.19–20  62n.47
   F 6 Fr. 39 col. xi  65n.59
   F 6 Fr. 39 col. xiii.23–38  64
   F 6 Fr. 39 col. xiv.31  62n.47
   F 6 Fr. 39 col. xv.13–14  62n.47
   F 6 Fr. 39 col. xxiii.1–6  62n.44
   F 19  27

*Scholia in Apoll. Rhod.*
   I 645  105n.47

*Scholia vet. in Hom. Od.*
   10.492  67n.65

Seneca
*Apocol.*
   5.4  208n.45

*Ben.*
   4.2.1  221

*Ep.*
   9.1  194n.5
   88.5  221

Sextus Empiricus
*Adv. math.*
   1.252–3  96n.22
   1.263–5  96n.22
   1.305  231n.108
   9.108  194n.5
   11.1  231n.108
   11.51–8  116–17

*Pyr.*
   1.224  231

Simplicius
*In Phys.*
   8.16  166n.10
   8.17  166n.11

Sophocles
*Aj.*
   233–44  39
   296–310  39

Speusippus (ed. Tarán)
   F 5a  112
   F 5b  112
   F 80a–81b  111n.67
   F 86–7  109n.62
   T 1  109–10

Stilpo
   *SSR* II O 17  19, 20

Stobaeus
   1.49.47  156n.114
   2.15.47  208
   3.1.98  208
   3.3.25  56n.29
   3.6.63  195
   3.8.20  209–10
   3.40.8  197, 208
   4.22a.25  159n.124
   4.22d.103  159n.124
   4.29a  170n.23
   4.29a.13  207
   4.29a.24  170
   4.29a.25  171
   4.29c.52  171
   4.31b.51  145
   4.31c.64  118n.87
   4.31d.117  145
   4.32a.21  208
   4.32b.33  118n.87
   4.33.6  118n.87
   4.33.11  118n.87
   4.33.31  208

4.33.33 145
4.34.72 208
4.34.75 156n.114
4.44.82 208
4.44.83 208
4.52b.54 156n.114
4.53.38 156n.114
4.67.22 159n.124

Strabo

1.1.10 95n.18
1.2.2 234
1.2.3 95n.18
2.3.4 102
10.4.8 135n.30
12.3.1 92
13.2.4 180
14.1.28 231n.105
15.1.28 204
15.1.63-5 204
15.1.64 206
15.1.65 204n.30
16.2.29 212, 214n.60

Suda

s.v. Ἀντισθένης (a 2723) 155n.107, 177n.44
s.v. ἀπ' αἰγείρου θέα καὶ ἐπ' αἴγειρον (a 2952) 39n.67
s.v. αἴγειρος (αι 35) 39n.67
s.v. Αἰσχίνης (αι 346) 145
s.v. διαλεκτική (δ 627) 7n.17
s.v. Ἐμπεδότιμος (ε 1007) 107n.55
s.v. Ἐρατοσθένης (ε 2898) 143, 143n.66
s.v. Ἑρμαγόρας (ε 3023) 217
s.v. Εὐκλείδης (ε 3539) 194, 195
s.v. Ἡρακλείδης (η 461) 93
s.v. Λακύδης (λ 72) 91
s.v. Λέων (λ 265) 157n.116
s.v. Πολέμων (π 1887) 90
s.v. Στίλπων (σ 1114) 196
s.v. τὰ τρία τῶν εἰς τὸν θάνατον (τ 154) 35n.58
s.v. Φαιός (φ 180) 213
s.v. Φιλίσκος (φ 359) 204
s.v. φιλόσοφος (φ 418) 132

Tacitus
*Ann.*
16.34 209n.51

Teles (ed. Fuentes González)
F 1 208, 211
F 2 208, 209, 209n.47
F 3 197-8, 208, 209n.47, 210-11

F 4a 208, 209n.47, 212
F 4b 208, 212
F 5 208
F 6 208
F 7 208

Tertullian
*De praescr. haeret.*
39.4 235n.118

Themistius
*Or.*
23.295 176

Theodoretus of Cyrus
*Eranistes*
62 7n.17

Theognis
*Eleg.*
1.198 133n.23

Theon
*Progymn.*
60 69n.72
89-90 69n.72
101 22n.26
103 22n.26

Thucydides
1.6.3 100n.31
1.20.2 134n.25
5.4-5 146
6.15.3 71n.77
6.54.2-55 134n.25

Timon of Phlius
*SH* 775 230n.104
*SH* 833 231
*SH* 841 231n.108

*Trag. Adesp.*
*TrGF* F 92 34n.55

Tzetzes, *Chil.*
10.355.783-5 7n.17

Valerius Maximus
5.1(ext)2 72n.79

Vita Aesopi
65 80

Vita Marciana
4 177

Xenocrates (ed. Isnardi Parente)
F 264-6 114n.77
F 267 114n.77

Xenophon
*Hell.*
4.2.11-12 146

Xenophon (cont.)
  Mem.
    1.2.48  196n.11
    1.3.1  14n.5
    1.3.2  141n.56
    1.3.9–13  84n.111
    1.4.1  139
    1.6  84
    2.1.21–34  40, 118, 153n.100, 209
    2.3.1–19  196n.11
    2.9.4  114n.78
    3.1  160n.127
    3.3  160n.127
    3.8  84
    3.8.2  55n.28
    3.9.1  13
    3.9.6–7  141n.56
    3.9.14  14
    3.11.1  22
    3.12.1–8  196n.11
    3.13.1  14
    3.13.2  14
    3.13.2–4  25n.32
    3.13.3  14
    3.13.5  14
    3.13.6  14
    3.14  25n.32
    3.14.2–3  160n.127
    3.14.4  21
    4.1.1  14n.5
    4.2  143
    4.2.12–19  148n.81
    4.2.34  55n.28
    4.2.34–35  55
    4.4  84
    4.4.6  143
  *Oec.*
    1.7–14  147
    7.1  147
    14.10.3  133n.23
  *Symp.*
    1.1–3  70n.75
    2.1  221n.77
    2.22  33n.51
    2.26–7  33n.51
    4.12–26  153n.98

Zeno
  *SVF* 1.47 F 190  119n.91

Zenobius
  6.11 s.v. τὰ τρία τῶν εἰς τὸν θάνατον  35n.58

Ps.-Zonaras
  s.v. διαλεκτική  7n.17

# Index of Greek Terms

ἀκροαματικός 166
ἀπομνημονεύματα 14
αὐτοπρόσωπος 166
διάλογος 3, 7
διατριβή 3–4, 206, 220
ἐξωτερικός 165–6
μυθολογία 95
προοίμια 98, 179

συγγράμματα 3–4
συνταγματικά 111
σχολαί 120
ὑπομνήματα 3–4, 17, 110, 131n.16
ὑπομνηματικά 111
χρεία 13n.2, 17
ψυχαγωγία 94
ψυχρός 196

# General Index

Abaris 94, 95, 96, 106, 155
Abdera 36, 39
Academy 89–125, 126n.2, 132, 136, 137n.39, 138, 140, 143, 148n.82, 152, 158n.119, 164, 180, 184, 189n.75, 206, 212, 239, 244–5
  *see also* Middle Platonism
Achilles 47n.7, 68, 172–3
Achilles Tatius 236
Acicharus 103, 180
Acragas 103
acroamatic works 165n.7, 8, 166–7, 172, 178, 191
Aelian 158
Aeschines of Sphettus 48, 51, 64, 145–6, 156n.114
Aeschylus 15, 61, 108, 118n.89
Aesop 95, 180
Aethalides 105
afterlife 105, 107, 155, 185, 192
  *see also* Hades; underworld
Ahiquar *see* Acicharus
Aï Khanoum 57, 59, 181
Ajax 39, 202
Alcibiades 48, 71n.77, 140, 141n.56, 141n.57, 161
Alcyone 157–9
Alexander of Aphrodisias 167
Alexander the Great 16–17, 22, 31n.45, 32, 40, 69–70, 85–6, 88, 108, 127, 141, 144n.67, 154n.102, 180, 182, 184, 195, 204–6, 238, 242
Alexander of Pherae 76, 172
Alexander, Tiberius Julius 236
Alexandria 5, 29, 75, 242
Alexinus of Elis 15, 16–17, 194n.5, 195, 238, 242
allegorical interpretation 31, 68n.69, 98, 235
Amphion 143
Anacreon 133, 134n.26
Anaxagoras 63
Anaximenes of Lampsacus 196
anecdote 9, 10, 13–27, 40–2, 63, 78–82, 101, 109, 137, 196–7, 200, 202–4, 238, 242–3
animals 29, 31, 37, 39, 60, 86, 109n.60, 111, 112n.70, 114, 157, 158, 236–7
anonymity *see* interlocutor, anonymous
Antagoras of Rhodes 115
Antigonus I Monophthalmus 76n.88
Antigonus II Gonatas 17, 23n.27, 32n.50, 206–8, 216–7, 238

Antiochus of Ascalon 89, 92, 125
Antipater (general) 76, 86
Antipater of Tarsus 23, 159n.124, 203, 215, 219, 245
Antipater of Tyre 159n.124
Antiphon 20, 84
Antisthenes 34, 48, 50, 57n.32, 64n.53, 65n.57, 82, 100, 136, 148n.82, 155n.107, 177n.44, 202–3
Anytus 150
Apollo 54, 106, 113, 186
Apollophanes 216
*apomnemoneumata* 13n.2, 15–17, 18n.19, 23, 25, 27, 197, 216, 231n.108, 238, 242
apotheosis 106
Arcesilaus 26–7, 89, 91, 115, 120–3, 124n.105, 182, 212, 213, 231, 232, 234, 239
Archedemus of Syracuse 114–5
Archelaus (philosopher) 15n.7
Archelaus I 63, 140, 141n.57
Archetimus of Syracuse 24
Archilochus 94, 108
Archytas of Tarentum 41, 102, 114–15, 187–8
Aristeas *see Letter of Aristeas*
Aristides of Alopece (I) 148, 149
Aristides of Alopece (II) 137
Aristippus of Cyrene 3n.5, 17, 20, 51, 84, 111, 196, 199–200
Aristippus the Younger 102, 111
Aristo of Ceos 106, 190, 216n.67, 242
Aristo of Chios 15, 17, 190, 216, 232, 233–4
Aristocles of Messene 16–17, 231–2
aristocracy 49
Aristogeiton 134
Aristotle 2, 3, 5, 6, 10n.28, 16–17, 23, 24n.29, 29, 56–7, 59, 61, 65, 68, 72, 93, 94, 103, 105n.46, 108, 113, 116, 131, 154, 159, 164–81, 183–5, 191, 195, 196, 231, 242, 244
  *see also* dialogue, Aristotelian
Aristophanes 54n.26, 64, 112, 118n.89, 209
Aristophanes of Byzantium 126, 128
Aristoxenus of Tarentum 23, 24, 41, 42, 102, 103, 159, 187
Arrian 76n.88, 121
Arsinoe III Philopator 232–3
Artemon 29

Asclepiades (author of *Apomnemoneumata of Plato*) 15, 16
Asclepiades of Myrleia 96n.22
Aspasia 63, 64, 199
astronomy 130, 132, 142
Athenaeus 21–2, 24, 27n.36, 36, 101n.33, 245
Athenians 63, 71, 76, 80–1, 99–100, 147, 177
Athens 5, 11, 15, 33, 49, 63, 72, 74–5, 76, 89, 92–3, 111, 133–4, 144, 146, 178n.44, 195, 207
Atlantis 119, 155

Bacchius of Tanagra 16
banquet *see* dialogue, sympotic
beauty 22, 46–8, 54–6, 119n.91
Bernays, Jacob 164, 169
biographical literature 11n.30, 13, 14n.3, 15, 41–2, 61, 63, 65, 82, 104, 159, 187, 190, 203, 243
Bion of Borysthenes 170n.23, 206–8, 209, 234
birth *see* noble birth
Brandis, Christian August 169

Calanoi 183–4
Calanus 183, 205
Callias 100, 196
Callicles 41, 112n.71, 114, 141, 143n.64, 188
Callimachus 115, 155, 189, 201–2
Callisthenes 159, 180
Carneades 89, 91, 120–2, 123n.104, 244–5
Carneiscus 189, 226, 228
Carthage 91, 122
Cassander 76, 86
Cato the Elder 41, 190
Cebes 234–5
Cephalus 110, 156
Chaerecrates 196
Chaerephon 157–9, 161
Chaeroneia 186
Chaldaeans 103, 132
Chamaeleon of Heraclea 188
characterization 7–8, 10, 169
 *see also* ethopoiia
Charmides 47, 137, 147, 153
Chion of Heraclea 102n.37
*chreia* 9, 13–14, 17, 20–2, 79, 205, 231n.108, 243
Cicero 1, 28–9, 61, 64, 65n.61, 70, 92n.9, 96–8, 119–24, 165–6
Cimon 15, 25
Circe 66, 68
Cleanthes 24n.29, 118, 202n.24, 203, 209, 215, 217–8, 237
Clearchus of Heraclea 102n.37

Clearchus of Soli 31, 33n.53, 34–5, 57, 59, 103, 105n.47, 181–5
Cleinias 107, 153–4, 161
Cleinias of Cnossus 129, 131
Cleinomachus 110, 195
Cleitophon 138–9, 160, 161, 162
Cleombrotus 155, 201
Cleonymus 185, 244
Clitomachus 89, 91, 120, 122, 124n.105
Colotes 194n.5
comedy 33n.53, 63, 90, 96, 118n.89, 208, 214, 230n.104
 *see also* drama; theatre
commemorative literature 82, 227, 242
consolation 11, 12, 91, 115–16, 122, 154, 156, 176, 243
Corinth 24, 73–4, 176, 186
courtesan 24n.29, 34, 105n.47 214–15
 *see also hetaira*
Crantor of Soli 91, 115–19, 140n.54, 146, 154, 176, 180, 209, 242
Crates (head of the Academy) 90–1
Crates of Thebes 15, 83, 202n.24, 206, 209
Critias (father of Callaeschrus) 155
Critias (son of Callaeschrus) 47, 146, 161
Croesus 24, 31, 175, 214
Cynics 19, 33–6, 38, 100, 136, 140, 147, 155n.107, 197, 202–15, 216, 217, 230n.104, 235, 239
Cypselus 24, 73, 74
Cyrenaics 52, 102, 111, 155, 196, 199–202, 206
Cyrus 202, 204n.31, 205n.36

*daimon* 107, 130, 138, 154, 195, 235
*daimonion* of Socrates 136n.36, 137, 138n.41
Damon 153
dance 33n.51, 213
Dandamis 85, 205
 *see also* Mandanis
death, fear of 50–1, 153–4
 *see also* dialogue, on death; starvation; suicide
Deinarchus 76–7
Deinias 100, 101
deliberation 49, 144–5
Delphi 24, 59, 134, 181, 232
Demades 69, 76–7
Demetrius the Cynic 209
Demetrius of Phaleron 17, 29–31, 159, 188
Demetrius Poliorcetes 32n.50, 196
democracy 6n.12, 48–50
Democritus 36–40, 170n.23, 237
Demodocus 136, 150–1, 160
Demosthenes 76, 77
desires 41, 79, 222

dialectic 111, 121, 122-3, 194, 197, 199, 203, 219n.71
dialogue
   ancient terminology 3-4
   Aristotelian 62, 84, 97, 165, 167-8, 191
   bloom, decline, revival 1, 2, 4-6, 164
   on death 18, 35, 104, 113, 116, 154, 172-5, 180, 201-2, 228
   definitions 7-8
   diegetic, dramatic, mixed 9n.26, 43-4
   historical 24, 30-1, 69-77, 85, 88, 96-7, 102, 238, 241
   on Homer 66-8, 94, 108, 188
   question-and-answer format 7-8, 20, 32, 42, 81, 123, 164-5, 166, 194, 198, 202, 230
   Plato's 2, 3, 5, 7-8, 9-10, 90, 241
   Socratic 9-10, 13, 20, 45, 64, 69, 121-3, 139, 154, 160-1, 241
   sympotic 2, 5, 23-7, 33-6, 104, 113, 179, 187, 190, 213, 215, 216-17, 219, 220-2, 240
   titles 3-4, 17, 126, 177, 178n.44, 191
   *see also* erotapocritic format; interlocutor
diatribe 3-4, 85n.114, 118n.90, 206
Dicaearchus of Messana 93, 105n.47, 185-7, 191
Didymus Chalcenterus 24
*diegesis* 8, 9n.26, 37n.62, 85
   *see also* narration
digression 10, 133, 184
Dio Chrysostom 2, 3, 8, 17n.15, 22, 31n.45, 61, 64, 70, 109, 116, 204, 205, 235, 238
Diodorus (author of *Apomnemoneumata*) 15
Diodorus Cronus 196, 199
Diogenes of Babylon 219
Diogenes the Cynic 8-9, 17, 19, 20n.22, 21n.23, 22, 40, 79-82, 83, 84, 170n.23, 181n.52, 195, 197, 200, 202-4, 205-6, 209, 213, 242
Diogenes of Oenoanda 41n.70, 228-30, 239
Diogenes of Tarsus 120n.98
Dion of the Academy 2, 23
Dion of Syracuse 29n.39, 133n.22, 175
Dionysius of Heraclea 93, 202n.24
Dionysius of Syracuse 29n.39, 41, 75, 80, 102, 114, 144, 175, 188, 200
Dioscurides (author of *Apomnemoneumata*) 16
Diotima 63
*Dissoi logoi* 149n.84, 152
Doric dialect 200
drama 39, 63, 96, 118
   *see also* comedy; theatre; tragedy
dream 39-40, 172, 175, 183, 184, 195
   *see also* sleep
Droysen, Johann Gustav 2n.2
Düring, Ingemar 6, 164

education 54-5, 81, 85, 86, 88, 129-31, 132, 136, 141n.56, 142, 204, 206
   *see also* erudition; polymathy
Egypt 74, 75, 114, 196
*ekphrasis* 29, 235
Empedocles 60, 63n.51, 103-4, 107n.52, 237
Empedotimus 96, 106-7, 109, 185
Empedus (author of *Apomnemoneumata*) 16
Ephorus 24, 135n.30
Epictetus 121, 202
Epicureans 89, 95, 124, 153, 163, 189, 194, 213, 219-30, 237, 239
Epicurus 2, 23, 33n.53, 95n.19, 120, 194n.5, 213, 219-30, 231, 239-40
Epigenes 196
epiphany 107, 158, 185
epistolography 28-41, 42, 114n.78, 196, 204, 220
   *see also* letter
Er 107n.53, 185, 244
Erastus (author of *Apomnemoneumata of Plato*) 15, 16
Eratosthenes of Cyrene 143, 216, 232-4, 242
eristic 123, 152, 194
erotapocritic format 32, 200
   *see also* dialogue, question-and-answer format
erudition 36, 88, 142-3
   *see also* polymathy
*ethopoiia* 69, 178, 241
   *see also* characterization
Eubulides 195
Euclides of Megara 110-1, 153n.97, 194-5
Eudoxus of Cnidus 102, 103, 111, 113-14
Euphorbus 105, 106n.49
Eupolis 189n.75
Euripides 63-5, 93, 115, 118, 140, 141, 143n.64, 170n.23, 171, 178, 181, 186
Eusebius of Caesarea 3
Euthydemus 55, 143, 148n.81
Euxitheus 182
exile 197-9, 208, 210-11
exoteric works 164-7, 169, 178, 179, 181, 191

fable 86, 95, 114
fame 54-5, 105
farming 176-7
feast 15, 32n.50, 33, 34, 103-4, 233
   *see also* dialogue, sympotic; funeral feast
food 23, 25, 33, 34-5, 60, 185, 214, 217
   *see also* feast; meal
Forms *see* Ideas
Fronto 218-19
funeral feast 113, 199, 232

Gelon 31n.45, 102, 105
genre blending 10–11, 12, 29, 38–9, 77, 158, 163, 243–4
Glycera 27, 197
Gnathaena 24n.29
Gobryas 103, 154–5
gods 130–1, 140–1, 149, 157–8, 221, 231
goods 55–6, 116–19, 146, 147, 153, 170, 198
Gregory of Nyssa 245
grief 115–16, 154, 156, 180, 185
Gymnosophists 32, 85, 184, 204–5

Hades 51, 105, 107, 213
 see also afterlife; underworld
Hagnon of Tarsus 120
happiness 55–6, 118, 132, 175, 200–1
Harmodius 134
health 55, 118–19, 146
Hecato of Rhodes 17, 219
hedonism 41, 51–2, 100, 102, 111, 113, 200, 216, 218
Hegesias of Cyrene 52, 155, 200–2
Hellenistic
 aesthetics 156, 162, 163, 243
 literature 1–2, 4–7, 8, 11–12, 243–4
 prose genres 1–3, 5 10–11, 61, 89–90, 227n.96
Heraclea 102n.37
Heracles 35–6, 40, 118, 202, 209
Heraclides of Pontus 3, 31n.45, 59, 61, 65, 68, 69, 75, 92–109, 113, 138, 154, 155, 177n.43, 179, 185, 241, 242
Heraclides of Tarentum 23
Herillus 215, 217
Hermagoras of Amphipolis 217
Hermarchus 60, 194n.5
Hermetic literature 106n.51
Hermodorus of Syracuse 103
Hermotimus 105, 106n.49, 107n.52
Herophilus 16
Hesiod 135, 195, 230, 237
*hetaira* 18, 20n.22, 22, 27
 see also courtesan
Hiero 31, 102, 144n.67
Hierocles 159n.124
Hieronymus of Rhodes 2, 23, 159, 190
Hipparchus 133–4
Hippias (tyrant) 134n.25
Hippias of Elis 84, 168
Hippocrates 36–40
Hippolochus of Macedon 32–3
Hirzel, Rudolf 1, 4–6, 43
history 69–70, 74, 88, 96

Homer 34, 61, 63, 64, 66–8, 74, 91, 93, 99, 108, 115, 133, 134n.26, 135, 141, 165, 172–3, 178, 186, 195, 207–8, 214, 220, 230, 237
Hyperboreans 95, 106, 154–5
Hyperochides 31, 183
*hypomnemata* 17, 110–11, 115, 187

Iamblichus 105n.46, 106, 177
Ichthyas 83, 195, 203
Ideas 57–8
Idomeneus of Lampsacus 224, 227n.97
Ilissus 158, 162
imitation 77, 140, 160, 162, 164, 230, 237–8, 244
 see also mimetic techniques
immortality of the soul 104, 107, 153, 172, 175, 180
impiety 60, 130–1
India 103, 183–4, 204
interlocutor
 anonymous 124, 128, 142, 160, 161, 243
 an author 10, 62, 97, 167–8, 175n.33, 181, 191, 237, 242
 contemporary 96, 167–8, 242
 female 34, 62–5, 199
 mythological 96, 186, 190, 202, 242
Ion of Chios 14–15, 25, 120n.96
Irus 67
Ischomachus 64, 100, 147
Isocrates 4, 158, 177n.43, 189, 191

Jaeger, Werner 164, 168
Jerusalem 29, 183
Jews 29–32, 103, 182–4, 236
Julian the Apostate 107n.55, 245
justice 60, 65n.57, 138, 142, 147–8
Justin the Martyr 245

kingship 32, 75, 136, 169, 177, 202
 see also monarchy

Lacydes 91, 120
laughter 26, 33n.51, 34, 36–8, 67, 213, 214n.60
law 29–30, 135
Lebadeia 186
lentils 34–5, 215
Leon (tyrant) 31n.45, 102, 104, 109
Leon the Academic 157
Lesbos 186, 191
letter 5, 12, 28–42, 77, 219–20, 230
 see also epistolography
*Letter of Aristeas* 29–32, 42
Libya 102, 200
literary criticism 12, 61, 65, 188–9
Longus 236

## 294 GENERAL INDEX

love 25, 46–7, 67, 181, 194, 217, 222
Lucian 8, 9n.23, 11n.30, 36, 69n.72, 86n.118, 109, 157, 204, 208n.45, 212–14, 231, 245
luxury 54, 99–100, 182, 233
Lyco of Troas 190
Lynceus of Samos 16, 32
Lysias 110–11, 138, 238

Macedonia 33, 63, 76, 85–6, 172, 174–5, 189
Machon 17–18, 19n.20, 20
madness 36, 39, 100–1, 141n.56
Magi 31n.45, 102–3, 105, 154–5, 178n.44
Mandanis 205–6
  see also Dandamis
Mandroboulus 112
Marathon 100
*Margites* 141
marriage 159–60, 219
  see also wife
Matro of Pitane 33n.53
meal 21, 25, 215, 221n.76, 222, 227, 233
  see also feast; food
medical themes 16, 24, 37, 104, 154, 221
Megarians 16, 83, 152, 194–9
Melanippe 65
Meleager of Gadara 23, 34, 214–15, 239, 240
memoir literature 10, 13–16, 25, 242
Menander 29, 80, 82, 170n.23
Menedemus the Cynic 213n.54
Menedemus of Eretria 32n.48, 202n.24
Menippean satire 5, 208, 212n.53, 214, 215
Menippus of Gadara 23, 34n.54, 208, 212–14, 215, 239, 240, 242
Meno 145, 148n.83, 149–50, 162
metamorphosis myths 157–8
Methodius of Olympus 245
Metrocles 17, 19–20, 82–4, 88, 196, 197, 202n.24
Metrodorus 95n.19, 225–6, 227n.98, 230n.102
Midas 116, 174–5, 214
midday 107, 109, 158
Middle Platonism 89, 125, 237
mime 9
mimetic techniques 37, 42, 128, 238, 243
  see also imitation
Minos 112, 135–6
miraculous stories 92, 103, 158, 184–5, 187
miscellanies 16, 24, 187
monarchy 16, 32, 75, 238
  see also kingship
Moschus 196
music 49, 81n.100, 94, 103, 158, 179, 187
Musonius Rufus 159n.124
Myrto 137, 158–9, 171n.25

myths 8, 54, 96, 107n.53, 108, 116, 154–5, 157–8, 174n.30, 185, 244
  see also interlocutor, mythological
Mytilene 186

narration 7–8, 10, 29, 44, 70, 161
  see also *diegesis*
nature 79, 157–8, 159, 205
Neocles 226, 227, 230n.102, 240
Nicagoras (tyrant of Zeleia) 16–17, 195
Nicias 69, 100
Nicion 34–6, 214, 215
noble birth 169–71
noon see midday
Numenius 245

Odysseus 66–8, 73, 202
old age 181, 188, 190, 229n.100, 242
oligarchy 48–50
Olympia 186
Onesicritus 184, 204–6
oral discourse 120, 216n.67, 244–5
Orphism 153

pain 51, 100, 111n.67, 232, 234
painting 22, 218, 235, 236
Panaetius 159, 190, 194, 215, 216n.67, 219
paradoxography 11, 158, 243
paraenetic discourse 12, 38, 89, 169n.22, 193, 235, 239
Parmenides 40, 69, 194, 231, 237
Parmeniscus 33–6, 214–15, 239, 240
parody 18, 23, 24n.29, 33–36, 105n.47, 109, 113, 139, 156, 193, 206, 208, 213–15, 230, 232, 239, 240, 242
Peisistratus 69, 70–5, 133, 134n.25, 26, 180
Pella 76
Perdiccas 76–7
Periander 24, 69, 73–5, 108
Pericles 140, 148, 149
*perideipnon* see funeral feast
*periegesis* 235, 243
Peripatetics 2, 45, 57, 59, 61, 65, 93, 94, 103, 104, 143, 164–92, 242
Persaeus of Citium 15, 17, 25–6, 120n.98, 197, 207, 215, 216–17, 222n.80, 238, 240
Persephone 107, 185
Persia 102n.36, 154n.102
  see also wisdom, non-Greek
personifications 116–19, 125, 209, 218, 235, 239, 242
Petronius 33, 36
Phaedo of Elis 196
Phaedrus 158, 189, 238

GENERAL INDEX 295

Phaenias 120n.98
Phalaris 76, 106
Phaleron 157, 162
Pharsalus 144–5
Pherae 172, 174
Philip II of Macedon 16–17, 108, 109, 143, 144n.67, 174–5, 195, 238
Philip of Opus 103, 128, 132
Philiscus of Aegina 203, 204
Philo of Alexandria 2, 3, 6, 11, 158, 236–8, 239, 242, 244
Philodemus 90, 228
Philo the Dialectitian 199
Philo of Larissa 89, 92, 125
philology 12, 61, 68, 88, 241
  *see also* literary criticism
Philosopher mosaic 245
Philostratus 245
Philoxenus 18–19, 33n.53
Phrynichus 15
Phthia 172–3, 186
piety 60, 94, 95, 98, 130, 181
Plato *see* dialogue, Plato's
pleasure 41, 51–2, 98, 99–102, 110, 111, 117–18, 119n.91, 153, 177, 182, 188, 208, 218, 228, 233
Plutarch 1, 2, 3, 9, 22–3, 24, 31n.44, 31n.45, 32, 36, 60, 61, 64, 70, 125, 136n.35, 158, 178n.44, 186–7, 236, 237, 238, 245
Pluto 107
Polemo 90–1, 138n.42, 143
Polyaenus (Epicurean) 221–2, 228
Polyarchus 41, 102, 188
polymathy 142–3, 232
  *see also* erudition
Porphyry 60, 202n.24
Poseidon 107
Posidonius 102, 120n.98, 215, 219
poverty 79, 118n.87, 118n.89, 209, 212, 234, 239, 242
Praxiphanes 4, 65, 188–9, 191, 242, 244
prayer 140, 141n.56, 169, 177
prefaces 98, 167, 178, 191
pre-Socratic philosophy 94, 103, 108, 231
Prodicus 146, 147, 153, 155n.110
prophecies 66–7, 106, 137, 172–3, 187
prosimetric texts 214
Protagoras 107, 108, 168
protreptic 12, 52, 59n.39, 89, 131–2, 139, 177
proverbs 39, 46, 47n.7, 54, 56, 57n.32, 112, 180
providence 236–7
Prytanis 2, 23, 190
Ptolemy I Soter 196, 199, 238
Ptolemy II Philadelphus 29–32, 155, 188, 201–2

Ptolemy IV Philopator 217, 233n.110
Pyrrho of Elis 120n.97, 230, 231–2, 239
Pythagoras 31n.45, 102, 104–6, 107n.52, 55, 108–9, 187, 205, 231
Pythagoreans 34–5, 60, 93, 94, 111, 115, 153, 182, 187, 235
Pythodorus 120

question-and-answer format *see* dialogue, question- and-answer format

reincarnation 105, 109
Rhadamantus 135
rhetoric 48–9, 69, 75–7, 183–4, 223–4
Rome 2, 6, 11, 89, 92, 95
Rose, Valentinus 169
ruler *see* wise man, encounter with a ruler

Sardanapalus 214
Satyrus of Callatis 3, 27, 41, 61–6, 159, 190–1
school compositions 69, 77n.90, 85–6, 148, 150, 152, 241
Seneca the Younger 3, 116n.82, 209, 212, 214, 237
Septuagint 29
Seven Sages 15n.6, 23, 24, 32, 85, 245n.2
Sextus Empiricus 91, 120, 237n.129
*Shepherd of Hermas* 235
Sicily 102, 146–7, 172
Silenus 116, 174–6
Simonides 15, 31, 75, 99, 102, 133, 134n.26, 141, 171, 178
skepticism 52n.19, 91, 92n.9, 119–20, 125, 150, 157, 230–1, 239, 242
sleep 104, 184, 195
  *see also* dream
Socrates 9, 13–14, 15n.7, 21–2, 25, 45, 47–8, 50–2, 55, 63, 64–5, 69, 78–9, 84, 103, 104, 121, 123, 133–51, 153–63, 171, 172–3, 175, 176, 178, 187, 189, 194, 195, 196, 199, 201, 205, 227n.97, 231, 238, 242, 243, 244
  see also *daimonion* of Socrates
Socratic dialogue *see* dialogue, Socratic
Socratics 2, 5, 6, 13, 23, 25, 45, 48, 61, 148n.82, 149n.84, 154n.106, 231
Solon 16, 31, 70, 71–2, 74–5, 108, 175
Sophocles 15, 25, 39, 61, 91, 94, 170n.23
soul 47, 56, 94, 95, 99–100, 104, 105, 106, 107, 119, 135, 153–5, 172, 175, 176, 184–7, 209n.51
Sparta 49, 140
speeches 7, 9, 77, 101, 164, 168, 171
Speusippus 2, 15, 23, 59, 90, 93, 102, 109–13, 119, 195, 200, 232

Sphaerus 215, 217
starvation 201-2
Stilpo of Megara 19-20, 25, 27, 82-4, 110n.65, 194n.5, 195-8, 199, 200, 210, 217, 238
Stoics 89, 119, 136, 140, 150, 159, 194n.4, 215-19, 231, 237, 238
story-telling 95, 97, 106
strength 54-5
suicide 34-5, 155, 201-2, 215
    see also starvation
*symposion see* dialogue, sympotic
Syracuse 75, 146, 172, 175

*Tabulae Iliacae* 236
Teles 79, 197-8, 206, 208-12, 239, 243
Thales 24, 231
Theages 136-8, 150, 160
theatre 39, 118
    see also drama
Themistocles 148, 149, 198
Theodoridas of Lindus 228-9, 239
Theodorus the Atheist 206
Theodote 21-2, 27, 63
Theognis 171, 178
theology 130, 132, 221n.78
Theophrastus 23, 57, 59, 60, 93, 98, 103, 116, 120n.98, 154, 167, 168-9, 176, 179-81, 191, 244
Thrasea Paetus 209
Thrasyllan canon 126
Thrasyllus of Aexone 100-1
Thrasymachus 41, 138, 162, 168, 188
Thucydides 7, 132n.22, 148, 189
Timocrates 226
Timon of Phlius 113, 189n.75, 230-2, 239, 240, 242
Tithonus 190, 191, 242
titles *see* dialogue, titles
tragedy 16n.11, 34, 64n.54, 94, 96, 109, 118n.89, 203, 208n.45, 215
    see also drama; theatre

Trophonius 186-7
tyranny 72, 74, 102n.37, 133, 136, 141

underworld 94, 95, 213, 231
    see also afterlife; Hades

Varro 97n.24, 212-13, 214
virtue(s) 64, 118, 130, 139, 149-50, 209, 218, 233

walking conversations 158, 222-3
wealth 54-5, 56, 63, 79, 100, 117-19, 146-7, 209, 212
wife 64, 157, 158-9
    see also marriage
wine 25, 26, 33, 181, 217, 221-2
wisdom 119n.91, 129-30, 132, 133-4, 146, 154
    non-Greek 31-2, 103, 155, 180, 184, 205
    and power *see* wise man, encounter with a ruler
    see also Seven Sages
wise man, encounter with a ruler 31, 32, 41, 85, 102, 105, 175, 188
women *see* interlocutor, female

Xanthippe 64, 78, 156, 158, 159
Xenocrates 4n.5, 24n.29, 59, 60, 90, 93, 114-15, 119, 138, 149n.84, 150, 208n.45
Xenophanes 230-1, 237, 242
Xenophon 2, 10, 13-15, 17n.16, 19, 20, 23, 31, 33, 64, 69, 75, 78, 79, 82, 102, 115, 127, 137, 148, 150n.88, 160n.127, 177, 178n.44, 199, 203-4, 220, 222n.80

Zeno of Alexandria 120
Zeno of Citium 15, 16, 17, 25, 119n.91, 120n.98, 196, 197, 202n.24, 215-17, 231
Zeno of Elea 237
Zeno of Sidon 223
*zetemata* 11, 61, 68, 108, 241
Zethus 143
Zeus 107, 135, 141, 205, 208n.45, 218n.69
Zoroaster 94, 102, 103